The Theater Essays of
ARTHUR MILLER

Edited with Introductions by
ROBERT A. MARTIN
and
STEVEN R. CENTOLA

Foreword by
ARTHUR MILLER

Revised and Expanded

DA CAPO PRESS • NEW YORK

Library of Congress Cataloging in Publication Data

Miller, Arthur, 1915–
    The theater essays of Arthur Miller / edited with introductions by Robert
A. Martin and Steven R. Centola; foreword by Arthur Miller.—Rev. and expanded.
        p.   cm.
    Includes bibliographical references and index.
    ISBN 0-306-80732-7 (alk. paper)
    1. Miller, Arthur, 1915–   —Aesthetics. 2. American drama—20th cen-
tury—History and criticism—Theory, etc. 3. Dramatists, American—20th
century—Interviews. 4. Drama—Technique. I. Martin, Robert A. II. Centola, Steve, 1952–   . III. Title.
PS3525.I5656T5   1996
809.2—dc20   96-16452
                                                                         CIP

First Da Capo Press edition 1996

This Da Capo Press paperback edition of *The Theater Essays of Arthur Miller*
is a republication of the edition first published in New York in 1978.
It has been extensively expanded with eighteen new selections as well as a
new literary chronology, introduction, bibliography, and updated play casts
and production information. It is reprinted by arrangement with Viking
Penguin, a division of Penguin Books USA, Inc., and Arthur Miller.

Published by Da Capo Press, Inc.
A Subsidiary of Plenum Publishing Corporation
233 Spring Street, New York, N.Y. 10013

To *Kenneth Thorpe Rowe*
—teacher, friend, scholar—
whose lifelong devotion to drama
and the theater has made a difference

ROBERT A. MARTIN AND ARTHUR MILLER

*I would like to thank Arthur Miller for recommending
that I expand and revise this collection and for guiding
me in the selection of new material; Robert A. Martin
for first recognizing the value of a collection of theater
essays by Arthur Miller; Michael Dorr, editor at
Da Capo Press; Marjorie Warmkessel, librarian at
Ganser Library, Millersville University; and my wife,
Susan, and my children, Tamara, Paul, and Devon,
for their love, patience, and understanding. I dedicate
this edition to them.*

STEVEN R. CENTOLA

Acknowledgments

For their encouragement, support, and research assistance, I would like to thank the following individuals who in different ways have contributed substantially to the completion of this collection of essays:

Professors William Halstead, Kenneth Rowe, and Erich Walter of The University of Michigan, all of whom have generously shared information and documentation on Arthur Miller's student days in Ann Arbor; Mary Cooley, Hilda Bonham, and Professor John W. Aldridge of the Hopwood Room at The University of Michigan; Harriet C. Jameson and her capable staff of the Rare Book Room at The University of Michigan; Professor Richard D. Meyer, Director of Theatre Programs at The University of Michigan; the late Phyllis Jackson of International Creative Management, New York City; Bill Decker, editor and expeditor, of The Viking Press; Arthur Miller for his interest and assistance in preparing this collection for publication; my wife, Peggy, and my children, John, Doug, Carole, and Christy, for their assistance, patience, and support.

—ROBERT A. MARTIN

Contents

I. *Death of a Salesman* to *A View from the Bridge*

II. The *Collected Plays* to *The Misfits*

III. *After the Fall* to Lincoln Center

IV. *The Creation of the World and Other Business* to *Timebends*

V. *Danger: Memory!* to *Broken Glass*

A Literary Chronology

1915   Arthur Asher Miller, the second child of Isidore (owner of the Miltex Coat and Suit Company) and Augusta Barnett Miller, is born on October 17 on East 112th Street in New York City.

1920–28   He attends public school in Harlem.

1923   At about the age of eight, Miller goes to the Shubert Theater with his mother and sees his first stage play.

1929   The Millers move to East Third Street in Brooklyn after Isidore's women's clothing business sustains severe financial losses as a result of the Great Depression.

1932   Miller graduates from Abraham Lincoln High School, where he earns a reputation for being more interested in athletics than academics.

1932–34   After graduation Miller works at various jobs, ranging from singer on a local radio station to truck driver to clerk in an automobile-parts warehouse on Tenth Avenue in Manhattan. He writes about his work experience at his father's garment business in a memoir entitled "In Memorium," which describes his reaction to an indigent salesman's suicide. He later recounts his bittersweet memory of his work at the automobile-parts warehouse in the nostalgic one-act play, *A Memory of Two Mondays*.

1934–35   Miller enrolls as a student in journalism at the University of Michigan. He becomes a reporter and night editor for the student newspaper, *The Michigan Daily*, and supplements his income by caring for mice in the University's laboratories.

1936   Miller launches his playwriting career by writing *No Villain* in just six days during spring vacation. In May *No Villain* receives a Hopwood Award in Drama from the Avery Hopwood Writing Awards Contest. In September, Miller transfers his degree program from journalism to English. He revises *No Villain* for the Theater Guild's Bureau of New Plays Contest and renames the new version *They Too Arise*. He also begins work on another play, *Honors at Dawn*, for the 1937 Hopwood Contest.

1937   In February, Miller enrolls in a playwriting class taught by Professor Kenneth T. Rowe. *They Too Arise* receives a major award of $1250 from the Bureau of New Plays and is produced in Ann Arbor and Detroit. In June *Honors at Dawn* receives a Hopwood Award in Drama. Miller continues to study playwriting with Professor Rowe and to work as a reporter and editor for *The Michigan Daily*. In October he begins a new play, *The Great Disobedience*, for entry in the 1938 Hopwood Contest.

1938   In March, Miller enters *The Great Disobedience* in the Hopwood Contest and sends a copy to the Bureau of New Plays. In April he begins the revision of *They Too Arise* with a new title, *The Grass Still Grows,* for anticipated production by a theater group in New York City. In May *The Great Disobedience* places second in the Hopwood Contest, and receives a laboratory production from the University of Michigan Theatre Department. In June, Miller graduates with a Bachelor of Arts Degree in English Language and Literature.

1938–43   Miller joins the Federal Theater Project in New York City in the fall. He writes radio plays and scripts for numerous programs, including the *Columbia Workshop* (CBS) and the

Cavalcade of America (NBC). He continues to write stage plays while looking for a producer.

1940   Miller marries Mary Grace Slattery. He also writes *The Golden Years*, a historical play about the Cortés/Montezuma conflict.

1941   Miller continues working on scripts, but supplements his income by taking a job as a shipfitter's helper at the Brooklyn Navy Yard. He writes two radio plays, *William Ireland's Confession* and *The Pussycat and the Expert Plumber Who Was a Man*.

1943   Miller completes another new play, *The Half-Bridge*, and sees *That They May Win*, a one-act supporting the United States war effort, produced in New York City.

1944   On September 7, Miller's daughter, Jane, is born. He tours army camps to gather material for the film, *The Story of G. I. Joe*, and publishes a book about his tour with the title *Situation Normal* on November 27. His first Broadway play, *The Man Who Had All the Luck*, premieres at the Forrest Theater on November 23. Although the play closes after just six performances, it receives the Theater Guild National Award and is selected for inclusion in *Cross-Section: A Collection of New American Writing*.

1945   On October 30, Miller publishes *Focus*, a novel attacking anti-Semitism in American society.

1947   *All My Sons* premieres on January 29 at the Coronet Theater in New York City and is published on February 7. The play enjoys a successful production and receives the New York Drama Critics' Circle Award, the Donaldson Award, and professional recognition for Miller. On May 31, Miller's son, Robert, is born.

1949   *Death of a Salesman* premieres on February 10 at the Morosco Theater in New York City and is published on May 18. The play receives the Pulitzer Prize, the New York Drama Critics' Circle Award, the Antoinette Perry Award, the Donaldson Award, and the Theater Club Award, among

many others. "Tragedy and the Common Man" is published in *The New York Times* on February 27.

1950   While in Hollywood for a meeting with producers about
the Columbia Pictures film version of *Death of a Salesman*,
Miller meets Marilyn Monroe. *An Enemy of the People* (his
adaptation of Ibsen's play) premieres on December 28 at
the Broadhurst Theater in New York City and is published
on March 2, 1951. *The Hook*, a screenplay about waterfront
corruption for Columbia Pictures, fails to reach production
because of pressure on Hollywood filmmakers by the
House Committee on Un-American Activities.

1953   *The Crucible* premieres on January 22 at the Martin Beck
Theater in New York City and is published on April 1. The
play wins the Antoinette Perry Award and the Donaldson
Award.

1955   *A View from the Bridge* premieres along with *A Memory of
Two Mondays* (both one-act plays) on September 29 at the
Coronet Theater in New York City and is published on
November 14.

1956   Miller divorces Mary Grace Slattery, and marries Marilyn
Monroe on June 29. In the same month he is subpoenaed
to appear before the House Committee on Un-American
Activities and receives an honorary Doctor of Humane Letters (L.H.D.) from the University of Michigan. An expanded version of *A View from the Bridge* (two acts)
premieres on October 11 at the Comedy Theater in London, England and is published on March 11, 1957.

1957   *Arthur Miller's Collected Plays* is published on May 23.
Miller is convicted of contempt of Congress for having re-
fused to name writers suspected of Communist sympathies.
"The Misfits," a short story, appears in *Esquire*.

1958   The United States Court of Appeals overturns Miller's contempt conviction. Miller is elected to the National Institute
of Arts and Letters.

1959   Miller receives the Gold Medal for Drama from the National Institute of Arts and Letters.

1961   Miller divorces Marilyn Monroe on January 20. Following publication of the screenplay on January 31, *The Misfits,* a film, premieres in February in New York City.

1962   Miller marries Inge Morath, a professional photographer, on February 17.

1963   In August, Miller's daughter, Rebecca, is born. His children's book, *Jane's Blanket,* is published.

1964   *After the Fall* premieres on January 23 at the ANTA-Washington Square Theater in New York City and is published on February 11. In March, Miller covers the Nazi trials in Frankfurt, Germany for the *New York Herald Tribune. Incident at Vichy* premieres on December 3 at the same theater as *After the Fall* and is published on January 12, 1965.

1965   Miller is elected President of International P.E.N., an organization of playwrights, poets, essayists, and novelists.

1967   *I Don't Need You Anymore,* a collection of short stories, is published on February 15.

1968   *The Price* premieres on February 7 at the Morosco Theater in New York City and is published on March 7. Miller attends the Democratic National Convention in Chicago as a delegate.

1969   *In Russia,* a book of reportage with photographs by Inge Morath, is published on November 19.

1970   In November *Fame* and *The Reason Why,* one-act plays, are produced at the New Theater Workshop in New York City.

1971   *The Portable Arthur Miller,* edited by Harold Clurman, is published on June 2.

1972   *The Creation of the World and Other Business* premieres on November 30 at the Shubert Theater in New York City and is published on June 23, 1973. Miller attends the Democratic National Convention in Miami as a delegate.

1974   *Up from Paradise,* a musical version of *The Creation of the World and Other Business,* premieres on April 23 at the Power Center for the Performing Arts, The University of Michigan, Ann Arbor.

1977   *In the Country*, a book of reportage with photographs by
        Inge Morath, is published on February 22. *The Archbishop's
        Ceiling* premieres on April 23 at the Kennedy Center for
        the Performing Arts, Washington, D.C.

1978   *The Theater Essays of Arthur Miller*, edited by Robert A.
        Martin, is published on March 10. On November 30 *Fame*
        appears on NBC.

1979   *Chinese Encounters*, a book of reportage with photographs
        by Inge Morath, is published.

1980   On September 30 *Playing for Time*, Miller's adaptation of
        Fania Fenelon's memoirs, appears on CBS. After premier-
        ing at the Spoleto Festival in South Carolina, *The American
        Clock* opens on November 20 at the Biltmore Theater in
        New York City. *Elegy for a Lady* appears in the December
        issue of *Esquire*.

1981   The second volume of *Arthur Miller's Collected Plays* is
        published.

1982   *Elegy for a Lady* and *Some Kind of Love Story* appear as
        2 by A.M. on October 26 at the Long Wharf Theater in
        New Haven, Connecticut. *The American Clock* is pub-
        lished.

1983   Miller directs *Death of a Salesman* at the People's Art Thea-
        ter in Beijing, the People's Republic of China.

1984   *Salesman in Beijing* is published. *Two-Way Mirror*, Miller's
        new title for the anthology consisting of *Elegy for a Lady*
        and *Some Kind of Love Story*, is published. Miller re-
        ceives Kennedy Center Honors for his lifetime achieve-
        ment.

1985   *Death of a Salesman*, starring Dustin Hoffman as Willy
        Loman, appears on CBS in September.

1986   Miller publishes two one-act plays, *Clara* and *I Can't Re-
        member Anything*, as *Danger: Memory!*

1987   *Danger: Memory!* opens on February 8 at the Mitzi E.
        Newhouse Theater, Lincoln Center, in New York City.
        Miller publishes his autobiography, *Timebends: A Life*.

The Golden Years receives its world premiere on BBC Radio on November 6.

1989   *The American Clock* and *The Archbishop's Ceiling* are published in a single volume. *The Golden Years* and *The Man Who Had All the Luck* are also published in a single volume.

1990   *Everybody Wins*, Miller's screenplay of his play *Some Kind of Love Story*, is released in movie theaters in February and is later published.

1991   *The Last Yankee*, a one-act, is given a studio production in June at the Ensemble Studio Theater in New York City. *The Ride Down Mount Morgan* premieres on October 11 at Wyndham's Theater in London and is later published. In November, Miller receives the Mellon Bank Award for his lifetime achievement in the humanities.

1992   *Homely Girl*, a novella, is published by Peter Blum in New York.

1993   An expanded version of *The Last Yankee* premieres on January 21 at the Manhattan Theater Club in New York City and is later published.

1994   After a short run in March at the Long Wharf Theater in New Haven, Connecticut, *Broken Glass* premieres on April 24 at the Booth Theater in New York City and is later published.

1995   In April, Miller receives the William Inge Festival Award for distinguished achievement in American theater. During the summer, production starts on a film version of *The Crucible* near Crane's Beach on Hog Island Reservation in Essex, Massachusetts. Arthur Miller celebrates his eightieth birthday in October. Tributes to the playwright are held at the National Theatre in London and at the Town Hall in New York City. *Homely Girl, A Life and Other Stories*, a collection containing Miller's novella and the short stories "Fame" and "Fitter's Night," is published. A revised edition of *The Portable Arthur Miller*, edited by Christopher Bigsby, is published.

1996   In August, Miller receives the Edward Albee Last Frontier Playwright Award (presented by Albee) at the Fourth Annual Prince William Sound Community College Theatre Conference in Valdez, Alaska. A revised and expanded edition of *The Theater Essays of Arthur Miller*, edited by Steven R. Centola, is published in October.

Introduction to the Original Edition
by Robert A. Martin

I

DURING the thirty years since *All My Sons* premiered on January 29, 1947, Arthur Miller's reputation and stature as a writer of unusual talent and insight have increased steadily with the appearance of each of his plays, books, and films. He has been variously described as a moralist, a playwright of ideas, or a social dramatist; his contributions to the theater have been of a consistently high quality during a period when many critics apparently believed that the theater was, at best, a dying institution, slowly giving way to the demands of commercialization, sex and sadism, movies and television. That such has not been the case with the plays of Arthur Miller is, however, readily apparent through his continuing appeal to theater audiences and readers in virtually every civilized country in the world. Along with the plays of Eugene O'Neill and Tennessee Williams, Arthur Miller's plays have been responsible in large part for extending the significance of the American theater beyond the horizons of its national origins, and for providing a standard of dramatic achievement for contemporary playwrights everywhere.

Miller's plays have always been surrounded by controversy, and he has been well aware of his position as one of America's most important living dramatists ever since *Death of a Salesman* brought him instant recognition. In spite of the obvious difficulties, Miller has managed to keep his public life and image separate from his life as an artist. Few writers have, in fact, managed quite as successfully to remain both a private and a public person while maintaining an active engagement with the problems and issues of contemporary society and of their craft.

Following the popular and critical success of *Death of a Salesman* in 1949, Miller has continued to write plays that reflect his belief in "the theater as a serious business, one that makes or should make man more human, which is to say, less alone." Miller's conviction that the theater should be a "serious business," one that places serious issues before the public, appears in various forms again and again in his prefaces and essays, which set forth his beliefs against the background of his plays. It is, I believe, through his prefaces and essays that Miller speaks most directly of his social and dramatic convictions, and of his craftsmanship as a playwright; they comprise a body of critical commentary that is both distinguished and significant in the history of American drama and culture. Collectively, Arthur Miller's essays on drama and the theater may well represent the single most important statement of critical principles to appear in England and America by a major playwright since the Prefaces of George Bernard Shaw.

It is as a result of this belief that the present collection has been selected and assembled. Several of these important essays have been reprinted in whole or in part in studies dealing with a particular play, such as *Death of a Salesman* or *The Crucible,* or in more general collections dealing with Miller's overall achievement as a playwright, but their scattered locations in separate books, newspapers, and magazines have made it difficult for all but the most determined reader to see them as a sustained and comprehensive commentary on his art and craft, his theory and practice, and his ideas on why the theater is important. In a few cases I have deleted an interviewer's opening phrase or comment that did not seem particularly relevant, and in one instance, at the end of his "Preface" to *An Enemy of the People,* Miller has added a note to the original essay. With Miller's approval, I have edited his theater comments from *In Russia* to create a new essay from the book's much broader range. In all other pieces, the text is identical to its original appearance, edited lightly only to correct misprints. One essay, originally published as "The Playwright in the Atomic World," has been retitled for this collection as "1956 and All This" since neither Arthur Miller nor I felt that the original title accurately reflected the contents.

In sifting through all of Miller's essays with an eye toward selecting those that would best represent a career that has spanned over thirty years in the theater, I was often struck by the range of his interests and by the intensity with which he has pursued the twin concepts of truth and morality as the highest priority in his work. In a press interview at the premiere of *All My Sons* in 1947, Miller quite clearly set forth his basic theoretical view on drama and his pragmatistic approach to playwriting:

> In all my plays and books I try to take settings and dramatic situations from life which involve real questions of right and wrong. Then I set out, rather implacably and in the most realistic situations I can find, the moral dilemma and try to point a real, though hard, path out. I don't see how you can write anything decent without using the question of right and wrong as the basis.

While this statement would appear to anticipate Miller's larger themes in *Death of a Salesman, The Crucible,* and *A View from the Bridge,* it actually moves backward and forward simultaneously. Between his graduation from The University of Michigan in 1938 and the production of *All My Sons* nine years later, Miller had written and published a novel (*Focus,* 1945), a book of reportage (*Situation Normal,* 1944), numerous radio plays and scripts, a play (*The Man Who Had All the Luck,* 1944) that closed after four performances, as well as "a dozen or more plays earlier which hadn't been produced," plus the three plays he wrote as a student for the Hopwood Writing Awards Contest, two of which had won major awards. Looking back on this crucial period from the perspective of ten years later in the "Introduction" to his *Collected Plays,* Miller wrote:

> I was turning thirty then, the author of perhaps a dozen plays, none of which I could truly believe were finished. I had written many scenes, but not a play. A play, I saw then, was an organism of which I had fashioned only certain parts. The decision formed to write one more, and if again it turned out to be unrealizable, I would go into another line of work.

The one more play, of course, was *All My Sons,* which turned out to be "realizable" enough to encourage Miller to continue as a dramatist. The difference between *The Man Who Had All the Luck* and *All My Sons,* dramatically at least, was that in the period between 1944 and 1946 Miller's disappointment in the reception of *The Man Who Had All the Luck* forced him to reconsider both his objectives in writing a play ("I had tried to grasp wonder," he has said) and his technique in conveying the play's objective meaning to an audience. If, in *The Man Who Had All the Luck,* he had been betrayed by "wonder," his next play would have to be built on the bedrock of logic so as to "make sense to common-sense people." The result, Miller has said, was a determination to forgo the impulse to create wonder:

> But wonder had betrayed me and the only other course I had was the one I took—to seek cause and effect, hard actions, facts, the geometry of relationships, and to hold back any tendency to express an idea in itself unless it was literally forced out of a character's mouth; in other words, to let wonder rise up like a mist, a gas, a vapor from the gradual and remorseless crush of factual and psychological conflict.

This is, of course, a comment on method and not meaning. But Miller's thematic emphasis on "questions of right and wrong" and his attempt to locate "the moral dilemma" in realistic situations suggest his theoretical inclination to merge objective and subjective forces that extends from *All My Sons* into *Death of a Salesman,* and that continues, with only minor modifications, into *The Crucible* and *A View from the Bridge.* The lessons of a dozen unfinished and unproduced plays, along with the failure of *The Man Who Had All the Luck,* were undoubtedly on his mind at the premiere of *All My Sons,* and lay just beneath the surface of his comments during the press interview.

All My Sons ran for nine months, from January 29 to November 8, 1947, for a total of 328 performances, and is generally considered Miller's first successful play. Although critics have been intent on tracing the influences of Ibsen in the play's content and structure, Miller has continually emphasized that Ibsen was important to him not so much for his mastery of the realistic form as for his ability to construct a dramatic fact from an idea, and to make audiences listen to what he had to say.

As a self-acknowledged playwright of social plays, one who defines social drama as "the drama of the whole man," Miller also believes that "society is inside man and man is inside society, and you cannot even create a truthfully drawn psychological entity on the stage until you understand his social relations...." In his more theoretical essays, Miller again and again turns to the social relationship to stress that drama and the playwright, as exemplified primarily by Ibsen, are reflections of the social barometer. Ibsen, Shaw, Chekhov, Brecht, and Miller share in common the philosophy that the fate of man is social, and that the stage should be considered as a medium more important for ideas than for mere entertainment, and should serve a serious purpose intellectually. In his "Preface" to *An Enemy of the People,* for one of many examples, Miller defends the right of the playwright to engage his audiences in serious issues, and places Ibsen in the tradition of playwright-as-philosopher and dramatic *provocateur:*

> The dramatic writer has, and must again demonstrate, the right to entertain with his brains as well as his heart. It is necessary that the public understand again that the stage is *the* place for ideas, for philosophies, for the most intense

discussions of man's fate. One of the masters of such a discussion is Henrik Ibsen, and I have presumed to point this out once again.

And so the critical debate over Ibsen's influence on *All My Sons* continues to flourish in the numerous critical essays and articles that regularly appear in *The New York Times* and in various academic journals and quarterlies, such as *Modern Drama* and *Educational Theatre Journal*. Evidence to the contrary, it would appear that interest in the Miller-Ibsen relationship might well survive the play that generated the discussion in the first place. To say that Miller's engagement with the theater as "a serious business" continues to reverberate loudly from his prefaces and essays seems equally apparent as a consequence of his willingness early in his career to raise questions of form and method—not to mention social issues—that continue to engage lively and intelligent debate among critics and scholars to the present day. To suggest that the question is one not taken lightly by Miller himself is perhaps indicated by his interest in adding, at my invitation, a current note to his "Preface" to *An Enemy of the People* in which he replies to criticism (unspecified) that he misused Ibsen "as an easy way to make contemporary points."

That such issues were not contemporary during the initial run of *All My Sons* is, however, reflected in the simple fact that, aside from a few interviews, Miller did not publish any essays that could be seen as controversial—with one exception. In *The New York Times* of June 22, 1947, there appeared an article titled "Subsidized Theatre," in which Miller argued that the only hope for the theater as an art form was to establish theater companies that would be supported by local public and private subsidy (not Federal) and that would provide a permanent home for playwrights, actors, directors, and scene designers. Calling for an end to the commercial demands and standards of the marketplace and businessmen in the theater, Miller issued a call for a *Theater* as an organization: one in which the artist would be more responsible to himself and his profession. Such a Theater,

Miller contended, would constitute a group for whom a successful production would lead to increasing challenges and higher production standards. Defining a Theater as a collection of talented people "who share a common outlook upon life and art, and are permanently joined together for the purpose of producing dramatic art," as opposed to theaters, which are "buildings for rent, real estate," Miller outlined his hope for its contribution to the art:

> Furthermore, this Theater will have demonstrated—and it unquestionably will—that there is a vast audience for art. If nothing else, therefore, a Theater in America would call forth new works as nothing else has been able to do. It would re-establish the stage as a medium worthy of a serious writer. It would set a new standard for success which would soon dominate and overwhelm the present standard of cheap, circus entertainment and reveal the latter in its true light to critics and to audiences. Finally, it would require of actors that they become more than one-man corporations and get down to satisfying the true requisites of the acting art, which cannot be met, as at present, with no training and no study.

If *All My Sons* allowed Miller a tentative entry into the ranks of American playwrights, his next play propelled him not only into the forefront of his profession but into the center of the most sustained critical debate quite possibly ever to take place in the history of the American theater. *Death of a Salesman* opened on February 10, 1949. While *All My Sons* was timely in 1947, *Salesman* struck at the timeless nerve of the post–World War II American preoccupation with success and money, home and family. The play met with immediate popular and critical acclaim, although not without some reservations concerning the status of Willy Loman as tragic hero, and enjoyed an initial production of 742 performances extending from February 10, 1949, to November 18, 1950.

Miller has said in his "Introduction" to the *Collected Plays* that "*Salesman* is a slippery play to categorize because nobody in it stops to make a speech objectively stating the great issues which I believe it embodies." This is, in my view, the most understated sentence in the entire "Introduction," for during the twenty-eight years since the play opened there has been an impressively large number of books, articles, prefaces, essays, dissertations, and panel discussions attempting to evaluate, to categorize, to explain, to attack, and to defend in a variety of ways the meaning and methods of *Death of a Salesman*. And the discussions, like the play, continue in a lively fashion on and on. As Miller said, it is a slippery play to categorize.

In a new essay written especially for this volume, the "Author's Foreword: Sorting Things Out," Miller says that he has "often wished that [he] had never written a word on the subject of tragedy." Calling the tragic phenomenon "an arena of near-theological devoutness," he sets forth his current view of the nature of the tragic emotion, the society that it reflects, and his appraisal of the theater as he has seen it develop throughout his career. I point this out to emphasize that the essays and interviews selected for this collection are collectively a record of his views on the same subjects written during different stages of his career, documents that represent a continuing process of growth and development—if not struggle—to define and clarify the principles of his craft. One does not, of course, reasonably expect an artist to maintain precisely the same views on his work over a period of five years, let alone thirty. And it is also true that what one does in a play meant for the stage is somewhat different from what one does in an essay meant for a reader. That such considerations apply to Arthur Miller in particular is, I believe, self-evident to anyone who follows the thread of commentary that weaves throughout these essays like a dominant color in a tapestry. The theme of his work is most often reflected in these essays by the repetition of such key words as conscience, commitment, responsibility, identity, hope, faith, courage—words that, in effect, may be used to describe Miller himself as both a public and private individual.

But if Miller has been consistent in attempting to articulate his basic beliefs, his many theoretical statements on tragedy have in no small part contributed to the controversy surrounding his most important work. The first essay to appear in this collection is "Tragedy and the Common Man," which appeared in *The New York Times* on February 27, 1949, a little over two weeks after the opening performance of *Death of a Salesman*. This essay was primarily motivated by the initial critical response to the play, and represents Miller's first major statement on the tragic potential of serious modern drama. It was, in the setting of the late 1940s, received with mixed blessings, and has continued to evoke the most extreme reactions of practically anything he has written of a theoretical nature. The statement replied indirectly to such critics as John Gassner and Joseph Wood Krutch, who (along with Aristotle) held the belief that tragedy involved questions of rank and stature and awareness that were by implication beyond the dramatic character of the play's protagonist, Willy Loman. Although the question of tragedy has been considered by numerous commentators for at least twenty-five hundred years, it was not Miller's entry into the critical arena that created the difficulty, but his insistence that previous definitions were not necessarily definitive in 1949. The statement that I suspect brought down an avalanche of criticism upon Miller's unsuspecting head appears early in the essay:

> I believe that the common man is as apt a subject for tragedy in its highest sense as kings were. On the face of it this ought to be obvious in the light of modern psychiatry, which bases its analysis upon classic formulations, such as the Oedipus and Orestes complexes, for instances, which were enacted by royal beings, but which apply to everyone in similar emotional situations.

Taken in the context of the times, this pronouncement was guaranteed to invoke the wrath of critics, academic and otherwise, many of whom were not convinced that there *was* an American drama worth discussing. If not heresy, it was at least close enough to challenge some traditional and basic assumptions on the nature of tragedy in much the same way that Darwin's *Origin of Species* had earlier challenged the assumptions of a fairly complacent religious establishment in the nineteenth century, although to a much lesser degree. Together with another paragraph buried inconspicuously in the middle of the essay, Miller's statement on the common man clearly presented a challenge to current ideologies:

> Insistence upon the rank of the tragic hero, or the so-called nobility of his character, is really but a clinging to the outward forms of tragedy. If rank or nobility of character was indispensable, then it would follow that the problems of those with rank were the particular problems of tragedy. But surely the right of one monarch to capture the domain from another no longer raises our passions, nor are our concepts of justice what they were to the mind of an Elizabethan king.

I have no idea whether or not Arthur Miller would care to defend these lines, but I suspect from his comments in his new essay for this book that he would not be entirely reluctant to do so. In comparison with two other essays I have included in this collection, "The Nature of Tragedy" and "The *Salesman* Has a Birthday," his comments on tragedy in "Tragedy and the Common Man" may be seen as more absolute, however, than was actually the case at the time of their publication. In "The Nature of Tragedy," published in the *New York Herald Tribune* on March 27, 1949 (one month after "Tragedy and the Common Man"), he proposed several definitions of tragedy, and distinguished between drama and melodrama, drama and tragedy, in terms of "order of feeling":

> Tragedy, first of all, creates a certain order of feeling in the audience. The pathetic creates another order of feeling. Again, as with drama and melodrama, one is higher than the other. But while drama may be differentiated psychologically from melodrama—the higher entailing a conflict *within* each character—to separate tragedy from the mere pathetic is much more difficult. It is difficult because here society enters in.

There is a fairly good game in these early essays for the reader who wishes to follow Miller's theoretical—and sometimes conflicting—comments: in how many ways and under what conditions does he define tragedy as a form and in relation to his own work as playwright? The answer to this question involves a great deal of comparison between essays. It is not to be found, however, entirely within the essays written between 1949 ("Tragedy and the Common Man") and 1956 ("The Family in Modern Drama"). Although *Death of a Salesman* and *The Crucible* are, by my count, the two plays most frequently referred to by Miller in this collection, his major contribution critically for the literature of his time is unquestionably his "Introduction" to the *Collected Plays*. Perhaps no longer concerned with definitions after he wrote the "Introduction," Miller's essays after 1957 concern themselves less and less with the theoretical aspects of his craft and more and more with commentary on the issues and problems of the contemporary theater and production aspects of specific plays.

II

As important and interesting as Miller's early essays on the theoretical nature of drama and tragedy may be for the illumination of his thinking at the time, it is generally recognized that they culminate in the more profound and fully developed commentary of the "Introduction" to the *Collected Plays,* published in 1957. The advance in critical judgment and insight is apparent to even the most casual of readers, especially those who may not have previously considered the very direct relationship between Miller's theory and practice from *Death of a Salesman* to *A View from the Bridge* and his "Introduction." Along with "On Social Plays" (1955), "The Family in Modern Drama" (1956), and "The Shadows of the Gods" (1958), Miller's "Introduction" stands as one of the most important documents in the history of the American theater, if not the most important. Relationships and ideas that were previously developed only partially or passed over in haste are in the "Introduction" expanded and clarified, defined and analyzed as only a playwright of considerable maturity and experience could possibly accomplish within the framework of an essay setting forth first principles and fundamental concepts concerning the nature of his own work.

That such an advance was possible in the relatively short period of five years can be accounted for theoretically purely in terms of the maturation of a playwright who has mastered the fundamental concepts of his craft and who has surpassed his contemporaries in applying form to meaning in its broader philosophical application. While I would not totally disagree with this explanation of Miller's obvious advance in his thought and understanding of dramatic principles, especially as they are brought to bear on his own work, neither am I inclined to agree without some reservation. The factors that contribute to the intellectual maturity and expression of any artist are, as often as not, obscured by a series of social and psychological events that are not always apparent in the reconstruction of artistic creativity. Arthur Miller is an example rather than an exception to this notion, and obviously has survived as an individual and an artist in spite of a succession of crises that occurred during the same five years as his so-called period of rapid intellectual growth and maturity.

Between 1952 and 1957, the years in which some of his most important work was accomplished, Miller saw *The Crucible* through its writing and production in 1953; was denied a passport by the State Department to attend the Brussels premiere of *The Crucible* in 1954; wrote the one-act version of *A View from the Bridge* along with *A Memory of Two Mondays,* and participated in their production; had his political beliefs investigated by the New York City Youth Board after it had cancelled a contract for a film script on juvenile delinquency; was publicly accused of having leftist political connections (all in 1955); was called to testify before the House Committee on Un-American Activities in the time between his divorce from his first wife, Mary Slattery, and his marriage to film actress Marilyn Monroe; wrote and saw produced the expanded two-act version of *A View from the*

Bridge in London, England (all in 1956); and was convicted for contempt of Congress (decision later reversed) for refusing to testify against others in 1957.

In spite of the "Faulknerian" appearance of this chronology stylistically, I have compressed the events into a single sentence within a single paragraph to emphasize that during the same period in which Miller wrote his most important theoretical essays, he also experienced a series of events in his personal life that can hardly be summarized as conducive to philosophical introspection. And yet, numerous critics have pointed out that it was during this period that Miller came to his intellectual maturity as a dramatic critic and theorist of major importance to American drama. The conclusion is right, but if one takes into account the events listed in the above paragraph as well, the phenomenon of Miller's sudden maturity suggests that the experience was equally the result of factors not entirely of an intellectual nature. Miller has implied as much in his comments on *The Crucible* in his "Introduction," but without detailing the full background of the fifties, the Korean War, or his own difficulties politically as a liberal opponent of "McCarthyism." His world, he wrote, changed.

If the reception of *All My Sons* and *Death of a Salesman* had made the world a friendly place for me, events of the early fifties quickly turned that warmth into an illusion. It was not only the rise of "McCarthyism" that moved me, but something which seemed much more weird and mysterious. It was the fact that a political, objective, knowledgeable campaign from the far Right was capable of creating not only a terror, but a new subjective reality, a veritable mystique which was gradually assuming even a holy resonance. The wonder of it all struck me that so practical and picayune a cause, carried forward by such manifestly ridiculous men, should be capable of paralyzing thought itself, and worse, causing to billow up such persuasive clouds of "mysterious" feelings within people. It was as though the whole country had been born anew, without a memory even of certain elemental decencies which a year or two earlier no one would have imagined could be altered, let alone forgotten. Astounded, I watched men pass me by without a nod whom I had known rather well for years; and again, the astonishment was produced by my knowledge, which I could not give up, that the terror in these people was being knowingly planned and consciously engineered, and yet that all they knew was terror. That so interior and subjective an emotion could have been so manifestly created from without was a marvel to me. It underlies every word in *The Crucible*.

Miller's essays have rarely been concerned with simply a technical account of an issue or a description of a process. His comments, although always in relation to his work, become after the "Introduction" to the *Collected Plays* more general reflections on his life and work in relation to the larger issues of the time. It is perhaps indicative of the times rather than Miller that *The Crucible*, set in the days of Salem witchcraft in 1692, was initially received as a political allegory, intended to remind contemporary audiences of the dangers of handing over conscience to the state. In short, the play's subject was apparently, to many critics, not about witchcraft at all, but about the congressional investigations then being conducted by Senator Joseph McCarthy. Miller has said that he could not have written *The Crucible* at any other time, a statement that reflects his reaction both to the McCarthy era and to the creative process by which he finds his way to the thematic center of a play. The two essays in this collection that deal most directly with the historical background of *The Crucible* ("Journey to *The Crucible*," published February 8, 1953, and "Brewed in *The Crucible*," published March 9, 1958) are both newspaper pieces, published soon after the premiere production in 1953 and on the occasion of a revival in 1958. They should be taken in conjunction with Miller's other comments on the play that appear throughout many of his essays, but specifically in his "Introduction," "On Recognition," and in "Arthur Miller: An Interview." These pieces are separated by a span of some thirteen years, and contain slightly different statements from Miller on the play's meaning, origin, and development as it receded into the background of his life.

The Crucible as a play and not a political allegory, however, has always had its supporters and detractors. This is not the place to enter into that discussion, but to point out that since its premiere production in 1953 several generations of theater audiences and readers have appeared for many of whom the term "McCarthyism" has little or no meaning. This is perhaps as it should be, since the play contains significantly larger issues and is more important than merely as a passing commentary on the political moment of the fifties. But the play did open in an atmosphere of suspicion and political witch-hunting, which should not be disregarded as a factor in its history. The critics, Miller has said, were afraid of the theme of the play, which may account for an initial production engagement of only 197 performances between January 22 and July 11, 1953. To Miller, looking back ten years later in the Hopwood lecture "On Recognition," the play had finally become a play and was no longer entangled in the political atmosphere that accompanied its opening.

> *The Crucible* opened in New York in 1954 [1953], at the height of the McCarthy hysteria. It got respectful notices, the kind that bury you decently. It ran a few months and closed. In 1960 [1958], I believe it was, an Off-Broadway production of the play was put on. The same critics reviewed it again, this time with what are called hit notices, which is to say they were fairly swept away, the drama was as real to them as it had seemed cold and undramatic before. Reasons were given for the new impression; the main one was that the script had been improved.
>
> This rather astonished me, since the scripts were exactly the same in both productions. Worse yet, the cast of the original was all in all far superior to the second production. The answer is quite simple; when McCarthy was around, the critics, reflecting the feeling in the audience, were quite simply in fear of the theme of the play, which was witch hunting. In 1960 [1958] they were not afraid of it and they began to look at the play.

If *The Crucible* has become a play instead of a political allegory, it is seen by contemporary audiences more nearly as a cultural and historical study, one that defines and interprets the American character in terms of its past transgressions and diabolical delusions. For many people of a certain age and experience, however, *The Crucible* represents a political and social fact upon which is based the central experience of the fifties—an experience exemplified by John Proctor's question in the play, "Is the accuser always holy now?" And as the political background of *The Crucible* gradually fades away into footnotes, the play's theme and essential theatricality continue to attract new audiences wherever it is presented. Given its vitality and increasing popularity, *The Crucible* may well eventually emerge as Arthur Miller's most enduring play.

Miller has said that nothing in the *Collected Plays* "was written with greater love" than the short and autobiographical *A Memory of Two Mondays*. In many ways, the play looks forward to the full-length exploration of his past in *After the Fall*, and—along with the one-act version of *A View from the Bridge*—was the final play Miller would write for production during the next nine years. Following his expansion of *A View from the Bridge* into two acts in 1956, Miller entered into a period of silence on the stage that has frequently puzzled critics and the general public. Miller has never been prone to write a play simply for production or for its own sake, and has insisted on his artistic prerogative to remain silent when he has nothing to say. There is no particular reason, in my view, to divide a writer's work into periods or to pursue whatever reasons may lie behind periods of either exceptional artistic productivity or a lack of it. It is clear, however, that the publication of the *Collected Plays* marked the end of the first phase of Miller's career.

During his nine-year hiatus from the stage, Miller wrote many plays, none of which he felt would contribute substantially to his previous work or to his current views of society. The essays in this collection that represent that period of Miller's career from

1957 to 1964 are considerably more varied and "occasional" than their predecessors; they generally speak to a specific point such as the revival in 1958 of *The Crucible,* or the publication in 1960 of the revised version of *A View from the Bridge.* I have also included in this section two interviews that seem to raise issues and questions concerning Miller and his work that are unexplored elsewhere in his own writings. It might also be useful to point out that during this same period Miller wrote and had published a fairly large number of social and fictional works, including the screenplay of *The Misfits,* all of which fall outside the subject of this collection of theater essays.

The theater is never far from Miller's thoughts, however, and in "The Shadows of the Gods," written in 1958, he set forth one of his most important statements on his craft and the literary and social conditions that have influenced its development throughout the history of the theater. It was also during his period of silence that Miller's marriage to Marilyn Monroe came to an end in 1960, and a new marriage to his present wife, Inge Morath, began in 1962. Both of these events were to figure prominently in ending the extended silence when his next play appeared in 1964.

III

If the shadow of McCarthyism had fallen over *The Crucible,* the ghost of Marilyn Monroe descended even more heavily on *After the Fall* when the play opened on January 23, 1964. Although Miller had two-thirds of the play written before her death in 1962, the biographical and autobiographical overtones of the Miller-Monroe relationship quickly became the subject of journalistic commentary that was primarily focused on issues and personalities extraneous to the value of the play itself. Miller's return to the Broadway stage with his first play in nine years was more than dramatic, in several ways, and thrust him once again into the center of the critical acclaim and controversy that has consistently surrounded his major work.

In an article not included in this collection ("With Respect for Her Agony—but with Love," published in *Life* magazine on February 7, 1964), Miller attempted to respond to some of the more personal criticism that had been directed against him rather than the play. Although the character of Maggie, he pointed out, may have suggested Marilyn Monroe, she "is not in fact Marilyn Monroe."

> Maggie is a character in a play about the human animal's unwillingness or inability to discover in himself the seeds of his own destruction. Maggie is in this play because she most perfectly exemplifies the self-destructiveness which finally comes when one views oneself as pure victim. And she most perfectly exemplifies this view because she comes so close to being a pure victim—of parents, of a Puritanical sexual code and of her exploitation as an entertainer.

The basis for such "extra-dramatic identification of themes and persons in them," he continued, is the literary "game of Find the Author: Tolstoy, barely concealed behind Pierre in *War and Peace;* Fitzgerald behind Dick Diver; Hemingway behind all his heroes; Goethe, behind Dr. Faustus."

> It is as though fiction, whether in play or novel form, ought to be derived from the thinnest air or it loses its right to some aesthetic category. The fact is that the identification of the artist in his work, while sometimes interesting as gossip, has nothing at all to do with the value of the work— which depends, or ought to, on its general application to other men besides himself.

Despite Miller's statements—defense perhaps is a better term— attempting to return critical discussion to *After the Fall* as a literary and not autobiographical work, the play has continued to suffer or benefit somewhat—depending on the viewpoint— from the association of the character of Maggie with Marilyn Monroe. Perhaps in anticipation of that "identification" as a distraction in future productions, Miller emphatically stated that he believed the play represented "a vision of life":

I believe *After the Fall* to be a dramatic statement of a hidden process which underlies the destructiveness hanging over this age. That elements of my life have been publicized to the point where, in some minds, fiction and design seem to have given way to reportage cannot have prevented me from using my own evidence, any more than if my life were unknown. The time may be close or far away, I do not know, but it will come—as it has for certain other of my plays—when the extra-dramatic identification of themes and persons in them will no longer matter.

I would say now that despite appearances, this play is no more and no less autobiographical than *All My Sons, Death of a Salesman, The Crucible* or *A View from the Bridge.*

In his earlier comments in the "Foreword to *After the Fall,*" published in *The Saturday Evening Post* and which appears in this collection, Miller called the play "a trial; the trial of a man by his own conscience, his own values, his own deeds." The metaphor is appropriate, especially for *After the Fall,* which has as its narrator and central character Quentin, a lawyer who is no longer interested in the law. Miller had used the law and lawyers in his previous plays, but was unaware of the broader legal analogy that extended through his plays indirectly and through his essays directly. In 1963, I happened to mention to him that in all his plays, with the exception of *A Memory of Two Mondays,* and in his novel, *Focus,* he had used the law, lawyers, a policeman, courtrooms, or judges as representatives of truth, justice, and morality. At the time, Miller was nearing completion of *After the Fall,* which, although very different thematically and structurally, also places the protagonist on trial in much the same way that Joe Keller in *All My Sons,* Willy Loman in *Death of a Salesman,* John Proctor in *The Crucible,* and Eddie Carbone in *A View from the Bridge* had also undergone moral and legal litigation.

Although it has not been sufficiently recognized by critics, Miller's dramatic method of contrasting and exemplifying the social and moral dilemmas of American society has always been achieved through a lawyer figure or a representative of the law. His novel *Focus* begins with a man who wakes up in the middle of the night when a woman outside his bedroom window cries, "Police! Police! Please, police!" Later, he is himself beaten and harassed on the street when he is mistakenly believed to be a Jew. The final scene in the novel takes place in a police station as Lawrence Newman reports the incident to a policeman, who also assumes wrongly that he is Jewish. In *All My Sons*, it is the arrival of George Deever, a lawyer, that brings to bear retribution and punishment to Joe Keller for his misdeeds (Kate Keller ends Act One by saying: "He's a lawyer now, Joe. George is a lawyer. ... Be smart now, Joe. The boy is coming. Be smart."); and it is the figure of Bernard in *Death of a Salesman* who functions as a counterbalance to the failure of Biff when he displays a compassion and mercy for Willy Loman on the eve of his departure to argue a case before the Supreme Court. ("The Supreme Court!" Willy says. "And he didn't even mention it!" "He don't have to," Bernard's father replies, "he's gonna do it.")

Although the Puritans did not believe in lawyers or legal training, *The Crucible,* as in the history behind it, is complete with judges, a courtroom, prosecutors, and witnesses. Through the figure of the Reverend Hale, Miller offsets the perversion and betrayal of justice by the court as Hale assumes the role of counselor for the defense, and emerges as a beacon of the middle way upon which justice—moral and social—is finally balanced. In *A View from the Bridge*, it is the lawyer-narrator figure of Alfieri who represents justice not as retribution but as quest. *A View from the Bridge* represents a turning point for Miller in that Alfieri is an observer rather than a participant, and can do nothing to prevent the tragedy he sees about to happen. The law as a social contract is less absolute in *Bridge*, less definable as the ultimate truth. Instead, it is the law of the Sicilian vendetta that places Alfieri in an impossible position in the dispute between Eddie and Marco. In a scene that anticipates Quentin's dilemma over the law by some nine years in *After the Fall*, Alfieri tells

Marco that "not to kill is not dishonorable," to which Marco replies:

MARCO: Then what is done with such a man?
ALFIERI: Nothing. If he obeys the law, he lives. That's all.
MARCO: The law? All the law is not in a book.
ALFIERI: Yes. In a book. There is no other law.
MARCO: He degraded my brother. My blood. He robbed
           my children, he mocks my work. I work to come
           here, mister!
ALFIERI: I know, Marco—
MARCO: There is no law for that? What is the law for
           that?
ALFIERI: There is none.

Miller's increasing emphasis on lawyers and his use of legal analogies as representatives of secular and moral justice from *All My Sons* through *A View from the Bridge* are reflected and refined in his essays written during the corresponding period, and suggest the importance of his intellectual identification with the law as a symbolic and affirmative system of values. There is, again, a rather interesting game here for readers who might wish to follow Miller's extended legal analogies and references throughout this collection of essays. They are his most consistent references, and illuminate his theory in relation to his dramatic practices more clearly than anything else in these pages. For only a few examples, consider the following, all written before he became aware of the legal background in either his plays or essays:

> Now, if it is true that tragedy is the consequence of a man's total compulsion to evaluate himself justly, his destruction in the attempt posits a wrong or an evil in his environment. And this is precisely the morality of tragedy and its lesson. The discovery of the moral law, which is what the enlightenment of tragedy consists of, is not the discovery of some abstract or metaphysical quantity.
>   —From "Tragedy and the Common Man," 1949

> In one sense a play is a species of jurisprudence, and some
> part of it must take the advocate's role, something else must
> act in defense, and the entirety must engage the Law.
>   —From the "Introduction" to the *Collected Plays*, 1957

> A great drama is a great jurisprudence. Balance is all. It
> will evade us until we can once again see man as whole,
> until sensitivity and power, justice and necessity are utterly
> face to face. . . .
>   —From "The Shadows of the Gods," 1958

If in *After the Fall* Miller openly questions the nature of the
law itself, he was at the time of its writing unconscious of the
string of lawyers and legal analogies behind him. Nor does
the open issue of the play appear as the law or even justice. But
Quentin is a lawyer by profession, and the legal metaphor of the
play as a trial is central to understanding the thematic intensity
of his quest for meaning in the midst of chaos. A fluid and flowing play, *After the Fall* is novelistic—a stream-of-consciousness
approach to Quentin's mind, thought, and memory. Perhaps not
so surprisingly, Quentin says he had perceived his past life "like
a case at law. It was a series of proofs," until he reached the point
where the law and his life lost its necessity:

> I think now that my disaster began when I looked up one
> day . . . and the bench was empty. No judge in sight. And all
> that remained was the endless argument with oneself, this
> pointless litigation of existence before an empty bench.

It is perhaps inevitable that *After the Fall* will continue to be
seen and discussed as autobiography and not drama. Miller's
strength as a playwright, however, lies in his ability to give dramatic life to the fundamental assumptions concerning the American experience, its values and inflated sense of self-importance,
through an imaginative and coherent vision of its immense potential for the individual life and consciousness. Like Joseph
Heller, following his success with *Catch-22*, Miller achieved
prominence early in his career, and could have quite easily
chosen to continue his recognition as the author of *Death of a*

Salesman by writing alternate versions such as *Death of a Lawyer, Death of a Doctor,* or perhaps even *Death of a President*—the possibilities seem endless. That he has not chosen to retread the same ground is evidence that, like Heller, who could have continued with *Catch-23, Catch-24, 25, ad infinitum,* he is possessed of courage and insight exceptional for the artistic atmosphere of his time. His further explorations of the present in terms of the past in *Incident at Vichy, The Price,* and *The Creation of the World* have demonstrated once again that he views the theater and his contribution to it as "a serious business, one that makes or should make man more human, which is to say, less alone."

And it is to the "aloneness" of contemporary society that Miller has increasingly directed his thought and plays. *Incident at Vichy* has as its resolution the embodiment of not being alone as an act of individual choice when Von Berg, an Austrian prince, hands his pass to freedom over to Leduc, a Jewish doctor. In *The Price,* Miller returned to his family theme to point out the psychological price they pay for their inability to resolve misunderstandings from the past. Two brothers who have been separated for sixteen years come together briefly, but leave singly and alone by the end of the play. *The Creation of the World* is also about aloneness, the kind that results from moments nearly existential when man stands on the brink between murder and forgiveness, innocence and guilt. And it may be worth pointing out that if Miller has relied less directly on the legal analogies and lawyer figures in his plays since *After the Fall, Incident at Vichy* takes place in a detention room for suspected Jews in Vichy, France, in 1942, and is structured around a police investigation complete with guards and detectives, while *The Price* has as one of its two central characters a policeman, Victor Franz, whose only comment, after spending twenty-five years of his life in the New York City Police Department, is "I've hated every minute of it." Although *The Creation of the World* is based on the Biblical account of Adam and Eve, Cain and Abel, it too is predicated on the consequences of a legal violation that occurred some time ago in the Garden of Eden, and which can be seen metaphorically or literally as a legal precedent of considerable significance to present-day society.

In the essays collected for this volume that appeared following *After the Fall*'s premiere production, Miller's commentary ranges variously and individually from "What Makes Plays Endure?", published in 1965, to "Arthur Miller *vs.* Lincoln Center," published in 1972. Along with his new essay, "Sorting Things Out," that appears on the next few pages, Miller has continued to speak out on whatever issue and subject draws his attention. There is one interview included in this section that is especially informative and penetrating, and serves as a transition between Miller's earlier comments on his work and his later views, looking back from 1966.

As a final note, this collection of twenty-three essays and three interviews has been prepared in the firm belief that Arthur Miller's critical commentaries on drama and the theater should be more accessible to interested readers than they have been in the past. As a continuing expression of a major playwright's engagement with the important issues of his life and art, they represent a major contribution to the criticism and literature of our time. That they are significant seems obvious; that they speak with erudition and cogency to a wide variety of readers is further evidence of their range and authenticity as reflections of the social and theatrical milieu that produced them. It should be equally obvious that in spite of his established position as a playwright and essayist, Arthur Miller is still very much a man in motion, constantly exploring new territories—social and dramatic. Even as I write the final sentences of this introduction, I am reminded of this fact by a letter in which Miller informs me that plans are now underway for the premiere production of a new play, *The Archbishop's Ceiling,* and a new production of *Up from Paradise,* for which he has written twenty-three song lyrics.

The tone of the letter is cautiously optimistic. There is also a piece of fiction nearly completed—a novella, perhaps—as well as several scenes from another play that just might turn out to be a comedy. But there are also problems: problems of production, casting, rehearsals, scheduling difficulties and, above all, time to do the work still in progress.

The letter reflects the man, a playwright first and foremost, who continues to be fully involved and committed to the highest professional standards of his art and craft. A new play and a new musical are ready for production, other works are in various stages of completion, and along with it all, new problems and new difficulties. As a man named Charley once remarked in a different context, "It comes with the territory."

—ROBERT A. MARTIN
The University of Michigan
Ann Arbor, Michigan
April 1977

Introduction to the Expanded Edition

EIGHTEEN years have passed since Robert A. Martin edited *The Theater Essays of Arthur Miller*. In his superb introduction to the original edition Martin celebrates Miller's numerous accomplishments and reports that "Miller's reputation and stature as a writer of unusual talent and insight have increased steadily with the appearance of each of his plays, books, and films." What was true in 1977 is no less true today. Since that time, Miller has written nine new plays, *Fame* (1978), *The American Clock* (1980), *Elegy for a Lady* (1980), *Some Kind of Love Story* (1982), *Clara* (1987), *I Can't Remember Anything* (1987), *The Ride Down Mount Morgan* (1991), *The Last Yankee* (1993), and *Broken Glass* (1994); a screenplay, *Everybody Wins* (1990); an adaptation of Fania Fenelon's memoirs, *Playing for Time* (1980); a book of reportage, *Chinese Encounters* (1979); a memoir about his experiences directing *Death of a Salesman* in the People's Republic of China, *Salesman in Beijing* (1983); his autobiography, *Timebends* (1987); and a novella, *Homely Girl* (1992). In actuality, if 1972—the publication date of the last essay in the original collection—were used as a dividing line instead, Miller's artistic output in this more recent phase of his career would seem even greater, as the number of plays published or produced between 1972 and 1994 actually exceeds what had appeared either in print or on stage before this time period. During the past two decades Miller's enlarged presence in the world theater is also evident in the steady increase in the number of productions of his plays around the globe. On virtually any night one can find a production of his plays on some stage in a major European city. In fact, by Miller's count, in 1989 there were 52 different productions of his plays in Germany alone. His enormous popularity abroad, particularly in Europe and Japan, testifies to his tremendous ability to transcend cultural, ideological, and societal differences with his enlightened vision of the eternal struggle to give authentic meaning to human existence.

Although Miller has always given fresh and rich expression to his artistic vision in plays that are remarkably different from each other in form, style, mood, theme, setting, characterization, plot, and even language, the plays of this later period have noticeable similarities with much of his earlier work. Within their tight constructions and riveting depictions of intense social and psychological conflicts, Miller subtly explores crucial questions that have troubled humankind from time immemorial, but that seem to have even greater relevance to modern life. *Fame* and *The Last Yankee* examine the impact of external forces—social myths in particular—on human identity and mental health; *The American Clock* questions how social dislocation can trigger identity crises; *The Ride Down Mount Morgan* considers the effects of betrayal and guilt on the individual and society. *Playing for Time* and *Broken Glass* explore anti-Semitism, genocide, and the link between public and private acts of cruelty, while *Elegy for a Lady*, *Some Kind of Love Story*, *Clara*, *I Can't Remember Anything*, and *The Ride Down Mount Morgan* question the symbolic nature of reality. With only a few exceptions the family remains the matrix of his drama, for it is here that the individual first experiences the anguish that derives from the inevitable and necessary discovery of one's separateness and personal stance toward the world. As with his early successes, what gives his later work its popular appeal is that, while developing significant thematic concerns, Miller speaks directly about inherent conditions and problems tied specifically to his audiences' personal experiences. In almost all of his plays Miller explodes the myth of private life and emphasizes the value of social responsibility. He extols individuality while simultaneously suggesting that only democratic principles can provide moral solutions to the problems of our age. He espouses a doctrine of freedom that confers upon the individual the power to make independent choices and to convert those choices into noble actions. In Miller's world, freedom necessitates social responsibility. Regardless of the often overwhelming external and internal forces in his characters' lives and their success or failure in meeting personal challenges, the individual in Miller's plays generally has the ability to oppose deterministic forces; to resist destructive impulses from within oneself; to raise oneself from inertia; to oppose any form of injustice; to construct a society based on humanitarian and democratic principles, creating order out of chaos and giving meaning and dignity to human existence.

These issues are also the subjects of Miller's theater essays and interviews. Whether discussing his art form, the modern theater, his literary counterparts, or his own plays, Miller regularly injects his prose with personal comments that expose the values that inspire and shape his artistic vision. While his greatest artistic achievements have undoubtedly occurred in the theater, he has also continued to write insightful, provocative essays that illuminate his stage work and offer compelling perspectives on life and society. This revised and expanded edition of *The Theater Essays* adds fourteen essays and four interviews (published between 1972 and 1994) to the original collection in an effort to update the record of Miller's contribution to the field of theater criticism. This contribution is indeed substantial, for as Bob Martin accurately points out in his introduction, "Arthur Miller's essays on drama and the theater may well represent the single most important statement of critical principles to appear in England or America by a major playwright since the Prefaces of George Bernard Shaw."

The new additions to this collection have been divided into two groups: Part IV, *The Creation of the World and Other Business* to *Timebends,* containing essays and interviews published from 1972 to 1987, and Part V, *Danger: Memory!* to *Broken Glass,* consisting of pieces published between 1988 and 1994. Part IV ends in 1987, the year in which Miller published his extraordinary autobiography, *Timebends.* Not since his introduction to his *Collected Plays* in 1957 has Miller written so lucidly and comprehensively about his craft and his plays. *Timebends,* therefore, stands apart from the rest of his nonfiction in that it provides Miller's principal commentary on his distinguished career. Unfortunately, space limitations necessitate that just an excerpt from this remarkable book be included here. Likewise, only a brief selection from Miller's Salesman *in Beijing* appears in this collection. While not as inclusive as *Timebends* in its discussion of the playwright's art, Salesman *in Bejing* is important for the many insights Miller provides about the play's themes, conflict, and characters as well as for his fascinating discussion of various performance issues raised in *Death of a Salesman* and of the challenges he faced in staging the play in China.

As was the case with the original selections, the new material continues to focus on certain subjects that have interested Miller throughout his career: the nature of tragedy, various forms of realism, theater language, the American theater in the 1930s, problems with theater in America, the demise of Broadway, and the enormous contributions to the modern stage by such playwrights as Ibsen, Strindberg, O'Neill, Odets, and Williams. He also discusses the Greeks and their influence, along with that of Russian writers like Tolstoy and Dostoevsky, on his own artistic vision and sense of dramatic form. Miller comments frequently on several themes that reverberate throughout his drama: the problem with power, the need for personal and social responsibility, the importance of hope, the tension between the individual and society, the past and its unforeseen consequences in the present, the inevitability of alienation, and the problematic nature of reality. While interesting in their own right, these new selections are particularly valuable for the light they shed on the playwright's craft and dramatic work.

The first essay, "Arthur Miller on *The Crucible*" (1972), presents his commentary on Jean-Paul Sartre's screenplay for the 1957 film, *Les Sorcieres de Salem*. Miller develops a motif that recurs in many of these selections: the problem of translating word-based plays into image-based films. While appreciating the visual qualities of the film and the strong performances by its actors, Miller regrets Sartre's Marxist oversimplification of the Salem hysteria. The Marxist approach fails to address the moral issues in his play and the individual's ultimate struggle with himself. This commitment to "truth" and "the moral" in his drama accounts for Bob Martin's astute identification of these twin concepts as "the highest priority in his work."

Miller delivered the speech "The American Writer: The American Theater" (1982) at the University of Michigan on the fiftieth anniversary of the Avery Hopwood Awards. Discussing the state of American theater in the 1930s and his early exposure to stage productions, he credits Clifford Odets with first inspiring him to become a playwright. Miller then addresses other recurring themes: the problem with popular escapist theater and the demise of Broadway. Blaming *The New York Times*'s monopoly of theater criticism, drama critics' inflated sense of their own self-importance, and the exorbitant production costs and high ticket prices in New York City, Miller concludes that American playwrights must now write for audiences in regional theaters.

The March 22 entry from *Salesman in Beijing* (1984) deals primarily with the Chinese cast's first reading of the play. Distinct cultural differences present the playwright-director with a huge obstacle, but he takes comfort in the actors' consistent interpretation of his characters. To help them understand his characters, Miller discusses the way their inner tensions and concerns affect and motivate their behavior. Most of his remarks center on Willy Loman and the inherent nobility in his futile struggle to alter reality. Miller ultimately decides that the play can only succeed if the actors find the Lomans in themselves and help the audience discover our common humanity. This excerpt reveals Miller's interest in performance issues as he regularly comments on his characters' speech rhythms and style of presentation.

The interview "The Will to Live" (1984) identifies striking parallels between the generalized core of meaning in Miller's plays and Jean-Paul Sartre's existentialist philosophy. Rejecting the social-realist tag with which he has been labeled, Miller describes the "dialectic" of existence as the underlying source of tension and conflict in his drama. Offering provocative views of "the Fall" as "the threat of freedom" and guilt as "the consent that one gives to superior power," he also explains how evidence in nature of "the will to live" constantly renews his hope.

In "The Mad Inventor of Modern Drama" (1985) Miller credits August Strindberg with having the greatest impact on modern theater. Without excusing the man's excesses and bizarre traits, he praises Strindberg's dramatic method. According to Miller, the mad Swede derived his power from his unflinching confrontation with the terrors of his soul. His imaginative release of unconscious truths enabled Strindberg to create a drama unshackled by the fetters of rational thought. His boldly innovative style advanced the cause of modernism, freeing others like Eugene O'Neill and Miller himself to experiment with dramatic form. (Miller's appreciation for O'Neill is evident in "A Fabulous Appetite for Greatness" [1988], as he compliments O'Neill's ability to fuse character and theme, style and substance.)

The playwright comments again on the moral point of view in his plays and his characters' search for truth in "An Interview with Arthur Miller" (1985). Miller insists that he is interested in "reality," not "realism," and explains why form is the body that holds the soul of the play. He reserves his most trenchant commentary for his characterization of the American Dream as an "ironical pole" for all storytelling in America. It is an irony that pervades all writing in America, says Miller, including his own.

In the excerpt from *Timebends* (1987) he praises Tennessee Williams and *A Streetcar Named Desire* for opening the possibility for a full range of expression in the theater. According to Miller, Williams's appreciation of words and their power liberated other dramatists and gave Miller the confidence he needed to breathe life into Willy Loman. Miller recalls, however, that before he could work on *Death of a Salesman*, he felt compelled to build a studio in which he could write. Once the construction was done, a two-day burst of creative energy resulted in the composition of Act 1, and six weeks later he finished the play. He then discusses how Lee J. Cobb was cast in the role of Willy Loman for the original Broadway production and makes an interesting comparison between the actor's accommodation to the role and his own creative process.

In "Again They Drink from the Cup of Suspicion" (1989) Miller discusses the origin and nature of his most frequently produced play, *The Crucible*. The guilt he observed in people who feared persecution by Senator McCarthy and his investigators led Miller to the Salem witch trials. What he discovered in both situations was "the dread of social isolation." He then lists successful productions worldwide—including those in the People's Republic of China and in Soviet Georgia as well as Olivier's 1965 National Theatre production and Sartre's screenplay for the French film, *Les Sorcieres de Salem*—and attributes his play's popularity to two factors: its frighteningly real depiction of the irrational that lurks beneath the semblance of order in society, and its confirmation that individual conscience can courageously oppose tyranny.

His introduction (1989) to *The Golden Years* and *The Man Who Had All the Luck* explains how the Great Depression and the spread of Fascism affected his early artistic development. Against this general threat to democracy and individual existence Miller created dramas that asserted the value of individuality and the possibility for freely chosen acts. Not coincidentally, "Conditions of Freedom: Two Plays of the Seventies" (1989) presents a similar view. Approximately 35 years after writing his apprentice plays, *The Golden Years* and *The Man Who Had All the Luck*, Miller again returned to the subject of the Great Depression in *The American Clock* and the debilitating effect of a totalitarian state on individual liberties in *The Archbishop's Ceiling*. Pointing out striking similarities between the 1930s and the 1970s, Miller says *The American Clock* reflects his personal search for a resolution to the Great Depression. His mixture of epic and intimate, comic and tragic, subjective and objective elements in the play's vaudeville-like form achieves a balance without imposing a resolution—precisely the right method, the playwright concludes, to depict the paradoxes of the age. Miller reports that work on *The Archbishop's Ceiling* started at the time of disclosures of the government's electronic bugging efforts at Watergate and various government buildings in Washington, D.C. Inspired by these events and by his own experiences behind the Iron Curtain with Eastern European writers who knew their homes were wiretapped, Miller raises provocative questions about the effects of surveillance on the consciousness of people. Both plays, he asserts, capture the spirit of the 1970s—a time of disillusionment over "the failure to penetrate Power with a more humane and rational point of view."

"A Conversation with Arthur Miller" (1990) reveals his continued interest in morality, the reach of the past, and the symbolic nature of reality. He cogently defends his rejection of absurdism and wryly comments on the absence of the past in contemporary drama and film. Perhaps the most fascinating part of the discussion, however, is his identification of writers and works that most inspired him: the Greeks, particularly Sophocles; Shakespeare's *Hamlet* and *Lear*; Melville's *Moby Dick*; Synge's *The Playboy of the Western World*; O'Casey's *Juno and The Paycock*; and the Russian writers like Tolstoy, Gogol, and Dostoevsky, especially his novel *The Brothers Karamazov*. In the excerpt from *Arthur Miller and Company* (1990) Miller acknowledges his preference for certain actors who have played Willy Loman. Selecting Warren Mitchell, Lee J. Cobb, and Dustin Hoffman for the individual talents and perspectives they brought to the role, Miller concludes that Hoffman's Willy is the best.

Miller's whimsical introduction to *Plays: Three* (1990) amply displays his tremendous skill in sustaining an ironic tone. Here he defines two kinds of theater: the Majority and the Other. The Majority consists of the standard fare of musicals, comedies, melodramas, and farces that routinely make their way to Broadway, while the Other embraces non-escapist drama that shakes the audience from its tired complacency and challenges it to think critically about the play's themes and the prevailing, typically tragic, conditions of life. Miller wrote this essay while preparing to premiere *The Ride Down Mount Morgan* in London, the only time in his career that he chose to introduce a new play outside the United States. That decision was due largely to his dissatisfaction with the state of the theater profession in New York City. In keeping with his past concerns over the disturbing and ever-worsening conditions on Broadway, this essay leaves no doubt about Miller's position. In a more muted tone a similar perspective appears in the essay "We Are Probably in an Art That Is—Not Dying" (1993). Miller blames the decline of American theater on several factors: high production and tickets costs, restricted audiences, and the difficulty in finding actors for stage productions due to the theater's competition with higher paying and less demanding work in television and films. He grimly concludes that while the theater profession in New York is not dead, the problem, if left unaddressed, could become terminal.

"On Screenwriting and Language," Miller's preface to *Everybody Wins* (1990), examines the inherent difference between playwriting and screenwriting. Confessing his bias against screenwriting, he points out the essential difference between writing for theater and writing for cinema: plays suggest through words, whereas films indicate through images. A screenplay, says Miller, serves other elements in the film, but in theater other people serve the play. Even more significantly, the powerful presentation of images in cinema requires only a passive audience response. The emphasis on words in the theater demands an active and imaginative involvement from the audience.

"About Theater Language" (1994), one of Miller's most valuable contributions from this later phase of his career, clarifies a distinction first raised in 1955 in his "On Social Plays": the difference between prose and poetry in the theater. By Miller's definition prose realism deals with the real and requires the language of the private person. Its aim and main achievement is "verisimilitude." Social drama, on the other hand, deals with the symbolic and requires a "poetic dramatic language." Miller credits Odets with first expanding the range of poetic dialogue in American theater. His unconventional, stylized expressions represented a departure from the realistic theater of his day. Miller then relates these observations to his own style in *The Last Yankee*. While the play appears to be realistic on the surface, "its action is overtly stylized rather than 'natural.'" The "split vision" evident in this play, Miller notes, can be found in all of his dramatic output. It is created by the reciprocal repulsion exerted upon his work by the realistic surface tone and the underlying "thematic selectivity."

Appropriately enough, the last essay, "Ibsen and the Drama of Today" (1994), pays homage to the writer who most influenced Miller at the start of his career. He explains that people read Ibsen in America in the 1930s for his ideas, not his language, which did not translate well into English. He then credits Ibsen with teaching him how to show the present consequences of past actions in his dramas. Expressing this lesson in one of his favorite sayings, Miller writes: "Every catastrophe was the story of how the birds came home to roost." Even though Ibsen has been out of fashion because of the influence of Absurdism and the disappearance of the past in contemporary film and theater, Miller concludes that the great Norwegian will be rediscovered by playwrights who turn to life for inspiration and find in life ample evidence that the past is always present.

The essays and interviews added to this edition in no way constitute the full body of critical writings by Arthur Miller during this later phase of his career. The list of his nonfiction is long and continues to grow, for he regularly publishes essays on a host of subjects in various periodicals. These pieces were chosen because they complement and comment on his work in the theater; they chronicle major developments in his art and in the American theater; they shed light on his intentions and provide insight into the dramatic methods he employs; and they give us a personal glimpse of Arthur Miller, whose values and vision inform and define the shape and content of his drama. I regret that anything had to be left out due to space limitations, but hope that the present selections sufficiently convey the range and style of his theater criticism, and that this new edition of *The Theater Essays* will lead the reader to a greater appreciation and understanding of the tremendous talents of this outstanding American playwright.

—Steven R. Centola
Millersville University
Millersville, Pennsylvania
March 1996

Author's Foreword:
Sorting Things Out

I FIND it hard to read through these essays without wanting to make changes on each page and often in each sentence. Nothing written about the theater ever comes out right, the thing is forever escaping its commentators.

I am a little surprised that I have written so much on the subject in the past thirty years, and it is hard now to remember what drove me to it. I think it may have been the feeling that it was being trivialized in most published commentary at a time when I thought it the most important thing in the world. It could be of some great importance, I still think, if we ever get it beyond the childish delights of the commercial hit-flop situation.

I have not so much changed my opinions about certain issues as added to what I believed, but I have often wished that I had never written a word on the subject of tragedy. I am not a scholar, not a critic, and my interest in the phenomenon was and is purely practical, so that having delivered myself of certain views I only unwittingly entered an arena of near-theological devoutness which I had not known existed. The damage having been done, however, there is no further reason to withhold new thoughts, which may or may not line up with those of the ancients and their modern heirs.

I have not yet seen a convincing explanation of why the tragic mode seems anachronistic now, nor am I about to attempt one. But it has often seemed to me that what tragedy requires—

of the artist first and of the audience thereafter—is a kind of grief without which the tragic area somehow cannot be approached. Instead of grief we have come to substitute irony and even comedy, black or otherwise. I am too lazy to go back to Aristotle, but I do not recall his mentioning grief; most probably because he took for granted that his hero's catastrophe would entail that emotion all by itself.

It is probably not that we have lost the capacity to grieve, but that we have misplaced the ritual through which grief can be shown to others and shared. Of course the waning of organized religion is a factor, but I wonder if it is not more a result than a cause. And I wonder, too, if we are awkward about grieving because the loss of one person evokes in us only the paradoxical fact of death without the straightforward and clear image of a sacred identity that has vanished. Rather, we know that nothing and no one is truly sacred, but that a biological set of forces have been used up so that there is something faintly fatuous, something perhaps operatic, in the kind of grief-outbreak which underlies the real tragedies as they approach their moments of terror and death.

If we are this way—rationalized and beyond the reach of public grief—it is interesting to wonder why it has happened. And inevitably there arise the images of the carnage of two world wars, the many revolutions and counter-revolutions, the Nazi Holocaust—this, after all, has been the most spendthrift of all centuries with human lives. Perhaps the public psyche has simply been overloaded and, like an electrical circuit, has blown its fuse and gone cold under the weight of too many impulses. So that the tragic proposal is simply presumptuous—this making so much out of one death when we know it is meaningless. In other words, in an important respect we have ceased to feel.

I would agree, except that we can still respond to the old tragedies as much as people apparently did in early times. Is this merely nostalgia? It doesn't seem so in the theater.

My own view, or at least my leaning, is toward a less alarming explanation. Clearly, however tragedy is defined or explained, it must allow the hero to speak for himself. This may sound so rudimentary as not to be worth discussing, but in contemporary drama few major characters are allowed this privilege, it being assumed that something like naturalism is one thing we can't have. What we have instead are forms of authorial ironical comment or directorial interpretation of the character's situation total enough to wipe out his autonomy entirely. We are being spared the incoherence of the character's feeling for the coherence of our own interpretation, which allows us to observe the outlines of suffering without very much participation in it. Thus, it is absurd to attempt the kind of protest that tragedy always has entailed, a cry against heaven, fate, or what you will. That cry may still be implicit, but it has been stylized into a glance upwards or even a grin and a cough. From one or another philosophical points of view this makes lots of sense, but is it really the viewpoint of the sufferer or of the one observing him? If we could get this sorted out, we might well see tragic emotions forming again.

What I think has been forgotten is that the objectivity of a Shakespeare is expressed through his form—the balancing of responsibility between various persons, interests, and forces—but that the sufferings that result are not at all objectified, dried up, or gentled. It may be we have lost the art of tragedy for want of a certain level of self-respect, finally, and are in disgrace with ourselves. Compared to the tragic emotion, the others are covered with a certain embarrassment, even shame, as though suffering were a sign of one's failure or a loss of dignity, like being caught with a hole in one's stocking at an affair of state. People not free enough to weep or cry out are not fit subjects for tragedy, at least not on the stage, and weeping without self-respect is mere self-pity.

As for the sociology in these pieces, I still support its main point, the need to subsidize the American theater. I have had far more experience with such theaters abroad than I had decades ago, and I would add now that a mixed private and public theater would be the most useful rather than a monopoly by either type.

A subsidy is a form of power that always tends toward bureau-cratization and needs challenging from outside the organization. We are still, at this writing, paying less for the upkeep of theater art than any other viable nation.

Finally, there is a question of tone in these pieces—an over-emphasis here and there on what has already been proved. I would ask the reader to remember that an unspoken gentleman's agreement was prevalent in the 1940s and 50s, if not earlier, under which every playwright had to present himself to critics and the public as a pure entertainer, a man in an aesthetic daze who barely knew the name of the president or how to negotiate a sub-way turnstile. This image was good for business, conforming to the Anglo-Saxon tradition of the separation of church and state, poesy and instruction, form and meaning. A play, needless to say, could not teach without exploding into its several parts, so that the most authentically aesthetic of experiences was necessarily the one without any perceptible reference to society or life as it was lived. The exception was George Bernard Shaw, but only because he was funny, and funny in a definitely aristocratic man-ner that gave him license to preach the virtues of a socialism of wits and a capitalism whose horrors were familiar, somehow warm, and somehow bearable after all.

Thus, the lessons of a play, its meaning and theme, had to spread out like a contagion if they were to be aesthetic, in which case few would be aware they were even infected. In a word, what I was trying to do was to objectify the social situation of our theater, and even of some of the creative procedures that pro-duced one style of playwriting or another, rather than leaving these matters—as our critics normally did—to temperament and taste without deeper reason or cause.

Nevertheless and notwithstanding, the theater is first of all imitation, mimickry. If anything contrary is found in these pieces, it was not intended to be there. We need food, sex, and an image. The rest is commentary on these.

—ARTHUR MILLER

1977

I

Death of a Salesman to *A View from the Bridge*

"I am not a dime a dozen! I am Willy Loman, and you are Biff Loman!"
—Willy Loman in *Death of a Salesman*

"Charley, the man didn't know who he was."
—Biff Loman at Willy's grave

Tragedy and the Common Man

In this age few tragedies are written. It has often been held that the lack is due to a paucity of heroes among us, or else that modern man has had the blood drawn out of his organs of belief by the skepticism of science, and the heroic attack on life cannot feed on an attitude of reserve and circumspection. For one reason or another, we are often held to be below tragedy—or tragedy above us. The inevitable conclusion is, of course, that the tragic mode is archaic, fit only for the very highly placed, the kings or the kingly, and where this admission is not made in so many words it is most often implied.

I believe that the common man is as apt a subject for tragedy in its highest sense as kings were. On the face of it this ought to be obvious in the light of modern psychiatry, which bases its analysis upon classic formulations, such as the Oedipus and Orestes complexes, for instances, which were enacted by royal beings, but which apply to everyone in similar emotional situations.

More simply, when the question of tragedy in art is not at issue, we never hesitate to attribute to the well-placed and the exalted the very same mental processes as the lowly. And finally, if the exaltation of tragic action were truly a property of the

From *The New York Times,* February 27, 1949, Sec. 2, pp. 1, 3. The appearance of this essay followed closely upon the opening of *Death of a Salesman* at the Morosco Theatre on February 10, 1949. Copyright 1949 by Arthur Miller, Copyright © renewed 1977 by Arthur Miller.

high-bred character alone, it is inconceivable that the mass of mankind should cherish tragedy above all other forms, let alone be capable of understanding it.

As a general rule, to which there may be exceptions unknown to me, I think the tragic feeling is evoked in us when we are in the presence of a character who is ready to lay down his life, if need be, to secure one thing—his sense of personal dignity. From Orestes to Hamlet, Medea to Macbeth, the underlying struggle is that of the individual attempting to gain his "rightful" position in his society.

Sometimes he is one who has been displaced from it, sometimes one who seeks to attain it for the first time, but the fateful wound from which the inevitable events spiral is the wound of indignity, and its dominant force is indignation. Tragedy, then, is the consequence of a man's total compulsion to evaluate himself justly.

In the sense of having been initiated by the hero himself, the tale always reveals what has been called his "tragic flaw," a failing that is not peculiar to grand or elevated characters. Nor is it necessarily a weakness. The flaw, or crack in the character, is really nothing—and need be nothing—but his inherent unwillingness to remain passive in the face of what he conceives to be a challenge to his dignity, his image of his rightful status. Only the passive, only those who accept their lot without active retaliation, are "flawless." Most of us are in that category.

But there are among us today, as there always have been, those who act against the scheme of things that degrades them, and in the process of action everything we have accepted out of fear or insensitivity or ignorance is shaken before us and examined, and from this total onslaught by an individual against the seemingly stable cosmos surrounding us—from this total examination of the "unchangeable" environment—comes the terror and the fear that is classically associated with tragedy.

More important, from this total questioning of what has previously been unquestioned, we learn. And such a process is not beyond the common man. In revolutions around the world, these past thirty years, he has demonstrated again and again this inner dynamic of all tragedy.

Insistence upon the rank of the tragic hero, or the so-called nobility of his character, is really but a clinging to the outward forms of tragedy. If rank or nobility of character was indispensable, then it would follow that the problems of those with rank were the particular problems of tragedy. But surely the right of one monarch to capture the domain from another no longer raises our passions, nor are our concepts of justice what they were to the mind of an Elizabethan king.

The quality in such plays that does shake us, however, derives from the underlying fear of being displaced, the disaster inherent in being torn away from our chosen image of what and who we are in this world. Among us today this fear is as strong, and perhaps stronger, than it ever was. In fact, it is the common man who knows this fear best.

Now, if it is true that tragedy is the consequence of a man's total compulsion to evaluate himself justly, his destruction in the attempt posits a wrong or an evil in his environment. And this is precisely the morality of tragedy and its lesson. The discovery of the moral law, which is what the enlightenment of tragedy consists of, is not the discovery of some abstract or metaphysical quantity.

The tragic right is a condition of life, a condition in which the human personality is able to flower and realize itself. The wrong is the condition which suppresses man, perverts the flowing out of his love and creative instinct. Tragedy enlightens— and it must, in that it points the heroic finger at the enemy of man's freedom. The thrust for freedom is the quality in tragedy which exalts. The revolutionary questioning of the stable environment is what terrifies. In no way is the common man debarred from such thoughts or such actions.

Seen in this light, our lack of tragedy may be partially accounted for by the turn which modern literature has taken toward the purely psychiatric view of life, or the purely sociological. If all our miseries, our indignities, are born and bred within our minds, then all action, let alone the heroic action, is obviously impossible.

And if society alone is responsible for the cramping of our lives, then the protagonist must needs be so pure and faultless as to force us to deny his validity as a character. From neither of these views can tragedy derive, simply because neither represents a balanced concept of life. Above all else, tragedy requires the finest appreciation by the writer of cause and effect.

No tragedy can therefore come about when its author fears to question absolutely everything, when he regards any institution, habit or custom as being either everlasting, immutable or inevitable. In the tragic view the need of man to wholly realize himself is the only fixed star, and whatever it is that hedges his nature and lowers it is ripe for attack and examination. Which is not to say that tragedy must preach revolution.

The Greeks could probe the very heavenly origin of their ways and return to confirm the rightness of laws. And Job could face God in anger, demanding his right and end in submission. But for a moment everything is in suspension, nothing is accepted, and in this stretching and tearing apart of the cosmos, in the very action of so doing, the character gains "size," the tragic stature which is spuriously attached to the royal or the highborn in our minds. The commonest of men may take on that stature to the extent of his willingness to throw all he has into the contest, the battle to secure his rightful place in his world.

There is a misconcepion of tragedy with which I have been struck in review after review, and in many conversations with writers and readers alike. It is the idea that tragedy is of necessity allied to pessimism. Even the dictionary says nothing more about the word than that it means a story with a sad or unhappy ending. This impression is so firmly fixed that I almost hesitate to claim that in truth tragedy implies more optimism in its author than does comedy, and that its final result ought to be the reinforcement of the onlooker's brightest opinions of the human animal.

For, if it is true to say that in essence the tragic hero is intent upon claiming his whole due as a personality, and if this struggle must be total and without reservation, then it automatically demonstrates the indestructible will of man to achieve his humanity.

The possibility of victory must be there in tragedy. Where pathos rules, where pathos is finally derived, a character has fought a battle he could not possibly have won. The pathetic is achieved when the protagonist is, by virtue of his witlessness, his insensitivity or the very air he gives off, incapable of grappling with a much superior force.

Pathos truly is the mode for the pessimist. But tragedy requires a nicer balance between what is possible and what is impossible. And it is curious, although edifying, that the plays we revere, century after century, are the tragedies. In them, and in them alone, lies the belief—optimistic, if you will, in the perfectibility of man.

It is time, I think, that we who are without kings, took up this bright thread of our history and followed it to the only place it can possibly lead in our time—the heart and spirit of the average man.

The Nature of Tragedy

THERE are whole libraries of books dealing with the nature of tragedy. That the subject is capable of interesting so many writers over the centuries is part proof that the idea of tragedy is constantly changing, and more, that it will never be finally defined.

In our day, however, when there seems so little time or inclination to theorize at all, certain elemental misconceptions have taken hold of both critics and readers to a point where the word has often been reduced to an epithet. A more exact appreciation of what tragedy entails can lead us all to a finer understanding of plays in general, which in turn may raise the level of our theater.

The most common confusion is that which fails to discriminate between the tragic and the pathetic. Any story, to have validity on the stage, must entail conflict. Obviously the conflict must be between people. But such a conflict is of the lowest, most elementary order; this conflict purely *between* people is all that is needed for melodrama and naturally reaches its apogee in physical violence. In fact, this kind of conflict defines melodrama.

The next rung up the ladder is the story which is not only a conflict between people, but at the same time within the minds of the combatants. When I show you why a man does what he

From *The New York Herald Tribune*, March 27, 1949, Sec. 5, pp. 1, 2. Copyright 1949 by Arthur Miller, Copyright © renewed 1977 by Arthur Miller.

does, I may do so melodramatically; but when I show why he almost did not do it, I am making drama.

Why is this higher? Because it more closely reflects the actual process of human action. It is quite possible to write a good melodrama without creating a single living character; in fact, melodrama becomes diffused wherever the vagaries and contradictions of real characterizations come into play. But without a living character it is not possible to create drama or tragedy. For as soon as one investigates not only why a man is acting, but what is trying to prevent him from acting—assuming one does so honestly—it becomes extremely difficult to contain the action in the forced and arbitrary form of melodrama.

Now, standing upon this element of drama we can try to reach toward tragedy. Tragedy, first of all, creates a certain order of feeling in the audience. The pathetic creates another order of feeling. Again, as with drama and melodrama, one is higher than the other. But while drama may be differentiated psychologically from melodrama—the higher entailing a conflict *within* each character—to separate tragedy from the mere pathetic is much more difficult. It is difficult because here society enters in.

Let me put it this way. When Mr. B., while walking down the street, is struck on the head by a falling piano, the newspapers call this a tragedy. In fact, of course, this is only the pathetic end of Mr. B. Not only because of the accidental nature of his death; that is elementary. It is pathetic because it merely arouses our feelings of sympathy, sadness, and possibly of identification. What the death of Mr. B. does not arouse is the tragic feeling.

To my mind the essential difference, and the precise difference, between tragedy and pathos is that tragedy brings us not only sadness, sympathy, identification and even fear; it also, unlike pathos, brings us knowledge or enlightenment.

But what sort of knowledge? In the largest sense, it is knowledge pertaining to the right way of living in the world. The manner of Mr. B.'s death was not such as to illustrate any principle of living. In short, there was no illumination of the ethical in it. And to put it all in the same breath, the reason we confuse the tragic with the pathetic, as well as why we create so few tragedies, is twofold: in the first place many of our writers have given up trying to search out the right way of living, and secondly, there is not among us any commonly accepted faith in a way of life that will give us not only material gain but satisfaction.

Our modern literature has filled itself with an attitude which implies that despite suffering, nothing important can really be learned by man that might raise him to a happier condition. The probing of the soul has taken the path of behaviorism. By this method it is sufficient for an artist simply to spell out the anatomy of disaster. Man is regarded as essentially a dumb animal moving through a preconstructed maze toward his inevitable sleep.

Such a concept of man can never reach beyond pathos, for enlightenment is impossible within it, life being regarded as an immutably disastrous fact. Tragedy, called a more exalted kind of consciousness, is so called because it makes us aware of what the character might have been. But to say or strongly imply what a man might have been requires of the author a soundly based, completely believed vision of man's great possibilities. As Aristotle said, the poet is greater than the historian because he presents not only things as they were, but foreshadows what they might have been. We forsake literature when we are content to chronicle disaster.

Tragedy, therefore, is inseparable from a certain modest hope regarding the human animal. And it is the glimpse of this brighter possibility that raises sadness out of the pathetic toward the tragic.

But, again, to take up a sad story and discover the hope that may lie buried in it, requires a most complete grasp of the characters involved. For nothing is so destructive of reality in literature as thinly motivated optimism. It is my view—or my prejudice—that when a man is seen whole and round and so characterized, when he is allowed his life on the stage over and beyond the mould and purpose of the story, hope will show its face in his, just as it does, even so dimly, in life. As the old saying has it, there is some good in the worst of us. I think that the tragedian, supposedly the saddest of citizens, can never forget this fact, and must strive always to posit a world in which that good might have been allowed to express itself instead of sucumbing to the evil. I began by saying that tragedy would probably never be wholly defined. I end by offering you a definition. It is not final for me, but at least it has the virtue of keeping mere pathos out.

You are witnessing a tragedy when the characters before you are wholly and intensely realized, to the degree that your belief in their reality is all but complete. The story in which they are involved is such as to force their complete personalities to be brought to bear upon the problem, to the degree that you are able to understand not only why they are ending in sadness, but how they might have avoided their end. The demeanor, so to speak, of the story is most serious—so serious that you have been brought to the state of outright fear for the people involved, as though for yourself.

And all this, not merely so that your senses shall have been stretched and your glands stimulated, but that you may come away with the knowledge that man, by reason of his intense effort and desire, which you have just seen demonstrated, is capable of flowering on this earth.

Tragedy arises when we are in the presence of a man who has missed accomplishing his joy. But the joy must be there, the promise of the right way of life must be there. Otherwise pathos reigns, and an endless, meaningless, and essentially untrue picture of man is created—man helpless under the falling piano, man wholly lost in a universe which by its very nature is too hostile to be mastered.

In a word, tragedy is the most accurately balanced portrayal of the human being in his struggle for happiness. That is why we revere our tragedies in the highest, because they most truly portray us. And that is why tragedy must not be diminished through confusion with other modes, for it is the most perfect means we have of showing us who and what we are, and what we must be—or should strive to become.

The *Salesman* Has a Birthday

EXPERIENCE tells me that I will probably know better next year what I feel right now about the first anniversary of *Death of a Salesman*—it usually takes that long to understand anything. I suppose I ought to try to open some insights into the play. Frankly, however, it comes very fuzzily to mind at this date. I have not sat through it since dress rehearsal and haven't read it since the proofs went to the publisher. In fact, it may well be that from the moment I read it to my wife and two friends one evening in the country a year ago last fall, the play cut itself off from me in a way that is incomprehensible.

I remember that night clearly, best of all. The feeling of disaster when, glancing up at the audience of three, I saw nothing but glazed looks in their eyes. And at the end, when they said nothing, the script suddenly seemed a record of a madness I had passed through, something I ought not admit to at all, let alone read aloud or have produced on the stage.

I don't remember what they said, exactly, excepting that it had taken them deeply. But I can see my wife's eyes as I read a—to me—hilarious scene, which I prefer not to identify. She was weeping. I confess that I laughed more during the writing of this play than I have ever done, when alone, in my life. I laughed

From *The New York Times*, February 5, 1950, Sec. 2, pp. 1, 3. Copyright 1950 by Arthur Miller.

because moment after moment came when I felt I had rapped it right on the head—the non sequitur, the aberrant but meaningful idea racing through Willy's head, the turn of story that kept surprising me every morning. And most of all the form, for which I have been searching since the beginning of my writing life.

Writing in that form was like moving through a corridor in a dream, knowing instinctively that one would find every wriggle of it and, best of all, where the exit lay. There is something like a dream's quality in my memory of the writing and the day or two that followed its completion.

I remember the rehearsal when we had our first audience. Six or seven friends. The play working itself out under the single bulb overhead. I think that was the first and only time I saw it as others see it. Then it seemed to me that we must be a terribly lonely people, cut off from each other by such massive pretense of self-sufficiency, machined down so fine we hardly touch any more. We are trying to save ourselves separately, and that is immoral, that is the corrosive among us.

On that afternoon, more than any time before or since, the marvel of the actor was all new to me. How utterly they believed what they were saying to each other!

To watch fine actors creating their roles is to see revealed the innocence, the naïve imagination of man liberated from the prisons of the past. They were like children wanting to show that they could turn themselves into anybody, thus opening their lives to limitless possibilities.

And Elia Kazan, with his marvelous wiles, tripping the latches of the secret little doors that lead into the always different personalities of each actor. That is his secret; not merely to know what must be done, to know the way to implement the doing for actors trained in diametrically opposite schools, or not trained at all. He does not "direct," he creates a center point, and then goes to each actor and creates the desire to move toward it. And they all meet, but for different reasons, and seem to have arrived there by themselves.

Was there ever a production of so serious a play that was carried through with so much exhilarating laughter? I doubt it. We were always on the way, and I suppose we always knew it.

There are things learned—I think, by many people—from this production. Things which, if applied, can bring much vitality to our theater.

There is no limit to the expansion of the audience's imagination so long as the play's internal logic is kept inviolate. It is not true that conventionalism is demanded. They will move with you anywhere; they will believe right into the moon so long as you believe who tell them this tale. We are at the beginning of many explosions of form. They are waiting for wonders.

A serious theme is entertaining to the extent that it is not trifled with, not cleverly angled, but met in head-on collision. They will not consent to suffer while the creators stand by with tongue in cheek. They have a way of knowing. Nobody can blame them.

And there have been certain disappointments, one above all. I am sorry the self-realization of the older son, Biff, is not a weightier counterbalance to Willy's disaster in the audience's mind.

And certain things are more clearly known, or so it seems now. We want to give of ourselves, and yet all we train for is to take, as though nothing less will keep the world at a safe distance. Every day we contradict our will to create, which is to give. The end of man is not security, but without security we are without the elementary condition of humaneness.

A time will come when they will look back at us astonished that we saw something holy in the competition for the means of existence. But already we are beginning to ask of the great man, not what has he got, but what has he done for the world. We ought to be struggling for a world in which it will be possible to lay blame. Only then will the great tragedies be written, for where no order is believed in, no order can be breached, and thus all disasters of man will strive vainly for moral meaning.

And what have such thoughts to do with this sort of reminiscence? Only that to me the tragedy of Willy Loman is that he gave his life, or sold it, in order to justify the waste of it. It is the tragedy of a man who did believe that he alone was not meeting the qualifications laid down for mankind by those clean-shaven frontiersmen who inhabit the peaks of broadcasting and advertising offices. From those forests of canned goods high up near the sky, he heard the thundering command to succeed as it ricocheted down the newspaper-lined canyons of his city, heard not a human voice, but a wind of a voice to which no human can reply in kind, except to stare into the mirror at a failure.

So what is there to feel on this anniversary? Hope, for I know now that the people want to listen. A little fear that they want to listen so badly. And an old insistence—sometimes difficult to summon, but there nonetheless—that we will find a way beyond fear of each other, beyond bellicosity, a way into our humanity.

Preface to
an Adaptation of Ibsen's
An Enemy of the People

AT the outset it ought to be said that the word "adaptation" is very distasteful to me. It seems to mean that one writer has ventured into another's chickencoop, or worse, into the sacred chamber of another's personal creations and rearranged things without permission. Most of the time an adaptation is a playwright's excuse for not writing his own plays, and since I am not yet with my back against that particular wall, I think it wise to set down what I have tried to do with *An Enemy of the People,* and why I did it.

There is one quality in Ibsen that no serious writer can afford to overlook. It lies at the very center of his force, and I found in it—as I hope others will—a profound source of strength. It is his insistence, his utter conviction, that he is going to say what he has to say, and that the audience, by God, is going to listen. It is the very same quality that makes a star actor, a great public speaker, and a lunatic. Every Ibsen play begins with the unwritten words: "Now listen here!" And these words have shown me a path through the wall of "entertainment," a path that leads beyond the formulas and dried-up precepts, the pretense and fraud, of the business of the stage. Whatever else Ibsen has to teach, this is his first and greatest contribution.

From *An Enemy of the People* (New York: Viking, 1951), pp. 7–12. Miller's adaptation of Henrik Ibsen's play. Copyright 1950, 1951 by Arthur Miller.

In recent years Ibsen has fallen into a kind of respectful obscurity that is not only undeserved but really quite disrespectful of culture—and a disservice to the theater besides. I decided to work on *An Enemy of the People* because I had a private wish to demonstrate that Ibsen is really pertinent today, that he is not "old-fashioned," and, implicitly, that those who condemn him are themselves misleading our theater and our playwrights into a blind alley of senseless sensibility, triviality, and the inevitable waste of our dramatic talents; for it has become the fashion for plays to reduce the "thickness" of life to a fragile facsimile, to avoid portraying the complexities of life, the contradictions of character, the fascinating interplay of cause and effect that have long been part of the novel. And I wished also to buttress the idea that the dramatic writer has, and must again demonstrate, the right to entertain with his brains as well as his heart. It is necessary that the public understand again that the stage is *the* place for ideas, for philosophies, for the most intense discussion of man's fate. One of the masters of such a discussion is Henrik Ibsen, and I have presumed to point this out once again.

I have attempted to make *An Enemy of the People* as alive to Americans as it undoubtedly was to Norwegians, while keeping it intact. I had no interest in exhuming anything, in asking people to sit respectfully before the work of a celebrated but neglected writer. There are museums for such activities; the theater has no truck with them, and ought not to have.

And I believe this play could be alive for us because its central theme is, in my opinion, the central theme of our social life today. Simply, it is the question of whether the democratic guarantees protecting political minorities ought to be set aside in time of crisis. More personally, it is the question of whether one's vision of the truth ought to be a source of guilt at a time when the mass of men condemn it as a dangerous and devilish lie. It is an enduring theme—in fact, possibly the most enduring of all Ibsen's themes—because there never was, nor will there ever be, an organized society able to countenance calmly the individual who insists that he is right while the vast majority is absolutely wrong.

The play is the story of a scientist who discovers an evil and, innocently believing that he has done a service to humanity, expects that he will at least be thanked. However, the town has a vested interest in the perpetuation of that evil, and his "truth," when confronted with that interest, must be made to conform. The scientist cannot change the truth for any reason disconnected with the evil. He clings to the truth and suffers the social consequences. At rock bottom, then, the play is concerned with the inviolability of objective truth. Or, put more dynamically, that those who attempt to warp the truth for ulterior purposes must inevitably become warped and corrupted themselves. This theme is valid today, just as it will always be, but some of the examples given by Ibsen to prove it may no longer be.

I am told that Ibsen wrote this play as a result of his being practically stoned off the stage for daring to present *Ghosts*. The plot is supposed to have come from a news item which told of a Hungarian scientist who had discovered poisoned water in the town's water supply and had been pilloried for his discovery. If this was the case, my interpretation of the theme is doubly justified, for it then seems beyond doubt that Ibsen meant above and beyond all else to defend his right to stand "at the outpost of society," alone with the truth, and to speak from there to his fellow men.

However, there are a few speeches, and one scene in particular, which have been taken to mean that Ibsen was a fascist. In the original meeting scene in which Dr. Stockmann sets forth his—and Ibsen's—point of view most completely and angrily, Dr. Stockmann makes a speech in which he turns to biology to prove that there are indeed certain individuals "bred" to a superior apprehension of truths and who have the natural right to lead, if not to govern, the mass.

If the entire play is to be understood as the working-out of this speech, then one has no justification for contending that it is other than racist and fascist—certainly it could not be thought of as a defense of any democratic idea. But, structurally speaking, the theme is not wholly contained in the meeting scene alone. In fact, this speech is in some important respects in contradiction to the actual dramatic working-out of the play. But that Ibsen never really believed that idea in the first place is amply proved by a speech he delivered to a workers' club after the production of *An Enemy of the People*. He said then: "Of course I do not mean the aristocracy of birth, or of the purse, or even the aristocracy of the intellect. I mean the aristocracy of character, of will, of mind—that alone can free us."

I have taken as justification for removing those examples which no longer prove the theme—examples I believe Ibsen would have removed were he alive today—the line in the original manuscript that reads: "There is no established truth that can remain true for more than seventeen, eighteen, at most twenty years." In light of genocide, the holocaust that has swept our world on the wings of the black ideology of racism, it is inconceivable that Ibsen would insist today that certain individuals are by breeding, or race, or "innate" qualities superior to others or possessed of the right to dictate to others. The man who wrote *A Doll's House*, the clarion call for the equality of women, cannot be equated with a fascist. The whole cast of his thinking was such that he could not have lived a day under an authoritarian regime of any kind. He was an individualist sometimes to the point of anarchism, and in such a man there is too explosive a need for self-expression to permit him to conform to any rigid ideology. It is impossible, therefore, to set him beside Hitler.

On reading the standard translation of Ibsen's work it quickly became obvious that the false impressions that have been connected with the man would seem to be justified were he to be produced in "translated" form. For one thing, his language in English sounds impossibly pedantic. Combine this with the fact that he wore a beard and half-lenses in his eyeglasses, and that his plays have always been set forth with yards of fringe on every tablecloth and drapery, and it was guaranteed that a new production on the traditional basis would truly bury the man for good.

I set out to transform his language into contemporary English. Working from a pidgin-English, word-for-word rendering of the Norwegian, done by Mr. Lars Nordenson, I was able to gather the meaning of each speech and scene without the obstruction of any kind of English construction.

For instance, Mr. Nordenson, working from the original Norwegian manuscript, set before me speeches such as: "But, dear Thomas, what have you then done to him again?" Or: "The Mayor being your brother, I would not wish to touch it, but you are as convinced as I am that truth goes ahead of all other considerations." Or: "Well, what do you say, Doctor? Don't you think it is high time that we stir a little life into the slackness and sloppiness of halfheartedness and cowardliness?" This last speech now reads: "Well, what do you say to a little hypodermic for these fence-sitting deadheads?"

It was possible to peer into the original play with as clear an eye as one could who knew no Norwegian. There were no English sentences to correct and rewrite, only the bare literalness of the original. This version of the play, then, is really in the nature of a new translation into spoken English.*

But it is more too. The original has a tendency to indulge in transitions between scenes that are themselves uninteresting, and although as little as possible of the original construction has been changed and the play is exactly as it was, scene for

---

* It might be added, however, that I did not "use" Ibsen as an easy way to make contemporary points, as more than one critic has complained. The glaring example is my alleged invention of the idea that Dr. Stockmann emigrate to America where tolerance and liberality will make his life easier, which was taken as my jab at our own anti-radicalism. In fact, emigration to liberal America is in the original, and is not at all an ironical suggestion but seriously intended as a contrast with Norwegian narrowness. (A.M., 1977.)

scene, I have made each act seem of one piece, instead of separate scenes. And my reason for doing this is simply that the tradition of Ibsen's theater allowed the opera-like separation of scenes, while ours demands that the audience never be conscious that a "scene" has taken place at all.

Structurally the largest change is in the third act—Ibsen's fifth. In the original the actual dramatic end comes a little past the middle of the act, but it is followed by a wind-up that keeps winding endlessly to the curtain. I think this overwriting was the result of Ibsen's insistence that his meaning be driven home—and from the front door right through to the back, lest the audience fail to understand him. Generally, in this act, I have brought out the meaning of the play in terms of dramatic action, action which was already there and didn't need to be newly invented, but which was separated by tendentious speeches spoken into the blue.

Throughout the play I have tried to peel away its trappings of the moment, its relatively accidental details which ring the dull green tones of Victorianism, and to show that beneath them there still lives the terrible wrath of Henrik Ibsen, who could make a play as men make watches, precisely, intelligently, and telling not merely the minute and the hour but the age.

Many Writers: Few Plays

It is impossible for anyone living in the midst of a cultural period to say with certainty why it is languishing in its produce and general vitality. This is especially true of the theater, where we tend to compare our usually vapid present with "Chekhov's period," or "Ibsen's," or our own previous decades, much to our disadvantage, forgetting that the giants usually stood alone in their time. Nevertheless, even optimists now confess that our theater has struck a seemingly endless low by any standard. I cannot hope to try to explain the reasons for this but certain clues keep recurring to me when thinking on the matter.

We can find no solace in the fact that there never have been more than a handful of first-class playwrights in any one country at any one time, for we have more than the usual number in America now, but few plays from them, and fewer still of any weight. A lizardic dormancy seems to be upon us; the creative mind seems to have lost its heat. Why?

I think the answers will be found in the nature of the creative act. A good play is a good thought; a great play is a

From *The New York Times,* August 10, 1952, Sec. 2, p. 1. This essay was written during the final stages of revising *The Crucible* for its premiere production on Broadway. The play opened at the Martin Beck Theatre on January 22, 1953, during what Miller has elsewhere called "the height of the McCarthy hysteria." Copyright 1952 by Arthur Miller.

great thought. A great thought is a thrust outward, a daring act. Daring is of the essence. Its very nature is incompatible with an undue affection for moderation, respectability, even fairness and responsibleness. Those qualities are proper for the inside of the telephone company, not for creative art.

I may be wrong, but I sense that the playwrights have become more timid with experience and maturity, timid in ethical and social idea, theatrical method, and stylistic means. Because they are unproduced, no firm generalization can be made about the younger playwrights, but from my personal impressions of scripts sent me from time to time, as well as from talks I have had with a few groups of them, I have been struck and dismayed by the strangely high place they give to inoffensiveness.

I find them old without having been young. Like young executives, they seem proudest of their sensibleness—what they call being practical. Illusion is out; it is foolish. What illusion? The illusion that the writer can save the world. The fashion is that the world cannot be saved. Between the determinism of economics and the iron laws of psychiatrics they can only appear ridiculous, they think, by roaring out a credo, a cry of pain, a point of view. Perhaps they really have no point of view, or pain either. It is incomprehensible to me.

Recently a young Chilean director, who has put on more than thirty plays in his own country, and spent the past three years studying theater on a fellowship in France, in Britain, and in two of our leading universities, told me this: "Your students and teachers seem to have no interest at all in the meanings of the ideas in the plays they study. Everything is technique. Your productions and physical apparatus are the best in the world, but among all the university people I came to know, as well as the professionals, scarcely any want to talk about the authors' ethical, moral, or philosophical intentions. They seem to see the theater almost as an engineering project, the purpose being to study successful models of form in order, somehow, to reproduce them with other words."

All this means to me, if true, is that this generation is turning Japanese. The Japanese are said to admire infinite repetitions of time-hallowed stories, characters, and themes. It is the triumph of the practical in art. The most practical thing to do is to repeat what has been done and thought before. But the very liquor of our art has always been originality, uniqueness. The East is older. Perhaps this sterile lull is therefore the sign of our aging. Perhaps we are observing several seasons of hush and silence to mark the passage through our youth. Our youth that was Shaw and Ibsen and O'Neill and all the great ones who kept turning and turning the central question of all great art—how may man govern himself so that he may live more humanly, more alive?

Japanism, so to speak, took over Hollywood long ago, and now the movie is ritual thinly veiled. The practical took command. The "showman" won. High finance took sterility by the hand, and together they rolled the product smooth, stripped off all its offensive .edges, its individuality, and created the perfect circle—namely, zero.

I think the same grinding mill is at work in the theater, but more deceptively because we have no big companies enforcing compliance to any stated rules. But we have an atmosphere of dread just the same, an unconsciously—or consciously—accepted party line, a sanctified complex of moods and attitudes, proper and improper. If nothing else comes of it, one thing surely has: it has made it dangerous to dare, and, worse still, impractical. I am not speaking merely of political thought. Journalists have recently made studies of college students now in school and have been struck by the absence among them of any ferment, either religious, political, literary, or whatever. Wealthy, powerful, envied all about, it seems the American people stand mute.

We always had with us the "showman," but we also had a group of rebels insisting on thrusting their private view of the world on others. Where are they? Or is everybody really happy now? Do Americans really believe they have solved the problems of living for all time? If not, where are the plays that reflect the soul-racking, deeply unseating questions that are being inwardly asked on the street, in the living room, on the subways? Either the playwrights are deaf to them, which I cannot believe, or they are somehow shy of bringing them onto the stage. If the last is true we are unlikely to have even the "straight" theater again—the melodramas, the farces, the "small" plays. It is hard to convince you of this, perhaps, but little thoughts feed off big thoughts; an exciting theater cannot come without there being a ferment, a ferment in the colleges, in the press, in the air. For years now I seem to have heard not expressions of thought from people but a sort of oblong blur, a reflection in distance of the newspapers' opinions.

Is the knuckleheadedness of McCarthyism behind it all? The Congressional investigations of political unorthodoxy? Yes. But is that all? Can an artist be paralyzed except he be somewhat willing? You may pardon me for quoting from myself, but must one always be not merely liked but well liked? Is it not honorable to have powerful enemies? Guardedness, suspicion, aloof circumspection—these are the strongest traits I see around me, and what have they ever had to do with the creative act?

Is it quixotic to say that a time comes for an artist—and for all those who want and love theater—when the world must be left behind? When, like some pilgrim, he must consult only his own heart and cleave to the truth it utters? For out of the hectoring of columnists, the compulsions of patriotic gangs, the suspicions of the honest and the corrupt alike, art never will and never has found soil.

I think of a night last week when a storm knocked out my lights in the country, and it being only nine o'clock it was unthinkable to go to bed. I sat a long time in the blacked-out living room, wide awake, a manuscript unfinished on the table. The idea of lying in bed with one's eyes open, one's brain alive, seemed improper, even degrading. And so, like some primitive man discovering the blessings of fire, I lit two candles and experimentally set them beside my papers. Lo! I could read and work again.

Let a storm come, even from God, and yet it leaves a choice with the man in the dark. He may sit eyeless, waiting for some unknown force to return him his light, or he may seek his private flame. But the choice, the choice is there. We cannot yet be tired. There is work to be done. This is no time to go to sleep.

Journey to *The Crucible*

The Crucible is taken from history. No character is in the play who did not take a similar role in Salem, 1692. The basic story is recorded, if briefly, in certain documents of the time. It will be a long time before I shall be able to shake Rebecca Nurse, John Proctor, Giles Corey and the others out of my mind. But there are strange, even weird memories that have connected themselves to this play, and these have to do with the present, and it has all got mixed up together.

I went to Salem for the first time early last spring. I already knew the story, and had thought about it for a long time. I had never been to Salem before and, driving alone up the brand-new superhighway, I felt a shock at seeing the perfectly ordinary, steel sign reading, "Salem 3 mi." I confess it—some part of my mind had expected to see the old wooden village, not the railroad tracks, the factories, the trucks. These things were not real, suddenly, but intruders, as tourists are in the halls of Versailles. Underneath, in the earth, was the reality. I drove into the town.

I asked the courthouse clerk for the town records for 1692. A lawyer-looking man in an overcoat asked for 1941. A lady, who looked like she was planning to sue somebody, asked for 1913. The clerk handed over a volume to each of us and we sat at separate tables, the three of us, turning pages.

From *The New York Times,* February 8, 1953, Sec. 2, p. 3. Copyright 1953 by Arthur Miller.

The lawyer began copying—possibly from a deed. The woman read perhaps a will—and got angrier. I looked into 1692. Here were wills, too, and deeds, and warrants sworn out, and the usual debris a town leaves behind it for the legal record.

And then . . . dialogue! Prosecutor Hathorne is examining Rebecca Nurse. The court is full of people weeping for the young girls who sit before them strangling because Rebecca's spirit is out tormenting them. And Hathorne says, "It is awful to see your eye dry when so many are wet." And Rebecca replies, "You do not know my heart. I never afflicted no child, never in my life. I am as clear as the child unborn."

They hanged her. She was in her seventies. They had hesitated to go and arrest her because of her high reputation; but they took her from her sickbed, they took her from her lovely house that stands in the countryside yet, and they hanged her by the neck over the long Salem Bay.

The lawyer in the overcoat was copying his deed; the lady was back at the counter, asking the clerk for 1912. Did they know what had happened here?

In the museum all is silent. An old man, looking like a retired professor, is reading a document. Two middle-aged couples come in from their automobile outside and ask to see the pins: the pins the spirits stuck the children with. The pins are in the courthouse, they are told. They look about at the books, the faded fragments of paper that once meant Proctor must hang tomorrow, paper that came through the farmhouse door in the hand of a friend who had a half-determined, half-ashamed look in his eyes.

The tourists pass the books, the exhibits, and no hint of danger reaches them from the quaint relics. I have a desire to tell them the significance of those relics. It is the desire to write.

Day after day in the courthouse, until the evenings begin to arrive with forebodings in the night breeze. The locations of the old farmhouses are in my mind, their directions from the spot on which I stand; on Essex Street was a house, perhaps a few yards from here, where Reverend Parris lived and at night discussed with certain others who in the town was acting suspiciously, who might have shown signs of the Devil's touch. Salem was taken from the Hebrew, Sholom, meaning peace, but now in my mind and in the streets it is a dark word.

The stroll down Essex Street I remember, and the empty spaces between the parking meters, the dark storefronts—but further down a lighted store, and noise. I take a look. A candy store. A mob of girls and boys in their teens running in and out, ganging around on the vacant street; a jalopy pulls up with two wet-haired boys, and a whispered consultation with a girl on the running board; she runs into the store, comes out with a friend, and off they go into the night, the proud raccoon tail straightening from the radiator cap. And suddenly, from around a corner, two girls hopping with a broomstick between their legs, and a general laughter going up at the special joke. A broomstick. And riding it. And I remember the girls of Salem, the only Salem there ever was for me—the 1692 Salem—and how they purged their sins by embracing God and pointing out His enemies in the town.

And a feeling of love at seeing Rebecca Nurse's house on its gentle knoll; the house she lay in, ill, when they came, shuffling their feet, ashamed to have to ask her to come to court because the children said she had sent her spirit out.

And the great rock, standing mum over the bay, the splintered precipice on which the gibbet was built. The highway traffic endlessly, mindlessly humming at its foot, but up here the barrenness, the clinkers of broken stones, and the vast view of the bay; here hung Rebecca, John Proctor, George Jacobs—people more real to me than the living can ever be. The sense of a terrible marvel again; that people could have such a belief in themselves and in the rightness of their consciences as to give their lives rather than say what they thought was false. Or, perhaps, they only feared Hell so much? Yet, Rebecca said, and it is written in the record, "I cannot belie myself." And she knew it would kill her. They knew who they were.

My friends return, the men of my own life—in the hotel tap-room a circle of salesmen sitting around, waiting for bedtime. I listen. They are comparing the sizes of their television screens. Which one is the big-earner? Yep, that one. He says less, but they listen more when he says it. They are all wishing they were him. And all a little lost in the eyes, and nice fellas, so damned eager, and men-among-men, and around the eyes ever so faintly lost; laughing a little more than they want to, listening longer than they want to, sorry without sorrow, laughing with less than joy, until up in the hotel room alone there is only one certainty— tomorrow will come. Another day, another chance to find out— who they are. How they got there. Where they're going.

The rock stands forever in Salem. They knew who they were. Nineteen.

The American Theater

THE American theater occupies five side streets, Forty-fourth to Forty-ninth, between Eighth Avenue and Broadway, with a few additional theaters to the north and south and across Broadway. In these thirty-two buildings every new play in the United States starts its life and ends it. There will undoubtedly be many objections to this statement—you cannot say anything about our theater without fear of contradiction—and demurrers will come from professors of drama, stock-company directors, and little-theater people in New York, Texas, California, and elsewhere who will claim that Broadway is not the United States and that much theatrical production is going on in other places. I agree, and repeat only that with practically no exceptions, the *new* American plays originate on Broadway. I would add that I wish they didn't, but they do. The American theater is five blocks long, by about one and a half blocks wide.

It would seem a simple matter to characterize so limited an area, but I write this with the certainty that whatever I say will appear not only new and strange to many theater people but utterly untrue. And this is because the man or woman whose tapping shoes you hear from the second-story dance studio over the delicatessen on Forty-sixth Street is in the theater, the ballet

From *Holiday,* 17 (January 1955), pp. 90–104. Copyright 1954 by Arthur Miller.

girl hurrying to rehearsal in her polo coat with a copy of Rimbaud in her pocket is in the theater, the peasant-faced Irish stagehand sunning himself on the sidewalk with a *Racing Form* in his hand is in the theater, the slow-staring, bald-headed ticket broker blinking out through his agency window is in the theater, the wealthy, Park-Avenue-born producer is in the theater, and his cigar-smoking colleague from the West Bronx is in the theater.

In the audience itself, though the bulk of it is of the middle class, there is no uniformity either. There will be the businessman in town from Duluth sitting beside Marlene Dietrich, whom he will probably not recognize, and behind them two esthetes from Harvard. The word theater means different things to different groups. To some its very pinnacle is *South Pacific,* which is despised by the esthetes, who in turn cherish a wispy fantasy whose meaning escapes the Duluth man. There is a vast group of people for whom the theater means nothing but amusement, and amusement means a musical or light comedy; and there are others who reserve their greatest enthusiasm for heavy dramas that they can chew on.

The actors, directors, and writers themselves are just as varied. There are playwrights who are as illiterate as high-school boys, and there are playwrights like Maxwell Anderson, who have spent a good deal of their lives studying the Elizabethan drama and attempting to recreate its mood and luxuriance on Broadway. There are fine actors who are universally admired but who have absolutely no theory of acting and there are other actors, equally good or equally bad, who have spent years studying the history of acting, taking voice lessons, and learning how to dance in order to walk more gracefully.

The theater, obviously, is an entirely different animal to each of these groups. As for myself, I cannot pretend to any Olympian viewpoint about it either. I believe there is a confusion in many minds between Show Business and the Theater. I belong to the Theater, which happens at the moment to be in a bad way, but since this word, when capitalized, usually implies something uplifting and boring, I must add that the rarely seen but very real Theater is the most engrossing theater of all; and when it isn't it is nothing. I make the distinction so that the reader will be warned where my prejudice lies and discount accordingly.

The "glamour of the theater," which is and always will be its most powerful attraction, is a subject of daily reporting by almost every newspaper, gossip columnist, and radio station. Every year, around the first cool days of fall, the illustrated sections of the press and the picture magazines and newsreels run the familiar photographs of the limousines gliding up to the lighted marquees, the taxis and cars pressing into Forty-fourth Street for the opening of some musical or drama, the inevitable montage of Sardi's restaurant at dinner time, and so on. For anyone who has made the slightest mark in this occupation there is a line of type waiting when he so much as pays his rent on time. Soon after *Death of a Salesman* opened, it was reported that I was a millionaire, which was pleasant news, if not true, and that despite my new affluence I still rode the subways. I keep wondering who was watching me going through the turnstiles. And the importance of this news still escapes me.

In fact, while everybody in the business is worried about its future—and if there is a heart of uncertainty in the country its loudest beat may be heard on these five blocks—to read the columns and the usual sources of theatrical information you would think it was all a continuous carnival of divorce, practical jokes, hilarious wit, elopements, and sudden acquisition of enormous wealth.

But there is evidently no way of glamourizing the often inspiring and heart-lifting experiences of the work itself, a kind of labor that began in the Western world about three thousand years ago, and which has provided some of the most powerful insights we possess into the way men think and feel.

The net result of this image of our theater, the carnival image, is that the out-of-towner strolling these streets may quickly sense that he has been bilked. He will discover, especially if he arrives in midday, that the theater buildings themselves are tawdry-looking, and may well be disillusioned when he sees that some of the marquees do not have even the electrically lit signs of his home movie house—only temporary cardboards painted with the title of the show within. When he ventures into the outer lobby he will perhaps be shocked to discover that a seat costs six—or even eight—dollars and, if the show is a hit, that he won't get a ticket for six months or a year unless he pays a scalper twenty-five to a hundred dollars. If it is not a hit, and he buys a ticket legitimately, he may learn that he could have bought two for the price of one; and by the time he gets inside for the performance, some of the glamour of it all may have worn a bit thin.

Once inside, however, our visitor may find certain compensations. He may recognize very important people, from statesmen to movie stars, sitting nearby, whom he would not see in the home-town movie house. He will notice a certain dressed-up air about people, a few even wearing evening clothes. There are ushers to show him to his seat, and there is a program, and possibly a little more surprising is the coat-check man waiting as he passes through the outer door. There is still a vestigial ceremony about playgoing from which one may derive a sense of self-importance if not careful, and it all may lead our visitor to feel that he is, indeed, among ladies and gentlemen.

Then, as the lights go down and the curtain rises, our visitor may feel a certain strange tension, an expectancy, and an intense curiosity that he never knew in a theater before. Instead of the enormity of the movie image before which he could sit back and relax, he is confronted by human beings in life-size, and since their voices do not roar out at him from a single point to which his ear may tune in once and then relax, he must pay more attention, his eyes must rove over a thirty-foot expanse; he must, in other words, *discover*. And if there happens to be something real up there, something human, something true, our visitor may come away with a new feeling in his heart, a sense of having been a part of something quite extraordinary and even beautiful. Unlike the movies, unlike television, he may feel he has been present at an *occasion*. For outside this theater, no one in the world heard what he heard or saw what he saw this night. I know that, for myself, there is nothing so immediate, so actual, as an excellent performance of an excellent play. I have never known the smell of sweat in a movie house. I have known it in the theater—and they are also air-conditioned. Nor have I known in a movie house the kind of audience unity that occasionally is created in the theater, an air of oneness among strangers that is possible in only one other gathering place—a church.

Nevertheless, by every account our theater is a vanishing institution. We have some thirty-two houses going today in New York as against forty or more ten years ago, and between seventy and eighty in the twenties. I could weave you such a tapestry of evil omens as to make it a closed case that we will have no theater in America in two decades. What I should like to do instead, however, is wonder aloud, as it were, why it is that each year thousands of aspiring actors, directors, and playwrights continue to press into these five blocks from every corner of the country when they know, or learn very quickly, that ninety percent of the professional actors are normally unemployed, that most of the producers are dead broke or within three cigars of being broke, and that to become a director of a Broadway show one must be prepared to gamble five to ten to fifteen years of one's life. And yet, on all the trains they keep coming, aspiring actors and eager audiences both.

As for the aspiring actors, I will not pretend to hunt for an answer, because I know it. It is simply that there are always certain persons who are born without all their marbles. Even so, the full-blown actors are merely the completed types of the secret actors who are called producers, backers, directors, yes, and playwrights. The rest of us would have been actors had we had the talent, or a left and right foot instead of two left ones, or straight teeth, or self-assurance. The actor himself is the lunacy in full profusion—the lunacy which in the others is partially concealed.

All over the country there are nine-year-old girls, for instance, who are walking around the house as my daughter is at this very moment, in high-heeled shoes with the lace tablecloth trailing from their shoulders. If mine doesn't recover before she is sixteen she will wake up one morning and something will click inside her head and she will go and hang around some producer's office, and if he talks to her, or just asks her what time it is, she may well be doomed for life.

The five blocks, therefore, are unlike any other five blocks in the United States, if only because here so many grown people are walking around trailing the old lace tablecloth from their shoulders.

If you know how to look you will find them waiting on you in Schrafft's, or behind the orange-drink counter at Nedick's. As a matter of fact, I have got so attuned to a certain look in their eyes that I can sometimes spot them on Sixth Avenue, which is not in the theater district. I was passing a truck being loaded there one day when I noticed a boy, unshaven, his hair uncombed, wearing paratroop boots; he was pitching boxes into the truck. And he looked at me, just a glance, and I thought to myself that he must be an actor. And about three days later I was sitting in my producer's office interviewing actors for *The Crucible,* when in he walked. Characteristically, he did not remember seeing me before—actors rarely do, since they are not looking at anyone but rather are being looked *at*. When asked the usual questions about his experience he just shrugged, and when asked if he wanted to read for us he shrugged again, quite as though the questions were impertinent when addressed to a great artist, and I knew then why I had tabbed him for an actor. It was the time when all the young actors were being Marlon Brando. He was being Marlon Brando even when loading the truck, for a real truck driver would never show up for work looking so unkempt.

The blessed blindness of actors to everything around them, their intense preoccupation with themselves, is the basic characteristic of all Broadway, and underlies most of its troubles, which, in another industry, would have been solved long ago.

But since it is glamour which brings the young to Broadway, as well as the audience, it cannot be so quickly dismissed. The fact is, it exists. But it is not the glamour you are probably thinking of.

The time is gone when the Great Producer kept four or five Great Stars in ten-room apartments on Park Avenue, and they waited in their gilded cages for days and weeks for the Impresario to call for them—for without him they were forbidden to be seen in public lest they lose their "distance," their altitude above the common things of life. The time is gone when the leading lady dared not arrive at the theater in anything but a limousine with chauffeur and lap robe, while a line of stove-pipe-hatted men waited in the stage-door alley with flowers in their manicured hands. There are a few hangovers, of course, and I remember a show in Boston a few years ago whose leading lady, an hour before curtain time, phoned the producer to say she was ill and could not play. The poor man was desperate, but there was an old-time doorman in that theater who happened to be near the phone and he said, "Get a limousine and a chauffeur." The producer, a contemporary type who was as familiar with gallantry as any other businessman, mastered his uncertainty and hired a car and chauffeur and sent a mass of roses to the lady's hotel room. Her fever vanished in roughly four minutes and she played better than she ever had, and I must confess I couldn't blame her for wanting the glamour even if she had had to make it herself.

But leading ladies, nowadays, arrive in a taxi, and a lot of them come in by bus or subway.

I have been around only ten years or so and I never knew the kind of glamour that evidently existed. But a few years ago I had occasion to visit John Golden in his office, and I saw then that there was, in fact, a kind of bravado about being in the theater, a declaration of war against all ordinariness that I can find no more.

The average theatrical producer's office today consists mainly of a telephone, a girl to answer it, an outer room for actors to wait in, and an inner room with a window for the producer to stare out of when he has nothing to produce. John Golden's office is different. It rests on top of the St. James Theatre; you rise in a private elevator, and come out in a dark, paper-cluttered reception room where an elderly and very wise lady bars you—with the help of a little gate—from entry. You know at once that behind her is not merely a man, but a Presence.

In his office the walls are painted with smoke. They are very dark and covered with hundreds of photographs, plaques, statuettes, hanging things, and jutting things of gold, silver, and shiny brass. There is an Oriental rug on the floor, an ornate desk at the distant end of the room, and there sits John Golden, who is now eighty years old. Behind him stands an imposing ascent of bookshelves filled with leather-bound plays he has produced. In a smaller adjoining room is a barber chair where his hair is cut, his beard shaved, and, I presume, his shoes shined. The windows are covered with drapes and obstructing statuary, because when this office was created, the man who worked in it had no time to look out into the street.

It was a time when the railroads were freighting out one after another of his productions, winter and summer, to all sections of the country. It was a time when, unlike now, important performers and even playwrights were kept on long-term contracts, when a producer owned his own theater and used his own money and was therefore not an accountant, nor even a businessman, but an impresario. In short, it was the time before the masses had left the theater for the new movies, and the theater was the main source of American popular entertainment. This office is now a kind of museum. There were once many like it, and many men like John Golden.

Their counterparts, the reflected images of Ziegfeld, Frohman, Belasco, and the others, appeared only later in Hollywood, for the masses are needed to create impresarios, or more precisely, a lucrative mass market. In Golden's office I saw the genesis of so much we have come to associate with Hollywood: the stars under long-term contract, the planning of one production after another instead of the present one-shot Broadway practice, the sense of permanence and even security. None of these are part of Broadway now, and they appear in their afterglow above the St. James; for it is not the masses we serve any more, not the "American People," but a fraction of one class—the more or less better-educated people, or the people aspiring to culture.

Golden's eyes blazed with pleasure as he talked of plays long since gone, like *Turn to the Right* and *Lightnin'* and others I remember my father raving about when I was a boy, and finally he sat back and mused about playwriting.

"You fellows have a much harder time," he said, "much harder than in the old days; nowadays every show has to seem new and original. But in the old days, you know, we had what you might call favorite scenes. There was the scene where the mother puts a candle on the window sill while she waits for her long-lost boy to come home. They loved that scene. We put that scene in one play after another. You can't do things like that any more. The audience is too smart now. They're more educated, I suppose, and sophisticated. Of course it was all sentimental, I guess, but they were good shows."

He was right, of course, except you *can* do that now; the movies have been doing it for thirty or forty years and now television is doing it all over again. I remember a friend who had worked in Hollywood writing a picture. The producer called him in with a bright new idea for a scene to be inserted in the script. My friend listened and was amazed. "But just last month you released a picture with that same scene in it," he reminded the producer.

"Sure," said the producer, "and didn't it go great?"

The Golden species of glamour is gone with the masses; it went with the big money to Hollywood, and now it is creating itself all over again in television. The present-day actors and directors would probably seem tame and dull to their counterparts of thirty and forty years ago. David Belasco, for instance, had even convinced himself that his was a glamorous profession, and took to dressing in black like a priest—the high priest of the theater—and turned his collar around to prove it. He carried on as no contemporary director would dare to do. Toward the last days of rehearsal, when he wanted some wooden but very beautiful leading lady to break down and weep, he would take out a watch, the watch he had been displaying for weeks as the one his mother gave him on her deathbed, and smash it on the floor in a high dudgeon, thus frightening the actress to tears and making her putty in his hands. It need hardly be added that he kept a large supply of these watches, each worth one dollar.

The traditional idea of the actor with his haughty stance, his peaked eyebrows, elegant speech, artistic temperament, and a necessary disdain for all that was common and plain, has long since disappeared. Now they are all trying to appear as ordinary as your Uncle Max. A group of actors sitting at a bar these days could easily be mistaken for delegates to a convention of white-collar people. They are more likely, upon landing in a hit show, to hurry over to the offices of a tax consultant than to rush out and buy a new Jaguar. For a few years after the war a certain amount of effort was put into aging their dungarees and wearing turtle-neck sweaters, and some of them stopped combing their hair, like the boy I noticed loading the truck. But you don't get Marlon Brando's talent by avoiding a bath, and gradually this fad has vanished. There are more "colorful" personalities up here in the tiny Connecticut village where I spend summers than you will find on all Broadway. The only real showman I know of is Joshua Logan, who can throw a party for a hundred people in his Park Avenue apartment and make it appear a normal evening. Logan is the only director I can name who would dare to knock a stage apart and build into it a real swimming pool, as he did for the musical *Wish You Were Here,* and can still talk about the theater with the open, full-blown excitement of one who has no reservations about it. The other directors, at least the half-dozen I know—and there are not many more—are more likely to be as deadly serious as any atomic physicist, and equally worried.

There is a special aura about the theater, nevertheless, a glamour, too, but it has little connection with the publicity that seeks to create it. There is undoubtedly as much sexual fooling around as there is in the refrigerator business, but I doubt if there is much more. The notion of theatrical immorality began when actors were socially inferior by common consent; but now a Winnifred Cushing (of the Boston Cushings), the loose woman in *Death of a Salesman,* hurries home to her mother after each show.

Not that it is an ordinary life. There is still nothing quite like it, if only because of the fanaticism with which so many respond to its lure. One cannot sit in a producer's office day after day interviewing actors for a play without being struck by their insistence that they belong in the theater and intend to make their lives in it. In the outer reception rooms of any producer's office at casting time is a cross section of a hundred small towns and big cities, the sons and daughters of the rich families and of the middle-class families and of families from the wrong side of the tracks. One feels, on meeting a youngster from a way-station town or a New Mexico ranch, that the spores of this poor theater must still possess vitality to have flown so far and rooted so deep. It is pathetic, it is saddening, but a thing is dead only when nobody wants it, and they do want it desperately. It is nothing unusual to tell a girl who has come to a casting office that she looks too respectable for the part, and to be greeted by her an hour later dressed in a slinky black dress, spike heels, outlandishly overdone make-up, and blond dye in her hair that has hardly had time to dry. One of our best-known actresses had her bowlegs broken in order to appear as she thought she must on the stage, and there is an actor who did the same to his knees in order to play Hamlet in tights.

There is, it must be admitted, an egotism in this that can be neither measured nor sometimes even stomached, but at casting time, when one spends hour after hour in the presence of human beings with so powerful a conviction and so great a desire to be heard and seen and judged as artists, the thing begins to surpass mere egotism and assumes the proportion of a cause, a belief, a mission. And when such sacrifices are made in its name one must begin to wonder at the circumstances that have reduced it to its present chaos. It might be helpful to take a look at how the whole thing is organized—or disorganized.

Everything begins with a script. I must add right off that in the old mass theater that came to an end somewhere in the late twenties, when the movies took over, the script was as often as not a botch of stolen scenes, off-the-cuff inventions of the producer or director, or simply pasted-together situations designed for some leading player. The audience today, however, demands more, and so the script has become the Holy Grail for which a producer dreams, prays, and lives every day of his life. Being so valuable, and so difficult to write, it is leased by the author on a royalty basis and never sold outright. He receives, I am happy to report, roughly ten percent of the gross receipts, or between two and three thousand dollars a week if he has a hit. (I would add that he resolves not to change his standard of living but he has a wife, and that is that.)

Three or four times a year the playwrights have a meeting of the Dramatists Guild, their union, in a private dining room of the St. Regis Hotel. Moss Hart, the author of *The Climate of Eden* and, with George Kaufman, of a string of successes like *The Man Who Came to Dinner* and *You Can't Take It With You,* is the current president of the Guild. There is probably more money represented here than at most union luncheons, the only trouble being that with a few exceptions none of the playwrights has any assets; that is, you can't write a hit every time so the three thousand a week begins to look smaller and smaller when it is averaged out over a period of unfruitful years. Oscar Hammerstein, another Guild member, put an ad in *Variety* after his *South Pacific* opened, listing a dozen or so of his failures that everyone had forgotten, and at the bottom of the page repeated the legend of show business, "I did it before and I can do it again."

Between the turtle soup and the veal scaloppine, various issues are discussed, all of which are usually impossible to solve, and the luncheons roll by and we know that our profession is on the edge of an abyss because the theater is contracting; and we all go home to write our plays. Occasionally we meet with a group of producers, and Max Gordon can usually be relied on to demand the floor; and red in the face, full of his wonderful fight, he will cut to the heart of the problem by shouting at the playwrights, "The producers are starving, you hear me? Starving!" Leland Hayward, who has scraped by on *South Pacific, Mister Roberts,* and other such titbits, will accuse me of making too much money, and Herman Shumlin, the producer of *The Little Foxes, The Children's Hour, Watch on the Rhine,* will solemnly avow that he is leaving the business forever unless we writers cut our royalties; and then we all go home. Once the late Lee Shubert came with the others to discuss the problems of the theater, and when he was asked if he would reduce the rentals of his many theaters, since the playwrights were willing to reduce their royalties, he looked as though the butter was, indeed, melting in his mouth, so he didn't open it. And we all went home again.

There are seemingly hundreds of producers, but actually only fifteen or twenty go on year after year. Few are wealthy, and money is usually promoted or lured out of any crack where it can be found. It is a common, although not universal, practice to hold a gathering of potential backers before whom either the playwright or the director reads the script. Established producers regard this as beneath their dignity, but some don't, or can't afford to. These readings usually take place either on Park Avenue or on swank Beekman Place, for some reason, and while I never attended one, I have known many playwrights who have, but never heard of one dollar being raised in that way.

Script in hand, then, and money either raised or on its way— usually in amounts under five hundred dollars per backer—the producer hires a director, also on a percentage with a fee in advance, and a scene designer; the set is sketched, approved, and ordered built. Casting begins. While the author sits home revising his script—for some reason no script can be produced as the author wrote it—agents are apprised of the kinds of parts to be filled, and in the producer's reception room next morning all hell breaks loose.

The basis upon which actors are hired or not hired is sometimes quite sound; for example, they may have been seen recently in a part which leads the director to believe they are right for the new role; but quite as often a horde of applicants is waiting beyond the door of the producer's private office and neither he nor the director nor the author has the slightest knowledge of any of them. It is at this point that things become painful, for the strange actor sits before them, so nervous and frightened that he either starts talking and can't stop, and sometimes *says* he can't stop, or is unable to say anything at all and says *that*. During the casting of one of my plays there entered a middle-aged woman who was so frightened she suddenly started to sing. The play being no musical, this was slightly beside the point, but the producer, the director, and myself, feeling so guilty ourselves, sat there and heard her through.

To further complicate matters there is each year the actor or actress who suddenly becomes what they call "hot." A hot performer is one not yet well-known, but who, for some mysterious reason, is generally conceded to be a coming star. It is possible, naturally, that a hot performer really has talent, but it is equally possible, and much more likely, that she or he is not a whit more attractive or more talented than a hundred others. Nevertheless, there comes a morning when every producer in these five blocks—some of them with parts the performer could never play —simply has to have him or her. Next season, of course, nobody hears about the new star and it starts all over again with somebody else.

All that is chancy in life, all that is fortuitous, is magnified to the bursting point at casting time; and that, I suspect, is one of the attractions of this whole affair, for it makes the ultimate winning of a part so much more zesty. It is also, to many actors, a most degrading process and more and more of them refuse to submit to these interviews until after the most delicate advances of friendship and hospitality are made to them. And their use of agents as intermediaries is often an attempt to soften the awkwardness of their applying for work.

The theatrical agents, in keeping with the unpredictable lunacy of the business, may be great corporations like the Music Corporation of America, which has an entire building on Madison Avenue, and will sell you anything from a tap dancer to a movie star, a symphony orchestra, saxophonists, crooners, scene designers, actors, and playwrights, to a movie script complete with cast; or they may be like Jane Broder, who works alone and can spread out her arms and touch both walls of her office. They may even be like Carl Cowl, who lives around the corner from me in Brooklyn. Carl is an ex-seaman who still ships out when he has no likely scripts on hand to sell, and when things get too nerve-racking he stays up all night playing Mozart on his flute. MCA has antique desks, English eighteenth-century prints, old broken clocks and inoperative antique barometers hanging on its paneled walls, but Carl Cowl had a hole in his floor that the cat got into, and when he finally got the landlord to repair it he was happy and sat down to play his flute again; but he heard meowing, and they had to rip the floor open again to let out the cat. Still, Carl is not incapable of landing a hit play and neither more nor less likely than MCA to get it produced, and that is another handicraft aspect of this much publicized small business, a quality of opportunity which keeps people coming into it. The fact is that theatrical agents do not sell anyone or anything in the way one sells merchandise. Their existence is mainly due to the need theater people have for a home, some semblance of order in their lives, some sense of being wanted during the long periods when they have nothing to do. To have an agent is to have a kind of reassurance that you exist. The actor is hired, however, mainly because he is wanted for the role.

By intuition, then, by rumor, on the recommendation of an agent—usually heartfelt; out of sheer exhaustion, and upsurge of sudden hope or what not, several candidates for each role are selected in the office of the producer, and are called for readings on the stage of a theater.

It is here that the still unsolved mystery begins, the mystery of what makes a stage performer. There are persons who, in an office, seem exciting candidates for a role, but as soon as they step onto a stage the observers out front—if they are experienced—know that the blessing was not given them. For myself, I know it when, regardless of how well the actor is reading, my eyes begin to wander up to the brick wall back of the stage. Conversely, there are many who make little impression in an office, but once on the stage it is impossible to take one's attention from them. It is a question neither of technique nor of ability, I think, but some quality of surprise inherent in the person.

For instance, when we were searching for a woman to play Linda, the mother in *Death of a Salesman,* a lady came in whom we all knew but could never imagine in the part. We needed a woman who looked as though she had lived in a house dress all her life, even somewhat coarse and certainly less than brilliant. Mildred Dunnock insisted she was that woman, but she was frail, delicate, not long ago a teacher in a girl's college, and a cultivated citizen who probably would not be out of place in a cabinet post. We told her this, in effect, and she understood, and left.

And the next day the line of women formed again in the wings, and suddenly there was Milly again. Now she had padded herself from neck to hem line to look a bit bigger, and for a moment none of us recognized her, and she read again. As soon as she spoke we started to laugh at her ruse; but we saw, too, that she *was* a little more worn now, and seemed less well-maintained, and while she was not quite ordinary, she reminded you of women who were. But we all agreed, when she was finished reading, that she was not right, and she left.

Next day she was there again in another getup, and the next

and the next, and each day she agreed with us that she was wrong; and to make a long story short when it came time to make the final selection it had to be Milly, and she turned out to be magnificent. But in this case we had known her work; there was no doubt that she was an excellent actress. The number of talented applicants who are turned down because they are unknown is very large. Such is the crap-shooting chanciness of the business, its chaos, and part of its charm. In a world where one's fate so often seems machined and standardized, and unlikely to suddenly change, these five blocks are like a stockade inside which are people who insist that the unexpected, the sudden chance, must survive. And to experience it they keep coming on all the trains.

But to understand its apparently deathless lure for so many it is necessary, finally, to have participated in the first production of a new play. When a director takes his place at the beaten-up wooden table placed at the edge of the stage, and the cast for the first time sit before him in a semicircle, and he gives the nod to the actor who has the opening lines, the world seems to be filling with a kind of hope, a kind of regeneration that, at the time, anyway, makes all the sacrifices worth while.

The production of a new play, I have often thought, is like another chance in life, a chance to emerge cleansed of one's imperfections. Here, as when one was very young, it seems possible again to attain even greatness, or happiness, or some otherwise unattainable joy. And when production never loses that air of hope through all its three-and-a-half-week rehearsal period, one feels alive as at no other imaginable occasion. At such a time, it seems to all concerned that the very heart of life's mystery is what must be penetrated. They watch the director and each other and they listen with the avid attention of deaf mutes who have suddenly learned to speak and hear. Above their heads there begins to form a tantalizing sort of cloud, a question, a challenge to penetrate the mystery of why men move and speak and act.

It is a kind of glamour that can never be reported in a newspaper column, and yet it is the center of all the lure theater has.

It is a kind of soul-testing that ordinary people rarely experience except in the greatest emergencies. The actor who has always regarded himself as a strong spirit discovers now that his vaunted power somehow sounds querulous, and he must look within himself to find his strength. The actress who has made her way on her charm discovers that she appears not charming so much as shallow now, and must evaluate herself all over again, and create anew what she always took for granted. And the great performers are merely those who have been able to face themselves without remorse.

In the production of a good play with a good cast and a knowing director a kind of banding together occurs; there is formed a fraternity whose members share a mutual sense of destiny. In these five blocks, where the rapping of the tap-dancer's feet and the bawling of the phonographs in the record-shop doorways mix with the roar of the Broadway traffic; where the lonely, the perverted, and the lost wander like the souls in Dante's hell and the life of the spirit seems impossible, there are still little circles of actors in the dead silence of empty theaters, with a director in their center, and a new creation of life taking place.

There are always certain moments in such rehearsals, moments of such wonder that the memory of them serves to further entrap all who witness them into this most insecure of all professions. Remembering such moments the resolution to leave and get a "real" job vanishes, and they are hooked again.

I think of Lee Cobb, the greatest dramatic actor I ever saw, when he was creating the role of Willy Loman in *Death of a Salesman*. When I hear people scoffing at actors as mere exhibitionists, when I hear them ask why there must be a theater if it cannot support itself as any business must, when I myself grow sick and weary of the endless waste and the many travesties of this most abused of all arts, I think then of Lee Cobb making that role and I know that the theater can yet be one of the chief glories of mankind.

He sat for days on the stage like a great lump, a sick seal, a mourning walrus. When it came his time to speak lines, he whispered meaninglessly. Kazan, the director, pretended certainty, but from where I sat he looked like an ant trying to prod an elephant off his haunches. Ten days went by. The other actors were by now much further advanced: Milly Dunnock, playing Linda, was already creating a role; Arthur Kennedy as Biff had long since begun to reach for his high notes; Cameron Mitchell had many scenes already perfected; but Cobb stared at them, heavy-eyed, morose, even persecuted, it seemed.

And then, one afternoon, there on the stage of the New Amsterdam way up on top of a movie theater on Forty-second Street (this roof theater had once been Ziegfeld's private playhouse in the gilded times, and now was barely heated and misty with dust), Lee rose from his chair and looked at Milly Dunnock and there was a silence. And then he said, "I was driving along, you understand, and then all of a sudden I'm going off the road...."

And the theater vanished. The stage vanished. The chill of an age-old recognition shuddered my spine; a voice was sounding in the dimly lit air up front, a created spirit, an incarnation, a Godlike creation was taking place; a new human being was being formed before all our eyes, born for the first time on this earth, made real by an act of will, by an artist's summoning up of all his memories and his intelligence; a birth was taking place above the meaningless traffic below; a man was here transcending the limits of his body and his own history. Through the complete concentration of his mind he had even altered the stance of his body, which now was strangely not the body of Lee Cobb (he was thirty-seven then) but of a sixty-year-old salesman; a mere glance of his eye created a window beside him, with the gentle touch of his hand on this empty stage a bed appeared, and when he glanced up at the emptiness above him a ceiling was there, and there was even a crack in it where his stare rested.

I knew then that something astounding was being made here. It would have been almost enough for me without even opening the play. The actors, like myself and Kazan and the producer, were happy, of course, that we might have a hit; but there was a good deal more. There was a new fact of life, there was an alteration of history for all of us that afternoon.

There is a certain immortality involved in theater, not created by monuments and books, but through the knowledge the actor keeps to his dying day that on a certain afternoon, in an empty and dusty theater, he cast a shadow of a being that was not himself but the distillation of all he had ever observed; all the unsingable heartsong the ordinary man may feel but never utter, he gave voice to. And by that he somehow joins the ages.

And that is the glamour that remains, but it will not be found in the gossip columns. And it is enough, once discovered, to make people stay with the theater, and others to come seeking it.

I think also that people keep coming into these five blocks because the theater is still so simple, so old-fashioned. And that is why, however often its obsequies are intoned, it somehow never really dies. Because underneath our shiny fronts of stone, our fascination with gadgets, and our new toys that can blow the earth into a million stars, we are still outside the doorway through which the great answers wait. Not all the cameras in Christendom nor all the tricky lights will move us one step closer to a better understanding of ourselves, but only, as it always was, the truly written word, the profoundly felt gesture, the naked and direct contemplation of man which is the enduring glamour of the stage.

On Social Plays

A GREEK living in the classical period would be bewildered by the dichotomy implied in the very term "social play." Especially for the Greek, a drama created for public performance had to be "social." A play to him was by definition a dramatic consideration of the way men ought to live. But in this day of extreme individualism even that phrase must be further defined. When we say "how men ought to live," we are likely to be thinking of psychological therapy, of ridding ourselves individually of neurotic compulsions and destructive inner tendencies, of "learning how to love" and thereby gaining "happiness."

It need hardly be said that the Greek dramatist had more than a passing interest in psychology and character on the stage. But for him these were means to a larger end, and the end was what we isolate today as social. That is, the relations of man as a social animal, rather than his definition as a separated entity, was the dramatic goal. Why this should have come to be is a large historical question which others are more competent to explain, as several already have. For our purposes it will be sufficient to

From the original edition of *A View from the Bridge* (New York: Viking, 1955), pp. 1–18, in which this essay appeared as the preface to the one-act version of *A View from the Bridge,* along with *A Memory of Two Mondays.* Miller subsequently expanded *A View from the Bridge* into a two-act version, which opened in London, England, on October 11, 1956, and is reprinted in the *Collected Plays.* Copyright © 1955 by Arthur Miller.

indicate one element in the life of classical Greece that differs so radically from anything existing in the modern world as to throw a bright light on certain of our attitudes which we take for granted and toward which we therefore are without a proper perspective.

The Greek citizen of that time thought of himself as belonging not to a "nation" or a "state" but to a *polis*. The polis were small units, apparently deriving from an earlier tribal social organization, whose members probably knew one another personally because they were relatively few in number and occupied a small territory. In war or peace the whole people made the vital decisions, there being no profession of politics as we know it; any man could be elected magistrate, judge, even a general in the armed forces. It was an amateur world compared to our stratified and specialized one, a world in which everyone knew enough about almost any profession to practice it, because most things were simple to know. The thing of importance for us is that these people were *engaged,* they could not imagine the good life excepting as it brought each person into close contact with civic matters. They were avid argufiers. Achilles was blessed by the gods with the power to fight well and make good speeches. The people had a special sense of pride in the polis and thought that it in itself distinguished them from the barbarians outside who lived under tyrannies.

The preoccupation of the Greek drama with ultimate law, with the Grand Design, so to speak, was therefore an expression of a basic assumption of the people, who could not yet conceive, luckily, that any man could long prosper unless his polis prospered. The individual was at one with his society; his conflicts with it were, in our terms, like family conflicts the opposing sides of which nevertheless shared a mutuality of feeling and responsibility. Thus the drama written for them, while for us it appears wholly religious, was religious for them in a more than mystical way. Religion is the only way we have any more of expressing our genuinely social feelings and concerns, for in our bones we as a people do not otherwise believe in our oneness with a larger group. But the religiousness of the Greek drama of the classical time was more worldly; it expressed a social concern, to be sure, but it did so on the part of a people already unified on earth rather than the drive of a single individual toward personal salvation. The great gap we feel between religious or "high" emotion and the emotions of daily life was not present in their mass affairs. The religious expression was not many degrees higher for them than many other social expressions, of which their drama is the most complete example.

It is necessary to add that as the polis withered under the impact of war and historical change, as commerce grew and a differentiation of interest separated man from man, the Greek drama found it more and more difficult to stand as a kind of universal mass statement or prayer. It turned its eye inward, created more elaborated characterizations, and slowly gave up some of its former loftiness. Men, as H. D. F. Kitto has said in *The Greeks,* replaced Man in the plays. Nevertheless, to the end the Greek drama clearly conceived its right function as something far wider than a purely private examination of individuality for the sake of the examination or for art's sake. In every dramatic hero there is the idea of the Greek people, their fate, their will, and their destiny.

In today's America the term "social play" brings up images which are historically conditioned, very recent, and, I believe, only incidentally pertinent to a fruitful conception of the drama. The term indicates to us an attack, an arraignment of society's evils such as Ibsen allegedly invented and was later taken up by left-wing playwrights whose primary interest was the exposure of capitalism for the implied benefit of socialism or communism. The concept is tired and narrow, but its worst effect has been to confuse a whole generation of playwrights, audiences, and theater workers.

If one can look at the idea of "social drama" from the Greek viewpoint for one moment, it will be clear that there can be only either a genuinely social drama or, if it abdicates altogether, its true opposite, the antisocial and ultimately antidramatic drama.

To put it simply, even oversimply, a drama rises in stature and intensity in proportion to the weight of its application to all manner of men. It gains its weight as it deals with more and more of the whole man, not either his subjective or his social life alone, and the Greek was unable to conceive of man or anything else except as a whole. The modern playwright, at least in America, on the one hand is importuned by his most demanding audience to write importantly, while on the other he is asked not to bring onto the stage images of social function, lest he seem like a special pleader and therefore inartistic. I am not attempting a defense of the social dramas of the thirties, most of which were in fact special pleadings and further from a consideration of the whole man than much of the antisocial drama is. I am trying only to project a right conception of what social drama was and what it ought to be. It is, I think, the widest concept of drama available to us thus far.

When, however, a contemporary dramatist is drawn for but a moment toward a concept of form even remotely Greek, certain lacks become evident—a certain abyss even begins to appear around him. When you are writing in the name of a people unified in a self-conscious and rather small band, when yourself as a writer are not an individual entrepreneur offering wares to a hostile marketplace but a member of a group who is in other ways no different from the rest—when, in short, the dramatic form itself is regarded as inevitably a social expression of the deepest concerns of all your fellow men—your work is bound to be liberated, freed of even the hypothesis of partisanship, if only because partisanship cannot thrive where the idea of wholeness is accepted. Thus in such a situation what we call social matters become inseparable from subjective psychological matters, and the drama is once again whole and capable of the highest reach.

If one considers our own drama of the past forty years in comparison with that of classical Greece, one elemental difference —the difference which seems to me to be our crippling hobble —will emerge. The single theme to which our most ambitious plays can be reduced is frustration. In all of them, from O'Neill's through the best of Anderson, Sidney Howard, and the rest, the underlying log jam, so to speak, the unresolvable paradox, is that, try as he will, the individual is doomed to frustration when once he gains a consciousness of his own identity. The image is that of the individual scratching away at a wall beyond which stands society, his fellow men. Sometimes he pounds at the wall, sometimes he tries to scale it or even blow it up, but at the end the wall is always there, and the man himself is dead or doomed to defeat in his attempt to live a human life.

The tragic victory is always denied us because, I believe, the plays cannot project with any conviction what the society, in the playwrights' views at any rate, has failed to prove. In Greece the tragic victory consisted in demonstrating that the polis—the whole people—had discovered some aspect of the Grand Design which also was the right way to live *together*. If the American playwrights of serious intent are in any way the subconscience of the country, our claims to have found that way are less than proved. For when the Greek thought of the right way to live it was a whole concept; it meant a way to live that would create citizens who were brave in war, had a sense of responsibility to the polis in peace, and were also developed as individual personalities.

It has often seemed to me that the Soviet Russians have studied classical Greece and have tried to bridge with phraseology profound differences between their social organization and that of Greece, while demanding of their writers what in effect is a Greek social drama. The word "cosmopolitan," as Kitto points out, was invented in Greece when the small polis were disintegrating, and when the drama itself was beginning to turn inward, away from the largest questions of social fate to the fate of individuals alone. It was invented to describe a new kind of man, a man whose allegiance was not primarily to his society, his polis, but to others of like mind anywhere in the world. With it goes an intimation—or more—of skepticism, of self-removal, that presages the radical separation of man from society which the American drama expresses ultimately through themes of frustration. To supplant the polis and allegiance to it, the Soviets have a thousand kinds of social organizations, and, for all one knows, the individual Russian might well feel a sense of connection with civic affairs which the West does not afford its citizens. The crucial difference, however, is that only the most theoretical Russian can trace the effects, if any, of his personality upon the policies of his country, while the Greek could literally see what he had done when he made his speech and swayed or failed to sway his fellow men.

Thus the Russian drama after the Revolution, much as ours, is a drama of frustration, the inability of industrialized men to see themselves spiritually completed through the social organization. But in the Soviet case the frustration is not admitted; it is talked away in large phrases having to do with a victory of the people through tragic sacrifice. The fact remains, however, that nowhere in the world where industrialized economy rules—where specialization in work, politics, and social life is the norm—nowhere has man discovered a means of connecting himself to society except in the form of a truce with it. The best we have been able to do is to speak of a "duty" to society, and this implies sacrifice or self-deprivation. To think of an individual fulfilling his subjective needs through social action, to think of him as living most completely when he lives most socially, to think of him as doing this, not as a social worker acting out of conscientious motives, but naturally, without guilt or sense of oddness—this is difficult for us to imagine, and when we can, we know at the same time that only a few, perhaps a blessed few, are so constructed as to manage it.

As with Greece, so with us—each great war has turned men further and further away from preoccupation with Man and drawn them back into the family, the home, the private life and the preoccupation with sexuality. It has happened, however, that at the same time our theater has exhausted the one form that was made to express the private life—prose realism. We are bored with it; we demand something more, something "higher," on the stage, while at the same time we refuse, or do not know how, to live our private lives excepting as ego-centers. I believe it is this paradox that underlies the kind of struggle taking place in the drama today—a struggle at one and the same time to write of private persons privately and yet lift up their means of expression to a poetic—that is, a social—level. You cannot speak in verse of picayune matters—at least not on the stage—without sounding overblown and ridiculous, and so it should be. Verse reaches always toward the general statement, the wide image, the universal moment, and it must be based upon wide concepts—it must speak not merely of men but of Man. The language of dramatic verse is the language of a people profoundly at one with itself; it is the most public of public speech. The language of prose is the language of the private life, the kind of private life men retreat to when they are at odds with the world they have made or been heirs to.

The social drama, then—at least as I have always conceived it—is the drama of the whole man. It seeks to deal with his differences from others not *per se,* but toward the end that, if only through drama, we may know how much the same we are, for if we lose that knowledge we shall have nothing left at all. The social drama to me is only incidentally an arraignment of society. *A Streetcar Named Desire* is a social drama; so is *The Hairy Ape,* and so are practically all O'Neill's other plays. For they ultimately make moot, either weakly or with full power, the ancient question, how are we to live? And that question is in its Greek sense, its best and most humane sense, not merely a private query.

The social drama, as I see it, is the main stream and the antisocial drama a bypass. I can no longer take with ultimate seriousness a drama of individual psychology written for its own sake, however full it may be of insight and precise observation. Time is moving; there is a world to make, a civilization to create that will move toward the only goal the humanistic, democratic mind can ever accept with honor. It is a world in which the human being can live as a naturally political, naturally private, naturally engaged person, a world in which once again a true tragic victory may be scored.

But that victory is not really possible unless the individual is more than theoretically capable of being recognized by the powers that lead society. Specifically, when men live, as they do under any industrialized system, as integers who have no weight, no *person*, excepting as either customers, draftees, machine tenders, ideologists, or whatever, it is unlikely (and in my opinion impossible) that a dramatic picture of them can really overcome the public knowledge of their nature in real life. In such a society, be it communistic or capitalistic, man is not tragic, he is pathetic. The tragic figure must have certain innate powers which he uses to pass over the boundaries of the known social law—the accepted mores of his people—in order to test and discover necessity. Such a quest implies that the individual who has moved onto that course must be somehow recognized by the law, by the mores, by the powers that design—be they anthropomorphic gods or economic and political laws— as having the worth, the innate value, of a whole people asking a basic question and demanding its answer. We are so atomized socially that no character in a play can conceivably stand as our vanguard, as our heroic questioner. Our society—and I am speaking of every industrialized society in the world—is so complex, each person being so specialized an integer, that the moment any individual is dramatically characterized and set forth as a hero, our common sense reduces him to the size of a complainer, a misfit. For deep down we no longer believe in the rules of the tragic contest; we no longer believe that some ultimate sense can in fact be made of social causation, or in the possibility that any individual can, by a heroic effort, make sense of it. Thus the man that is driven to question the moral chaos in which we live ends up in our estimate as a possibly commendable but definitely odd fellow, and probably as a compulsively driven neurotic. In place of a social aim which called an all-around excellence—physical, intellectual, and moral—the ultimate good, we have set up a goal which can best be characterized as "happiness"—namely, staying out of trouble. This concept is the end result of the truce which all of us have made with society. And a truce implies two enemies. When the truce is broken it means either that the individual has broken out of his ordained place as an integer, or that the society has broken the law by harming him unjustly—that is, it has not left him alone to be a peaceful integer. In the heroic and tragic time the act of questioning the-way-things-are implied that a quest was being carried on to discover an ultimate law or way of life which would yield excellence; in the present time the quest is that of a man made unhappy by rootlessness and, in every important modern play, by a man who is essentially a victim. We have abstracted from the Greek drama its air of doom, its physical destruction of the hero, but its victory escapes us. Thus it has even become difficult to separate in our minds the ideas of the pathetic and of the tragic. And behind this melting of the two lies the overwhelming power of the modern industrial state, the ignorance of each person in it of anything but his own technique as an economic integer, and the elevation of that state to a holy, quite religious sphere.

What, after all, are our basic social aims as applied to the individual? Americans are often accused of worshiping financial success, but this is, first of all, not an American monopoly, and, second, it does not as a concept make clear what is causing so much uneasiness and moral pain. My own belief, at any rate, is that America has merely arrived first at the condition that awaits every country that takes her economic road without enforcing upon every development of industrial technique certain quite arbitrary standards of value.

The deep moral uneasiness among us, the vast sense of being only tenuously joined to the rest of our fellows, is caused, in my view, by the fact that the person has value as he fits into the pattern of efficiency, and for that alone. The reason *Death of a Salesman,* for instance, left such a strong impression was that it set forth unremittingly the picture of a man who was not even especially "good" but whose situation made clear that at bottom we are alone, valueless, without even the elements of a human person, when once we fail to fit the patterns of efficiency. Under the black shadow of that gigantic necessity, even the drift of some psychoanalytic practice is toward the fitting-in, the training of the individual whose soul has revolted, so that he may once again "take his place" in society—that is, do his "work," "function," in other words, accommodate himself to a scheme of things that is not at all ancient but very new in the world. In short, the absolute value of the individual human being is believed in only as a secondary value; it stands well below the needs of efficient production. We have finally come to serve the machine. The machine must not be stopped, marred, left dirty, or outmoded. Only men can be left marred, stopped, dirty, and alone. Our pity for the victim is mixed, I think. It is mixed with an air of self-preserving superiority—we, thank God, know how to fit in, therefore this victim, however pitiful, has himself to thank for his fate. We believe, in other words, that to fit into the patterns of efficiency is the ultimate good, and at the same time we know in our bones that a crueler concept is not easy to arrive at.

Nor may the exponents of socialism take heart from this. There is no such thing as a capitalist assembly line or drygoods counter. The disciplines required by machines are the same everywhere and will not be truly mitigated by old-age pensions and social-security payments. So long as modern man conceives of himself as valuable only because he fits into some niche in the machine-tending pattern, he will never know anything more than a pathetic doom.

The implications of this fact spread throughout our culture, indeed, throughout the culture of the industrialized parts of the world. Be it in music, literature, drama, or whatever, the value of a work is, willy nilly, equated with its mass "acceptance," i.e., its efficiency. All the engines of economic law are, like the mills of the gods, working toward that same end. The novel of excellence that could once be published without financial loss if it sold two or three thousand copies can no longer be published, because the costs of production require that every book sell at least ten, twelve, or fifteen thousand copies. The play that might have been produced at a decent profit if it could fill half a house for a few months can no longer be produced, for the costs of production require a play to draw packed houses from the first night.

When one has the temerity to suggest that the Greek theater was subsidized, that so much of the world's great music, art, and literature was stubbornly patronized by people who found honor in helping to bring beauty onto the earth, one is not quite suspect, to be sure, but the suggestion nevertheless has an unreal air, an air of being essentially at odds and possibly in dangerous conflict with some unspoken sense of values. For we do believe that a "good" thing, be it art or toothpaste, proves its goodness by its public acceptance. And at the same time we know, too, that something dark and dreadful lies within this concept.

The problem, then, of the social drama in this generation is not the same as it was for Ibsen, Chekhov, or Shaw. They, and the left-wing playwrights of the thirties who amplified their findings and repeated their forms, were oriented either toward an arraignment of some of the symptoms of efficiency men or toward the ultimate cure by socialism. With the proliferation of machine techniques in the world, and the relative perfection of distributing techniques, in America first and the rest of the world soon, the time will shortly be upon us when the truth will dawn. We shall come to see, I think, that Production for Profit and Production for Use (whatever their relative advantages— and each has its own) leave untouched the problem which the Greek drama put so powerfully before mankind. How are we to live? From what fiat, from what ultimate source are we to derive a standard of values that will create in man a respect for himself, a real voice in the fate of his society, and, above all, an aim for his life which is neither a private aim for a private life nor one which sets him below the machine that was made to serve him?

The social drama in this generation must do more than analyze and arraign the social network of relationships. It must delve into the nature of man as he exists to discover what his needs are, so that those needs may be amplified and exteriorized in terms of social concepts. Thus, the new social dramatist, if he is to do his work, must be an even deeper psychologist than those of the past, and he must be conscious at least of the futility of isolating the psychological life of man lest he fall always short of tragedy, and return, again and again and again, to the pathetic swampland where the waters are old tears and not the generative seas from which new kinds of life arise.

It is a good time to be writing because the audience is sick of the old formulations. It is no longer believed—and we may be thankful for it—that the poor are necessarily virtuous or the rich necessarily decayed. Nor is it believed that, as some writers would put it, the rich are necessarily not decayed and the poor necessarily the carriers of vulgarity. We have developed so democratic a culture that in America neither the speech of a man nor his way of dressing nor even his ambitions for himself inevitably mark his social class. On the stage social rank tells next to nothing about the man any more. The decks are cleared. There is a kind of perverse unity forming among us, born, I think, of the discontent of all classes of people with the endless frustration of life. It is possible now to speak of a search for values, not solely from the position of bitterness, but with a warm embrace of mankind, with a sense that at bottom every one of us is a victim of this misplacement of aims.

The debilitation of the tragic drama, I believe, is commensurate with the fracturing and the aborting of the need of man to maintain a fruitful kind of union with his society. Everything we learn, everything we know or deem valuable for a man to know, has been thrown into the creation of a machine technology. The nuclear bomb, as a way of waging war, is questioned only now—because we have it, because we have invented it: not before both sides knew how to make it. Both sides have the bomb and both sides have the machine. Some day the whole world will have both and the only force that will keep them from destructive use will be a force strange to machine psychology, a force born of will—the will of man to survive and to reach his ultimate, most conscious, most knowing, most fulfilled condition, his fated excellence.

History has given the social drama its new chance. Ibsen and Shaw had to work through three acts to prove in the fourth that, even if we are not completely formed by society, there is little left that society does not affect. The tremendous growth in our consciousness of social causation has won for these writers their victory in this sense: it has given to us a wider consciousness of the causes that form character. What the middle of the twentieth century has taught us is that theirs was not the whole answer. It is not enough any more to know that one is at the mercy of social pressures; it is necessary to understand that such a sealed fate cannot be accepted. Nor is courage alone required now to question this complex, although without courage nothing is possible, including real dramatic writing. It is necessary to know that the values of commerce, values which were despised as necessary but less than noble in the long past, are now not merely perversely dominant everywhere but claimed as positive moral goodness itself. The question must begin to be asked; not whether a new thing will work or pay, not whether it is more efficient than its predecessor, more popular, and more easily accepted; but what it will do to human beings. The first invention of man to create that response in all nations was the atomic bomb. It is the first "improvement" to have dramatized for even the numbest mind the question of value. Over the past decade this nation and this world have been gripped by an inner debate on many levels, a debate raised to consciousness by this all-destroying "improvement." Alongside it is the "improvement" called automation, which will soon displace workers who mass-produce in industry. The conquest of poverty and hunger is the order of the day; the refusal of the dark peoples to live in subjection to the white is already a fact. The world, I think, is moving toward a unity, a unity won not alone by the necessities of the physical developments themselves, but by the painful and confused re-assertion of man's inherited will to survive. When the peace is made, and it will be made, the question Greece asked will once again be a question not reserved for philosophers and dramatists; it will be asked by the man who can live out his life without fear of hunger, joblessness, disease, the man working a few hours a day with a life-span probability of eighty, ninety, or perhaps a hundred years. Hard as it is for most people, the sheer struggle to exist and to prosper affords a haven from thought. Complain as they may that they have no time to think, to cultivate themselves, to ask the big questions, most men are terrified at the thought of not having to spend most of their days fighting for existence. In every sphere, and for a hundred hard reasons, the ultimate questions are once again becoming moot, some because without the right answers we will destroy the earth, others because the peace we win may leave us without the fruits of civilized life. The new social drama will be Greek in that it will face man as a social animal and yet without the petty partisanship of so much of past drama. It will be Greek in that the "men" dealt with in its scenes—the psychology and characterizations—will be more than ends in themselves and once again parts of a whole, a whole that is social, a whole that is Man. The world, in a word, is moving into the same boat. For a time, their greatest time, the Greek people were in the same boat—their polis. Our drama, like theirs, will, as it must, ask the same questions, the largest ones. Where are we going now that we are together? For, like every act man commits, the drama is a struggle against his mortality, and meaning is the ultimate reward for having lived.

A NOTE ON THESE PLAYS

A Memory of Two Mondays is about several things. It is about mortality, first, in that the young man caught in the warehouse cannot understand what point there can be, beyond habit and necessity, for men to live this way. He is too young to find out, but it is hoped that the audience will glimpse one answer.

It is that men live this way because they must serve an industrial apparatus which feeds them in body and leaves them to find sustenance for their souls as they may.

This play is a mortal romance. It expresses a preoccupation with the facts that everything we do in this fragmented world is so quickly wiped away and the goals, when won, are so disappointing. It is also the beginning of a further search and it lays the basis for a search. For it points the different roads people do take who are caught in warehouses, and in this play the warehouse is our world—a world in which things are endlessly sent and endlessly received; only time never comes back.

It is an abstract realism in form. It is in one act because I have chosen to say precisely enough about each character to form the image which drove me to write the play—enough and no more.

It is in one act, also, because I have for a long time wished I could turn my back on the "demands" of the Broadway theater in this regard. There are perfectly wonderful things one can say in one sentence, in one letter, one look, or one act. On Broadway this whole attitude has been suspect, regarded as the means taken by fledglings to try their wings. My ambition is to write shorter and shorter plays. It is harder to hit a target with one bullet—perhaps that is why.

A View from the Bridge is in one act because, quite simply, I did not know how to pull a curtain down anywhere before its end. While writing it, I kept looking for an act curtain, a point of pause, but none ever developed. Actually it is practically a full-length play in number of pages, needing only the addition of a little material to make it obvious as such.

That little material, that further elaboration, is what seemed to me, however, exactly what it ought not to have. Like *A Memory of Two Mondays,* this play has been in the back of my head for many years. And, as with the former, I have been asking of it why it would not get any longer. The answer occurred finally that one ought to say on the stage as much as one knows, and this, quite simply, is what I know about these subjects.

This is not to say that there is nothing more I could tell about any of the people involved. On the contrary, there is a great deal—several plays' worth, in fact. Furthermore, all the cues to great length of treatment are there in *A View from the Bridge*. It is wide open for a totally subjective treatment, involving, as it does, several elements which fashion has permitted us to consider down to the last detail. There are, after all, an incestuous motif, homosexuality, and, as I shall no doubt soon discover, eleven other neurotic patterns hidden within it, as well as the question of codes. It would be ripe for a slowly evolving drama through which the hero's antecedent life forces might, one by one, be brought to light until we know his relationships to his parents, his uncles, his grandmother, and the incident in his life which, when revealed toward the end of the second act, is clearly what drove him inevitably to his disaster.

But as many times as I have been led backward into Eddie's life, "deeper" into the subjective forces that made him what he evidently is, a counter-impulse drew me back. It was a sense of form, the shape of this work which I saw first sparely, as one sees a naked mast on the sea, or a barren cliff. What struck me first about this tale when I heard it one night in my neighborhood was how directly, with what breathtaking simplicity, it did evolve. It seemed to me, finally, that its very bareness, its absolutely unswerving path, its exposed skeleton, so to speak, was its wisdom and even its charm and must not be tampered with. In this instance to cleave to his story was to cleave to the man, for the naïveté with which Eddie Carbone attacked his apparent enemy, its very directness and suddenness, the kind of blatant confession he could make to a near-stranger, the clarity with which he saw a wrong course of action—these *qualities* of the events themselves, their texture, seemed to me more psychologically telling than a conventional investigation in width which would necessarily relax that clear, clean line of his catastrophe.

This play falls into a single act, also, because I saw the characters purely in terms of their action and because they are a kind of people who, when inactive, have no new significant definition as people. I use the word "significant" because I am tired of documentation which, while perfectly apt and evidently reasonable, does not add anything to our comprehension of the tale's essence. In so writing, I have made the assumption that the audience is like me and would like to see, for once, a fine, high, always visible arc of forces moving in full view to a single explosion.

There was, as well, another consideration that held ornamentation back. When I heard this tale first it seemed to me that I had heard it before, very long ago. After a time I thought that it must be some re-enactment of a Greek myth which was ringing a long-buried bell in my own subconscious mind. I have not been able to find such a myth and yet the conviction persists, and for that reason I wished not to interfere with the myth-like march of the tale. The thought has often occurred to me that the two "submarines," the immigrants who come to Eddie from Italy, set out, as it were, two thousand years ago. There was such an iron-bound purity in the autonomic egocentricity of the aims of each of the persons involved that the weaving together of their lives seemed almost the work of a fate. I have tried to press as far as my reason can go toward defining the objective and subjective elements that made that fate, but I must confess that in the end a mystery remains for me and I have not attempted to conceal that fact. I know a good many ways to explain this story, but none of them fills its outline completely. I wrote it in order to discover its meanings completely, and I have not got them all yet, for there is a wonder remaining for me even now, a kind of expectation that derives, I think, from a sense of having somehow stumbled upon a hallowed tale.

The form of this play, finally, had a special attraction for me because once the decision was made to tell it without an excess line, the play took a harder, more objective shape. In effect, the form announces in the first moments of the play that only that will be told which is cogent, and that this story is the only part of Eddie Carbone's life worth our notice and therefore no effort will be made to draw in elements of his life that are beneath these, the most tense and meaningful of his hours. The form is what it is because its aim is to recreate my own feeling toward this tale—namely, wonderment. It is not designed primarily to draw tears or laughter from an audience but to strike a particular note of astonishment at the way in which, and the reasons for which, a man will endanger and risk and lose his very life.

The Family in Modern Drama

MOST people, including the daily theater reviewers, have come to assume that the forms in which plays are written spring either from nowhere or from the temperamental choice of the playwrights. I am not maintaining that the selection of a form is as objective a matter as the choice of let us say a raincoat instead of a linen suit for a walk on a rainy day; on the contrary, most playwrights, including myself, reach rather instinctively for that form, that way of telling a play, which seems inevitably right for the subject at hand. Yet I wonder whether it is all as accidental, as "free" a choice, as it appears to be at a superficial glance. I wonder whether there may not be within the ideas of family on the one hand, and society on the other, primary pressures which govern our notions of the right form for a particular kind of subject matter.

It has gradually come to appear to me over the years that the spectrum of dramatic forms, from Realism over to the Verse Drama, the Expressionistic techniques, and what we call vaguely the Poetic Play, consists of forms which express human relationships of a particular kind, each of them suited to express either a primarily familial relation at one extreme, or a primarily social relation at the other.

From *The Atlantic Monthly,* 197 (April 1956), pp. 35–41. Based on an address delivered at Harvard University in memory of Theodore Spencer. Copyright © 1956 by Arthur Miller.

When we think of Realism we think of Ibsen—and if we don't we ought to, because in his social plays he not only used the form but pressed it very close to its ultimate limits. What are the main characteristics of this form? We know it by heart, of course, since most of the plays we see are realistic plays. It is written in prose; it makes believe it is taking place independently of an audience which views it through a "fourth wall," the grand objective being to make everything seem true to life in life's most evident and apparent sense. In contrast, think of any play by Aeschylus. You are never under an illusion in his plays that you are watching "life"; you are watching a play, an art work.

Now at the risk of being obvious I must remind you that Realism is a style, an artful convention, and not a piece of reportage. What, after all, is real about having all the furniture in a living room facing the footlights? What is real about people sticking to the same subject for three consecutive hours? Realism is a style, an invention quite as consciously created as Expressionism, Symbolism, or any of the other less familiar forms. In fact, it has held the stage for a shorter period of time than the more poetic forms and styles which dominate the great bulk of the world repertoire, and when it first came into being it was obvious to all as a style, a poet's invention. I say this in order to make clear that Realism is neither more nor less "artistic" than any other form. The only trouble is that it more easily lends itself in our age to hack work, for one thing because more people can write passable prose than verse. In other ages, however, as for instance in the lesser Elizabethan playwrights, hack work could also make of the verse play a pedestrian and uninspired form.

As with any artist, Ibsen was writing not simply to photograph scenes from life. After all, at the time he wrote *A Doll's House* how many Norwegian or European women had slammed the door upon their hypocritical relations with their husbands? Very few. So there was nothing, really, for him to photograph. What he was doing, however, was projecting through his personal interpretation of common events what he saw as their concealed significance for society. In other words, in a perfectly "realistic" way he did not report so much as project or even prophesy a meaning. Put in playwriting terms, he created a symbol on the stage.

We are not ordinarily accustomed to juxtaposing the idea of a symbol with the idea of Realism. The symbolic action, symbolic speech, have come to be reserved in our minds for the more poetic forms. Yet Realism shares equally with all other ways of telling a play this single mission. It must finally arrive at a meaning symbolic of the underlying action it has set forth. The difference lies in its method of creating its symbol as opposed to the way the poetic forms create theirs.

Now then, the question arises: Why, if Ibsen and several other playwrights could use Realism so well to make plays about modern life, and if in addition the modern American audience is so quickly at home with the form—why should playwrights over the past thirty years be so impatient with it? Why has it been assaulted from every side? Why do so many people turn their backs on it and revere instead any kind of play which is fanciful or poetic? At the same time, why does Realism always seem to be drawing us all back to its arms? We have not yet created in this country a succinct form to take its place. Yet it seems that Realism has become a familiar bore; and by means of cutout sets, revolving stages, musical backgrounds, new and more imaginative lighting schemes, our stage is striving to break up the old living room. However, the perceiving eye knows that many of these allegedly poetic plays are Realism underneath, tricked up to look otherwise. I am criticizing nobody, only stating that the question of form is a deeper one, perhaps, than we have been willing to admit.

As I have indicated, I have come to wonder whether the force or pressure that makes for Realism, that even requires it, is the magnetic force of the family relationship within the play, and the pressure which evokes in a genuine, unforced way the un-realistic modes is the social relationship within the play. In a generalized way we commonly recognize that forms do have some extra-theatrical, common-sense criteria; for instance, one of the prime difficulties in writing modern opera, which after all is lyric drama, is that you cannot rightly sing so many of the common thoughts of common life. A line like "Be sure to take your bath, Gloria," is difficult to musicalize, and impossible to take seriously as a sung concept. But we normally stop short at recognition of the ridiculous in this problem. Clearly, a poetic drama must be built upon a poetic idea, but I wonder if that is the whole problem. It is striking to me, for instance, that Ibsen, the master of Realism, while writing his realistic plays in quite as serious a frame of mind as in his social plays, suddenly burst out of the realistic frame, out of the living room, when he wrote *Peer Gynt*. I think that it is not primarily the living room he left behind, in the sense that this factor had made a poetic play impossible for him, but rather the family context. For Peer Gynt is first of all a man seen alone; equally, he is a man confronting non-familial, openly social relationships and forces.

I warn you not to try to apply this rule too mechanically. A play, like any human relationship, has a predominant quality, but it also contains powerful elements which, although secondary, may not be overlooked, and may in fact be crucial in the development of that relationship. I offer this concept, therefore, as a possible tool and not as a magic key to the writing or understanding of plays and their forms.

I have used Ibsen as an example because he wrote in several forms; another equally experimental dramatist was O'Neill. It ought to be noted that O'Neill himself described his preoccupation as being not with the relations between man and man, but with those between man and God. What has this remark to do with dramatic form? Everything, I think. It is obvious, to begin with, that Ibsen's mission was to create not merely characters, but a context in which they were formed and functioned as people. That context, heavily and often profoundly delineated, was his society. His very idea of fate, for instance, was the inevitability residing in the conflict between the life force of his characters struggling with the hypocrisies, the strangling and abortive effects of society upon them. Thus, if only to create a climax, Ibsen had to draw society in his plays as a realistic force embodied in money, in social mores, in taboos, and so on, as well as an internal, subjective force within his characters.

O'Neill, however, seems to have been seeking for some fate-making power behind the social force itself. He went to ancient Greece for some definition of that force; he reached toward modern religion and toward many other possible sources of the poetic modes. My point here, however, is that so long as the family and family relations are at the center of his plays his form remains—indeed, it is held prisoner by—Realism. When, however, as for instance in *The Hairy Ape* and *Emperor Jones,* he deals with men out in society, away from the family context, his forms become alien to Realism, more openly and self-consciously symbolic, poetic, and finally heroic.

Up to this point I have been avoiding any question of content except that of the family relation as opposed to relations out in the world—social relations. Now I should like to make the bald statement that all plays we call great, let alone those we call serious, are ultimately involved with some aspect of a single problem. It is this: How may a man make of the outside world a home? How and in what ways must he struggle, what must he strive to change and overcome within himself and outside himself if he is to find the safety, the surroundings of love, the ease of soul, the sense of identity and honor which, evidently, all men have connected in their memories with the idea of family?

One ought to be suspicious of any attempt to boil down all the great themes to a single sentence, but this one—"How may a man make of the outside world a home?"—does bear watching as a clue to the inner life of the great plays. Its aptness is most evident in the modern repertoire; in fact, where it is not the very principle of the play at hand we do not take the play quite seriously. If, for instance, the struggle in *Death of a Salesman* were simply between father and son for recognition and forgiveness it would diminish in importance. But when it extends itself out of the family circle and into society, it broaches those questions of social status, social honor and recognition, which expand its vision and lift it out of the merely particular toward the fate of the generality of men.

The same is true—although achieved in different ways—of a play like *A Streetcar Named Desire,* which could quite easily have been limited to a study of psychopathology were it not that it is placed clearly within the wider bounds of the question I am discussing. Here Blanche Dubois and the sensitivity she represents has been crushed by her moving out of the shelter of the home and the family into the uncaring, anti-human world outside it. In a word, we begin to partake of the guilt for her destruction, and for Willy's, because the blow struck against them was struck outside the home rather than within it—which is to say that it affects us more because it is a social fact we are witnessing.

The crucial question has an obverse side. If we look at the great plays—at *Hamlet, Oedipus, Lear*—we must be impressed with one fact perhaps above all others. These plays are all examining the concept of loss, of man's deprivation of a once-extant state of bliss unjustly shattered—a bliss, a state of equilibrium, which the hero (and his audience) is attempting to reconstruct or to recreate with new, latter-day life materials. It has been said often that the central theme of the modern repertoire is the alienation of man, but the idea usually halts at the social alienation—he cannot find a satisfying role in society. What I am suggesting here is that while this is true of our plays, the more or less hidden impulse antedating social alienation, the unsaid premise of the very idea of "satisfaction," is the memory of both playwright and audience of an enfolding family and of childhood. It is as though both playwright and audience believed that they had once had an identity, a *being,* somewhere in the past which in the present has lost its completeness, its definitiveness, so that the central force making for pathos in these large and thrusting plays is the paradox which Time bequeaths to us all: we cannot go home again, and the world we live in is an alien place.

One of the forms most clearly in contrast to Realism is Expressionism. I should like now to have a look at its relevancy to the family-social complex.

The technical arsenal of Expressionism goes back to Aeschylus. It is a form of play which manifestly seeks to dramatize the conflict of either social, religious, ethical, or moral forces *per se,* and in their own naked roles, rather than to present psychologically realistic human characters in a more or less realistic environment. There is, for instance, no attempt by Aeschylus to create the psychology of a violent "character" in *Prometheus Bound,* or of a powerful one; rather he brings on two figures whose names are Power and Violence, and they behave as the *idea* of Power and the *idea* of Violence ought to behave, according to the laws of Power and Violence. In Germany after the First World War, playwrights sought to dramatize and unveil the social condition of man with similar means. For instance, in *Gas I* and *Gas II* Georg Kaiser placed the figure of man against an image of industrial society but without the slightest attempt to characterize the man except as a representative of one or the other of the social classes vying for control of the machine. There are, of course, numerous other examples of the same kind of elimination of psychological characterization in favor of what one might call the presentation of forces. In *The Great God Brown,* for instance, as well as in *The Hairy Ape,* O'Neill reached toward this very ancient means of dramatization without psychology—without, one might say, behavior as we normally know it. *Everyman* is another work in that long line.

In passing, I must ask you to note that expressionist plays—which is to say plays preoccupied with the open confrontation of moral, ethical, or social forces—seem inevitably to cast a particular kind of shadow. The moment realistic behavior and psychology disappear from the play all the other appurtenances of

Realism vanish too. The stage is stripped of knickknacks; instead it reveals symbolic *designs,* which function as overt pointers toward the moral to be drawn from the action. We are no longer under quite the illusion of watching through a transparent fourth wall. Instead we are constantly reminded, in effect, that we are watching a theater piece. In short, we are not bidden to lose our consciousness of time and place, the consciousness of ourselves, but are appealed to through our intelligence, our faculties of knowing rather than of feeling.

This difference in the area of appeal is the difference between our familial emotions and our social emotions. The two forms not only spring from different sectors of human experience but end up by appealing to different areas of receptivity within the audience. Nor is this phenomenon confined to the play.

When one is speaking to one's family, for example, one uses a certain level of speech, a certain plain diction perhaps, a tone of voice, an inflection suited to the intimacy of the occasion. But when one faces an audience of strangers, as a politician does, for instance—and he is the most social of men—it seems right and proper for him to reach for the well-turned phrase, even the poetic word, the aphorism, the metaphor. And his gestures, his stance, his tone of voice, all become larger than life; moreover, his character is not what gives him these prerogatives, but his role. In other words, a confrontation with society permits us, or even enforces upon us, a certain reliance upon ritual. Similarly with the play.

The implications of this natural wedding of form with inner relationships are many, and some of them are complex. It is true to say, I think, that the language of the family is the language of the private life—prose. The language of society, the language of the public life, is verse. According to the degree to which the play partakes of either relationship, it achieves the right to move closer or further away from either pole. I repeat that this "right" is given by some common consent which in turn is based upon our common experience in life.

It is interesting to look at a couple of modern plays from this viewpoint and to see whether critical sense can be made of them. T. S. Eliot's *The Cocktail Party,* for instance, drew from most intelligent auditors a puzzled admiration. In general, one was aware of a struggle going on between the apparencies of the behavior of the people and what evidently was the preoccupation of the playwright. There were a Husband and a Wife whom we were evidently expected to accept in that commonly known relationship, especially since the setting and the mode of speech and much of its diction were perfectly real if inordinately cultivated for a plebeian American audience. Even the theme of the play was, or should have been, of importance to most of us. Here we were faced with the alternative ways of giving meaning to domestic existence, one of them being through the cultivation of self, partly by means of the psychoanalytic ritual; the other and victorious method being the martyrization of the self, not for the sake of another, or as a rebuke to another, as martyrdom is usually indulged in in family life, but for the sake of martyrdom, of the disinterested action whose ultimate model was, according to the author, Jesus Christ. The heroine is celebrated for having been eaten alive by ants while on a missionary work among savages, and the very point is that there was no point—she converted nobody at all. Thus she gained her self by losing self or giving it away. Beyond the Meaningless she found Meaning at last.

To say the least, Eliot is manifestly an apt writer of verse. The inability of this play to achieve a genuine poetic level cannot therefore be laid to the usual cause—the unpoetic nature of the playwright's talent. Indeed, *Murder in the Cathedral* is a genuine poetic play, so he had already proved that he could achieve a wholeness of poetic form. I believe that the puzzlement created by *The Cocktail Party,* the sense of its being drawn in two opposite directions, is the result of the natural unwillingness of our minds to give to the Husband-Wife relation—a family relation— the prerogatives of the poetic mode, especially when the relationship is originally broached, as it is in this play, through any means approaching Realism.

Whether consciously or not, Eliot himself was aware of this

dichotomy and wrote, and has said that he wrote, a kind of line
which would not seem obtrusively formal and poetic to the listening ear. The injunction to keep it somehow unpoetic was issued
by the central family situation, in my opinion. There was no need
to mask his poetry at all in *Murder in the Cathedral,* because the
situation is social, the conflict of a human being with the world.
That earlier play had the unquestioned right to the poetic because it dealt with man as a public figure and could use the public
man's style and diction.

We recognize now that a play can be poetic without verse, and it
is in this middle area that the complexities of tracing the influence of the family and social elements upon the form become
more troublesome. *Our Town* by Thornton Wilder is such a
play, and it is important not only for itself but because it is the
progenitor of many other works.

This is a family play which deals with the traditional family
figures, the father, mother, brother, sister. At the same time it
uses this particular family as a prism through which is reflected
the author's basic idea, his informing principle—which can be
stated as the indestructibility, the everlastingness, of the family
and the community, its rhythm of life, its rootedness in the essentially safe cosmos despite troubles, wracks, and seemingly
disastrous, but essentially temporary, dislocations.

Technically, it is not arbitrary in any detail. Instead of a family
living room or a house, we are shown a bare stage on which actors
set chairs, a table, a ladder to represent a staircase or an upper
floor, and so on. A narrator is kept in the foreground as though
to remind us that this is not so much "real life" as an abstraction of it—in other words, a stage. It is clearly a poetic rather than
a realistic play. What makes it that? Well, let us first imagine
what would make it more realistic.

Would a real set make it realistic? Not likely. A real set
would only discomfit us by drawing attention to what would
then appear to be a slightly unearthly quality about the characterizations. We should probably say, "People don't really act like

that." In addition, the characterization of the whole town could not be accomplished with anything like its present vividness if the narrator were removed, as he would have to be from a realistic set, and if the entrances and exits of the environmental people, the townspeople, had to be justified with the usual motives and machinery of Realism.

The preoccupation of the entire play is quite what the title implies—the town, the society, and not primarily this particular family—and every stylistic means used is to the end that the family foreground be kept in its place, merely as a foreground for the larger context behind and around it. In my opinion, it is this larger context, the town and its enlarging, widening significance, that is the bridge to the poetic for this play. Cut out the town and you will cut out the poetry.

The play is worth examining further against the Ibsen form of Realism to which it is inevitably related if only in contrast. Unlike Ibsen, Wilder sees his characters in this play not primarily as personalities, as individuals, but as forces, and he individualizes them only enough to carry the freight, so to speak, of their roles as forces. I do not believe, for instance, that we can think of the brother in this play, or the sister or the mother, as having names other than Brother, Sister, Mother. They are not given that kind of particularity or interior life. They are characterized rather as social factors, in their roles of Brother, Sister, Mother, in Our Town. They are drawn, in other words, as forces to enliven and illuminate the author's symbolic vision and his theme, which is that of the family as a timeless, stable quantity which has not only survived all the turmoil of time but is, in addition, beyond the possibility of genuine destruction.

The play is important to any discussion of form because it has achieved a largeness of meaning and an abstraction of style that created that meaning, while at the same time it has moved its audiences subjectively—it has made them laugh and weep as abstract plays rarely if ever do. But it would seem to contradict my contention here. If it is true that the presentation of the family on the stage inevitably forces Realism upon the play, how did this family play manage to transcend Realism to achieve its symbolistic style?

Every form, every style, pays its price for its special advantages. The price paid by *Our Town* is psychological characterization forfeited in the cause of the symbol. I do not believe, as I have said, that the characters are identifiable in a psychological way, but only as figures in the family and social constellation, and this is not meant in criticism, but as a statement of the limits of this form. I would go further and say that it is not *necessary* for every kind of play to do every kind of thing. But if we are after ultimate reality we must make ultimate demands.

I think that had Wilder drawn his characters with a deeper configuration of detail and with a more remorseless quest for private motive and self-interest, for instance, the story as it stands now would have appeared oversentimental and even sweet. I think that if the play tested its own theme more remorselessly, the world it creates of a timeless family and a rhythm of existence beyond the disturbance of social wracks would not remain unshaken. The fact is that the juvenile delinquent is quite directly traced to the breakup of family life and, indeed, to the break in that ongoing, steady rhythm of community life which the play celebrates as indestructible.

I think, further, that the close contact which the play established with its audience was the result of its coincidence with the deep longing of the audience for such stability, a stability which in daylight out on the street does not truly exist. The great plays pursue the idea of loss and deprivation of an earlier state of bliss which the characters feel compelled to return to or to recreate. I think this play forgoes the loss and suffers thereby in its quest for reality, but that the audience supplies the sense of deprivation in its own life experience as it faces what in effect is an idyl of the past. To me, therefore, the play falls short of a form that will press into reality to the limits of reality, if only because it could not plumb the psychological interior lives of its characters and still keep its present form. It is a triumph in that it does open a way toward the dramatization of the larger truths of existence while using the common materials of life. It is a truly poetic play.

Were there space, I should like to go into certain contemporary works with a view to the application in them of the forces of society and family—works by Clifford Odets, Tennessee Williams, Lillian Hellman, William Saroyan, and others. But I will jump to the final question I have in mind. If there is any truth in the idea of a natural union of the family and Realism as opposed to society and the poetic, what are the reasons for it?

First, let us remind ourselves of an obvious situation, but one which is often overlooked. The man or woman who sits down to write a play, or who enters a theater to watch one, brings with him in each case a common life experience which is not suspended merely because he has turned writer or become part of an audience. We—all of us—have a role anteceding all others: we are first sons, daughters, sisters, brothers. No play can possibly alter this given role.

The concepts of Father, Mother, and so on were received by us unawares before the time we were conscious of ourselves as selves. In contrast, the concepts of Friend, Teacher, Employee, Boss, Colleague, Supervisor, and the many other social relations came to us long after we gained consciousness of ourselves, and are therefore outside ourselves. They are thus in an objective rather than a subjective category. In any case, what we feel is always more "real" to us than what we know, and we feel the family relation while we only know the social one. Thus the former is the very apotheosis of the real and has an inevitability and a foundation indisputably actual, while the social relation is always relatively mutable, accidental, and consequently of a profoundly arbitrary nature to us.

Today the difficulty in creating a form that will unite both elements in a full rather than partial onslaught on reality is the reflection of the deep split between the private life of man and his social life. Nor is this the first time in history that such a separation has occurred. Many critics have remarked upon it, for instance, as a probable reason for the onset of Realism in the later Greek plays, for it is like a rule of society that, as its time of troubles arrives, its citizens revert to a kind of privacy of life that excludes society, as though man at such times would like to banish society from his mind. When this happens, man excludes poetry too.

All of which, while it may provide a solution, or at least indicate the mansion where the solution lives, only serves to point to the ultimate problem more succinctly. Obviously, the playwright cannot create a society, let alone one so unified as to allow him to portray man in art as a monolithic creature. The playwright is not a reporter, but in a serious work of art he cannot set up an image of man's condition so distant from reality as to violate the common sense of what reality is. But a serious work, to say nothing of a tragic one, cannot hope to achieve truly high excellence short of an investigation into the whole gamut of causation of which society is a manifest and crucial part. Thus it is that the common Realism of the past forty or fifty years has been assaulted—because it could not, with ease and beauty, bridge the widening gap between the private life and the social life. Thus it is that the problem was left unsolved by Expressionism, which evaded it by forgoing psychological realism altogether and leaping over to a portrayal of social forces alone. Thus it is that there is now a certain decadence about many of our plays; in the past ten years they have come more and more to dwell solely upon psychology, with little or no attempt to locate and dramatize the social roles and conflicts of their characters. For it is proper to ascribe decay to that which turns its back upon society when, as is obvious to any intelligence, the fate of mankind is social.

Finally, I should say that the current quest after the poetic as poetic is fruitless. It is the attempt to make apples without growing trees. It is seeking poetry precisely where poetry is not: in the private life viewed entirely within the bounds of the subjective, the area of sensation, or the bizarre and the erotic. From these areas of the private life have sprung the mood plays, the plotless plays for which there is much admiration as there is much relief when one turns from a problem to a ramble in the woods. I do not ask you to disdain such plays, for they are within the realm of art; I say only that the high work, the tragic work, cannot be forged waywardly, while playing by ear. There is a charm in improvisation, in letting one chord suggest the other and ending when the moment wanes. But the high order of art to which drama is fated will come only when it seeks to account for the total condition of man, and this cannot be improvised.

Whatever is said to describe a mood play, one point must be made: such plays all have in common an air of self-effacement—which is to say that they wish to seem as though they had not only no plot but no writer. They would convince us that they "just happen," that no directing hand has arranged matters—contrary to the Ibsen plays, for instance, or, for that matter, the Shakespearean play or the Greek.

Furthermore, the entire operation is most moody when the characters involved have the least consciousness of their own existence. The mood play is a play in hiding. A true plot is an assertion of meaning. The mood play is not, as it has been mistaken for, a rebellion of any kind against the so-called well-made play, especially when Ibsen is widely held to be a writer of well-made plays. For there is as much subjectivity and inner poetry in *Hedda Gabler*—I daresay a lot more—as in any of these mood plays. What is really repulsive in Ibsen to one kind of contemporary mind is not openly mentioned: it is his persistent search for an organizing principle behind the "moods" of existence and not the absence of mood in his work.

An art form, like a person, can achieve greatness only as it accepts great challenges. Over the past few decades the American theater, in its best moments, has moved courageously and often beautifully into the interior life of man, an area that had most often been neglected in the past. But now, I think, we are in danger of settling for tears, as it were—for any play that "moves" us, quite as though the ultimate criterion of the art were lachrymosity. For myself, I find that there is an increasing reliance upon what pass for realistic, even tough, analytical picturizations of existence, which are really quite sentimental underneath; and the sentiment is getting thicker, I think, and an end in itself. Sentimentalism is perfectly all right, but it is nowhere near a great challenge, and to pursue it, even under the guise of the exotic atmosphere and the celebration of the sensuous, is not going to bring us closer to the fated mission of the drama.

What, after all, is that mission? I may as well end with such a question because it underlies and informs every word I have written. I think of it so: Man has created so many specialized means of unveiling the truth of the world around him and the world within him—the physical sciences, the psychological sciences, the disciplines of economic and historical research and theory. In effect, each of these attacks on the truth is partial. It is within the rightful sphere of the drama—it is, so to speak, its truly just employment and its ultimate design—to embrace the many-sidedness of man. It is as close to being a total art as the race has invented. It can tell, like science, what is—but more, it can tell what ought to be. It can depict, like painting, in designs and portraits, in the colors of the day or night; like the novel it can spread out its arms and tell the story of a life, or a city, in a few hours—but more, it is dynamic, it is always on the move as life is, and it is perceived like life through the motions, the gestures, the tones of voice, and the gait and nuance of living people. It is the singer's art and the painter's art and the dancer's art, yet it may hew to fact no less tenaciously than does the economist or the physician. In a word, there lies within the dramatic form the ultimate possibility of raising the truth-consciousness of mankind to a level of such intensity as to transform those who observe it.

The problem, therefore, is not simply an aesthetic one. As people, as a society, we thirst for clues to the past and the future; least of all, perhaps, do we know about the present, about what *is*. It is the present that is always most evasive and slippery, for the present always threatens most directly our defenses against seeing what we are, and it is the present, always the present, to which the dramatic form must apply or it is without interest and a dead thing, and forms do die when they lose their capacity to open up the present. So it is its very nature to bring us closer to ourselves if only it can grow and change with the changing world.

In the deepest sense, I think, to sophisticated and unsophisticated alike, nothing is quite so real to us, so extant, as that which has been made real by art. Nor is this ironical and comic. For the fact is that art is a function of the civilizing act quite as much as is the building of the water supply. American civilization is only recently coming to a conscious awareness of art not as a luxury but as a necessity of life. Without the right dramatic form a genuine onslaught upon the veils that cloak the present is not possible. In the profoundest sense I cannot create that form unless, somewhere in you, there is a wish to know the present and a demand upon me that I give it to you.

For at bottom what is that form? It is the everlastingly sought balance between order and the need of our souls for freedom; the relatedness between our vaguest longings, our inner questions, and private lives and the life of the generality of men which is our society and our world. How may man make for himself a home in that vastness of strangers and how may he transform that vastness into a home? This, as I have repeated, is the question a form must solve anew in every age. This, I may say, is the problem before you too.

1956 and All This

I OBVIOUSLY can have no special competence in the field of foreign policy. I only know what I read in the papers, and the fact that I am a creative writer does not make my opinions either wiser or more persuasive than those of any other man. But it seems to me that there might be some good purpose in one of my profession expressing himself on this kind of problem. A certain awareness of attitudes outside our borders has been forced on me over the past ten years. My plays are regularly produced on the stages of Europe, Asia, Australia, and other areas. I have not traveled extensively abroad for some seven years now, but I do receive a steady mail from artists, producers, and audiences in foreign countries; there are visits and a steady correspondence with them and frequent newspaper reviews and articles concerning my work.

From all these sources I have a certain group of impressions, especially of Europe, which have at least one rather unusual basis, namely, the comparative foreign reaction to works written for the American audience.

Through these varying reactions to the same object, national

Originally published as "The Playwright and the Atomic World" in the *Colorado Quarterly*, 5 (Autumn 1956), pp. 117–137. Reprinted with the same title in the *Tulane Drama Review*, 5 (June 1961), pp. 3–20. Neither Arthur Miller nor I find that the original title accurately reflects the contents of the essay, and have retitled it for this collection.—(R.A.M.)

attitudes can be examined in a perspective less turbulent and possibly of more lasting truth than purely political studies will elicit. In a theater, people are themselves; they come of their own volition; they accept or reject, are moved or left cold not by virtue of reason alone or of emotion alone, but as whole human beings.

A communion through art is therefore unusually complete; it can be a most reliable indication of a fundamental unity; and an inability to commune through art is, I think, a stern indication that cultures have not yet arrived at a genuine common ground. Had there been no Flaubert, no Zola, no Proust, de Maupassant, Stendhal, Balzac, Dumas; had there been no Mark Twain, or Poe, Hawthorne, Emerson, Hemingway, Steinbeck, Faulkner, or the numerous other American artists of the first rank, our conviction of essential union with France and of France with us would rest upon the assurances of the two Departments of State and the impressions of tourists. I think that had there been no Tolstoy, no Gogol, no Turgenev, no Chekhov or Dostoyevsky, we should have no assurance at all nor any faint hope that the Russian heart was even ultimately comprehensible to us. Just recently the new government of Ceylon, which has just replaced the avowedly pro-British, pro-American regime, was and is still thought to be anti-American. The program is to nationalize foreign-owned plantations, and for the first time in history they will exchange Ambassadors with Moscow and Peking. The Prime Minister, an Oxford graduate, took pains to correct the idea he was anti-Western. He said, "How could I be against a country that produced Mark Twain?"

There is more than a literary appreciation behind this remark, I think. Literature of the first rank is a kind of international signaling service, telling all who can read that wherever that distant blinker is shining live men of a common civilization.

Now, at the outset, I want to make clear that I disagree with those who believe the United States has entirely failed in its foreign policy since the close of World War II. But I think that the values this country has stood for in the past, more than in the present, have helped to keep alive a promise of a democratic future for the world. I do not believe, however, that our policy has stopped communism. I think that our armament has been a deterrent. But that is all. A policy of merely deterring anything is negative. I believe the time is upon us, and has been for some time now, when an entirely new approach has to be taken to the whole problem of what the future is to be. I base this upon the assumption that the atomic and armament statement is a historic fact which will remain for an indefinite period. In short, the policy was justified, if it was at all, on the basis of an imminence of war. I am proceeding on the ground that there will not be a war and cannot be. I summarize these conclusions at the outset so that the criticisms I may level now will be taken as they are intended—as guides to a positive foreign policy, and not an exercise in sarcasm. For good or ill, what the government has done in the world we have done; equally, what it will do in the future must represent, more than ever before, the real feelings and the judgments of the people. My quarrel, in fact, is that our policy has ceased to reflect the positive quality of the American people, and rests basically on their fears, both real and imaginary. We are much more than our fears, but the world does not often know that. And now to certain observations from my experience as a dramatist.

To begin with, I have often been struck, in foreign reviews of my plays, by the distinct difference in the foreign critic's attitudes toward meaning in a play, toward the theater as an institution. Here, our critics and most of the people in our audiences are pragmatists. As in our scientific tradition, our industrial tradition, in most of the things we do, we are almost wholly absorbed by the immediate impact of an idea or an invention. A thing is judged almost exclusively by whether it works, or pays, or is popular. In the scientific fields, my understanding is that this has been both an advantage and a liability, because our traditionally meager interest in theoretical, pure science has held back our scientific advance. At the same time, of course, our concentration upon practical, applied science has helped to give us a highly developed industry and a profusion of consumers' goods. The

roster of those scientists who developed the atomic bomb is, as
we know, very heavily weighted with foreign names, for this was
a child of pure research. The opposing emphasis here and abroad
is probably accounted for by the smallness of the European
market for the products of applied science, for one thing. From
this lack they have in this case made a virtue. But the irony
remains that despite our enormous scientific establishment and
our admitted superiority in many applied fields, there is evidently
an impression abroad, founded until recently on fact, that we
have little intellectual interest in science. I believe there is now a
consciousness here of that need which is long past due.

In the field of the drama the same sort of irony prevails, and
I think its operating principle has a certain effect upon a rather
wide sector of European opinion. On the one hand, one feels
the European writer, the critic, and from my mail the audience
too are more interested in the philosophic, moral and principled
values of the play than we are. One senses that they rather look
askance at our lack of interest in these matters, and I often think
that for this among other reasons they so often regard us as
essentially a people without seriousness. The truth is that while
our plays move much more rapidly than theirs do, are less likely
to dwell on long conversations woven around piquant paradox
and observation for its own sake, and while they strive more to
be actions than thoughts, it is often admitted that if there is a
leadership in the contemporary play since the Second World
War, at least in terms of international public appeal, America
has it. Put simply, we write plays for people and not for professors or philosophers; the people abroad accept and love many
of our plays, and in some cases, even the philosophers do too.
The point I would make here is that without any special consciousness of the attempt, we have created in the past few decades
a kind of American dramatic style. We have also created an
American movie style, an American style of dress, and probably
architecture, and a style of shopping, and a style of comic books,
and a style of novel writing and popular music—in a word, we
have spontaneously created methods of reaching the great mass

of the people whose effectiveness and exportability, if one may use an ugly word, are not equaled anywhere else.

This has had a multiple effect and it is not easy to separate the good from the bad. But I know, for instance, that there is great resentment among thinking people in Europe at the inroads made by *Reader's Digest* and comic books. One finds Dick Tracy all over the place. As a result of this particular kind of export, we are unwittingly feeding the idea that we incline ever so slightly to the moronic. The idea, for instance, of publishing an abridged novel is barbaric to them, and I'm not sure they're wrong. At the same time, however, our best writers are in many cases their secret or admitted models.

It is time to interject here some word about the importance of what is vaguely called culture in our foreign relations, a matter to which our government, to put it gently, is stupendously indifferent. In 1950, I was interviewed by the press in Copenhagen. It was an entirely literary interview. But when the reporters had left, one man stayed behind. Unlike the others who were of an intellectual sort, he wanted to know where I lived, what sort of a house, whether I played with my children, owned a car, dressed for dinner, and so forth. He turned out to have been from a tabloid paper which was read mainly by what he termed shop-girls. Now, I have yet to be interviewed by the New York *Daily News,* for instance, so I asked him what interest his readers could have in a person who wrote such morose and dreary plays. "It is very important for them to know that there are writers in America," he said. I could hardly believe they doubted that. "Oh yes," he said, "they will be very surprised to read about you, that you exist." But if they were that ignorant, I said, what difference would it make to them whether writers exist in America? What importance could the whole question have for them? "Very important," he said. "They are not intellectuals, but they think anyway that it is necessary for a country to have intellectuals. It will make them more sympathetic to America."

This is but one of many similar incidents which have made me wonder whether we are struggling, unknowingly, with a difference in cultural attitudes which may even warp and change purely political communication at any particular moment.

It is not that we are a people without seriousness. It is that we measure seriousness in an entirely different way than they do. They are the inheritors of a culture which was established, and I believe still exists, on an essentially aristocratic concept, which is to say, out of societies whose majority was nearly illiterate, education was for the few and the artist a kind of adornment to the political state, a measure of its glory and its worth. The artist for us, even as we may pay him much better than they do and cheat him much less, is more of an odd duck, and even among his fellow artists here he does not really exist except when he gains a great popular following. Again, our pragmatism is at work. I think that more Americans than not concede an artist his importance in proportion to his ability to make money with what he creates, for our measure of value is closely attuned to its acceptance by the majority. The artistic product has traditionally had little if any intrinsic justification for most of us. And this has presented our artists with a very lonely and frustrating life on the one hand, but on the other with a worthy if nearly impossible challenge. We regard it as our plain duty to make high art, if we are able, but to make it for all the people. More often than not, however, the art that *is* made sacrifices art for popularity partly because popularity pays fabulously among us. But the challenge is the right one anyway, I believe. The thing of importance now, however, is that even as we have produced some of the best works of literature of this era, we yet stand accused with perfect sobriety of being a mindless country. In this area the Russians have an inherited advantage over us. Despite all their differences from the Western tradition, their inherited attitude toward the artist and the intellectual has essentially the same sort of consciousness as that of the European. I think, for instance, of the time Dostoyevsky died. The entire Russian nation went into mourning for a novelist. I think of the endless lines of people who came to sit at Tolstoy's feet in his later years. I think too of the time a few years ago when I visited the Royal Dramatic Theater in Stockholm and saw an announcement of a forthcoming cycle of Strindberg's plays. I asked the director whether Strindberg was a popular writer in his native Sweden, and the director said he was not. Still for at least one period in each season, Strindberg's plays are regularly produced. "But why do you do this if he is not very popular?" I asked. "That isn't the point," he said. "He was our greatest dramatist and one of the best in the world; it is up to us to keep his plays alive and before the public." Later, we walked through the vast dressing room area of the theater, and there was one which, he said, is not often used. It belonged to a great actor who was now too aged to play. Yet they kept his dressing room solely for his use just in case he might drop in to rest of an afternoon. They needed dressing rooms badly, but it was inconceivable to take this once-great actor's name off his door until he had died.

This is not the occasion to examine the right and wrong of that system; I only wish to say that there is in Europe at least the strong remnant of the idea that the artist is the vessel of his country's selfhood, the speaker who has arisen among his countrymen to articulate if not to immortalize their age. I believe, as well, that because this reverence remains, it leads them to believe that they care more for art than we do, and that it follows we have no real life of the spirit but only a preoccupation with commodities. I would go even further and say that often our immense material wealth is the cue for them to believe that we care less for people than for things. I will not comment here on how much we care for people or how little; I am trying to avoid the question of the civilizing value of this kind of reverence for art. I will only say that at least in one country, Germany, its alleged pride in its artists did not seem to mitigate its ferocity in two world wars. But this is not the whole story either, and I leave it to go on with my observations.

In the different attitudes toward art can be detected attitudes which may be of significance politically. The reviews and comments upon my own play, *Death of a Salesman,* are of interest in this connection. When the play opened in New York it was taken for granted that its hero, the Salesman, and the story itself, were so American as to be quite strange if not incomprehensible to people of other nations; in some countries there is, for instance, no word that really conveys the idea of the salesman in our sense. Yet, wherever it has been shown there seems to have been no difficulty at all in understanding and identifying with the characters, nor was there any particular notice taken of the hero's unusual occupation. It seems to me that if this instantaneous familiarity is any guide, we have made too much of our superficial differences from other peoples. In Catholic Spain, where feudalism is still not a closed era; among fishermen in Norway at the edge of the Arctic Circle; in Rome, Athens, Tokyo—there has been an almost disappointing similarity of reaction to this and other plays of mine in one respect at least. They all seem to feel the anxieties we do; they are none of them certain of how to dissolve the questions put by the play, questions like —what ultimate point can there be for a human life? What satisfaction really exists in the ideal of a comfortable life surrounded by the gadgets we strive so hard to buy? What ought to be the aim for a man in this kind of a world? How can he achieve for himself a sense of genuine fulfillment and an identity? Where, in all the profusion of materiality we have created around us, is the cup where the spirit may reside? In short, what is the most human way to live?

I have put these questions because the commentators around the world have put them, but also because they do inform the play and I meant them to. Yet, no American reviewer actually brought up any of these questions. A play is rarely discussed here as to its philosophic meanings, excepting in a most cursory way; yet the basic effect upon us and the effect upon foreign audiences is evidently very similar. What I am trying to point out, again, is that it is less often the fact itself, the object itself about which we differ, than our unwillingness to rationalize how we feel. I sense that even as we do create the things of the spirit it seems to them rather an accident, rather a contradiction of our real character. I would add that had my plays not worked in Europe, which is to say that had they really been only philosophical works and not infused with the American pragmatic need for scenes to move with a pace and with characters made clear and familiar, the European would not be likely to be interested in them either.

I think it is true to say that for the most part as a nation we do not understand, we do not see that art, our culture itself, is a very sinew of the life we lead. Truly, we have no consciousness of art even as it has changed our tastes in furniture, in the houses we buy, in the cars we want. Only as it is transformed into things of daily use have we the least awareness of its vital functioning among us, and then it is only as its by-products appear in the most plain aspects of usefulness. As an example, even while abstract art is gazed at without comprehension, if not with hatred, its impact upon our linoleum designs, our upholsteries, our drapes, our women's dresses, our buildings, our packages, our advertising—these uses or misuses are quickly accepted without a thought. We have made in real life a most modern environment in many cases and have little conscious awareness of modernity; they have kept an outmoded environment in many cases and have a heightened awareness of what is modern.

This whole antipathy for theorizing, of knowing intellectually what we are doing, has very often crippled our ability to appraise reality. We so often become drowned in our own actions. For instance, it seems to me that this government has acted time and again as though its reasons would be automatically accepted without question or suspicion. In recent months we have armed Pakistan, a nation imbedded in the Indian nation, and one with which India has some potentially explosive disagreements. The reason given for arming Pakistan was security against Russia and China. For the Indian government, however, there could only be one result of this arming and it would be to strengthen Pakistan against India. To defend our act by claiming naïveté will simply not do under the circumstances. We intended the arms for defense against Russia and China, therefore that is all

they will be used for. To rise above our immediate action and
interest, to see beyond the moment and through the eyes of
another country—this requires a kind of imagination which, to
be sure, is not very difficult to achieve, but one must be accustomed to using it. In general, it seems to me, speaking as an
artist and not a politician, this government has proceeded at
times quite as though individual actions could have no larger
meaning; quite as though, in dramatic terms, each moment of
the play we are writing were to be judged for itself and separately
from the play as a whole.

This evident inability to see a context behind an action does
not stop at Politics. I think it is part of our method of seeing life.
Again, I will use the theater as an example. Our critics will be
inclined to see the hero of a play as a psychological figure, as
an individual, a special case always, and their interest flags
beyond that point. It is even said that, strictly speaking, it is not
their business as to the larger significance of a character portrayed on the stage. They are present to discern whether he is
interesting, logically formed, persuasive as a fiction, and so forth.
The European, however, while interested in the character's manifest surface, is equally intent upon discovering what generality
he represents. It is not the business of our critics to decide or
most often to even discuss whether a play is built upon a tattered
and outworn idea; if an old and worn idea is made to work
on the stage once again in terms of effects and suspense and so
forth, it is enough. In the European review one will inevitably
find some estimate of the value of the concept behind the play.
In other words, it is assumed to begin with that a thing is always
made with an intention and that the intention is as important to
evaluate as the effects it manages to create.

Thus it is that we find ourselves unable to meet the suspicions
of Europeans in many situations, and find ourselves puzzled and
even angered as a result. For instance, it is no secret to anyone
in Europe that our borders are, in effect, sealed. And when, as
happened recently, a writer of the eminence of Graham Greene
is denied entry here for a visit in transit to the Far East, I am

sure that most Americans cannot find the slightest patriotic interest in the situation. It happens that for a short time some decades ago, Mr. Greene, a converted Catholic, belonged to the Communist Party and has been an anti-Communist ever since. More importantly, his works are known around the world, and they are regarded by tens of thousands of people as sincere attempts to wrestle with some of the most serious moral and religious and ethical problems of this age. I can only ascribe his exclusion to a complete unwillingness, perhaps even an inability, to admit that Mr. Greene is not any Greene but a very particular Greene existing in a definite Red context; that being a writer of his stature is not a fact of any consequence but a politically important consideration; that for millions of people in the world his profession and the high seriousness with which he has practiced it lend him a certain dispensation, the dispensation of the truth-seeker; and finally, that to refuse him entry into this country implied that this country feared what he might see here. I am sure that given these considerations, our officials would reply that the law is the law; that a writer is only another name to them. Yet it is impossible not to conclude that the real interests of the United States, to say nothing of its dignity, are transgressed by such an action.

I believe that this attitude toward culture is a disservice to us all because it lays us open to extremely dangerous suspicions which can spread out to stain our whole effort to preserve the democratic idea in the world, especially when we have had to create so large a military machine. A display of force is always a generator of fear in others, whether it be in private or public, local or international affairs. We consent to the policeman's carrying a gun not because we have lost our fear of the bullet but because we have agreed to suspend that fear on the assurance that the policeman carrying it is acculturated with us, that he shares our values, that he holds high what we hold high. But at the same time he must be willing to use that gun, he must be psychologically able to commit violence if we are to believe in his protection, and his willingness to slay, if it is not securely hedged about by his very clearly displayed respect for our values, quickly becomes a fearful thing. It is no different with a nation which would convince the world of its peaceful intentions even as it is heavily armed and its troops are stationed around the world. In the final analysis a reliance on force is always a confession of moral defeat, but in the affairs of nations it is tragically necessary sometimes to confess that defeat and to gather and rely on force. But to forget even for a moment that only the most persuasively demonstrated belief in civilized values can keep the image of force from being distorted into a menacing image—to forget this is to invite the easy demolition of our efforts for peace.

To prove an assertion whose implications are so vast is impossible, yet I must say that in a very profound way the differences I have indicated in our attitudes toward culture itself have often made it possible for Russian propaganda to raise fear of us in foreign peoples.

In passing, I should like to touch for a moment on a minor but I think indicative paradox inherent here. A recent article in *The New York Times Magazine* on Russian education and another group of photographs in *Life* described the high seriousness of the Russian college students, their evident dedication to their work, a picture so intense as to throw up in the mind the counter-image of so many American students for whom college is quite another thing. Unless I am entirely mistaken, the same article and the same photographs would not appear extraordinary to the European. What would be strange to him and cause him to wonder on his community with us, would be pictures of some of the shenanigans indulged in by some of our students. What I am trying to indicate here again is that there are superficial differences in our attitudes to culture in this particular area which show us to be less intimately connected to the European than the Russian is. The same is true of our kind of theater as contrasted with the German, let us say, and the Russian. I emphasize that the official attitude toward these manifestations of culture is extremely weighty outside this country. Yet the fact remains, and

I believe it to be a demonstrable fact, that with all our absence of apparent awe, we have produced more than a decent quota of cultural works in the past two decades. The crucial importance of the image we cast in the world is not appreciated among us and, in my opinion, is one of the wounds through which the blood of our influence and our dignity is constantly seeping out. I go back once again to the image of our force. If our enormous power to destroy—and whatever else it is, military force is a destructive force—if we are content to allow it to appear in the hands of a people who make nothing of culture, who are content to appear solely as businessmen, technicians, and money-makers, we are handing to the Russian, who appears to make so much of culture, an advantage of regiments. And the further irony is that the serious Russian, both student and artist, has been so hamstrung by the tyrannical strictures on thought in his country, that his intellectual production has in recent years been brought to nearly a standstill, excepting in those scientific pursuits connected with militarily valuable science. It is, in their case, an irony which does not escape the notice of the world, in fact, it is precisely their tyranny that has kept nations out of their grasp. I believe, in short, that if we could only recognize and admit to our successes in culture, if the policy of our government and our people toward the things of the mind and the spirit were especially conscious and made serious, we have at hand a means of coming into closer harmony with other peoples who at bottom share our basic values.

But lest I seem to advocate a new advertising campaign, let me quickly correct the impression. To be sure, the object of a business or a nation in its relations with the world outside is to show its best qualities. More precisely, the obvious thing to do is to exhibit to the world whatever the world will most easily take to its heart for its own, those things which will make other peoples fear us less and love us more, those things with which they can identify themselves. For it is easier to misunderstand and hate that which seems alien and strange.

Our most popular, most widely seen cultural export is the

American movie. It is a powerful convincer because hardly any-body in the world doesn't like to go to the movies. More im-portant, however, it is spontaneously made, it appears without an ulterior political motive. So the man who sees it does so volun-tarily and with his resistance down.

The trouble with the movies, however, is the same sort of trouble which Americans themselves often create when they go to Europe. Our movies draw the affections of people, their admiration, and envy for the opulence they generally portray, and also their disgust—as for instance, when a woman douses a cigarette in a perfectly good, uneaten, fried egg. At the same time, the movie star is beloved, his private life is followed with the interest long ago reserved for the minor gods. As such, we can only be glad so many foreigners like to see our pictures.

But even as we gain by them, we lose something of tremen-dous importance. Most movies are admittedly and even proudly brainless. When you have as much destructive power as we do, it is of the first importance that the world be continuously made aware not merely of how silly we can be, and at times how vulgar, but of how deep an attachment the American people have for the nicest cultivation of humane values.

It is in our novels, our poems, our dance, our music, and some of our plays, primarily, that we can and do reveal a better preoccupation. Yet, I can say from personal experience and from the experiences of other writers, that the work of art in which we really examine ourselves, or which is critical of society, is not what this government regards as good propaganda. I am not aware, for instance, that the export of any comic book has been interfered with, but only recently a nonfiction book was refused a congressional appropriation for inclusion in our over-seas libraries because it showed a dust storm and a picture of an old-time country schoolhouse. In my opinion, it is not only not bad to show such things, nor bad to send our critical works around the world, but a necessity. For it is clearly one of our handicaps that we somehow insist, at least officially, that we have no inkling of a tragic sense of life. We posture before the world at times as though we had broken with the entire human race and had hold of a solution to the enigma of existence that was beyond questioning. As a dramatist I know that until the audience can identify itself with the people and the situations presented on the stage, it cannot be convinced of anything at all; it sits before an utterly uncomprehensible play of shadows against an unseeable wall. Thus, when a work or an action or a speech or a declaration of the world is presented without a trace of decent humility before the unsolved problems of life, it is not only that we do not really reflect our real selves, but that we must inevitably alienate others. For the truth is that we have not discovered how to be happy and at one with ourselves, we have only gone far in abolishing physical poverty, which is but one single element in the solution. And by harping only on that, we in effect declare a want of spirituality, a want of human feeling, a want of sympathy in the end. I believe we have solutions for poverty which the world must eventually come to adopt or adapt to other conditions, and we are obligated to demonstrate always what we have accomplished, obligated not only to ourselves but to humanity, which hungers for ways to organize production and create material wealth. But along with our success we have created a body of art, a body of literature which is markedly critical, which persists in asking certain human questions of the patterns we have created, and they are questions whose ultimate answers will prove or disprove our claims to having built a genuine civilization and not merely a collection of dominating inventions and bodily comforts. We are too often known abroad as dangerous children with toys that can explode the planet for us to go on pretending that we are not conscious of our underlying ethical and moral dilemmas.

It is no disgrace to search one's soul, nor the sign of fear. It is rather the first mark of honesty and the pool from which all righteousness flows. The strength of a Lincoln as he appeared in the eye of the world was not compounded of a time-bound mastery of military force alone, nor of an image monolithic and beyond the long reach of doubt. That man could lead and in our best moments leads us yet because he seemed to harbor in his soul an ever-renewing tear for his enemies and an indestructible desire to embrace them all. He commanded armies in the cruelest kind of war between brothers, yet his image is of a peaceful man. For even as history cast him as a destroyer of men, as every leader in war must always be, he seemed never to have lost that far-off gaze which cannot obliterate the tragic incompleteness of all wisdom and must fill with sympathy the space between what we know and what we have to do. For me, it is a reassuring thing that so much attention and appreciation is shown our novels and plays of high seriousness, for it signifies, I think, that others wish to see us more humanly and that the world is not as satisfied as we sometimes wish to appear that we have come to the end of all philosophy and wonderment about the meaning of life. It is dangerous to be rich in a world full of poverty. It is dangerous in obvious ways and in ways not so obvious.

During the war I worked for some time in the Brooklyn Navy Yard repairing and building ships for our fleet. The ships of many allied nations were often repaired there and we got to know many of the foreign crews. I remember one afternoon standing on the deck of a British destroyer with a British sailor at my side, when alongside us an American destroyer was passing out into the harbor. It was a boiling hot summer day. As the American ship moved slowly beside us a sailor appeared on her deck and walked over to a water cooler on the deck and drank. On British destroyers a thirsty man went below to a tap and drank lukewarm water; when he bathed it was out of a portable basin, the same one he washed his clothes in. I glanced at the British seaman sweating on the deck beside me and I said, "That's what you guys ought to have, eh?" "Oh," he said, with an attempt at a sneer, "your ships are built for comfort." It was not that he couldn't bear the idea of ice water on a hot day. I feel reasonably sure he would not have joined a demonstration against the British Admiralty had a water cooler been installed on his deck. But the mere fact that we had coolers on our decks did not at once overwhelm him with a reverence for our superiority. The essential emotion in his mind was a defense of his own dignity and the dignity of his country in the face of what ought to have been a promising hope for himself but was taken as a challenge, if not a kind of injury to his own pride. I am not saying we ought not to have water coolers, either in our ideas or on our ships, but a foreign policy based solely on water coolers and water coolers alone may create as much envy, distrust, and even hatred as anything else. As a matter of fact, his deprivation he made into a positive virtue. It was common to hear Britishers say that their fleet was made to fight, unlike ours, that they had no comforts, no shower baths, plenty of cockroaches, and what to us would be miserable food, because they had no time and ought to have no time for anything but their guns, and because a ship of the fleet had no right to be anything but a floating gun platform. And finally, they convinced themselves that we couldn't hit anything anyway.

It is important for us to recall that there was a time not long ago when the positions were almost exactly reversed. It was the time of our frontier, the time when for the European, America was an uncomfortable place, without the amenities of his civilization. And at that time a stock situation in our plays and novels and our folklore was the conflict between the elegant but effete European or Englishman being outwitted or mocked or in some other way overcome morally by the inelegant, poor, roughhewn Yankee the mark of whose superiority was his relative poverty, an inability to spell, and a rugged, even primitive jealousy of his own independence. I was reminded of this irony by the latest novel of the aforementioned Graham Greene called *The Quiet American*. This is the story of an American working in Asia for a cloak and dagger bureau in Washington, and his friendship and conflict with a British newspaperman. One is struck time and again by the Britisher's resentment of the American's precautions again disease or dirt—a veritable phobia of contamination—quite like the old literature in which the Englishman appears in tweeds and cap to shoot buffalo in the West, his sandwich hamper neat and ready, the napkin included. It is not merely the resentment which is important, but Greene's evident conviction that the American's relative wealth insulates him from any interest or insight into the realities around him, particularly the stubborn problem of the meanings of existence, meanings which transcend the victory over material want. And Greene reflects as well a kind of grudging admiration for the Asiatic Communists compared to the smooth-faced, naïve American, for the Communist, he says, knows how to talk to his fellow poor. In contrast, the Americans are prosperous and spiritually blank-eyed; they walk with the best of intentions in the impenetrable delusion that theirs is the only civilized way to live; in this book they walk in a closed circle outside of which the alien millions of the world, especially the poor, lead a life unknown and unknowable to them, and they are forced, the Americans are in this book, finally to rely upon devious policies of political opportunism and terroristic force. I will add that there is a pronounced quality of the caricature in this book, a caricature which quite astounded me coming from the pen of Graham Greene. It is easy to cast a stone at him and walk away, but there it is, a book which evidently appears quite accurate to the British and presumably to the European, whose reviewers took no note of the caricature in it; the work of a man who has not shown himself to be a fool in the past and is surely not against democracy.

It is time, I think, for us to step back and with open eyes, and a dignified humility, to look at where we are. How does it come to pass that so successful a system and so free should so steadily lose its hold upon the hearts of men over a single decade, when its competition is a tyranny whose people live in comparative poverty and under the rule of men instead of law? Is it truly possible that everything can be laid to the success of Communist propaganda? If that is true, then I think the jig is up, for then history is truly made of words, and words that lie. But it is demonstrably untrue, for there has never been a Communist revolution in a country with parliamentary government, except for Czechoslovakia, which was a revolution under Russian bayonets. Nevertheless, there is a sense in the world that somehow we are help-less, except for our armament, against a positive ideology which moves forward as we stand still or move backward. The convic-tion grows, it seems, that we have nothing really to say that we haven't said, and nothing to do except to stand by our guns.

I would make certain simple and self-evident observations and leave the largest conclusions to you. There is a revolution going on every single day in this era. Sometimes it erupts only in North Africa, sometimes in Iran, sometimes in a less obvious way in Greece, sometimes in the heart of Africa itself. By and large the foreign policy of the United States has gone on the assumption that things ought to remain as they are. By and large we have adopted a posture of resistance to change and have linked our fate and our dignity and our idea of safety to those regimes and forces which are holding things down. It is as though the misery of most of the world would not exist had the Communists not given it a name. We have, in more ways than one, made them into magicians. We had a Point Four program. We were going to buy the friendship of peoples with a few hundred million dollars. But the basic conditions of misery, the basic setup under which this misery is perpetuated and will continue to be perpetuated—for this we have no official word. The deepest hope, and we must come to admit it, was that they would take our aid and stop shouting. As a consequence, even by our own admission, enor-mous amounts of our aid have made the rich richer, as in Greece, and the poor no better off. Nor is this entirely our fault in a tech-nical sense. It is not our fault that thieves steal for themselves, but there is a possibility which lies in another direction, a possibility which costs money to realize, but in my view presents our one great hope. One, but only one element in it, involves our resolu-tion as a people and as a government that abject poverty and human freedom cannot coexist in the world. It is the despera-tion born of poverty that makes freedom a luxury in men's minds. Were this country to place as the first object in its foreign policy a resolution, a call, a new dedication to the war on poverty, a new wind would, I think, begin to blow through the stifled atmosphere of international relations.

I believe such a program set at the very forefront of our work in the world would have not economic consequences alone, but ultimately political and institutional changes would occur. There ought to be in training here technicians and experts for loan wherever they are needed, an army of them ready to move into any land asking for them. We ought to be building as many atomic power reactors as we can build, and we ought to be offering them to any nation asking for them. And above all, we ought to make clear that there are no strings attached.

The objection will be that we have already tried this and what have we got in return? I say that we have not tried it un-politically. In India, in Italy, in Greece and other places, we have given aid on conditions of political fealty, and there is no blinking that fact. We have said, in effect, your misery does not move our hearts if you do not believe as we do. I say that it is the peoples of the world more than their governments who must be reached and raised up, and if that is the aim, if the love of the American people and their sympathy is permitted to surround this aid, instead of the fear of the American people turning all help into a species of bribery, we shall have reason for hope. Nehru is not suspicious of America because we have given India help in the past but because we have withheld it at times and threatened to at others when he says something we don't like. We ought to make it absolutely clear to the world that we are precisely what has never been before, a nation devoting itself now to the international onslaught on poverty, a nation eager for change, not in fear of it. Certainly we shall be greeted with cynicism, but if we adopt cynicism we are falling into the trap set for us, as we so often have over the past ten years.

But along with economic and technical aid on a scale far beyond that of the past, our entire attitude toward cultural matters must be revolutionized. There ought to be an army of teachers in training here for foreign service, people who can teach languages, mathematics, science, and literature. We ought to appear in the world as the source and pool from which the nations may draw for the new age that is to come. Our own gates must be thrown open to the musicians, the players, the writers, the literature of these countries, and our own artists must be invited to perform wherever there is an audience for them. And what do we get in return? Nothing. Nothing but the slow, but I believe inevitable, understanding of the peoples of the world, nothing but the gradual awakening to the fact that we are not a fearful country, nor a country that knows all the answers, but a country with an understanding for the poor, a country which has such an abundance of materials and talents that it wishes to reach out its hand to others less favored.

But whatever the technical aspects of this approach, however difficult they may be to put into force, they are simple compared to the change in spirit required of us. I think the single most important alteration that has occurred among us since the Second World War is an insidious infusion of cynicism. No more were we going to be naïve, not again taken in by large visions and giveaways and the whole social-worker, Rooseveltian panorama of idealism. We were dealing now with sharks, and we must know how.

Yet, when was it that we held our undisputed moral leadership in the world? When did we start to lose it? It is simply no good laying the blame on communist propaganda because it was no more wily after the war than before. We have lost sight of the context in which we are living. We have come to imagine that because there are two major powers there can only be one of two ways the social and economic organization of the world can materialize. But already there are three. There is Tito's Yugoslavia, striving to remain independent, trying to establish a kind of socialism and at the same time to put forth at least a root from which may grow a tradition of civil liberty. And there are four. There is India, insistent upon social planning and a high degree of government supervision of economic life, yet tolerant of private property and private business, but rejecting the American system of unrestricted private enterprise. And there are five, with Israel mixing completely socialized villages and farms with a private economy developing in the cities. And there will probably be six, seven, eight, or a dozen different combinations of social and economic forces in as many areas before the next decade is finished. Only one rule can guide us if we are to be wise, and it is, again, that misery does not breed freedom but tyranny.

We have long since departed from any attempt to befriend only democratic nations and not others. The police states included by us in what we call the Free World are too numerous to mention. The Middle East and certain states in South America are not noteworthy for their respect for civil rights, nor is Franco Spain or the Union of South Africa. All these states promise only one thing in common—an allegiance to the West. But if we are not to be taken in by our own propaganda we shall have to see that they have other less amiable traits in common. They are economically backward and their regimes have vested interests in backwardness. Why then do we include them in the Free World? Because they claim in common a hatred of socialism and a willingness to fight with our side in case of war. But what if there is not to be war in our generation? Then we have only collected deserts that might have been watered but were not.

This brings me to my final point and it is the most vital and the most debatable of all. I believe that the world has now arrived, not at a moment of decision, but two minutes later. When Russia exploded her atom bomb the decision of history was made, and it was that diplomacy based either on the fear or the confidence that the final decision would be made by war, is no longer feasible. I believe the arms stalemate is with us for an indefinite time to come, and that to base a foreign policy upon an ingathering of states willing to side with us in war is to defeat ourselves in the other contest, the main contest, the crucial contest. I believe that the recent shift of Russian emphasis to economic, social, and cultural penetration rather than revolutionary tactics issuing in ultimate war, is based on this new situation. I believe that literally the hands, or more precisely, the fists, of the nations are tied if they only knew it, and that it is their hearts and minds which are left with the struggle. I believe that in its own devious way history has placed the nations squarely in a moral arena from which there is no escape.

But the implications go even further. The whole concept of Russian-type socialism and American capitalism competing for the allegiance of mankind is going to fall apart. There will be no pure issue from this struggle. There will be so many mutations and permutations of both systems, that it will be impossible to untangle them and call them one or the other.

The danger, I believe, is that the Communist idea will, in fact, be able to accommodate itself to the new complexity, but that we shall not, because we shall have refused to see that great social changes can be anything but threats to us. The danger is that without our participation in the reorganization of the backward sections of the world, our central value, the dignity of the human being based upon a rule of law and civil liberty, will never become part of the movement of peoples striving to live better at any cost.

For that and that alone ought to be our mission in this world. There are many mansions not only in heaven but on earth. We have or ought to have but one interest, if only for our safety's sake, and it is to preserve the rights of man. That ought to be our star and none other. Our sole aim in the past ten years was the gathering in of states allied against the Soviet Union, preparing for an attack from that source. As from some fortress town of the Middle Ages, we have seen the world. But now as then history is making fortresses ridiculous, for the movement of man is outside and his fate is being made outside. It is being made on his farm, in his hut, in the streets of his cities, and in his factories.

In the period of her so-called naïveté, America held the allegiance of people precisely because she was not cynical, because her name implied love and faith in people, and because she was the common man's country. In later years we have gone about forgetting our simplicity while a new ideology has risen to call for justice, however cynically, and imparting the idea that Russia stood for the working man. Meanwhile in a small voice we have spoken of justice and in a big voice of arms and armaments, wars and the rumors of wars. Now we must face ourselves and ask—what if there is to be no more war? What is in us that the world must know of? When we find this, the essence of America, we shall be able to forge a foreign policy capable of arousing the hopes and the love of the only force that matters any more, the force that is neither in governments nor armies nor banks nor institutions, the force that rests in the heart of man. When we come to address ourselves to this vessel of eternal unrest and eternal hope, we shall once again be on our way.

II

The *Collected Plays* to *The Misfits*

ROSLYN: Oh, Gay, what is there? Do you know? What is there that stays?

GAY: God knows. Everything I ever see was comin' or goin' away. Same as you. Maybe the only thing is ... the knowin'. 'Cause I know you now, Roslyn, I do know you. Maybe that's all the peace there is or can be.

—From *The Misfits*

Introduction to
the *Collected Plays*

I

As a writer of plays I share with all specialists a suspicion of generalities about the art and technique of my craft, and I lack both the scholarly patience and the zeal to define terms in such a way as to satisfy everyone. The only other course, therefore, is to stop along the way to say what *I* mean by the terms I use, quite certain as I do so that I will be taken to task by no small number of people, but hopeful at the same time that something useful may be said about this art, a form of writing which generates more opinions and fewer instructive critical statements than any other. To be useful it seems impossible not to risk the obvious by returning always to the fundamental nature of theater, its historic human function, so to speak. For it seems odd, when one thinks of it, that an art which has always been so expensive to produce and so difficult to do well should have survived in much the same general form that it possessed when it began. This is especially striking now, when almost alone among the arts the theater has managed to live despite the devouring mechanization of the age, and, in some places and instances, even to thrive and grow. Under these circumstances of a very long if frequently interrupted history, one may make

From *Arthur Miller's Collected Plays* (New York: Viking, 1957), pp. 3–55. Copyright © 1957 by Arthur Miller.

the assumption that the drama and its production must represent a well-defined expression of profound social needs, needs which transcend any particular form of society or any particular historic moment. It is therefore possible to speak of fundamentals of the form too when its only tools of importance never change, there being no possibility of drama without mimicry, conflict, tale, or speech.

My approach to playwriting and the drama itself is organic; and to make this glaringly evident at once it is necessary to separate drama from what we think of today as literature. A drama ought not be looked at first and foremost from literary perspectives merely because it uses words, verbal rhythm, and poetic image. These can be its most memorable parts, it is true, but they are not its inevitable accompaniments. Nor is it only convention which from Aristotle onward decreed that the play must be dramatic rather than narrative in concept and execution. A Greek's seat was harder than an American's and even he had to call a halt to a dramatic presentation after a couple of hours. The physiological limits of attention in a seated position enforce upon this art an interconnected group of laws, in turn expressed by aesthetic criteria, which no other writing art requires. But it is not my intention here to vivisect dramatic form or the techniques of playwriting. I only want to take advantage of this rare opportunity—a collected edition—to speak for myself as to my own aims; not to give my estimates of what can portentously be called the dramatic problem in this time, but simply to talk in workaday language about the problem of how to write so that one's changing vision of people in the world is more accurately represented in each succeeding work.

A few of the inevitable materials of the art dictate to me certain aesthetic commitments which may as well be mentioned at the outset, for they move silently but nevertheless with potent influence through the plays in this book as well as in my thoughts about them. These plays were written on the assumption that they would be acted before audiences. The "actor" is a person, and he no sooner appears than certain elementary questions are broached. Who is he? What is he doing here? How does he live or make his living? Who is he related to? Is he rich or poor? What does he think of himself? What do other people think of him, and why? What are his hopes and fears; and what does he say they are? What does he claim to want, and what does he really want?

The actor brings questions onto the stage just as any person does when we first meet him in our ordinary lives. Which of them a play chooses to answer, and how they are answered, are the ruling and highly consequential imperatives which create the style of the play, and control what are later called the stylistic levels of its writing. If, for instance, the actor is masked as he appears and his body movements are constricted and highly ordered, we instantly expect that the common surfaces of life will also be breached by the kinds of questions he or the play will respond to. He will very probably speak about the theme or essential preoccupation of the play directly and without getting to it by circuitous routes of naturalistic detail. If he appears in the costume of his trade, class, or profession, however, we expect that he or the play will give us the answers to his common identity, and if they do not they risk our dissatisfaction and frustration. In a word, the actor's appearance on the stage in normal human guise leads us to expect a realistic treatment. The play will either be intent upon rounding out the characters by virtue of its complete answers to the common questions, or will substitute answers to a more limited group of questions which, instead of being "human," are thematic and are designed to form a symbol of meaning rather than an apparency of the "real." It is the nature of the questions asked and answered, rather than the language used—whether verse, ordinary slang, or colorless prose —that determines whether the style is realistic or non-realistic. When I speak of style, therefore, this is one of the relationships I intend to convey. In this sense the tragedies of Shakespeare are species of realism, and those of Aeschylus and Sophocles are not. We know a great deal more about Macbeth and Hamlet, apart from their functions as characters in their particular given dramas, than we can ever surmise about Oedipus the king, or the heroes and heroines of Strindberg's plays. To put it another way, when the career of a person rather than the detail of his motives stands at the forefront of the play, we move closer to non-realistic styles, and vice versa. I regard this as the one immovable and irremediable quality which goes to create one style or another. And there is always an organic connection rather than a temperamental choice involved in the style in which a play is written and must be performed. The first two plays in this book were written and performed with the intention of answering as many of the common questions as was possible. *The Crucible, A Memory of Two Mondays,* and *A View from the Bridge* were not so designed, and to this extent they are a departure from realism.

Another decisive influence upon style is the conception and manipulation of time in a play. Broadly speaking, where it is conceived and used so as to convey a natural passage of hours, days, or months, the style it enforces is pressed toward realism. Where action is quite openly freed so that things mature in a moment, for instance, which would take a year in life, a true license for non-realistic styles is thereby won. As is obvious, the destruction of temporal necessity occurs in every play if only to a rudimentary degree; it is impossible that in life people should behave and speak in reference to a single thematic point for so continuous a time. Events, therefore, are always collapsed and drawn together in any drama. But as the collapsing process becomes more self-evident, and as the selection of events becomes less and less dominated by the question of their natural maturation, the style of the play moves further and further away from realism. *All My Sons* attempts to account for time in terms of months, days, and hours. *Death of a Salesman* explodes the watch and the calendar. *The Crucible* is bound by natural time —or strives to appear so.

The compacting of time destroys the realistic style not only because it violates our sense of reality, but because collapsing time inevitably emphasizes an element of existence which in life is not visible or ordinarily felt with equivalent power, and this is its symbolic meaning. When a criminal is arraigned, for instance, it is the prosecutor's job to symbolize his behavior for the jury so that the man's entire life can be characterized in one way and not in another. The prosecutor does not mention the accused as a dog lover, a good husband and father, a sufferer from eczema, or a man with the habit of chewing tobacco on the left and not the right side of his mouth. Nor does he strive to account for the long intervals of time when the accused was behaving in a way quite contrary to that symbolic characterization. The prosecutor is collapsing time—and destroying realism—by fastening only on those actions germane to the construction of his symbol. To one degree or another every play must do this or we should have to sit in a theater for years in order to appreciate a character and his story. But where the play does pretend to give us details of hours, months, and years which are not clearly and avowedly germane to the symbolic meaning, we come closer and closer to what is called a realistic style. In passing, I should say that the Greek "unity" of time imposed on the drama was not arbitrary but a concomitant of the preponderant Greek interest in the fate and career of the hero rather than his private characteristics, or, to put it another way, his social and symbolic side rather than his family role.

Another material, so to speak, of drama is not describable in a word, and has a less direct influence on style. I mention it, however, because it is probably the single most powerful influence on my way of writing and enforces on me a kind of taste and approach to the art which marks these plays. It is necessary, if one is to reflect reality, not only to depict why a man does what he does, or why he nearly didn't do it, but why he cannot simply walk away and say to hell with it. To ask this last question of a play is a cruel thing, for evasion is probably the most developed technique most men have, and in truth there is an extraordinarily small number of conflicts which we must, at any cost, live out to their conclusions. To ask this question is immediately to impose on oneself not, perhaps, a style of writing but at least a kind of dramatic construction. For I understand the symbolic meaning of a character and his career to consist of the kind of commitment he makes to life or refuses to make, the kind of challenge he accepts and the kind he can pass by. I take it that if one could know enough about a human being one could discover some conflict, some value, some challenge, however minor or major, which he cannot find it in himself to walk away from or turn his back on. The structure of these plays, in this respect, is to the end that such a conflict be discovered and clarified. Idea, in these plays, is the generalized meaning of that discovery applied to men other than the hero. Time, characterizations, and other elements are treated differently from play to play, but all to the end that that moment of commitment be brought forth, that moment when, in my eyes, a man differentiates himself from every other man, that moment when out of a sky full of stars he fixes on one star. I take it, as well, that the less capable a man is of walking away from the central conflict of the play, the closer he approaches a tragic existence. In turn, this implies that the closer a man approaches tragedy the more intense is his concentration of emotion upon the fixed point of his commitment, which is to say the closer he approaches what in life we call fanaticism. From this flows the necessity for scenes of high and open emotion, and plays constructed toward climax rather than the evocation of a mood alone or of bizarre spectacle. (The one exception among these plays is *A Memory of Two Mondays*—as will be seen later.)

From such considerations it ought to be clear that the common tokens of realism and non-realism are in themselves not acceptable as criteria. That a play is written prosaically does not make it a realistic play, and that the speech is heightened and intensified by imagery does not set it to one side of realism necessarily. The underlying poem of a play I take to be the organic necessity of its parts. I find in the arbitrary not poetry but indulgence. (The novel is another matter entirely.) A very great play can be mimed and still issue forth its essential actions and their rudiments of symbolic meaning; the word, in drama, is the transformation into speech of what is *happening,* and the fiat for intense language is intensity of happening. We have had more than one extraordinary dramatist who was a cripple as a writer, and this is lamentable but not ruinous. Which is to say that I prize the poetic above else in the theater, and because I do I insist that the poem truly be there.

II

The assumption—or presumption—behind these plays is that life has meaning. I would now add, as their momentary commentator, that what they meant to me at the time of writing is not in each instance the same as what they mean to me now in the light of further experience. Plato, by banning artists from citizenship in his ideal republic, expressed at least a partial truth; the intention behind a work of art and its effects upon the public are not always the same. Worse yet, in his conscious intention the artist often conceals from himself an aim which can be quite opposed to his fondest beliefs and ideas. Those more tempted by an evil, for instance, are more likely to feel deeply about it than those who have only known the good. From this, two ironic propositions logically flow. The first is that a play's "idea" may be useful as a unifying force empowering the artist to evoke a cogent emotional life on the stage, but that in itself it has no aesthetic value, since, after all, it is only a means to an end. The second is that since every play means something—even the play which denies all meaning to existence—the "idea" of a play is its measure of value and importance and beauty, and that a play which appears merely to exist to one side of "ideas" is an aesthetic nullity.

Idea is very important to me as a dramatist, but I think it is time someone said that playwrights, including the greatest, have not been noted for the new ideas they have broached in their plays. By new I mean an original idea invented by the playwright, quite as such things are created, if infrequently, by scientists, and occasionally by philosophers. Surely there is no known philosophy which was first announced through a play, nor any ethical idea. No social concept in Shaw's plays could have been much of a surprise to the Webbs and thousands of other Socialists of the time; nor can Ibsen, Chekhov, Strindberg, or O'Neill be credited with inventing any new thoughts. As a matter of fact, it is highly unlikely that a new idea could be successfully launched through a play at all, and this for several good reasons.

A genuine invention in the realm of ideas must first emerge as an abstruse and even partial concept. Be it Christianity, Darwinism, Marxism, or any other that can with reason be called original it has always been the product of proofs which, before they go to form a complete and new concept, require years and often generations of testing, research, and polemic. At first blush a new idea appears to be very close to insanity because to be new it must reverse important basic beliefs and assumptions which, in turn, have been institutionalized and are administered by one or another kind of priesthood with a vested interest in the old idea. Nor would the old idea be an idea at all, strictly speaking, if some goodly section of the population did not believe in it. If only because no dramatic structure can bear the brunt of the incredulity with which any really new idea is greeted, the play form would collapse under the burdens of having to deliver up the mountain of proof required for a new idea to be believed. And this would be true even if the audience were all philosophers—perhaps even truer, for the philosopher requires proofs even more exact than the layman does.

The dramatic form is a dynamic thing. It is not possible to dally in it for reflection. The polemical method, as well as the scientific exposition, the parable, or the ethical teaching, all depend upon a process which, in effect, says, "What you believe is wrong for these reasons; what the truth is is as follows." Tremendous energy must go into destroying the validity of the ancient proposition, and destroying it from an absolutely opposite viewpoint. An idea, if it is really new, is a genuine humiliation for the majority of the people; it is an affront not only to their sensibilities but to their deepest convictions. It offends against the things they worship, whether God or science or money.

The conflict between a new idea and the very notion of drama is remorseless and not resolvable because, among other things, plays are always performed before people sitting en masse and not alone. To a very large degree, much greater than is generally realized, we react *with* a surrounding crowd rather than against it; our individual criteria of truth are set to one side and we are no longer at the mercy of a performance alone, but of the surrounding reaction to it. A man walking down a deserted street sees another man beating a horse; he does not like this, he is possibly revolted by it, even angered. Perhaps he walks on, or perhaps he stops to remonstrate with the horsewhipper, who then perhaps threatens *him* with the same whip. Depending on the character of the man, he either fights or decides it is none of his business, really, and goes on about his life. The same man on the same street, but this time a busy street with many people, sees the same scene of cruelty. He is now behaving in public; he cries out and hears his cries echoed; he is encouraged; he moves in to stop the cruelty and when he himself is threatened the conflict in him over whether to back off or to fight is much higher and more intense, for now he is surrounded by the administrators of shame or the bestowers of honor—his fellow men. He is no longer looking at the same scene in the same way; the very significance of the experience is changed and more likely than not his own actions. So it is in the theater. Inevitably, to one degree or another, we see what we see on the stage not only with our own eyes but with the eyes of others. Our standards of right and wrong, good taste and bad, must in some way come into either conflict or agreement with social standards, and a truth, however true, is no longer merely itself, but itself plus the conventional reaction to it; and in the case of a genuinely new idea the conventional reaction, by definition, will come down on it like a ton of bricks, and it is finished, however beautifully written.

If plays have not broached new ideas, they have enunciated not-yet-popular ideas which are already in the air, ideas for which there has already been a preparation by non-dramatic media. Which is to say that once an idea is "in the air" it is no longer an idea but a feeling, a sensation, an emotion, and with these the drama can deal. For one thing, where no doubt exists in the hearts of the people, a play cannot create doubt: where no desire to believe exists, a play cannot create a belief. And again, this springs from the nature of dramatic form and its inevitable dynamism; it must communicate as it proceeds and it literally has no existence if it must wait until the audience goes home to think before it can be appreciated. It is the art of the present tense par excellence.

Thus it is that the forms, the accents, the intentions of the plays in this book are not the same from play to play. I could say that my awareness of life was not the same and leave it at that, but the truth is wider, for good or for ill. It is also that the society to which I responded in the past decade was constantly changing, as it is changing while I write this sentence. These plays, in one sense, are my response to what was "in the air," they are one man's way of saying to his fellow men, "This is what you see every day, or think or feel; now I will show you what you really know but have not had the time, or the disinterestedness, or the insight, or the information to understand consciously." Each of these plays, in varying degrees, was begun in the belief that it was unveiling a truth already known but unrecognized as such. My concept of the audience is of a public each member of which is carrying about with him what he thinks is an anxiety, or a hope, or a preoccupation which is his alone and isolates him from mankind; and in this respect at least the function of a play is to reveal him to himself so that he may touch others by virtue of the revelation of his mutuality with them. If only for this reason I regard the theater as a serious business, one that makes or should make man more human, which is to say, less alone.

III

When *All My Sons* opened on Broadway, it was called an "Ibsenesque" play. Some people liked it for this reason and others did not. Ibsen is relevant to this play but what he means to me is not always what he means to others, either his advocates or his detractors. More often than not, these days, he is thought of as a stage carpenter with a flair for ideas of importance. The whole aim of shaping a dramatic work on strict lines which will elicit a distinct meaning reducible to a sentence is now suspect. "Life" is now more complicated than such a mechanical contrasting of forces can hope to reflect. Instead, the aim is a "poetic" drama, preferably one whose ultimate thought or meaning is elusive, a drama which appears not to have been composed or constructed, but which somehow comes to life on a stage and then flickers away. To come quickly to the point, our theater inclines toward the forms of adolescence rather than analytical adulthood. It is not my place to deal in praise or blame, but it seems to me that a fair judge would be compelled to conclude, as a minimum, that the run of serious works of the past decade have been written and played under an intellectually—as well as electrically—diffused light. It is believed that any attempt to "prove" something in a play is somehow unfair and certainly inartistic, if not gauche, more particularly if what is being proved happens to be in any overt way of social moment. Indeed, one American critic believes that the narrowness of the theater audience—as compared with that for the movies and television —is the result of the masses' having been driven away from the theater by plays that preached.

This is not, of course, a new attitude in the world. Every major playwright has had to make his way against it, for there is and always will be a certain amount of resentfulness toward the presumption of any playwright to teach. And there will never be a satisfactory way of explaining that no playwright can be praised for his high seriousness and at the same time be praised for not trying to teach; the very conception of a dramatic theme inevitably means that certain aspects of life are selected and others left out, and to imagine that a play can be written disinterestedly is to believe that one can make love disinterestedly.

The debatable question is never whether a play ought to teach but whether it is art, and in this connection the basic criterion—purely technical considerations to one side—is the passion with which the teaching is made. I hasten to add the obvious—that a work cannot be judged by the validity of its teaching. But it is entirely misleading to state that there is some profound conflict between art and the philosophically or socially meaningful theme. I say this not out of a preference for plays that teach but in deference to the nature of the creative act. A work of art is not handed down from Olympus from a creature with a vision as wide as the world. If that could be done a play would never end, just as history has no end. A play must end, and end with a climax, and to forge a climax the forces in life, which are of infinite complexity, must be made finite and capable of a more or less succinct culmination. Thus, all dramas are to that extent arbitrary—in comparison with life itself—and embody a viewpoint if not an obsession on the author's part. So that when I am told that a play is beautiful and (or because) it does not try to teach anything, I can only wonder which of two things is true about it: either what it teaches is so obvious, so inconsiderable as to appear to the critic to be "natural," or its teaching has been embedded and articulated so thoroughly in the action itself as not to appear as an objective but only a subjective fact.

All My Sons was not my first play but the eighth or ninth I had written up to the mid-forties. But for the one immediately preceding it, none of the others were produced in the professional theater, and since the reader can have little knowledge of this one—which lasted less than a week on Broadway—and no knowledge at all of the others, a word is in order about these desk-drawer plays, particularly the failure called *The Man Who Had All the Luck*.

This play was an investigation to discover what exact part a man played in his own fate. It deals with a young man in a small town who, by the time he is in his mid-twenties, owns several growing businesses, has married the girl he loves, is the father of a child he has always wanted, and is daily becoming convinced that as his desires are gratified he is causing to accumulate around his own head an invisible but nearly palpable fund, so to speak, of retribution. The law of life, as he observes life around him, is that people are always frustrated in some important regard; and he conceives that he must be too, and the play is built around his conviction of impending disaster. The disaster never comes, even when, in effect, he tries to bring it on in order to survive it and find peace. Instead, he comes to believe in his own superiority, and in his remarkable ability to succeed.

Now, more than a decade later, it is possible for me to see that far from being a waste and a failure this play was a preparation, and possibly a necessary one, for those that followed, especially *All My Sons* and *Death of a Salesman,* and this for many reasons. In the more than half-dozen plays before it I had picked themes at random—which is to say that I had had no awareness of any inner continuity running from one of these plays to the next, and I did not perceive myself in what I had written. I had begun with a play about a family, then a play about two brothers caught on either side of radicalism in a university, then a play about a psychologist's dilemma in a prison where the sane were inexorably moving over to join the mad, a play about a bizarre ship's officer whose desire for death led him to piracy on the seas, a tragedy on the Cortes-Montezuma conflict, and others. Once again, as I worked on *The Man Who Had All the Luck,* I was writing, I would have said, about what lay outside me. I had heard the story of a young man in a midwestern town who had earned the respect and love of his town and great personal prosperity as well, and who, suddenly and for no known reason, took to suspecting everyone of wanting to rob him, and within a year of his obsession's onset had taken his own life.

In the past I had rarely spent more than three months on a play. Now the months went by with the end never in sight. After nearly ten years of writing, I had struck upon what seemed a bottomless pit of mutually canceling meanings and implications. In the past I had had less difficulty with forming a "story" and more with the exploration of its meanings. Now, in contrast, I was working with an overwhelming sense of meaning, but however I tried I could not make the drama continuous and of a piece; it persisted, with the beginning of each scene, in starting afresh as though each scene were the beginning of a new play. Then one day, while I was lying on a beach, a simple shift of relationships came to mind, a shift which did not and could not solve the problem of writing *The Man Who Had All the Luck,* but, I think now, made at least two of the plays that followed possible, and a great deal else besides.

What I saw, without laboring the details, was that two of the characters, who had been friends in the previous drafts, were logically brothers and had the same father. Had I known then what I know now I could have saved myself a lot of trouble. The play was impossible to fix because the overt story was only tangential to the secret drama its author was quite unconsciously trying to write. But in writing of the father-son relationship and of the son's search for his relatedness there was a fullness of feeling I had never known before; a crescendo was struck with a force I could almost touch. The crux of *All My Sons,* which would not be written until nearly three years later, was formed; and the roots of *Death of a Salesman* were sprouted.

The form of *All My Sons* is a reflection and an expression of several forces, of only some of which I was conscious. I desired above all to write rationally, to write so that I could tell the story of the play to even an unlettered person and spark a look of recognition on his face. The accusation I harbored against the earlier play was that it could not make sense to common-sense people. I have always been in love with wonder, the wonder of how things and people got to be what they are, and in *The Man Who Had All the Luck* I had tried to grasp wonder, I had tried to make it on the stage, by writing wonder. But wonder had betrayed me and the only other course I had was the one I took—to seek cause and effect, hard actions, facts, the geometry of relationships, and to hold back any tendency to express an idea in itself unless it was literally forced out of a character's mouth; in other words, to let wonder rise up like a mist, a gas, a vapor from the gradual and remorseless crush of factual and psychological conflict. I went back to the great book of wonder, *The Brothers Karamazov,* and I found what suddenly I felt must be true of it: that if one reads its most colorful, breath-taking, wonderful pages, one finds the thickest concentration of hard facts. Facts about the biographies of the characters, about the kind of bark on the moonlit trees, the way a window is hinged, the exact position of Dmitri as he peers through the window at his father, the precise description of his father's dress. Above all, the precise collision of inner themes during, not before or after, the high dramatic scenes. And quite as suddenly I noticed in Beethoven the holding back of climax until it was ready, the grasp of the rising line and the unwillingness to divert to an easy climax until the true one was ready. If there is one word to name the mood I felt it was *Forgo.* Let nothing inter-fere with the shape, the direction, the intention. I believed that I had felt too much in the previous play and understood too little.

I was turning thirty then, the author of perhaps a dozen plays, none of which I could truly believe were finished. I had written many scenes, but not a play. A play, I saw then, was an organism of which I had fashioned only certain parts. The decision formed to write one more, and if again it turned out to be unrealizable, I would go into another line of work. I have never loved the brick and mortar of the theater, and only once in my life had I been truly engrossed in a production—when Ruth Gordon played in the Jed Harris production of *A Doll's House.* The sole sense of connection with theater came when I saw the productions of the Group Theatre. It was not only the brilliance of ensemble acting, which in my opinion has never been equaled since in America, but the air of union created between actors and the audience. Here was the promise of prophetic theater which suggested to my mind the Greek situation when religion and belief were the heart of drama. I watched the Group Theatre from fifty-five-cent seats in the balcony, and at intermission time it was possible to feel the heat and the passion of people moved not only in their bellies but in their thoughts. If I say that my own writer's ego found fault with the plays, it does not detract from the fact that the performances were almost all inspiring to me, and when I heard that the Group was falling apart it seemed incredible that a society of saints—which they were to me, artistically, even as I had never met one of them— should be made up of people with less than absolute dedication to their cause.

All My Sons was begun several years after the Group had ceased to be, but it was what I can only call now a play written for a prophetic theater. I am aware of the vagueness of the term but I cannot do very well at defining what I mean. Perhaps it signifies a theater, a play, which is meant to become part of the lives of its audience—a play seriously meant for people of common sense, and relevant to both their domestic lives and their daily work, but an experience which widens their awareness of connection—the filaments to the past and the future which lie concealed in "life."

My intention in this play was to be as untheatrical as possible. To that end any metaphor, any image, any figure of speech, however creditable to me, was removed if it even slightly brought to consciousness the hand of a writer. So far as was possible nothing was to be permitted to interfere with its artlessness.

It seems to me now that I had the attitude of one laying siege to a fortress in this form. The sapping operation was to take place without a sound beneath a clear landscape in the broad light of a peaceful day. Nor was this approach arbitrary. It grew out of a determination to reverse my past playwriting errors, and from the kind of story I happened to have discovered.

During an idle chat in my living room, a pious lady from the Middle West told of a family in her neighborhood which had been destroyed when the daughter turned the father into the authorities on discovering that he had been selling faulty machinery to the Army. The war was then in full blast. By the time she had finished the tale I had transformed the daughter into a son and the climax of the second act was full and clear in my mind.

I knew my informant's neighborhood, I knew its middle-class ordinariness, and I knew how rarely the great issues penetrate such environments. But the fact that a girl had not only wanted to, but had actually moved against an erring father transformed into fact and common reality what in my previous play I had only begun to hint at. I had no awareness of the slightest connection between the two plays. All I knew was that somehow a hard thing had entered into me, a crux toward which it seemed possible to move in strong and straight lines. Something was crystal clear to me for the first time since I had begun to write plays, and it was the crisis of the second act, the revelation of the full loathesomeness of an anti-social action.

With this sense of dealing with an existing objective fact, I began to feel a difference in my role as a writer. It occurred to me that I must write this play so that even the actual criminal, on reading it, would have to say that it was true and sensible and as real as his life. It began to seem to me that what I had written until then, as well as almost all the plays I had ever seen, had been written for a theatrical performance, when they should have been written as a kind of testimony whose relevance far surpassed theatrics.

For these reasons the play begins in an atmosphere of undisturbed normality. Its first act was later called slow, but it was designed to be slow. It was made so that even boredom might threaten, so that when the first intimation of the crime is dropped a genuine horror might begin to move into the heart of the audience, a horror born of the contrast between the placidity of the civilization on view and the threat to it that a rage of conscience could create.

It took some two years to fashion this play, chiefly, I think now, because of a difficulty not unconnected with a similar one in the previous play. It was the question of relatedness. The crime in *All My Sons* is not one that is about to be committed but one that has long since been committed. There is no question of its consequences' being ameliorated by anything Chris Keller or his father can do; the damage has been done irreparably. The stakes remaining are purely the conscience of Joe Keller and its awakening to the evil he has done, and the conscience of his son in the face of what he has discovered about his father. One could say that the problem was to make a fact of morality, but it is more precise, I think, to say that the structure of the play is designed to bring a man into the direct path of the consequences he has wrought. In one sense, it was the same problem of writing about David Beeves in the earlier play, for he too could not relate himself to what he had done. In both plays the dramatic obsession, so to speak, was with the twofold nature of the individual—his own concept of his deeds, and what turns out to be the "real" description of them. *All My Sons* has often been called a moral play, and it is that, but the concept of morality is not quite as purely ethical as it has been made to appear, nor is it so in the plays that follow. That the deed of Joe Keller at issue in *All My Sons* is his having been the cause of the death of pilots in war obscures the other kind of morality in which the play is primarily interested. Morality is probably a faulty word to use in the connection, but what I was after was the wonder in the fact that consequences of actions are as real as the actions themselves, yet we rarely take them into consideration as we perform actions, and we cannot hope to do so fully when we must always act with only partial knowledge of consequences. Joe Keller's trouble, in a word, is not that he cannot tell right from wrong but that his cast of mind cannot admit that he, personally, has any viable connection with his world, his universe, or his society. He is not a partner in society, but an incorporated member, so to speak, and you cannot sue personally the officers of a corporation. I hasten to make clear here that I am not merely speaking of a literal corporation but the concept of a man's becoming a function of production or distribution to the point where his personality becomes divorced from the actions it propels.

The fortress which *All My Sons* lays siege to is the fortress of unrelatedness. It is an assertion not so much of a morality in terms of right and wrong, but of a moral world's being such because men cannot walk away from certain of their deeds. In this sense Joe Keller is a threat to society and in this sense the play is a social play. Its "socialness" does not reside in its having dealt with the crime of selling defective materials to a nation at war—the same crime could easily be the basis of a thriller which would have no place in social dramaturgy. It is that the crime is seen as having roots in a certain relationship of the individual to society, and to a certain indoctrination he embodies, which, if dominant, can mean a jungle existence for all of us no matter how high our buildings soar. And it is in this sense that loneliness is socially meaningful in these plays.

To return to Ibsen's influence upon this play, I should have to split the question in order to make sense of it. First, there was the real impact of his work upon me at the time: this consisted mainly in what I then saw as his ability to forge a play upon a factual bedrock. A situation in his plays is never stated but revealed in terms of hard actions, irrevocable deeds; and sentiment is never confused with the action it conceals. Having for so long written in terms of what people felt rather than what they did, I turned to his works at the time with a sense of homecoming. As I have said, I wanted then to write so that people of common sense would mistake my play for life itself and not be required to lend it some poetic license before it could be believed. I wanted to make the moral world as real and evident as the immoral one so splendidly is.

But my own belief is that the shadow of Ibsen was seen on this play for another reason, and it is that *All My Sons* begins very late in its story. Thus, as in Ibsen's best-known work, a great amount of time is taken up with bringing the past into the present. In passing, I ought to add that this view of action is presently antipathetic to our commonly held feeling about the drama. More than any other quality of realism, or, to be more exact, of Ibsenism as a technique, this creates a sense of artificiality which we now tend to reject, for in other respects realism is still our reigning style. But it is no longer acceptable that characters should sit about discussing events of a year ago, or ten years ago, when in "life" they would be busy with the present. In truth, the effort to eliminate antecedent material has threatened to eliminate the past entirely from any plays. We are impatient to get on with it—so much so that anyone making a study of some highly creditable plays of the moment would be hard put to imagine what their characters were like a month before their actions and stories begin. *All My Sons* takes its time with the past, not in deference to Ibsen's method as I saw it then, but because its theme is the question of actions and consequences, and a way had to be found to throw a long line into the past in order to make that kind of connection viable.

That the idea of connection was central to me is indicated again in the kind of revision the play underwent. In its earlier versions the mother, Kate Keller, was in a dominating position; more precisely, her astrological beliefs were given great prominence. (The play's original title was *The Sign of the Archer.*) And this, because I sought in every sphere to give body and life to connection. But as the play progressed the conflict between Joe and his son Chris pressed astrology to the wall until its mysticism gave way to psychology. There was also the impulse to regard the mystical with suspicion, since it had, in the past, given me only turgid works that could never develop a true climax based upon revealed psychological truths. In short, where in previous plays I might well have been satisfied to create only an astrologically obsessed woman, the obsession now had to be opened up to reveal its core of self-interest and intention on the character's part. Wonder must have feet with which to walk the earth.

But before I leave this play it seems wise to say a few more words about the kind of dramatic impulse it represents, and one aspect of "Ibsenism" as a technique is the quickest path into that discussion. I have no vested interest in any one form—as the variety of forms I have used attests—but there is one element in Ibsen's method which I do not think ought to be overlooked, let alone dismissed as it so often is nowadays. If his plays, and his method, do nothing else they reveal the evolutionary quality of life. One is constantly aware, in watching his plays, of process, change, development. I think too many modern plays assume, so to speak, that their duty is merely to show the present countenance rather than to account for what happens. It is therefore wrong to imagine that because his first and sometimes his second acts devote so much time to a studied revelation of antecedent material, his view is static compared to our own. In truth, it is profoundly dynamic, for that enormous past was always heavily documented to the end that the present be comprehended with wholeness, as a moment in a flow of time, and not—as with so many modern plays—as a situation without roots. Indeed, even though I can myself reject other aspects of his work, it nevertheless presents barely and unadorned what I believe is the biggest single dramatic problem, namely, how to dramatize what has gone before. I say this not merely out of technical interest, but because dramatic characters, and the drama itself, can never hope to attain a maximum degree of consciousness unless they contain a viable unveiling of the contrast between past and present, and an awareness of the process by which the present has become what it is. And I say this, finally, because I take it as a truth that the end of drama is the creation of a higher consciousness and not merely a subjective attack upon the audience's nerves and feelings. What is precious in the Ibsen method is its insistence upon valid causation, and this cannot be dismissed as a wooden notion.

This is the "real" in Ibsen's realism for me, for he was, after all, as much a mystic as a realist. Which is simply to say that while there are mysteries in life which no amount of analyzing will reduce to reason, it is perfectly realistic to admit and even to proclaim that hiatus as a truth. But the problem is not to make complex what is essentially explainable; it is to make understandable what is complex without distorting and oversimplifying what cannot be explained. I think many of his devices are, in fact, quite arbitrary; that he betrays a Germanic ponderousness at times and a tendency to over-prove what is quite clear in the first place. But we could do with more of his basic intention, which was to assert nothing he had not proved, and to cling always to the marvelous spectacle of life forcing one event out of the jaws of the preceding one and to reveal its elemental consistencies with surprise. In other words, I contrast his realism not with the lyrical, which I prize, but with sentimentality, which is always a leak in the dramatic dike. He sought to make a play as weighty and living a fact as the discovery of the steam engine or algebra. This can be scoffed away only at a price, and the price is a living drama.

IV

I think now that the straightforwardness of the *All My Sons* form was in some part due to the relatively sharp definition of the social aspects of the problem it dealt with. It was conceived in wartime and begun in wartime; the spectacle of human sacrifice in contrast with aggrandizement is a sharp and heartbreaking one. At a time when all public voices were announcing the arrival of that great day when industry and labor were one, my personal experience was daily demonstrating that beneath the slogans very little had changed. In this sense the play was a response to what I felt "in the air." It was an unveiling of what I believed everybody knew and nobody publicly said. At the same time, however, I believed I was bringing news, and it was news which I half expected would be denied as truth.

When, in effect, it was accepted, I was gratified, but a little surprised. The success of a play, especially one's first success, is somewhat like pushing against a door which is suddenly opened from the other side. One may fall on one's face or not, but certainly a new room is opened that was always securely shut until then. For myself, the experience was invigorating. It suddenly seemed that the audience was a mass of blood relations, and I sensed a warmth in the world that had not been there before. It made it possible to dream of daring more and risking more. The Wonderful was no longer something that would inevitably trap me into disastrously confusing works, for the audience sat in silence before the unwinding of *All My Sons* and gasped when they should have, and I tasted that power which is reserved, I imagine, for playwrights, which is to know that by one's invention a mass of strangers has been publicly transfixed.

As well, the production of the play was an introduction to the acting art and its awesome potentials. I wanted to use more of what lay in actors to be used. To me, the most incredible spectacle of this first successful production was the silence it enforced. It seemed then that the stage was as wide and free and towering and laughingly inventive as the human mind itself, and I wanted to press closer toward its distant edges. A success places one among friends. The world is friendly, the audience is friendly, and that is good. It also reveals, even more starkly than a failure—for a failure is always ill-defined—what remains undone.

The wonder in *All My Sons* lay in its revelation of process, and it was made a stitch at a time, so to speak, in order to weave a tapestry before our eyes. What it wanted, however, was a kind of moment-to-moment wildness in addition to its organic wholeness. The form of the play, I felt, was not sensuous enough in itself. Which means that its conception of time came to appear at odds with my own experience.

The first image that occurred to me, which was to result in *Death of a Salesman,* was of an enormous face the height of the proscenium arch which would appear and then open up, and we would see the inside of a man's head. In fact, *The Inside of His Head* was the first title. It was conceived half in laughter, for the inside of his head was a mass of contradictions. The image was in direct opposition to the method of *All My Sons*—a method one might call linear or eventual in that one fact or incident creates the necessity for the next. The *Salesman* image was from the beginning absorbed with the concept that nothing in life comes "next" but that everything exists together and at the same time within us; that there is no past to be "brought forward" in a human being, but that he is his past at every moment and that the present is merely that which his past is capable of noticing and smelling and reacting to.

I wished to create a form which, in itself as a form, would literally be the process of Willy Loman's way of mind. But to say "wished" is not accurate. Any dramatic form is an artifice, a way of transforming a subjective feeling into something that can be comprehended through public symbols. Its efficiency as a form is to be judged—at least by the writer—by how much of the original vision and feeling is lost or distorted by this transformation. I wished to speak of the salesman most precisely as I felt about him, to give no part of that feeling away for the sake of any effect or any dramatic necessity. What was wanted now was not a mounting line of tension, nor a gradually narrowing cone of intensifying suspense, but a bloc, a single chord presented as such at the outset, within which all the strains and melodies would already be contained. The strategy, as with *All My Sons,* was to appear entirely unstrategic but with a difference. This time, if I could, I would have told the whole story and set forth all the characters in one unbroken speech or even one sentence or a single flash of light. As I look at the play now its form seems the form of a confession, for that is how it is told, now speaking of what happened yesterday, then suddenly following some connection to a time twenty years ago, then leaping even further back and then returning to the present and even speculating about the future.

Where in *All My Sons* it had seemed necessary to prove the connections between the present and the past, between events and moral consequences, between the manifest and the hidden, in this play all was assumed as proven to begin with. All I was doing was bringing things to mind. The assumption, also, was that everyone knew Willy Loman. I can realize this only now, it is true, but it is equally apparent to me that I took it somehow for granted then. There was still the attitude of the unveiler, but no bringing together of hitherto unrelated things; only pre-existing images, events, confrontations, moods, and pieces of knowledge. So there was a kind of confidence underlying this play which the form itself expresses, even a naïveté, a self-disarming quality that was in part born of my belief in the audience as being essentially the same as myself. If I had wanted, then, to put the audience reaction into words, it would not have been "What happens next and why?" so much as "Oh, God, of course!"

In one sense a play is a species of jurisprudence, and some part of it must take the advocate's role, something else must act in defense, and the entirety must engage the Law. Against my will, *All My Sons* states, and even proclaims, that it is a form and that a writer wrote it and organized it. In *Death of a Salesman* the original impulse was to make that same proclamation in an immeasurably more violent, abrupt, and openly conscious way. Willy Loman does not merely suggest or hint that he is at the end of his strength and of his justifications, he is hardly on the stage for five minutes when he says so; he does not gradually imply a deadly conflict with his son, an implication dropped into the midst of serenity and surface calm, he is avowedly grappling with that conflict at the outset. The ultimate matter with which the play will close is announced at the outset and is the matter of its every moment from the first. There is enough revealed in the first scene of *Death of a Salesman* to fill another kind of play which, in service to another dramatic form, would hold back and only gradually release it. I wanted to proclaim that an artist had made this play, but the nature of the proclamation was to be entirely "inartistic" and avowedly unstrategic; it was to hold back nothing, at any moment, which life would have revealed, even at the cost of suspense and climax. It was to forgo the usual preparations for scenes and to permit—and even seek—whatever in each character contradicted his position in the advocate-defense scheme of its jurisprudence. The play was begun with only one firm piece of knowledge and this was that Loman was to destroy himself. How it would wander before it got to that point I did not know and resolved not to care. I was convinced only that if I could make him remember enough he would kill himself, and the structure of the play was determined by what was needed to draw up his memories like a mass of tangled roots without end or beginning.

As I have said, the structure of events and the nature of its form are also the direct reflection of Willy Loman's way of thinking at this moment of his life. He was the kind of man you see muttering to himself on a subway, decently dressed, on his way home or to the office, perfectly integrated with his surroundings excepting that unlike other people he can no longer restrain the power of his experience from disrupting the superficial sociality of his behavior. Consequently he is working on two logics which often collide. For instance, if he meets his son Happy while in the midst of some memory in which Happy disappointed him, he is instantly furious at Happy, despite the fact that Happy at this particular moment deeply desires to be of use to him. He is literally at that terrible moment when the voice of the past is no longer distant but quite as loud as the voice of the present. In dramatic terms the form, therefore, *is* this process, instead of being a once-removed summation or indication of it.

The way of telling the tale, in this sense, is as mad as Willy and as abrupt and as suddenly lyrical. And it is difficult not to add that the subsequent imitations of the form had to collapse for this particular reason. It is not possible, in my opinion, to graft it onto a character whose psychology it does not reflect, and I have not used it since because it would be false to a more integrated—or less disintegrating—personality to pretend that the past and the present are so openly and vocally intertwined in his mind. The ability of people to down their past is normal, and without it we could have no comprehensible communication among men. In the hands of writers who see it as an easy way to elicit anterior information in a play it becomes merely a flashback. There are no flashbacks in this play but only a mobile concurrency of past and present, and this, again, because in his desperation to justify his life Willy Loman has destroyed the boundaries between now and then, just as anyone would do who, on picking up his telephone, discovered that this perfectly harmless act had somehow set off an explosion in his basement. The previously assumed and believed-in results of ordinary and accepted actions, and their abrupt and unforeseen—but apparently logical—effects, form the basic collision in this play, and, I suppose, its ultimate irony.

It may be in place to remark, in this connection, that while the play was sometimes called cinematographic in its structure, it failed as a motion picture. I believe that the basic reason—aside from the gross insensitivity permeating its film production—was that the dramatic tension of Willy's memories was destroyed by transferring him, literally, to the locales he had only imagined in the play. There is an inevitable horror in the spectacle of a man losing consciousness of his immediate surroundings to the point where he engages in conversations with unseen persons. The horror is lost—and drama becomes narrative—when the context actually becomes his imagined world. And the dream evaporates because psychological truth has been amended, a truth which depends not only on what images we recall but in what connections and contexts we recall them. The setting on the stage was never shifted, despite the many changes in locale, for the precise reason that, quite simply, the mere fact that a man forgets where he is does not mean that he has really moved. Indeed, his terror springs from his never-lost awareness of time and place. It did not need this play to teach me that the screen is time-bound and earth-bound compared to the stage, if only because its preponderant emphasis is on the visual image, which, however rapidly it may be changed before our eyes, still displaces its predecessor, while scene-changing with words is instantaneous; and because of the flexibility of language, especially of English, a preceding image can be kept alive through the image that succeeds it. The movie's tendency is always to wipe out what has gone before, and it is thus in constant danger of transforming the dramatic into narrative. There is no swifter method of telling a "story" but neither is there a more difficult medium in which to keep a pattern of relationships constantly in being. Even in those sequences which retained the real backgrounds for Willy's imaginary confrontations the tension between now and then was lost. I suspect this loss was due to the necessity of shooting the actors close-up —effectively eliminating awareness of their surroundings. The basic failure of the picture was a formal one. It did not solve, nor really attempt to find, a resolution for the problem of keeping the past constantly alive, and that friction, collision, and tension between past and present was the heart of the play's particular construction.

A great deal has been said and written about what *Death of a Salesman* is supposed to signify, both psychologically and from the socio-political viewpoints. For instance, in one periodical of the far Right it was called a "time bomb expertly placed under the edifice of Americanism," while the *Daily Worker* reviewer thought it entirely decadent. In Catholic Spain it ran longer than any modern play and it has been refused production in Russia but not, from time to time, in certain satellite countries, depending on the direction and velocity of the wind. The Spanish press, thoroughly controlled by Catholic orthodoxy, regarded the play as commendable proof of the spirit's death where there is no God. In America, even as it was being cannonaded as a piece of Communist propaganda, two of the largest manufacturing corporations in the country invited me to address their sales organizations in conventions assembled, while the road company was here and there picketed by the Catholic War Veterans and the American Legion. It made only a fair impression in London, but in the area of the Norwegian Arctic Circle fishermen whose only contact with civilization was the radio and the occasional visit of the government boat insisted on seeing it night after night —the same few people—believing it to be some kind of religious rite. One organization of salesmen raised me up nearly to patronsainthood, and another, a national sales managers' group, complained that the difficulty of recruiting salesmen was directly traceable to the play. When the movie was made, the producing company got so frightened it produced a sort of trailer to be shown before the picture, a documentary short film which demonstrated how exceptional Willy Loman was; how necessary selling is to the economy; how secure the salesman's life really is; how idiotic, in short, was the feature film they had just spent more than a million dollars to produce. Fright does odd things to people.

On the psychological front the play spawned a small hill of doctoral theses explaining its Freudian symbolism, and there were innumerable letters asking if I was aware that the fountain pen which Biff steals is a phallic symbol. Some, on the other hand, felt it was merely a fountain pen and dismissed the whole play. I received visits from men over sixty from as far away as California who had come across the country to have me write the stories of their lives, because the story of Willy Loman was exactly like theirs. The letters from women made it clear that the central character of the play was Linda; sons saw the entire action revolving around Biff or Happy, and fathers wanted advice, in effect, on how to avoid parricide. Probably the most succinct reaction to the play was voiced by a man who, on leaving the theater, said, "I always said that New England territory was no damned good." This, at least, was a fact.

That I have and had not the slightest interest in the selling profession is probably unbelievable to most people, and I very early gave up trying even to say so. And when asked what Willy was selling, what was in his bags, I could only reply, "Himself." I was trying neither to condemn a profession nor particularly to improve it, and, I will admit, I was little better than ignorant of Freud's teachings when I wrote it. There was no attempt to bring down the American edifice nor to raise it higher, to show up family relations or to cure the ills afflicting that inevitable institution. The truth, at least of my aim—which is all I can speak of authoritatively—is much simpler and more complex.

The play grew from simple images. From a little frame house on a street of little frame houses, which had once been loud with the noise of growing boys, and then was empty and silent and finally occupied by strangers. Strangers who could not know with what conquistadorial joy Willy and his boys had once re-shingled the roof. Now it was quiet in the house, and the wrong people in the beds.

It grew from images of futility—the cavernous Sunday afternoons polishing the car. Where is that car now? And the chamois cloths carefully washed and put up to dry, where are the chamois cloths?

And the endless, convoluted discussions, wonderments, arguments, belittlements, encouragements, fiery resolutions, abdications, returns, partings, voyages out and voyages back, tremendous opportunities and small, squeaking denouements—and all in the kitchen now occupied by strangers who cannot hear what the walls are saying.

The image of aging and so many of your friends already gone and strangers in the seats of the mighty who do not know you or your triumphs or your incredible value.

The image of the son's hard, public eye upon you, no longer swept by your myth, no longer rousable from his separateness, no longer knowing you have lived for him and have wept for him.

The image of ferocity when love has turned to something else and yet is there, is somewhere in the room if one could only find it.

The image of people turning into strangers who only evaluate one another.

Above all, perhaps, the image of a need greater than hunger or sex or thirst, a need to leave a thumbprint somewhere on the world. A need for immortality, and by admitting it, the knowing that one has carefully inscribed one's name on a cake of ice on a hot July day.

I sought the relatedness of all things by isolating their unrelatedness, a man superbly alone with his sense of not having touched, and finally knowing in his last extremity that the love which had always been in the room unlocated was now found.

The image of a suicide so mixed in motive as to be unfathomable and yet demanding statement. Revenge was in it and a power of love, a victory in that it would bequeath a fortune to the living and a flight from emptiness. With it an image of peace at the final curtain, the peace that is between wars, the peace leaving the issues above ground and viable yet.

And always, throughout, the image of private man in a world full of strangers, a world that is not home nor even an open battleground but only galaxies of high promise over a fear of falling.

And the image of a man making something with his hands being a rock to touch and return to. "He was always so wonderful with his hands," says his wife over his grave, and I laughed when the line came, laughed with the artist-devil's laugh, for it had all come together in this line, she having been made by him though he did not know it or believe in it or receive it into himself. Only rank, height of power, the sense of having won he believed was real—the galaxy thrust up into the sky by projectors on the rooftops of the city he believed were real stars.

It came from structural images. The play's eye was to revolve from within Willy's head, sweeping endlessly in all directions like a light on the sea, and nothing that formed in the distant mist was to be left uninvestigated. It was thought of as having the density of the novel form in its interchange of viewpoints, so that while all roads led to Willy the other characters were to feel it was their play, a story about them and not him.

There were two undulating lines in mind, one above the other, the past webbed to the present moving on together in him and sometimes openly joined and once, finally, colliding in the showdown which defined him in his eyes at least—and so to sleep.

Above all, in the structural sense, I aimed to make a play with the veritable countenance of life. To make one the many, as in life, so that "society" is a power and a mystery of custom and inside the man and surrounding him, as the fish is in the sea and the sea inside the fish, his birthplace and burial ground, promise and threat. To speak commonsensically of social facts which every businessman knows and talks about but which are too prosaic to mention or are usually fancied up on the stage as philosophical problems. When a man gets old you fire him, you have to, he can't do the work. To speak and even to celebrate the common sense of businessmen, who love the personality that wins the day but know that you've got to have the right goods at the right price, handsome and well-spoken as you are. (To some, these were scandalous and infamous arraignments of society when uttered in the context of art. But not to the businessmen themselves; they knew it was all true and I cherished their clear-eyed talk.)

The image of a play without transitional scenes was there in the beginning. There was too much to say to waste precious stage time with feints and preparations, in themselves agonizing "structural" bridges for a writer to work out since they are not why he is writing. There was a resolution, as in *All My Sons,* not to waste motion or moments, but in this case to shear through everything up to the meat of a scene; a resolution not to write an unmeant word for the sake of the form but to make the form give and stretch and contract for the sake of the thing to be said. To cling to the process of Willy's mind as the form the story would take.

The play was always heroic to me, and in later years the academy's charge that Willy lacked the "stature" for the tragic hero seemed incredible to me. I had not understood that these matters are measured by Greco-Elizabethan paragraphs which hold no mention of insurance payments, front porches, refrigerator fan belts, steering knuckles, Chevrolets, and visions seen not through the portals of Delphi but in the blue flame of the hot-water heater. How could "Tragedy" make people weep, of all things?

I set out not to "write a tragedy" in this play, but to show the truth as I saw it. However, some of the attacks upon it as a pseudo-tragedy contain ideas so misleading, and in some cases so laughable, that it might be in place here to deal with a few of them.

Aristotle having spoken of a fall from the heights, it goes without saying that someone of the common mould cannot be a fit tragic hero. It is now many centuries since Aristotle lived. There is no more reason for falling down in a faint before his *Poetics* than before Euclid's geometry, which has been amended numerous times by men with new insights; nor, for that matter, would I choose to have my illnesses diagnosed by Hippocrates rather than the most ordinary graduate of an American medical school, despite the Greek's genius. Things do change, and even a genius is limited by his time and the nature of his society.

I would deny, on grounds of simple logic, this one of Aristotle's contentions if only because he lived in a slave society. When a vast number of people are divested of alternatives, as slaves are, it is rather inevitable that one will not be able to imagine drama, let alone tragedy, as being possible for any but the higher ranks of society. There is a legitimate question of stature here, but none of rank, which is so often confused with it. So long as the hero may be said to have had alternatives of a magnitude to have materially changed the course of his life, it seems to me that in this respect at least, he cannot be debarred from the heroic role.

The question of rank is significant to me only as it reflects the question of the social application of the hero's career. There is no doubt that if a character is shown on the stage who goes through the most ordinary actions, and is suddenly revealed to be the President of the United States, his actions immediately assume a much greater magnitude, and pose the possibilities of much greater meaning, than if he is the corner grocer. But at the same time, his stature as a hero is not so utterly dependent upon his rank that the corner grocer cannot outdistance him as a tragic figure—providing, of course, that the grocer's career engages the issues of, for instance, the survival of the race, the relationships of man to God—the questions, in short, whose answers define humanity and the right way to live so that the world is a home, instead of a battleground or a fog in which disembodied spirits pass each other in an endless twilight.

In this respect *Death of a Salesman* is a slippery play to categorize because nobody in it stops to make a speech objectively stating the great issues which I believe it embodies. If it were a worse play, less closely articulating its meanings with its actions, I think it would have more quickly satisfied a certain kind of criticism. But it was meant to be less a play than a fact; it refused admission to its author's opinions and opened itself to a revelation of process and the operations of an ethic, of social laws of action no less powerful in their effects upon individuals than any tribal law administered by gods with names. I need not claim that this play is a genuine solid-gold tragedy for my opinions on tragedy to be held valid. My purpose here is simply to point out a historical fact which must be taken into account in any consideration of tragedy, and it is the sharp alteration in the meaning of rank in society between the present time and the distant past. More important to me is the fact that this particular kind of argument obscures much more relevant considerations.

One of these is the question of intensity. It matters not at all whether a modern play concerns itself with a grocer or a president if the intensity of the hero's commitment to his course is less than the maximum possible. It matters not at all whether the hero falls from a great height or a small one, whether he is highly conscious or only dimly aware of what is happening, whether his pride brings the fall or an unseen pattern written behind clouds; if the intensity, the human passion to surpass his given bounds, the fanatic insistence upon his self-conceived role—if these are not present there can only be an outline of tragedy but no living thing. I believe, for myself, that the lasting appeal of tragedy is due to our need to face the fact of death in order to strengthen ourselves for life, and that over and above this function of the tragic viewpoint there are and will be a great number of formal variations which no single definition will ever embrace.

Another issue worth considering is the so-called tragic victory, a question closely related to the consciousness of the hero. One makes nonsense of this if a "victory" means that the hero makes us feel some certain joy when, for instance, he sacrifices himself for a "cause," and unhappy and morose because he dies without one. To begin at the bottom, a man's death is and ought to be an essentially terrifying thing and ought to make nobody happy. But in a great variety of ways even death, the ultimate negative, can be, and appear to be, an assertion of bravery, and can serve to separate the death of man from the death of animals; and I think it is this distinction which underlies any conception of a victory in death. For a society of faith, the nature of the death can prove the existence of the spirit, and posit its immortality. For a secular society it is perhaps more difficult for such a victory to document itself and to make itself felt, but, conversely, the need to offer greater proofs of the humanity of man can make that victory more real. It goes without saying that in a society where there is basic disagreement as to the right way to live, there can hardly be agreement as to the right way to die, and both life and death must be heavily weighted with meaningless futility.

It was not out of any deference to a tragic definition that Willy Loman is filled with a joy, however broken-hearted, as he approaches his end, but simply that my sense of his character dictated his joy, and even what I felt was an exultation. In terms of his character, he has achieved a very powerful piece of knowledge, which is that he is loved by his son and has been embraced by him and forgiven. In this he is given his existence, so to speak—his fatherhood, for which he has always striven and which until now he could not achieve. That he is unable to take this victory thoroughly to his heart, that it closes the circle for him and propels him to his death, is the wage of his sin, which was to have committed himself so completely to the counterfeits of dignity and the false coinage embodied in his idea of success that he can prove his existence only by bestowing "power" on his posterity, a power deriving from the sale of his last asset, himself, for the price of his insurance policy.

I must confess here to a miscalculation, however. I did not realize while writing the play that so many people in the world do not see as clearly, or would not admit, as I thought they must, how futile most lives are; so there could be no hope of consoling the audience for the death of this man. I did not realize either how few would be impressed by the fact that this man is actually a very brave spirit who cannot settle for half but must pursue his dream of himself to the end. Finally, I thought it must be clear, even obvious, that this was no dumb brute heading mindlessly to his catastrophe.

I have no need to be Willy's advocate before the jury which decides who is and who is not a tragic hero. I am merely noting that the lingering ponderousness of so many ancient definitions has blinded students and critics to the facts before them, and not only in regard to this play. Had Willy been unaware of his separation from values that endure he would have died contentedly while polishing his car, probably on a Sunday afternoon with the ball game coming over the radio. But he was agonized by his awareness of being in a false position, so constantly haunted by the hollowness of all he had placed his faith in, so aware, in short, that he must somehow be filled in his spirit or fly apart, that he staked his very life on the ultimate assertion. That he had not the intellectual fluency to verbalize his situation is not the same thing as saying that he lacked awareness, even an overly intensified consciousness that the life he had made was without form and inner meaning.

To be sure, had he been able to know that he was as much the victim of his beliefs as their defeated exemplar, had he known how much of guilt he ought to bear and how much to shed from his soul, he would be more conscious. But it seems to me that there is of necessity a severe limitation of self-awareness in any character, even the most knowing, which serves to define him as a character, and more, that this very limit serves to complete the tragedy and, indeed, to make it at all possible. Complete consciousness is possible only in a play about forces, like *Prometheus,* but not in a play about people. I think that the point is whether there is a sufficient awareness in the hero's career to make the audience supply the rest. Had Oedipus, for instance, been more conscious and more aware of the forces at work upon him he must surely have said that he was not really to blame for having cohabited with his mother since neither he nor anyone else knew she was his mother. He must surely decide to divorce her, provide for their children, firmly resolve to investigate the family background of his next wife, and thus deprive us of a very fine play and the name for a famous neurosis. But he is conscious only up to a point, the point at which guilt begins. Now he is inconsolable and must tear out his eyes. What is tragic about this? Why is it not even ridiculous? How can we respect a man who goes to such extremities over something he could in no way help or prevent? The answer, I think, is not that we respect the man, but that we respect the Law he has so completely broken, wittingly or not, for it is that Law which, we believe, defines us as men. The confusion of some critics viewing *Death of a Salesman* in this regard is that they do not see that Willy Loman has broken a law without whose protection life is insupportable if not incomprehensible to him and to many others; it is the law which says that a failure in society and in business has no right to live. Unlike the law against incest, the law of success is not administered by statute or church, but it is very nearly as powerful in its grip upon men. The confusion increases because, while it is a law, it is by no means a wholly agreeable one even as it is slavishly obeyed, for to fail is no longer to belong to society, in his estimate. Therefore, the path is opened for those who wish to call Willy merely a foolish man even as they themselves are living in obedience to the same law that killed him. Equally, the fact that Willy's law—the belief, in other words, which administers guilt to him—is not a civilizing statute whose destruction menaces us all; it is, rather, a deeply believed and deeply suspect "good" which, when questioned as to its value, as it is in this play, serves more to raise our anxieties than to reassure us of the existence of an unseen but humane metaphysical system in the world. My attempt in the play was to counter this anxiety with an opposing system which, so to speak, is in a race for Willy's faith, and it is the system of love which is the opposite of the law of success. It is embodied in Biff Loman, but by the time Willy can perceive his love it can serve

only as an ironic comment upon the life he sacrificed for power
and for success and its tokens.

v

A play cannot be equated with a political philosophy, at least
not in the way a smaller number, by simple multiplication, can
be assimilated into a larger. I do not believe that any work of art
can help but be diminished by its adherence at any cost to a
political program, including its author's, and not for any other
reason than that there is no political program—any more than
there is a theory of tragedy—which can encompass the complexities of real life. Doubtless an author's politics must be
one element, and even an important one, in the germination
of his art, but if it is art he has created it must by definition bend
itself to his observation rather than to his opinions or even his
hopes. If I have shown a preference for plays which seek causation not only in psychology but in society, I may also believe in
the autonomy of art, and I believe this because my experience
with *All My Sons* and *Death of a Salesman* forces the belief upon
me. If the earlier play was Marxist, it was a Marxism of a strange
hue. Joe Keller is arraigned by his son for a willfully unethical
use of his economic position; and this, as the Russians said when
they removed the play from their stages, bespeaks an assumption that the norm of capitalist behavior is ethical or at least
can be, an assumption no Marxist can hold. Nor does Chris
propose to liquidate the business built in part on soldiers' blood;
he will run it himself, but cleanly.

The most decent man in *Death of a Salesman* is a capitalist
(Charley) whose aims are not different from Willy Loman's.
The great difference between them is that Charley is not a
fanatic. Equally, however, he has learned how to live without
that frenzy, that ecstasy of spirit which Willy chases to his end.
And even as Willy's sons are unhappy men, Charley's boy,
Bernard, works hard, attends to his studies, and attains a worth-

while objective. These people are all of the same class, the same background, the same neighborhood. What theory lies behind this double view? None whatever. It is simply that I knew and know that I feel better when my work is reflecting a balance of the truth as it exists. A muffled debate arose with the success of *Death of a Salesman* in which attempts were made to justify or dismiss the play as a Left-Wing piece, or as a Right-Wing manifestation of decadence. The presumption underlying both views is that a work of art is the sum of its author's political outlook, real or alleged, and more, that its political implications are valid elements in its aesthetic evaluation. I do not believe this, either for my own or other writers' works.

The most radical play I ever saw was not *Waiting for Lefty* but *The Madwoman of Chaillot*. I know nothing of Giradoux's political alignment, and it is of no moment to me; I am able to read this play, which is the most open indictment of private exploitation of the earth I know about. By the evidence of his plays, Shaw, the socialist, was in love not with the working class, whose characters he could only caricature, but with the middle of the economic aristocracy, those men who, in his estimate, lived without social and economic illusions. There is a strain of mystic fatalism in Ibsen so powerful as to throw all his scientific tenets into doubt, and a good measure besides of contempt—in this radical—for the men who are usually called the public. The list is long and the contradictions are embarrassing until one concedes a perfectly simple proposition. It is merely that a writer of any worth creates out of his total perception, the vaster part of which is subjective and not within his intellectual control. For myself, it has never been possible to generate the energy to write and complete a play if I know in advance everything it signifies and all it will contain. The very impulse to write, I think, springs from an inner chaos crying for order, for meaning, and that meaning must be discovered in the process of writing or the work lies dead as it is finished. To speak, therefore, of a play as though it were the objective work of a propagandist is an almost biological kind of nonsense, provided, of course, that it is a play, which is to say a work of art.

VI

In the writing of *Death of a Salesman* I tried, of course, to achieve a maximum power of effect. But when I saw the devastating force with which it struck its audiences, something within me was shocked and put off. I had thought of myself as rather an optimistic man. I looked at what I had wrought and was forced to wonder whether I knew myself at all if this play, which I had written half in laughter and joy, was as morose and as utterly sad as its audiences found it. Either I was much tougher than they, and could stare at calamity with fewer terrors, or I was harboring within myself another man who was only tangentially connected with what I would have called my rather bright viewpoint about mankind. As I watched and saw tears in the eyes of the audience I felt a certain embarrassment at having, as I thought then, convinced so many people that life was not worth living—for so the play was widely interpreted. I hasten to add now that I ought not have been embarrassed, and that I am convinced the play is not a document of pessimism, a philosophy in which I do not believe.

Nevertheless, the emotionalism with which the play was received helped to generate an opposite impulse and an altered dramatic aim. This ultimately took shape in *The Crucible,* but before it became quite so definite and formed into idea, it was taking hold of my thoughts in a purely dramatic and theatrical context. Perhaps I can indicate its basic elements by saying that *Salesman* moves with its arms open wide, sweeping into itself by means of a subjective process of thought-connection a multitude of observations, feelings, suggestions, and shadings much as the mind does in its ordinary daily functions. Its author chose its path, of course, but, once chosen, that path could meander as it pleased through a world that was well recognized by the audience. From the theatrical viewpoint that play desired the audience to forget it was in a theater even as it broke the bounds, I believe, of a long convention of realism. Its expressionistic elements were consciously used as such, but since the approach to Willy Loman's characterization was consistently and rigorously subjective, the audience would not ever be aware—if I could help it—that they were witnessing the use of a technique which had until then created only coldness, objectivity, and a highly styled sort of play. I had willingly employed expressionism but always to create a subjective truth, and this play, which was so manifestly "written," seemed as though nobody had written it at all but that it had simply "happened." I had always been attracted and repelled by the brilliance of German expressionism after World War I, and one aim in *Salesman* was to employ its quite marvelous shorthand for humane, "felt" characterizations rather than for purposes of demonstration for which the Germans had used it.

These and other technical and theatrical considerations were a preparation for what turned out to be *The Crucible,* but "what was in the air" provided the actual locus of the tale. If the reception of *All My Sons* and *Death of a Salesman* had made the world a friendly place for me, events of the early fifties quickly turned that warmth into an illusion. It was not only the rise of "McCarthyism" that moved me, but something which seemed much more weird and mysterious. It was the fact that a political, objective, knowledgeable campaign from the far Right was capable of creating not only a terror, but a new subjective reality, a veritable mystique which was gradually assuming even a holy resonance. The wonder of it all struck me that so practical and picayune a cause, carried forward by such manifestly ridiculous men, should be capable of paralyzing thought itself, and worse, causing to billow up such persuasive clouds of "mysterious" feelings within people. It was as though the whole country had been born anew, without a memory even of certain elemental decencies which a year or two earlier no one would have imagined could be altered, let alone forgotten. Astounded, I watched men pass me by without a nod whom I had known rather well for years; and again, the astonishment was produced by my knowledge, which I could not give up, that the terror in these people was being knowingly planned and consciously engineered, and yet that all they knew was terror. That so interior and subjective an emotion could have been so manifestly created from without was a marvel to me. It underlies every word in *The Crucible*.

I wondered, at first, whether it must be that self-preservation and the need to hold on to opportunity, the thought of being exiled and "put out," was what the fear was feeding on, for there were people who had had only the remotest connections with the Left who were quite as terrified as those who had been closer. I knew of one man who had been summoned to the office of a network executive and, on explaining that he had had no Left connections at all, despite the then current attacks upon him, was told that this was precisely the trouble; "You have nothing to give them," he was told, meaning he had no confession to make, and so he was fired from his job and for more than a year could not recover the will to leave his house.

It seemed to me after a time that this, as well as other kinds of social compliance, is the result of the sense of guilt which individuals strive to conceal by complying. Generally it was guilt, in this historic instance, resulting from their awareness that they were not as Rightist as people were supposed to be; that the tenor of public pronouncements was alien to them and that they must be somehow discoverable as enemies of the power overhead. There was a new religiosity in the air, not merely the kind expressed by the spurt in church construction and church attendance, but an official piety which my reading of American history could not reconcile with the free-wheeling iconoclasm of the country's past. I saw forming a kind of interior mechanism of confession and forgiveness of sins which until now had not been rightly categorized as sins. New sins were being created monthly. It was very odd how quickly these were accepted into the new orthodoxy, quite as though they had been there since the beginning of time. Above all, above all horrors, I saw accepted the notion that conscience was no longer a private matter but one of state administration. I saw men handing conscience to other men and thanking other men for the opportunity of doing so.

I wished for a way to write a play that would be sharp, that would lift out of the morass of subjectivism the squirming, single, defined process which would show that the sin of public terror is that it divests man of conscience, of himself. It was a theme not unrelated to those that had invested the previous plays. In *The Crucible,* however, there was an attempt to move beyond the discovery and unveiling of the hero's guilt, a guilt that kills the personality. I had grown increasingly conscious of this theme in my past work, and aware too that it was no longer enough for me to build a play, as it were, upon the revelation of guilt, and to rely solely upon a fate which exacts payment from the culpable man. Now guilt appeared to me no longer the bedrock beneath which the probe could not penetrate. I saw it now as a betrayer, as possibly the most real of our illusions, but nevertheless a quality of mind capable of being overthrown.

I had known of the Salem witch hunt for many years before "McCarthyism" had arrived, and it had always remained an inexplicable darkness to me. When I looked into it now, however, it was with the contemporary situation at my back, particularly the mystery of the handing over of conscience which seemed to me the central and informing fact of the time. One finds, I suppose, what one seeks. I doubt I should ever have tempted agony by actually writing a play on the subject had I not come upon a single fact. It was that Abigail Williams, the prime mover of the Salem hysteria, so far as the hysterical children were concerned, had a short time earlier been the house servant of the Proctors and now was crying out Elizabeth Proctor as a witch; but more —it was clear from the record that with entirely uncharacteristic fastidiousness she was refusing to include John Proctor, Elizabeth's husband, in her accusations despite the urgings of the prosecutors. Why? I searched the records of the trials in the courthouse at Salem but in no other instance could I find such a careful avoidance of the implicating stutter, the murderous, ambivalent answer to the sharp questions of the prosecutors. Only here, in Proctor's case, was there so clear an attempt to differentiate between a wife's culpability and a husband's.

The testimony of Proctor himself is one of the least elaborate in the records, and Elizabeth is not one of the major cases either. There could have been numerous reasons for his having been ultimately apprehended and hanged which are nowhere to be found. After the play opened, several of his descendants wrote to me; and one of them believes that Proctor fell under suspicion because, according to family tradition, he had for years been an amateur inventor whose machines appeared to some people as devilish in their ingenuity, and—again according to tradition— he had had to conceal them and work on them privately long before the witch hunt had started, for fear of censure if not worse. The explanation does not account for everything, but it does fall in with his evidently liberated cast of mind as revealed in the record; he was one of the few who not only refused to admit consorting with evil spirits, but who persisted in calling the entire business a ruse and a fake. Most, if not all, of the other victims were of their time in conceding the existence of the immemorial plot by the Devil to take over the visible world, their only reservation being that they happened not to have taken part in it themselves.

It was the fact that Abigail, their former servant, was their accuser, and her apparent desire to convict Elizabeth and save John, that made the play conceivable for me.

As in any such mass phenomenon, the number of characters of vital, if not decisive, importance is so great as to make the dramatic problem excessively difficult. For a time it seemed best to approach the town impressionistically, and, by a mosaic of seemingly disconnected scenes, gradually to form a context of cause and effect. This I believe I might well have done had it not been that the central impulse for writing at all was not the social but the interior psychological question, which was the question of that guilt residing in Salem which the hysteria merely unleashed, but did not create. Consequently, the structure reflects that understanding, and it centers in John, Elizabeth, and Abigail.

In reading the record, which was taken down verbatim at the trial, I found one recurring note which had a growing effect upon my concept, not only of the phenomenon itself, but of our modern way of thinking about people, and especially of the treatment of evil in contemporary drama. Some critics have taken exception, for instance, to the unrelieved badness of the prosecution in my play. I understand how this is possible, and I plead no mitigation, but I was up against historical facts which were immutable. I do not think that either the record itself or the numerous commentaries upon it reveal any mitigation of the unrelieved, straightforward, and absolute dedication to evil displayed by the judges of these trials and the prosecutors. After days of study it became quite incredible how perfect they were in this respect. I recall, almost as in a dream, how Rebecca Nurse, a pious and universally respected woman of great age, was literally taken by force from her sickbed and ferociously cross-examined. No human weakness could be displayed without the prosecution's stabbing into it with greater fury. The most patent contradictions, almost laughable even in that day, were overridden with warnings not to repeat their mention. There was a sadism here that was breathtaking.

So much so, that I sought but could not at the time take hold of a concept of man which might really begin to account for such evil. For instance, it seems beyond doubt that members of the Putnam family consciously, coldly, and with malice aforethought conferred in private with some of the girls, and told them whom it was desirable to cry out upon next. There is and will always be in my mind the spectacle of the great minister, and ideological authority behind the prosecution, Cotton Mather, galloping up to the scaffold to beat back a crowd of villagers so moved by the towering dignity of the victims as to want to free them.

It was not difficult to foresee the objections to such absolute evil in men; we are committed, after all, to the belief that it does not and cannot exist. Had I this play to write now, however, I might proceed on an altered concept. I should say that my own —and the critics'—unbelief in this depth of evil is concomitant with our unbelief in good, too. I should now examine this fact of evil as such. Instead, I sought to make Danforth, for instance, perceptible as a human being by showing him somewhat put off by Mary Warren's turnabout at the height of the trials, which caused no little confusion. In my play, Danforth seems about to conceive of the truth, and surely there is a disposition in him at least to listen to arguments that go counter to the line of the prosecution. There is no such swerving in the record, and I think now, almost four years after the writing of it, that I was wrong in mitigating the evil of this man and the judges he represents. Instead, I would perfect his evil to its utmost and make an open issue, a thematic consideration of it in the play. I believe now, as I did not conceive then, that there are people dedicated to evil in the world; that without their perverse example we should not know the good. Evil is not a mistake but a fact in itself. I have never proceeded psychoanalytically in my thought, but neither have I been separated from that humane if not humanistic conception of man as being essentially innocent while the evil in him represents but a perversion of his frustrated love. I posit no metaphysical force of evil which totally possesses certain individuals, nor do I even deny that given infinite wisdom and patience and knowledge any human being can be saved from himself. I believe merely that, from whatever cause, a dedication to evil, not mistaking it for good, but knowing it as evil and loving it as evil, is possible in human beings who appear agreeable and normal. I think now that one of the hidden weaknesses of our whole approach to dramatic psychology is our inability to face this fact—to conceive, in effect, of Iago.

The Crucible is a "tough" play. My criticism of it now would be that it is not tough enough. I say this not merely out of deference to the record of these trials, but out of a consideration for drama. We are so intent upon getting sympathy for our characters that the consequences of evil are being muddied by sentimentality under the guise of a temperate weighing of causes. The tranquility of the bad man lies at the heart of not only moral philosophy but dramaturgy as well. But my central intention in this play was to one side of this idea, which was realized only as the play was in production. All I sought here was to take a step not only beyond the realization of guilt, but beyond the helpless victimization of the hero.

The society of Salem was "morally" vocal. People then avowed principles, sought to live by them and die by them. Issues of faith, conduct, society, pervaded their private lives in a conscious way. They needed but to disapprove to act. I was drawn to this subject because the historical moment seemed to give me the poetic right to create people of higher self-awareness than the contemporary scene affords. I had explored the subjective world in *Salesman* and I wanted now to move closer to a conscious hero.

The decidedly mixed reception to the play was not easily traceable, but I believe there are causes for it which are of moment to more than this play alone. I believe that the very moral awareness of the play and its characters—which are historically correct—was repulsive to the audience. For a variety of reasons I think that the Anglo-Saxon audience cannot believe the reality of characters who live by principles and know very much about their own characters and situations, and who say what they know. Our drama, for this among other reasons, is condemned, so to speak, to the emotions of subjectivism, which, as they approach knowledge and self-awareness, become less and less actual and real to us. In retrospect I think that my course in *The Crucible* should have been toward greater self-awareness and not, as my critics have implied, toward an enlarged and more pervasive subjectivism. The realistic form and style of the play would then have had to give way. What new form might have evolved I cannot now say, but certainly the passion of knowing is as powerful as the passion of feeling alone, and the writing of the play broached the question of that new form for me.

The work of Bertolt Brecht inevitably rises up in any such quest. It seems to me that, while I cannot agree with his concept of the human situation, his solution of the problem of consciousness is admirably honest and theatrically powerful. One cannot watch his productions without knowing that he is at work not on the periphery of the contemporary dramatic problem, but directly upon its center—which is again the problem of consciousness.

VII

The Crucible, then, opened up a new prospect, and, like every work when completed, it left behind it unfinished business. It made a new freedom possible, and it also threw a certain light upon the difference between the modern playwriting problem of meaning and that of the age preceding the secularization of society. It is impossible to study the trial record without feeling the immanence of a veritable pantheon of life values in whose name both prosecution and defense could speak. The testimony is thick with reference to Biblical examples, and even as religious belief did nothing to temper cruelty—and in fact might be shown to have made the cruel crueler—it often served to raise this swirling and ludicrous mysticism to a level of high moral debate; and it did this despite the fact that most of the participants were unlettered, simple folk. They lived and would die more in the shadow of the other world than in the light of this one (and it is no mean irony that the theocratic prosecution should seek out the most religious people for its victims).

The longer I dwelt on the whole spectacle, the more clear became the failure of the present age to find a universal moral sanction, and the power of realism's hold on our theater was an aspect of this vacuum. For it began to appear that our inability to break more than the surfaces of realism reflected our inability —playwrights and audiences—to agree upon the pantheon of forces and values which must lie behind the realistic surfaces of life. In this light, realism, as a style, could seem to be a defense against the assertion of meaning. How strange a conclusion this is when one realizes that the same style seventy years ago was the prime instrument of those who sought to illuminate meaning in the theater, who divested their plays of fancy talk and improbable locales and bizarre characters in order to bring "life" onto the stage. And I wondered then what was true. Was it that we had come to fear the hard glare of life on the stage and under the guise of an aesthetic surfeited with realism were merely expressing our flight from reality? Or was our condemned realism only the counterfeit of the original, whose most powerful single impetus was to deal with man as a social animal? Any form can be drained of its informing purpose, can be used to convey, like the Tudor façades of college dormitories, the now vanished dignity and necessity of a former age in order to lend specious justification for a present hollowness. Was it realism that stood in the way of meaning or was it the counterfeit of realism?

Increasingly over the past five years and more the poetic plays, so-called, some of them much admired by all sorts of critics, were surprisingly full of what in the university years ago was called "fine" writing. If one heard less of the creak of plot machinery there was more of the squeak of self-pity, the humming of the poetic poseur, the new romance of the arbitrary and the uncompleted. For one, I had seen enough of the "borrowings" of the set, the plot, the time-shifting methods, and the lighting of *Death of a Salesman* to have an intimate understanding of how a vessel could be emptied and still purveyed to the public as new wine. Was realism called futile now because it needed to illuminate an exact meaning behind it, a conviction that was no more with us? Confusion, the inability to describe one's sense of a thing, often issues in a genuine poetry of feeling, and feeling was now raised up as the highest good and the ultimate attainment in drama. I had known that kind of victory myself with *Salesman;* but was there not another realm even higher, where feeling took awareness more openly by the hand and both equally ruled and were illuminated? I had found a kind of self-awareness in the bloody book of Salem and had thought that since the natural, realistic surface of that society was one already immersed in the questions of meaning and the relations of men to God, to write a realistic play of that world was already to write in a style beyond contemporary realism. That more than one critic had found the play "cold" when I had never written more passionately was by this time an acceptable and inevitable detail of my fate, for, while it will never confess to it, our theater is trained—actors, directors, audience, and critics—to take to its heart anything that does not prick the mind and to suspect everything that does not supinely reassure.

If *Salesman* was written in a mood of friendly partnership with the audience, *The Crucible* reminded me that we had not yet come to terms. The latter play has been produced more often than any of the others, and more successfully the more time elapses from the headline "McCarthyism" which it was supposed to be "about." I believe that on the night of its opening, a time when the gale from the Right was blowing at its fullest fury, it inspired a part of its audience with an unsettling fear and partisanship which deflected the sight of the real and inner theme, which, again, was the handing over of conscience to another, be it woman, the state, or a terror, and the realization that with conscience goes the person, the soul immortal, and the "name." That there was not one mention of this process in any review, favorable or not, was the measure of my sense of defeat, and the impulse to separate, openly and without concealment, the action of the next play, *A View from the Bridge,* from its generalized significance. The engaged narrator, in short, appeared.

I had heard its story years before, quite as it appears in the play, and quite as complete, and from time to time there were efforts to break up its arc, to reshuffle its action so that I might be able to find what there was in it which drew me back to it again and again—until it became like a fact in my mind, an unbreakable series of actions that went to create a closed circle impervious to all interpretation. It was written experimentally not only as a form, but as an exercise in interpretation. I found in myself a passionate detachment toward its story as one does toward a spectacle in which one is not engaged but which holds a fascination deriving from its monolithic perfection. If this had happened, and if I could not forget it after so many years, there must be some meaning in it for me, and I could write what had happened, why it had happened, and to one side, as it were, express as much as I knew of my sense of its meaning for me. Yet I wished to leave the action intact so that the onlooker could seize the right to interpret it entirely for himself and to accept or reject my reading of its significance.

That reading was the awesomeness of a passion which, despite its contradicting the self-interest of the individual it inhabits, despite every kind of warning, despite even its destruction of the moral beliefs of the individual, proceeds to magnify its power over him until it destroys him.

I have not dealt with the business of production until now because it is a subject large enough for separate treatment, but at this point it is unavoidable. *A View from the Bridge* was relatively a failure in New York when it was first produced; a revised version, published in this volume, became a great success in London not long afterward. The present version is a better play, I think, but not that much better; and the sharp difference between the impressions each of the productions created has a bearing on many themes that have been treated here.

Certain objective factors ought to be mentioned first. In New York, the play was preceded by *A Memory of Two Mondays*. That one of its leading performers on opening night completely lost his bearings and played in a state bordering on terror destroyed at the outset any hope that something human might be communicated by this evening in the theater. *A Memory of Two Mondays* was dismissed so thoroughly that in one of the reviews, and one of the most important, it was not even mentioned as having been played. By the time *A View from the Bridge* came on, I suppose the critics were certain that they were witnessing an aberration, for there had been no suggestion of any theatrical authority in the first play's performance. It was too much to hope that the second play could retrieve what had been so completely dissipated by the first.

A Memory of Two Mondays is a pathetic comedy; a boy works

among people for a couple of years, shares their troubles, their victories, their hopes, and when it is time for him to be on his way he expects some memorable moment, some sign from them that he has been among them, that he has touched them and been touched by them. In the sea of routine that swells around them they barely note his departure. It is a kind of letter to that sub-culture where the sinews of the economy are rooted, that darkest Africa of our society from whose interior only the sketchiest messages ever reach our literature or our stage. I wrote it, I suppose, in part out of a desire to relive a sort of reality where necessity was open and bare; I hoped to define for myself the value of hope, why it must arise, as well as the heroism of those who know, at least, how to endure its absence. Nothing in this book was written with greater love, and for myself I love nothing printed here better than this play.

Nevertheless, the fact that it was seen as something utterly sad and hopeless as a comment on life quite astonishes me still. After all, from this endless, timeless, will-less environment, a boy emerges who will not accept its defeat or its mood as final, and literally takes himself off on a quest for a higher gratification. I suppose we simply do not want to see how empty the lives of so many of us are even when the depiction is made hopefully and not at all in despair. The play speaks not of obsession but of rent and hunger and the need for a little poetry in life and is entirely out of date in those respects—so much so that many took it for granted it had been written a long time ago and exhumed.

It shares with *A View from the Bridge* the impulse to present rather than to represent an interpretation of reality. Incident and character are set forth with the barest naïveté, and action is stopped abruptly while commentary takes its place. The organic impulse behind *Salesman,* for instance, and *All My Sons* is avowedly split apart; for a moment I was striving not to make people forget they were in a theater, not to obliterate an aware-ness of form, not to forge a pretense of life, but to be abrupt, clear, and explicit in setting forth fact as fact and art as art so that the sea of theatrical sentiment, which is so easily let in to drown all shape, meaning, and perspective, might be held back and some hard outline of a human dilemma be allowed to rise and stand. *A Memory of Two Mondays* has a story but not a plot, because the life it reflects appears to me to strip people of alternatives and will beyond a close and tight periphery in which they may exercise a meager choice.

The contradiction in my attitude toward these two plays and what was hoped for them is indicated by the experience of the two productions of *A View from the Bridge,* the one a failure and "cold," the other quite the opposite. In writing this play originally I obeyed the impulse to indicate, to telegraph, so to speak, rather than to explore and exploit what at first had seemed to me the inevitable and therefore unnecessary emotional implications of the conflict. The Broadway production's setting followed the same impulse, as it should have, and revealed nothing more than a platform to contain the living room, the sea behind the house, and a Grecian-style pediment overhanging the abstract doorway to the house. The austerity of the production, in a word, expressed the reticence of the writing.

This version was in one act because it had seemed to me that the essentials of the dilemma were all that was required, for I wished it to be kept distant from the empathic flood which a realistic portrayal of the same tale and characters might unloose.

On seeing the production played several times I came to understand that, like the plays written previously, this one was expressing a very personal preoccupation and that it was not at all apart from my own psychological life. I discovered my own relationships to what quite suddenly appeared as, in some part, an analogy to situations in my life, a distant analogy but a heartening proof that under the reticence of its original method my own spirit was attempting to speak. So that when a new production was planned for London it was not possible to let the original go on as it was. Now there were additional things to be said which it became necessary to say because I had come to the awareness that this play had not, as I had almost believed before, been "given" to me from without, but that my life had created it.

Therefore, many decisive alterations, small in themselves but nonetheless great in their over-all consequences, began to flow into the conception of the play. Perhaps the two most important were an altered attitude toward Eddie Carbone, the hero, and toward the two women in his life. I had originally conceived Eddie as a phenomenon, a rather awesome fact of existence, and I had kept a certain distance from involvement in his self-justifications. Consequently, he had appeared as a kind of biological sport, and to a degree a repelling figure not quite admissible into the human family. In revising the play it became possible to accept for myself the implication I had sought to make clear in the original version, which was that however one might dislike this man, who does all sorts of frightful things, he possesses or exemplifies the wondrous and humane fact that he too can be driven to what in the last analysis is a sacrifice of himself for his conception, however misguided, of right, dignity, and justice. In revising it I found it possible to move beyond contemplation of the man as a phenomenon into an acceptance for dramatic purposes of his aims themselves. Once this occurred the autonomous viewpoints of his wife and niece could be expressed more fully and, instead of remaining muted counterpoints to the march of Eddie's career, became involved forces pressing him forward or holding him back and eventually forming, in part, the nature of his disaster. The discovery of my own involvement in what I had written modified its original friezelike character and the play moved closer toward realism and called up the emphatic response of its audience.

The conception of the new production was in accordance with this new perspective. Peter Brook, the London director, designed a set which was more realistically detailed than the rather bare, if beautiful, New York background, and at the same time emphasized the environment of the neighborhood. Its central idea was to bring the people of the neighborhood into the foreground of the action. Two high wings closed to form the face of the house where Eddie lived, a brick tenement, and when opened revealed a basement living room. Overhead and at the sides and across the back were stairways, fire escapes, passages, quite like a whole neighborhood constructed vertically. The easier economics of the London theater made it possible to use many more neighbors than the three or four extras we could hire in New York, and there was a temperate but nevertheless full flow of strangers across the stage and up and down its stairways and passages. The maturing of Eddie's need to destroy Rodolpho was consequently seen in the context which could make it of real moment, for the betrayal achieves its true proportions as it flies in the face of the mores administered by Eddie's conscience—which is also the conscience of his friends, co-workers, and neighbors and not just his own autonomous creation. Thus his "oddness" came to disappear as he was seen in context, as a creature of his environment as well as an exception to it; and where originally there had been only a removed sense of terror at the oncoming catastrophe, now there was pity and, I think, the kind of wonder which it had been my aim to create in the first place. It was finally possible to mourn this man.

Perhaps more than any other production experience, this helped to resolve for me one important question of form and meaning. I warn, however, that like everything else said here this is highly personal, and even as I avow it I know that there are other paths and other standards which can issue in a worthwhile kind of dramatic experience. For myself, the theater is above all else an instrument of passion. However important considerations of style and form have been to me, they are only means, tools to pry up the well-worn, "inevitable" surfaces of experience behind which swarm the living thoughts and feelings whose expression is the essential purpose of art. I have stood squarely in conventional realism; I have tried to expand it with an imposition of various forms in order to speak more directly, even more abruptly and nakedly of what has moved me behind the visible facades of life. Critics have given me more praise than a writer can reasonably hope for, and more condemnation than one dares believe one has the power to survive. There are certain distillations which remain after the dross rises to the top and boils away, certain old and new commitments which, despite the heat applied to them and the turmoil that has threatened to sweep them away, nevertheless remain, some of them purified.

A play, I think, ought to make sense to common-sense people. I know what it is to have been rejected by them, even unfairly so, but the only challenge worth the effort is the widest one and the tallest one, which is the people themselves. It is their innate conservatism which, I think, is and ought to be the barrier to excess in experiment and the exploitation of the bizarre, even as it is the proper aim of drama to break down the limits of conventional unawareness and acceptance of outmoded and banal forms.

By whatever means it is accomplished, the prime business of a play is to arouse the passions of its audience so that by the route of passion may be opened up new relationships between a man and men, and between men and Man. Drama is akin to the other inventions of man in that it ought to help us to know more, and not merely to spend our feelings.

The ultimate justification for a genuine new form is the new and heightened consciousness it creates and makes possible—a consciousness of causation in the light of known but hitherto inexplicable effects.

Not only in the drama, but in sociology, psychology, psychiatry, and religion, the past half century has created an almost overwhelming documentation of man as a nearly passive creation of environment and family-created psychological drives. If only from the dramatic point of view, this dictum cannot be accepted as final and "realistic" any more than man's ultimate position can be accepted as his efficient use by state or corporate apparatus. It is more "real," however, for drama to "liberate" itself from this vise by the route of romance and the spectacle of free will and a new heroic formula than it is "real" now to represent man's defeat as the ultimate implication of an overwhelming determinism.

Realism, heightened or conventional, is neither more nor less an artifice, a species of poetic symbolization, than any other form. It is merely more familiar in this age. If it is used as a covering of safety against the evaluation of life it must be overthrown, and for that reason above all the rest. But neither poetry nor liberation can come merely from a rearrangement of the lights or from leaving the skeletons of the flats exposed instead of covered by painted cloths; nor can it come merely from the masking of the human face or the transformation of speech into rhythmic verse, or from the expunging of common details of life's apparencies. A new poem on the stage is a new concept of relationships between the one and the many and the many and history, and to create it requires greater attention, not less, to the inexorable, common, pervasive conditions of existence in this time and this hour. Otherwise only a new self-indulgence is created, and it will be left behind, however poetic its surface.

A drama worthy of its time must first, knowingly or by instinctive means, recognize its major and most valuable traditions and where it has departed from them. Determinism, whether it is based on the iron necessities of economics or on psychoanalytic theory seen as a closed circle, is a contradiction of the idea of drama itself as drama has come down to us in its fullest developments. The idea of the hero, let alone the mere protagonist, is incompatible with a drama whose bounds are set in advance by the concept of an unbreakable trap. Nor is it merely that one wants arbitrarily to find a hero and a victory. The history of man is a ceaseless process of overthrowing one determinism to make way for another more faithful to life's changing relationships. And it is a process inconceivable without the existence of the will of man. His will is as much a fact as his defeat. Any determinism, even the most scientific, is only that stasis, that seemingly endless pause, before the application of man's will administering a new insight into causation.

The analogy to physics may not be out of place. The once-irreducible elements of matter, whose behavior was seen as fixed and remorseless, disintegrated under the controlled bombardment of atomic particles until so fine a perception as the scale of atomic weights appears as a relatively gross concept on the road to man's manipulation of the material world. More to the point: even as the paths, the powers, and the behavior of smaller and smaller elements and forces in nature are brought into the fields of measurement, we are faced with the dialectical irony that the act of measurement itself changes the particle being measured, so that we can know only what it is at the moment when it receives the impact of our rays, not what it was before it was struck. The idea of realism has become wedded to the idea that man is at best the sum of forces working upon him and of given psychological forces within him. Yet an innate value, an innate will, does in fact posit itself as real not alone because it is devoutly to be wished, but because, however closely he is measured and systematically accounted for, he is more than the sum of his stimuli and is unpredictable beyond a certain point. A drama, like a history, which stops at this point, the point of conditioning, is not reflecting reality. What is wanted, therefore, is not a poetry of escape from process and determinism, like that mood play which stops where feeling ends or that inverted romanticism which would mirror all the world in the sado-masochistic relationship. Nor will the heightening of the intensity of language alone yield the prize. A new poem will appear because a new balance has been struck which embraces both determinism and the paradox of will. If there is one unseen goal toward which every play in this book strives, it is that very discovery and its proof—that we are made and yet are more than what made us.

Brewed in *The Crucible*

ONE afternoon last week I attended a rehearsal of the imminent Off-Broadway production of *The Crucible*. For the first time in the five years since its opening on Broadway, I heard its dialogue, and the experience awakened not merely memories but the desire to fire a discussion among us of certain questions a play like this ought to have raised.

Notoriously, there is what is called a chemistry in the theater, a fusion of play, performance, and audience temper which, if it does not take place, leaves the elements of an explosion cold and to one side of art. For the critics, this seems to be what happened with *The Crucible*. It was not condemned; it was set aside. A cold thing, mainly, it lay to one side of entertainment, to say nothing of art. In a word, I was told that I had not written another *Death of a Salesman*.

It is perhaps beyond my powers to make clear, but I had no desire to write another *Salesman,* and not because I lack love for that play but for some wider, less easily defined reasons that have to do with this whole question of cold and heat and, indeed, with the future of our drama altogether. It is the question of whether we—playwrights and audiences and critics—are to de-

From *The New York Times,* March 9, 1958, Sec. 2, p. 3. An Off-Broadway production of *The Crucible* opened at the Martinique Theatre on March 11, 1958. After a successful run of 633 performances, the revival closed on June 14, 1959. Copyright © 1958 by Arthur Miller.

clare that we have reached the end, the last development of dramatic form. More specifically, the play designed to draw a tear; the play designed to "identify" the audience with its characters in the usual sense; the play that takes as its highest challenge the emotional relations of the family, for that, as it turns out, is what it comes to.

I was disappointed in the reaction to *The Crucible* not only for the obvious reasons but because no critic seemed to sense what I was after. In 1953 McCarthyism probably helped to make it appear that the play was bounded on all sides by its arraignment of the witch hunt. The political trajectory was so clear—a fact of which I am a little proud—that what to me were equally if not more important elements were totally ignored. The new production, appearing in a warmer climate, may, I hope, flower, and these inner petals may make their appropriate appearance.

What I say now may appear more technical than a writer has any business talking about in public. But I do not think it merely a question of technique to say that with all its excellences the kind of play we have come to accept without effort or question is standing at a dead end. What "moves" us is coming to be a narrower and narrower aesthetic fragment of life. I have shown, I think, that I am not unaware of psychology or immune to the fascinations of the neurotic hero, but I believe that it is no longer possible to contain the truth of the human situation so totally within a single man's guts as the bulk of our plays presuppose. The documentation of man's loneliness is not in itself and for itself ultimate wisdom, and the form this documentation inevitably assumes in playwriting is not the ultimate dramatic form.

I was drawn to write *The Crucible* not merely as a response to McCarthyism. It is not any more an attempt to cure witch hunts than *Salesman* is a plea for the improvement of conditions for traveling men, *All My Sons* a plea for better inspection of airplane parts, or *A View from the Bridge* an attack upon the Immigration Bureau. *The Crucible* is, internally, *Salesman's* blood brother. It is examining the questions I was absorbed with before—the conflict between a man's raw deeds and his conception of himself; the question of whether conscience is in fact an organic part of the human being, and what happens when it is handed over not merely to the state or the mores of the time but to one's friend or wife. The big difference, I think, is that *The Crucible* sought to include a higher degree of consciousness than the earlier plays.

I believe that the wider the awareness, the felt knowledge, evoked by a play, the higher it must stand as art. I think our drama is far behind our lives in this respect. There is a lot wrong with the twentieth century, but one thing is right with it—we are aware as no generation was before of the larger units that help make us and destroy us. The city, the nation, the world, and now the universe are never far beyond our most intimate sense of life. The vast majority of us know now—not merely as knowledge but as feeling, feeling capable of expression in art—that we are being formed, that our alternatives in life are not absolutely our own, as the romantic play inevitably must presuppose. But the response of our plays, of our dramatic form itself, is to faint, so to speak, before the intricacies of man's wider relationships and to define him further and redefine him as essentially alone in a world he never made.

The form, the shape, the meaning of *The Crucible* were all compounded out of the faith of those who were hanged. They were asked to be lonely and they refused. They were asked to deny their belief in a God of all men, not merely a god each individual could manipulate to his interests. They were asked to call a phantom real and to deny their touch with reality. It was not good to cast this play, to form it so that the psyche of the hero should emerge so "commonly" as to wipe out of mind the process itself, the spectacle of that faith and the knowing will which these people paid for with their lives.

The "heat" infusing this play is therefore of a different order from that which draws tears and the common identifications. And it was designed to be of a different order. In a sense, I felt, our situation had thrown us willy-nilly into a·new classical period. Classical in the sense that the social scheme, as of old, had reached the point of rigidity where it had become implacable as a consciously known force working in us and upon us. Analytical psychology, when so intensely exploited as to reduce the world to the size of a man's abdomen and equate his fate with his neurosis, is a re-emergence of romanticism. It is inclined to deny all outer forces until man is only his complex. It presupposes an autonomy in the human character that, in a word, is false. A neurosis is not a fate but an effect. There is a higher wisdom, and if truly there is not, there is still no aesthetic point in repeating something so utterly known, or in doing better what has been done so well before.

For me *The Crucible* was a new beginning, the beginning of an attempt to embrace a wider field of vision, a field wide enough to contain the whole of our current awareness. It was not so much to move ahead of the audience but to catch up with what it commonly knows about the way things are and how they get that way. In a word, we commonly know so much more than our plays let on. When we can put together what we do know with what we feel, we shall find a new kind of theater in our hands. *The Crucible* was written as it was in order to bring me, and the audience, closer to that theater and what I imagine can be an art more ample than any of us has dared to strive for, the art of Man among men, Man amid his works.

The Shadows of the Gods

I SEE by the papers that I am going to talk today on the subject of the literary influences on my work. It is probably a good subject, but it isn't what Harold Clurman and I discussed when he asked if I would speak here. What he had in mind was something else. I am supposed to widen your horizons by telling something about the frame of reference I used when I started to write, and that included books I read, or music I heard, or whatnot.

I doubt whether anybody can widen horizons by making a speech. It is possible, perhaps, by writing a play. Still, I may be able to suggest an approach to our theater which—even if it is not valid for everyone—will not be quite the same as that of the various critics; and if nothing else is accomplished here maybe it will at least appear that there is another way of looking at drama.

Tolstoy wrote a book called *What Is Art?* The substance of it is that almost all the novels, plays, operas, and paintings were not art but vanity, and that the rhythm with which a Russian peasant swung a scythe was more artful than all the dance on Moscow stages, and the paintings of peasants on the sides of their wagons more genuine than all the paintings in the museums. The thing that disheartened him most, I believe, was that inevitably

From *Harper's,* 217 (August 1958), pp. 35–43. Based on a talk prepared for a meeting of Miller's co-workers in the theater. Copyright © 1958 by Arthur Miller.

artistic creation became a profession, and the artist who may have originated as a natural quickly became self-conscious and exploited his own gifts for money, prestige, or just for want of an honest profession.

Yet, Tolstoy went on writing. The truth, I suppose, is that soon or late we are doomed to know what we are doing, and we may as well accept it as a fact when it comes. But the self-knowledge of professionalism develops only as a result of having repeated the same themes in different plays. And for a whole theater the time for self-appraisal comes in the same way. We are, I believe, at the end of a period. Certain things have been repeated sufficiently for one to speak of limitations which have to be recognized if our theater is not to become absurd, repetitious, and decayed.

Now one can no sooner speak of limitations than the question of standards arises. What seems like a limitation to one man may be an area as wide as the world to another. My standard, my viewpoint, whether it appears arbitrary, or true and inevitable, did not spring out of my head unshaped by any outside force. I began writing plays in the midst of what Allan Seager, an English teacher friend of mine at Michigan, calls one of the two genuinely national catastrophes in American history—the Great Depression of the thirties. The other was the Civil War. It is almost bad manners to talk about depression these days, but through no fault or effort of mine it was the ground upon which I learned to stand.

There are a thousand things to say about that time but maybe one will be evocative enough. Until 1929 I thought things were pretty solid. Specifically, I thought—like most Americans—that somebody was in charge. I didn't know exactly who it was, but it was probably a businessman, and he was a realist, a no-nonsense fellow, practical, honest, responsible. In 1929 he jumped out of the window. It was bewildering. His banks closed and refused to open again, and I had twelve dollars in one of them. More precisely, I happened to have withdrawn my twelve dollars to buy a racing bike a friend of mine was bored with, and the

next day the Bank of the United States closed. I rode by and saw
the crowds of people standing at the brass gates. Their money
was inside! And they couldn't get it. And they would never
get it. As for me, I felt I had the thing licked.

But about a week later I went into the house to get a glass
of milk and when I came out my bike was gone. Stolen. It
must have taught me a lesson. Nobody could escape that disaster.

I did not read many books in those days. The depression was
my book. Years later I could put together what in those days
were only feelings, sensations, impressions. There was the sense
that everything had dried up. Some plague of invisible grass-
hoppers was eating money before you could get your hands on
it. You had to be a Ph. D. to get a job in Macy's. Lawyers were
selling ties. Everybody was trying to sell something to everybody else. A past president of the Stock Exchange was sent to
jail for misappropriating trust funds. They were looking for
runaway financiers all over Europe and South America. Practically everything that had been said and done up to 1929
turned out to be a fake. It turns out that there had never been
anybody in charge.

What the time gave me, I think now, was a sense of an
invisible world. A reality had been secretly accumulating its
climax according to its hidden laws to explode illusion at the
proper time. In that sense 1929 was our Greek year. The gods
had spoken, the gods, whose wisdom had been set aside or
distorted by a civilization that was to go onward and upward
on speculation, gambling, graft, and the dog eating the dog.
Before the crash I thought "Society" meant the rich people in
the Social Register. After the crash it meant the constant visits
of strange men who knocked on our door pleading for a chance
to wash the windows, and some of them fainted on the back
porch from hunger. In Brooklyn, New York. In the light of
weekday afternoons.

I read books after I was seventeen, but already, for good or
ill, I was not patient with every kind of literature. I did not
believe, even then, that you could tell about a man without

telling about the world he was living in, what he did for a living, what he was like not only at home or in bed but on the job. I remember now reading novels and wondering, What do these people do for a living? When do they work? I remember asking the same questions about the few plays I saw. The hidden laws of fate lurked not only in the characters of people, but equally if not more imperiously in the world beyond the family parlor. Out there were the big gods, the ones whose disfavor could turn a proud and prosperous and dignified man into a frightened shell of a man whatever he thought of himself, and whatever he decided or didn't decide to do.

So that by force of circumstance I came early and unawares to be fascinated by sheer process itself. How things connected. How the native personality of a man was changed by his world, and the harder question, how he could in turn change his world. It was not academic. It was not even a literary or a dramatic question at first. It was the practical problem of what to believe in order to proceed with life. For instance, should one admire success—for there were sucessful people even then. Or should one always see through it as an illusion which only existed to be blown up, and its owner destroyed and humiliated? Was success immoral?—when everybody else in the neighborhood not only had no Buick but no breakfast? What to believe?

An adolescent must feel he is on the side of justice. That is how human indignation is constantly renewed. But how hard it was to feel justly, let alone to think justly. There were people in the neighborhood saying that it had all happened because the workers had not gotten paid enough to buy what they had produced, and that the solution was to have Socialism, which would not steal their wages any more the way the bosses did and brought on this depression. It was a wonderful thought with which I nearly drove my grandfather crazy. The trouble with it was that he and my father and most of the men I loved would have to be destroyed.

Enough of that. I am getting at only one thought. You can't

understand anything unless you understand its relations to its context. It was necessary to feel beyond the edges of things. That much, for good or ill, the Great Depression taught me. It made me impatient with anything, including art, which pretends that it can exist for its own sake and still be of any prophetic importance. A thing becomes beautiful to me as it becomes internally and externally organic. It becomes beautiful because it promises to remove some of my helplessness before the chaos of experience. I think one of the reasons I became a playwright was that in dramatic form everything must be openly organic, deeply organized, articulated from a living center. I used long ago to keep a book in which I would talk to myself. One of the aphorisms I wrote was, "The structure of a play is always the story of how the birds came home to roost." The hidden will be unveiled; the inner laws of reality will announce themselves; I was defining my impression of 1929 as well as dramatic structure.

When I was still in high school and ignorant, a book came into my hands, God knows how, *The Brothers Karamazov*. It must have been too rainy that day to play ball. I began reading it, thinking it was a detective story. I have always blessed Dostoevsky for writing in a way that any fool could understand. The book, of course, has no connection with the depression. Yet it became closer, more intimate to me, despite the Russian names, than the papers I read every day. I never thought to ask why, then. I think now it was because of the father and son conflict, but something more. It is always probing beyond its particular scenes and characters for the hidden laws, for the place where the gods ruminate and decide, for the rock upon which one may stand without illusion, a free man. Yet the characters appear liberated from any systematic causation.

The same yearning I felt all day for some connection with a hidden logic was the yearning in this book. It gave me no answers but it showed that I was not the only one who was full of this kind of questioning, for I did not believe—and could not after 1929—in the reality I saw with my eyes. There was an invisible world of cause and effect, mysterious, full of surprises, implacable in its course. The book said to me:

"There is a hidden order in the world. There is only one reason to live. It is to discover its nature. The good are those who do this. The evil say that there is nothing beyond the face of the world, the surface of reality. Man will only find peace when he learns to live humanly, in conformity to those laws which decree his human nature."

Only slightly less ignorant, I read Ibsen in college. Later I heard that I had been reading problem plays. I didn't know what that meant. I was told they were about social problems, like the inequality of women. The women I knew about had not been even slightly unequal; I saw no such problem in *A Doll's House*. I connected with Ibsen not because he wrote about problems, but because he was illuminating process. Nothing in his plays exists for itself, not a smart line, not a gesture that can be isolated. It was breath-taking.

From his work—read again and again with new wonders cropping up each time—as well as through Dostoevsky's, I came to an idea of what a writer was supposed to be. These two issued the license, so to speak, the only legitimate one I could conceive, for presuming to write at all. One had the right to write because other people needed news of the inner world, and if they went too long without such news they would go mad with the chaos of their lives. With the greatest of presumption I conceived that the great writer was the destroyer of chaos, a man privy to the councils of the hidden gods who administer the hidden laws that bind us all and destroy us if we do not know them. And chaos, for one thing, was life lived oblivious of history.

As time went on, a lot of time, it became clear to me that I was not only reporting to others but to myself first and foremost. I wrote not only to find a way into the world but to hold it away from me so that sheer, senseless events would not devour me.

I read the Greeks and the German Expressionists at the same

time and quite by accident. I was struck by the similarity of their dramatic means in one respect—they are designed to present the hidden forces, not the characteristics of the human beings playing out those forces on the stage. I was told that the plays of Aeschylus must be read primarily on a religious level, that they are only lay dramas to us now because we no longer believe. I could not understand this because one did not have to be religious to see in our own disaster the black outlines of a fate that was not human, nor of the heavens either, but something in between. Like the howling of a mob, for instance, which is not a human sound but is nevertheless composed of human voices combining until a metaphysical force of sound is created.

I read O'Neill in those days as I read everything else—looking to see how meaning was achieved. He said something in a press conference which in the context of those years seemed to be a challenge to the social preoccupations of the thirties. He said, "I am not interested in the relations of man to man, but of man to God." I thought that very reactionary. Until, after repeated and repeated forays into one play of my own after another, I understood that he meant what I meant, not ideologically but dramatically speaking. I too had a religion, however unwilling I was to be so backward. A religion with no gods but with godlike powers. The powers of economic crisis and political imperatives which had twisted, torn, eroded, and marked everything and everyone I laid eyes on.

I read for a year in economics, discovered my professors dispensing their prejudices which were no better founded than my own; worse yet, an economics that could measure the giant's footsteps but could not look into his eyes.

I read for a year in history, and lost my last illusion on a certain afternoon at two-thirty. In a lecture class a student at question time rose to ask the professor if he thought Hitler would invade Austria. For fifteen minutes the professor, by no means a closet historian but a man of liberal and human interests, proved why it was impossible for Hitler to invade Austria. It seems there were treaties forbidding this which went back to the Congress of Vienna, side agreements older than that, codicils, memoranda, guarantees—and to make a long story short, when we got out at three o'clock there was an extra being hawked. Hitler had invaded Austria. I gave up history. I knew damned well Hitler was going to invade Austria.

In that sense it was a good time to be growing up because nobody else knew anything either. All the rules were nothing but continuations of older rules. The old plays create new plays, and the old histories create new histories. The best you could say of the academic disciplines was that they were breathlessly running after the world. It is when life creates a new play that the theater moves its limbs and wakens from its mesmerized fixation on ordinary reality; when the present is caught and made historic.

I began by speaking of standards. I have labored the point long enough to state it openly. My standard is, to be sure, derived from my life in the thirties, but I believe that it is as old as the drama itself and was merely articulated to me in the accent of the thirties. I ask of a play, first, the dramatic question, the carpenter-builder's question—What is its ultimate force? How can that force be released? Second, the human question—What is its ultimate relevancy to the survival of the race?

Before proceeding with these two queries I want to jump ahead to say that my object remains to throw some light on our dramatic situation today, the challenge, so to speak, which I think lies before us. I will pause for a moment or two in order to say a few things about a writer who has been, along with Ibsen, an enormous influence upon our theater whether we know it or not.

It is hard to imagine any playwright reading Chekhov without envying one quality of his plays. It is his balance. In this, I think he is closer to Shakespeare than any dramatist I know. There is less distortion by the exigencies of the telescoping of time in the theater, there is less stacking of the cards, there is less fear of the ridiculous, there is less fear of the heroic. His touch is tender, his eye is warm, so warm that the Chekhovian legend in our theater has become that of an almost sentimental man and writer whose plays are elegies, postcripts to a dying age. In passing, it must be said that he was not the only Russian writer who seemed to be dealing with all his characters as though he were related to them. It is a quality not of Chekhov alone but of much Russian literature, and I mention it both to relate him to this mood and to separate him from it.

Chekhov is important to us because he has been used as a club against two opposing views of drama. Sometimes he seems —as he evidently does to Walter Kerr—to have encouraged dramatists to an overly emphasized introspection if not self-pity. To this kind of viewpoint, he is the playwright of inaction, of perverse self-analysis, of the dark blue mood. In the thirties he was condemned by many on the Left as lacking in militancy, and he was confused with the people he was writing about.

His plays, I think, will endure, but in one sense he is as useless as a model as the frock coat and the horse and carriage. Our civilization is immeasurably more strident than his and to try to recreate his mood would be to distort our own. But more important, I think, is that—whatever the miseries of his characters— their careers are played out against a tradition of which they are quite conscious, a tradition whose destruction is regarded by them as the setting of their woes. Whether or not it was ever objectively true is beside the point, of course; the point is that they can look back to a time when the coachman was young and happy to be a coachman, when there was a large, firmly entrenched family evenly maturing over the slow-passing years, when, in a word, there was an order dominated by human relations. Now—to put it much more briefly than its complexity warrants—the Cherry Orchard is cut down by a real estate man, who, nice fellow that he may be, simply has to clear land for a development.

The closest we have ever gotten to this kind of relation to a tradition is in Tennessee Williams, when a disorganized refugee from a plantation arrives in our civilization some eighty years after the plantation itself has been destroyed. We cannot reproduce Chekhov if only because we are long past the time when we believe in the primacy of human relations over economic necessity. We have given up what was still in his time a live struggle. We believe—or at least take it completely for granted —that wherever there is a conflict between human relations and necessity, the outcome is not only inevitable but even progressive when necessity wins, as it evidently must.

The main point I would make here in relation to our theater, however, is that while Chekhov's psychological insight is given full play, and while his greatest interest is overwhelmingly in the spiritual life of his characters, his farthest vision does not end with their individual psychology. Here is a speech to remind you —and it is only one of a great many which do not at all fit with the conventional characterization of these allegedly wispy plays —concerned with nothing more than realistic character drawing and introspection. In *Three Sisters* Vershinin speaks:

> What else am I to say to you at parting? What am I to theorize about? (Laughs) Life is hard. It seems to many of us blank and hopeless; but yet we must admit that it goes on getting clearer and easier, and it looks as though the time were not far off when it will be full of happiness. (Looks at his watch.) It's time for me to go! In old days men were absorbed in wars, filling all their existence with marches, raids, victories, but now all that is a thing of the past, leaving behind it a great void which there is so far nothing to fill; humanity is searching for it passionately, and of course will find it. Ah, if only it could be quickly. If, don't you know, industry were united with culture and culture with industry.... (Looks at his watch.) But, I say, it's time for me to go. ...

In other words, these plays are not mere exercises in psychology. They are woven around a very critical point of view, a point of view not only toward the characters, but toward the social context in which they live, a point of view which—far from being some arbitrary angle, as we have come to call such things—is their informing principle. I haven't the time here to investigate the plays one by one and it is not the business of the moment. All I have said comes down to this: that with all our technical dexterity, with all our lighting effects, sets, and a theater more solvent than any I know about, yes, with all our freedom to say what we will—our theater is narrowing its vision year by year, it is repeating well what it has done well before.

I can hear already my critics complaining that I am asking for a return to what they call problem plays. That criticism is important only because it tells something important about the critic. It means that he can only conceive of man as a private entity, and his social relations as something thrown at him, something "affecting" him only when he is conscious of society. I hope I have made one thing clear to this point—and it is that society is inside of man and man is inside society, and you cannot even create a truthfully drawn psychological entity on the stage until you understand his social relations and their power to make him what he is and to prevent him from being what he is not. The fish is in the water and the water is in the fish.

I believe we have arrived in America at the end of a period because we are repeating ourselves season after season, despite the fact that nobody seems to be aware of it. In almost every success there is a striking similarity of mood and of mode. There is one play after another in which a young person, usually male, usually sensitive, is driven either to self-destructive revolt or impotency by the insensitivity of his parents, usually the father. A quick and by no means exhaustive look brings to mind, *Look Homeward Angel, Dark at the Top of the Stairs, Cat on a Hot Tin Roof, A Hatful of Rain*. I wish to emphasize at once that I am not here as a critic of these plays as plays, nor do I intend to equate their worth one with the other. I am rather looking at them as a stranger, a man from Mars, who would surely have to wonder at so pervasive a phenomenon.

Now I am not saying there is anything "wrong" with this theme, if only because I have written more than once on it myself. It lies at the heart of all human development, and its echoes go to *Hamlet*, to *Romeo and Juliet*, to *Oedipus Rex*. What I am critical of is that our theater is dealing almost exclusively with affects. Where the parent stands the world ends, and where the son stands is where the world should begin but cannot because he is either made impotent, or he revolts, or more often runs away. What is there wrong with this? Does it not happen all the time? It must, or so many playwrights would not be repeating the theme, and it would not have the fascination it evidently does for so many audiences.

What is wrong is not the theme but its failure to extend itself so as to open up ultimate causes. The fact, for one thing, is not merely the frustration of the children, or even the bankruptcy of moral authority in the parents, but also their common awareness in our time of some hidden, ulterior causation for this. If only because this theme is so recurrent, the phenomenon has the right to be called a generalized social one. Therefore, it is proper in this instance to say that the potential vision of these plays is not fulfilled and their potential aesthetic size and perfection is left unrealized. And perhaps even more important, there is implicit in this cut-down vision a decay of nerve, a withering of power to grasp the whole world on the stage and shake it to its foundations as it is the historic job of high drama to do. The mystery of our condition remains, but we know much more about it than appears on our stage.

I am not asking for anything new, but something as old as the Greek drama. When Chekhov, that almost legendary subjectivist, has Vershinin—and many others in his plays—objectifying the social questions which his play has raised, he is merely placing himself within the great tradition which set its art works fully in view of the question of the survival of the race. It is we who are the innovators, or more precisely, the sports, when we refuse to reflect on our stage a level of objective awareness at least as great as exists commonly in our lives outside.

I am asking for the world to be brought into the stage family, to be sure, but I begin and I end from the viewpoint of the dramatist, the dramatist seeking to intensify the power of his plays and his theater. There is something dramatically wrong, for instance, when an audience can see a play about the Nazi treatment of a group of Jews hiding in an attic, and come away feeling the kind of—I can only call it gratification—which the audiences felt after seeing *The Diary of Anne Frank*. Seeing this play I was not only an audience or even a Jew, but a dramatist, and it puzzled me why it was all so basically reassuring to watch what must have been the most harrowing kind of suffering in real life.

As a constructor of plays I had nothing technical of consequence to add. And I found myself putting to this play the question I have put to you—what is its relevancy to the survival of the race? Not the American race, or the Jewish race, or the German race, but the human race. And I believe the beginning of an answer has emerged. It is that with all its truth the play lacks the kind of spread vision, the over-vision beyond its characters and their problems, which could have illuminated not merely the cruelty of Nazism but something even more terrible. We see no Nazis in this play. Again, as with the plays I have mentioned, it is seen from the viewpoint of the adolescent, a poignant and human viewpoint to be sure, but surely a limited one. The approach of the Nazi is akin to the approach of a childhood Demon.

What was necessary in this play to break the hold of reassurance upon the audience, and to make it match the truth of life, was that we should see the bestiality in our own hearts, so that we should know how we are brothers not only to these victims but to the Nazis, so that the ultimate terror of our lives should be faced—namely our own sadism, our own ability to obey orders from above, our own fear of standing firm on humane principle against the obscene power of the mass organization. Another dimension was waiting to be opened up behind this play, a dimension covered with our own sores, a dimension revealing us to ourselves.

Once this dimension had been unveiled we could not have watched in the subtly perverse comfort of pathos; our terror would no longer be for these others but for ourselves, once that part of ourselves which covertly conspires with destruction was made known. Then, for one thing, even tragedy would have been possible, for the issue would not have been why the Nazis were so cruel, but why human beings—ourselves, us—are so cruel. The pathetic is the refusal or inability to discover and face ultimate relevancy for the race; it is therefore a shield against ultimate dramatic effect.

In this instance the objection will be raised that I am demanding a different kind of play than *Diary* was intended to be. I am. I make this demand, if one can presume so far, even though I believe that the original book was very faithfully followed by the dramatists who adapted it. Who am I to argue with the martyred girl who wrote the original document? Her right to her point of view is irreproachable. I agree that it is irreproachable. I repeat, as a matter of fact, what I said earlier—that the adolescent viewpoint is and should be precious to us. In this instance, first of all, I am treating the play as a separate work, as another play opening in New York. Secondly, I am using it to show that even when the adolescent viewpoint is most perfectly announced and movingly dramatized, it nevertheless has a nature, an inner dynamic which prevents it from seeing what it cannot see and still be itself.

It is necessary, in short, to be able to appreciate a thing for what it is, and to see what it is not and what it might be. Our present failure to distinguish between low and high altitude, between amplitude and relative narrowness, leaves us—as it leaves the critics for the most part—at the mercy of "affects"; which is to say that if a small play of minor proportions achieves its affects well, it is as good as a large play of greater proportions.

One consequence of this inability to distinguish between the sizes of things, so to speak, is to condemn ourselves ultimately to minor art. For it is always more likely that small things of shallow breath will show fewer defects than the large, and if the perfecting of affects, regardless of their larger relevancies or irrelevancies, is to be our criterion, as it threatens now to be, we shall turn the theater into a kind of brooding conceit, a showplace for our tricks, a proving ground for our expertise, a shallows protected from the oceans.

I repeat that I am not here as a critic of individual plays but of the dramatic viewpoint which I believe imposes by no means unbreakable limitations upon them. They are limitations which tend to force repetitions of mood, mode, style, yes, and even the lighting and setting of one play after another, even as they are written by writers in their individual isolation. While on the one hand we prize the original work, the new creation, we are surprisingly unconscious of the sameness of so much that passes for new. But the new, the truly new dramatic poem will be, as it has always been, a new organization of the meaning, the generalized significance of the action.

A moment ago I threw together several plays for the purposes of this discussion, one of which I should like now to set apart. In every way but one *Cat on a Hot Tin Roof* differs from *Diary of Anne Frank,* as well as from the others mentioned. Williams has a long reach and a genuinely dramatic imagination. To me, however, his greatest value, his aesthetic valor, so to speak, lies in his very evident determination to unveil and engage the widest range of causation conceivable to him. He is constantly pressing his own limit. He creates shows, as all of us must, but he possesses the restless inconsolability with his solutions which is inevitable in a genuine writer. In my opinion, he is properly discontented with the total image some of his plays have created. And it is better that way, for when the image is complete and self-contained it is usually arbitrary and false.

It is no profound thing to say that a genuine work of art creates not completion, but a sustained image of things in tentative balance. What I say now is not to describe that balance as a false or illusory one, but one whose weighing containers, so to speak, are larger and greater than what has been put into them. I think, in fact, that in *Cat on a Hot Tin Roof,* Williams in one vital respect made an assault upon his own viewpoint in an attempt to break it up and reform it on a wider circumference.

Essentially it is a play seen from the viewpoint of Brick, the son. He is a lonely young man sensitized to injustice. Around him is a world whose human figures partake in various ways of grossness, Philistinism, greed, money-lust, power-lust. And—with his mean-spirited brother as an example—it is a world senselessly reproducing itself through ugly children conceived without the grace of genuine affection, and delivered not so much as children but as inheritors of great wealth and power, the new perpetuators of inequity.

In contrast, Brick conceives of his friendship with his dead friend as an idealistic, even gallant and valorous and somehow morally elevated one, a relationship in which nothing was demanded, but what was given was given unasked, beyond the realm of price, of value, even of materiality. He clings to this image as to a banner of purity to flaunt against the world, and more precisely, against the decree of nature to reproduce himself, to become in turn the father, the master of the earth, the administrator of the tainted and impure world. It is a world in whose relations—especially between the sexes—there is always the element of the transaction, of materiality.

If the play confined itself to the psychiatry of impotence, it could be admired or dismissed as such. Williams' plays are never really that, but here in addition, unlike his other plays, there is a father. Not only is he the head of a family, but the very image of power, of materiality, of authority. And the problem this father is given is how he can infuse his own personality into the prostrated spirit of his son so that a hand as strong as his own will guide his fortune when he is gone—more particularly, so that his own immortality, his civilization will be carried on.

As the play was produced, without the surface realism of living-room, bedroom, walls, conventional light—in an atmosphere, instead, of poetic conflict, in a world that is eternal and not merely this world—it provided more evidence that Williams' preoccupation extends beyond the surface realities of the relationships, and beyond the psychiatric connotations of homosexuality and impotence. In every conceivable fashion there was established a goal beyond sheer behavior. We were made to see, I believe, an ulterior pantheon of forces and a play of symbols as well as of characters.

It is well known that there was difficulty in ending this play, and I am certainly of no mind to try it. I believe I am not alone in saying that the resolutions wherein Brick finally regains potency was not understandable on the stage. But my feeling is that even if this were more comprehensively motivated so that the psychiatric development of the hero were persuasively completed, it in itself could not embrace the other questions raised in the play.

We are persuaded as we watch this play that the world around Brick is in fact an unworthy collection of unworthy motives and greedy actions. Brick refuses to participate in this world, but he cannot destroy it either or reform it and he turns against himself. The question here, it seems to me, the ultimate question is the right of society to renew itself when it is, in fact, unworthy. There is, after all, a highly articulated struggle for material power going on here. There is literally and symbolically a world to win or a world to forsake and damn. A viewpoint is necessary, if one is to raise such a tremendous issue, a viewpoint capable of encompassing it. This is not a study in cynicism where the writer merely exposes the paradoxes of all sides and is content to end with a joke. Nor, again, is it mere psychiatry, aiming to show us how a young man reclaims his sexuality. There is a moral judgment hanging over this play which never quite comes down. A tempting analogy would be that of a Hamlet who takes up his sword and neither fights nor refuses to fight but marries an Ophelia who does not die.

Brick, despite his resignation from the race, has thrown a challenge to it which informs the whole play, a challenge which the father and the play both recognize and ignore. But if it is the central challenge of the play—as the play seems to me to emphasize—then the world must either prove its worthiness to survive, or its unworthiness must lie dramatically proved, to justify Brick's refusal to renew it—or, like a Hamlet who will neither do battle nor put down his sword, it must condemn Brick to inaction and perhaps indifference to its fate.

Because of Williams' marvelous ability, I for one would be willing to listen—and perhaps to him alone—even as he pronounced ultimate doom upon the race—a race exemplified in his play by the meanest of motives. This is a foundation grand enough, deep enough, and worthy of being examined remorselessly and perhaps even shaken and smashed. Again, as with *The Diary of Anne Frank*, had the implicit challenge ripened, we should no longer be held by our curiosity or our pity for someone else, but by that terror which comes when we must in truth justify our most basic assumptions. The father in this play, I think, must be forced to the wall in justification of his world, and Brick must be forced to his wall in justification of his condemning that world to the ultimate biological degree. The question of society's right to insist upon its renewal when it is unworthy is a question of tragic grandeur, and those who have asked this question of the world know full well the lash of its retaliation.

Quite simply, what I am asking is that the play pursue the ultimate development of the very questions it asks. But for such a pursuit, the viewpoint of the adolescent is not enough. The father, with the best will in the world, *is* faced with the problem of a son he loves best refusing to accept him and his spirit. Worse yet, it is to the least worthy son that that spirit must be handed if all else fails. Above the father's and the son's individual viewpoints the third must emerge, the viewpoint, in fact, of the audience, the society, and the race. It is a viewpoint that must weigh, as I have said, the question of its own right to biological survival—and one thing more, the question of the fate of the sensitive and the just in an impure world of power. After all, ultimately someone must take charge; this is the tragic dilemma, but it is beyond the viewpoint of adolescence. Someone must administer inequity or himself destroy that world by refusing to renew it, or by doing battle against its injustice, or by declaring his indifference or his cynicism. The terms upon which

Brick's potency returns are left waiting to be defined and the play is thus torn from its climax.

Again, I am not criticizing this play, but attempting to mark the outlines of its viewpoint—which is an extension of our theater's viewpoint to its present limits. Nor is this an entirely new and unheralded idea. Be it Tolstoy, Dostoevsky, Hemingway, you, or I, we are formed in this world when we are sons and daughters and the first truths we know throw us into conflict with our fathers and mothers. The struggle for mastery—for the freedom of manhood or womanhood as opposed to the servility of childhood—is the struggle not only to overthrow authority but to reconstitute it anew. The viewpoint of the adolescent is precious because it is revolutionary and insists upon justice. But in truth the parent, powerful as he appears, is not the source of injustice but its deputy.

A drama which refuses or is unable to reach beyond this façade is denying itself its inherited chance for greatness. The best of our theater is standing tiptoe, striving to see over the shoulders of father and mother. The worst is exploiting and wallowing in the self-pity of adolescence and obsessive keyhole sexuality. The way out, as the poet has said, is always *through*. We will not find it by huddling closer to the center of the charmed circle, by developing more and more naturalism in our dialogue and our acting, that "slice-of-life" reportage which is to life what an overheard rumor is to truth; nor by setting up an artificial poetic style, nor by once again shocking the householders with yet other unveilings of domestic relations and their hypocrisies. Nor will we break out by writing problem plays. There is an organic aesthetic, a tracking of impulse and causation from the individual to the world and back again which must be reconstituted. We are exhausting the realm of affects, which is the world of adolescence taken pure.

The shadow of a cornstalk on the ground is lovely, but it is no denial of its loveliness to see as one looks on it that it is telling the time of the day, the position of the earth and the sun, the size of our planet and its shape, and perhaps even the length of its life and ours among the stars. A viewpoint bounded by affects cannot engage the wider balance of our fates where the great climaxes are found.

In my opinion, if our stage does not come to pierce through affects to an evaluation of the world it will contract to a lesser psychiatry and an inexpert one at that. We shall be confined to writing an *Oedipus* without the pestilence, an *Oedipus* whose catastrophe is private and unrelated to the survival of his people, an *Oedipus* who cannot tear out his eyes because there will be no standard by which he can judge himself; an *Oedipus,* in a word, who on learning of his incestuous marriage, instead of tearing out his eyes, will merely wipe away his tears thus to declare his loneliness. Again, where a drama will not engage its relevancy for the race, it will halt at pathos, that tempting shield against ultimate dramatic effect, that counterfeit of meaning.

Symbolically, as though sensing that we are confined, we have removed the doors and walls and ceilings from our sets. But the knowing eye still sees them there. They may truly disappear and the stage will open to that symbolic stature, that realm where the father is after all not the final authority, that area where he is the son too, that area where religions are made and the giants live, only when we see beyond parents, who are, after all, but the shadows of the gods.

A great drama is a great jurisprudence. Balance is all. It will evade us until we can once again see man as whole, until sensitivity and power, justice and necessity are utterly face to face, until authority's justifications and rebellion's too are tracked even to those heights where the breath fails, where—because the largest point of view as well as the smaller has spoken—truly the rest is silence.

Morality and Modern Drama

INTERVIEW BY PHILLIP GELB

GELB: Mr. Miller, what about the apparent lack of moral values in modern drama?

MILLER: Not only modern drama, but literature in general—and this goes back a long, long distance in history—posits the idea of value, of right and wrong, good and bad, high and low, not so much by setting forth these values as such, but by showing, so to speak, the wages of sin. In other words, when for instance, in *Death of a Salesman,* we are shown a man who dies for the want of some positive, viable human value, the play implies, and it could not have been written without the author's consciousness, that the audience did believe something different. In other words, by showing what happens when there are no values, I, at least, assume that the audience will be compelled and propelled toward a more intense quest for values that are missing. I am assuming always that we have a kind of civilized sharing of what we would like to see occur within us and in the world; and I think that the drama, at least mine, is not so much an attack but an exposition, so to speak, of the want of value, and you can only do this if the audience itself is constantly trying to supply what is missing. I don't say that's a new thing. The Greeks did the same thing. They may have had a chorus

From the *Educational Theatre Journal,* 10 (October 1958), pp. 190–202. Reprinted by permission of Phillip Gelb.

which overtly stated that this is what happens when Zeus' laws are abrogated or broken, but that isn't what made their plays great.

GELB: Reverend John Bachman at the Union Theological Seminary said something similar. He said that the *Death of a Salesman* is moral to the extent that it is a negative witness. Now at the same time he felt that your play could not do any kind of a job in terms of presenting positive answers; this, of course, in his view, was the job of religion. Do you feel that that dichotomy actually—

MILLER: It isn't always so. Ibsen used to present answers. Despite the fashion that claims he never presented answers, he of course did. In the *Doll's House* and even in *Hedda Gabler,* we will find—and in Chekhov, too—we will find speeches toward the ends of these plays which suggest, if they don't overtly state, what the alternative values are to those which misled the heroes or heroines of the action shown. The difference is that we are now a half century beyond that probably more hopeful time, and we've been through social revolution which these people hadn't witnessed yet. We have come to a kind of belated recognition that the great faith in social change as an ameliora-tion or a transforming force of the human soul leaves something to be wanted. In other words, we originally, in the late nineteenth century, posed the idea that science would, so to speak, cure the soul of man by the eradication of poverty. We have eradicated poverty in large parts—well, in small parts of the world, but in significant parts of the world—and we're just as mean and ornery as we ever were. So that the social solution of the evil in man has failed—it seems so, anyway—and we are now left with a kind of bashful unwillingness to state that we still believe in life and that we still believe there is a conceivable standard of values. My feeling is, though, that we are in a transition stage between a mechanistic concept of man and an amalgam of both the rationalistic and what you could call the mystical or spiritual-istic concept of him. I don't think either that man is without will or that society is impotent to change his deepest, most private self-conceptions. I think that the work of art, the great work of art, is going to be that work which finds space for the two forces to operate. So far, I will admit, the bulk of literature, not only on the stage but elsewhere, is an exposition of man's failure: his failure to assert his sense of civilized and moral life.

GELB: A situation came up just the other day—I teach speech at Hunter College—in which somebody made a speech proclaiming the values of deceit: manipulative techniques, sophistry, and the rest. Most everybody went along with it to the extent that they felt that the use of techniques was automatically deceitful. Techniques were equated with trickery and the negative. I pointed out that integrity and honor, responsibility, rationality, logic—a lot of these things can be used as techniques, too.

MILLER: That reminds me of a book by Thomas Mann about Moses, in which, with his tongue in his cheek probably, but certainly with high seriousness, he portrays Moses as being a man bedeviled by the barbaric backwardness of a stubborn people and trying to improve them and raise up their sights. He disappears into the wilderness, up on the mountain, and comes down after a considerable period of time with the Ten Commandments. Now the Ten Commandments, from the point of view that you've just been speaking about, is a technique. It is purely and simply a way of putting into capsule form what probably the most sensitive parts of the society were wishing could be stated so that people could memorize it and people could live by it. I am sure that there must have been a number of people that said it was a kind of deceit or dishonesty to try to pinpoint things that way, things that were otherwise amorphous and without form and which probably some old Jews felt were even irreligious to carve into stone—but it is a technique. The whole Bible is a technique; it has got a form. If you read the three Gospels of Matthew, Mark, and Luke you will see the tremendous effort being made to dramatize, to make vivid, an experience which probably none of them really saw—except possibly one. It was a job almost of spiritual propaganda. Why would they have to write this down? Why would they strive for the *mot juste,* for the perfect paragraph, for the most vivid image, which quite evidently they do? Technique is like anything else; it is deceitful only when it is used for deceitful purposes.

GELB: Mr. John Beaufort, the critic for the *Christian Science Monitor,* attacked Willy Loman as a sad character, a vicious character, who couldn't figure in dramatic tragedy because he never starts with any ideals to begin with.

MILLER: The trouble with Willy Loman is that he has tremendously powerful ideals. We are not accustomed to speaking of ideals in *his* terms, but if Willy Loman, for instance, had not had a very profound sense that his life as lived had left him hollow, he would have died contentedly polishing his car on some Sunday afternoon at a ripe old age. The fact is that he has values. The fact that they cannot be realized is what is driving him mad, just as, unfortunately, it is driving a lot of other people mad. The truly valueless man, the man without ideals, is always perfectly at home anywhere because there cannot be conflict between nothing and something. Whatever negative qualities there are in the society or in the environment don't bother him because they are not in conflict with any positive sense that he may have. I think Willy Loman is seeking for a kind of ecstasy in life which the machine civilization deprives people of. He is looking for his selfhood, for his immortal soul, so to speak, and people who don't know the intensity of that quest think he is odd, but a lot of salesmen, in a line of work where ingenuity and individualism are acquired by the nature of the work, have a very intimate understanding of his problem; more so, I think, than literary critics who probably need strive less, after a certain point. A salesman is a kind of creative person. It is possibly idiotic to say so in a literary program, but they are; they have to get up in the morning and conceive a plan of attack and use all kinds of ingenuity all day long just like a writer does.

GELB: I think this idea of "a plan of attack" comes back to what we were talking about before, about techniques that become deceitful. The whole concept of present advertising is involved. By techniques the public is sold things they don't really need. Your plan of attack therefore becomes vicious; only the technique makes them buy.

MILLER: Well, that's true. I see the point now. But compared to, let's say, the normal viciousness, if you want to use that term, of standard advertising techniques. Willy is a baby. I mean, Willy is naive enough to believe in the goodness of his mission. There are highly paid advertising people who are utterly cynical about this business, and probably a lot of people call Willy vicious who would think of themselves as simply the pillars of society. Willy is a victim; he didn't originate this thing. He believes that selling is the greatest thing anybody can do.

GELB: This would seem to imply that Willy Loman, at least in terms of his problems and his anxieties, could be a lot of people. Now, Beaufort makes the statement, "If Willy Loman represented the whole mass of American civilization today, I think the country would be in a terrible state. I just can't accept Willy Loman as the average American citizen."

MILLER: It is obvious that Willy *can't* be an average American man, at least from one point of view; he kills himself. That's a rare thing in society, although it is more common than one could wish, and it's beside the point. As a matter of fact, that standard of "averageness" is not valid. It neither tells whether the character is a truthful character as a character, or a valid one. I can't help adding that that is the standard of socialist realism—which of course wasn't invented by socialists. It is the idea that a character in a play or in a book cannot be taken seriously unless he reflects some statistical average, plus his ability to announce the official aims of the society; and it is ridiculous. Hamlet isn't a typical Elizabethan, either. Horatio probably is. What is the difference? It has no point unless you are talking about, not literature, but patriotism. I didn't write *Death of a Salesman* to announce some new American man, or an old American man. Willy Loman is, I think, a person who embodies in himself some of the most terrible conflicts running through the streets of America today. A Gallup Poll might indicate that they are not the majority conflicts; I think they are. But what's the difference?

GELB: Maybe I should have read this statement first. This was made by the critic for *Progressive* magazine, Martin Dworkin, and he considers that *Death of a Salesman* makes a strong message for an average American man because "Willy Loman is such a particular Willy Loman. He is not simply a slogan out of the 1930s; he is not a banner to be waved to liberate people; he is not a criticism of society." And then Dworkin points out that because Willy is so particular, therefore he does these other universal things. What about the theory of art and drama here that the best way to present a universal is in terms of a really specific story?

MILLER: It is the best. It is the hardest way, too, and it isn't given to many authors or to any single author many times to be able to do it. Namely, to create the universal from the particular. You have to know the particular in your bones to do that. As the few plays that are repeatedly done over generations and centuries show, they are generally, in our western culture anyway, those plays which are full of the most particular information about people. We don't do many Greek plays any more, in my opinion not because they lack wonderful stories—they have wonderful stories—but in our terms, in terms of particularization of characters, they are deficient. It doesn't mean the Greeks were bad playwrights. It means their aims were different. But we do do *Hamlet,* we do do *Macbeth,* we do a number of more mediocre plays as well; but the ones that last are the ones that we recognize most immediately in terms of the details of real human behavior in specific situations.

GELB: How do you apply that to T. S. Eliot and George Bernard Shaw? Do you feel that their people are very real or specific?

MILLER: I don't think T. S. Eliot would even claim that he is creating characters, in the realistic sense of the word. It is a different aim. It doesn't mean that he can't do it; I don't think he can, but I don't think he is trying to do it. I think he is trying to dramatize quite simply a moral, a religious dilemma. The same is true of Bernard Shaw excepting for occasional characters, usually women, in his plays. They are more psychologically real than anything, of course, T. S. Eliot has done to my knowledge, excepting perhaps for *Murder in the Cathedral*. But the aim in these plays is not the aim of *Salesman* or most American work. It is the setting forth of an irony, a dilemma, more or less in its own terms. I think all the characters in Shaw can be reduced to two or three, really, and nobody would mind particularly. You always know that it's Shaw speaking no matter what side of the argument is being set forth, and that is part of the charm. I think his great success is due to the fact that he made no pretense to do otherwise; he was observing the issues in the dilemma of life rather than the psychology of human beings.

GELB: I'd like to take issue with that and simply say that Shaw might be writing real people but they speak more eloquently, more intellectually than real people. Essentially, I am not sure that in *Pygmalion* the father isn't real. I don't think anybody would talk like that, but I think his motives are real. I think Higgins is a real person. I think Shaw simply is not happy with the inability of people to express themselves and so he says I will do it for them; but I never really felt that Shaw's people were not people.

MILLER: I would put it this way. Shaw is impatient with the insignificance of most human speech, most human thought, and most human preconceptions. It's not that his characters are not people, it is that they aren't insignificant people the way people usually are. When you strip from the human being everything that is not of significance, you may get a valid moment out of him, a valid set of speeches, a valid set of attitudes, but in the normal, naturalistic concept, they aren't real because the bulk of reality is, of course, its utter boredom, and its insignificance, and its irrelevancy, and Shaw is absolutely uninterested in that. Consequently, if you just take the significant part of the character, it will be true but if this is lifted out of the rest of the character's psychology, you can no longer speak in terms of normal psychological writing. I happen to like this sort of thing; I am not criticizing it. I think it is a great thing to be able to do. But it isn't the tapestry work, let us say, of a *Hamlet* where you are carried through moment to moment, from one thought to the next, including the boredom, including the irrelevancy, including the contradictions within him which are not thematic. That is to say, they have very little to do with his conflict with the king or his mother, but they have much to do with creating a background for the major preconceptions of the play. Shaw is always eliminating the insignificant background, and it's possibly because he had so much to say and there was so little time to say it. But you mentioned one of the minor characters in *Pygmalion,* like the father. I think, in general, aside from the women, it *is* the minor characters who are most realistically drawn. The major characters are too completely obsessed with the issues that are being set forth. One of the signs of an abrogation of regular psychology is that people stay on the theme. You know and I know, even in this little interview, that it is very difficult, if not impossible, to spontaneously stay on the subject. You read Shaw's plays and see how rarely people get off the subject; and that's what I mean when I say that it isn't psychology he is following, it is the theme.

GELB: Let's assume that Shaw is concerned with the intellectual or social significances and chooses his material accordingly. The statement has been made by anthropologist Solon Kimball that Tennessee Williams chooses materials by their psychological significances. Dr. Kimball says that while Williams' picture of a Southern community in part may be true, that this psychological orientation gives a distorted picture of the whole. Evidently even some truth to the community and to the psychology of characters is not enough. Do you feel that is true of Williams, or what do you think of the general idea?

MILLER: Williams is a realistic writer; realistic in the sense that I was just referring to—that is to say, realistic in the way that Shaw is not. I think Williams is primarily interested in passion, in ecstasy, in creating a synthesis of his conflicting feelings. It is perfectly all right, of course, for an anthropologist to make an observation that Williams' picture of the South is unrepresentative. It probably is, but at the same time, the intensity with which he feels whatever he does feel is so deep, is so great, that we do end up with a glimpse of another kind of reality; that is, the reality in the spirit rather than in the society. I think, as I said before, that the truly great work is that work which will show at one and the same time the power and force of the human will working with and against the force of society upon it. Probably Williams is less capable of delivering the second than he might be. Everybody has some blind spot. But, again, as with Willy Loman, I'm not ready to criticize a writer because he isn't delivering a typical picture. The most typical pictures of society I know are probably in *The Saturday Evening Post,* or on the soap operas. It is more likely to be typical of people to be humdrum and indifferent and without superb conflicts. When a writer sets out to create high climaxes, he automatically is going to depart from the typical, the ordinary, and the representative. The pity is, of course, that Williams works out of Southern material, I work out of big city material, so instantly our characters are compared in a journalistic sense to some statistical norm. Truly, I have no interest in the selling profession, and I am reasonably sure that Williams' interest in the sociology of the South is only from the point of view of a man who doesn't like to see brutality, unfairness, a kind of victory of the Philistine, etc. He is looking at it emotionally, and essentially I am, too. Inevitably, people are going to say that Willy Loman is not a typical salesman, or that Blanche Dubois is not a typical something else, but to tell you the truth, the writer himself couldn't be less interested.

GELB: You point out Shaw as dealing with the intellectual, the social, the moral; Eliot with the moral, the religious; Williams with the psychological. Eric Bentley made the statement that he thought, perhaps, Arthur Miller was the one writer today who had the most possibility of combining all of these things, and yet he also thought that this was impossible. Can it be done?

MILLER: Well, whether it can be done remains for me or somebody else to prove. But let me put it this way: we are living, or I'm living anyway, with a great consciousness of the incredible force of objective thought. As we speak, there is an object flying around in the sky, passing over this point, I think it is every hundred and some minutes, which was put there by thinking men who *willed* it to go up there. The implications of this are as enormous as any statement by or on the part of Zeus, or Moses, or Shakespeare, or any feeling man. Now it may be a great bite to take, but I think the only thing worth doing—whether one can do it or not is an entirely different story, but aims are important—the only thing worth doing today in the theater, from my point of view, is to synthesize the subjective drives of the human being with what is now demonstrably the case, namely, that by an act of will man can and has changed the world. Now it is said that nothing is new under the sun: this is. It is right under the sun and it is new. And it is only one of the things that are new. I have seen communities transformed by the act of a committee. I have seen the interior lives of people transformed by the decision of a company, or of a man, or of a school. In other words, it is old fashioned, so to speak, and it is not moot simply to go on asserting the helplessness of the individual. The great weight of evidence is upon the helplessness of man. This is true, I think, with variations: the great bulk of the weight of evidence is that we are not in command. And we're not, I'm not saying we are. But we surely have much more command than anybody, including Macbeth's Witches, could ever dream of, and somehow a form has to be devised which will account for this. Otherwise the drama is doomed to repeating and repeating *ad nauseam* the same pattern of striving, disillusion, and defeat. And I don't think it is a modern day phenomenon.

GELB: Gore Vidal made a statement similar to yours with almost an exact opposite conclusion. His point was that he felt the only influence he could be was in terms of man's ability to destroy and despair, and so he wrote a play in which he is going to destroy the world. He said this facetiously, but since he didn't present any positive point of view, this led to the general topic of "the artist as the enemy"—perhaps the thing behind it is that many artists like to see the world destroyed. This isn't just a reporting; this is their own feeling.

MILLER: The enemy is the wrong word to me, although I would concede it. The artist is the outcast; he always will be. He is an outcast in the sense that he is to one side of the stream of life and absorbs it and is, in some part of himself, reserved from its implications; that is to say, a man like Vidal says we're out to destroy everything. I think that you can't see a thing when you are in the middle of it. To some extent, an artist has to step to one side of what is happening, divorce himself from his role as a citizen, and in that sense he becomes the enemy because he does not carry forth in himself and believe what is being believed around him. He is the enemy usually, I suppose, of the way things are, whatever way they are.

GELB: Does that mean, though, that he is always an inadequate reporter, too, because he is not a part? Is the artist perhaps in the least likely position to tell what might be true to most people?

MILLER: The trouble with literature is that writers have to be the ones who write it. It's always partial; it's always partisan, and it's always incomplete. When I say that writers have to be the ones to write it, I mean that in order to generate the energy to create a big novel, a big play, an involved poem, one has to be a specie of fanatic. You have to think that that is really the only thing worth doing. Otherwise, you can't generate the intensity to do it well. And to that degree, by generating that intensity, you are blinding yourself to what does not fit into some preconceived pattern in your own mind. There's no doubt about that to me, and I think that probably lay behind Plato's prohibition of the artist in society. He was right in the sense that the artist doesn't know what he is doing, to some extent. That is, we pretend, or like to believe, that we are depicting the whole truth of some situation, when as a matter of fact, the whole truth is, by definition, made impossible by the fact that we are obsessed people. I don't know of a first class piece of work written by what I would call, or a psychologist would call, a balanced, adjusted fellow who could easily be, let us say, a good administrator for a complicated social mechanism of some sort. It doesn't work that way. We are not constituted that way; so consequently, to be sure, it will have to be partial. The impulse to do it is obsessive; it always is. One of the fairest, most just writers was Tolstoy, who was, to make it short, quite mad. I mean, you can't pretend that as a person he was judicious, balanced: he wasn't. Neither was Dostoevsky. Neither, certainly, was Ibsen. Probably the most generously balanced man I know of was Chekhov. And I suspect that half of his psychological life we will never know. He was very reticent, and in those days there were no interviews of this sort, and if he didn't choose to write some essays describing his methods and personal life, you'd just know nothing about him.

GELB: I can get obsessive once or twice a year and maybe write a one-act play or something. The students have asked me this, "How do you take this obsessiveness and channel it into a discipline whereby you sit down and write regularly? Or is this always an individual problem?"

MILLER: I don't know how to write regularly. I wish I did. It's not possible to me. I suppose if one were totally dependent upon one's writing for a living and one's writing was of a kind that could be sold, like Dostoevsky's was—he seems about the only big writer I know that wrote regularly, but he wrote regularly because he had to pay his gambling debts half the time and the sheriff was on his tail. I don't know what would have happened if he had been given a stipend of $10,000 a year. Well, he probably would have gambled it away and been in debt again, I guess. So he would have written regularly.

GELB: Now you're very well established. You don't have to look for a theater, I imagine, just to see a play done. But do you feel that you might write more, or at least more regularly, if you were part of a group? I am thinking of the tradition of the writer as part of a theater group—as it was with Shakespeare, the

Greeks, Molière, even Shaw usually worked for some kind of company.

MILLER: I think that in the early life of a writer, in his beginning work—and this would go for Shaw, O'Neill, and anybody you wanted to mention—a connection with a group of actors could be very valuable. But I think you will find that as he grows older a playwright dreads the prospect of his play being produced. I mean that seriously. There are so many stupid things that happen which destroy the most valuable, the most sensitive parts of a manuscript that, truthfully, if I seriously contemplated the production of a play as I was writing it, I don't know that I could write it. It is too dreadful a risk, and I don't care how well established you are; it is always the same risk. Your work can go down the drain because you have happened to hire an actor who simply does not have the sensitivity for that role and you didn't know it until the night before you opened. Think of that when you put in two, three, four years on a play, and you pick up a team of actors, so to speak, and put one guy in to pitch and another in to catch, and the catcher can't catch and the pitcher can't pitch, and there's your manuscript. And there's no critic alive who can tell the difference between a bad production and a bad script unless they are extremely bad in either direction. But where there is some reasonable excellence, nobody knows the difference. I have had plays that have failed in New York—*View from the Bridge* was one of them. I am sure that anybody who saw *View from the Bridge* in New York would not have recognized it in London. I had a great deal to do with the production there; it was a different mood, a different key, a different production, and I am sure anybody would have said it was a different play.

GELB: In your case, your plays are going to be done for years and years, and you just can't be around, you don't know what kind of actors are going to do them. Any good playwright is at the mercy of a hundred and one different kinds of people, and personalities, and places. Why does one write for the theater then?

MILLER: It is one of the minor curses of mankind, I suppose. I have a feeling that it is a way of seeing existence in terms of audible scenes. I was always a playwright. I was a playwright before I'd ever been in the theater. I wrote my first play, which was produced in various places and was a play, after having seen only two.

GELB: From viewing current plays, one might conclude that maybe what makes most people write is antagonism, negative qualities: despair, getting even, spite.

MILLER: For myself, I can't write anything if I am sufficiently unhappy. A lot of writers write best when they are most miserable. I suppose my sense of form comes from a positive need to organize life and not from a desire to demonstrate the inevitability of defeat and death. If I feel miserable enough, I can't work. A lot of writers, I am aware, then are spurred on to express their disillusion. All I know about that really comes down to this— that we are doomed to live, and I suppose one had better make the best of it. I imagine that Vidal shares that fate with me and will continue to. He is probably taking some perverse pleasure in positing the destruction of the world, but I suspect he wouldn't enjoy it as much as he says he would.

GELB: You feel your need is to organize life and not to present the case for death and despair?

MILLER: It is a basic commitment for me, sitting here now in America. For another writer who is, let's say, a French writer, an Italian writer, and who has been through a sufficiently profound social cataclysm, such as two world wars and a depression in-between in Europe, where he was faced with the ultimate disaster, it might seem foolish. My experience, though, is as valid as theirs. In other words, I can't pretend things are worse than they are, any more than they can pretend things are better. It is a commitment on my part that I don't see the point in proving again that we must be defeated. I didn't intend that—since you have mentioned *Salesman* so much in this interview—I didn't intend it in *Salesman*. I was trying in *Salesman*, in this respect, to set forth what happens when a man does not have a grip on the forces of life and has no sense of values which will lead him to that kind of a grip; but the implication was that there must be such a grasp of those forces, or else we're doomed. I was not, in other words, Willy Loman, I was the writer, and Willy Loman is there because I could see beyond him.

GELB: Mr. Miller, in an interview I had with George Freedley of the New York Drama Critics Circle, Mr. Freedley stated that he thought some Broadway producers and investors shied away from your plays because they were too liberal, that perhaps some of your plays had difficulty in getting productions. Now has anything like that ever occurred?

MILLER: Soon after *Salesman* I tried to do a new version of *An Enemy of the People,* which is a play by Ibsen, and which I had felt was never properly put on, and it was very difficult to raise the money. The reason was quite openly stated, at that time—this was back in 1951—that it was too evidently a counter-statement to McCarthy and at that time he was looking like he might be president of the United States and people were wary about supporting such a play. There's no question about that. It exists today. I have never had a play that was not produced for that reason, but I know that the pressure exists. I don't want to appear as somebody who is carrying the firebrand, but there's no question about it, the climate of opinion over the past ten years has been opposed to what we call an openly liberal approach. I suppose a demonstration could be made, however, that the bulk of the plays, rather than being reactionary, are liberal. There's a contradiction there, but it simply means that it is a small minority who do lead an attack on liberal things. The bulk of the people in the theater, and in my opinion, the bulk of the audience, are liberals. I think it is sad from many points of view to have to say that, because it means the enemy is almost non-existent, but that is the case, I think. I would be happier if there were more reactionary playwrights who were willing to put in the theater what they really feel about mankind and about the state of the world.

GELB: It was Eric Bentley's statement that what he thought

was lacking in Arthur Miller's plays was a character who could present the McCarthy point of view. Do you feel that it is the job of the playwright himself to introduce such a reasonable case?

MILLER: I never attempted to do that because there was never any point in it, excepting in one play, and that is in *The Crucible* and through the judge who condemned the victims of the witch hunt. The trouble with doing that, though, was as follows: In all truth, the real backward, knuckleheaded reactionary is ridiculous. Now you can say this is merely Miller's viewpoint, but if I showed you the record of the Salem witch hunt and reproduced verbatim from the court record taken in 1692 in Salem, Massachusetts, what the judge said and what he did, you would simply not believe it. You would burst into laughter. I was charged, if not openly then by implication, with not giving the judge his due. The truth of the matter is that I was at my wit's end to give him some respectable viewpoint which one could listen to without simply throwing it out the window. I made a statement in the introduction to my play that we no longer believe in the positiveness of evil, that is to say that people will, with malice aforethought, go about creating bad situations for other people. It's a failure, perhaps, in our point of view, but it's true what Bentley says in that respect. That is to say, I wish there were a way of showing the conqueror, who is usually the bad one, in his own justifications. Think of writing a play about Hitler.

GELB: I am sure the inquisitor in Shaw's *Saint Joan* is much more understanding and human than the real human.

MILLER: We don't dare set forth evil in its full bloom in a person; we don't quite believe it. I go back again to *The Crucible*. Believe me, I think now my mistake in *The Crucible* was that I didn't make the judge evil enough. I think I should have gone the whole hog. I should have shown him conspiring with the witnesses to take evidence, which he did, still being a deeply religious man, a man who could quote any part of the Bible at will, who prayed at every opportunity, and met, as is known, with the girls who were hysterical and fed them cues as to what they should testify to an hour hence. He did that; there were others who did that. It was cooked up from their point of view. The hysteria, however, was not cooked up from the point of view of the average person in Salem. He believed it. And the judge was a great actor; he could get himself into a froth and a frenzy knowing, at the same time, that he had manufactured the whole thing. And one of the judges ended a drunk and probably insane as a result of the conflicts aroused in his mind by the behavior of this other judge and by his own behavior. I am trying to deal with that now, to tell you the truth. I am trying to deal with it because I can't see the problem of will evolving fruitfully unless the existence of evil is taken into account.

GELB: So far you've been talking about this immensity of evil, its potential, within an individual. But something even worse and more immense occurs when this evil becomes social, when everybody says, "Well, I was obeying orders," or "I did what others did." Is this a problem that we should do nothing about; but simply mention that it exists, in terms of the theater? Well, I suppose what I am really asking is, can this kind of evil be understood dramatically in any way, the Nazi evil, for example?

MILLER: It can be understood in one way. I'm not saying that this is *the* way to understand it, of course. A point arrives in the evolution of a society when a goodly number of people take a position knowingly in opposition to what we would call civilized values. I think it has been an old story with us. After all, Lincoln Steffens' autobiography is filled with the observation that the evildoers in his day, the early twentieth century, the political bosses in the big city, with absolute consciousness and awareness of what they were doing, faked elections, bought votes, engaged in every conceivable kind of corruption. And Steffens was probably one of the few reporters who ever confronted them with the facts of their deeds because he was philosophically interested in it. Their answer was that they were no more dishonest than the reformers who refused to understand what they were doing. The reformers had a stake in the graft and refused to see it; refused to see that, in many cases, reformers were professionals, or businessmen, or whatever, and their very professions and businesses were in some way dependent upon the favors that could be gotten from money.

GELB: Think of *Major Barbara*.

MILLER: Yes, it's Shaw's irony again, and so the admission of evil occurs. We blanked it out in this last generation, I think, as a result of the thirties. The depression taught us that we were all equally victims. Suddenly we were all the victims of something unseen and unknowable, and none of us was any worse than the other guy. We were all primarily in a situation; we were no longer individuals. And then along came psychology to tell us that we were again the victim of drives that we weren't even conscious of, so that the idea of a man being willfully good or willfully bad evaporated. We are nothing but what we were born and what we were taught to be up to the age of six, and we are essentially irresponsible. I think that's the situation we're in now.

GELB: What about Germany?

MILLER: Well, the Germans have been notoriously irresponsible since they formed the first states in Germany because of the fact that they never had a social revolution. The people of Germany never rose up, as the people of America did, and asserted a form of government; the form of government was always given them from above. They were essentially in the position of a servant; they were essentially in the position of a son, you might say, and consequently, the father idea, the idea of a strong leader, from Bismark through Hitler, was a given quality. It was always there, and consequently they are irresponsible from that point of view. They tell the truth when they say they only did what they were told. They've always been doing what they were told. Every nation that does not establish its own government, by its own efforts, like France, like England, like America, creates that kind of irresponsibility below because the individual has had no say in the way things are.

GELB: What are the possible alternatives? Is there a necessity of maintaining very consciously the importance of democratic institutions? I am thinking, for example, of people who object to Governor Faubus of Arkansas. Their reaction is, "Shut him up." It strikes me, "Let him hang himself," would be better. The one who is shut up, if I'm not mistaken, in the South today is the integrationist.

MILLER: We have Faubus because the Civil War wasn't completed. Lincoln was shot about two years too early. The victory was given away in many respects, the victory of education that should have followed, and which undoubtedly would have followed, had Lincoln lived. In a sense, in a wider sense, it is good that Faubus exists because a lot of people will have to examine their own attitudes toward Negroes. People who disapprove of them in the North, for example, and are at heart, or in part of their hearts, not ready to give the Negro his rights, either. But of course, the field of action must be maintained: that is to say, the democratic situation, where this battle can be fought out through the educational process.

GELB: I think that last statement's very important because I think you are implying here that the only alternative to the use of the democratic process is violence. Now maybe that's too extreme a conclusion; but, in addition to Little Rock forcing people to clarify in their own hearts how they feel about Negroes, maybe it might force some people to clarify how they feel about democratic institutions, and maybe it's the system that's continually being tested.

MILLER: I suppose what the lesson is, if there is one, of the current struggle in the South is that an edict was given which reaffirmed the rights of all men to be equal and that for a very long time, not only in the South but in the North, all men have not been equal. What this has done creates no new situation, it simply is a firecracker under an old, old situation. I think it is being well worked out. I think that the suffering involved there is less than would be the case if this were being treated in a dictatorial way. It isn't being treated in a dictatorial way. The use of troops down there was the enforcement of a law, democratically arrived at, and democratically asserted in a normal democratic way. The reaction to it, in my opinion, is the dictatorial reaction. That is, there's no question any more that the threat of violence came not from the United States government but from probably a small minority of people who are fanatically interested in the subject. I'm not in Arkansas, but from up here it would seem that the solution to a deficiency in democracy is—I think Lord Bryce said it—is more democracy. I think that struggle, the struggle to raise up men, is part of the given situation of man. It will never end.

On Adaptations

THE presentation in the same week of television adaptations of *Don Quixote* and *A Doll's House* raises questions concerning the propriety of laying hands on classic works without investigating the full depth of responsibility entailed.

The vast majority of viewers has not read or seen these works in their original forms. Therefore, television must face the fact that it is really presenting not adaptations of them but, in reality, the works themselves—so far as the public knows.

In its original form *A Doll's House* would need close to three hours of playing time, or thereabouts. You cannot cut it in half without cutting in half its emotional, philosophical and human value. Specifically, a profound work, the orchestration of whose themes is quite marvelous, becomes a superficial "story" at worst, and a hint of something more at best, when it is told by leaping from one high point to another.

The adapters of these classics are neither guilty nor innocent, nor are the sponsors. The illusion is overpowering among us that it is possible to reduce everything to a painless capsule without losing its meaning. Nor is television alone in this. I happened on a paperback edition of Tolstoy's *War and Peace*, which the publishers proudly declared was shorn of all its political and

From *The New York Times*, November 29, 1959, Sec. 2, p. 13. A letter to the Radio-Television Editor.

social speculation, leaving its "human" story uncluttered by the author's thought. There are digests of novels published with their authors' consent, and the movies have for years purveyed adaptations of great books and plays.

Only one thing is lost by "digesting" great works, and it is possibly the main thing, namely, the depth of experience one might find in the originals. However skillfully one "cuts to the story," eliminating the gradual development of motive and meaning, one is of necessity cutting the reason for the story to a greater or lesser extent. Literature is reduced to what E. M. Forster has called the cave man element—the "what happens next?" Why it happened; why it had to happen, what significance the happenings might have—these questions are the crucial ones for the creator and for mankind, and we are being deprived of them by digesting them out of the great works we see.

However well they are played and directed, these truncated versions must inevitably confirm the opinion of those who cannot tell why they should bother with real literature or drama, for they are being given basically the plots at best, the skeletons of living organisms. The person who has always heard of *Don Quixote* and *A Doll's House* but never got around to reading them, has now "seen them." Worse than utter ignorance is the knowledge that is not knowledge but its shadow.

We are breaking the continuity of culture by passing on its masterpieces through mutilated distortions. This is not "better than nothing." The wholeness of viewpoint, the completeness of the human beings in certain masterpieces is being fragmented so that the marvel of a complete experience—which a great work is—is denied millions of people who, worse yet, go forth under the illusion that they have actually had it.

The fault seems to be the question of adequate time. Do you imagine you have heard the Fifth Symphony of Beethoven, let us say, when the orchestra has eliminated everything but its main and most thunderous themes? A fine work is wedded to the time it takes to perform or read it.

Perhaps it might be excusable if, instead of using the titles of *Don Quixote* and *A Doll's House,* we were told that what we are about to see are themes from these works, and warned before and after their presentations that only the broad outlines have been suggested, and that the originals are far more challenging and interesting. As it is, nothing less than a deception is being carried on, a positive act of misinformation and mis-education.

I said above that the adapters and sponsors are neither guilty nor innocent, given the power of the tendency to digest everything. I take it back. After all, those who are knowledgeable enough to adapt classics are to that degree in charge of them for the moment, so to speak, and are as responsible as a librarian who tears out half the pages of a work in order to get more busy people to read it. The justification that half is better than nothing does not hold when one knows the humanizing power of the originals. You cannot digest a real work of art because it is digested in the first place; it is the ultimate distillation of the author's vision by definition.

When television spends all day and all night purveying junk, is it really too much to ask that two, two and a half, or three hours be set aside once in a while for the full-length presentation of a masterpiece?

Failing this, the digests of such works ought not bear their original titles any more than diluted beer or perfume can be sold with the brand name of the manufacturer who makes the real thing. The integrity of a masterpiece is at least equal to that of a can of beans.

Introduction to
A View from the Bridge
(TWO-ACT VERSION)

A PLAY is rarely given a second chance. Unlike a novel, which may be received initially with less than enthusiasm, and then as time goes by hailed by a large public, a play usually makes its mark right off or it vanishes into oblivion. Two of mine, *The Crucible* and *A View from the Bridge,* failed to find large audiences with their original Broadway productions. Both were regarded as rather cold plays at first. However, after a couple of years *The Crucible* was produced again Off-Broadway and ran two years, without a line being changed from the original. With McCarthy dead it was once again possible to feel warmly toward the play, whereas during his time of power it was suspected of being a special plea, a concoction and unaesthetic. On its second time around its humanity emerged and it could be enjoyed as drama.

At this writing I have not yet permitted a second New York production of *A View from the Bridge* principally because I have not had the desire to see it through the mill a second time. However, a year or so after its first production it was done with great success in London and then in Paris, where it ran two years. It is done everywhere in this country without any apparent difficulty in reaching the emotions of the audience. This play, however,

From the two-act version of *A View from the Bridge* (New York: Viking, Compass Edition, 1960), pp. *v–x*. Copyright © 1960 by Arthur Miller.

unlike *The Crucible*, I have revised, and it was the revision which London and Paris saw. The nature of the revisions bears directly upon the questions of form and style which interest students and theater workers.

The original play produced on Broadway (Viking, 1955) was in one act. It was a hard, telegraphic, unadorned drama. Nothing was permitted which did not advance the progress of Eddie's catastrophe in a most direct way. In a Note to the published play, I wrote:

> What struck me first about this tale when I heard it one night in my neighborhood was how directly, with what breathtaking simplicity, it did evolve. It seemed to me, finally, that its very bareness, its absolutely unswerving path, its exposed skeleton, so to speak, was its wisdom and even its charm and must not be tampered with. . . . These *qualities* of the events themselves, their texture, seemed to me more psychologically telling than a conventional investigation in width which would necessarily relax that clear, clean line of his catastrophe.

The explanation for this point of view lies in great part in the atmosphere of the time in which the play was written. It seemed to me then that the theater was retreating into an area of psycho-sexual romanticism, and this at the very moment when great events both at home and abroad cried out for recognition and analytic inspection. In a word, I was tired of mere sympathy in the theater. The spectacle of still another misunderstood victim left me impatient. The tender emotions, I felt, were being overworked. I wanted to write in a way that would call up the faculties of knowing as well as feeling. To bathe the audience in tears, to grip people by the age-old methods of suspense, to theatricalize life, in a word, seemed faintly absurd to me if not disgusting.

In *The Crucible* I had taken a step, I felt, toward a more self-aware drama. The Puritan not only felt, but constantly referred his feelings to concepts, to codes and ideas of social and ethical importance. Feeling, it seemed to me, had to be made of importance; the dramatic victory had to be more than a triumph over the audience's indifference. It must call up a concept, a new awareness.

I had known the story of *A View from the Bridge* for a long time. A waterfront worker who had known Eddie's prototype told it to me. I had never thought to make a play of it because it was too complete, there was nothing I could add. And then a time came when its very completeness became appealing. It suddenly seemed to me that I ought to deliver it onto the stage as fact; that interpretation was inherent in the very existence of the tale in the first place. I saw that the reason I had not written it was that as a whole its meaning escaped me. I could not fit it into myself. It existed apart from me and seemed not to express anything within me. Yet it refused to disappear.

I wrote it in a mood of experiment—to see what it might mean. I kept to the *tale,* trying not to change its original shape. I wanted the audience to feel toward it as I had on hearing it for the first time—not so much with heart-wringing sympathy as with wonder. For when it was told to me I knew its ending a few minutes after the teller had begun to speak. I wanted to create suspense but not by withholding information. It must be suspenseful because one knew too well how it would come out, so that the basic feeling would be the desire to stop this man and tell him what he was really doing to his life. Thus, by knowing more than the hero, the audience would rather automatically see his life through conceptualized feelings.

As a consequence of this viewpoint, the characters were not permitted to talk about this and that before getting down to their functions in the tale; when a character entered he proceeded directly to serve the catastrophe. Thus, normal naturalistic acting techniques had to be modified. Excessive and arbitrary gestures were eliminated; the set itself was shorn of every adornment. An atmosphere was attempted in which nothing existed but the purpose of the tale.

The trouble was that neither the director, the actors, nor I had had any experience with this kind of staging. It was difficult to know how far to go. We were all aware that a strange style was called for which we were unsure how to provide.

About a year later in London new conditions created new solutions. Seemingly inconsequential details suggested these solutions at times. For one, the British actors could not reproduce the Brooklyn argot and had to create one that was never heard on heaven or earth. Already naturalism was evaporated by this much: the characters were slightly strange beings in a world of their own. Also, the pay scales of the London theater made it possible to do what I could not do in New York—hire a crowd.

These seemingly mundane facts had important consequences. The mind of Eddie Carbone is not comprehensible apart from its relation to his neighborhood, his fellow workers, his social situation. His self-esteem depends upon their estimate of him, and his value is created largely by his fidelity to the code of his culture. In New York we could have only four strategically placed actors to represent the community. In London there were at least twenty men and women surrounding the main action. Peter Brook, the British director, could then proceed to design a set which soared to the roof with fire escapes, passageways, suggested apartments, so that one sensed that Eddie was living out his horror in the midst of a certain normality, and that, invisibly and without having to speak of it, he was getting ready to invoke upon himself the wrath of his tribe. A certain size accrued to him as a result. The importance of his interior psychological dilemma was magnified to the size it would have in life. What had seemed like a mere aberration had now risen to a fatal violation of an ancient law. By the presence of his neighbors alone the play and Eddie were made more humanly understandable and moving. There was also the fact that the British cast, accustomed to playing Shakespeare, could incorporate into a seemingly realistic style the conception of the play—they moved easily into the larger-than-life attitude which the play demanded, and without the self-conscious awkwardness, the uncertain stylishness which hounds many actors without classic training.

As a consequence of not having to work at making the play

seem as factual, as bare as I had conceived it, I felt now that it could afford to include elements of simple human motivation which I had rigorously excluded before—specifically, the viewpoint of Eddie's wife, and *her* dilemma in relation to him. This, in fact, accounts for almost all the added material which made it necessary to break the play in the middle for an intermission. In other words, once Eddie had been placed squarely in his social context, among his people, the mythlike feeling of the story emerged of itself, and he could be made more human and less a figure, a force. It thus seemed quite in keeping that certain details of realism should be allowed; a Christmas tree and decorations in the living room, for one, and a realistic make-up, which had been avoided in New York, where the actor was always much cleaner than a longshoreman ever is. In a word, the nature of the British actor and of the production there made it possible to concentrate more upon realistic characterization while the universality of Eddie's type was strengthened at the same time.

But it was not only external additions, such as a new kind of actor, sets, and so forth, which led to the expansion of the play. As I have said, the original was written in the hope that I would understand what it meant to me. It was only during the latter part of its run in New York that, while watching a performance one afternoon, I saw my own involvement in this story. Quite suddenly the play seemed to be "mine" and not merely a story I had heard. The revisions subsequently made were in part the result of that new awareness.

In general, then, I think it can be said that by the addition of significant psychological and behavioral detail the play became not only more human, warmer and less remote, but also a clearer statement. Eddie is still not a man to weep over; the play does not attempt to swamp an audience in tears. But it is more possible now to relate his actions to our own and thus to understand ourselves a little better not only as isolated psychological entities, but as we connect to our fellows and our long past together.

The State of the Theater

INTERVIEW BY HENRY BRANDON

BRANDON: What stimulates you into writing a play?

MILLER: If I knew, I could probably control the inception of it better. I'm at the mercy of it; I don't really know. I cannot write anything that I understand too well. If I know what something means to me, if I have already come to the end of it as an experience, I can't write it because it seems like a twice-told tale. I have to astonish myself, and that's of course a very costly way of going about things, because you can go up a dead end and discover that it's beyond your capacity to discover some organism underneath your feeling, and you're left simply with a formless feeling which is not itself art. It's inexpressible and one must leave it until it is hardened and becomes something that has form and has some possibility of being communicated. It might take a year or two or three or four to emerge.

BRANDON: So you really don't know how your play is going to end when you start it.

MILLER: I don't. I have a rough notion... for instance, if a play has a hero in it who will die, I know that. And I must know the core of irony involved. But little else in terms of the progression of the story. The shape and, so to speak, the tempo of the development are created within the play itself.

From *Harper's*, 221 (November 1960), pp. 63–69. Miller's initial, brief comment on trends in the postwar American and British theaters has been deleted. Copyright © 1960 by *Harper's Magazine*.

BRANDON: When you, for instance, wrote your new film script, *The Misfits,* did you write it with your wife in mind for a part in it?

MILLER: I was of two minds about that, because I happen to believe that she can do anything on the screen. But it's impossible for me to write for a person, inasmuch as my vision is concentrated on something quite different, on some evolving paradox. The question of an actress, an actor, is the furthest thing from my mind at that time. Only toward the end of *The Misfits* did I become thankfully aware that this would be wonderful for Marilyn.

A play is made by sensing how the forces in life simulate ignorance—you set free the concealed irony, the deadly joke.

BRANDON: So it's really a rather tortuous birth, isn't it?

MILLER: I can write very quickly, but that's simply the last stage of the process. By that time, I have found the walls of life and I can feel them, and I can fill that room now and I can proceed. It's when there is no inner evolution that I am lost.

BRANDON: Do you think that American drama has been an authentic expression of life in this country?

MILLER: It depends on the level on which you're thinking of American life. Any people has a conventional idea of what they're like. Americans fancy themselves, for instance, to be openhanded, on the side of justice, a little bit careless about what they buy, wasteful, but essentially good guys, optimistic. But under that level of awareness there is another one, which gets expressed in very few movies and very few plays, but in more plays in proportion than in the movies: the level which confronts our bewilderment, our lonely naïveté, our hunger for purpose.

BRANDON: Some critics think that the Angry Young Men in England were influenced by American writing on that deeper level.

MILLER: I think that there is an American note in their writing. I don't mean that a play like John Osborne's *Look Back in Anger* could not have been done without the American influence, but there's a certain straightforward, even brash, thrust to these works which in tone is very American, and which to my mind does not typify modern English letters—which are much more oblique and remote. I found myself very much at home with the writing. Osborne's attitudes were always those of the plain fellow kicking through the conventional class lines in all directions—something that has become commonplace in this country since even Mark Twain.

The American play is pre-eminently active, relatively unreflective as such. It deals with nothing it cannot act out. It rarely comments on itself; like the people, it always pretends it does not know what it is doing. It must *be* something rather than be *about* something. But when a play does both at once it is most highly prized. It is a hard school to go to, but in my opinion the best one at the present time.

BRANDON: Do you see anything as "indigenous" in the American theater as is the Westerner in films?

MILLER: Literally speaking, the Westerner as he appears in Westerns is the last "indigenous" person in the United States today. The number of people involved, let's say, in cattle raising, in being cowboys, is very small. The number of people in the West, however, who are involved in trade and industry is much greater. What the Westerner in the Western is, of course, is a folk hero, but he doesn't typify anything any more except escape and a memory of what people like to believe the past was like. I think the salesman is much more typical of American life, both in viewpoint and numbers. God knows, for every cowboy there are one million salesmen.

BRANDON: To switch for a moment to a more modern character: As one who had a brush with McCarthyism, do you think that this phenomenon is now dead in America?

MILLER: As such it is. Two things happened: one was that the Army defeated him, not—I'm sad to say—liberals or the Left— not the people who knew what he was about. It was another conservative authority that knocked him down. I don't think one can push an attack on the integrity of the United States government itself to the lengths that he did and get away with it. However, the legacy of McCarthy is still with us. But it doesn't have the mass backing that it could call up at any juncture a few years ago.

BRANDON: You mean he was defeated for the wrong reasons.

MILLER: Yes. He gained the antagonism of people who essentially didn't disagree with him very much—not all of them, but a good many of them. My own opinion is that he may have been demented toward the end; he misjudged his position and his power.

BRANDON: Well, do you mean to imply, then, that you think it could recur?

MILLER: If an international crisis sufficiently intense gripped us, I think something like it could happen again, yes.

BRANDON: Still he stands basically in most American eyes exposed as a bad influence.

MILLER: He does, but what he did doesn't. Guilt-by-association, for instance—I would say quite as many people believe that as believed it before. I don't think they'd recognize it as McCarthyism, if it were presented in another form. When you don't defeat somebody on the basis of principle, he is only personally defeated, but that's all.

BRANDON: Not long ago I discussed with Peter Ustinov a complaint of yours that American playwrights write important social plays, but that they fail to grasp the total social problem. Peter felt that there was a lack of sensitivity involved in what you said, that you could say the same thing about Chekhov— that he was only dealing with a cross section of weary landlords on the point of bankruptcy, but as soon as the revolution broke out these things were accepted as very valid criticism. After all, Peter said, the writer's job is to stimulate—to ask questions, not to provide solutions.

MILLER: Ustinov is wrong about Chekhov and he is wrong about me. I have never been able to understand why one is insensitive because one looks beyond the individual to society for certain causations and certain hopes. It seems quite the reverse to me. I never had the illusion that Chekhov was only writing about some weary landlords. Bolsheviks, indeed, accused him of this, and defensive conservatives hoped it was true, but if it were he would be known now merely as a genre painter, a curio. It is an almost international mistake, even now, to see him as a writer satisfied to reveal life's absurdities, even as a celebrant of futility. But, in fact, Chekhov was tortured by his inability to settle on solutions—he accused himself of deceiving his public because he could not tell them what they must do. The plays are great, for one thing, not because they do not give answers but because they strive so mightily to discover them, and in the process draw into view a world that is historical.

It is not right to confuse Chekhov's modesty with his accomplishments. In *The Cherry Orchard* when the real-estate developer destroys with his axe the lovely but unproductive basis of the characters' lives, Chekhov was not merely describing a picturesque piquancy, but the crude thrust of materialism taking command of an age. His plays are full of speeches about having to go to work and somehow to become part of productive society. He was seeking some reconciliation for these much-loved people and the forces displacing them. A playwright provides answers by the questions he chooses to ask, by the exact conflicts in which he places his people. Chekhov wrote: "A conscious life without a definite philosophy is no life, rather a burden and nightmare." A writer who has not spent his life trying to find and articulate "answers" could not have written this.

I am not calling for more ideology, as Ustinov implies. I am simply asking for a theater in which an adult who wants to live can find plays that will heighten his awareness of what living in our time involves. I am tired of a theater of sensation, that's all. I am tired of seeing man as merely a bundle of nerves. That way lies pathology, and we have pretty well arrived.

BRANDON: Talking about ideology, how does the religious drama of Graham Greene impress you?

MILLER: I must confess that as a dramatist I find his work faintly formularized. His philosophic dilemma is real, but it seems to end in a bald assertion. He's caught between two needs. On the one hand, he has to keep his works on a lay level, because that's his style as well as the level on which life is lived in this age. On the other hand, he has to broach a spiritual solution, which has no embodiment in the course of the play. God escapes realism. I find them to be good plays until they have approached the point where what is most important to him enters into them—the leap to another form of consciousness. I don't see how that leap is possible within his realistic form. To make it you would have to create an inspired world from the beginning; I could believe in that. I don't think I could explain it, but I could believe in it. I admire the quality of his conviction, even of his dilemma, but he has forced it into a geometry at the end. I have to look at his experience from the standpoint of the daylight world because Greene is presenting his vision as, so to speak, a daylight vision.

BRANDON: The American theater has no religious content; do you have an explanation?

MILLER: There's one possible clue in this schizophrenia of the American mind in that respect. We're probably the most church-going nation in history. But there is a sharp line drawn between going to church and thinking that way. In daily economic life, there is no more materialistic or efficient population. However, on Sunday it's quite the other way. Life is lived, so to speak, without reference to a religious ideology, excepting the weekly nodding toward the sky.

Now I suppose our theater naturally reflects this. I think the big change for the American theater came when it was no longer possible to contain the increasingly absurd contradictions of existence within the formula of a play which simply presented a more or less evil influence, and a more or less good influence, and batted it out between them. The evil influences had become so pervasive and so ill-defined that we were left with, I think, a hero whose enemies were invisible: the victim *as* victim came to the fore. The story of almost every important American play is how the main character got his corners knocked off.

So, I would say, our main tradition from O'Neill to the present revolves around the question of integrity—not moral integrity alone, but the integrity of the personality. The difficulty is to locate the forces of disintegration. I have to believe they exist and can be unveiled.

I wrote *The Crucible* in this frame of mind. It happened that it was written at the time of McCarthyism so that a kind of personification of disintegration existed among us again. But it was an attempt to create the old ethical and dramaturgic order again, to say that one couldn't passively sit back and watch his world being destroyed under him, even if he did share the general guilt. In effect, I was calling for an act of will. I was trying to say that injustice has features, that the amorphousness of our world is so in part because we have feared through guilt to unmask its ethical outlines.

The plays of the forties, which began as an attempt to analyze the self in the world, are ending as a device to exclude the world. Thus self-pity and sentimentality rush in, and sexual sensationalism. It is an anti-dramatic drama, and it reflects the viewpoint of a great many people who seem to feel that's the way life is today. To me it's a challenge to define what is creating these effects among us.

BRANDON: American drama is really still very young. How do you see its evolution?

MILLER: We had a very slight indigenous American drama until the first world war. By that I mean a direct reflection of American manners, American life, barely existed on the stage. The plays were melodramas, for the most part, with a very few exceptions. It's after the first world war that real attempts were made to create a modern drama that reflects the life of the people at the moment. And I think O'Neill has to be set aside from the main stream because his preoccupation was not so much with the journalistic reportage of what was going on—which is, I think, true of most of the other writers in the twenties and thirties—but with the quest for the relationship between an individual, and for want of a better word, fate. At bottom their world was rational, his a mystery.

BRANDON: Which writers are you thinking of?

MILLER: Well, you take plays like Anderson and Stallings' *What Price Glory?* and Hecht and MacArthur's *The Front Page,* which were great influences, I think, and Elmer Rice's *Street Scene.* For the first time, for instance, profanity was used in the way that it's used commonly in the United States. The old hokum of sentimental idealism was destroyed. The war was viewed without the usual ballyhoo of past plays, which made a glorification of it. It was now looked at as a dirty business. A new, brash iconoclasm entered, the contemporaneous cynicism and the gaiety.

I think a great influence was probably David Belasco, who was a naturalist, what we would think of as corny because his plots were frightful. There were scenes in his plays such as the one where the hero is about to be executed and the heroine runs onto the stage with the American flag and throws it over him— and the United States Army could not fire through the flag, naturally.

However, in the making of the productions he was enormously inventive in naturalistic terms. He created volcanoes on the stage —and Child's Restaurant down to the flies on the mince pie. Stanislavsky saw his work and thought Belasco was a very great director. He seized on a tool which the American theater is still using and to much better effect—the naturalistic actor. What was added subsequently was the story whose proportions were closer to the reality as the audience knew it. Robert Sherwood, Maxwell Anderson, S. N. Behrman, Philip Barry, Elmer Rice, George Kelly, Sidney Howard—all began or had their roots in the thirties. They brought it of age.

BRANDON: How does their work strike you now?

MILLER: Today a lot of their work seems mild, a bit too play-conscious and even innocent, despite their efforts to break with the older tradition of pose and stage sham. Some of their work is very fine—the workmanship is good, perhaps too good for our current taste. But some of O'Neill seems more valid now, perhaps because we share his neuroticism. O'Neill spoke like a minority man, like us; the others were more public speakers. We prize the subjective now; they prized craft, wit, comment on manners, iconoclasm.

Some of the best work of these men was done in the thirties, but that epoch was characterized for many people by the minority voices, mainly Clifford Odets and Lillian Hellman. The social playwrights were still trying to be craftsmen, still spoke publicly, but in Odets and Hellman the inner voice broke through in that they personally felt the public anguish of the Fascist years. In Odets a new lyricism; a prose larger than life. In Hellman a remorseless rising line of action in beautifully articulated plays. Both these writers expressed personality—their works identified them. But the symbols were often so tuned to the particulars of the thirties that when that brief cataclysm passed into wartime, their world seemed out of date. It remains to be seen whether this is really so. I am not the one to judge this because I was deeply moved by these plays and remember them with love.

One ought to remember that it was by no means only the "Left" writers who wrote social plays. Maxwell Anderson, Sherwood, Rice, Sidney Howard, even Behrman and Barry were involved with the themes of social and economic disaster, Communism and Fascism. But Odets and Hellman made these themes personal to themselves. They matured with the depression; the others before.

BRANDON: And what followed then?

MILLER: Since the forties, the line of development has been toward more and more intimacy of statement by playwrights and less attention to the older idea of craft, of stage logic. In this sense O'Neill remains the leader. His work is just as full of ill-digested Freudianism as the others, just as absorbed with questions like Socialism, the Negro problem, social justice, etc., and as weighted down as any other with out-of-date slang and mawkish devices and melodrama. But he could not for long be drowned in his moment—we hear his inner voice, we respond to many of its tones. His self-pity, his tortured questing, his relentless doubts, overwhelm his often stagy solutions; the other writers too often were sealed up in their plays.

The fifties became an era of gauze. Tennessee Williams is responsible for this in the main. One of my own feet stands in this stream. It is a cruel, romantic neuroticism, a translation of current life into the war within the self. All conflict tends to be transformed into sexual conflict. The sets have therefore become less and less defined in realistic terms, for the society is more and more implied, or altogether blotted out. Its virtue is it ability to intensify the sensual—using that word to mean the senses, feeling.

It has all moved now to a dangerous extreme of triviality. It is a theater with the blues. The genuine original cry has become a rehearsed scream of a self-conscious whimper. The drama will have to find its way back into the daylight world without losing its inner life. I sometimes long to see a set with a ceiling again. The drama will have to re-address itself to the world beyond the skin, to fate.

BRANDON: Did you see Samuel Beckett's *Waiting for Godot?*

MILLER: I've read it. I never got to see it. I admire that play for the rebellion in it. It is an intimate statement—a very hard thing to do on the stage, and at the same time an abstract of the time. It has feeling and it has a brain. I find it necessary, however, to ask what are its limits—its viability for the future. It enforces upon us a sense of the desolate—which is just what it is designed to do. But I do not think it flexible enough to embrace other moods, so to speak. A criticism of it would be that it is addressed, I think, exclusively to its own cultural level. That is legitimate and proper. But, for myself anyway, the challenge is still the Elizabethan one, the public address on the street corner.

BRANDON: I think that you and Sartre are the two most powerful dramatists today. The difference between you and him, it seems to me, is that his writings are dominated by ideas....

MILLER: There is a great difference between us. For one, I'm writing in a culture that does not truck with ideas; it resists knowing what it is doing. This goes for an ordinary individual and a gigantic corporation.

In France—to a much greater degree—the people are aware that if they don't know what they're doing, it is possible to characterize it objectively anyway; that is, they will concede that *somebody* knows what they're doing, and that this is a legitimate kind of work, so to speak. Here, this sort of approach is a luxury, which a few cloistered people may indulge in, but it's of no consequence. What the hell is the difference if you do know? We believe in necessity here; we're loyal slaves of it. The necessary, here in America, is mistaken for the right. But sometimes men must interfere with the inevitable.

BRANDON: Is this partly due to a certain anti-intellectualism?

MILLER: I would like to make clear my attitude toward the charge of anti-intellectualism in this country. I believe some of this feeling among Europeans and Englishmen is based on a distortion.

My own feeling is that foreigners are overly impressed with the fact that we have no sense here of an intellectual *class*.

I am not at all sure, for instance, that there are more people in other countries who understand what an intellectual *does*. There are more people abroad who have learned to tip their hats to the idea of an intellectual. It reminds me of a barber I used to go to. He'd been cutting my hair for years and never said more than Hello and Thank you until my picture got into the *Daily News* when I won some prize or other. Then he asked me if I had heard of D'Annunzio. (He was an old Italian who could barely speak any English at all.) I said I knew his work. From this time the barber's eyes lit up whenever I came into the shop, and when I sat in his chair, he would give me a warm, rather intimate smile, nod his head, and say, "D'Annunzio." He knew nothing, really, of D'Annunzio's work, but had attached to "D'Annunzio" a feeling of national pride and accomplishment. "D'Annunzio" made the barber feel more valuable.

BRANDON: You had become an intellectual in the eyes of your barber because you knew D'Annunzio.

MILLER: Writers here have no such connotation for the masses as D'Annunzio had for the Italians. Nor would any writer regard himself—as Russian writers have and many French—as spokesman for the national spirit or something of the kind. In a word, we have no status excepting that we are makers of entertainment, or heavy thinkers, or earners of big money.

In the profoundest sense, of course, this is an anti-intellectual attitude, but it is neither hateful nor contemptuous for the most part. The truth is that no other occupation is regarded symbolically as a national adornment, so to speak, excepting, possibly, that of the soldier in wartime. Nor do we have a consciousness of an "American Culture" in the way the French have, and other European nations. But it does not mean we do not value our plays, movies, paintings, music. It is simply that they are enjoyed without being called manifestations of the national spirit.

This has both good and bad consequences. Most obviously, it makes the country appear from outside like a nest of peddlers. Denial of public recognition makes some intellectuals take on an unnatural defensiveness toward themselves, an inferior feeling which breeds isolation and hopelessness and weakness. Perhaps the worst effect is that when, as during the McCarthy period, it is necessary for basic principles of human existence to be upheld, the natural upholders—the intellectuals—are face to face with a population that is unused to listening to their advice.

In a word, we are not so much persecuted as ignored. But everybody else is ignored too. I doubt there is a single professional class in this country which feels it gets due public thanks or recognition. This even includes businessmen who are always revealing a sense of occupational inferiority, and who envy and resent how artists are all the time being publicly acclaimed!

The benefits, if one may call them that, are not inconsiderable. Art here is irrelevant to life, in the minds of most, so it is free to do what it will with life.

BRANDON: Doesn't that depress an artist?

MILLER: Yes. The artist is hard put to reassure himself that his occupation is anything but trivial. And this, I think, is the biggest wound the American attitude inflicts. To survive it, an artist has to cling to his dignity with his teeth sometimes, often at the very moment he is being acclaimed, for it is a rare thing to be acclaimed excepting for irrelevant reasons. But will a public cult of intellectualism really result in a higher understanding of art's relevance to life? If Europe is an example, I wonder.... I have heard, in my very limited experience, some of the loudest avowals of pro-intellectualism from some of the most corrupt and unphilosophical people.

The single important advantage of the attitude, I think, is that it presses the artist the more to overcome it. You have to hit the public when it is not looking, so to speak; you have to make it real to them the way the subway is real. You can't depend on their embracing your work because it is art, but only because it somehow reaches into the part of them that is still alive and questing. This kind of challenge can almost destroy a delicate art like poetry, but for the drama and the novel it can muscularize them. It can also make them musclebound, and strident, and screaming, and sensational. But all I want to make clear at the moment is that the thing is not a dead loss by any means.

BRANDON: Where, do you think, are we moving?

MILLER: One thing the theater will not stand for too long—at least not in this country—is boredom. The blue play is now becoming predictable in mood. We expect a pathetic defeat in the play and the documentation of alienated loneliness. I think they're quite suddenly going to become old hat.

Perhaps it is only my feeling; but I think life is now perhaps less impossible than it was, say, even two years ago. And this is as much a political and social fact as it is a theatrical fact. I mean to say that the possibility of the survival of the human race now appears to be a reasonable hope for a person to take hold of. Certain steps have been taken that would indicate that a rapprochement of some sort can be made between two civilizations.

The theater as yet has not got the reach, the breadth of vision to see much more than the center of the web in which we struggle. But I think there are indications that we may have a right to state once again that all is not lost. And as soon as that really happens, the black air surrounding many plays may appear unjustified; it will not long seem the way things are; and the style itself will seem willful and self-conscious.

On Recognition

I ACCEPTED the Hopwood Committee's invitation to speak today with misgivings. In fact, many years ago I swore that if I were ever asked to, I would never speak on the occasion of the award ceremonies. This, because I recalled too vividly how I sat where you are sitting now, listening to I think it was Christopher Morley droning on and on in what was probably a fascinating way, while on the table were the envelopes with the winners' names inside. If there was ever a captive audience, this is it. You have to listen to me or you don't get your money, and who knows, I could go on for an hour. It is even worse when I know that the very people I am most interested in reaching—namely the best writers among you and presumably the ones who are going to win today—are least likely to be paying me any attention.

So in the hope of flagging down your greedily racing thoughts, I am going to speak today on a subject which, along with money, must surely be on your minds. On Recognition. It may not sound like a particularly literary subject, but you would be amazed at how powerful a force it is in literary affairs. Offhand, I should say that if everybody who expressed a desire to be a

From the *Michigan Quarterly Review*, 2 (October 1963), pp. 213–220. An address delivered at The University of Michigan on May 23, 1963, for the annual Hopwood Awards in creative writing. While a student at the University, Miller won two Hopwood Awards in Drama in 1936 and 1937. Copyright © 1963 by the Regents of The University of Michigan.

writer were automatically recognized and were given a lapel button saying "Writer," approximately eighty percent of those who devote their lives to some form of writing or another would not have bothered. I can even imagine a society in which practically everybody is born a writer, and there is a contest each year in some university where prizes are given for the most persuasive *business proposition*. I can imagine the winners' parents going around boasting, "Imagine, my son won a prize for not writing!" I can imagine the genius businessman in such a society surrounded after his lecture by envious people all asking the same questions—"How did you start? What is it like not to be stuck at home every day, having to write a poem or a play like everybody else, but to go off by yourself into a nice busy office where all you've got to deal with are other people?"

It's hard, but I can imagine it. Distinction, after all, is relative. More precisely, distinction abhors relatives. In some cases it despises just about everybody. The other day I got a pamphlet containing three speeches by writers delivered at the Library of Congress, under some grant or other, and one of them, McKinlay Kantor's, I may as well say, was almost wholly taken up with an attack on other historical novelists who fail to do enough research to justify the honor of being called a historical novelist. It turns out that Lincoln did not have a deep baritone, as some writer had written in a recent best-seller, but a high nasal twang, and that the belt-buckle worn by Union soldiers did not say U.S.A. on it but U.S. He was also mad at Stephen Crane because *The Red Badge of Courage* could have been about any war and was not specifically what it claimed, a book about the Civil War. In short, distinction in itself is no guarantee of anything in particular.

The trouble is that the writer has to win recognition almost before he is recognizable. Before, that is, he is distinct. He needs recognition in order to win it. He therefore has to invent it first in the hope that his invention will be pronounced a fact by the outside world. The effort to first invent one's own distinction, and then to get others to agree to it, is so strenuous that in a great many cases the man is exhausted just when he ought to be starting. But having won his own reality, so to speak, having won his public license to practice his recognition, he faces the danger—possibly the greatest danger writers face in this particular time of enormous publicity and big money—the danger of placing himself in the service of his continuing recognition. In that service he is tempted to repeat with greater polish, perhaps, or louder stridency, what he has done before, in which case his trade mark burns a little deeper into his soul. To the need for recognition, as to the making of books, there is no end. It is finally not enough even to be distinct from others; the time comes when you have to be distinct from yourself, too. That is, it must not be too apparent that you are always writing the same book or play, but on the other hand it is also bad if your work appears to be written by three, four, or six different people. That way you may distinguish yourself as a wonderfully varied writer, but the danger is that you may vary your style out of recognition.

Now this is hardly the time in your lives to be warning you to beware of a mindless pursuit of recognition. In any case, a man who somewhere in his soul does not feel, however shyly, a burning desire to put himself forward, has no business trying to become a writer. I speak on this subject only because of the times in which we live. They are extraordinarily treacherous for a writer. Never was publicity so remorselessly in search of the least signal of a successful author; never was money more plentiful for a successful book or play. The writer motivated by the wish to shine, by that mainly, can very quickly mistake himself for a finished product when in fact he has only begun his rightful and ordained struggle to perfect his art. The pressures of exploitation of literature, the photographic reporter, the television interview, the newspaper and magazine columnists —all these forces tend to press the writer closer to the position of performer. What comes to matter is less his work than the cult which comes to surround his personality.

Obviously, this is hardly the first time or place in history that has sought to celebrate writers, but the quality of celebration has taken on a new tone, not only among us but in a different way in Europe too. The writer, as far as the mass publication and media are concerned, is of interest in much the same way as an actor is, or God save the mark, a politician. He has made himself known and that is all.

Now we have had Hemingway, and Samuel Clemens, and Charles Dickens, and Bernard Shaw, and a long line of writers who were or could easily have been actors had they not been too embarrassed too early in life. Sinclair Lewis actually made the jump and acted in his own plays toward the end of his career, and even so careful a workman and so jealous a man of his own privacy as James Thurber made the eight-thirty curtain night after night in the year or two before he died. Shakespeare was an actor too, but it is important to note that he started as an actor, he did not end as one. I am a pretty good actor myself, despite the impression I may be giving today, and I would probably have become one except that I could never remember lines, and worse yet, have a tendency to change everything I hear. You can't revise with an audience watching, so I act alone in a room, perform all the parts, and come away with the lion's share of the glory.

There is nothing wrong in recognition providing it is not permitted to devaluate, finally, what it is supposed to elevate. Nor is this an entirely esoteric problem. I think it true that fewer American writers have won the mature growth of their art and talent than writers anywhere in the world. As with everyone else, the writer in America is in a country that fits him only when he is young and starting out; as he grows to maturity, or what should be maturity, he is much more likely to have lost his way than to have more securely discovered it. I think one reason for this is the quality of the recognition we give to writers. We recognize him as a success rather than as a writer. It is hard to earn success, but much harder to keep it; evidently it is nearly impossible to forget all about it and keep on calling oneself a writer, but I think it is the only way to earn that much-abused title, that much-abused recognition—it is, for one thing, to never turn pro. In short, to remain a failure, forever unrecognized in one's heart.

This may sound easy, but it is immeasurably more difficult to really admit failure while still accepting the rewards of success —harder than to believe that those rewards truly have a connection with oneself as a writer. To come directly to the point, of how many writers can it be said that their later work was wiser, deeper, more beautiful than what came earlier? Extraordinarily few. As a class, especially in America, the writer is a great beginner and a very bad finisher.

I do not propose to solve this problem today, but some totally ignored fundamentals of what I can only call the fact of the writer seem to me to need repeating. To start at the end of my thought and work backwards, I believe that so many fine and truly talented writers fail of their promise because they adopt the perspective of their society toward themselves. Before I mention an alternative perspective, let me tell you what I think the American perspective—and gradually the European perspective—is toward the writer.

To begin at the absurd extreme, we cannot believe that a writer who is not known is really a writer. Ergo, the more known he is the more writer he is.

There are various proofs that he is known, which is to say, that he is a writer. He has published a book with his name on it, a play has been produced on the stage. He is more of a writer, however, if he has another attribute—if he has made money with his book or play. He is most writer if he has made a fortune. And this will become truer and truer as time passes because it has dawned on publishers now, just as it did on the patent medicine industry in the eighties of the past century, that the more the product is publicized the more reliable it will come to appear.

The distortions forced upon writers by baths of publicity are not all the same. A Salinger reacts by evidently refusing to see or speak to anyone at all. Other writers are busy speaking to everyone on radio, television, and over expensive restaurant tables. You can be driven mad in many different directions by the same cause.

The worst of this distortion is that it undermines the only recognition worth the name: a recognition that a book or a play or a poem has delivered up a genuine insight into the nature of man and the human condition. That you or I happen to have been the author of it is extremely pleasant, but it is not the point. I try to read a work or see a play as though I did not know who the author was. I try to see and read not in order to lay praise on a person or to blame him, but to receive into myself whatever that work is purporting to say to me. The uses of publicity are such that this kind of seeing and reading has become impossible; in fact, it is unimaginable to ninety-nine percent not only of the public but of the critics as well. At the risk of immodesty, warranted I think by the proof it can give, I will say that I try to write in the same mood. To ask of myself, either at the beginning of a work or in the middle, and certainly by the end—what will this add, if anything, to what is known?

Admittedly, this is an old man's question. When I was much younger it would never have occurred to me. I was too eager to find the proof in others' eyes that I in fact was a playwright, and this indeed ought to be so. As I said at the beginning, we must first invent a recognition before it can be recognized, and it matters less what its contribution might be to what has gone before than to what *we* were before we wrote it. But the time does come, or should, I think, when one admits that one has learned one's job and that it is not enough merely to prove it once again. There are and have been writers who have done more through middle and old age and up to the end, and Faulkner is perhaps the most noteworthy, and I say this without being one of his fans. For the most part, however, it seems to me that by far the majority of writers have done and are doing perhaps a little better, perhaps a little worse, what they did before. A writer ought to have the right to shut up when he has nothing he feels he must say; to shut up and still be considered a writer. To consider and still be a writer; to nose about as long as it takes until he can once again enslave himself to some voice that has entered him. I wonder if the destruction of many writers is in part the fear of silence E. M. Forster found; the clarity of aim which can turn back the whorish demand that at all costs he say something, even something not worth the saying, rather than face a deeper suffering, however, which may honestly open out into wisdom and a new art.

The perspective of society, of the world, is the perspective of competition. Again, this is invaluable for the young, who always live in a world of comparisons. It is a way of dying, however, for those no longer young. Hemingway was forever comparing; one year he had "taken on" Dostoevsky; then he was about to "take on" Tolstoy. I strongly doubt that Dostoevsky "took on" any writer, and I know Tolstoy could not have kept such an idea in his head for more than ten minutes. And yet both these men were pursued by a sense of their own failure, but in the correct, if one may use such a word, the proper way. They had failed, as certainly Tolstoy's diaries make clear, and knew they were doomed forever to fail to hear with absolute clarity the voice of their people's suffering. Not the voice of *Time* Magazine, or the voice of the latest fashionable critic, or the voice of the salon, but the only voice whose expression literature was invented for. Which is to say that a writer is a writer not because he is known, and not by how much he is known, but by how truly he hears and sees the essentials of the human situation in his time.

Now it will be objected that there is no contradiction between excellence and the wish to excel, and certainly if proof is needed it is supplied by the competitions among the Greek dramatists at the festival performances of their plays. Nor is King of the Hill a game confined to this age; battles of the books have been fought in many places and in many different times. But there are battles which enliven literature and battles which are non-battles, such as we have today, in which nothing is at stake, neither a literary viewpoint, a social ideal, or any other question of value but who stands on top of the heap. This was finally institutionalized, as it were, in a long article in *The New York Times Book Review* a few months ago. Who, it was asked, will be the new Hemingway and the new Faulkner? Whereupon some ten or so young and middle-aged writers were presented as contenders for the title. The conclusion, as one must expect in the *Times Book Review,* was of course a loud shrug of the shoulders. But even if there could be a conclusion where there cannot be an argument, who should care? And supposing, unbelievable as it sounds, supposing neither Hemingway nor Faulkner twenty years from now, or fifty or ten, turns out to be the best writers of their time? Then truly the crown would not exist at all and the vacuousness of the whole competitive concept would be laughably obvious.

But if the printed consensus and the word-of-mouth augmentation of that opinion is not to guide a young man toward his models and finally toward an evaluation of himself and his work, where can he look? The only answer I know to be unassailable is also unacceptable; it is *nowhere.* Nor am I lamenting this; we live in an age bankrupt of a truly independent public criticism. In one sense it is a fine opportunity, for the new writer today has no critical institution to overthrow. In writing there is no ruling idea to buck or go with, there is no particular style or form either frowned on or overwhelmingly fashionable. The simple truth is that a terribly small number of Americans read books or see plays; I will not even speak of poetry. If fifty thousand copies of a new book are sold it is regarded as a triumph in a country of over a hundred and eighty million. If half a million people see a play it is a monstrous hit and probably a masterpiece, at least that year. So that these readers and playgoers are really tight little islands in a sea of real Americans who don't know they are there and couldn't care less. The pond, as big as it seems, is really quite small, which need not mean that its quality is bad but that the victory it can offer is not the victory it appears to offer. The American people do not play a part in the art works of our time. The working class is all but illiterate, the middle class is mostly sheep frightened of not liking what it should and liking what it shouldn't. As a consequence, I think, of the narrowness of the audience, there is no body of peers worthy of your creative respect. Nobody writing public criticism today represents anybody, at least not anybody with a real crown to give you. I don't like bandying about the names of other writers so I'll use my own work and give you an example.

The Crucible opened in New York in 1954, at the height of the McCarthy hysteria. It got respectful notices, the kind that bury you decently. It ran a few months and closed. In 1960, I believe it was, an Off-Broadway production of the play was put on. The same critics reviewed it again, this time with what are called hit notices, which is to say they were fairly swept away, the drama was as real to them as it had seemed cold and undramatic before. Reasons were given for the new impression; the main one was that the script had been improved.

This rather astonished me, since the scripts were exactly the same in both productions. Worse yet, the cast of the original was all in all far superior to the second production. The answer is quite simple; when McCarthy was around, the critics, reflecting the feeling in the audience, were quite simply in fear of the theme of the play, which was witch hunting. In 1960 they were not afraid of it and they began to look at the play. It is perfectly natural and not even particularly reprehensible. My only point is that had I been a new playwright in 1954, and *The Crucible* my first professional production, and had I looked outside myself for recognition, I would not have found it.

But let us not get too romantic; it is all very well to tell you to look within yourself for your values. The lonely genius ahead of his time is a hallowed image which probably infects more writers with monomania than inspiration. The truth, I think, is that at its best and at its highest, literature is not the monologue the age has made it out to be but a personal conversation beween a people and its artists. Whether it be our educational system, our Puritan tradition suspicious of art, or simply the mechanization of man and his dehumanized nervous system, it cannot be said that a dialogue exists today between the American people and the American artist, excepting the kind who decorate packages.

Nor is this news, of course. Everybody knows about the lonely Melville trudging back and forth to his customs house, unrecognized by anyone around him, even he the author of America's great epic. Everybody knows about Hart Crane, and Sherwood Anderson and God knows how many others who tried to speak to America and got no answer. Some people even know about Samuel Clemens trying to hoist some flag of spirit over an America he saw turning to iron and iron values. There is one word traditional for the American writer—alone. Alone as a failure, alone as a success. But what does it mean? What, you may ask, is the opposite of being alone? Well, the average answer is, together. Like perhaps a movie star is together with his fans, or a ball player, or some other species of entertainer. In other words, the usual response is some kind of recognition. Like wouldn't it be more cultured if a good novelist were mobbed in the street instead of somebody who needs a haircut and plays a guitar? And to be sure, on a much more austere level, the present administration has sought now and then to supply a new recognition. A lot of us have been to the White House. Well then, maybe the solution is to have us all to the White House every other Wednesday or something like that. We might even have a National Writers' Day.

Obviously, recognition of the writer, of his person, is not the issue. Recognition of writing is. Recognition of what writing is for, of why it has a mission, of what its mission is, this kind of recognition is unknown among the people and, for the most part, among those whose business it is to criticize. What is that mission?

Now, I am not going to wax poetic about, let's say, the writer as the conscience of mankind or the voice of the nation's spirit. No one can set out to be a conscience or a voice for anyone but himself, and if he succeeds in even that he is going a long way already. But we are faced with a curious situation; I think it is probably true to say that there are more young writers today than there used to be who have a command of the forms they write in, but are at a loss for something to say. I am sure of this in the theater, and I judge it to be little different in fiction. From my painter friends I get the same sense of bafflement. There is no longer a battle to establish a new form, at least not west of the Russian border. Certainly on the stage you can now do anything from the point of view of form, anything you can possibly imagine. The shape of realism has been shattered; like all the fixed social ideas of the past our art lies in pieces, and some of them are quite beautiful.

Now part of the work of art is to say something to art; Hemingway's early stylistic discoveries spoke not only to the reader but to all the books that had been written before. Joyce spoke to all of literature, Pound to all of poetry. The speech one can make to art itself has been made.

What has not been made, and can never be completed, is the speech one can make to mankind. It seems to me that possibly because most of America does not hear us we have ceased to try to engage a vast attention and have been backed up into the invisible salon of art. There opinions are made, discoveries are registered, the imprimatur is given or withheld, but it is not the source of something to say. The source is in the way men live. But since the mass of men cannot hear us or will not, how can one address the multitude? There is no answer excepting to say that one can imagine doing it. One can write as though the many were in fact listening. Or, if not actually listening, as though the fate of all were at stake on one's pages even as they do not know and cannot know. For the time being the dialogue can only go on from the artist's side; but it is better than to let it die.

All of which is said in face of a certain number of books which in fact have attempted to carry on that dialogue. The underlying scheme of *Lolita* is a painting of American adolescence as it appears in the middle-aged man; *Catch 22* is a frontal attack on the idiocies not only of modern warfare but of society itself; the work of Saul Bellow has reached out beyond the preoccupation with salable sexuality into the investigation of what man might become, which is what *Henderson the Rain King* is especially about. It would be easy to list twenty books, at least, in the past few years, which are in the tradition of the dialogue with mankind, and his general condition; I am not, in other words, attacking writers. It is simply that if we even had National Writers' Week, and open house at the Kennedys' every Thursday, the other half of the dialogue would not have begun. The people, in short, do not read books, do not answer books, and consequently are not in a position to answer for the truth or validity of books. A National Book Award has about the same importance among us as the Grand Prize for the Best Table Setting. I say this in face of the much greater number of paperbacks sold as compared to former years; I say this, moreover, with no assurance whatever that if everybody read two books a week the country would be a better place in which to live. The Germans, for example, have always read an immense number of books, and the Russians too.

So I am concerned not with the sociology of book reading or publishing, or even with improving the country in this context, but with the weight and the maturity of our literature. To make the statement as unvarnished, as clear as I can: I believe the mission of writing is tragedy. I think that in the works in which man is most human, in addition to being the works that last, and reflect most deeply and most truthfully the situation of man on this earth, tragedy must confront the work itself, the artist himself, and the country itself. I believe at bottom, that the word has not yet entered the blood stream of America because it is a country which as yet has no tragic sense of itself. Without that sense, without that longing, a people does not, strictly speaking, need the answers and the formulations which art was made to give. If a people conceives that death is a kind of accident or, worse yet, an inconvenience to be remedied by insurance policies; if its religion is designed to ameliorate suffering rather than to make it meaningful; if its soul-searching is self-blame and psychoanalysis, it is not yet ready to ask the questions a tragic literature can give.

I am not going to launch into what tragedy is, or what I think it is, beyond saying that when Christ hung on the cross it was not tragic until He spoke and asked why God had forsaken Him, and having spoken that shattering doubt, nevertheless did not ask to be taken down, nor wish He had His life to live over again, nor express remorse or a resolution to do differently. Above all, He did not say that He felt nothing, that He was not really on the cross, that His faith had vanquished pain, and that He was sure He had done what He was fated to do.

It is not tragic, which is to say it lacks humanity, which is to say it lacks human meaning, when a people presumes to possess the final answer for all mankind as to what life is for and how to live it. It lacks human meaning, equally, when a people, and a literature, seizes only on doubt and will not accept the torture of trying to believe in the midst of doubt. It lacks human meaning if a literature merely exemplifies what dies and what shows the signs of death, quite as meaninglessly although less obviously than when life and what gives life is all that vision can see. The literature I am talking about engages the tension between an event and the human experience of it; between the meaningless particular career and the situation of the race.

The battle of the writer today is not primarily a battle to break through old forms but against a world-wide conspiracy to call things by their wrong names; it is a battle against human presumption whose end will be, for one thing, the destruction of the planet under the banner of saving mankind. I think that so few American writers have matured because only in the tragic confrontation is there the possibility of escaping from the themes and attitudes and controlling visions of adolescence, that time in a writer's life when his usable sources of wonder and originality are richest, newest, and most deeply embedded in his heart. Our literature, its deepest stamp and line, is the adventure of the young, the young man, the young spirit, the

voyage begun, the first arrival. Two authors come to mind—
three perhaps—who went beyond: Faulkner, Melville, and
O'Neill. But is it not worth noting that Faulkner had to create,
literally, a world in which tragedy was possible, a world manifestly his own and not industrial America? And Melville and
O'Neill had to cut loose to the sea for an arena of tragic action?
Only there, I think, did O'Neill feel at home with his sense
of life. Whatever is mawkish, contrived, learned and unworthy
in his work comes to the high surface whenever he is on land,
where social institutions rule, where Americans really live, and
where the landscape is always inhuman.

I shudder at the thought of giving advice to anyone, let
alone young writers. To paraphrase an old Army poster, your
country needs you, but it doesn't know it. But you have a way
around that: you can pretend it does. You can pretend you are
not at all alone but in a community, a community of mutes,
and you the only one around with the gift of speech. In this
dream you alone have the responsibility for proving to your
people what they are doing, and perhaps what they ought to
do in order to be glorious and true to their nature. Remember,
the writer has one gift from life which nothing can take from
him—he is describing a species that has to die. So when the
mutes signal to you that this world or this country is bound for
glory and you are nothing but a pest, you can always ask if
that's enough to die with, and if not, is it enough to live with?
And if they signal that man is worthless, you, standing at the
lip of the grave, you, with time pouring through your fingers,
meaningless without your shaping hand, you can reply similarly,
that if we are indeed worthless how is it possible that we can
know it when the very concept requires a concept of worth.
You are writers because you have inherited the ageless tension
between despair and faith, the two arms of the tragic cross. The
situation never changes; but man does. How and why is what
you have to say.

Now, forgive me this delay before your moment of recognition. I have kept you in tension between you own self-doubts

and the faith which others may give you in these prizes. Permit me to say that I have won Hopwoods and also lost them, and I know the power that winning gives and the way the soul shakes when, all ears, you hear silence instead of your name. Either way it matters very much and always will, but not as much as knowing that it is not one another we must finally vanquish, but life's brute fist clamped around the reason for our being. To bend back one finger and glimpse what it conceals, and harder yet, to dare remember what one has seen inside that hand—this is the power you have a right to seek and the only recognition worth the work.

III

After the Fall to Lincoln Center

Is the knowing all? To know, and even happily
that we meet unblessed; not in some garden of
wax fruit and painted trees, that lie of Eden,
but after, after the Fall, after many, many
deaths. Is the knowing all?

—Quentin in *After the Fall*

Foreword to *After the Fall*

THIS play is not "about" something; hopefully, it is something. And primarily it is a way of looking at man and his human nature as the only source of the violence which has come closer and closer to destroying the race. It is a view which does not look toward social or political ideas as the creators of violence, but into the nature of the human being himself. It should be clear now that no people or political system has a monopoly on violence. It is also clear that the one common denominator in all violent acts is the human being.

The first real "story" in the Bible is the murder of Abel. Before this drama there is only a featureless Paradise. But in that Eden there was peace because man had no consciousness of himself nor any knowledge of sex or his separateness from plants or other animals. Presumably we are being told that the human being becomes "himself" in the act of becoming aware of his sinfulness. He "is" what he is ashamed of.

After all, the infraction of Eve is that she opened up the knowledge of good and evil. She presented Adam with a choice. So that where choice begins, Paradise ends, Innocence ends, for what is Paradise but the absence of any need to choose this action? And two alternatives open out of Eden. One is

From *The Saturday Evening Post,* 237 (February 1, 1964), p. 32. Copyright © 1964 by Arthur Miller.

Cain's alternative—or, if you will, Oswald's; to express without limit one's unbridled inner compulsion, in this case to murder, and to plead unawareness as a virtue and a defense. The other course is what roars through the rest of the Bible and all history —the struggle of the human race through the millennia to pacify the destructive impulses of man, to express his wishes for greatness, for wealth, for accomplishment, for love, but without turning law and peace into chaos.

The question which finally comes into the open in this play is, how is that pacification to be attained? Quentin, the central character, arrives on the scene weighed down with a sense of his own pointlessness and the world's. His success as an attorney has crumbled in his hands as he sees only his own egotism in it and no wider goal beyond himself. He has lived through two wrecked marriages. His desperation is too serious, too deadly to permit him to blame others for it. He is desperate for a clear view of his own responsibility for his life, and this because he has recently found a woman he feels he can love, and who loves him; he cannot take another life into his hands hounded as he is by self-doubt. He is faced, in short, with what Eve brought to Adam—the terrifying fact of choice. And to choose, one must know oneself, but no man knows himself who cannot face the murder in him, the sly and everlasting complicity with the forces of destruction. The apple cannot be stuck back on the Tree of Knowledge; once we begin to see, we are doomed and challenged to seek the strength to see more, not less. When Cain was questioned, he stood amazed and asked, "Am I my brother's keeper?" Oswald's first words on being taken were, "I didn't do anything." And what country has ever gone into war proclaiming anything but injured innocence? Murder and violence require Innocence, whether real or cultivated. And through Quentin's agony in this play there runs the everlasting temptation of Innocence, that deep desire to return to when, it seems, he was in fact without blame. To that elusive time, which persists in all our minds, when somehow everything was part of us and we so pleasurably at one with others, and everything merely "happened" to us. But the closer he examines those seemingly unified years the clearer it becomes that his Paradise keeps slipping back and back. For there was always his awareness, always the choice, always the conflict between his own needs and desires and the impediments others put in his way. Always, and from the beginning, the panorama of human beings raising up in him and in each other the temptation of the final solution to the problem of being a self at all—the solution of obliterating whatever stands in the way, thus destroying what is loved as well.

This play, then, is a trial; the trial of a man by his own conscience, his own values, his own deeds. The "Listener," who to some will be a psychoanalyst, to others God, is Quentin himself turned at the edge of the abyss to look at his experience, his nature and his time in order to bring to light, to seize and—innocent no more—to forever guard against his own complicity with Cain, and the world's.

But a work of fiction, like an accident witnessed in the street, inevitably gives rise to many differing accounts. Some will call it a play "about" Puritanism, or "about" incest, or "about" the transformation of guilt into responsibility, or whatever. For me it is as much a fact in itself as a new bridge. And in saying this I only dare to express what so many American writers are trying to bring to pass—the day when our novels, plays, pictures and poems will indeed enter into the business of the day, the mindless flight from our own actual experience, a flight which empties out the soul.

What Makes Plays Endure?

MORE than any other art, theater asks for relevance. A play that convinces us that "this is the way it is now" can be excused many shortcomings. At any one moment there is a particular quality of feeling which dominates in human intercourse, a tonality which marks the present from the past, and when this tone is struck on the stage, the theater seems necessary again, like self-knowledge. Lacking this real or apparent contemporaneity, many well-written plays pass quickly into oblivion, their other virtues powerless to convince us of their importance.

Before a play is art it is a kind of psychic journalism, a mirror of its hour, and this reflection of contemporary feeling is exactly what makes so many plays irrelevant to later times. For the last generation was always naïve to this one; all strong feelings tend finally to form into squares as time goes by. For nearly a decade O'Neill had little appeal. When life seemed enslaved to Economics, it was old-fashioned and pointless to stare so at Fate.

But "conditions" change rather swiftly and nothing is harder to remember, let alone convey to a later generation, than the quality of an earlier period. What finally survives, when any-

From *The New York Times,* August 15, 1965, Sec. 2, pp. 1, 3. Copyright 1965 © by Arthur Miller.

thing does, are archetypal characters and relationships which can be transferred to the new period.

Ibsen's focal point of attack, his contemporaneity, was rebellion against small-town narrowness, smugness, the sealed morality whose real fruit was spiritual death. But we cannot bring *his* context to *Hedda Gabler* any more. Society, conditions, have melted away and she lives autonomously now, a recognizable neurotic who transcends her historical moment. The journalistic shell of a play—its reflective mirror surface—is its mortal part without which it could not be born. But its transcendency springs from the author's blindness rather than his sight, from his having identified himself with a character or a situation rather than from his criticism of it.

Thus, history unveils the painful irony, the irony without which no play continues to live: that without a certain love for what he hates, without a touch of hands with his adversary, his work will not outlive its necessary journalism, its mortal frame. Perhaps this is why the seeing of old works is always underscored by a kind of consolation, a conciliation at least. It is like reading of old wars in which the heroism of the enemy is finally conceded and something like Truth seems to appear.

The relations of a particular play to its time are therefore shifting and complicated. Consciously or not, a writer is addressing not only his audience, his own past or his present agonies, but also other plays, his wife's mood, an item in the paper, a lost lover, a face he saw in a crowd. "Why" a play was written is really unanswerable, the more so as it survives its first moment at all. But some things can be said about the genesis of *A View from the Bridge,* which, at least, throw some light on theatrical conditions and one man's reaction to them ten years ago, and possibly on the play itself.

The first condition that ought to be mentioned is that the play was not written for Broadway or the commercial theater. A man I hardly knew then—Martin Ritt—was acting in *The Flowering Peach* by Clifford Odets; the play was losing business and the cast wanted to use the theater, which was closed on Sundays, to put on one-act plays for invited audiences free of charge. I had never written one-acters, but I said I would think about it.

Within the next three or four weeks I wrote *A Memory of Two Mondays* and *A View from the Bridge*. By the time they were finished *The Flowering Peach* had closed, and the project ended up on Broadway as a regular commercial production. I mention this genesis only to indicate why both plays, for different and even opposite reasons, were to one side of the then reigning ideas in the theater.

Memory is a plotless and leisurely play, an exploration of a mood, the mood of the thirties and the pathos of people forever locked into the working day. Some people paid me the inverse compliment of saying it had been written twenty years earlier and dredged out of the drawer, but, in fact, it was a reaching toward some kind of bedrock reality at a time, in 1954, when it seemed to me that the very notion of human relatedness had come apart.

It was McCarthy's time, when even the most remote conception of human solidarity was either under terrific attack or forgotten altogether. *A Memory of Two Mondays,* however lyrical and even nostalgic, was the evocation of a countervailing idea, the idea, quite simply, of "other people," of sympathy for others, and finally of what I believed must come again lest we lose our humanity—a sense of sharing a common fate even as one escaped from it.

Bridge, written in the same month, was the other side of the same coin. What kills Eddie Carbone is nothing visible or heard, but the built-in conscience of the community whose existence he has menaced by betraying it. Whatever both plays are, they are at bottom reassertions of the existence of the community. A solidarity that may be primitive but which finally administers a self-preserving blow against its violators. In both plays there is a search for some fundamental fiat, not moral in itself but ultimately so, which keeps a certain order among us, enough to keep us from barbarism.

It was still a time when Absurdity had a pejorative connotation, and was a kind of moral insanity; for when a senator, waving empty file cards in his hand, could strike terror into the highest government officials, how could one relish Absurdity, how could one simply stop there and merely report, in a play, that life had turned out to be utterly senseless? The Absurd was something one had to be able to afford. The abrogation of cause and effect was entertaining so long as one had never felt the effects.

This pressure of the time's madness is reflected in the strict and orderly cause-and-effect structure of *A View from the Bridge*. Apart from its meaning, the manner in which the story itself is told was a rejection of that enervated "acceptance" of illogic which was the new wisdom of the age. Here, actions had consequences again, betrayal was not greeted with a fashionably lobotomized smile.

To be sure, any such considerations lie to one side of an evaluation of any play as a play, but they are not entirely personal either. A few nights before the play's opening in London, for example, I asked Peter Brook, who was directing it, whether its locale and characters would be comprehensible to the British. "They may find it bizarre, but they like that sort of thing," he said. "What may put them off, though, is its logical inevitability. The British are terribly disturbed by any suggestion that the future is so closely determined by the present. If that were so, you see, we should have to blow our brains out. Of course, this is all happening in Brooklyn, and they may allow it there."

In France, where he also directed the play, its logic was of course taken for granted and, with Raf Vallone as Eddie, it became a tale of sexual passion. *Cavalleria Rusticana* cropped up in the Italian reviews. In Russia last winter I saw it and was astounded to hear Eddie, in the first ten minutes of the play, facing Catherine in the presence of his wife, and announcing that he was in love with the girl—they had simply eliminated anything subconscious from the whole story.

A phone call from an actor in a failing play, the temper of the American fifties, my own relationships to the time—none of it matters, excepting that it all went into the writing of the play whose present relevance or irrelevance stems from God knows what shifting forces of the hour. *Death of a Salesman* was hardly noticed when it opened in Paris some fifteen years ago. A new production now is a great success. In 1950, Willy was a man from Mars. Today, the French are up to their necks in time payments, broken washing machines, dreams of fantastic success, new apartment houses shading out the vegetables in the back-yard, and the chromed anxiety of a society where nothing deserves existence that doesn't pay.

Recently, as I watched Ulu Grosbard's production of *A View from the Bridge* downtown, it was striking how the passage of time, the shifting of social context and even the theatrical context, both reinforces the original impulse behind the writing of a play and distorts it. Ironically, the play written for a Sunday night and an informal group of actors rather than a Broadway production, was finally being done more or less that way and it was simpler than the original, authentic and plain.

The audience that night was very young, sprawled in the current attitudes of the cool. Characters get excited at the prospect of buying a rug, making forty dollars a week, a girl is untouched at the age of seventeen.

The laughter, at first, seems to come at the wrong moments, full of strange surprise. And Eddie enters the play not like a tragic character but a longshoreman scratching himself after a long day on the ships. The audience seems to be watching it from a British distance, an exotic workers' world where people do get caught in a dilemma and not stylishly but for real, and as the plot unfolds and the silence deepens in the little theater, the cool goes, the sprawls tighten up, and one knows that even though Catherine and Rodolpho now do the frug to the rock 'n' roll phonograph record instead of the original, sedate-seeming dance, and the question of informers no longer means very much, something human is working all by itself, sprung free of the original context, perhaps even purified of any of its author's preoccupations at the time of writing.

And yet one knows that, while this purely human spectacle is the ultimate fruit of any work, one will, nevertheless, sit down to write again at a particular hour pressed by the unique weight of a particular day, addressing that day and that hour whose consequences will not even appear to the audience a year or two hence, to say nothing of a decade or in another country. It is the kind of lesson one must remember and forget at the same time.

Arthur Miller: An Interview

INTERVIEW BY OLGA CARLISLE AND ROSE STYRON

INTERVIEWER: After reading your short stories, especially "The Prophecy" and "I Don't Need You Any More," which have not only the dramatic power of your plays but also the description of place, the *foreground,* the intimacy of thought hard to achieve in a play, I wonder: is the stage much more compelling for you?

MILLER: It is only very rarely that I can feel in a short story that I'm right on top of something, as I feel when I write for the stage. I am then in the ultimate place of vision—you can't back me up any further. Everything is inevitable, down to the last comma. In a short story, or any kind of prose, I still can't escape the feeling of a certain arbitrary quality. Mistakes go by—people consent to them more—more than mistakes do on the stage. This may be my illusion. But there's another matter; the whole business of my own role in my own mind. To me the great thing is to write a good play, and when I'm writing a short story it's as though I'm saying to myself, Well, I'm only doing this because I'm not writing a play at the moment. There's guilt connected with it. Naturally I do enjoy writing a short story; it is a form that has a certain strictness. I think I reserve for plays those

From *The Paris Review,* 10 (Summer 1966), pp. 61–98. Copyright © 1967 by The Paris Review, Inc. The first few lines of the interview on the quality of the Connecticut landscape surrounding Miller's home have been deleted.

things which take a kind of excruciating effort. What comes easier goes into a short story.

INTERVIEWER: Would you tell us a little about the beginning of your writing career?

MILLER: The first play I wrote was in Michigan in 1935. It was written on a spring vacation in six days. I was so young that I dared do such things, begin it and finish it in a week. I'd seen about two plays in my life, so I didn't know how long an act was supposed to be, but across the hall there was a fellow who did the costumes for the University theater and he said, "Well, it's roughly forty minutes." I had written an enormous amount of material and I got an alarm clock. It was all a lark to me, and not to be taken too seriously . . . that's what I told myself. As it turned out, the acts were longer than that, but the sense of the timing was in me even from the beginning, and the play had a form right from the start.

Being a playwright was always the maximum idea. I'd always felt that the theater was the most exciting and the most demanding form one could try to master. When I began to write, one assumed inevitably that one was in the mainstream that began with Aeschylus and went through about twenty-five hundred years of playwriting. There are so few masterpieces in the theater, as opposed to the other arts, that one can pretty well encompass all of them by the age of nineteen. Today, I don't think playwrights care about history. I think they feel that it has no relevance.

INTERVIEWER: Is it just the young playwrights who feel this?

MILLER: I think the young playwrights I've had any chance to talk to are either ignorant of the past or they feel the old forms are too square, or too cohesive. I may be wrong, but I don't see that the whole tragic arch of the drama has had any effect on them.

INTERVIEWER: Which playwrights did you most admire when you were young?

MILLER: Well, first the Greeks, for their magnificent form, the symmetry. Half the time I couldn't really repeat the story because the characters in the mythology were completely blank to me. I had no background at that time to know really what was involved in these plays, but the architecture was clear. One looks at some building of the past whose use one is ignorant of, and yet it has a modernity. It had its own specific gravity. That form has never left me; I suppose it just got burned in.

INTERVIEWER: You were particularly drawn to tragedy, then?

MILLER: It seemed to me the only form there was. The rest of it was all either attempts at it, or escapes from it. But tragedy was the basic pillar.

INTERVIEWER: When *Death of a Salesman* opened, you said to *The New York Times* in an interview that the tragic feeling is evoked in us when we're in the presence of a character who is ready to lay down his life, if need be, to secure one thing—his sense of personal dignity. Do you consider your plays modern tragedies?

MILLER: I changed my mind about it several times. I think that to make a direct or arithmetical comparison between any contemporary work and the classic tragedies is impossible because of the question of religion and power, which was taken for granted and is an a priori consideration in any classic tragedy. Like a religious ceremony, where they finally reached the objective by the sacrifice. It has to do with the community sacrificing some man whom they both adore and despise in order to reach its basic and fundamental laws and, therefore, justify its existence and feel safe.

INTERVIEWER: In *After the Fall,* although Maggie was "sacrificed," the central character, Quentin, survives. Did you see him as tragic or in any degree potentially tragic?

MILLER: I can't answer that, because I can't, quite frankly, separate in my mind tragedy from death. In some people's minds I know there's no reason to put them together. I can't break it— for one reason, and that is, to coin a phrase: there's nothing like death. Dying isn't like it, you know. There's no substitute for the impact on the mind of the spectacle of death. And there is no possibility, it seems to me, of speaking of tragedy without it.

Because if the total demise of the person we watch for two or three hours doesn't occur, if he just walks away, no matter how damaged, no matter how much he suffers—

INTERVIEWER: What were those two plays you had seen before you began to write?

MILLER: When I was about twelve, I think it was, my mother took me to a theater one afternoon. We lived in Harlem and in Harlem there were two or three theaters that ran all the time and many women would drop in for all or part of the afternoon performances. All I remember was that there were people in the hold of a ship, the stage was rocking—they actually rocked the stage—and some cannibal on the ship had a time bomb. And they were all looking for the cannibal: it was thrilling. The other one was a morality play about taking dope. Evidently there was much excitement in New York then about the Chinese and dope. The Chinese were kidnapping beautiful blond, blue-eyed girls who, people thought, had lost their bearings morally; they were flappers who drank gin and ran around with boys. And they inevitably ended up in some basement in Chinatown, where they were irretrievably lost by virtue of eating opium or smoking some pot. Those were the two masterpieces I had seen. I'd read some others, of course, by the time I started writing. I'd read Shakespeare and Ibsen, a little, not much. I never connected playwriting with our theater, even from the beginning.

INTERVIEWER: Did your first play have any bearing on *All My Sons,* or *Death of a Salesman?*

MILLER: It did. It was a play about a father owning a business in 1935, a business that was being struck, and a son being torn between his father's interests and his sense of justice. But it turned into a near-comic play. At that stage of my life I was removed somewhat. I was not Clifford Odets: he took it head on.

INTERVIEWER: Many of your plays have that father-son relationship as the dominant theme. Were you very close to your father?

MILLER: I was. I still am, but I think, actually, that my plays don't reflect directly my relationship to him. It's a very primitive thing in my plays. That is, the father was really a figure who incorporated both power and some kind of a moral law which he had either broken himself or had fallen prey to. He figures as an immense shadow....I didn't expect that of my own father, literally, but of his position, apparently I did. The reason that I was able to write about the relationship, I think now, was because it had a mythical quality to me. If I had ever thought that I was writing about my father, I suppose I never could have done it. My father is, literally, a much more realistic guy than Willy Loman, and much more successful as a personality. And he'd be the last man in the world to ever commit suicide. Willy is based on an individual whom I knew very little, who was a salesman; it was years later that I realized I had only seen that man about a total of four hours in twenty years. He gave one of those impressions that is basic, evidently. When I thought of him, he would simply be a mute man: he said no more than two hundred words to me. I was a kid. Later on, I had another of that kind of a contact, with a man whose fantasy was always overreaching his real outline. I've always been aware of that kind of an agony, of someone who has some driving, implacable wish in him which never goes away, which he can never block out. And it broods over him, it makes him happy sometimes or it makes him suicidal, but it never leaves him. Any hero whom we even begin to think of as tragic is obsessed, whether it's Lear or Hamlet or the women in the Greek plays.

INTERVIEWER: Do any of the younger playwrights create heroes —in your opinion?

MILLER: I tell you, I may be working on a different wave length, but I don't think they are looking at character any more, at the documentation of facts about people. All experience is looked at now from a schematic point of view. These playwrights won't let the characters escape for a moment from their preconceived scheme of how dreadful the world is. It is very much like the old strike plays. The scheme then was that someone began a play with a bourgeois ideology and got involved in some area of experience which had a connection to the labor movement— either it was actually a strike or, in a larger sense, it was the collapse of capitalism—and he ended the play with some new positioning vis-à-vis that collapse. He started without an enlightenment and he ended with some kind of enlightenment. And you could predict that in the first five minutes. Very few of those plays could be done any more, because they're absurd now. I've found over the years that a similar thing has happened with the so-called absurd theater. Predictable.

INTERVIEWER: In other words, the notion of tragedy about which you were talking earlier is absent from this preconceived view of the world.

MILLER: Absolutely. The tragic hero was supposed to join the scheme of things by his sacrifice. It's a religious thing, I've always thought. He threw some sharp light upon the hidden scheme of existence, either by breaking one of its profoundest laws, as Oedipus breaks a taboo, and therefore proves the existence of the taboo, or by proving a moral world at the cost of his own life. And that's the victory. We need him, as the vanguard of the race. We need his crime. That crime is a civilizing crime. Well, *now* the view is that it's an inconsolable universe. Nothing is proved by a crime excepting that some people are freer to produce crime than others, and usually they are more honest than the others. There is no final reassertion of a community at all. There isn't the kind of communication that a child demands. The best you could say is that it is intelligent.

INTERVIEWER: Then it's aware—

MILLER: It's aware, but it will not admit into itself any moral universe at all. Another thing that's missing is the positioning of the author in relation to power. I always assumed that underlying any story is the question of who should wield power. See, in *Death of a Salesman* you have two viewpoints. They show what would happen if we all took Willy's viewpoint toward the world, or if we all took Biff's. And took it seriously, as almost a political fact. I'm debating really which way the world ought to be run; I'm speaking of psychology and the spirit, too. For example, a play that isn't usually linked with this kind of problem is Tennessee Williams' *Cat on a Hot Tin Roof*. It struck me sharply that what is at stake there is the father's great power. He's the owner, literally, of an empire of land and farms. And he wants to immortalize that power, he wants to hand it on, because he's dying. The son has a much finer appreciation of justice and human relations than the father. The father is rougher, more Philistine; he's cruder; and when we speak of the fineness of emotions, we would probably say the son has them and the father lacks them. When I saw the play I thought, This is going to be simply marvelous because the person with the sensitivity will be presented with power and what is he going to do about it? But it never gets to that. It gets deflected onto a question of personal neurosis. It comes to a dead end. If we're talking about tragedy, the Greeks would have done something miraculous with that idea. They would have stuck the son with the power, and faced him with the racking conflicts of the sensitive man having to rule. And then you would throw light on what the tragedy of power is.

INTERVIEWER: Which is what you were getting at in *Incident at Vichy*.

MILLER: That's exactly what I was after. But I feel today's stage turns away from any consideration of power, which always lies at the heart of tragedy. I use Williams' play as an example because he's that excellent that his problems are symptomatic of the time—*Cat* ultimately came down to the mendacity of human relations. It was a most accurate personalization but it bypasses the issue which the play seems to me to raise, namely the mendacity in social relations. I still believe that when a play questions, even threatens, our social arrangement, that is when it really shakes us profoundly and dangerously, and that is when you've got to be great; good isn't enough.

INTERVIEWER: Do you think that people in general now rationalize so, and have so many euphemisms for death, that they can't face tragedy?

MILLER: I wonder whether there isn't a certain—I'm speaking now of all classes of people—you could call it a softness, or else a genuine inability to face the tough decisions and the dreadful results of error. I say that only because when *Death of a Salesman* went on again recently, I sensed in some of the reaction that it was simply too threatening. Now there were probably a lot of people in the forties, when it first opened, who felt the same way. Maybe I just didn't hear those people as much as I heard other people—maybe it has to do with my own reaction. You need a certain amount of confidence to watch tragedy. If you yourself are about to die, you're not going to see that play. I've always thought that the Americans had, almost inborn, a primordial fear of falling, being declassed—you get it with your driver's license, if not earlier.

INTERVIEWER: What about Europeans?

MILLER: Well, the play opened in Paris again only last September; it opened in Paris ten years earlier, too, with very little effect. It wasn't a very good production, I understand. But now suddenly they discovered this play. And I sensed that their reaction was quite an American reaction. Maybe it comes with having...having the guilt of wealth; it would be interesting if the Russians ever got to feel that way!

INTERVIEWER: *Death of a Salesman* has been done in Russia, hasn't it?

MILLER: Oh, many times.

INTERVIEWER: When you were in Russia recently did you form any opinion about the Russian theater public?

MILLER: First of all, there's a wonderful naïveté that they have; they're not bored to death. They're not coming in out of the rain, so to speak, with nothing better to do. When they go to the theater, it has great weight with them. They come to see something that'll change their lives. Ninety percent of the time, of course, there's nothing there, but they're open to a grand experience. This is not the way we go to the theater.

INTERVIEWER: What about the plays themselves?

MILLER: I think they do things on the stage which are exciting and deft and they have marvelous actors, but the drama itself is not adventurous. The plays are basically a species of naturalism; it's not even realism. They're violently opposed to the theater of the absurd because they see it as a fragmenting of the community into perverse individuals who will no longer be under any mutual obligation at all, and I can see some point in their fear. Of course, these things should be done if only so one can rebut them. I know that I was very moved in many ways by German expressionism when I was in school: yet there too something was perverse in it to me. It was the end of man, there are no people in it any more; that was especially true of the real German stuff: it's the bitter end of the world where man is a voice of his class function, and that's it. Brecht has a lot of that in him, but he's too much of a poet to be enslaved by it. And yet, at the same time, I learned a great deal from it. I used elements of it that were fused into *Death of a Salesman*. For instance, I purposefully would not give Ben any character, because for Willy he *has* no character—which is, psychologically, expressionist because so many memories come back with a simple tag on them: somebody represents a threat to you, or a promise.

INTERVIEWER: Speaking of different cultures, what is your feeling about the French Théâtre National Populaire?

MILLER: I thought a play I saw by Corneille, *L'Illusion Comique,* one of the most exciting things I've ever seen. We saw something I never thought I could enjoy—my French is not all that good. But I had just gotten over being sick, and we were about to leave France, and I wanted to see what they did with it. It was just superb. It is one of Corneille's lesser works, about a magician who takes people into the nether regions. What a marvelous mixture of satire, and broad comedy, and characterizations! And the acting was simply out of this world. Of course, one of the best parts about the whole thing was the audience. Because they're mostly under thirty, it looked to me; they pay very little to get in; and I would guess there are between twenty-five hundred and three thousand seats in that place. And the vitality of the audience is breathtaking. Of course the actors' ability to speak that language so beautifully is just in itself a joy. From that vast stage, to talk quietly, and make you *feel* the voice just wafting all over the house...

INTERVIEWER: Why do you think we haven't been able to do such a thing here? Why has Whitehead's Lincoln Center Repertory Theater failed as such?

MILLER: Well, that is a phenomenon worthy of a sociological study. When I got into it, *After the Fall* was about two-thirds written. Whitehead came to me and said, "I hear you're writing a play. Can we use it to start the Lincoln Center Repertory Company?" For one reason or another I said I would do it. I expected to take a financial beating (I could hope to earn maybe twenty percent of what I normally earn with a play, but I assumed that people would say, "Well, it's a stupid but not idiotic action"). What developed, before any play opened at all, was a hostility which completely dumfounded me. I don't think it was directed against anybody in particular. For actors who want to develop their art, there's no better place to do it than in a permanent repertory company, where you play different parts and you have opportunities you've never had in a lifetime on Broadway. But the actors seemed to be affronted by the whole thing. I couldn't dig it! I could understand the enmity of commercial producers who, after all, thought they were threatened by it. But the professional people of every kind greeted it as though it were some kind of an insult. The only conclusion I can come to is that an actor was now threatened with having to put up or shut up. He had always been able to walk around on Broadway, where conditions were dreadful, and say, "I'm a great actor but I'm unappreciated," but in the back of his mind he could figure, "Well, one of these days I'll get a starring role and I'll go to Hollywood and get rich." This he couldn't do in a repertory theater where he signed up for several years. So the whole idea of that kind of quick success was renounced. He didn't want to face an opportunity which threatened him in this way. It makes me wonder whether there is such a profound alienation among artists that any organized attempt to create something that is not based upon commerce, that has sponsorship, automatically sets people against it. I think that's an interesting facet. I also spoke to a group of young playwrights. Now, if it had been me, I would have been knocking at the door, demanding that they read my play, as I did unsuccessfully when the Group Theatre was around. Then every playwright was banging on the door and furious and wanted the art theater to do what *he* thought they should do. We could do that because it belonged to us all—you know—we thought of the Group Theatre as a public enterprise. Well, that wasn't true at all here. Everyone thought the Lincoln Theater was the property of the directors, of Miller and Whitehead and Kazan and one or two other people. Of course, what also made it fail was, as Laurence Olivier suggested, that it takes years to do anything. But he also made the point that with his English repertory theater he got encouragement from the beginning. There were people who pooh-poohed the whole thing, and said it was ridiculous, but basically the artistic community was in favor of it.

INTERVIEWER: How about the actors themselves? Did Lee Strasberg influence them?

MILLER: I think Strasberg is a symptom, really. He's a great force, and (in my unique opinion, evidently) a force which is not for the good in the theater. He makes actors secret people and he makes acting secret, and it's the most communicative art known to man; I mean, that's what the actor's *supposed* to be doing. But I wouldn't blame the Repertory Theater failures on him, because the people in there were not Actors Studio people at all; so he is not responsible for that. But the Method is in the air: the actor is defending himself from the Philistine, vulgar public. I had a girl in my play I couldn't hear, and the acoustics in that little theater we were using were simply magnificent. I said to her, "I can't hear you," and I kept on saying, "I can't hear you." She finally got furious and said to me, in effect, that she was acting the truth, and that she was not going to prostitute herself to the audience. That was the living end! It reminded me of Walter Hampden's comment—because we had a similar problem in *The Crucible* with some actors—he said they play a cello with the most perfect bowing and the fingering is magnificent but there are no strings on the instrument. The problem is that the actor is now working out his private fate through his role, and the idea of communicating the meaning of the play is the last thing that occurs to him. In the Actors Studio, despite denials, the actor is told that the text is really the framework for his emotions; I've heard actors change the order of lines in my work and tell me that the lines are only, so to speak, the libretto for the music—that the actor is the main force that the audience is watching and that the playwright is his servant. They are told that the analysis of the text, and the rhythm of the text, the verbal texture, is of no importance whatever. This is Method, as they are teaching it, which is, of course, a perversion of it, if you go back to the beginning. But there was always a tendency in that direction. Chekhov, himself, said that Stanislavsky had perverted *The Seagull*.

INTERVIEWER: What about Method acting in the movies?

MILLER: Well, in the movies, curiously enough, the Method works better. Because the camera can come right up to an actor's nostrils and suck out of him a communicative gesture; a look in the eye, a wrinkle of his grin, and so on, which registers nothing on the stage. The stage is, after all, a verbal medium. You've got to make large gestures if they're going to be seen at all. In other words, you've got to be unnatural. You've got to say, I am out to move into that audience; that's my job. In a movie you don't do that; as a matter of fact, that's bad movie acting, it's overacting. Movies are wonderful for private acting.

INTERVIEWER: Do you think the movies helped bring about this private acting in the theater?

MILLER: Well, it's a perversion of the Chekhovian play and of the Stanislavsky technique. What Chekhov was doing was eliminating the histrionics of his actors by incorporating them in the writing: the internal life was what he was writing about. And Stanislavsky's direction was also internal: for the first time he was trying to motivate every move from within instead of imitating an action; which is what acting should be. When you eliminate the vital element of the actor in the community and simply make a psychiatric figure on the stage who is thinking profound thoughts which he doesn't let anyone know about, then it's a perversion.

INTERVIEWER: How does the success of Peter Weiss's *Marat/Sade* play fit into this?

MILLER: Well, I would emphasize its production and direction. Peter Brook has been trying for years, especially through productions of Shakespeare, to make the bridge between psychological acting and theater, between the private personality, perhaps, and its public demonstration. *Marat/Sade* is more an oratorio than a play; the characters are basically thematic relationships rather than human entities, so the action exemplified rather than characterized.

INTERVIEWER: Do you think the popularity of the movies has had any influence on playwriting itself?

MILLER: Yes. Its form has been changed by the movies. I think certain techniques, such as the jumping from place to place, although it's as old as Shakespeare, came to us not through Shakespeare, but through the movies, a telegraphic, dream-constructed way of seeing life.

INTERVIEWER: How important is the screenwriter in motion pictures?

MILLER: Well, you'd be hard put to remember the dialogue in some of the great pictures that you've seen. That's why pictures are so international. You don't have to hear the style of the dialogue in an Italian movie or a French movie. We're watching the film, so that the vehicle is not the ear or the word, it's the eye. The director of a play is nailed to words. He can interpret them a little differently, but he has limits: you can only inflect a sentence in two or three different ways, but you can inflect an image on the screen in an infinite number of ways. You can make one character practically fall out of the frame; you can shoot it where you don't even see his face. Two people can be talking, and the man talking cannot be seen, so the emphasis is on the reaction to the speech rather than on the speech itself.

INTERVIEWER: What about television as a medium for drama?

MILLER: I don't think there is anything that approaches the theater. The sheer presence of a living person is always stronger than his image. But there's no reason why TV shouldn't be a terrific medium. The problem is that the audience watching TV shows is always separated. My feeling is that people in a group, en masse, watching something, react differently, and perhaps more profoundly, than they do when they're alone in their living rooms. Yet it's not a hurdle that couldn't be jumped by the right kind of material. Simply, it's hard to get good movies, it's hard to get good novels, it's hard to get good poetry—it's *impossible* to get good television because in addition to the indigenous difficulties there's the whole question of it being a medium that's controlled by big business. It took TV seventeen years to do *Death of a Salesman* here. It's been done on TV in every country in the world at least once, but it's critical of the business world and the content is downbeat.

INTERVIEWER: A long time ago, you used to write radio scripts. Did you learn much about technique from that experience?

MILLER: I did. We had twenty-eight and a half minutes to tell a whole story in a radio play, and you had to concentrate on the words because you couldn't see anything. You were playing in a dark closet, in fact. So the economy of words in a good radio play was everything. It drove you more and more to realize what the power of a good sentence was, and the right phrase could save you a page you would otherwise be wasting. I was always sorry radio didn't last long enough for contemporary poetic movements to take advantage of it, because it's a natural medium for poets. It's pure voice, pure words. Words and silence; a marvelous medium. I've often thought, even recently, that I would like to write another radio play, and just give it to someone and let them do it on WBAI. The English do radio plays still, very good ones.

INTERVIEWER: You used to write verse drama too, didn't you?

MILLER: Oh yes, I was up to my neck in it.

INTERVIEWER: Would you ever do it again?

MILLER: I might. I often write speeches in verse, and then break them down. Much of *Death of a Salesman* was originally written in verse, and *The Crucible* was all written in verse, but I broke it up. I was frightened that the actors would take an attitude toward the material that would destroy its vitality. I didn't want anyone standing up there making speeches. You see, we have no tradition of verse, and as soon as an American actor sees something printed like verse, he immediately puts one foot in front of the other—or else he mutters. Then you can't hear it at all.

INTERVIEWER: Which of your own plays do you feel closest to now?

MILLER: I don't know if I feel closer to one than another. I suppose *The Crucible* in some ways. I think there's a lot of myself in it. There are a lot of layers in there that I know about that nobody else does.

INTERVIEWER: More so than in *After the Fall?*

MILLER: Yes, because although *After the Fall* is more psychological it's less developed as an artifice. You see, in *The Crucible* I was completely freed by the period I was writing about—over three centuries ago. It was a different diction, a different age. I had great joy writing that, more than with almost any other play I've written. I learned about how writers felt in the past when they were dealing almost constantly with historical material. A dramatist writing history could finish a play Monday and start another Wednesday, and go right on. Because the *stories* are all prepared for him. Inventing the story is what takes all the time. It takes a year to invent the story. The historical dramatist doesn't have to invent anything, except his language, and his characterizations. Oh, of course, there's the terrific problem of condensing history, a lot of reshuffling and bringing in characters who never lived, or who died a hundred years apart—but basically if you've got the story, you're a year ahead.

INTERVIEWER: It must also be tempting to use a historical figure whose epoch was one of faith.

MILLER: It is. With all the modern psychology and psychiatry and the level of literacy higher than it ever was, we get less perspective on ourselves than at almost any time I know about. I have never been so aware of clique ideas overtaking people—fashions, for example—and sweeping them away, as though the last day of the world had come. One can sometimes point to a week or month in which things changed abruptly. It's like women's clothing in a certain issue of *Vogue* magazine. There is such a wish to be part of that enormous minority that likes to create new minorities. Yet people are desperately afraid of being alone.

INTERVIEWER: Has our insight into psychology affected this?

MILLER: It has simply helped people rationalize their situation, rather than get out of it, or break through it. In other words—you've heard it a hundred times—"Well, I am this type of person, and this type doesn't do anything but what I'm doing."

INTERVIEWER: Do you think the push toward personal success dominates American life now more than it used to?

MILLER: I think it's far more powerful today than when I wrote *Death of a Salesman*. I think it's closer to a madness today than it was then. Now there's no perspective on it at all.

INTERVIEWER: Would you say that the girl in *After the Fall* is a symbol of that obsession?

MILLER: Yes, she is consumed by what she does, and instead of it being a means of release, it's a jail. A prison which defines her, finally. She can't break through. In other words, success, instead of giving freedom of choice, becomes a way of life. There's no country I've been to where people, when you come into a room and sit down with them, so often ask you, "What do you do?" And, being American, many's the time I've almost asked that question, then realized it's good for my soul not to know. For a while! Just to let the evening wear on and see what I think of this person without knowing what he does and how successful he is, or what a failure. We're *ranking* everybody every minute of the day.

INTERVIEWER: Will you write about American success again?

MILLER: I might, but you see, as a thing in itself, success is self-satirizing; it's self-elucidating, in a way. That's why it's so difficult to write about. Because the very people who are being swallowed up by this ethos nod in agreement when you tell them, "You are being swallowed up by this thing." To really wrench them and find them another feasible perspective is therefore extremely difficult.

INTERVIEWER: In your story "The Prophecy," the protagonist says this is a time of the supremacy of personal relations, that there are no larger aims in our lives. Is this your view too?

MILLER: Well, that story was written under the pall of the fifties, but I think there's been a terrific politicalization of the people these past four or five years. Not in the old sense, but in the sense that it is no longer gauche or stupid to be interested in the fate of society and in injustice and in race problems and the rest of it. It now becomes aesthetic material once again. In the fifties it was *out* to mention this. It meant you were really not an artist. That prejudice seems to have gone. The Negroes broke it up, thank God! But it has been an era of personal relations—and now it's being synthesized in a good way. That is, the closer you get to any kind of political action among young people, the more they demand that the action have a certain fidelity to human nature, and that pomposity, and posing, and role-taking not be allowed to strip the movement of its veracity. What they suspect most is gesturing, you know, just making gestures, which are either futile, or self-serving, or merely conscientious. The intense personal-relations concentration of the fifties seems now to have been joined to a political consciousness, which is terrific.

INTERVIEWER: Do you feel politics in any way to be an invasion of your privacy?

MILLER: No, I always drew a lot of inspiration from politics, from one or another kind of national struggle. You live in the world even though you only vote once in a while. It determines the extensions of your personality. I lived through the McCarthy time, when one saw personalities shifting and changing before one's eyes, as a direct, obvious result of a political situation. And had it gone on, we would have gotten a whole new American personality—which in part we have. It's ten years since McCarthy died, and it's only now that powerful senators dare to suggest that it might be wise to learn a little Chinese, to talk to some Chinese. I mean, it took ten years, and even those guys who are thought to be quite brave and courageous just now dare to make these suggestions. Such a pall of fright was laid upon us that it truly deflected the American mind. It's part of a paranoia which we haven't escaped yet. Good God, people still give their lives for it; look what we're doing in the Pacific.

INTERVIEWER: Yet so much of the theater these last few years has had nothing to do with public life.

MILLER: Yes, it's got so we've lost the technique of grappling with the world that Homer had, that Aeschylus had, that Euripides had. And Shakespeare. How amazing it is that people who adore the Greek drama fail to see that these great works are works of a man confronting his society, the illusions of the society, the faiths of the society. They're social documents, not little piddling private conversations. We just got educated into thinking this is all "a story," a myth for its own sake.

INTERVIEWER: Do you think there'll be a return to social drama now?

MILLER: I think there will be, if theater is to survive. Look at Molière. You can't conceive of him except as a social playwright. He's a social critic. Bathes up to his neck in what's going on around him.

INTERVIEWER: Could the strict forms utilized by Molière appear again?

MILLER: I don't think one can repeat old forms as such, because they express most densely a moment of time. For example, I couldn't write a play like *Death of a Salesman* any more. I couldn't really write any of my plays now. Each is different, spaced sometimes two years apart, because each moment called for a different vocabulary and a different organization of the material. However, when you speak of a strict form, I believe in it for the theater. Otherwise you end up with anecdotes, not with plays. We're in an era of anecdotes, in my opinion, which is going to pass any minute. The audience has been trained to eschew the organized climax because it's corny, or because it violates the chaos which we all revere. But I think that's going to disappear with the first play of a new kind which will once again pound the boards and shake people out of their seats with a deeply, intensely organized climax. It can only come from a strict form: you can't get it except as the culmination of two hours of development. You can't get it by raising your voice and yelling, suddenly—because it's getting time to get on the train for Yonkers.

INTERVIEWER: Have you any conception of what your own evolution has been? In terms of form and themes?

MILLER: I keep going. Both forward and backward. Hopefully, more forward than backward. That is to say, before I wrote my first *successful* play, I wrote, oh, I don't know, maybe fourteen or fifteen other full-length plays and maybe thirty radio plays. The majority of them were nonrealistic plays. They were metaphorical plays, or symbolistic plays; some of them were in verse, or in one case—writing about Montezuma—I turned out a grand historical tragedy, partly in verse, rather Elizabethan in form. Then I began to be known really by virtue of the single play I had ever tried to do in completely realistic Ibsen-like form, which was *All My Sons*. The fortunes of a writer! The others, like *Salesman,* which are a compound of expressionism and realism, or even *A View from the Bridge,* which is realism of a sort (though it's broken up severely), are more typical of the bulk of the work I've done. *After the Fall* is really down the middle, it's more like most of the work I've done than any other play— excepting that what has *surfaced* has been more realistic than in the others. It's really an impressionistic kind of a work. I was trying to create a total by throwing many small pieces at the spectator.

INTERVIEWER: What production of *After the Fall* do you think did it the most justice?

MILLER: I saw one production which I thought was quite marvelous. That was the one Zeffirelli did in Italy. He understood that this was a play which reflected the world as one man saw it.

Through the play the mounting awareness of this man was the issue, and as it approached agony the audience was to be enlarged in its consciousness of what was happening. The other productions that I've seen have all been really *realistic* in the worst sense. That is to say, they simply played the scenes without any attempt to allow the main character to develop this widened awareness. He has different reactions on page ten than he does on page one, but it takes an actor with a certain amount of brains to see that evolution. It isn't enough to feel them. And as a director, Zeffirelli had an absolutely organic viewpoint toward it. The play is about someone desperately striving to obtain a viewpoint.

INTERVIEWER: Do you feel in the New York production that the girl allegedly based on Marilyn Monroe was out of proportion, entirely separate from Quentin?

MILLER: Yes, although I failed to foresee it myself. In the Italian production this never happened; it was always in proportion. I suppose, too, that by the time Zeffirelli did the play, the publicity shock had been absorbed, so that one could watch Quentin's evolution without being distracted.

INTERVIEWER: What do you think happened in New York?

MILLER: Something I never thought could happen. The play was never judged as a play at all. Good or bad, I would never know what it was from what I read about it, only what it was supposed to have been.

INTERVIEWER: Because they all reacted as if it were simply a segment of your personal life?

MILLER: Yes.

INTERVIEWER: Do you think contemporary American critics tend to regard the theater in terms of literature rather than theater?

MILLER: Yes, for years theatrical criticism was carried on mainly by reporters. Reporters who, by and large, had no references in the aesthetic theories of the drama, except in the most rudimentary way. And off in a corner, somewhere, the professors, with no relation whatsoever to the newspaper critics, were regarding the drama from a so-called academic viewpoint—with its relentless standards of tragedy, and so forth. What the reporters had very often was a simple, primitive love of a good show. And if nothing else, you could tell whether that level of mind was genuinely interested or not. There was a certain naïveté in the reportage. They could destroy plays which dealt on a level of sensibility that was beyond them. But by and large, you got a playback on what you put in. They knew how to laugh, cry, at least a native kind of reaction, stamp their feet—they loved the theater. Since then, the reporter-critics have been largely displaced by academic critics or graduates of that school. Quite frankly, two-thirds of the time I don't know what they really feel about the play. They seem to feel that the theater is an intrusion on literature. The theater as theater—as a place where people go to be swept up in some new experience—seems to antagonize them. I don't think we can really do away with *joy:* the joy of being distracted altogether in the service of some aesthetic. That seems to be the general drift, but it won't work: sooner or later the theater outwits everybody. Someone comes in who just loves to write, or to act, and who'll sweep the audience, and the critics, with him.

INTERVIEWER: Do you think these critics influence playwrights?

MILLER: Everything influences playwrights. A playwright who isn't influenced is never of any use. He's the litmus paper of the arts. He's got to be, because if he isn't working on the same wave length as the audience, no one would know what in hell he was talking about. He is a kind of psychic journalist, even when he's great; consequently, for him the total atmosphere is more important in this art than it is probably in any other.

INTERVIEWER: What do you think of a certain critic's statement that the success of a really contemporary play, like *Marat/Sade,* makes Tennessee Williams and his genre obsolete?

MILLER: Ridiculous. No more than that Tennessee's remarkable success made obsolete the past before him. There are some biological laws in the theater which can't be violated. It should not be made into an activated chess game. You can't have a theater based upon anything other than a mass audience if it's going to succeed. The larger the better. It's the law of the theater. In the Greek audience fourteen thousand people sat down at the same time, to see a play. Fourteen thousand people! And nobody can tell me that those people were all readers of *The New York Review of Books!* Even Shakespeare was smashed around in his time by university people. I think for much the same reasons—because he was reaching for those parts of man's make-up which respond to melodrama, broad comedy, violence, dirty words, and blood. Plenty of blood, murder, and not very well motivated at that.

INTERVIEWER: What is your feeling about Eugene O'Neill as a playwright?

MILLER: O'Neill never meant much to me when I was starting. In the thirties, and for the most part in the forties, you would have said that he was a finished figure. He was not a force any more. *The Iceman Cometh* and *Long Day's Journey into Night,* so popular a few years ago, would not have been successful when they were written. Which is another example of the psychic journalism of the stage. A great deal depends upon when a play is produced. That's why playwriting is such a fatal profession to take up. You can have everything, but if you don't have that sense of timing, nothing happens. One thing I always respected about O'Neill was his insistence on his vision. That is, even when he was twisting materials to distortion and really ruining his work, there was an image behind it of a possessed individual, who, for good or ill, was himself. I don't think there is anything in it for a young man to learn technically; that was probably why I wasn't interested in it. He had one virtue which is not technical, it's what I call "drumming"; he repeats something up to and past the point where you say, "I know this, I've heard this ninety-three different ways," and suddenly you realize you are being swept up in something that you thought you understood and he has drummed you over the horizon into a new perception. He doesn't care if he's repeating. It's part of his insensitivity. He's a very insensitive writer. There's no finesse at all: he's the Dreiser of the stage. He writes with heavy pencils.

His virtue is that he insists on his climax, and not the one you would want to put there. His failing is that so many of his plays are so distorted that one no longer knows on what level to receive them. His people are not symbolic; his lines are certainly not verse; the prose is not realistic—his is the never-never land of a quasi-Strindberg writer. But where he's wonderful, it's superb. The last play is really a masterpiece. But, to give you an example of timing: *The Iceman Cometh* opened, it happened, the same year that *All My Sons* opened. It's an interesting sociological phenomenon. That was in forty-seven, soon after the war. There was still in the air a certain hopefulness about the organization of the world. There was no depression in the United States. McCarthyism had not yet started. There was a kind of…one could almost speak of it as an atmosphere of good will, if such a term can be used in the twentieth century. Then a play comes along which posits a world *really* filled with disasters of one kind or another. A cul-de-sac is described, a bag with no way out. At that time it didn't corroborate what people had experienced. It corroborated what they were *going* to experience, and pretty soon after, it became very timely. We moved into the bag that he had gotten into first! But at the time it opened, nobody went to see *Iceman*. In a big way, nobody went. Even after it was cut, the thing took four or five hours to play. The production was simply dreadful. But nobody made any note that it was dreadful. Nobody perceived what this play was. It was described simply as the work of a sick old man of whom everybody said, "Isn't it wonderful that he can still spell?" When I went to see that play not long after it opened, there must have been thirty people in the audience. I think there were a dozen people left by the end of the play. It was quite obviously a great piece of work which was being mangled on the stage. It was obvious to me. And to a certain number of directors who saw it. Not all of them. Not all directors can tell the difference between the production and the play. I can't do it all the time, either, though *Iceman* was one where I could. But as for the critics I don't think there is anybody alive today, with the possible exception of Harold

Clurman, whom I would trust to know the difference between production and play. Harold can do it—not always, but a lot of the time—because he has directed a good deal.

INTERVIEWER: Could this question of timing have affected the reaction here to *After the Fall?*

MILLER: Look, *After the Fall* would have been altogether different if by some means the hero was killed, or shot himself. Then we would have been in business. I knew it at the time. As I was saying before, there's nothing like death. Still, I just wasn't going to do it. The ironical thing to me was that I heard cries of indignation from various people who had in the lifetime of Marilyn Monroe either exploited her unmercifully, in a way that would have subjected them to peonage laws, or mocked her viciously, or refused to take any of her pretensions seriously. So consequently, it was impossible to credit their sincerity.

INTERVIEWER: They were letting you get them off the hook.

MILLER: That's right. That's exactly right.

INTERVIEWER: And they didn't want Quentin to compromise.

MILLER: I think Günter Grass recently has said that art is uncompromising and life is full of compromises. To bring them together is a near impossibility, and that is what I was trying to do. I was trying to make it as much like life as it could possibly be and as excruciating—so the relief that we want would not be there: I denied the audience the relief. And of course all these hard realists betrayed their basic romanticism by their reaction.

INTERVIEWER: Do you think if you had done it in poetry that would have removed the threat more?

MILLER: Yes, I suppose so. But I didn't want to remove it. It would have seduced people in a way I didn't want to. Look, I know how to make 'em go with me—it's the first instinct of a writer who succeeds in the theater at all. I mean by the time you've written your third play or so you know which buttons to push; if you want an easy success there's no problem that way once you've gotten a story. People are pretty primitive—they really want the thing to turn out all right. After all, for a century and a half *King Lear* was played in England with a happy ending. I wrote a radio play about the boy who wrote that version—William Ireland—who forged Shakespeare's plays, and edited *King Lear* so that it conformed to a middle-class view of life. They thought, including all but Malone, who was the first good critic, that this was the real Shakespeare. He was an expert forger. He fixed up several of the other plays, but this one he really re-wrote. He was seventeen years old. And they produced it—it was a big success—and Boswell thought it was the greatest thing he'd ever seen, and so did all the others. The only one was Malone, who on the basis of textual impossibilities—aside from the fact that he sensed it was a bowdlerization—proved that it couldn't have been Shakespeare. It's what I was talking about before: the litmus paper of the playwright: you see, Ireland sensed quite correctly what these people really wanted from *King Lear,* and he gave it to them. He sentimentalized it; took out any noxious references.

INTERVIEWER: And did it end with a happy family reunion?

MILLER: Yes, kind of like a Jewish melodrama. A family play.

INTERVIEWER: To go back to *After the Fall*. Did the style in which this play was presented in New York affect its reception?

MILLER: Well, you've hit it right on the head. You see, what happened in Italy with Zeffirelli was— I can describe it very simply: there was a stage made up of steel frames; it is as though one were looking into the back of a bellows camera—you know, concentric oblong steel frames receding toward a center. The sides of these steel frames were covered, just like a camera is, but the actors could enter through openings in these covers. They could appear or disappear on the stage at any depth. Further-more, pneumatic lifts silently and invisibly raised the actors up, so that they could appear for ten seconds—then disappear. Or a table would be raised or a whole group of furniture, which the actors would then use. So that the whole image of all this happen-ing inside a man's head was there from the first second, and re-mained right through the play. In New York the difficulty was partly due to the stage which was open, rounded. Such a stage has virtues for certain kinds of plays, but it is stiff—there is no place to hide at all. If an actor has to *appear* stage center, he makes his appearance twenty feet off the left or right. The laborious nature of these entrances and exits is insuperable. What is supposed to "appear" doesn't appear, but lumbers on stage toward you.

INTERVIEWER: Did that Italian production have a concentration camp in the background? I remember a piece by Jonathan Miller complaining of your use of the concentration camp in New York.

MILLER: Oh yes. You see in Italy the steel frame itself *became* the concentration camp, so that the whole play in effect was taking place in the *ambiance* of that enclosure. This steel turned into a jail, into a prison, into a camp, into a constricted mechanical environment. You could light those girders in such a way that they were forbidding—it was a great scenic idea.

INTERVIEWER: Why did you choose to use a concentration camp in the first place?

MILLER: Well, I have always felt that concentration camps, though they're a phenomenon of totalitarian states, are also the logical conclusion of contemporary life. If you complain of people being shot down in the streets, of the absence of communication or social responsibility, of the rise of everyday violence which people have become accustomed to, and the dehumanization of feelings, then the ultimate development on an organized social level is the concentration camp. Camps didn't happen in Africa where people had no connection with the basic development of Western civilization. They happened in the heart of Europe, in a country, for example, which was probably less anti-Semitic than other countries, like France. The Dreyfus case did not happen in Germany. In this play the question is, what is there between people that is indestructible? The concentration camp is the final expression of human separateness and its ultimate consequence. It is organized abandonment...one of the prime themes of *After the Fall*.

Even in *Salesman* what's driving Willy nuts is that he's trying to establish a connection, in his case, with the world of power; he is trying to say that if you behave in a certain way, you'll end up in the catbird seat. That's your connection; then life is no longer dangerous, you see. You are safe from abandonment.

INTERVIEWER: What is the genesis of *The Crucible?*

MILLER: I thought of it first when I was at Michigan. I read a lot about the Salem witch trials at that time. Then when the McCarthy era came along, I remembered these stories and I used to tell them to people when it started. I had no idea that it was going to go as far as it went. I used to say, you know, McCarthy is actually saying certain lines that I recall the witch-hunters saying in Salem. So I started to go back, not with the idea of writing a play, but to refresh my own mind because it was getting eerie. For example, his holding up his hand with cards in it, saying, "I have in my hand the names of so-and-so." Well, this was a standard tactic of seventeenth-century prosecutors confronting a witness who was reluctant or confused, or an audience in a church which was not quite convinced that this particular individual might be guilty. He wouldn't say, "I have in my hand a list"; he'd say, "We possess the names of all these people who are guilty. But the time has not come yet to release them." He had nothing at all—he simply wanted to secure in the town's mind the idea that he saw everything, that everyone was transparent to him. It was a way of inflicting guilt on everybody, and many people responded genuinely out of guilt; some would come and tell him some fantasy, or something that they had done or thought that was evil in their minds. I had in my play, for example, the old man who comes and reports that when his wife reads certain books, *he* can't pray. He figures that the prosecutors would know the reason, that they can see through what to him was an opaque glass. Of course he ends up in a disaster because they prosecuted his wife. Many times completely naïve testimony resulted in somebody being hanged. And it was because they originally said, "We really know what's going on."

INTERVIEWER: Was it the play, *The Crucible* itself, do you think, or was it perhaps that piece you did in *The Nation*—"A Modest Proposal"—that focused the Un-American Activities Committee on you?

MILLER: Well, I had made a lot of statements and I had signed a great many petitions. I'd been involved in organizations, you know, putting my name down for fifteen years before that. But I don't think they ever would have bothered me if I hadn't married Marilyn. Had they been interested, they would have called me earlier. And, in fact, I was told on good authority that the then chairman, Francis Walter, said that if Marilyn would take a photograph with him, shaking his hand, he would call off the whole thing. It's as simple as that. Marilyn would get them on the front pages right away. They had been on the front page for years, but the issue was starting to lose its punch. They ended up in the back of the paper or on the inside pages, and here they would get right up front again. These men would time hearings to meet a certain day's newspaper. In other words, if they figured the astronauts were going up, let's say, they wouldn't have a hearing that week; they'd wait until they'd returned and things had quieted down.

INTERVIEWER: What happened at the committee hearing?

MILLER: Well, I was indicted for contempt for having refused to give or confirm the name of a writer, whether I had seen him in a meeting of communist writers I had attended some eight or ten years earlier. My legal defense was not on any of the Constitutional amendments but on the contention that Congress couldn't drag people in and question them about anything on the Congressman's mind; they had to show that the witness was likely to have information relevant to some legislation then at issue. The committee had put on a show of interest in passport legislation. I had been denied a passport a couple of years earlier. Ergo, I fitted into their vise. A year later I was convicted after a week's trial. Then about a year after that the Court of Appeals threw out the whole thing. A short while later the committee's chief counsel, who had been my interrogator, was shown to be on the payroll of a racist foundation and was retired to private life. It was all a dreadful waste of time and money and anger, but I suffered very little, really, compared to others who were driven out of their professions and never got back, or who did get back after eight and ten years of black-listing. I wasn't in TV or movies, so I could still function.

INTERVIEWER: Have your political views changed much since then?

MILLER: Nowadays I'm certainly not ready to advocate a tightly organized planned economy. I think it has its virtues, but I'm in deadly fear of people with too much power. I don't trust people that much any more. I used to think that if people had the right idea they could make things move accordingly. Now it's a day-to-day fight to stop dreadful things from happening. In the thirties it was, for me, inconceivable that a socialist government could be really anti-Semitic. It just could not happen, because their whole protest in the beginning was against anti-Semitism, against racism, against this kind of inhumanity; that's why I was drawn to it. It was accounted to Hitler; it was accounted to blind capitalism. I'm much more pragmatic about such things now, and I want to know those I'm against and who it is that I'm backing and what he is like.

INTERVIEWER: Do you feel whatever Jewish tradition you were brought up in has influenced you at all?

MILLER: I never used to, but I think now that, while I hadn't taken over an ideology, I did absorb a certain viewpoint. That there is tragedy in the world but that the world must continue: one is a condition for the other. Jews can't afford to revel too much in the tragic because it might overwhelm them. Consequently, in most Jewish writing there's always the caution, "Don't push it too far toward the abyss, because you're liable to fall in." I think it's part of that psychology and it's part of me, too. I have, so to speak, a psychic investment in the continuity of life. I couldn't ever write a totally nihilistic work.

INTERVIEWER: Would you care to say anything about what you're working on now?

MILLER: I'd better not. I do have about five things started—short stories, a screenplay, et cetera. I'm in the process of collecting my short stories. But I tell myself, What am I doing. I should be doing a play. I have a calendar in my head. You see, the theater season starts in September, and I have always written plays in the summertime. Almost always—I did write *View from the Bridge* in the winter. So, quite frankly, I can't say. I have some interesting beginnings, but I can't see the end of any of them. It's usually that way: I plan something for weeks or months and suddenly begin writing dialogue which begins in relation to what I had planned and veers off into something I hadn't even thought about. I'm drawing down the lightning, I suppose. Somewhere in the blood you have a play, and you wait until it passes behind the eyes. I'm further along than that, but I'd rather leave it at that for now.

It Could Happen Here—And Did

I KEEP no file of reviews, but if memory serves, *The Crucible* was generally dismissed as a cold, anti-McCarthy tract, more an outburst than a play. A relatively small band of rooters kept it on the Broadway stage for six months or so.

It is certain that a reading now of those reviews would leave unexplained, to say the least, why the play has continued to be produced here and around the world these fifteen years, or why it should have run through several seasons in France and remains in many permanent repertories, including Olivier's National Theatre in Britain. There have been years when it was more often performed than *Death of a Salesman*. Something living must thrive in the play which, I was told on its opening, was a dead husk.

Perhaps its victory over adversities has made me prouder of it than of anything else I have written, and perhaps it is permissible to say why I think it has refused to be dismissed.

The prime point at issue in 1953 when it opened was whether the analogy was a sound one between the Massachusetts witch hunt and the then-current hysteria about Communists boring from within the government, labor, education, entertainment and the intellectual community. After all, there never

From *The New York Times,* April 30, 1967, Sec. 2, p. 17. Copyright © 1967 by Arthur Miller.

were any witches while there certainly were Communists, so that *The Crucible* appeared to some as a misreading of the problem at best—a "naïveté," or at worst a specious and even sinister attempt to whitewash the guilt of the Communists with the noble heroism of those in 1692 who had rather be hanged than confess to nonexistent crimes. Indeed, the critic Eric Bentley wrote that one never knew what a Miller play was about.

I believe that life does provide some sound analogies now and again, but I don't think they are any good on the stage. Before a play can be "about" something else, it has to be about itself. If *The Crucible* is still alive, it can hardly be due to any analogy with McCarthyism. It is received in the same way in countries that have never known such a wave of terror as those that have. The bulk of the audiences, for example, in the British National Theatre, are too young to have known McCarthyism, and England is not a hysterical country. Nor, quite rightly, is it for them a play about a "problem" to be "solved."

The truth is that as caught up as I was in opposition to McCarthyism, the playwriting part of me was drawn to what I felt was a tragic process underlying the political manifestation. It is a process as much a part of humanity as walls and food and death, and no play will make it go away. When irrational terror takes to itself the fiat of moral goodness, somebody has to die. I thought then that in terms of this process the witch hunts had something to say to the anti-Communist hysteria. No man lives who has not got a panic button and when it is pressed by the clean white hand of moral duty, a certain murderous train is set in motion. Socially speaking this is what the play is and was "about," and it is this which I believe makes it survive long after the political circumstances of its birth have evaporated in the public mind.

Is it a political play? It is, I think, but in a particular sense. It is very often done in Latin America just before a dictatorship is about to take over—as a warning—and just after one has been overthrown, as a reminder. It was one of the first foreign works to be done after Stalin's death, and I will wager that it will be done soon after Franco goes to his reward. As I say, it is very popular in England, where hysteria is not one of the national vices. I think it is a political play but not in terms of Left and Right. Its underlying reference is to political paranoia, whichever side makes use of that source of power.

But paranoid politics is not easy to discuss for the reason that *our* fears are always based on something quite palpable and real, while *theirs* are illusory. I realize now that it was probably impossible to have expected an audience and critics in 1953 to feel the heat of a play which so much as implied that a state of deep fear was not entirely new in the world, let alone that the evil plotters might just be worth some dispassionate examination. On top of this, to have treated this fear as a tragic thing rather than a necessary and realistic and highly moral sort of patriotism, was more than could be borne by liberals and conservatives alike.

We customarily think of paranoia as a craziness, a diseased delusionary state in which fears are obviously out of proportion to any conceivable stimulus. But if this were all, we should never be endangered by it. Paranoia has a power and it rises not basically from ravings about plots and hidden conspiracies, but from the grain of recognizable fact around which the fantasies are woven.

The paranoid feels endangered by some person or group mysteriously controlling his actions despite his will. His violence is therefore always defensive, trained against oppressors who mean to kill him before he can kill them. His job is therefore to unmask and disarm, to find the seemingly innocent traces of the pervading malevolence, and he comes to recognize hostility even in the way a person folds his hands or turns his head. His only hope is power, power to neutralize the dangers around him. Naturally, since those dangers can be anywhere, his power must also be total in order to work.

And of course it is true that to one degree or another we are, in fact, hostile to each other, and when we are accused of holding that hostility, we do indeed hate the accusation and the accuser. So that the paranoid creates the reality which proves him right. And this is why the paranoid, who in normal times might merely end in an institution, can rise to the leadership of a society which is really insecure and at a loss as to the causes of its spiritual debility. Nothing is as frightening as to not know why one is frightened. Given the "cause" we can act, and thus keep ourselves from flying apart altogether.

Paranoid politics is seductive, too, because all politics requires that we symbolize people, until individuals cease to exist and there are only compliant supporters or the opposition. The paranoid discovers the murderous potential in the opposition, which it therefore must destroy. When, during World War II, for example, we ripped 100,000 Japanese-Americans out of their California farms and shops and confined them to Midwestern camps, we were indulging the paranoid side of our realistic fears of Japan. But was it really probable that *all* these men, women and children were secret agents? The grain of truth was that some, or perhaps one of them, was. Their non-"whiteness" enhanced our irrationality; we never rounded up German-Americans even though crowds of them, unlike the Japanese, had been marching around with Nazi flags in Jersey right up to the day we declared war.

A few years after its original production, *The Crucible* opened again in New York, Off-Broadway, and the script was now judged by many of the same critics as an impassioned play rather than a cold tract, and it ran two years. It is true that the original production was formalized and rather ballet-like, but not by that much. It was simply that in 1958 nobody was afraid any more. Nor do I imagine that I can convince many people that this is basically what was changed and for good reason. Great fear, like great pain, is not easily recalled, it is self-healing, and the more of it we have felt the less of it we can really get ourselves to remember. And this forgetfulness is part of the tragedy.

But no amount of paranoids walking around has very great

political significance unless a partner appears who, naturally, is Interest. Hitler without the support of German big business would have merged with the legions of the mentally lost. Stalin in his last years slept in a different bed every night, employed food-tasters, and ordered the executions of people whose names he merely heard in conversation, but if the Revolution had created a healthy, ongoing society, it could not have tolerated such a chief. Had the witch-crying girls started their shenanigans in a stable community certain of itself and its future, they would have been soaked in cold water and put to bed.

But land titles were in dispute in Salem due to edicts from Boston and London; the repressions of the Puritan code no longer seemed holy to people born after the early deprivations of the militant pioneers. A host of socially disruptive pressures were upon Salem which seemed to threaten a disorder beyond the power of the mind to analyze. The girls lifted up a cause for it all out of the morass. Americans in the late forties and fifties felt paralyzed before a power of darkness expanding its reign; we had "lost" China (which we had never "had") and Eastern Europe. Enormous Communist parties existed in France and Italy. McCarthy solved the problem of our helplessness with a stroke—we were infiltrated by the enemy. Twenty years of conservative frustration with contemporary America was unleashed until, like the girls, McCarthy was in a position of such incredible authority that the greatest people in the land shuddered at the thought that their names might fall from his sniggering lips.

The fantasy of the fifties has rich documentation, but the Rosenberg case, because it ended in death, provides one insight which may throw some light on paranoid fear. In the final speech of the presiding judge is the statement that the defendants committed one of the gravest crimes in all history in giving the atom-bomb secret to Russia. Yet, no expert competent to make such a judgment had been called, and even more instructive— the defense attorney was so eager to prove *his* adherence to the reigning fear that he moved to impound the diagram of the bomb lens allegedly transmitted by the Rosenbergs, so that nobody in the future could steal it again—or, by the way, examine its validity. Recently, however, it was examined by a group of physicists who had actually worked on the lens, and their verdict was that it was scientifically a farce. I am reasonably sure that the passion of the judge's speech was real, and certainly he was not crazy. He was, however, afraid.

Can it all happen again? I believe it can. Will it?

The opposite of paranoid politics is Law and good faith. An example, the best I know, is the American Constitution, and the Bill of Rights, which de-symbolize the individual and consider him as the sum of his acts rather than his hidden thoughts and propensities for plotting evil.

And there are signs that somehow, someway, people in responsible positions have learned at least part of the lesson. Despite our being in a war, despite the immense opposition to it, the draft-card burning and demonstrations, the President and the leadership of the country as a whole have not rallied the unwashed to go hunting for people whose bad thoughts are cheating us of victory.

But what will happen if the American becomes more desperately frustrated, if this war goes on for years, if a sense of national powerlessness prepares the ground for cries of "Betrayal!" —the old paranoid cry to which the highly moral mad respond by seeing where others are blind?

Laws, as we know, are made of bendable stuff; panic systematized around a grain of fact waits forever in the human brain. The tragic reply, John Proctor's, is unfortunately no defense against this kind of social dissolution, but spoken in good time it is perhaps our only safety: "A fire, a fire is burning. I hear the boot of Lucifer, I see his filthy face. And it is my face, and yours, Danforth. For them that quail to bring men out of ignorance as I have quailed, and as you do now when you know in all your black hearts that this be fraud—God damns our kind especially...." A foisted analogy? Only if we are certain that the slide into darkness is far, far behind us. As things stand, Proctor's passion has its own life intact and will until Power is guaranteed against the temptations of the irrational. The surgeons say they work to make their job unnecessary. *The Crucible* was written in that spirit—that the coiled thing in the public heart might die of light. A reasonable thought, but an unreasonable hope which against all reason never disappears.

The Contemporary Theater

I THOUGHT that I might talk about the situation of the theater these days, rather than about plays and about the art of the theater, because there won't be any art of the theater if the situation doesn't change. It's an easy subject to talk about, the American theater is, because we hardly have any. And this has been a rhetorical statement for many years which is rapidly becoming a fact. We have shows in this country—I've been boring people with this for years—and I'll bore you with it now because it is boring but it is the truth. We have shows in New York, but we don't have any theater in New York.

As you know, in every country the theater is, for numerous reasons, usually the creation of a city. It is concentrated in the city, whether it be Paris or London or Moscow, and when it dies in the main city or diminishes, it generally diminishes in the whole country. Whatever was wrong with the Broadway set-up for many years since, let's say, the First World War, it also provided the plays of our time. It is just now over the edge, in my opinion, in being unable to even do that.

Specifically, I strongly doubt as of this year, whether a serious play—by that I mean a serious comedy or serious drama—but

From the *Michigan Quarterly Review*, 6 (Summer 1967). pp. 153–163. Miller's informal remarks in this piece were made before a large audience at The University of Michigan on February 28, 1967. Copyright © 1967 by the *Michigan Quarterly Review*.

one which is something more than trivial, whether such a play with terrific reviews—or I should say a terrific review, there being only one morning critic left in New York—could survive for a season. In other words, the old chestnut that a good play will always come through, is now, in my opinion, on the verge of not being the case. A good play with good reviews will not survive in New York today. That's almost the case. It may well be the case. There have been examples in the last two years of plays with pretty decent reviews, plays with some value, I'm told—I didn't see all of them—which simply could not find an audience any more. This shouldn't have surprised anybody, and indeed it hasn't, excepting the people most intimately involved.

There is no more irresponsible group of people I think in this country than people who are engaged in making theater. They are universally, almost, committed to the idea that while the general situation may be dreadful, there's still place for a good one. And it has become a den of gamblers, so to speak, who think that they're going to crack through that sound barrier and beat the system. And of course occasionally they do. And gradually the system degenerates and finally all that we have left now are a handful of showplaces, show houses in New York City.

The audience for any real theater in New York stays home because the student, the teacher, the serious person of any kind, or the joker who likes to see a good play but hasn't got thirty dollars to spend to go out at night with his wife or girl friend, can't come any more to this arena of the arts, and we are left with the expense-account people, who don't pay for their seats, whose companies give them a certain allowance for playing, and who are, of course, not in the mood, generally speaking, for anything but a musical or a quick laugh. And as Carl Sandburg once said, "Great poets need great audiences"—we don't have the audience, and we certainly don't have the poets.

So as students and as people presumably interested in this nearly lost art, it might behoove you to think about some of the perspectives which are now nearly totally lost, which the art requires if it is to survive, to say nothing of flourishing. Where there is no vision, as I think Thomas Jefferson may have said, the people perish. The same is true of the theater or anything else. We have gone as far as the real-estate business can carry us. There is nowhere else to go. What is the solution? It is easy to say that we need a government-subsidized theater. We do. In all likelihood, if there is a future, that will be it—some kind of national or state subsidy for repertory theaters scattered through the country and in New York.

A long time ago that sounded simple and sufficient. However, one lives and learns, and the solution has to be looked at with a certain amount of skepticism but at the same time with an insistence upon its positive aspects. I'll tell you what's wrong with it. We aren't mature enough in this country, in my humble opinion, to give away money to a bunch of lunatics, such as artists generally are, without some important kind of political interference. We had a publicly subsidized theater in the thirties, the WPA Theater, which was, of course, basically an attempt to alleviate the unemployment situation. But, nevertheless, it did create many theaters in many cities in the United States, and, in half a dozen instances, the government stepped in to stop particular productions because they were too left-wing, or something of that sort. And finally the thing was abandoned as the economic situation improved, and there was nothing left of it. But I'm just pointing that out as one kind of danger.

Worse yet is that a government theater tends to subsidize also a great many people who are hanging on who really aren't artists. They wouldn't be artists, excepting that there was a government payroll to call them artists. There's all that that goes on when a tremendous bureaucracy starts to move in. It's our curse. We will never be able to get rid of it. I see no hope of ever getting rid of it. But, with all that, it would still provide for that one man in a hundred, or maybe it's a thousand, who has a vision, an aesthetic vision, who wants to make theater because he is a theatrical man—a writer or director or an actor—and out of this morass of mediocrity can come something worthwhile. Out of the mass of mediocrity now something worthwhile can't come, for the simple reason that we have to face facts: the American public, only a minority of it, is ready to pay for the quality the drama can give. I think it could grow and be made to grow, but at the moment it's simply not there.

The public for that kind of theater isn't there. It has to be developed and can be developed. So that in a competitive situation such as exists on Broadway, the bad money drives out the good money. An investor facing the choice of investing in a trivial play, which he believes has a large audience, or in something different that has a small audience, the same dollar will generally go into the trivial play. In a subsidized theater, the principle involved is such, and it is hallowed enough in its usage, to require that something more than triviality be presented. People come into such a theater with a different attitude; they expect to be cultivated; they expect to be exalted; they don't expect merely to be tickled and entertained, and consequently there is the chance for something better.

We've had experience in New York with the Lincoln Center, which was such an attempt, and is such an attempt, and I find a few things about it which I'd like to speak about. I discovered to my astonishment, when the Lincoln Center was being organized —that is, before it had opened any plays or indeed had even selected any plays—that there was a quite unbelievable hostility to it, not on the part of the Philistines necessarily—that is, the Broadway producers naturally were very unhappy because they mistakenly assumed it was going to be a great success, and they thought, "Here go all the playwrights, and all the actors will be sucked in to this stupid artistic stuff, and we won't be able to get any good plays any more." They proved to be wrong. But the hostility also came from actors, from writers, from a good part of the public. I can't say that I understand it altogether, even now, but I have some clues, which we might as well face.

There is no prestige in this country at the moment in any kind of activity that doesn't earn the label of "commercial." The big prestige goes to where the money is. I had thought originally that when I had agreed to give a new play to this unproved theater, that the reaction of the people whom I knew and the people in the theater would be: "What a fool he is to give up a lot of money, which that entailed, to take a risk of this sort"—which it certainly was. I thought I would be blamed rather for an excess of idealism, which it certainly wasn't, I think. But, on the contrary, what that action generated was simply hostility, as though somehow one had turned one's back upon a valuable idealistic community of some sort, namely Broadway, for something quite unworthy. In other words, it all kind of . . . it turned itself up on its head. And I talked to people at length about it and finally discovered a little about what their hostility came to.

I still don't know altogether, but I think what was involved there was that a great many people have made a spiritual living, so to speak, on complaining about the state of the arts. They live on these complaints. And when you say to some of them, let us say, a writer, "Where is the play that has not been produced because of the terrible situation?" And he says, "Well, I can't get myself to write it, it's so discouraging." I'm exaggerating a little bit but, unfortunately, not much. Or the actor who can't get himself to speak up so that people in the back row can hear him. You say, "Well why don't you speak better?" And he says, "Well, they didn't build these theaters for actors, they built them for the real-estate people," meaning that the seats are too close together, the ceiling is too low, or something of the sort, so that whole aesthetic systems begin to develop as a result of the hostile attitude of the actor toward his environment, or the writer toward his environment.

Here suddenly comes a theater which threatens to eliminate the source of the irritation. In other words, here threatens to be a theater where no longer would the writer be at the mercy of tomorrow's reviews altogether, because, being a repertory theater, it would continue putting his plays on more or less independently of how they were critically received, within limits. In other words, you couldn't close him up altogether in a few days. He would have a chance with his play to go on for months at intervals during the season and maybe his play would make its effect later on. Here is a chance for an actor to play not just himself on the stage, which is the way actors are usually cast, for what they are rather than what they can do. He could be thirty years old and play Shylock, or he could play Romeo, or he could play some realistic role in a contemporary play in the same week or the same month. So it's a terrific opportunity, one would imagine.

But it wasn't looked at that way. It was looked at vaguely as some sort of a plot. A threat against the complaint. And the appreciation of what an art-theater might be—let's forget art-theater—repertory theater was, and I'm ashamed to say, still is, nearly nil. For example: I don't think you could get together twenty-five people in the New York theater to agree on whether a subsidized repertory theater should do new plays, whether any of those new plays should be plays that could have been done on Broadway, namely plays with a mass appeal, whether they should only do plays which are difficult to comprehend so that one could say no Broadway producer would do them, or plays which have a smaller amplitude of effect so that only a smaller audience would be—a more intellectualized audience so to speak—would be interested in them, or whether that theater should be devoting itself to classics only, or whether it should revive old American plays.

There would be no agreement primarily because we have been brainwashed to a degree unimaginable to me, before I went through this experience, by the commercial theater. We are as commercialized as what has been attacked all these years. And, of course, it has to be so because you can't live in an environment ... you can't put a fish in salty water and not have him absorb the salt, and you can't exist in a visionless community without losing some of your vision.

At the moment, it's a curious thing, I thought that this perhaps was only a question of New York, but just last week I was approached by another theater, which is in New Haven, Connecticut, a smaller city, which is subsidized by local businessmen and the same thing has exploded. Namely, there is no audience-comprehension, let alone that of the board of directors, as to what such a theater is and should be. And I think, at this stage, that we've got to stop pretending that we know answers and get very primitive and fundamental about this, or we're going to lose whatever remains of an artistic community of actors, writers, and directors. I think we will have some movies left and perhaps an occasional production that will be exciting, but nothing more.

There isn't much time for me to do this today, but I would just throw certain guidelines out and say, from my point of view, it has to be a theater that loses money because a repertory theater, the more successful it is, the more money it loses. The reason for that is simple: you don't expand the number of seats at all, but the more successful you are the more productions you do, which means the more sets you have to build, the more stage hands you have to have, and the more actors you have to have. As you're failing, it gets less expensive. As you're succeeding, it costs more. This is a deficit business. A hospital that's doing very well financially is usually on the rocks medically. A hospital that is expanding all the time, and always needs money because its services are improving, is in debt. The same thing is true with the theater. That's number one.

Number two is: what is its attitude toward the public? It must without question take the public unto itself. It has to educate people. We are extremely primitive in relation to this whole institution. We really don't know what to ask of the theater, and the theater doesn't know what to give us back. If the Lincoln Center continued, I wanted to have several weeks where there was no theater but simply the public coming in, and we'd have discussions as to what they expected from the theater. What they wanted from it. Was it simply that somebody had told them it was cultivated to go to the theater?—what they really thought about the avant-garde; how much of it they understood; how much of it mystified them; did it move anybody?—etc., etc.

There is no communication, as Saroyan said in a wise and foolish little play he wrote once, "There's no foundation all the way down the line." And there's no communication all the way down the line. There's a big shadow-play going on, with immensely expensive constructions going on all over this country—more to come—big mausoleums where...You see we have no spirit moving yet, and until we do, it comes down to a few people, perhaps like myself, who go on with this because we love it, because we figure one day somehow, somewhere there will be a theater that can really do these plays the way one imagines they exist, and you wait for the desert to bloom.

But I'm here today in part because I wanted to make you see that as ignorant as you are, you are as ignorant as *we* are, that you have to ask yourself fundamental questions as to why there should be a theater. Maybe there shouldn't be. Maybe it's a dead art. Maybe it ought to be dead. Maybe what we want is a sculpture of the automobile, which sometimes isn't bad, and the jazz that we have, which is sometimes wonderful, and the popular arts that we really take to, that take no effort on our parts to enjoy. I always dislike the idea of people having to go to these damned things, to the theater. It's like people wanting to be better. They shouldn't want to be better; they should need this thing the way they need food. And I'm not sure we do. Maybe there's something farcical and unreal about it all that we're trying to prop up with new buildings.

Well, that ought to depress you enough. I would only add a most important thing, which is that it can't die. It can't die because we must have, in order to live at all, some kind of symbolization of our lives. The theater is not like life. Life is like the theater. We have to have, whether it be in some deserted basement or in a great building, an art which expresses, more fully than any individual can, the collective consciousness of people, what they share with each other, and where they're different. So that we can become individuals again we have to become a spiritual unity again. That's what it can do, and the need for it will always be there. So I'm not ultimately pessimistic but simply trying to warn us all that we have not got the solution now, but it's worth thought if one cares about it at all. I'll take some questions, if there are any.

[*An inaudible question from the front row.*]

He asked if I liked *The Time of Your Life,* which I called foolish. It wasn't foolish, it was moving.

["*Why do you say there is only one critic on Broadway?*"]

Well, I give him the distinction because there's only one morning newspaper. We used to have several, because there were several newspapers, and, as you know, a play runs or closes in New York by the verdict of these critics, and gradually the attrition of the newspaper business has been such that only *The New York Times* is left, so we have one critic which is equivalent, if you can imagine such a thing, to all the books in the United States—history books, economics books, fiction, poetry, drama— being approved of or disapproved of by one man.

He is supposed to be the world's greatest expert on musical comedy, the avant-garde theater, classical theater, even ballet, and we're supposed to believe that. That's the way it is though. A few weeks ago I complained that this was perhaps not the most rational way to go about things, and *The New York Times* agreed that it wasn't. And in fact Mr. Kerr [Walter F. Kerr, dramatic critic, *The New York Times*] independently had expressed some worry about this situation, which was none of his doings, of course. He did not destroy the other newspapers. But they asked me if I would like the job of being the other critic on the newspaper. That's how desperate things are. What I suggested was that they have at least two critics per night, and they thought that would compromise the unified opinion of the newspaper. As though anybody thought that something called *The New York Times* wrote these reviews. And they wouldn't do that, but they did think that they could ultimately find two men to do Sunday pieces. By which time, of course, the play which has been destroyed on Monday isn't there any more. It's a holocaust, it is a major disaster. And this only demonstrated, or should have, that it *is* so. That it is a disaster.

[*An inaudible question from somewhere down front.*]

Well, I wish that were so. The curious thing is that the spirit of which I speak, and which I don't have to label because I think we understand what it is, is more likely to exist in provincial theaters (I don't use that word with any condescension, I mean theaters outside New York). That's really a European expression, it doesn't mean anything lower. It just means that generally speaking, and in our case it's certainly true, I couldn't take a new play of mine and hope to cast it in Chicago, with the available actors, with the degree of excellence that I could in New York. I couldn't cast in Los Angeles. I could there, possibly, because many of the actors work also in movies and television, most of which is done in California. But that's sort of a branch of New York. You can't get set designers for the most part. There are some in some university theaters that are pretty damned good. The level of performance, because our audience is perhaps more demanding, is higher. There are exceptions to this. I may seem to be contradicting myself, but I'm not, because when I say that much of it is not good, but enough of it is—I'm speaking now of performance—is beyond what any other city in this country could manage.

[*Another inaudible question.*]

I suppose it does, but my only demurrer there would be... you see, I believe, as of tomorrow morning, that if I had a theater (in New York, I am speaking, I don't know the other cities as well) where I could have a hundred actors, and be able to charge, due to subsidy, a maximum of three dollars a seat, that I wouldn't have an empty seat for as long as I wanted to play. That to me is the problem. I avoid going to the theater for a very simple reason. If I go to the theater, I'm paying enough to buy a pair of shoes. That's what it comes to, you know. If you park your car and you go to the theater and so on—many people tell me it's fifty dollars. Well, they have to have dinner somewhere in that area, and it's very expensive. Now how are you going to run any kind of an art form with the toll on people of fifty dollars? It's ridiculous. You're already weeding out probably something on the order of eighty-five percent of the American people. And who's left? The people who are left are the guys who are half asleep from having drunk too much. You can't find anybody who's still what I call young—I mean I'm just fifty. They're all blasted in there—they don't know what show they've seen.

[*A question about subsidized theater.*]

I think the British example is the most applicable to this country because they also don't believe in political interference with any art, and, as a matter of fact, they've sought to guard against that by having a kind of buffer committee between the government's treasury and the acting companies. So that you don't get a government minister actually handing the money over to an actor. He hands it over to a neutral committee, which is in between both of them. And that committee is made up of people who could be lawyers, they could be educators, they could be businessmen, or—a couple of writers are on it too—called the Arts Council, and those people have the confidence of the government and the confidence of the theaters. And they give out these subsidies in various amounts. I think we could end up with such a system to our advantage. The problem with us, of course, is that everything costs about ten to twenty times what it does in England. An actor in England will work for thirty pounds a week. That's less than eighty dollars, I guess. And I don't see anybody here working for eighty dollars a week. Not that he should. But I mean that their problem is that much less, but of course they have much less to hand around too.

[*"Mr. Miller, what do you think the purpose, the ultimate purpose, of the theater is, really?"*]

I couldn't even speak in those terms because it's like asking, "What is the ultimate purpose of the Universe?" To me the theater is not a disconnected entertainment, which it usually is to most people here. It's the sound and the ring of the spirit of the people at any one time. It is where a collective mass of people, through the genius of some author, is able to project its terrors and its hopes and to symbolize them. Now how that's done—there are thousands of ways to do it of course...I personally feel that the theater has to confront the basic themes always. And the faces change from generation to generation, but their roots are generally the same, and that is a question of man's increasing awareness of himself and his environment, his quest for justice and for the right to be human. That's a big order, but I don't know where else excepting at a playhouse, where there's reasonable freedom, one should hope to see that.

[*"Why do you think the theater is so important?"*]

I could give you a lot of reasons but I suppose the basic thing is that I'm a playwright. I suppose I hoped in some way to prove that, and also it's a way of changing my world.

[*"Mr. Miller, could you comment on the power of the critic in molding taste?"*]

The power of a critic is in direct proportion to the—in my opinion this is—his power is greater where there is more cliquism in the theater, where the audience is less generalized, where the audience comes from a small class of people. But if there were a big audience in New York and outside New York, there would be a greater sense of proportion as to the critic's value and what his importance is. People would not be overwhelmed by this. You see, if you have to pay seven, eight, or ten dollars for a ticket you want to be pretty sure you're going to get your money's worth. If it costs a dollar, two dollars, three dollars, well—you may be told that this is not a masterpiece, but you say, "Well, maybe it's interesting." I confess, three dollars is something interesting. You see, I may not get a masterpiece every week. It turns out that those masterpieces aren't masterpieces anyway, it's just that he felt good that night, and he got excited.

[*"Why don't we have a theatrical community in this country?"*]

We do have a theatrical community in this country. It's spread out over the United States to some degree but especially in New York. There are people who have a strong idea about what is valuable in the theater, and they have a very strong idea as to how it should be done, but there isn't the money to do it. It takes years to create a company, for example, that one could call a company, which could show what a repertory company could do, etc. The danger from the whole thing is that you sometimes ensconce mediocrity in such a thing, and it has to be blasted out, but that's the problem of living, anyway. You've got to do that in a university, you've got to do it in the Standard Oil Company, you've got to do it anywhere. Now we have no problems at all; there simply is no situation here.

[*"What is the value of the Off-Broadway movement, plays like* America Hurrah, *for instance?"*]

What is their value? Well, I didn't see that play, I couldn't get in, thank God. I mean, I'm glad it was so crowded. It was early on in the run, maybe it's not as crowded now. I've only heard about it, *America Hurrah*. But I'd just like to make one comment about what I think you think. And that is that I'm very much in favor of any kind of experimentation provided that ultimately, sooner rather than later, it gets past the early incubation stages of self-expression and starts to deal with feelings and concepts in an organic fashion. There's a tendency in the Off-Off-Broadway theater to simply blow off steam, to write anecdotes that are half finished, and to shock the bourgeoisie by the most infantile procedures. But I think that's rather inevitable as a starting point. I don't think they should be judged by any other standard than that they're fooling around. They *should* fool around, after all the word *play* means you play. And it should be playing. I wish there were more places where they could play. I assume there must be something fascinating about that play, or they wouldn't have gotten the kind of audiences they're getting, and I hope for everybody's sake that it's very good, but I don't know.

[*"What about the good run of* Marat-Sade*?"*]

It didn't have a good run. That play was put on for a limited engagement by David Merrick at government expense. In other words, this is a Foundation, so if they lose all the money, it's simply a tax deduction. Which is not to underestimate the idea he has of using tax money in this way. But it was a limited engagement. In other words, to make your money back in a commercial theater, that play would have to run, probably with that cast, paid on American standards, I would roughly judge two and a half years, to really make a pile at it, which is what they would require of it. That play was begun by the Royal Shakespeare Company, I believe, in England, which has a subsidized theater. So he can spread out about thirty-five or forty actors on his stage. Thirty-five to forty actors in New York City at two hundred and fifty dollars a man is quite expensive, and, believe me, if it had been produced in New York to start with, it would have ended up with about a dozen lunatics spread out over the stage. It would have gotten more insane.

[*"Do you think there is a credibility gap between the audience and modern playwrights? What do you think of Robert Brustein, for instance?"*]

I have found that in general Robert Brustein tends to take adamant postures against the obvious, as though we were about to hear a tremendous thought falling, and you look around and there's cornflakes on the floor. There's nothing there. I haven't read everything he's written by a long shot, but I just remember an article or two I've recently read. For example, he announced the Theater of Joy—you know—since we don't have any theater, we have slogans. There's a Theater of Cruelty, the Absurd Theater, there's a commercial theater, there's a Pious Theater, and now suddenly you have the Theater of Joy. He was the master of the revels, and out comes *Viet Rock,* which is just nothing but a lousy play. And then the next job was another one he discovered at the Yale Drama School, which is a sketch of some sort, but you don't make theater by making slogans. You have, it seems to me, to create organic plays. And these plays are not organic. They are effusions of one sort or another, usually in bad taste, in which dirty words are said to shock us all to death and somebody's against Viet Nam and that's supposed to be terrifically adventurous. Your question was whether there was a gap—you see, it's a meaningless question, but I can see where you got it, because he puts things that way.

[*A question about Robert Brustein's criticism of Edward Albee.*]

Yes, but why does he have to knock Edward Albee to do

that? It depends on who's got ahead that year. I have to warn you that this is all journalism. This is not criticism. I could be very critical of Albee, I'm not defending him here, I'm just attacking a method. So that happens to be there that year, and it casts a long shadow over everybody because there are so few plays and here's one that holds together and people come in droves, so he's got to say that it is not funny enough. Well, he's not trying to be funny. He was trying to be Albee. Sure there's room for something else. But I don't see the point of having to destroy one thing in order to raise up something else. Especially if it's of some value. This is just to show how superior he is to the whole thing, and I'm happy about one development in our theaters: that several critics have become theatrical producers and ringmasters of one kind or another, and without exception they have produced the most vapid stuff of the times. And, of course, it's one thing to be a critic—it's an honorable profession—but there is a tendency to edge criticism in and the artist out. And it's totally unnecessary. I don't think it's part of the game at all. I think all he desires is to have a stage in a theater and not to be blasted because he's not funny. He may be over-pious, that's possible, but it's not supposed to be funny.

["*Why does New York have a monopoly on the theater?*"]

We've got probably about ninety-five percent unemployment among the New York actors. So it's not a monopoly of any kind. It's in desperate straits. I don't care where it springs up. I have no vested interest in New York, I don't live there any more. It's all the same to me. But that's where the talent is collected, and if it doesn't happen there, generally it doesn't happen anywhere else. I wish it would happen in Ann Arbor, when you get a new theater.

[*Inaudible question.*]

The Lincoln Center problem is simple at this moment. They have solved it by—gradually they will be—turning the theater into a booking house. They won't admit it but—I'll tell you a secret—which probably won't get back to New York, but, when the original company was still playing, when there was no question that it was going to continue, it was filling the theater eighty-five percent of capacity all the time, which is more than almost any Broadway show could do. I discovered by the grapevine that the new building, the Vivian Beaumont Theater, which was still —at that time—incomplete, was to be completed the next year, that they were negotiating with a great star and a private producer to open this theater with a revival of a Shakespeare play, completely unconnected from the repertory company, the Lincoln Center company. It was a purely commercial operation. At which point I said that if that would turn out to be true, I was going to quit now and withdraw all my plays at once, so they stopped it. But I'm not there any more, of course, and now they've announced that they have forwarded the cause of repertory by letting out the theater to, again, a completely private production, and how this advances repertory nobody has explained. It is a complete abandonment of the idea, but they're not prepared yet to admit it. This is going to be little by little. They're not prepared to announce it yet.

[*Inaudible question about Robert Whitehead.*]

I think he's embittered about it. Anyone would be. He really did organize the whole business and was on the verge—well, I'll give you a quick statistic—you see he had money enough to hire 22 actors. The British National Theatre has 145, the Moscow Art Theater has about 175, the Munich Theater has about two hundred and something, etc. Since we understand numbers quicker, that will give you an idea as to what the financial backing of this thing was. It was smaller backing than you would get, let's say, at Erfurt in Germany—some small town—you know with a hundred thousand population. Well, he naturally couldn't get all the people he wanted the first year, but as a result of the operation of a year and a half, every decent actor in New York was on line trying to become a member of this company. And within, I would guess, six months of the time that he was bounced, we would have started to have a really first-class theater. There's no doubt about it.

[*"Did you run into more trouble at Lincoln Center than you expected?"*]

No, but I knew what I was in for. It was starting. You can't begin an automobile factory and hope to manufacture your first cars without bugs. It was difficult. I think that that break-in period was necessary, and what they did was they scrapped it just as they were learning.

[*"Don't you think there is some value in musical comedy?"*]

The musical comedy is obviously the one American invention, or—I wouldn't call it an invention, but an adaptation of European operetta—which is indigenous to us and has a terrific life and a viability, and there should certainly be a place for it. It is a real art and a good one. And there's no contradiction between that and any other kind of theater. I would hope that a repertory theater one day would be able to do terrific musicals. They should be able to do anything.

[*"Why do you find repertory theater so important?"*]

Even in the short experience that has been had at Lincoln Center, it gradually dawned on people—I'll give you a concrete example—there's a fellow named Hal Holbrook who does the Mark Twain impersonations. He was in our original company and he played in *After the Fall, Incident at Vichy,* and he played in *Tartuffe.* There were three different roles. I thought he was marvelous, but his publicity image hadn't been created. Then we broke up, and Hal went and did his act, which he's been doing for years all over the United States. He opened on Broadway with it and became a sensation. Now the repertory theater at that time—before it broke up—was about to ask Hal, and Hal would have agreed, to do his one-character job, which is fantastic, on certain evenings during the repertory year. Imagine what it does to you as an audience, to see Hal Holbrook standing there as Mark Twain, absolutely believable and quite marvelous, and then the next night he's playing a German officer in 1942, who is going out of his mind with an agonizing conflict; the third night he's playing Quentin in *After the Fall;* and the fourth night he's playing a part in *Tartuffe*. Now there's just one actor. You see what happens is that the audience begins to get involved in the transformations of these people. And the very changes from evening to evening throw perspectives on what the play is about that they're doing now—because you know it's Hal Holbrook, ex-Mark Twain, and now he's a Nazi officer. The changes from night to night are part of the theater. The changes from night to night add an immense perspective to any one of those shows. I think that what happens is that an audience begins to participate in the creation of that art in a way that is not quite possible if you've got a play running for two years and the same guy does the same thing every night. You have no relationship to the thing excepting that of a customer. I know that process began to happen, and of course it was aborted, but it will come back again, it'll start again. That's just one element of the audience relation to such a theater. And that's what repertory does.

On the Theater in Russia

Russia is the only country I know of where one writer will passionately extol the works of a competitor. This is rather a shock at first and nearly unbelievable—and indeed, in some cases it is merely politic, but it happens genuinely often enough to force one to think about it. Of course in my presence they are talking to a foreigner, but that is just the point: in any other country the ignorant foreigner is usually sold on the unique excellence of the writer he happens to be speaking to at the moment —there is never much else of value. And in Russia it is also true that the more acclaim the writer has earned, the more he is at pains to draw one's attention to others less renowned but equally talented.

It is otherwise in France, England, Germany, or the United States, and it seems at first like a pure generosity of spirit, which it may well be, but it is also mildly tactical as well. There is a deep division among Soviet writers which reflects two conflicting attitudes toward power itself. As in any other country, the majority is not about to get in the way of the powerful. Most writers, like most other people, know where their bread is buttered. But there is also a minority in league with the future, the growing tip of the tree, and a certain amount of danger is

From *In Russia* (New York: Viking, 1969), pp. 16–23; 41–47; 52–54; 57–61. Copyright © 1969 by Arthur Miller.

always at their side. This is one of the reasons why both kinds of writer—although the vanguard is more likely to do this—will direct attention to colleagues of the same persuasion. It is a kind of politicking, a way of strengthening the side.

But what exactly are both factions after, what—beyond the obvious advantages of supporting the regime—are the so-called conservatives aiming at in their works, and what in the vanguard enrages them so?

The obvious answers are ideological, but they are not altogether explanatory. The conservative writer sees himself in the tradition of the realistic work of Tolstoy, for example—although he will disassociate himself from the master's mysticism and religiosity. Art, he would say, is basically the higher consciousness of the people, immediately comprehensible to them, and an enhancement of the values of socialism. Socialism is the Soviet system, whose fundamental objectives are humane, progressive, and generally directed toward the welfare of all. In a word, art is like science, a servant of the community. In fact, the whole concept is Platonic and by no means uniquely Russian or even Communist.

The Puritan fathers of the Massachusetts Bay Colony, for instance, would not have countenanced novels and poems which unearthed the sexual repressions enforced by their semi-military discipline, let alone advocated freer sexuality. The colony was always in danger and a man who kept himself apart from its spiritual defense, a man who deeply questioned the underlying propositions of the society, would not and did not last very long. The famed Roger Williams objected too strongly to the theocratic suppression of variant religious ideas and on top of that preached the equality in spirit of the Indians whom the white men were deceiving and robbing—and was promptly put out in the dead of winter to die. It was the Indians who saved him, and in Rhode Island he set up the first society on the American continent where the freedom to think was guaranteed.

The conservative Russian writer—the honest one anyway—is moved by the fear that the high communal aims of the Communist state will be atomized, diluted, and ultimately destroyed by the individualistic vanguard. But the writer who feels this way also has attitudes, apparently little connected with ideology, which also place him firmly in this ideological camp. He is more than likely, for example, to enjoy the feeling of solidarity with the party, with workers, and with other non-writers whose reality he shares. He is another kind of worker and takes pride in it, a worker in literature or art. It is not onerous but a matter of duty and goodness to accept party revisions of his work. He is likely to emphasize the virtues of craftsmanship, solid construction, and thoroughness in a work of art. He wants, in short, to be part of what-is. He is rationalist in his explanation of man.

It needs to be said that many of these men, like their counterparts everywhere, have been neither suborned nor corrupted by superior force. Accepting the fundamental bases of Soviet society, they honestly regard what injustice they see as temporary error or at worst a lamentable necessity which does not prove the rule. They are men who desire authority and fear chaos. For them life can never be tragic because the individual who comes to a bad end has simply separated himself from the victorious path of the society. Stalin stated their viewpoint most aptly—the writer is the engineer of the soul. Rather than speaking truth to power, he justifies power to the people. His greatest justification is quite probably the career and works of Mikhail Sholokhov, whose trilogy of the Russian Civil War in the Don Cossack area seems to demonstrate that art and absolute fealty to the state can be combined without damage.

There are those, on the other hand, who point out that Sholokhov revised his masterwork to minimize the values of those Cossacks who opposed the Red Army, and so weakened his achievement. Some even suggest that Sholokhov did not write these works but stood in as the author while the real author was liquidated. This last, however, seems unlikely as new Sholokhov stories have recently appeared and their style is the same as the works of thirty years ago. But the imputation indicates the depth of bitterness between the two factions. Sholokhov is a rauchy old Cossack now, advocating that the whipper-snappers be fed to the sharks if they don't like the way things are in the Soviet Union. His identification, in all likelihood, is with those first heroic revolutionaries who stood up like men before the Czar's agents and firing squads, and despite unimaginable deprivation, betrayals, and hardships, dragged Russia out of feudalism and into the age of science and modernity. To a Sholokhov, the power he respects and upholds is the power that fends off the decadence of the West—the pornography, the effeminacy, the rootless, nationless, cryptic, private art whose supremacy anywhere means the end of community itself. There are millions of Sholokhovs everywhere, needless to say, the difference being that in the Soviet Union a writer is far more than an individual facing a piece of blank paper alone in a room; he is state property and accountable for his attitudes. But as revolutionary ideas move into the streets in the West, much the same sort of conflict is rising among writers there. A LeRoi Jones, committed to black militancy, has no patience with Negro writers whose work does not forward the cause, and he would surely regard as an enemy and betrayer a talented Negro who spent his time dealing with matters irrelevant to that cause. Any claim to the autonomy of art must collapse when a people is in danger or struggling to preserve itself, and the single theme of Soviet political and social discourse for half a century has been its imminent peril before foreign and domestic enemies. Actually, much the same emotions work inside us. Until very recently it was a rare Hollywood movie that ventured to question any basic American social premise, and the studio heads exercised an ironbound censorship of any such story. They were avowedly providing "wholesome" entertainment in which fundamental conservative American ideas always emerged victorious—or at a minimum were awarded a metaphoric justification. School boards all over the country screen out material from textbooks they deem subversive of national values, whatever the validity of that material, and on the most blatant level the House Un-American Activities Committee for more than thirty years has arraigned writers and others whom it regards as dangerous to accepted thinking. Among other questions asked me by the chairman of that committee was, "Why do you write so sadly about this country?" It is a truly Stalinist question, if you will, and there are millions of Americans who share the chairman's feelings. Given the right political atmosphere, the kind we had in the 1950s, these deeply angry people will come out on the streets to picket movies and plays by authors they regard as hostile to American values, and given the legal power would unquestionably clean up our production in a matter of weeks.

The difference, therefore, is not in the uniqueness of Russian feelings toward such matters but in the legal systems; all Russian literature is published by the state and must meet the requirements of the Communist Party. That a certain number of works have been published which criticize or imply that all is not on the right track, indicates that within the party are men who have come to recognize that the role of the writer may not be quite as simple as Stalin thought. Obviously some of them see that the writer's criticisms might even strengthen the state by bringing to light real shortcomings which ought not be continually rationalized away. There are even a few who understand that the heavy censorship has bled much of Soviet writing of its individuality and sheer interest.

It is not possible to begin to understand anything about the feelings of either young or old Soviet artists without keeping in mind Ehrenburg's admission— "The thought came to me that I should have to remain silent for a very long time...I should have no one with whom to share my experiences."

Nothing is easier than to read a bad conscience into this, and little more; he should have fled when he could, or spoken out against what he knew was wrong, and so forth. But there is something much more. It is a little like a man trying to explain how he fell in love with a perfect woman who turned out to be murderous, vain, even insane, and cared nothing for him, a woman to whom he had dedicated his works, his life, and his highest idealistic feelings. How can you explain that, when the

truth is now so obvious to your listener? It is impossible spiritually to tear oneself apart from a beloved without leaving a part
of yourself behind, and the Soviet scene is still under the tension
of this same paradox, even in the hearts of those too young to
have been touched by Stalinism. For the power of the Communist
ideal is on the level of the religious one, of any belief in sacrifice
to a higher and worthier ideal than one's own selfish interests.

And that is why so many of the Ehrenburg generation, any of
those who once felt the totality of belief, seem so saddened now
regardless of the fact that some, at least, of the truth of Stalinism
has been revealed and its excesses curbed—most of the time, anyway.

Konstantin Simonov is in his fifties now. He is the author of
good, workable plays, poems, and novels, and during the war
was a front-line correspondent who saw more action than a great
many soldiers. His line of communication to the highest levels
of the party is still open. He lives very well, sometimes in a
spacious Moscow apartment, sometimes in a country house where
the shelves are littered with icons, sculpture, and paintings from
Russia and from the many other countries he has visited. The
sentencing of Yuri Daniel to prison he does not agree with;
Daniel was a soldier and wounded at that. Sinyavsky is another
story, for he never served in the war, and worse, perhaps, knowingly had his manuscripts published abroad rather than standing
up for them at home and struggling to get them accepted. Still,
Simonov can swallow his resentment of Sinyavsky too, knowing that it was not intelligent, by even putting him on trial, to
give the world a club with which to beat the Soviet Union.
Simonov is caught, it seems, between a certain sense of honor,
which to him Sinyavsky violated, and the hard-learned lesson
that imprisonment is no longer the answer to literary dissidence.

At the same time Simonov will not forgo any chance to put
down bad writers, whatever their loyalty, or foreign partisans of
the Soviet whose works are empty. In short, he seems to have
arrived at substantive rather than relative values. And inevitably,
his journals of the war, a work he regards as perhaps the most

important of his career, have been refused publication for several years now. But apparently he is determined to think and work within the slowly changing system and to fight the battle as he can.

Simonov may still be *persona grata* with the regime, but he is at bottom a working writer and knows that censorship finally means an instruction to writers to lie. A patriot, as Russian as you can get and still stay sober, he has that double vision of his country which the awakened live with; he often seems nearly ashamed of what is still done in the name of national security and socialist truth. But he is not an official, and I wanted to hear the official attitude toward writers and censorship.

Madame Ekaterina Furtseva is the nominal chief of all cultural work in the Soviet Union. We met in her office, a long and impressive room with a green felt-covered table in the center surrounded by armchairs, and a working desk at one end beneath two tall windows. Behind the chair was a ten-foot-long table piled high with possibly two hundred manuscripts and books. Slips of paper stuck out of those books and manuscripts—indicating, I assumed, marked passages.

Madame Furtseva was then in her sixties, a sensitive and still handsome woman, attentive and intelligent. Suffering had carved deeply into her face. Indeed, one day a few years ago, in the midst of a business meeting, a man in working clothes had entered her office and with a pair of clippers cut the wire of the phone that connected her office directly with Khrushchev's. She went home and slashed her wrists. Having been raised under Stalin, she knew what this gesture must mean. She was saved, however, and Khrushchev ordered her restored to her position, for she had been a favorite of his. When it is said that Russia has not really changed much, one must keep in mind that "much" can sometimes mean everything. But what such an incident still leaves in the mind of the foreigner is that the restoration is still quite as arbitrary and unpredictable as the condemnation, resting on a leader's temperament rather than on legally secured rights.

I knew that writers rather liked her—all sorts of writers, conservative and vanguard alike, more or less. The general feeling was that she cared about literature and was basically humane, and was not simply a police agent in disguise. Four or five officials sat around the table, she at the head. These were chiefs of various departments, one in charge of theater, another of children's books, and so on. They said nothing and were clearly of a lower but still considerable rank. They wore dark, well-pressed suits, starched collars, and subdued ties. We might well have been in a bank, discussing a mortgage.

Madame Furtseva, arranging her long shawl over her shoulders, talked of the weather, of all our children, of plays she had seen—including my own. *A View from the Bridge* had been playing for a long time and I told her I had seen it the night before. She was immediately curious about my reaction to the production. I said that I thought some of the actors superb, but that certain excisions and changes in the script disturbed me. She was genuinely surprised at this—and as her office was in charge of translations, her responsibility was now on the agenda.

I went on to say that all the psychological motivation had been carefully removed from the play. Eddie Carbone, the hero, must *slowly* reveal an illicit attachment to his niece, a love which helps to move him toward a betrayal of his two brothers-in-law, who are illegal Sicilian immigrants. But in the Soviet version he has hardly entered the scene when he speaks of his love for his niece and whenever she appears he puts on an agony of frustration which makes any later revelation immaterial and foolish. One wondered why his wife remained in the house at all.

There were many other changes of the same sort—nothing is left to be developed and discovered, everything is stated at the outset, and rather crudely at that. I could not understand why the play was such a success.

Madame Furtseva was obviously appalled. She wanted to know from her assistants who had translated the play and why this had been allowed to happen. The matter would be looked into. Her sincerity emboldened me and I asked what the procedure was for selecting translators. To my astonishment she was quite vague about it. Not secretive, but genuinely vague, and even asked her assistants to help out with an explanation. The embarrassment now spread down the table. It turned out that translators in effect selected themselves; someone with a bit of English might hear of a foreign hit, get hold of a manuscript or a book, rush through a Russian version, and be the first to get to one of the Moscow or Leningrad theaters with a script. This, I said, sounded like arrant free enterprise, the rewards going not to the most able but to the most aggressive. We all had a good hollow laugh at this, but the problem remained.

After about an hour it seemed time to break up, and I said I did not want to keep her from her work any longer. She glanced behind her at the massive piles of books and manuscripts which awaited her perusal. Yes, she said, there was a vast amount of work to do. I asked if she had to read all those manuscripts and she said yes, she did have to; unfortunately it was necessary. What do you suppose would happen, I asked, if she just chucked it and didn't read them? Just let them go through. Would it really rock the country?

She laughed then, and I thought I detected a certain understanding in her laugh—as though the relaxation of censorship, even its abolition, had been discussed by her before this. I persisted; I had met some writers who were suspect to one degree or another, but their complaint was that the current system was not Communist enough rather than too Communist. As for Russia itself, their eyes melted at the mention of it. She nodded. She understood perfectly well. She knew it better than I did, I thought then.

Perhaps I was too taken with her and let myself read too much into that laugh—a certain recognition of at least a grain of absurdity in her exhausting attempts to keep the national mind loyal and clean and unquestioning. More, I thought at that moment that somewhere in her was the wish that the gates could open and that mistaken literature could be condemned by the people in their wisdom. But I could be wrong. I could also be right, however.

Two days later at a cocktail party one of her assistants sought me out. He handed me an envelope. It contained a chit for royalties due me on a story of mine which had been published in Moscow years before. I asked what this amount represented—was it all I was owed? He asked if I wanted more, the way you ask a guest if he wants more pickles. I said no, I wasn't here to dun them for royalties but was merely curious, although anything would be gratefully received. He then gave me the message which was obviously his chief business. Madame Furtseva had not spoken idly during our meeting; she wanted to assure me that she would personally see to it that from now on my translators would be the best that could be found. I thanked him. Then I asked, what about the translators for the other Americans they published and produced? He seemed taken aback, surprised; there had been no discussion of the others, or of the whole procedure of selecting translators. In short, this was irrelevant.

Perhaps I read too much into his reaction, but it seemed rather a harking back to the royal past. Rules applied to everyone excepting to those especially favored from on high, and his total and naïve acceptance of such a benign procedure was noteworthy, I thought—he saw nothing whatever unjust about it. I had earned a favor and would receive it. What could be better than that?

And yet—don't politicians do favors in Washington? Of course they do, but one imagines they are remotely ashamed. Perhaps one ought not imagine too much. Or is the moral simply that we are still laboring under some fringe of the old illusion which the great October Revolution raised before the world—that a government of and by the insulted and injured had finally risen on the earth, a society which had somehow abolished the motivations for immorality, the incarnation at long last of the human community. So that infractions here, any appearance of the Old Adam, are doubly scandalous, immensely more meaningful than anywhere else.

After the performance of *A View from the Bridge,* backstage talking to the actors, I kept looking around for the actor who had played Eddie, the hero of the play, and since he was not present I referred to his performance several times, saying, "The man who played Eddie..." until I noticed a certain shifting, an embarrassment among the actors, and it was pointed out finally that their Eddie was standing next to me. He was totally unrecognizable. For the characterization on stage he had built up a different nose.

At the Sovremennik (Contemporary) Theater the troupe is very young, but several characters in Efremov's dazzling production of Schwartz's *The Emperor's Clothes* are aged men. The oldest, a prime minister who trembles with senility, turned out to be a twenty-four-year-old actor, and on another night I watched him for two hours in a different role and never realized it was the same fellow. It is all in the nose, and the changes are not always gross. A widening of the bridge, a slight tilting of the tip, a new flare for the nostrils and the actor is catapulted into another age bracket and a new personality. Gogol, of course, was fascinated with noses, and physical description in Russian literature has traditionally been of great importance. People, whatever their psychological nature may be, are first of all bodies, and this fascination with the way people look is, I think, the foundation for the vividness of so much Russian acting.

A great deal has been made in the past twenty years of the staleness of Russian theater. Certainly it has kept out Ionesco, Beckett, the whole absurdist mode. But there is very little in the West that can match the vitality of the best Russian productions. Directors like Efremov and Lubimov would be of first importance anywhere. Their productions are highly finished and complete, yet imaginative and sometimes wild. Their actors are mostly young, full of enthusiasm and curiosity, and far better trained than the majority of Americans.

Even in plays with little distinction or novelty of form there is always some startling acting. *Uncle's Dream,* a dramatization of a Dostoevsky story, is a case in point. A great nobleman is passing through a provincial Russian town and his carriage breaks down. He must spend the night. The ladies of the best families vie with one another for the honor of sheltering him. The nobleman is unmarried, so naturally the mothers of eligible daughters are desperate to receive him. These are "the best people," and the nobleman is the incarnation of state authority and aristocratic distinction. The ladies meet in the living room of an important matron to decide who among them will have the honor. They have all agreed, however, not to invite Madame X (I have forgotten the character's name), who is universally regarded as a viper and a pest. Ten or twelve of them in satin and embossed velour dresses move about the stage, plotting, sweeping from couch to piano to the bust of Byron to the French doors opening on the garden, like a flock of excited geese, their words lengthening out into a kind of whining, half-sung chorale which nevertheless remains this side of reality. Comic as it is, it is somehow hair-raising. They sit down at last, sipping the drink of the cultivated—chocolate. In comes Madame X, who has gotten wind of this meeting to which she was denied admission.

Serafina Birman, the actress, as I later found out, was the age of the character—in her mid-seventies. She enters. The company falls silent in a hush of horror. The offended socialite stands center stage, surveying her betrayers. She begins to take them apart one by one, their private bad habits drawn upon their foreheads by her mocking, searing voice. For three minutes she continues without pause or mercy. Then four, then five, then six, then seven. Her breath begins to come hard, but she will not relent. She is unsteady on her feet now and takes a faltering step to the side as though about to collapse, but she goes right on. Suddenly—she goes down on one knee. Her brown satin gown, a veritable drapery, catches on her heel, her hair is falling into her eyes, but her bitterness flows on. She is losing her breath altogether, it seems, she is shaking in every bone, and she lies down on one side, propped up by her elbow, her free arm extended as she points from hated face to hated face. However collapsed, she never loses her nobility, her stertorous frightfulness, her righteous wrathfulness. She continues gasping out her curses, and now she lowers her free hand to the floor, turns over on her stomach, and points at the hostess, the arch culprit. "And as for you—I spit in your chocolate!" With which she sits upright, gets her feet under herself, and stands, swaying with exhaustion and a certain profound pleasure, and staggers out of the house. It is beyond acting, it is apocalypse, and backstage later I found for the first time in my life that I was pleased that someone had been given the Order of Lenin. She has been acting for over fifty years.

The physicalness of Russian acting, its mortal quality, was apparent also in what can only be called the disembodying of the nobleman. He appears at first as a caricature of an upper-class dandy. Obviously made-up to look young enough to attract women, he can barely move about in his patent-leather shoes, the lace pouring out from under his sleeves, the high stiff collar manacling his neck. Alone, finally, in a bedroom with his valet, he is being undressed for the night. The wide-chested jacket is removed, revealing a skinny torso; his gloves off show veined and aged hands. His fine head of hair goes into the wig box leaving him bald, his teeth go into a jar and his lips pucker up, and finally one eye comes out and there he sits, the mummy of the ruling class still chattering on about his possibilities as a lover. Of course the idea is not new, but the detail is so deftly etched that it still frightens and illusions the onlooker, who can only marvel at it.

No one who goes to the theater in Russia can fail to be struck by the audience. It is not bored and it is not uncritical, but it is passionately open to what it has come to see. Outside on the street there are always dozens of people pleading with each arrival for an extra seat. Young people make up the majority of the audiences, and particularly if the production offers something new and contemporary there is almost an atmosphere of adoration in the house, and open gratitude to the author, the actors, the director. It is as though there were still a sort of community in this country, for the feeling transcends mere admiration for professionals doing their work well. It is as though art were a communal utterance, a kind of speech which everyone present is delivering together.

The earthiness, the bodiliness, so to speak, of Russian acting even extends into its stylizations. Yuri Lubimov's production of *Ten Days That Shook the World* in his Taganka Theater is a sort of visualization of the atmosphere of the Revolution, rather than a play. From time to time a white screen is lowered over the whole stage, and, lit from behind, it shows the silhouettes of the actors, the people of the city caught up in the chaos. The detail of each silhouette instantly conveys not only that one is a prostitute, another a bourgeois, another a worker, another an old querulous gentleman, but somehow their attitudes toward the Revolution, and the impression comes from body postures, particularly of gestures, the way a head is held or a finger points. And as the light is moved back and more distant from the actor, his silhouette grows on the screen, so that at the end the figures of the new Red Army men, the defenders of the Revolution, move like giants as tall as the proscenium, dominating the whole theater.

Much of this production is sheer choreography and neither better nor worse than its counterparts elsewhere, but there is always some explosive conception which instantly speaks of this particular Russian genius for physicalizing. A young man is being held before a firing squad. He is let go to face his death. The rifles rise to sight him. There is no explosion of bullets, but the young man rises onto his toes, then comes down on his heels. Then he rises again, a little higher this time, and comes down harder. Now he jumps up a few inches off the floor and comes down; then he jumps up about a foot off the floor and comes down; now he is springing, higher and higher, his hands behind his back, until he is flying upward in a movement of both escape and pride, of death's agony and life's unbelievable end, until one imagines he will succeed in simply flying upward and away—and then he comes down and crumples to the earth, and no sound is heard.

It is wordless and physical, the diametric opposite of the poets' avant-garde theater which Yevtushenko and Voznesensky, among others, are attempting to create. Neither is primarily a dramatist but, as in most countries now, the theater has attracted poets as a public forum where contact with wide audiences can make poetry stretch itself toward its classic applicability to public discourse. By the accident of their appearance as spokesmen for the youth their names are usually coupled, but their talents and traditions are not at all the same.

It is impossible for a foreigner really to appraise Yevtushenko's *Bratsk Station* or *The Triangular Pear* by Voznesensky because they both depend almost totally on language. One can, however, speak of two different kinds of feeling that are quite apparent and distinctive in each. Voznesensky's is a first-person work, a series of stylized scenes allowing actors to speak broken-up sections of his poems as individual speeches. It is rather a staged recitative than a dialogue, but the power of his verse over the audience is unmistakable. The near-surrealism of the staging is sophisticated and charming, but it would probably seem rather tame in some far-out Western theaters. Immersed as one inevitably is in mass theater in Russia, which is basically realistic theater, this performance reminds one that there is an "in" culture and an "out," a split in the sensibilities of the country. *The Triangular Pear* celebrates personal emotions and an individual's singular reaction to his time rather than any group or public destiny and if it has a moral purpose it is to raise up to view the response of one individual to the world he has found. Its beauty of language apart, perhaps it is this quality of individuation which attracts the young to it and to Voznesensky's verse. He pretends to speak for no one but himself, his own nature. It is also probable that this is what unnerves the authorities about him.

Bratsk Station is of another order, a sort of cantata embracing the sacrifices, the endurance, the heroism of the Russian people as well as hints of the injustices they suffered in the gigantic construction of modern Russia. With a cast of perhaps thirty young actors, using Egyptian slavery as a symbol of Stalinism, the work strives toward a Whitmanesque celebration of the people's victory over their history, their betrayers, and those who would enslave them. The work opens with a movie projected over the entire back of the stage, showing on grainy 1920 film stock a long line of workers with arms linked around each other's waists, rhythmically tramping their immense felt boots on soft concrete into the forms of the Bratsk Dam. Moving en masse from side to side over the cement, they perform a kind of massive Hora of brute human power driving a twentieth-century structure into the ancient Russian earth. The film appears again at the end, after we have seen how this very discipline and faith was taken advantage of by slave-driving betrayers, but this time it is interrupted by a rush onstage of a line of well-dressed, shiny-faced young couples who break into an arm-linked dance to the same rhythm as the old Bratsk workers use in the film—now, however, with a rock musical accompaniment which joins both generations together in the present. The new young people throw off an air of free and joyous energy which inevitably seems to taunt any who would do to them what was done to their fathers. And the one refrain of *Bratsk Station* is, indeed, "Russians never will be slaves."

Seeing these plays it is difficult to understand why they should have met with such opposition from the party if it were not still torn between rather primitive Stalinist and liberative factions. There surely seems to be no split in the audience's enthusiasm, nor does there appear to be any sense of scandal or exposé in the audience reception. That Russians never will be slaves is hardly a revolutionary slogan, and a regime which permits such sentiments on its official stage would merely seem to be feeling rather secure about its passage through a dark time. But the fact is that *Bratsk Station* went through many party-imposed revisions and line-changes. Only recently it was even taken out of production for a time and then allowed back again.

Ultimately there is an absurdity about this alternation between repression and freedom, and beyond the absurdity a question as to whether the leadership is, or dares to be, in touch with the people at all. If the invasion of Czechoslovakia is any guide, it is not. Justifying the invasion on the need to rescue the Czech Communist Party from counterrevolutionaries, the Russian government was unable to find a single Czech Communist leader of any repute who would come forward as a representative of the rescued. The Russians found themselves forced to treat with the very leadership against whose betrayals of Communism they had come to save the country. This bespeaks either total cynicism or a hermetic, self-induced illusion of such proportions as to astound the foreigner—and doubtless many Russians too. (The problem came up in conversations with Czech intellectuals in Prague in March 1969. With Soviet soldiers occupying their city, they were under the gun, yet they were not entirely able to dismiss the possibility that the invasion was to some degree the result of self-delusion on the part of the Soviet party, a sign of its incapacity to recognize realities which its a priori theories denied existed. Russian officers and soldiers stopped people on the streets in the early days of the occupation, asking to be led to the "counterrevolutionaries," and were shocked by the hostility of the Czechs. Others believed they had landed in West Germany, because the people were so antagonistic, and as well because the shops were so full of gadgets unseen in Russia; the miniskirted girls and the general absence of fraternal sentiments helped this impression, too. The Czech intellectuals, however, filled with indignation and apprehension for their own futures, did not overlook the implicit naïveté, let alone the blind stupidity, of Russian pronouncements on the invasion. One lesson they seemed to draw from the experience was that in their own country— and, it is to be hoped, one day in the Soviet Union too—a legalized opposition must be allowed; not only to hedge power with law and law with the free-spoken opinions of the people, but also to prevent the party from atrophying. And finally—although they are neighbors, fellow Slavs, and fellow Communists—these Czechs find the atmosphere of religiosity surrounding the Soviet government as odd as it is to us. They did not, for example, admire the all but total silence of Russian intellectuals toward the fate of Czechoslovakia, but at the same time agreed when I said that for Russians to stand openly against their government is akin to heresy, with all its implications of guilt and sinfulness. Indeed, one could almost say that the rock on which Soviet moral presumptions broke apart in Czechoslovakia was that Czech socialism in its two liberalizing years had become anti-ritualistic, practical, and humane. In this view the purpose of the collective is the flowering of the individual; for the Soviets the collective is its own end and justification, the individual remaining a theoretically unaccounted-for, free-floating object whose real nature has never been fitted into the system.)

There is not supposed to be any anti-Semitism in the Soviet Union. It is all the more vehemently denied, especially as being part of state policy, because it was so blatantly a part of the Nazi ideology. A short time ago, however, a respected Soviet writer submitted for publication a series of memoirs of Russian writers of the twenties. The work was accepted with enthusiasm by the board of the publishing house, but, as always, there were a few editorial problems which needed talking about. One of the poets discussed in the work, a man who died in the early thirties, had been a Latvian German, and naturally had a German family name. His middle name, however—this, the editors felt, was an interesting variation of any German name they had ever heard of. In fact, they wondered aloud, it seemed to sound like a Jewish name.

The memoirist, a Russian of course, had never considered this at all. It was a name. He did not know if the middle name was Jewish, but if it was—did this represent a problem?

Not at all, the editors replied. But why must it be included? Why not call the man by his first and last names and simply leave out the middle name? The poems themselves were thoroughly Russian; why throw some sort of pall of misunderstanding over them? The poet's middle name was dropped.

Another Soviet writer—who shall also be nameless—wrote the story of the Bible for children. His rendition was also enthusiastically read by his editors. But, again, there were certain problems of a minor sort which required a conference, and one afternoon the author and his editors sat down to iron them out.

First of all, said the editors, there was this question of God. As we all know, God is a mythological construction, and in any strict sense mentioning God is really unnecessary.

But, replied the author, in the Bible . . .

Secondly, the editors went on, there is the whole business of "the Jewish People" cropping up again and again in your work, which is otherwise quite admirable. Why is that necessary?

Well, replied the author, the Bible, you see is . . .

Why not simply call them "the People"? After all, it comes to the same thing, and in fact it generalizes and enhances the significance of the whole story. Call them "the People." And there is one final question.

The author waited for the final question.

It is the title. "The Story of the Bible" is not a very exact title. What would you suggest? the author asked.

How about, "Myths of the People"?

And that was that.

The Opera House in Tashkent looked so inviting, and they were playing *Leila and Mezhdu,* based on the national epic. We must go. Some difficulty in arranging tickets on such short notice. We arrive promptly at seven for a seven-thirty curtain, in order to see what the crowd looks like.

The building is some combination of Moorish, Spanish, City-Center-type architecture, but nevertheless very white and imposing, with wide-open concrete aprons around it and a nice flat stairway rising up from the street level. A strange quiet, however, as we pass beneath the outer archways, and in fact there is nobody in the lobby. Did we misunderstand the curtain time? It appears not, for the large lady usher takes our ticket and bids us follow her inside. Perhaps Uzbeks do not speak before the curtain goes up?

In the auditorium there is not one soul. Immaculately clean, the seat-arms polished, the carpet soft and well-vacuumed—but not a soul. We sit in the third row center. It is a vast house, with perhaps four thousand seats. Endless balconies, galleries, boxes. All empty.

Ten minutes pass like an hour and a half. Another couple comes down the aisle. Action! They are English. One can tell after a few minutes because they don't speak to one another but sit at polite attention quite as though the seats around them were full. Nothing whatever is odd, remarkable, wrong. If water started rising above their ankles they would not move or take note. One loves them, their truly *interested* attention as they stare at the empty orchestra pit. England will never die.

Movement behind us. Turning around I spy a customer. An Uzbek worker, he wears a cap sideways, a red bandanna around his neck, no shirt, his black wrinkled jacket and pants and shoes caked with white cement. He is alone, lounging in his seat, staring at the curtain up ahead. Things are moving. Soon we may have the ushers outnumbered and could force a performance.

A disturbance in the orchestra pit. A musician enters from under the stage. A man of sixty, his eyeglasses badly bent, he has no tie, wears a sweater. He sits and opens his violin case. Something wrong with the bridge. He adjusts it for ten minutes.

More action behind us. For some reason about eight people have entered the second balcony. Five or six now spread out behind us in the orchestra, one man sits alone in a side box.

Two more musicians enter the pit. One of them tests his clarinet, the other reads a newspaper. How forlorn. Three or four more come into the pit now. They tune up, but only barely take any notice of one another. Perhaps they have been exiled here? One, for some reason, is wearing a tuxedo. Probably a recent arrival from Moscow, still unaccustomed to frontier mores.

The tuning-up is getting louder and is much better than nothing. Suddenly, as though on cue, they all stop, pack up their instruments, and walk out under the stage! Can it all be over?

Inge is now weeping with laughter, a certain hysteria having entered our relationship. Neither one of us can say anything that is not funny.

A small note of revolt—the audience begins to clap in unison. It is now a quarter past eight. The English couple remains fascinated by the curtain, takes no note of the demonstration. The clapping dies away. Begins all over again.

The house lights go down as the musicians hurry back in. A full orchestra, the members glance out over the gala audience. A kind of utter exhaustion emanates from the conductor, who makes a play at a rapid, sprightly entrance. Somebody up in the gallery claps once.

The curtain rises. An Arab-type chieftain sits before a cardboard tent surrounded by his court. He seems angry as he sings baritone. The others try to placate him. He is stubborn, refusing comfort. Moussorgsky weaves through Tchaikovsky through intermittent Rimsky-Korsakov. Ignorant of the story, one still knows that the chieftain's daughter must soon appear. She sure as hell does. Beautiful girl, but can't sing. Which is the hero? Two or three young bravos appear and one knows which is the hero because he is the shortest and stands at the center, and whenever he points at something he also takes a gliding step in the same direction, while the others only point without taking a step. Very gradually one's sympathy begins to go out to all of them knocking themselves out for the empty house. What dreams of glory they must have had once! It is terribly hard work, this opera. Queen Victoria would have adored the purity of its emotions, the sweep of the music. It is all Cultural. Somewhere in this city must be some guys and girls hiding in a cellar playing some stringed instrument and singing to each other without a committee. The public has vetoed this opera, is all one can say. It has definitely decided to risk everything and not come. There is something heartening and universal, finally. As the box-office man on Broadway once said to me, "There is no power on earth that can keep the public from staying home."

Intermission. The audience rises. The combined sound is like eleven chickens scratching in Madison Square Garden. We stroll idly, politely, toward the lobby. The English couple, still *interested,* appears a few yards away. I confide to Inge that we are not remaining for the second act, although there is no doubt the English couple will do their national duty. We stroll out the front door rather as though wanting a breath of the night air. We keep on strolling at a sort of trot. Glancing behind, we see the English couple also strolling, looking about at the non-existent native audience, but disappearing nevertheless into the bowels of Tashkent. And yet—what's the opera situation on a weekday night in Duluth, Minnesota?

There is an almost universal conviction that all hotel rooms are tapped, as well as many apartments. Visitors sometimes arrive with paper and pencil, communicating by writing while they carry on banter directed toward the bug, or at home play loud Beethoven passages while discussing anything of importance. The odd thing is that after a while one gets used to it oneself. Transistorized cartridge tape recordings are also good masking devices. One sits down to discuss some ordinary matter, and the host turns on a loud rock-and-roll number in his lap. Pretty soon, though, a sort of surrealistic mood develops, especially if the conversation is a sad one, or if both parties to it lapse into silent thought for a few moments while hillbilly music squeals on. When the recorder is turned off it is time to eat, or speak of happy or inconsequential things. But should the serious mood return again, on goes the tape recorder and the rock-and-roll. Ultimately it is an incredibly pleasurable thing simply to go to bed and think freely to oneself. Maybe this is why so many Russians seem so deep, and despite their gregariousness so solitary —perforce, they have done so much communing with themselves.

It may also be part of the explanation for the special importance of literature to them. So much that is ordinarily unsayable is given by the nuances of good writing, by its capacity to imply far more than its syntax, transmitting by definition a climactic social application. Thus the pressures on the writer and artist are compounded, and the contradictions too. Nowhere else are writers so close to being worshiped by their readers, nowhere does a regime go to such extremes to honor or hound them. The paradox is built into the writing craft itself, for on one hand nobody, not even the commissar, denies that writing to be any good must be personal, must be an individual's own thought and style. On the other, by expressing his individuality the writer takes hold of a certain power, a power which he must not use beyond the point where the regime feels comfortable with his use of it. Thus, periodically he must be humbled. It is as though there were an arena where the talented may venture at risk, and the seer or prophet at the risk of his life. The importance of literature stems, finally, from the penalties hanging over the practice of it. Thus a writer is always a step away from dread heroism and is worshiped like a sacrifice. After all, writing is almost the only act one cannot in Russia commit anonymously; even the great physicists and inventors are rarely credited by name, so that whatever power might accrue to individual scientists is waylaid. But a novel or play or poem cannot very well come into the world by itself, or as the result of a committee's resolution, and the power of authorship is thus unique; only the leaders can be so well known, and therefore in danger of such idolatry—or such humiliation, should conditions change.

Perhaps it is also why they so detest frivolous or fragmentary or self-indulgent writing. It is like telling bad jokes at a funeral or in a church. In a very real sense the national fate is in the writer's hands, the immortal fire of the race. And so the wrath is terrible when he appears to have some secret allegiance to foreign ideas, and it is very probable that that anger is not confined to the bureaucracy alone. Whatever the repressions it may use to perpetuate itself, there must surely be a deep strain of apathetic consent in the people or they could not possibly continue.

One could, and one ought to go even further, and face the fact that there is such a thing as working-class taste, or more precisely, an unalienated taste of whatever class. So many attempts have been made in England, America, and France, for example, to establish trade-union theater movements and thus to break through the ring of bourgeois audiences and middle-class prejudices and tastes. They have never come to anything. It seems as though people who are deeply immersed in the production process, people who spend their lives trying to make things work, and have, so to speak, invested themselves in sustaining and elaborating the productive process, are not going to enjoy a spectacle which lacks materiality, reality, purpose, and logic of an everyday kind. Every machine process moves from less to more, from nothing to something, from the imminent to the accomplished. Conflicts of thought, abstract symbolizations, much of the arsenal of what is called modern art, lack point for these people because, while these qualities may *be* something, they do not apparently *do* anything either to move such people, to educate them, or to give them an idea about themselves. The Soviet hierarchy may well be basing itself upon the innate conservatism of all producers, and especially those who have no reason to be revolutionary. After all, the fame and impact of a Brecht was created with and among the alienated bourgeoisie and not among the working class. Finally, Solzhenitsyn, the one writer in Russia who is universally regarded as a classic, a genius, precisely fits the ultimate categories. He is a seer, an absolute truth-teller, and he writes simply, realistically, in a style untouched by the past fifty or even seventy-five years of literary experiment, a style which any literate worker, engineer, or schoolteacher can bite into and find nourishing. His latest books circulate in typewritten drafts, but they are not published. Yet he is known everywhere. He alone has had the audacity openly to call not for a relaxation of censorship but for its total abolition. He has entered the arena of the saints. And it needs to be added that there are not many writers anywhere in the world with this kind of insight, to say nothing of his courage, a courage which is not only expressed in the political implications of what he is saying, but in a style which dares be comprehensible to the alienated and the unalienated alike.

Our last night in Russia, inevitably, brought all the incipient chaos of feelings and unanswered questions to a head. Andrei Voznesensky and his wife, Zoya, good friends of Maya Plisetskaya, prima ballerina of the Bolshoi Ballet, had arranged for us to see her performance. Yevtushenko's wife, Galia, insisted we could not leave the country without seeing a certain painter's work in his apartment far from the center of town. Inge had meanwhile misplaced her passport. A Russian journalist who had broken his back in an Army plane (he crashed in Siberia in an attempt to machine-gun a bear) had insisted I take home a jar of special honey for my cold and would meet us anywhere. Appointments we had been postponing with three other people now had to be met. And through all these meetings and conversations and gift-giving Inge had to try to get through the telephone system to all the places we had been in the last twenty-four hours to try to locate her passport—a difficulty, when a lot of Russians do not answer their phones unless they have been notified ahead of time as to who is calling.

On top of it all there was a curious mood of uncertainty because a writer-friend of the Voznesenskys had just turned up; he had recently come under attack by the Writers' Union, which had gone so far as to publish an article against him in the press. The man some weeks before had gotten so apprehensive that he had gone off to a small town in Siberia to get away from the mutterings against him in Moscow. Now, just back, he was wondering if it had been wise to return. Then again, maybe he should issue some intransigent statement which might rally support for him; on the other hand, *would* others support him? Should he perhaps return again to Siberia? Should he go back to his own Moscow room? On the other hand, maybe he was overreacting altogether, and the whole business was unnerving him more than it should.

Meanwhile we were all moving into the immense crowd pressing into the Bolshoi Theater. To strange eyes it seemed as though the crowd had never before seen a ballet, the eagerness was so intense. We said good-by to the pale, uncertain writer at the stage entrance. He also knew Plisetskaya well and would love to go up to her dressing room and say hello with us, but maybe it was better he did not. We wound our way through the back corridors of the great theater; the public-address-system loud-speakers connected with the auditorium were alive with the powerful rumbling of people excitedly greeting each other as they took their seats out there. We climbed stairs, wound through other corridors, opened doors through sitting rooms, and the Bill of Rights seemed unutterably precious then, the sheer ignobility of hounding the man we had left in the street was a choking, enraging thing. Nothing, no progress could be worth the fear in that writer's face.

A gentleman in frock coat led us into a sitting room to wait until Plisetskaya had dressed. The walls were red velour, the Louis Something furniture covered with white sheeting as though waiting to be unveiled on some occasion of state, the mirror frames gilt, deeply carved—the very flower of the great age of the cataclysmic Czars. Here too the sound of the auditorium could be heard through the speakers, like a sea waiting to be calmed by the holy power of this dancer dressing on the other side of the paneled door. We waited, talked of the decor and its playful silliness, which now, however, seemed so innocent and naïve. Perhaps a Czar had sat here, made to wait a few minutes by some primping ballerina, for it all smelled of Power and therein lay its impressiveness and fatuousness. The frock-coated gentleman, the impresario actually, passed through with a nod to Voznesensky sitting there in his pea jacket and sweater, and opened the paneled door, closing it behind him. In a moment the door opened again—she was ready now.

We filed into Plisetskaya's dressing room. A hall of mirrors. She kissed Andrei. Some time ago he had written one of his best poems about her. They were in league with a spirit that shone in their eyes. She bade us sit down. I had never seen a human being move like this. A racehorse, her muscles swathing the bones. The costume was deceptively casual and peasantlike; in fact, it was an athlete's, like a fighter's gloves, a runner's trunks, and she shifted the waistband of the skirt a quarter-inch as though that infinitesimal adjustment would in a few minutes release her from the pull of earth. She was working now as we talked, turning her feet, ever so slightly stretching her shoulders inside her skin, and the sound of the packed house flowed over her from the loudspeakers, the adoring and menacing sea-rumble of Moscow.

A separate balcony about thirty feet wide hangs over the orchestra of the Bolshoi, in it two high-backed thronelike chairs flanked by lower ones for the noble retainers, the great red drapes framing it all with immense loops and flowings of cloth. The Czar was not in either of the thrones. The stage is very brightly lighted, the faces of the audience await the magic. The curtain lumbers up and *Don Quixote* begins. As a non-fan of classical ballet I decided to sit back in our box just over the footlights and interest myself in the sociology of it all, but as soon as the Knight's soliloquy was over and the girls came on, sociology finished. Each seemed six feet tall, full-bodied, and light as air. What woman could dance more beautifully than these? And Plisetskaya materialized, her body arched forward, it seemed, and her legs and arms shot backward, like a speeding bow freed of the laws of physics. The audience seems to be under her feet, behind her back, over her head, watching every flicker of movement she makes as an infant watches its mother move.

The act is ending. The music stops. She turns to our box, and suddenly I remember that she will be dancing a special cadenza for us. She glances up and begins. The audience knows something unusual is on. A hum, a subdued roar of an oncoming cavalry shudders the house. Wild, noble, unbelievably concentrated inside herself and yet abandoned to a love of air and space, she greets all poets, and perhaps America, with a freed body.

The pleasure of the audience now is like a statement, and the seeming paradox of the Bolshoi is straightened out; there is a mood here different from that in any other place I saw in Russia: the archaism of the house and the classicism of the repertoire are really the forms in which people can simply face beauty, beauty without the measure of utility, cant, or rationalized social significance. Here you are Russian and here you are free, and all the rutted roads, the toilets that don't work, the moralizing posters, all progress and all decay are far, far away as this woman transcends the dialectic and the mortality of thought itself.

We cannot stay for the second act and in Plisetskaya's dressing room we are all, for some reason, kissing each other. And we are off in Galia's little car—from the Bolshoi, as it turns out, to the Bronx, a housing project where her painter friend lives—but it is necessary first to accept the jar of honey from the bear-hunting ex-pilot at the stage door and then to drop Voznesensky at his apartment because he is tired and needs sleep. And where has the pale writer gone to spend the night?

Broadway, From O'Neill to Now

As anything approaching a mass entertainment, theater in America ceased to exist in the twenties when the talking picture drew off the unsophisticated. Then O'Neill introduced the audience that remained—the somewhat better-educated urban bourgeoisie —to a new, alienated content, announcing the hollowness of the standard American credo and the doom of a civilization based on optimism, materialism-as-salvation and the superiority of appearances over perverse, underlying reality.

O'Neill was not alone, of course. Babbitt-baiting, the spoofing of the Booboisie, the contempt for booming America's cultural barbarism, were the stock-in-trade of many writers of the twenties. The point, however, is that while plays and authors regarded as important were to one degree or another alienated, the bulk of Broadway's merchandise still remained well this side of controversy. Thus an incipient inner split in the theater audience already existed even if it lacked self-consciousness. Proponents of an "Art" theater had to struggle against the conservatism of audience and critics who joyfully declared, "When philosophy comes in, I go out," or, "If you have a message, send it by Western Union." These aphorisms were the pride of what can be called the majority theater that wanted entertainment, not agony, although it could tip its hat to "culture" if it had to. The only weapons O'Neill or any other American playwright had against them were superior showmanship and the sheer force of talent.

In short, there have been two audiences in the American theater for forty years or more. These audiences merge around certain plays at certain moments, their edges obscured by the universal appeal of particular productions (*The Great White Hope* is a current example). However, the crisis now is more obvious than before because the ground has nearly disappeared upon which the alienated and the unalienated can appreciate the same kind of art.

Looking back now, I believe that the late forties and early fifties—in fact, just before the Cold War froze what had been the tolerance of the Broadway theater—saw the last moments when both kinds of sensibility could share the same theater. It was then that Tennessee Williams and I, each from different vantage points, sought to speak to both kinds of people. For myself, it was never possible again after *The Crucible*. For Williams, quite obviously, the only audience left is the one that has nothing in common with the majority.

What movements or ideas gave vitality to the theater in the years after the twenties?

In the thirties, the Left theater groups, inspired by Marxist militancy, gave the alienated theater a new self-awareness as a theater apart and opposed to the majority theater. Still, even *their* aim was to succeed in the big time, to capture "Broadway." If "Broadway" ultimately captured most of their artists, it also absorbed their social consciousness, stripping the Left theater of its more arrant Marxist coloration and transforming it into a Liberal theater. For the audience, like society as a whole, had to adopt progressive revisions of the old American credo, and it did the same within the theater.

But not only a social attitude was involved in this process. The Group Theatre, for example, even though it failed to survive after a few years, injected a new method of actor-training, new ideals of ensemble performance, new extra-theatrical social references for stage reality which still rule in many diluted forms. It in turn was the heir of the old Provincetown experiments, and of Eva Le Gallienne, whose Civic Repertory on Fourteenth Street for many years brought Ibsen, Strindberg, Chekhov and the alienated European theater to an audience which would not find them on the commercial stage.

The greatest and most successful drive to expand the audience beyond the small, compact class represented on Broadway was the WPA Federal Theater Project. Government-supported and aimed primarily at giving employment to actors and other theater people hit by the Depression, it also hoped to reclaim the audience the talkies had drawn away. It played in ghettos, slums, churches, stores and small towns to people who had never before seen theater. However, a certain portion of its repertory was alienated theater, and the project was annulled in 1939 by congressmen who saw it as un-American. Indeed, the WPA Living Newspaper created perhaps the only new form invented in America, holding up the social system as such to inspection. When WPA died, the threat of the masses entering the theater receded.

In the past twenty years or so, alienation in society at large has become a highly self-conscious life-view, particularly with the youth but not only with them by any means. From being the property of the intellectual minority, alienated attitudes toward America-as-advertised have become the dominant code of communication among a very wide class of people. Alienation has thrown up its own critics, newspapers, radio stations, and new conventions of expressing faith, disbelief, idealism and nihilism. Its modes and styles, if not its moral and political content, have spilled over into those of the majority. In its myriad variations it still focuses on the old enemy, the unalienated American Credist.

There is no space here to evaluate the art of this insurgency or that of "Broadway," and that is not at issue here in any case. What needs to be recognized, I believe, is that an audience, and a large one, does exist for live theater, that it has an intense spiritual vitality, and that several forces within the presently constituted Broadway theater set-up actively repel this audience. At the same time, Broadway does not any longer attract a large enough part of that majority on which its life always depended. (I should add that I do not think that movies have somehow made live actors on a stage outmoded.)

I do not know that it will be possible for any but a few musical spectacles to support the price of midtown real estate over the next few years. This is the underlying competition of values which, if no other pathology entered, would destroy any professional theater in New York. The rock bottom process is that a play must earn enough income to ward off the physical removal of the theater and its replacement by buildings that can earn more.

It is now quite evident that marketplace laws, if allowed to continue operating without interference, will by themselves destroy what remains of the New York theater. The only interference imaginable is public subsidy of some kind. I take this to be basic, and no conversation about the question of theater survival can proceed until the economic dilemma is faced and resolved. One admonition: government, being sworn to power, is always artistically reactionary and must not in itself be the direct source of funds, but only indirectly. What purity remains to government-supported science is there because scientists sometimes are able to dispense the money. Control must remain within the theater itself in principle.

But whether private producers end up as the managers of a reconstituted New York theater, or WPA-like public officers do the job of administration, the question of minority-majority theater will have to be faced as well. There is no reason why, for example, we cannot support two kinds of theater, providing we recognize them for what they are. At present, both suffer for lack of such recognition. For example, critics have for a long time been pulled and stretched and distorted in their attempts to bridge the gap, when reviewing certain plays, between the two sets of values implied in alienated and unalienated theater. They have by and large taken it upon themselves to keep alive the fiction that there is only one audience. Thus, when in effect they tell "you" whether the work at hand is worth the price of admission, the "you" is really two different people whose values are quite strange to each other, and a work which one group would admire is forced out of existence because it does not meet the standards of the other.

All this would do would be to recognize existing reality, which is being masked by such concepts as "Broadway" and "Off-Broadway," "professional" and "revolutionary," and so forth. There are shows Off-Broadway which should be "on," and shows which briefly appear "on" which belong "off." That is, if their ideas, attitudes, quality of performance and sophistication are any guide.

The most obvious gain in placing productions in their real relationships to either of the two audiences is that a play of either kind will not be wiped out critically because it fails to meet standards it never sought to meet, or to attract an audience it had no thought of entertaining or instructing. But beyond that, a subsidized theater, a theater no longer competing with industry for the right to occupy land, would be relieved at least of the particular kinds of pressure which this unacknowledged competition generates. If it were recognized by every element in the theater that two audiences had a right to exist, rather than one fictive monolith, each kind of theater could then reach its real level with the audience for which it was designed.

One might then hope to see the day when productions which are not striving to innovate could be judged for what they are, rather than for what they are not and have no wish to be. It is even possible that the strident anxiety in so much of the acting, writing and direction on Broadway would at least lessen, and the sheer mawkishness of so many insurgent productions would begin to vanish as their confidence grew that they were, indeed, playing to their rightful peers and not to enemies.

There is no particular aesthetic dividend, no incremental virtue for artists in facing audiences which in principle are hostile or even indifferent to everything those artists stand for. Nor is there any sign of self-indulgence in addressing like-minded communities which share the artists' aims and spirit.

The open recognition that there are two Americas—at least two—and two theatrical communities would perhaps break up the current race to see who can be further "out" and begin integrating the inventions of the last few years into a form or forms that would support more than the anecdotal short play. Similarly, the majority theater, relieved of its terror of being outmoded, could perhaps concentrate on its own strengths rather than try to imitate watered-down avant-garde ideas and theatrical propositions.

Ultimately, perhaps, a new synthesis will develop. The open recognition of a split theater in the institutional sense, and critically as well, can only be a way station. The biggest possible loss entailed in such a situation would be that both theaters would be indulging themselves in code communication solely with their respective cliques. Inconceivable as it may be at the moment, one ought still to recall that the two most fully articulated theaters were the ancient Greek and the Elizabethan, and both were forced—or had the blessed opportunity—to face relatively unfragmented, whole communities. For us now, however, it is better to face the split, to exploit it aesthetically as far as possible, and hope that, as the possibilities of each audience and each theater are run to earth, the need for a universally applicable theater will once again make itself felt, and a new theater will rise that can both address the majority and speak the truth of the time for every sort of man to understand.

Whether there will ever again be a "Broadway," a collection of expensive buildings housing a theatrical profession where actors, playwrights and the other artists will start young and practice the art through maturity, no one can say. At least one new office building, on the site of the Astor Hotel, will house a new theater and this bodes well, but the unacknowledged problem of the audience lies hidden here too—the thing will have

1,800 seats. That spells majority theater, a musical house, probably. What about the other audience? When the minority and majority one day combine, perhaps it will be useful, but now?

Broadway was originally the arena, so to speak, for the entertainment of the masses. Its whole structure—financing, labor arrangements, land-use practices—is still based on that mass-based enterprise, which no longer reflects reality. If it is going to continue to pretend, in effect, that the nature of its business is the same as it was before the talking picture was invented, it must of course disappear, as it has been doing at an escalating rate. But if it faces the changed content of its two audiences, it could conceivably make room for both. The time, it seems, has come for all concerned—the theater owner, the commercial producer, the unions, the artists, the Off-Broadway producers and groups—yes, and the audience—to sit down together and face the facts. I forgot the critics. They can come too.

Arthur Miller *vs.* Lincoln Center

I'LL say something I've never said before: the Lincoln Center board *never* intended to have a repertory theater—a theater doing several productions at the same time—and they don't intend to now because they cannot and will not supply the money for repertory. When they originally consulted Robert Whitehead about the plans for a theater, he explained that it would have to have a vast area for the storage of scenery and everything else that goes with a repertory theater. His one aim was a repertory theater, but he told them there was no rule which said they had to build a repertory theater and suggested that maybe they should just build a place to put on plays, which would cost much less than a repertory installation.

They told Whitehead, "No, don't bother your head about costs, just build the nicest theater you can imagine." But when the point arrived at which the operational budget began to come up, it turned out that they had never established a budget on how much money would be allotted to the building, and how much was to be reserved for paying salaries for actors, and so forth. It was as simple as that. They were building a twelve-million-dollar monument, period. It's like building a new department store with practically no merchandise or employees.

From *The New York Times*, April 16, 1972, Sec. 2, pp. 1, 5. Copyright © 1972 by Arthur Miller.

The smallest repertory company I know of in Europe has about seventy-five people in its company. Lincoln Center originally eked about twenty-three out of its budget. The city of Munich pays $750,000 a year for the salaries and scenery and costumes of one repertory company out of four in that city. When the time came for the Lincoln Center board to bring repertory into being, they had no budget anywhere near to sufficient for it (by the way, the Robert Whitehead–Elia Kazan operation of the ANTA Theater downtown cost some $200,000 *less* than anticipated).

The Vivian Beaumont Theater was ready to open three months earlier than expected, but instead of giving Whitehead and Kazan the extra rehearsal time, the board began secretly dealing with Alexander H. Cohen to bring Rex Harrison to open this theater in a revival of some British comedy instead of opening it with a repertory production. This charade went on for months, mind you; they were on the verge of signing a contract with Cohen. In other words, they wanted a show in there at which you could really *dress*.

The Lincoln Center board's persistent, adamantine refusal to admit the facts continues to the present moment. These great giants of industry, banking, and commerce can't get it through their heads that the more successful a repertory theater is, the more it must cost. It contradicts all business principles.

The only explanation of their behavior I've ever come up with that made any sense was that they see credit to themselves in building monuments but not in paying actors. In their favor, it can be said that they would like to have had a repertory theater but, once having seen what it would cost, they should not have assumed the responsibility and then refused to make good on it, while at the same time pretending that they were indeed subsidizing such a theater. Except for the few weeks in the 1968–69 season when *King Lear* and *A Cry of Players* alternated, Lincoln Center has never operated as a repertory theater.

It may be as stupid as this: donors like to have their names on the back of a seat. When you pay an actor's salary, your name doesn't get engraved on the back of his head. Who will ever know that Mr. Rockefeller helped develop some great actor? Donors not only want to do good, they want their good to be seen being done.

What was their idea of a solution in the Lincoln Center Repertory situation last fall? Moving concrete. That makes sense to them. They will raise money to break down an existing thing as long as they can see an object being moved from one place to another. But they cannot conceive that the man who acts on the stage has got to get paid, *especially* if some weeks he's not working. Now you run into the ultimate absurdity where they planned to tear down the Forum, the best theater in that mess over there, and eliminate it.

At first, the board was great with Kazan and Whitehead, because Whitehead had a reputation as a tasteful and successful producer, and Kazan—well, Kazan was Kazan. Then the New York City drama critics began to slam these men, and the board decided to get rid of them. When they canned Whitehead, there were fourteen of the best American actors about to sign with Lincoln Center. I don't want to use names now, but in a season or two you would have had a marvelous company that no Broadway show could afford to hire, and they were possibly going to act for salaries close to minimum. As it was, the core of the company was in being. Faye Dunaway, John Phillip Law, Joseph Wiseman, Zohra Lampert, Hal Holbrook, David Wayne, Barbara Loden, Michael Strong and Jason Robards are all first-class talents, and something alive could have begun with them.

I don't know Jules Irving at all, I only met him once, I have no opinion about him one way or another as an administrator. But why did they reach all the way to California for Irving and Herbert Blau to run a New York theater? At the time, I thought it was because of the onslaught by the so-called intellectual critics, and these two fellows were more or less on the academic side. They had run a small provincial repertory company which had gotten good reviews in the local press, and everybody loved them out there. I figured the board looked around and said, "Who is loved?" and found Irving and Blau, poor fellows.

But the answer is simpler, I think now. They'd be *cheaper* than Whitehead, who was not trying to build a San Francisco repertory company but something in America that would vie with the great companies of the world.

When Whitehead was fired, I challenged the board, and I lost. I was the only one to make a statement in *The New York Times*. Nobody else would, and nobody picked mine up. The critics went right on yelling at the actors. If the critics would criticize *them*—the members of the Lincoln Center board—for a change, they might start to get very nervous, and when they get nervous they start to listen to *everybody*. You can't imagine how insecure these guys are. They're afraid of publicity, they want people to at least not notice. As you start to home in on them, I believe something would happen.

The critic has a duty here, because this is a public business. It's not entirely the board's business how Lincoln Center is run, because public money is involved and it's New York City's land, our property, that they're sitting on. It doesn't belong to them. You will *never* have a repertory company so long as that board is in control, and that is where the critics should make their attack, carefully and coolly. The critics must stop regarding Lincoln Center as just another Broadway operation where you hit the producer or director. You can't reach them by criticizing Jules Irving, or the actors, or the scenery design—this just creates a diversion and allows them to sit back and explain, "Well, you see, we didn't get good scenery this time."

Remarkably enough, in this age of anti-establishment feeling, this is one establishment which has never been attacked, and they are at the root of the entire Lincoln Center disaster. Look at them up there, you've got the heads of some of the biggest banks and other institutions in this country—nobody takes a critical shot at them. The critics will beat up the actors, the author, the director, that's easy. But it never occurs to any critic to go after those board fellows. Why not? Because the surrounding sociology of repertory is unknown to us.

All of us are always complaining about the death of the theater, now here's an instance where we can conceivably exercise an influence because we're dealing with a public institution. Now is the time for all of us, including the press, to say to them, "Anything *doesn't* go. You can't have it this way."

Most critics and other Americans don't understand what a repertory theater is, anyway. What does it take to run a repertory theater? Is it possible within the budgets the Lincoln Center board has envisaged? Let's investigate. These aren't mysteries on the moon. There are hundreds of repertory theaters all over the world. A study could be made, we could then lay out some kind of schematic idea of what it really takes to run a repertory theater.

Start with that, and leave artistic matters aside for the moment. Tell them: "All right, gentlemen, this is what is required to run a repertory theater, according to every piece of evidence. Can you supply it? If not, get out and let people in who can and will."

We have to face the economic issue, or else let's stop fooling around and rent the damned building out for whatever it will bring. The present situation is merely perpetuating a demoralizing feeling, as if to say, "Look, repertory doesn't work." We've never *had* anything like real repertory, so the alternative to the commercial Broadway theater has never come to be. The board is only pretending that it can come to be, and is thus preventing it from happening.

When we first started at the ANTA Theater downtown, Laurence Olivier asked me, "What are the critics screaming about? We were in Chichester for seven years before we ever came in to London. Our company was weeded out from hundreds of actors before we ever faced the London critics." He was bowled over by the fact that nobody here understood the rudiments of what goes into making a repertory company. It's an extraordinarily difficult thing to do, but it is worthwhile and so we must be clear about what the difficulties are, what the aims are, what it really takes to do this job, instead of going on saying, "When are we going to have a good show at Lincoln Center?" That is not the way to do it.

Let's look at budgets of repertory companies anywhere. If, indeed, the public or the donors will *not* give the money it takes to run a repertory theater, then let's stop pretending we have anything called the Lincoln Center Repertory Company and get rid of it. Maybe our culture will not support a repertory theater, or maybe some day, when we are all dead, there will be a repertory theater when they make up their minds to have it.

If you go to German theaters, you see facilities that are much larger than ours. Some of them, as in Frankfurt, have two stages, one to rehearse on behind the one they play on, with a movable wall between. So we shouldn't imagine that the Vivian Beaumont is outstandingly elaborate.

It's simply an impossibility to run this kind of an operation anywhere by selling tickets, even though the response of the audience with their subscriptions and admissions at Lincoln Center has been immense, tremendous. Let's clear the air. There could be no Kabuki, No, ballet, theater, opera, hospitals or libraries without an act of will. No marketplace ever has or can support such things.

Our cultural life seems to be drying up, we're becoming a utilitarian society in the crudest sense, namely, that which is not bought cannot be art. Whole sections of the New York Public Library, one of the greatest libraries in the world, are closed. Museums have short hours. Even the hospitals have to curtail their services and are threatened with closing because they have no money. We are becoming a second-class cultural power and in theater we are neck and neck with the Congo.

But the Lincoln Center situation may be amenable to improvement, theoretically, because it is not a part of the government. These guys are not elected officials, and they do not have the defense of the elected official, "How many votes do actors have?" The constituency of the Lincoln Center board is public opinion in general, and therefore something might come of our efforts.

All of which presumes that a repertory theater is really wanted here. Objectively speaking, though, maybe we'd do more good trying to raise money for libraries and hospitals, but let that lie for the moment. Maybe repertory theater isn't wanted as yet because it isn't understood. The first thing we have to do is declare our ignorance, and I include the lot of us.

I would also like to mention a mystery, however. Before there was a single production at the ANTA Theater downtown, before an actor had walked onto that stage, the mere announcement of the project set off an incomprehensible eruption of ridicule, cynicism and outright hostility in many theater people and the press. I still am unable to understand why. Maybe something in our culture rejects the idea as some kind of foreign body. We can't seem to connect prestige with repertory as we do with Broadway, God save the mark, while at the same time we are on our knees before the Royal Shakespeare and British National Theatres.

Repertory is certainly no panacea. It often breeds bureaucracy, time-saving lethargy. It always stands or falls on far-seeing, talented and selflessly ambitious artists at its helm, and these are scarce anywhere. But these problems can wait. Right now we don't even have a problem, because we have nothing. So the first order of business now is to get clear in our own minds what such a theater is, what it can do, and what is financially needed to do it. Then if we are convinced of its value, a considered serious attempt must be made to transform Lincoln Center into such a theater.

I think it is time the Lincoln Center board is called to account, just as playwrights, directors, and actors are. The Dramatists Guild and all concerned parties should demand they come forward and explain why they have failed to provide what they implicitly claim to provide. What is their policy? Surely they have a defense; what is it? They must no longer be allowed to fob off their failure on the artists working for them.

I repeat that a real repertory company may be impossible in the social system of New York today. Or it might be possible. We don't have the facts to make a judgment. The first thing to do, I believe, is to go in and challenge those men, to face the realities together, and decide what is to become of a potentially great theater that belongs to all of us.

IV

The Creation of the World and Other Business to *Timebends*

"Cain, we are surrounded by the beasts! And God's not coming any more. Boy, we are all that's left responsible!" —Adam in *The Creation of the World and Other Business*

"We must lie, it is our only freedom. To lie is our slot machine—we know we cannot win, but it gives us the feeling of hope. Is like a serious play which no one really believes, but the technique is admirable. Our country is now a theater, where no one is permitted to walk out and everyone is obliged to applaud." —Sigmund in *The Archbishop's Ceiling*

"All I mean is that we may be innocent, but we have changed. I mean we know a little something about the human race that we didn't know before. And it's not good news." —Fania Fenelon in *Playing for Time*

Arthur Miller on *The Crucible*

I SAW the movie of *The Crucible* with some very mixed emotions. I have never thought that a screen adaptation of a play must or even should hew to the details of the play, the film being so different a form. In fact, I don't think it is a good idea as a general rule to try to make movies of plays because the play is based primarily on what words can make true, while the movie is our most directly dream-based art and dreams are mostly mute.

The sheer visualness of *The Crucible* film is its best feature. It was made by the French on the Baltic coast of East Germany at a time when no American film company would touch the story for fear of attack by our righteous Right. The barrenness of the locale and the hardbitten peasantlike crudeness of the townspeople—all Germans— did indeed create the sense of our Puritanical forebears and the hard territory they were trying to transform into the New Jerusalem. In fact, I was later told that when it came time to shoot the hanging of the "witches," the actors and director got some expert advice based on real experience from some of the actors about how a hanging man reacts. (His feet continue to twitch for one thing.)

The actors, especially Simone Signoret as Mrs. Proctor, had enormous authority. Inevitably in a French picture the man-woman rela-

From *Audience,* (July/August 1972), pp. 46–47. Reprinted by permission of Arthur Miller.

tionship took on marvelously tender and complicated shades of resentment. The twisted marital love between Proctor and his wife was not seen as a mere means to a political end, but as something natural and moving in itself, and the Proctors' disaster was a wonderful mixture of personal and social themes. The Abigail, Mylene Demongeot, was truly beautiful and so bursting with real sexuality as to become a generalized force whose effects on the community transcended herself. As I had intended, she personified that force which the society of the time in turn suppressed and worshipped, for witchcraft—whatever else it is—is revolt, the revolt of the blood.

I don't like criticizing the film, primarily because I was grateful that it was made when it had become a symbol of what the ruling American idea could not tolerate. Fundamentally, I thought that it was weakened and made less actual, rather than more pointed, by Sartre's overly Marxist screenplay. Or maybe it is less a Marxist distortion than a European one. It is made very clear, for example, that the hysteria is rather coolly manufactured by a ruling class of big proprietors whose aim is to enslave the poorer farmers and the indigent. The feudal class structure of seventeenth-century French society is the prism through which Massachusetts is viewed, and this works to oversimplify the reality of the time. The fact is that while the Putnam family was wealthy and did indeed spur on the hysteria and in all probability engineered certain aspects of it, the line of battle was not nearly so clear or straight. Some very respectable people, some of them even in the Putnam family's class, were among the victims.

The original play stresses individual conscience as the ultimate defense against a tyrannical authority, but conscience in the screenplay is more an expression of rebellion against a class oppressor than a transcendence of a man over himself. Thus my viewpoint in the play was probably regarded as overly romantic and even bourgeois. In the screenplay this conscience carries the freight, so to speak, of a social-political lesson, but I am not sure it convinced many people of the truth that lesson was supposed to bring out. It didn't convince me because it mechanized the process by which very particular individuals become murderers of their fellow townspeople and others choose to give their lives rather than join the pack. This process may despiritualize the story and make it more politically recognizable, but it also reduces man to a digit in the social dialectic and in the end leaves everything explained but not illuminated. A Marxist interpretation of the Salem witch hunt could well throw light on many still mysterious and incomprehensible social motivations, but this moral puzzle will not give way to it. The victims as well as the persecutors were socially mixed in their backgrounds. This does not mean that an analysis based on socioeconomic forces is useless in analyzing such outbreaks, but it serves no purpose if it cannot penetrate the crazily various—and often decisive—courses which people took because of or despite their economic interests.

But the movie set itself a different task than faced me when I sat down to write *The Crucible*. The movie's intent is to prove that a landholding class in fear of losing its privileges instituted a terror against its social opponents. My play was an investigation into the how and the why of resistance to terror. The French, so far away and so conscious of their own history, transferred their very different sophistication to another place and another time, but not, I think, with sufficient grace of imagination to keep their grasp on the primary historical materials. The play was made more intellectually satisfactory to the Left, perhaps, but moved us further away from that confrontation with that very difficult-to-explain phenomenon of the human spirit refusing to go on living at the price of a terrible lie. This has more to do with faith than bare economics or even politics. I do not mean necessarily a religious faith but a belief, one might call it, in man as a creature transcending his appetites. We are what has made us but we are also something more, which is unpredictable finally. What comes to mind here is the fact that the people who kept their morale best in the German concentration camps were the devout Communists and the Jehovah's Witnesses. Their common denominator is something to think about in times when whole societies are in the process of being degraded.

But despite all this, I found it a stimulating and even gripping picture, which was finally deeply moving and quite beautiful. It is not to me *The Crucible* but a version of it and a strong film in its own right.

The American Writer:
The American Theater

IT IS quite beyond me to really do justice to this great occasion. The fiftieth anniversary of the Avery Hopwood Awards deserves a thorough historical account of their impact on American literature. I do not mean a mere listing of the notable writers who were first recognized and encouraged by the Awards, but perhaps, as important, the impact of the idea itself of a university that has the nerve not only to teach contemporary writing but, in effect, to act as its sponsor and to administer money prizes for student writing. I am not sure that this was a first, but I am certain that there could not have been many precedents fifty years ago. In fact, a look at the lives of some of our more distinguished writers who were born around the turn of the century and were of college age when universities were far more conventional in their attitudes toward the arts, will show that a large number of them either never bothered to finish college or had no connection as writers with any such institution. The Hopwood Awards, I believe, announced not merely annual winners but an attitude that has since spread through many other universities—that the writer can be just as valuable during his lifetime as he is afterwards.

So rather than attempt some sort of historical appreciation, I think it wiser to stick to my own experience as a beginning writer, a more

From *Michigan Quarterly Review*, 21 (Winter 1982), pp. 4–20. Reprinted by permission of Arthur Miller.

modest strategy, to be sure, but one that I hope will throw a more certain light on a far larger scene.

I believe I had two reasons for choosing Michigan, apart from its educational repute. The first was that it did not require mathematics. By the time I graduated from high school I was possibly the world's greatest expert on Algebra; having failed it twice, and only been passed a third time because they could not bear to look at me any-more, I came to a certain intimacy with every problem in the text-book. All I lacked was the remotest idea of how to solve them. The second attraction was the astounding news of the Hopwood Awards. The idea of a university handing out cold cash to students was, I con-fess, almost too glorious to contemplate. The money itself was impor-tant of course—even on the lowest prize, $250, I would later manage to live for a semester. And, of course, with money so hard to come by in the Depression thirties, giving it away for nothing more than words on a piece of paper had miraculous overtones when I had been work-ing in industry for years for twelve and fifteen dollars a week. But the central attraction was even more mysterious—the fact that money was given out meant that the judges—unlike your mother or your friends—could really tell good writing from bad. Thus, the recogni-tion of an award touched more than the pocket; it might even point the future.

I am forced to wonder whether, if Avery Hopwood had been a nov-elist and had neglected to give prizes for plays, I would not have tried harder to become a novelist. For the theater meant little to me when I began to write. I had seen only a handful of plays and those had seemed so remote and artificial that I could find no connection with myself at all in them. It must be remembered that in the thirties there was nothing that could be called an Off-Broadway theater. It would have been inconceivable to draw a separation between dramatic art and show business, which were treated as one and the same. I had heard vaguely about a Provincetown Theater, an experimental place where Eugene O'Neill had started out, but he, after all, had headed for Broadway as soon as producers would accept his plays. Later in the thirties, there would be two or three left-wing theater groups, most notably the Group Theater, but they, too, strove to succeed on

Broadway, even as they pronounced anathema upon its commercial greed.

Whatever triggered my imagination toward the play form is lost to me now, but it may well have been a production of an early Odets play by the Group Theater. Oddly enough, I cannot recall which play; all I remember was seeing actors who for the first time in my experience were physically vivid, whose faces seemed to have commonplace outlines, palpable noses and eyes that moved, and hands with veins. The *moments*, so to speak, of the play seemed superheated, isolated one from the other so that they counted eloquently, while at the same time—and this was the weird paradox—everything flowed together. More than this, I found myself believing that offstage—and I had never set foot on a stage but could imagine what it must be like back there—offstage was not offstage at all but the city itself, the New York I knew. So that the play was not like a little isolated cell where things went on disconnected from the city around us, but was one cell among the myriad, part of the sound and the anxiety and almost universal frustration of life at that time. Had I been capable, as I was not, of rationalizing the experience, I should have called it an experience of theater as life, as much a part of life as going into the subway or bringing home a bottle of milk or sitting in the back yard and wondering anxiously what was ever going to become of me after failing Algebra three times.

It would be decades before I would see it all from the opposite side of the equation—life, that is, seen as theater. Politics as theater, love as theater, lecturing on Chaucer as theater, psychoanalysis as theater, the church as theater. But perhaps there won't be time to go into all that.

Anyway, having seen that acting was not, as it had seemed till then, the art of speaking with an English accent, and that a play had something to do with sweat and hunger, I was hooked. I am speaking personally, of course, but only to support my generalizations. For example, I am sure that had I come of age in any other time and had seen some other production of high excellence, I would also have been similarly inspired. But one can't really be sure. I can only be sure that it did happen then; and I know it was not only the acting or the crazy poetry of Odets's lines. It was also what he was saying and what this whole way of acting was saying. It is a convenience to call their message Marxist or revolutionary; but for me it was more like being provided with an emotion, an emotion appropriate to the frustrations of living in the early thirties, specifically, the verb, if you will, for protesting the cursed irrationality of our lives. For people were starving then in America, while food was being burned up on the farms for want of a price. Odets seemed to provide a license for outrage, which has to be the first step toward a moral view. To me, as to most of the critics and the media of the time, he was overwhelmingly the clarion playwright. It would be years until I discovered, quite by chance in a conversation with Harold Clurman, who had directed the Group, that Odets's plays themselves—I am not speaking of the royalties, but of his plays—never made any money. Nor, as a matter of fact, did most of O'Neill's, although his made more than Odets's. And I mention this crass subject for reasons that will be alarmingly clear in a moment, but one point needs making right now. The American theater at that time was not about O'Neill or Odets, quite obviously; it was about entertainment of a quite different kind, the kind that offers an escape from life rather than a confrontation with it. I would only add that this is what most theater in most places is about most of the time.

But when I set about writing a play for the first time, I shared a certain illusion of community, which, I think, is implicit in the act of writing for publication or production. I felt alone, of course, and I was scared of making myself ridiculous, and I felt light years away from any suggestion of professionalism, for I was painfully aware that I knew very little about plays and nothing at all about the theater. My only hope was that the other plays being written for the Hopwood contest would be worse. This thought was the only one I had at the time that approached reason. The Awards provided a world small enough to grapple with.

For the real world of theater was quite different than it is today. As I have suggested, it consisted of the commercial Broadway theater and, to all intents and purposes, that was it. How did one achieve the requisite professionalism? It was all a mystery too deep for me. I had by this time dipped into the contemporary Broadway plays, those that had been published, for very few were then, and found little I could relate myself to. For I did not understand about charm in those days. Unawares, I had come to connect plays and the theater with some sort of prophetic function. Again, I was not in the habit of rationalizing such things, but a playwright for me was a man with his own church. Not that it was a question of preaching but rather of being the vessel of a community's need to talk to itself and to the world. It was possibly my Jewish heritage that imposed such a burden, or, if you will, such a challenge. But O'Neill was not Jewish any more than Ibsen was, or Chekhov, Strindberg, or the Greeks. (And, parenthetically, none of those writers could run very long on Broadway either, then or now.) How odd, then, to even imagine them as spokesmen, as prophets, for such they were to me then, and conventionally are still, even though we all know that the vast majority of plays are and always have been rearrangements of trivia.

It had not seemed to me to be too short a time—the five days of spring vacation—to write a three-act play. When it won a Hopwood Award, it was like an artillery shell fired right through the ranks of my opposing army—down went all my old Algebra teachers, for one thing. Then, soon after, another award fell upon the same play, The Bureau of New Plays Prize, administered by the Theater Guild in New York. This was a nationwide contest for college students. Another winner was a Brooklyn student who is surely present today, Norman Rosten. Another was a fellow from St. Louis named Tennessee Williams.

The main thing about this prize was the money—$1,250. I had already earned more with my first play than I had in three years as a shipping clerk. Needless to say, the contrast was not lost to my mind. And if I seem to linger on the subject of money, it is, I assure you, at the center of the great tradition of playwriting. As George Bernard Shaw replied to a businessman who had asked to discuss art with him, "No, I am an artist, not a businessman; businessmen always want to talk about art, but artists only talk about money." But with all the luck I seem to have had with that first play, the idea of actually making a profession of the theater was still quite unreal.

One problem was that I had spilled out into that first play everything I knew or could imagine about life. For I had hardly lived at all. I must invent something, I thought with sinking heart, and for this I supposed one had to have some kind of objectified technique. So, I promptly groped my way into Professor Kenneth T. Rowe's playwriting class. Such were the times—such was our theater, I should say—that one assumed to begin with that a certain technique could be learned that would more or less, if properly utilized, insure success. Again, the Broadway theater loomed in the background, the only theater we had and that indeed, rewarded certain formulas, as theater inevitably does at all times, including the present. That formula had numerous variations, but if it had to have a name it might be the Theater of the Rational. A problem was put in Act I, complicated and brought to a crisis in Act II, and resolved or answered in Act III.

It is hard to define what I took from Professor Rowe's classes. Perhaps it was, above all, his enthusiasm for the catholicity of dramatic literature, the sheer variety of forms that time had developed. And indeed, there was no single overriding style of writing in his class as there would be in the coming decades when fashion, for some reason, has so dominated and, I think, in many cases crushed invention. People then were writing Realism, Impressionism, Expressionism, poetic drama, verse drama, and Bronx comedies. It did not yet seem that there had to be obeisance to a prevailing mode. Perhaps fewer people were reading the Arts section of the *New York Times* then.

I suppose it was somewhat like learning how to draw in order to go on to painting, liberated from the tyranny of line. In any event, I think I came to believe that if the dazzling glory of the masters was finally their poetry, the fundamental poem was the structure. The structure, indeed, *was* the poem, the one element whose removal or disturbance collapsed the whole. One knew how Chekhov or Ibsen or Sophocles felt and *sounded*—now it was necessary to know how they were made. Paradoxically—or maybe it was quite logical—in less than ten years I would arrive on Broadway with a play, *The Man Who Had All the Luck*, that began with a problem and ended not with a solution, but at the door of the mystery of fate—why one person is chosen to win and another to lose, a question unanswerable whatever technique might be applied to it. I might add that the play lasted four nights. There was one encouraging review, but that from an alcoholic critic who was well on his way to the big bottle in the sky.

And speaking of the big bottle, it is time, I think, to talk about the critics. It is futile to criticize critics. It is quite enough to condemn them totally. Suffice it to say, I have never met a playwright who claimed he had learned anything from a review. Perhaps it can all be summed up in a story, which may just possibly be true, told me by the late Jed Harris who was the first director of *The Crucible* and in his best time, the twenties, one of the most creative men in the American theater. When he was directing *Our Town*, the most important critic, as always, was the man who happened to be on the *Times*, Brooks Atkinson, the very dean himself. Harris, concerned that Atkinson would not understand the play, which had certain innovations in staging, asked him to lunch, and there proposed to him that he begin a course of theater training by attending a few rehearsals. "I told him," said Harris, "that he really did not know very much about acting, directing, and scene design, and that I would be glad to teach him. He sat there very sweetly, listening to me and agreeing with me. But he didn't come to rehearsals because he felt it would be unethical and might tilt his opinion of the finished production."

Harris's point was one that everyone would have accepted in the decades before and after World War II—the New York reviewer was not necessarily a man who knew anything, he merely had to react with common sense in a manner representative of his readers. Thus, among the seven or eight main reviewers from the clutch of daily papers that still existed then, one found a remarkable number who arrived at the theater opening night on a tilting sidewalk. Others were unwashed refugees from the sports department, and one or two prided themselves on being professional humorists. The intellectual critics, exemplified perhaps by Joseph Wood Krutch, mattered very little to the box office, having disliked everything since the early Euripides. The reigning intellect of the Broadway scene was George Jean Nathan who, indeed, displayed occasional insights, but whose reviews, it seemed to me, most often consisted of lengthy lists of plays going back into antiquity of which the play at hand reminded him. To read

American theater reviewing then and now is to be convinced that the reviewer owns a certain sacred space, which it is his moral duty to prevent the playwright from entering. It is quite as though the entire purpose of the whole theater enterprise, its very *raison d'être*, is to provide a subject for criticism. This might be acceptable if one could recall the name of a single critic who, for example, had wounded Chekhov, Ibsen, Strindberg, or O'Neill by dismissing their works out of hand.

I won a second Hopwood in my Junior year, but I failed to win the big one as a senior. Nevertheless, it seemed possible to hope that I might become a professional playwright. The theater I was trying to enter seemed as always to be dominated by its critics, just as our immortal souls are dominated by our decaying flesh. But there was a certain illusion, shared by everyone involved, that I think helped to form a certain kind of play, and that kind, if I am not mistaken, was in the high tradition of the art. The illusion I speak of was that there was one single audience containing within itself in some mystical fashion the whole variety of America and Americans. The same audience that went to the Ziegfeld Follies one night might flock to O'Neill the next. And so it was not quite as odd as it might seem now that some of the reviewers would have been more at home at a ball game or a prize fight, for the same was true of much of the audience. In actual fact, of course, the audience may have been *emblematic* of American taste, but it was certainly not representative in the absence of blacks and workers in general. Still, there was a certain rough and ready air to its acceptance or rejection of a show.

The consequence to playwriting, however, is what is important here. Facing such an audience, the playwright could not console himself with yearnings for another, more sensitive and cultivated audience. Balcony seats in the thirties cost 55 cents and in them, at least, if not in the orchestra, were the salt of the earth—the student and his teacher, the neighborhood intellectuals of modest means, the housewives, and the more culturally hip of the working class. Downstairs in the orchestra were the business people and the professionals and, for certain shows, the usual sprinkling of cafe society. It may have been a better mix than we have today, but on the whole it never thought it owed anything to anyone, including even a minimal acquaintance with its own historical or literary culture. If a play had an idea, it had to be embodied in action; speeches had to be short, muscular, direct. If you had a message, said the prevailing wisdom, send it by Western Union, for it did not belong in a play. Plays were for fun, for obliterating your troubles, a chance to live other people's lives. It was a pragmatic, fundamentally uneducated audience, and if it simply turned its back on the poetic and the philosophical far more often than it should have, it could also make a quite proper demand upon a play: specifically, that its theme flow effortlessly from its action, and that meaning and viewpoint not be smeared all over it like mustard on a hotdog. It may be because of this kind of confrontation that I would find many years later a tendentiousness in so many absurdist plays that seemed to crudely slant life in favor of the meaningless conclusion, the hero slipping on a banana peel. It is a fact, nevertheless, that in the earlier time there was a dangerous intolerance of the ineffable unless even *it* were made active and packed with emotion, as in *The Glass Menagerie*, for example. That play, I would remind you, was regarded as certain to fail on Broadway because it seemed so delicately inactive, so ineffable and talky, and when it did succeed, it proved yet again that this audience for prize fights and ball games could be stretched and lifted by poetry, if it aimed for the heart rather than the education. In effect, then, the playwright was speaking to his country, and he had no other audience nor was it thought that he should have.

So, he was compelled to find language and theatricality broad enough in its humanity to hold such an audience. He could not rely for support on a clique pre-tuned to his cultural signals. Alienation in itself, in other words, had not yet become synonymous with style, let alone high art. And if it was mostly a theater of extroversion, its desire to make contact with the mass was not really different from that of the New and Old Testaments, the Classical Greek theater, and the best of the Elizabethans. It was a brutal challenge and could be a brutal confrontation, even unfair; but to accept it was to know the difference between grace under pressure and grace before dinner.

Sometime in the mid-fifties the profound shift within the audience as well as in the organization of the Broadway theater changed all these elements forever. In a word, one became aware that the audience was losing even its former superficial unity; it had begun to atomize. In my case, it was at the opening night of *The Crucible* in 1952 that I realized I was no longer precisely among friends. I have written of this elsewhere at greater length; let it be enough to say now that I was obviously not to be a part of what was then extolled as The American Century, a dawning era when the United States was going to be the new imperium abroad while jumping with democratic prosperity at home. What it all looked like to me was fear and anxiety covered over with the same old self-infatuation that had always led us to our disasters.

I have always supposed, however, that it was *Waiting For Godot* that signalled this shift within the audience. Why precisely it should have occurred at that moment must be left to another time; it is sufficient to say now that the absurdities of life moved into the stage as well as into the common wisdom of the time. But if the majority of the audience had no taste for shaggy dog stories and remained loyal to Broadway, most of the young left to support what now became known as the Off-Broadway theater, a theater whose main stock in trade was the absurd. I cannot attempt a sociological explanation for that absurdist vogue, but I can say that until the mid-fifties it would have been impossible to have met an American who could believe that General Motors, Chrysler, and Ford would one day find themselves incapable of building an automobile competitive with, of all things, the Japanese. It would have been equally hard to convince anyone that not only a President but his brother would be gunned down one after the other. The inconceivable, in short, had not yet become commonplace. And so, where before the structures of cause and effect, of fate and character-as-fate had supported the arch of dramatic structure, now it was the inconceivable itself that was raised up and given the kind of obeisance reserved for first principles. And in one sense, it was indeed a kind of naturalistic reportage of how the world was, for the concept of the absurd tended to legitimize the common conviction that absolutely nothing followed necessarily from anything else. One of the doubtful virtues of this philosophy was to liberate some of us from having to understand anything at all, and that included dramatic structure.

There were several reasons why I would find myself somewhat uneasy with this style. In principle, for one thing, it seemed odd that, whether in Paris, London, Berlin, or New York, regardless of the great differences between these societies, precisely the same mode of feeling and writing should have spontaneously arisen. In short, it seemed too obviously a fashion rather than a truth that had taken hold of the Western imagination. Secondly, our American despair is not quite the same as the European variety, for we have never ceased to hope, awkward as that may be to explain to strangers. So, it seemed somehow wrong that you should enter a theater and not be sure what country you were in. And, finally, so long as a writer writes, he hopes; this is what tragic writing assumes to begin with and black humor denies. I suppose what I am saying is that a work ought to acknowledge its premises.

With the atomization of the audience between avant and rear garde, a new breed of critic came on the scene. He or she was far more literary than the roughnecks of the past, far better trained academically, making the new demand for a theater of ideas and, in many instances, the more revolutionary the better. Some were brilliant stylists, others merely wished to be; the best that might be said of them is that their appearance was doubtless inevitable in the evolution of sophistication in American society, and the worst, that on the whole they seemed unwilling or incapable of admitting the contradictions of their own positions. Was it enough, for example, to abandon the majority audience in a democracy, or should playwriting and theater in general persist in trying to find the key to that audience rather than to play reassuringly to enclaves of the washed, the already saved, and the elite?

Nor is it altogether wrong to note that some of these critics were not too revolutionary to resist the call to assume the role of critic for the better paying magazines and even the *New York Times*. But perhaps their most harmful work was done upon the truth of history, for by the sixties they had all but persuaded their public that nothing in American theater was to be discussed in the same breath as the British, French, German—indeed, nearly any other theater. Modernity was European; mere naive sentimentality belonged to us. This was more than misleading nonsense. In fact, it was almost diametrically the opposite of truth.

In the early winter of 1956 I happened to experience a moment of historical change that might throw some light on this question of the American contribution to international theater. I was in London at that time working with Peter Brook on his production of *A View From the Bridge*. At the same time, my wife was starting a film, *The Prince and the Showgirl*, with Laurence Olivier. One evening soon after we arrived, he asked if there was anything in the London theater I wished to see. I glanced down the nearly full page of theatre ads— there were many dozens of shows then—and was at a loss. Not only had I never heard of any of the titles, but they seemed to promise precisely the kind of precious, upper-middle class nursery tales that had relevance, perhaps, to life among the fox hunters, but not very much else. My eye fell at last upon one title that I found intriguing— *Look Back in Anger*. It was not, of course, the looking back but the anger that seemed so un-British then. But Olivier dismissed it as an ugly travesty on English society. This made it even more interesting, and I persisted, and he finally agreed to get me a ticket. When I arrived at the Royal Court Theatre the following evening, I found Olivier in the lobby awaiting me. He had decided to see the play again.

To be brief about it, here was the first English play I had any knowledge of that told me something about actually living in England. And I had a strange *deja vu* sensation when I realized that it was doing for the English rather precisely what Odets had done in the early thirties for New Yorkers—letting loose a cleansing invective, an unbridled anguish and fury at the hapless decrepitude of the social system, its injustices and its frustrating stupidities.

Whether the author had ever read an Odets play was beside the point; the quite similar style, a certain apt wedding of lyricism and social outrage, had flashed out of the English sky a quarter of a century after it had done the same thing in New York, and doubtless for similar social reasons—namely, because a deadly formalized, polite, and rather bloodless commercial play had dominated in both countries for several decades earlier. Incidentally, after his second viewing, Olivier ended at the bar with the young Osborne who had written the play, and while I talked with George Devine, the director of the Royal

Court Theatre, I overheard Olivier asking Osborne whether he could write something for him. Which he promptly did—*The Entertainer*.

I was invited to be one of the speakers at an informal rally a few nights later in the Royal Court Theatre, where hundreds of young actors and writers had jammed the place to discuss the state of their theater. One of the recurrent questions directed to me was what they might do to begin creating plays like the Americans, plays that seemed to them so vital, so alive to current American life. There could simply be no mistaking that for these young men and women it was the American play and the American actor that had grasped the hour and the style of contemporary existence. In a few short years, of course, to listen to some of our own critics, it would be quite as though the American play and the American playwright had two left feet and could barely manage to read the hands of the clock. Indeed, this self-rejection went to such an extreme that nothing would do but an English critic had to be imported to oversee the New York theater for the *New York Times*. Such is the ineluctable power of fashion, I suppose. Indeed, the only English-speaking place left where you could find any real critical understanding and enthusiasm for the American play, its vigor and its poetry, was precisely in Britain, especially among the British actors, authors, and directors.

I have talked far longer than I meant to, but before I finish I must complete the winding of the noose from which American theater currently hangs. I am speaking, of course, of the Broadway theater, the so-called professional theater. If it was once *the* theater in the sense that almost everything original began on Broadway to be imitated by repertory and amateur theaters, it is now quite the opposite. Nothing but musicals now originates on Broadway; what serious work is shown, and it is practically extinct, has been transferred from Off-Broadway or regional threaters across the country. Broadway is hostile to serious work, that is no exaggeration, and so it should be. It is really too much to ask that people should spend twenty-five to forty dollars a seat to watch painful scenes and troubled characters. If it makes any sense at all, which I doubt, it indeed is far more sensible for the entertainment-seeker to spend that kind of money on song and dance shows, and that is just what has happened. The great audiences, which it used to be said great poets required, are no more. The student, the teacher, the man of modest means, the working woman—these will hardly be found in a theater anymore, not at such prices. But, as if this were not enough, we have the monopoly of theatrical criticism exercised by the *New York Times*.

Now the *Times* would doubtless deny this, pointing out that its critic has sometimes praised a play that in short order has closed anyhow. This is true but not particularly heartening. The far more decisive truth is that when the *Times* condemns a play it closes, and this regardless of how many other papers may have praised it. In fact, in 1963, when the *Herald Tribune*, the last of the *Times*'s competitors, shut down, the editors of the *Times*, led by their chief, Clifton Daniel, were sufficiently worried about the monopoly that had befallen them to call a meeting of theater people, at which I was one of the panel of speakers, in order to gather suggestions as to how that monopoly could be mitigated. I suggested that they provide readers with a healthy variety of views, three, four, or more critics to each show, but Mr. Daniel feared that nobody would know *who represented the opinion of the New York Times*. I thought this quite astonishing. It sounded suspiciously like an unacknowledged desire to wield the very power that they denied wishing to possess. But no matter—the absurdity remains, and given the massive domination of the *Times* over the theater, it is by no means an exaggeration to say that if every book published by a major American publisher—poetry, history, fiction, or whatever—were to be judged by a single individual and his word taken as to whether it ought to live or die, it would be an equivalent situation to the one obtaining on Broadway right now. Even in the Soviet Union plays can only be killed by a committee and not one man.

And on the outside chance that some of you may think me biased against the *Times*, let me say that in 1947 my first successful play, *All My Sons*, was recognized almost alone by Brooks Atkinson of the *Times*, his colleagues having been either indifferent or hostile to it. Having said that, I ought to add that the serenity of my confidence in critics is what it is because the same group of negative reviewers turned themselves around by the end of that season and voted *All My Sons* best play of the year. Such is life among the playwrights.

It seems to me that after fifty years of Hopwood Awards a cycle has been closed. I am sure that when Avery Hopwood conceived of financing prizes for young writers it was in some part an act of subversion against the commercial system of theater. I am also sure he wanted to encourage and support writers who would not only entertain but prophesy, and to give them a couple of years to strengthen themselves for a hard life. The Broadway theater today is, if anything, even more hostile to serious work than it was a half century ago, but all is not by any means lost. Today, unlike in Hopwood's time, there is a truly decentralized system of theaters spread across this country. Much fine work is done in these theaters—indeed, much of their work is stolen by Broadway. If there is any note of lamentation in this speech, it is not for a lost glory—there was never very much of that. But there was a level of professionalism in production, design, and performance that is not easy to find anymore. We have it still in the musical theater on Broadway, which is the best of its kind in the world. But the origination of serious theater is a thing of the past. Nor can one imagine how this will soon change; how forty-dollar seats will ever again come down in price, or how the monopoly of the *Times* will be broken, given the ingrained habits of theater-goers who follow the lead of that paper's tastes.

But maybe there is a disguised blessing in all this. A decentralized theater may turn out to be closer to the people than the New York-based one was, and perhaps this closeness will reflect itself in a more mature drama that reflects more of the balance of light and darkness in the country as a whole. I can see but one long-term danger, and it comes down to the problem of subservience. It is something that has cropped up frequently in the American theater since the early nineteenth century when Washington Irving complained that American authors and producers seemed to need the reassurance of foreign models for their works. Except in the musical, our most democratic form in the sense of its being adored and understood by the vast majority of the people, we seem uncertain about both the value of our own works as compared to foreign ones, and, more importantly, what the nature of serious theater really ought to be at this historical moment.

That last, of course, is a subject all by itself. Right now, one fundamental point might be made: what is evil in the United States and what
is good, what is confused and what is clear, what is progressive and
what is retrograde and reactionary, this whole crazy house—apart from
this or that judgment upon it—is in the vanguard of history, and continues to create the century in ways that no other civilization can.
Whether into the morass or onto the higher altitudes, we do break the
ground. Our drama, therefore, has the right if not the obligation to see
itself as a vanguard, as confronting human situations as though they
had never existed before in quite the same fashion and bearing quite
the same significance. I have traveled a great deal and in every kind of
extant social system, and whatever may be the local opinion of us, it is
from this land that they wait for news, for what's coming up, for word
of our state of mind, our hopes, and our despair. Confronted by a professional theater that, between its greed and its irresponsibility, no
longer has use for him, the American writer must now write for his own
people, for the theaters he finds around him. There is no center anymore, and in this sense the writing of plays is no longer a profession but
a calling to be practiced for the love of it or not at all.

I hope that what I have said has some truth in it. But since it is of the
theater I have talked, and in a larger sense America herself, whatever is
true now probably has been changing as we sit here. All I can hope for
is that you will catch her on the wing, willing and ready to fly to wherever in her unpredictable wisdom she decides she wants to go.

Salesman in Beijing

ARRIVING at the rehearsal hall at exactly 9:00 a.m., I find Ying Ruo-cheng, Liu Housheng, General Secretary of the Chinese Dramatists Association, and an ebullient, strong, laughing woman of fifty whose name is Zhou Baoyou—Joe, for short—who is filled with bursting good health from her forty-five-minute bike ride to her office, which she does every morning, winter and summer.

She is the Mrs. Trouble of China's entertainment industry, solving everybody's transportation problems, health and food difficulties, getting them airport and railroad tickets, and in general making foreigners believe they are safe in the laps of the gods. (As I would learn later, she is the daughter of a banker who decided to cast his and his family's lot with the Revolution; she studied English in a Christian school; her enjoyment of life springs in part from the post-Cultural Revolution liberty, which she loves, and in part from her children's success—her son is studying music in the United States and her daughter studies in China. Above all, she wants, she says, "to contribute something," and feels this production will be the best thing she has ever had a chance to help into life.)

Liu Housheng is her boss, a diffident man with short-cropped gray hair, wearing a particularly much-laundered Mao jacket and a gentle,

From *Salesman* in Beijing, Viking Press, New York, 1984, pp. 18–30. Reprinted by permission of Viking Press, a division of Penguin Books USA, Inc. Copyright © 1984 by Arthur Miller.

rather humorous look. I take him to be—from his position—a Communist Party member and probably its representative to me, for he has a certain amount of power, I am sure, at the apex of the Dramatists Association. But at the moment I have no interest in pursuing the submerged world of political controls in my eagerness to have my first readings of the play today.

Joe's news is that we must decide what to do about some twenty-two foreign television and print correspondents—and many more than that from Chinese media—who want to interview me about the production. I have already in hand about a dozen requests routed through the Association. Joe, thank God, has kept my telephone number secret but doesn't know for how long this will be possible. After much back and forth it is clear the Chinese have been caught up in the publicity hunger and want me to honor all the requests—a faint surprise, since I had somehow assumed that media pressure would inflame their phobias about being used. Instead it has amplified mine and pleases them no end. This is a very different China. It is funny to hear them talking Chinese among themselves with "CBS, ABC, NBC" thrown in. I finally decide that I will give the journalists interviews independently provided they're kept short. This is not going to work, of course, but has to be tried, I guess.

By ten we have all assembled, the whole cast seated around an ample room in armchairs, scripts in their hands. There is a moment of dread as Linda says the first line—"Weelee!"—from the bedroom, having heard him enter the house. The first surprise is how easy it is for me to follow the scene in my Penguin paperback. It is a triumph of Ying's translation—even the rhythms seem the same, the flows to the peaks and the slopes toward the silences. In a few minutes it is obvious that Zhu Lin and he will easily seem related, husband and wife, and of this particular class. I cannot believe they have come this far in a few rehearsal days. Ying hardly looks at the script, and she only a little more often. What am I going to do with six weeks of rehearsal time!

Zhu Lin is an actress of awesome experience in classic Chinese as well as modern plays—"a heavyweight," in Ying's words. She already knows she must keep Willy from wandering too close to the edge, affects a happiness with his positive moments, insinuates the truth when he cannot bear hearing it, always reaching a hand out as to a child who cannot walk without falling down. I can detect no trace of the declamatory style in either of them, something I had feared and still do. On the contrary, seated side by side in chairs, they create the Lomans' bedroom. Ying has a kind of absolute control that brings Olivier to mind—he simply does what is called for, easily, directly, effortlessly. But a few of his shifts of temper are repetitious and we shall work on those. The shape of the first scene does not yet exist, but the main thing is almost palpable—the truth of where the Lomans are with each other as a couple. The reading approaches a read performance in that they already possess consistent attitudes and are not merely groping. What gratifies me is the absence of the distance I had supposed would separate them from the feelings in the roles, but whatever is lacking, it is never intimacy with their own feelings. Or so it seems. If they were merely posing, imitating "American," I don't think I could follow every speech as easily as I do.

With the reading over I ask the cast to tell me what, in their roles, if anything, they feel alien to. "What are you called on to do that a Chinese would not do?" There is a silence. Then the actor playing Happy says (in Ying's translation), "I can't imagine a Chinese continuing to talk to his brother once he says, as Biff does, that he is going to sleep."

Ying clarifies: "He is talking not so much about impoliteness as that a Chinese would not feel such pressure to continue talking once his listener has said he is going to sleep."

"Then an American, you mean, feels the need to speak more urgently?"

"Exactly, yes. An American feels he must say what he has to say no matter what. Whereas a Chinese would feel that to continue would be ineffectual."

"Is this politesse?"

"No, not really. It is probably a recognition of the limits. Once the limits are reached, that is all that can be done."

I feel there is some hidden relationship to this analysis in a question the actor playing Charley asks a few minutes later. Today he is wearing a sweater in two shades of gray and looks more elegant. "I don't understand why Charley is so kind to Willy," he says.

"He feels pity for him, perhaps."

"Ah." He nods. I don't think he is really convinced.

"Maybe there are people like this, who feel for others and try to help if they can."

"Yes," he says, still weighing the possibility. I like him—an actor who has to make his information work and asks a solid question.

"They are old friends, you know."

"Yes, I know." There is a pause, and then he says, "I don't think any man would be so good to another in China." The others show no reaction.

This reminds me of the problem we had in casting the part in the original production. Kazan had reached out into what seemed the totally wrong direction for Howard Smith, a shouting comic who had been in vaudeville for years before becoming a minor star in farces, where he played the standard bewildered father of teenage girls. *Dear Ruth* was his big current success. Howard had never been near a serious play and had no desire to be, when comedies ran so much longer. He was a stout, gruff, tall man with sparse blond hair and a loud, rather common baritone voice. He read the play and refused the part, surely the best he had ever been offered in his life. Kazan, Bloomgarden, and friends of his all tried to change his mind but to no avail. "That play is *terrible*," he'd say. "Who's going to want to see something that sad?"

Finally, in desperation, a meeting was fixed with him and me alone in Bloomgarden's office. I had learned from Kazan what his objection was, but pretending ignorance I asked him to tell me why he was so against the play. "The poor man, for God's sake; the rotten things his sons say to him. And his boss. Everybody's so down on him. It's just awful!"

"Except Charley," I said. I could see his eyes change. He stopped moving. "Charley gives Willy good advice, lends him money, always makes time for him during office hours. . . . Charley really tries, Howard."

He sat there staring. Finally he said, "I'll think about it." That night he accepted the role. His instincts were as right for it as his personality: a hardheaded, realistic, decent man; slightly dense, perhaps, but filled with human warmth. A mature actor, he was instantly credible, no matter what he did or said.

We had been rehearsing for more than two weeks, the play was fully blocked, and while Arthur Kennedy, Lee Cobb, Mildred Dunnock, Cameron Mitchell had all had their turns asking Kazan or me what something meant, Howard Smith had never asked a single question. He was especially glorious in the card-game scene, where Willy is beginning to talk both to Charley and to his vision of his brother Ben, who has materialized at his elbow as he plays. Charley is of course totally unaware that Willy is addressing a wraith as well as himself, and from his viewpoint Willy is making less and less sense. Howard Smith managed this mystification with subtlety and discretion, never overdoing his bewilderment, always curious as to what Willy means.

But on this day he surprised everyone. He broke off the scene, and raised his hand up to shade his eyes and look out into the dark theater. "Can I ask a question?" he said. "Gadg? Are you there?"

"I'm right here, Howard," Kazan answered. "What's your question?"

Pointing at the actor playing Ben—Thomas Chalmers, an immense man, formerly an heroic basso with the Metropolitan Opera—he asked with a certain super-intensity that told of a long conflict he had been living through over possibly many days, "Do I see him?"

Kazan kept a straight face. "No, Howard."

"I don't see him at all," Howard Smith confirmed—happily, it seemed.

"Not for a minute, not at all, never. You just don't see him, Howard."

"Good. Okay. That's what I thought."

Apparently Howard had simply been obeying Kazan's instruction never to look at Ben, for what reason he did not really know, and had been puzzling it out for the past days until he could no longer hold back his question. It was a comically embarrassing setback for all the Stanislavski actors in the cast, who, in order to make themselves real, had put all they had into studying the reasons why they did what they did, while the realest one on the stage had not known what he was doing—and it was one of the most difficult feats of acting in the play.

Now, a world away in space and 35 years later, here was an actor being Charley again. How odd, yet fitting, that in this time and this place, after revolution and civil war and cruelties beyond the mind's power to contain, this Charley should be asking not why everyone is so bad to Willy but why Charley is so good to him.

I raise the question with the cast whether this play would have been performed, let's say, in 1977 or 1978, and they quickly reply, as though it were obvious, that it could not have been understood by the audience then. I take this to mean that they would not have understood the unusual form. Under the Gang of Four through the Cultural Revolution, they had only Jiang Qing's "Eight Permissible Plays," demonstrations of problems. But in the past five years a few foreign plays have been performed, and the audience, especially the younger majority, are eager for new forms.

"I read *Salesman* to this company in 1978," says Ying, "but they rejected it, sure that it would be incomprehensible. The elements of American society in it had no preparation in the public mind; nowadays everybody knows foreign films and TV and a great deal about how the West lives. We think even the liquid form of *Salesman* has also been prepared for in their minds now. They will be eager for it."

All this reminds me of how much doubt there was about the play when I wrote it. In fact, Joshua Logan, who had invested a thousand dollars in it sight unseen, withdrew five hundred after he read the script. One day during rehearsal Kazan and I ran into him in the street. He was painfully embarrassed, thinking we knew—which was not the case as yet—of his expression of disbelief in the play, and he urged me to remove Uncle Ben and all the elements of Willy's hallucinatory life because the audience would be hopelessly uncertain whether they were in the past or the present. At that time American theatrical experience also was primarily realistic, in the pictorial sense of the word.

I keep pressing the cast to ask questions, not only for the questions themselves but to help me judge where their minds are in relation to the play and American culture. At last the actress playing the Woman in Boston, who occasionally sleeps with Willy when he is there, asks, "Is she a Bad Woman?" This actress has the right voluptuousness, the round Chinese face and a sexy solidity of flesh. Ying quickly interrupts to explain that to the Chinese a woman has to be "Bad" to be so promiscuous, and I detect no irony in his voice.

Considering how I am to reply, I think that the actress and perhaps Ying as well and maybe the whole cast are hoping that she is *not* Bad— a prostitute—so it is easy to tell them that she is a lonely woman who has a regular office job and is not at all a prostitute, and that she genuinely likes Willy and his line of gab and his pathos, and so she sees him for dinner perhaps twice a month and they talk and "behave like husband and wife for a night." Great relief on all sides. It would have been difficult to add that she might have a similar relation to a couple of other salesmen from time to time and still not be thought of as a prostitute or even Bad. But this would also be hard to explain in parts of the United States.

I am not sure they accept her behavior as truly non-Bad, but I leave it ambiguous in the hope that she will not try to play a Chinese vamp. I don't trust their notions of Western sexuality, even if I have no experience of the Chinese kind; I remember that on our last visit in 1978, couples did not so much as touch hands in public. Amazingly enough, nowadays they have had to clear a small, dense patch of shrubbery not far from the American Embassy because of its attraction for extrabotanical exercises.

Now that the subject of sexuality is opened up, Happy raises his hand to say that the Chinese would probably not understand his character. This actor's personality baffles me; he is rather small and slight, with straight black hair, longer than usual here, that flows down above his left eye, and a thoroughly pleasant but somehow indefinite, even evasive smile. He seems too young for Happy, about twenty-four, and far too passive for that sexually overheated character, but I keep telling myself that maybe these traits will appear different to Chinese and that I must give him his head. Ying's casting was so right in the other parts, it is hard to believe this fellow is as wrong as he seems at this point.

"What do you think they won't understand?"

Ying intervenes. "He means, I believe, that they will understand the workings of his character, but the play seems not to condemn his womanizing. In Chinese society a man talking about women as Happy does—bowling them over and so on—would be a rotter."

"You mean it will leave them uneasy because he is sympathetic?"

"Exactly. The *i*'s have to be dotted here."

Ying translates our little exchange and the cast laughs, but with a certain uneasiness, as though they are not sure themselves about the matter.

I decide to leave it right there, for the time being. Let their anxieties deepen, it will charge them up all the higher. And anyway I am leaving the country two days after we open.

I ask Linda how she feels about her character and whether such women are to be found in Chinese society today.

"Oh, many, many. There are a lot whose lives are wound around their husbands', and who think only of their men and very little about themselves." The cast nods reassuringly to me. The time has not yet come to tell her that this idea of Linda is mistaken. I am better at working in detail than in throwing out broad generalities.

But in an attempt to fill in my sense of the country—rather than to document the character, which I see somewhat differently than the actress does—I ask whether this attitude, even if so prevalent, is not regarded as old-fashioned now. The cast is emphatic—it certainly is old-fashioned. To pin it down, I ask Biff and Happy, who are seated together, if their generation has women in it like Linda, and they are incredulous that I can have imagined such a thing, and set up a cross talk directed at me through Ying.

"The women," he translates, "earn their own livings now and that's the basis of the whole relationship. In fact"—he grins, pursing his mouth comically again and popping his eyes behind his thick lenses—"it's usually the women who throw the men out, not the other way around." Everyone guffaws. They are aware of riding a wave of change that has by no means hit the beach and flattened out yet.

I have been catching a certain tone of condescension toward Willy's character coming from Linda and Willy—from him, especially—from time to time. Perhaps it is unconscious; or possibly I misunderstand. It came at me yesterday and again two or three times today, an indefinable but dangerous attitude that could lead to a satiric interpretation, which would leave Ying Ruocheng unable to sustain the role the whole length of the play. (I am not sure he has yet caught on to how physically difficult this part is going to be.) But most important, I cannot let the play become a satire.

"I want to say a few things about the play and Willy now," I announce. They become silent quickly. It is now clear, incidentally, that they normally discuss a play for days and sometimes weeks before trying to do scenes and, like all actors, would—up to a certain point—much prefer interesting general discussions to hard work. But I am coming to realize that in this type of theater there is no rush to do anything. "You are all aware, I'm sure, that Willy is foolish and even ridiculous sometimes. He tells the most transparent lies, exaggerates mercilessly, and so on. But I want you to see that the impulses behind him are not foolish at all. He cannot bear reality, and since he can't do much to change it, he keeps changing his ideas of it." I am veering close to ideology; I note some agreement here, but it is uneasy. Charley is especially rapt and unable, I believe, to come down on the side of my argument. "But the one thing he is not, is passive. Something in him knows that if he stands still he will be overwhelmed. These lies and evasions of his are his little swords with which he wards off the devils around him. But his activist nature is what leads mankind to progress, doesn't it. It can create disaster, to be sure, but progress also. People who are able to accept their frustrated lives do not change conditions, do they. So my point is that you must look behind his ludicrousness to what he is actually confronting, and that is as serious a business as anyone can imagine. There is a nobility, in fact, in Willy's struggle. Maybe it comes from his refusal ever to relent, to give up."

Silence. It worries me, their never having seen it in this light, the character of this screwball; quite probably they had been moving toward a satiric interpretation, or at least one that would let them off the hook as actors, and the audience as well. I see now why Ying was so insistent that I come and direct; he is especially still, especially open to this apparently novel line on the play, although I have no doubt he has always seen the role as basically a tragic one.

Now Ben has a question. This actor is a short fellow with a certain ferocity in his gaze; the outer corners of his eyes are curled up like those of the Chinese opera villain-masks, especially when he concentrates on what I am saying. Compact and quick-moving, he already has a certain pecky style. Even when he suddenly changes, and bursts out laughing, there is some danger in him—all of this is perfectly subjective, of course; he is doubtless sweet and kind.

"Is Uncle Ben a ghost?" he asks.

"A ghost?"

"Yes."

"I'm not sure what you want to know." I dread misleading him; it will take days to undo some mistaken but—to him—attractive image.

"Chinese plays," he explains, "do not have ghosts."

"Really? I had some idea they did, but it doesn't matter. I realize that you cannot play a 'ghost' but what you should play is Willy's brother."

"Ah!" This seems to please him. "But I am really dead?"

"Oh yes. And you exist in his memory with certain characteristics that are not necessarily realistic. I mean that you must play him as Willy recalls him. He carries tremendous meaning for Willy, and you must learn what that is as time goes by. But for now you can forget the 'ghost' and think of yourself as his elder brother who made a great success in South African diamond mines, okay?"

He has an image and he is happy. A real actor, thank God.

But Ying is not quite satisfied. "What Mr. Miller was trying to say, I believe, is that sometimes Ben has his own character and sometimes he simply voices Willy's thoughts. In other words, he is and is not a real person like the other people in the play."

"That's not a contradiction," I add. "We all remember actual people we once knew but we remember them in a nonobjective way, a way that emphasizes and even parodies some of their qualities. It depends on what they mean to us, doesn't it."

Ying understands, and translates this for Ben, who seems to sop it up, nodding eagerly. So Freud works here, too.

Now Charley is back with another question—I feel good about their being relaxed enough now to leave off raising their hands like students. "He wants to know," Ying says, "whether he and Willy play cards for money."

I had never thought of this before, but actually they would be putting down small bets, and so I ask, "Do Chinese play cards much?"

"Oh, we love cards but never play for money."

Which brings back a walk I took in Yanan five years ago, when I saw a pretty hot card game going on in the middle of a field on the edge of town, with money on the ground and guys yelling with every card played. I had learned then of the state's prohibition on card gambling, a national vice the government was trying to stamp out. Without raising the political issue, I ask, "Could you play for small stakes in that scene?"

"Certainly, if that's called for." (Whether by design or simply because the very complicated mechanics of the scene made it nearly impossible, no money was ever subsequently used. However, it wasn't in the first New York production either, but it is interesting that the political side of the question was not put to me.)

Still drugged by the worst jet lag I have ever experienced I return to the theater at seven o'clock in the evening for the first reading of Act Two. I believe they might well turn out to be quite fine, and allow myself a more or less total silence as the reading proceeds. Inge is in tears at the end.

The weirdest part of this day is that in the car on the way back to our lodgings at the end of the reading, I realize again that I had been able to follow the dialogue almost always without using my English script, staying with the actors line for line. Even the lengths of sentences are nearly the same. It is uncanny. Yet, on questioning Inge I learn that the *content* of the lines is very often quite different, involving as it does the imagistic Chinese vocabulary. For example, Willy reports to his boys on his vastly successful selling trip: "Knocked 'em cold in Providence, slaughtered 'em in Boston." This becomes "I tumbled them backwards in Providence-ah, and they fell on their faces in Bos-i-ton!" But it had an uncannily similar sound and almost precisely the same beat.

I fall asleep as soon as I contemplate the bed, but wake every few hours, startled. I am still drugged, numbed, but not unhappy. These will be fifteen-hour days for me, rising at seven to have breakfast and drive to the theater, with bedtime only after the ten o'clock finish of rehearsals at night. But I am looking forward.

The Will to Live

INTERVIEW BY STEVEN R. CENTOLA

THIS INTERVIEW, the transcript of a conversation I had with the playwright on June 25, 1982 at his Roxbury, Connecticut home, has been deliberately left in its colloquial form. I have tried to recreate as closely as possible the sound and spirit of our conversation in the hope of sharing with the reader the distinctive intonation, quick wit, and candor of Miller's responses.

CENTOLA: I've always been fascinated by your ability to maintain a singleness of vision in plays remarkably different from each other in form, style, mood, theme, characterization, plot, and even at times in language. Would you agree that this underlying continuity in your work derives from a vision of the human condition that can be described as a kind of existential humanism—a vision that emphasizes self-determinism and social responsibility and that is optimistic and affirms life by acknowledging man's possibilities in the face of his limitations and even sometimes in the dramatization of his failures?

MILLER: That's very good. I would agree with that. That's a fair summary of what I feel about it—my own views about it.

CENTOLA: The one play that seems to provide the clearest revelation of your vision is *After the Fall*.

MILLER: Just about, yes.

From *Modern Drama*, 27 (September, 1984), pp. 345–360. Reprinted by permission of Steven R. Centola.

CENTOLA: Not many people see it that way.

MILLER: Well, I think they were, to be quite frank—I've said this before; it's no news—but I think that they were blinded by the gossip and the easy way out. But it's not just in my work. I think people go for tags for any writer; you don't have to think about what he's doing any longer, especially if he's around a long time. But then simply you know what you think you want to expect. It may or may not have much to do with what he's doing. But they find whatever in the work fits that expectation, and the other is simply not dealt with or is rejected. This is an old story here that we all know.

CENTOLA: Your vision, what I've called your existential humanism, seems to have a lot in common with Jean-Paul Sartre's existentialist philosophy.

MILLER: You know that Sartre did the screenplay for *The Crucible*, and we were on the verge of meeting three or four times and never managed to because he was out of France when I was there. There was always a mix-up, and I always thought that there was more time than there actually turned out to be. But I think there was a relationship which was not programmatic in any way. It just means people leaning in the same kind of direction.

CENTOLA: So you wouldn't say it was a matter of influence?

MILLER: No, no.

CENTOLA: Would you feel as though I were going for a tag if I pointed out some of the similarities between your vision and Sartre's existentialism?

MILLER: Well, I don't think that's a danger because he certainly was always attractive to me in a vague way. But I'll tell you, I'm not a methodical, philosophical writer; I don't spring out of that kind of tradition. I work out of instinct. And so whatever similarities that there turn out to be, somebody's always related to something.

CENTOLA: Do you think an identification of these Sartrean correspondences in your plays could bring out the metaphysical issues in your work and help to put to rest the notion that you're merely a social realist, the tag which you seem to have been stuck with for some time now?

MILLER: The social realist thing is what they were doing with Ibsen all his life. He was supposed to be interested in sewers because of *An Enemy of the People*, or in syphilis because of *Ghosts*, or in women's rights or something like that because of *A Doll's House*, and all the rest of it. Of course, what is inevitable is that these are all, in a certain sense, metaphors, and had the writer merely been interested in sewers, violence, women's rights, and the rest of it, we would have long since lost track of his name. These are metaphorical situations of the human race as it goes on forever.

CENTOLA: The great writer gets at the universal through the particular.

MILLER: Sure. If you don't, you end up with a kind of blatantly philosophical dialogue of some sort that nobody really is interested in. It isn't the way these obtrude into experience. That's as simple as it can be.

CENTOLA: I read some of your unpublished works that I was able to get through the Humanities Research Center at the University of Texas. One of these was a letter you wrote called "Willy and the Helpless Giant," and in that letter you suggest that tragedy results when one tries to attain honor by putting on a mask and performing for the public instead of being what one really is and does best. In many ways, that idea parallels Sartre's distinction between being-for-itself and being-for-others. I'm wondering if that conflict isn't part of the tragedy of modern existence: individuals feel obligated to adopt poses or wear masks in order to make themselves feel significant or honorable?

MILLER: That's true. But the question is how old a procedure that is, how old that process is. Because the more class-structured a society is (for example, a royal society like, let's say, the eighteenth-century or seventeenth-century French society), people had to fit into a mold that was given them by the class that they felt they belonged to. And all costume, dress, manners, habits, and the mores were predetermined, in effect, so that sincerity was hardly a value at all. It's just that it wasn't necessarily cynical. It was simply that the society and sincerity could not comfortably coexist. So that for the sake of good order, one had to adopt some kind of persona, which is not necessarily the one that one really has. Now, for us, I think this is an old thing in the United States. Alexis de Tocqueville mentions the fact that we don't want to be set aside from the mob. That means people will adopt a mask in order to be like everybody else. And maybe it's implicit in that statement that Americans don't want to be separated from the mask.

CENTOLA: That's an interesting way of establishing a connection with others.

MILLER: But there's also a price to pay for that. And the price, obviously, is the loss of something. Society makes such a heavy demand upon the individual that he has to give up his individuality (and we do have a high percentage of mental breakdowns and neuroses and the rest of it). So, maybe it goes along with democracy, oddly enough.

CENTOLA: That's interesting.

MILLER: I think that the British, for example, are far more able and willing to endure characters than we are. (What would you call characters? People who don't necessarily abide by the rules.) We're much less tolerant. We won't lend them money; we won't see them through school sometimes. We impose a discipline on them because they are different, and so on.

CENTOLA: So we place a greater emphasis on conformity?

MILLER: Conformity is a terrific power here. To jump to another sector of this, I think it lay behind the power of the Un-American Activities Committee, because, after all, what they were threatening most people with was not jail, and it certainly wasn't shooting; it was being disgraced—social disgrace.

CENTOLA: What I was getting at in that question is whether tragedy could be considered as a fundamental condition of being. Take Hamlet as an example. Here's an individual who is obsessed with living up to the image expected of him by others. It's the same with Othello and Oedipus. It seems that all these characters find themselves torn between....

MILLER: Mask and reality. You ought to look into the whole question of the fact that the Greek plays were played in masks. I'm not sure where that fits here, but it just occurred to me. Well, of course, I have been very conscious of this as a writer, that is, of the conflict, the friction, the opposition between the individual and his social obligations, his social mask, his social self. And it always seemed to me that the perfect society would be one in which that gap, the friction, would be able to be minimized, but people don't seem to be driven crazy about it. It isn't that totally American kind of a thing, though, obviously. It's everywhere; it just takes different shapes. I suspect it's in tribal Africa. You see, there are social duties and social fears that can create a tragic event.

CENTOLA: That's why I mentioned Sartre; he's dealing with the fundamental condition of being human: being self-conscious.

MILLER: It's certainly in the center of it.

CENTOLA: Well, it seems that the tragedy of displacement, which you have discussed in your essays, is really a type of existential crisis that results when one has to make a conscious choice between his public self and his private one. You say that displacement results from a character's violation of his nature through compromises or mistakes. And then his effort to regain his sense of identity against overwhelming obstacles makes the play take on a tragic dimension.

MILLER: I think in the plays of mine that I felt were of tragic dimensions, the characters are obsessed with retrieving a lost identity, meaning that they were displaced by the social pressure, the social mask, and no longer could find themselves, or are on the verge of not being able to. There in the private man is the real one.

CENTOLA: In your introduction to your *Collected Plays*, Volume I, you say that the one unseen goal toward which almost all of your plays strive is the "discovery and its proof—that we are made and yet are more than what made us." That statement seems to pinpoint the central tension underlying all of your plays, a tension created by the antagonistic forces of fate and free will acting upon each other.

MILLER: Right. Did you ever read my first play on Broadway, which failed, called *The Man Who Had All the Luck*? In the line of this kind of discussion, that really was a very important play for me, because while the play failed, I learned in that play where I was positioned in the world, so to speak. And the play taught me something which I wasn't even aware of at the moment. But looking back—just this kind of a question is raised. He wants to know where he begins and the world begins; where he leaves off, the world begins. He's trying really to separate himself and to control his destiny.

CENTOLA: Or to make himself aware that he has been controlling it, and that he's not just a pawn of the forces around him.

MILLER: Yes, right. So, it goes right back to the beginning in the most vague part of my career.

CENTOLA: That play didn't get the justice it deserved because the critics misunderstood it. If I'm not mistaken, a major complaint at the time was that the play displayed "jumbled philosophies" because you didn't choose to advocate either fate or free will. But why should you choose one and not see the interplay?

MILLER: The interplay was the point! Well, you see, this was where they couldn't run with a tag. That's exactly what I started out by saying today. Had I been very clever and sophisticated about it, I would have thrown out a tag that they could run with and feel that they had it in their pocket. But I let the tension run on right through the end, instead of resolving it for them the way it never is in life.

CENTOLA: So you would say that dialectic exists also in your other plays?

MILLER: Oh, yeah. No question about it. It goes right on now.

CENTOLA: Like Sartre, you often seem to concern yourself with the alienation of the individual in your plays. Frequently, alienation has something to do with the individual's recognition of (and reluctance to accept) his separateness. Such alienation is perhaps most apparent in *After the Fall*, but it is also evident in your other plays. Willy Loman and other characters also cannot accept the fact that they are separate beings.

MILLER: That's right. You know, I have a line somewhere—oh, I think it's in an introduction I wrote to *A View from the Bridge* or one of the editions of *A View from the Bridge*, but I could be wrong about this because it's now twenty years or more—to the effect that the underlying tension is that man is looking for a home. In other words, he's looking for an unalienated existence, and this can be terribly attractive and seductive and is the root of a lot of mystery. See, one of the greatest appeals of Christianity as well as of Communism is that it promises to end alienation. If I want to subjugate man, I can declare alienation a sin, and anybody who is alienated or causes anybody else to be alienated should be punished. See, this is what the Puritans did among themselves. This is what the Communist party does in Russia. And this is what the loyal extreme patriots in every country do. They're always against aliens, just as simple as that. It's the root of antiforeignism; it's the root of this philistinism that we're always confronting. And everybody does it! The function of a group is to define itself, and its definition is: "We are us, and you are you." You see?

CENTOLA: Isn't that a type of psychological projection? Couldn't people who create these groups of others, or outsiders, just as easily say: "We are good, and you are evil?"

MILLER: Absolutely. "We are us."

CENTOLA: And they project everything they don't like about themselves onto others?

MILLER: Absolutely. That's what it's all about. It's a form of psychological warfare. My view from the beginning has more or less been (it has shifted with each play to a certain degree) to find a form, in effect, for the condition of tension, rather than resolution of this particular dichotomy through consciousness, through being aware that indeed I am alienated. I'm not you, but that doesn't mean because I'm not you that I can't sympathize with you. Well, to maintain that kind of tension in all of the thing, especially in political and social existence, we're without and refuse to resolve it. You might be able to, but the solution is always false. That's the difficulty. And in a play, it's very aggravating for the audience.

CENTOLA: Not for the dramatist?

MILLER: No. It's a condition of existence. In fact, you could almost say that the tragic view is that it is tragic because of the fact that it's unresolvable. We wish so for a pillow to lay our head upon, and it's a stone.

CENTOLA: So man is always alienated, and yet he is constantly striving to get beyond his condition.

MILLER: Right.

CENTOLA: There's something dignified in his effort though.

MILLER: I was just about to say that the whole point of it is that the aspiration is holy. See, the Biblical prophets are terrific because they refused to compromise. They maintained the tension through people like Ezekiel or Isaiah. Isaiah will project the plowshares and the peacemakers will be blessed and all the rest of it, but that's the aspiration. The implicit fact is that they're not around yet, these blessed people.

CENTOLA: So what makes the characters tragic is partially the fact that only a few people, perhaps, ever attain that kind of self-recognition, or get to the point where they try to transcend their condition?

MILLER: Right.

CENTOLA: So the great mass of people aren't moved this way, or at least aren't aware of it?

MILLER: The great mass of people are in the chorus. They perceive perfectly well what's happening, or very often. But, for whatever reason, they are bereft of the power or the lust for the power or the sacrificial nature that is required to go seeking. You know, the other day with that case, the Hinckley case, is a very good example of something like this. Now this was a jury, I think, of almost all black people, and they gave this perfectly horrible (to most people) verdict. And then people said, "Well, that's because they're so dumb, you know; they aren't educated people." Well, they interviewed them on television, and they were remarkably sophisticated. And they dug it very, very well. They were really on a knife-edge, and they reacted in a very sharp and profound way: they blamed the code. And they said: "That's the code, and that is all the choice we had by that code." Well, that's terrific. See, now there's an instance of people who perforce were put in a position of having to make moral decisions, which normally in ordinary life they wouldn't be required to do, not in a public way certainly. My point is that you don't have to be a "noble" creature. This is changing the subject slightly, but since you raised the question of most people, this is certainly most people. These were blacks in Washington, D.C. They dug it; they understood it perfectly.

CENTOLA: So, it's just that most people usually aren't placed in that position, or they prefer not to be?

MILLER: Or they prefer not to be!

CENTOLA: But everyone could experience this same fate, this same tragic existence?

MILLER: Sure. Absolutely everyone as far as social rank is concerned.

CENTOLA: In an interview a few years ago, you said that Americans seem to have a "primordial fear of falling." I was wondering if you thought Americans, more than anyone else, have that feeling because it goes with the territory?

MILLER: I think that that is more American than any other country, yeah, in my observation. I think we are more afraid of losing caste, losing our hard-won place in the middle class. People will kill for that. I think that that causes more racial hatred and hostility and fear than anything else. Incidentally, I regard racism as a class phenomenon. I was born in Harlem, and I saw it happen in Harlem—I think I did, anyway. That's been my reason for it: that blacks are not acceptable more for the fact that they are working-class or poor than because they are black. If in a short period of time by some miracle there were hundreds and hundreds of thousands of black professionals, middle-class people, the thing would begin to fade. We're seeing it now with the Arabs, the sheiks, the wealthy Arab who was formerly a creature of ridicule. Well, now he can come in and buy up a whole city. With a new class identity he starts to take on a new kind of persona, a new kind of dignity. It isn't so jokey any more to see somebody walking around in those funny clothes which might conceal millions.

CENTOLA: So most people chase their American dreams because they know that success determines how much they are accepted by others.

MILLER: No question about it.

CENTOLA: In *Incident at Vichy*, Leduc tells the others as they await examination that they have been trained to die, to be willing victims for their persecutors. I'm wondering if he implies in that statement that death is often preferable to life for those who would have to live without illusions. And, once again, isn't such self-deception a peculiarly American trait? Haven't we been trained to see the world through rose-tinted glasses? Aren't we essentially a nation of people incapable of coping with reality?

MILLER: Yes. I think that tremendous power does that to people, incidentally. The British did it for two centuries as their power got tremendous. They were able to enforce their wishes upon the world. So they wished more than they observed. I think they were primarily that way, and I think the Germans were able to do this once where they had the power to do it. It goes with power; it goes with the territory.

CENTOLA: I'm going to take a different direction here. Some critics have complained about Charley's speech in the Requiem in *Death of a Salesman*, saying that it's out of character for a realist like Charley to be making sentimental speeches about dreams.

MILLER: It's not even sentimental. You know that speech is almost a handbook of what you've got to think if you're going to be a salesman. Under the circumstances, of course, it is said over a grave, so naturally it is full of feeling and mourning. But it is objective information, so to speak; it is absolutely real. Those are the visionary qualities that make salesmen tick.

CENTOLA: Aren't you also doing in this play what Fitzgerald does with Nick in his portrayal of Gatsby? In other words, you have a character who is fairly objective throughout the work make that statement over the grave because it can carry more weight coming from him, a realist.

MILLER: You're right! That speech is the obverse of the early speech that Charley makes in the play to Willy when he says: "Why must everybody like you? Who liked J. P. Morgan?" Which is an absolutely dead-on, existentialist kind of way of looking at salesmanship. This is the obverse of it. He knows damn well what Willy was feeling; that's why he can make that speech to him. This is now said as the obverse of the other, but it's complementary. These are two halves of the same thing.

CENTOLA: In an interview with Ronald Hayman some years ago, you defined fate as "high probability" and said that it is what happens "when a man starts out to do what he intends to do . . . [and] creates forces which he never bargained for, but whose contradictions nevertheless spring directly from the force of his thrust." Would you say that this is the kind of fate that's in the background of plays like *All My Sons, Death of a Salesman,* and *The Price*?

MILLER: Yes.

CENTOLA: Many of the characters in these plays seem to believe that they have no free will. But don't they have free will and just fail to consider all the consequences when they commit themselves to certain courses of action?

MILLER: Right. And I would add that it's all but impossible to take into consideration most of the time.

CENTOLA: We can't be that farsighted?

MILLER: No, because the possibilities are too complex, too complicated, too infinite.

CENTOLA: But, eventually, we have to accept what we do; we can't say we are excused from responsibility because the consequence was beyond our realm of control.

MILLER: Right. You started it. For me, the typical case of our time is the Oppenheimer thing. I use him as the symbol of the scientists who put together this ferocious world-ending trick hat. And what they were exercising was technical curiosity, a time-honored civilizing trait of mankind. And then it goes off, and as Oppenheimer says, he starts to quote Hindu scripture: "I've taken the shape of death. I started the dance and I end it by killing everyone."

CENTOLA: I'm going to shift directions again. In *The Price*, Solomon says he would not know what to say to his daughter if she were to return from the grave. Isn't Solomon essentially saying that no one can transcend the bounds of human subjectivity?

MILLER: That's a good way to put it.

CENTOLA: Doesn't he imply that because each individual is totally and irremediably separated from the other, only each individual can take responsibility for what he is in life?

MILLER: That's a very good way to put it. Yes. He accepts something there, doesn't he? He says, in effect: "I was the way I am; she is the way she was; and what happened was the inevitable result of that. So what could have changed it?"

CENTOLA: "And if she comes back, I still can't change it. So just accept it as it is."

MILLER: Right. There's a kind of a cosmic acceptance of the situation.

CENTOLA: That kind of acceptance seems to occur in your plays where characters like Quentin, Leduc, Von Berg, or Solomon decide that they must accept what is and not try to mold reality to fit their perceptions of it.

MILLER: Exactly. And from that comes not passivity but strength.

CENTOLA: That sounds again very much like Sartre. Like you, he was also accused of being a pessimist, and he responded to the charge by saying: "I'm not a pessimist; I merely believe in optimistic toughness." Isn't that also what you're saying?

MILLER: Right.

CENTOLA: In *After the Fall* both Rose and Elsie seem to betray the men they love because they want to deny their complicity in their husbands' problems in order to maintain their own innocence, a counterfeit innocence that helps them see themselves as victims.

MILLER: Those particular women feel that they did not participate in the decision making (if you want to objectify the whole thing), so they are not going to submit to the victimization. And that separation takes place, in effect saying: "You made your bed, now lie in it; I'm not going to get in there with you." It's a reassertion of separateness, incidentally.

CENTOLA: With that kind of separateness, though, isn't there also some kind of betrayal?

MILLER: Sure. It's inevitable because the implicit, although largely unannounced, larceny behind their relationship is that they were irrevocably joined. Right? And it turns out, they're not. It turns out that when the interests change, the arrangement has to change. This isn't cynicism, though, to me. It's just the way it is.

CENTOLA: I see Maggie in that play as a perfect illustration of the individual who counterfeits her innocence to appear as the helpless victim of others. I know you have spoken about this in some of your essays.

MILLER: Yeah, right.

CENTOLA: Would you say that Maggie is guilty of bad faith, of lying to herself or of trying to see only the illusions, more or less?

MILLER: Sure. In a way she's dying of the lie, as Quentin says to her. It's the only time in the play that he's absolutely right. She's a slave to the idea of being victimized. Oddly enough, it's a paradox that the awareness of being enslaved becomes the principle of the person. Instead of a key to freedom, it's a lock on the door. I guess it all comes down to a pact of nonrecognition with all human nature, which is what enslaves us all. And all these philosophical attempts are really, in one way or another, attempts toward a confrontation with the dialectic of how we operate.

CENTOLA: So what she does is self-destructive because she makes herself be what she really doesn't want to be?

MILLER: It's conformity to a perverse image. In one way or another, we're all involved with that, but for some people it's terminal.

CENTOLA: In *After the Fall* you seem to suggest that the original Fall, the Biblical Fall, is perpetually reenacted with each individual's fall into consciousness, his conflict with others, his struggle with his egotism, and his fundamental choice between good and evil, or as you have called it, his choice between Cain's and Abel's alternatives. Do you think that with the fall into consciousness comes the dilemma of choosing to live either for oneself or for others?

MILLER: Well, people are threatened with freedom; it's the reaction to the threat of freedom. The fall is the fall from the arms of God, the right to live, to eat, to be conscious that there exists all the world. It's the fall from nonconscious existence and from the pleasant and unconscious slavery of childhood and so on. The fall is the threat of freedom, of having to make choices, instead of having them made for you.

CENTOLA: In a few different places, you say that man is in the society and society is in the man, just as the fish is in the water and the water is in the fish. That statement reminds me of Jung, and I was wondering if you believe his theory about the individual carrying around with him in the collective unconscious, deep within his psyche, the cargo of his ancestral past?

MILLER: Yeah. I've often been tempted to believe that, although, of course, it's unprovable. And in my own case, I think, for example, I was never really a religious person in any conventional sense. I didn't even make sense out of the Bible until fairly recent years, if you can make sense out of the Bible. Yet, all of the ideas that we are talking about now are stemming from the Old Testament. The more I live, the more I think that somewhere down the line it poured into my ear, and I don't even know when or how. But I'm reading it again now, and I'm amazed at how embedded it is in me, even though, as I say, I never dealt with it objectively before.

CENTOLA: Do you think that we also contain racial instincts?

MILLER: Yeah, I think so. I think that they're not racial instincts; that's kind of a gross way, a gross measure of it, calling it a racial instinct. There is a culture that is in gestures, in speech, in temperament, and in the reactions of one to another, which is certainly so basic that it is the first thing probably a kid, I think, is taught. And it goes right into the irrational of the unconscious before the child even gets asleep. We call this some kind of an ethnic or a racial inheritance. It doesn't matter, but I don't see how either one is saying that.

CENTOLA: That's interesting in light of recent studies which seem to prove that a very young child is extremely sensitive to his surroundings.

MILLER: Oh, I have no doubt about that, no doubt about it. See, it's an ingenuous example of schizophrenic people, of mothers especially who tend to have those traits even though they might not break down. They look in the bloodstream for it, and maybe sometimes it is there. But there is a certain schizophrenic reaction to life which the child is subjected to or lives with. They're going to have a schizophrenic frame of reference. I don't see how you can avoid that. That's how that damn thing, I think, gets carried on from generation to generation. For a part of them there is a question about the blood and how the blood can be a problem suddenly. But there is a predisposition as soon as that—excuse the term—mother starts to infect each child or reality. How is it avoided? Well, we can't avoid that.

CENTOLA: Is that why Quentin says something to the effect that the sins of the father are handed down to the sons?

MILLER: Yeah. There's a truth in it. It's true. The older one gets, the more of one's parents one recognizes in oneself. You'd think it would be the opposite; it isn't. The more purified it becomes, the more obvious it becomes.

CENTOLA: In a lot of your works, you deal with guilt and seem to suggest that guilt can become a type of bad faith if it provides an individual with an excuse for not acting or taking his life into his own hands.

MILLER: Yeah, it's a cop-out—guilt—in one sense if it doesn't mean anything underneath to that person. Guilt is not guilt if it is conscious. It is then something even more sinister. But I suppose the way I perceive it is that guilt is a sense of unusable responsibility; it's a responsibility that can't be expressed, that can't be utilized for one reason or another. On the other hand, it is a way of self-paralysis. It's a many-faceted thing. It's self-love, but I don't want to go on with a list of what it is. But it may be the most complicated phenomenon that a society embeds in it citizens. It's the consent that one gives to superior power. It's the way that we police ourselves in the name of the greater power. I could go on and on and on about what it consists of.

CENTOLA: Would you say that at the end of *After the Fall*, Quentin transforms his guilt into responsibility?

MILLER: He at least sees the need and feels the strength to attempt to do that, yeah.

CENTOLA: The fact that he accepts Holga's love and then their movement off the stage together certainly seem to symbolize that transformation.

MILLER: Yeah, right. See, I think, too, what is resented in that play is that he refuses to settle with being guilty. This is where most people stop, because if you don't stop there then you've got to act. It would have been far more palatable if he shot himself or jumped into the river with her. I would add that *After the Fall*, the title, is probably—I didn't think of it then, but I was very moved years earlier by *The Fall* by Camus. In Camus's *The Fall* the man is guilty for not having acted to save a woman he never even saw or knew. And that's his fall. He recognizes all kinds of culpability, a species of responsibility, you might say, that was unacknowledged by his actions. And he's given up judging people, etc. The question in my play is what happens if you do go to the rescue. Does this absolve? Does this prevent the fall? Supposing he had run over to the bridge where he thought he heard someone fall in and had become involved with her and found out that she had an inexorable lust for destruction, at what point and when would he see wisdom?

CENTOLA: The point at which one says to himself: "Self-determinism—everyone has to be responsible for himself."

MILLER: Exactly!

CENTOLA: I saw the connection between these two works, but I never saw it in these terms before.

MILLER: That's why it's *After the Fall*.

CENTOLA: In *Incident at Vichy*, do you choose to have the prisoners face their interrogations alone to underscore, through their physical separation from each other, the fact that man must ultimately confront absurdity alone?

MILLER: I hadn't thought of it in those terms. Actually, it was—what you say is true—but it is constructed that way because that's the way it was done in France.

CENTOLA: The play has a symbolic movement.

MILLER: Well, a lot of these things turn out to be symbolic—these symbolic bureaucratic processes that they invent. They do it instinctively; they're the great instinctive behavioral psychologists.

CENTOLA: Do the white feathers that escape from the Old Jew's bag in *Incident at Vichy* symbolize ineffectual religions and value systems that make one take a passive or resigned posture in the face of his persecution?

MILLER: I'll tell you that I didn't know myself what was in the bag, and that when I suddenly saw that they were feathers, it was totally out of some subconscious pocket in my mind. Then sometime later I saw a film, *The Shop on Main Street*, which is a Czech film, about a little town in Bohemia where all the Jews are rounded up. And they're told to bring a few things; they don't know where they're going, but they're going to their deaths, of course. They're loaded on the trucks, and the whole town in devastated; that is, it is emptied out of all the Jews that live in this town. And there's a shot of the town square where a little while ago we saw this crowd of people assembled and thrown into the vehicles. And what's blowing around on the square is the feathers. And this was a kind of race memory of mine, quite frankly, because nothing like that ever happened in my family. My mother was born in this country; my father was brought over here at the age of six. But feathers—you see, you carry your bedding. It's the refugees' only possible property. It's light, it's warm, it's something he might sell if he had to, it's a touch of home, x, x, x; it has all kinds of uses. And also it's the plumage of birds that are blown about. They're weak things—it does have an aspect of weakness, but also of domesticity, an uprooted domesticity. Then once they're released, you can't capture them any more. And there's a pathetic quality to that: the fact that the old guy's clutching what to our minds would be a practically valueless bag of nothing, of air. It's his identity, though. There's a lot of feed into that symbol.

CENTOLA: I identified it with religious systems because he just sits there praying instead of doing anything actively to try to change his situation.

MILLER: He's transcended it; he's got one foot in heaven. He knows that this is the ancient persecutor, the face of hell, that comes in every generation, and this is his turn with him. And it's been happening forever, and probably will go on happening forever. And he's praying against it. With one eye or the other, he's got his eye on God, who's reaching out His hands to him.

CENTOLA: But is that an effective way of dealing with that type of crisis?

MILLER: It's not effective; it's the last gasp of his limited range of possibilities.

CENTOLA: You present a lot of different characters in that play who have their own ways of coping with that crisis.

MILLER: That's right.

CENTOLA: But only Von Berg, after being enlightened by Leduc, takes the action that turns things around and gives him a momentary triumph over his oppressors.

MILLER: Yeah, right.

CENTOLA: Doesn't a similar triumph occur in *Playing for Time*, when Fania Fenelon refuses to play in the orchestra unless her friend is allowed to join her?

MILLER: Right. Well, she's pressing it to the limit there.

CENTOLA: Isn't her survival itself another expression of her resistance to her persecutors?

MILLER: Yeah, well I guess that story is the story of the survival of one who has a picked identity of herself. This is the survival of an alienated woman who knows she is alienated and has a vision of an unalienated world.

CENTOLA: How about one last question? Would you agree that affirmation in your plays stems from the fact that the individual has the potential for the kind of self-determinism that is found in Proctor's resistance in *The Crucible* and Von Berg's actions in *Incident at Vichy*?

MILLER: Absolutely! Yes. I think, incidentally, that what you choose to call optimism is interesting. See, it's interesting, isn't it, that I'm generally thought of as a pessimist, and I've always denied it, even though most of the time I feel pessimistic, personally. But I find that the more I investigate my own feelings, the less capable I am of conceding that in truth there is no hope to the extent that one logically should lie down and let evil triumph, because there is too much evidence that I see of the will to live. It's everywhere. Maybe it's because I've lived for 25 years out here where if you look around, life is just overwhelming. It is simply overwhelming. It's also in my relationship with children; one sees that struggle in the child, his wish to be taught. If the lesson of life was that we are hopeless, we should have to teach children to breathe, and to struggle for hunger, to teach them to be hungry, to teach them to multiply; in other words, to awaken them to that tropism until death. But it's on the contrary. So you can see from that why I still have hope.

CENTOLA: Thank you, Mr. Miller.

The Mad Inventor of
Modern Drama

It Wouldn't have been very difficult to dislike August Strindberg, even to hate him. As a friend he was insupportable, inevitably turning with deadly suspicion on those who helped him; as a lover he was lethal; as a husband and father unpredictable, to say the least. Olof Lagercrantz does not stoop to sparing his subject and perhaps that is why, by the last chapters of his absorbing and profound biography of the great nineteenth-century Swedish author, the question of admiration or condemnation simply ceases to exist. In his life's struggles Strindberg regarded himself as paradigmatic, mankind's leading edge cutting into the future, and he is one of the rare instances of a man with such a conviction who turned out to be right.

The impact of his dramatic method, reflected in his many plays, most notably *The Father* (1887), *Miss Julie* (1888), and *The Dance of Death* (1900), is probably greater and less acknowledged than that of any other modern writer. If his plays are much less frequently produced than Ibsen's, his playwriting personality, his way of approaching reality, is evidenced far more deeply and more frequently in our contemporary theater. Strindberg struck strongly into O'Neill, is quite directly mirrored in Beckett and Pinter, in Tennessee Williams and Edward Albee. Writing before Freud was published, he wanted to offer, in Mr. Lagercrantz's words, "the pure naked truth." And this meant his entering

From *The New York Times Book Review*, 6 January 1985, pp. 1, 30. Reprinted by permission of Arthur Miller.

into the world of the subconscious, where the sexual encounter especially was a fight to the death, a world where the mother did not nur-
ture but suffocated and destroyed her offspring, a world where
domination (usually female) was the key to life. And, of course, it is this
digging the unconscious for its terrors, its lawless desires, and its ultimately creative thrusts that has provided the fodder of literature in this
century. If Ibsen was the revolutionary, seeking new, refurbished social
institutions to order mankind, Strindberg was the rebel for whom no
order would ever be true enough.

Married three times—each time disastrously—involved with
women who would appear fairly undisguised as figures in his plays,
Strindberg was a walking scandal from his first burst onto the literary
scene with *The Red Room* (1879), his autobiographical novel, to his
death in 1912 at the age of 63. It is no mean feat to encompass, as
Mr. Lagercrantz has done, the life of an author as busy as Strindberg
must have been with his train of personal catastrophes—a manifestly
mad man and yet the author of over fifty volumes of plays, poetry,
histories, political and cultural commentary, scientific and pseudos-
cientific monographs and speculations on the occult. One of the great
virtues of this fascinating biography is its level-headed acceptance of
Strindberg's impossibly paradoxical nature. He was certainly insane
for long spells, actually striking with a knife at invisible enemies behind his back, lying perfectly still "in state" as though dead, a paranoid given to great swings of mood from exultation to the
contemplation of suicide in the space of a few hours.

Mr. Lagercrantz, a Swedish poet, critic, and editor, in effect considers insanity not quite as aberration but as integral to the insights of
the man's art and of his invention of so much that has come to seem
modern in the theater. He shows Strindberg both split by his madness
and simultaneously observing his own delusions. He was a trium-
phantly unhappy man, often unsure when he was living in life or in
one of his plays, and part of his modernism springs quite probably
from his awareness that he was dipping his pen directly into his unconscious where truth is of a kind that is unarguable. His emotional
nakedness is modern, his blatantly confessional and autobiographical

style, his having obviously witnessed what he was trying to express. Part of the persuasiveness of his plays is that their truths seemed to be driving him crazy.

Thus his dramatic method is obsessive, an endlessly repeated drumming on a kind of monomanic and fearsome vision. If O'Neill did not consciously imitate this feature, he paralleled it, but at far vaster length, Strindberg's major plays being quite short and for many mercifully so. For even in his own time, when the perverse news he brought was fresh and new, audiences often laughed in the wrong places because he was carrying things much too far. Nor, with the possible exception of *Miss Julie*, was he able to leaven the spectral unreality of his dialogue with a depth of characterization. In any meaningful sense there are no characters in his plays; there are lethal relationships, concatenations that illuminate the whole inside of Strindberg's head, if nothing else, a head that was filled with the fear and hatred of womankind.

In any other man without the physique of a horse and nerves of piano wires, it would have been a fear that might have perhaps left us with a play or two or a brilliant essay followed by the mourning silence of a brain sick to death. But, as Mr. Lagercrantz repeatedly demonstrates, the fecund Strindberg not only suffered what by most definitions would be madness, but managed it like a conductor managing an orchestra. It makes his suffering no less real and painful to say that it was always being turned over and over by the bloody fingers of his mind, unceasingly searching out the artistic possibilities inside his explosions.

Yet Mr. Lagercrantz sees the playwright's unbalanced mental state as something less than a self-contained phenomenon. Strindberg, the third of six children born to a Stockholm steamship merchant and his wife, matured into a Sweden that was tearing up its roots in the past and becoming increasingly "developed," to use a modern term, which is to say that people were becoming more and more anonymous and the solaces of religion less useful. Reason and progress, as elsewhere, were the lures to self-completion and happiness, and it was Strindberg's intellectual as well as temperamental choice to strike out at what he thought of as the prison of the rational. Nietzsche would then be his brother-in-arms, supporting his claims to lead the anti-bourgeois revolution to come.

Strindberg apparently hated Ibsen, especially for his elevating women to heroic stature but also, one suspects, as a competing prophet. Yet Ibsen, the feminist, kept Strindberg's picture hanging over his desk, and it is possible to imagine why. Both men were truth-seekers in a world perpetually chained by hypocrisy and by denial of the perverse in nature and, with it, a denial of the human potential. Strindberg took his role as social critic with intense seriousness, seeing himself in one of his poems as the fireman coming to save the burning house. But "you prefer to die in your burning house to being roused by one who does not belong to the brigade." It may be, I think, that Strindberg's paranoia was also his weapon against social resistance to his ideas, for he was in fact quite alone against the self-satisfaction and inertia of the Swedish society of his time.

Inevitably, his social context having vastly changed with time, he has come to seem a merely visceral playwright and a self-confronter, but he thought of himself as a social prophet and a healer, a brother to the Paris Commune of 1871. George Bernard Shaw perceived him that way too, and until 1886 Strindberg thought of himself as a social-ist. His later development, not unlike O'Neill's, was toward the oc-cult, the Swedenborgian mysticism that would support work like *The Ghost Sonata* and the other so-called Chamber Plays written for small audiences of adventurers into the unknown. One wonders, indeed, whether Strindberg was not right in claiming himself as the first of the modern writers if only because he came to destroy the linear-thinking drama of cause and effect, the story moving from point to provable point. His drama is the conflict of essences, not characters, and it lives where the sun hardly rises and a perpetual twilight reigns. Indeed, his longing for an ultimate, superhuman world of causation lends his work a tragic grandeur at times, quite as though it were an effort to scale human limits.

Of Mr. Lagercrantz's book it must be said that a certain telegraphic style may make the opening chapter too factually dense for the non-specialist, but the writing soon relaxes and one finally feels in the presence of the ultimate Strindberg biography. Maybe more important

than any other of its qualities is its refusal to regard the writer's novels, poems, essays, and plays as "nothing but" some kind of barely disguised reportage of his life experiences. This would be a powerful
temptation in a biography of a writer like Strindberg who lived in a
panic of libel and self-incrimination. Everyone knew who his characters "really were," but the gossip is gone and his art, in the end, is
what endures.

And it has endured, quite probably, because the hallucinatory world
Strindberg saw seems much closer now to being real. We really walk
the moon, and with the press of a button can really crack the planet,
and if we have mastered the physics of this magical power, the morals
of it all are, if anything, farther from us than from Strindberg who,
mad as he was, believed that his labors were essentially moral and in
God's service. Or at least should be. He could be vile, hypocritical,
opportunistic, violent, but one cannot avoid the hopefulness in him,
of which his boundless creativity was the manifestation. Mr. Lagercrantz, rather than turning this mass of paradox into a monument,
has brought him alive. His is a wonderful biography, worthy of a
maddeningly foolish, wrong, and presciently wise writer who was one
of the prime inventors of our theater and our time.

An Interview with Arthur Miller

BY MATTHEW C. ROUDANÉ

THE INTERVIEW took place on November 7, 1983 in the playwright's New York City apartment near Central Park. Throughout our conversation Miller spoke patiently and frankly about his work and modern drama in general. Eager to speak, Miller never stopped the conversation, not even while in the bathroom washing up, dressing for the evening, or walking the crowded streets later that evening.

ROUDANÉ: Reflecting back upon five decades of playwriting, which plays hold the fondest memories for you?

MILLER: Each play comes out of a quite different situation. Sometimes I feel proudest of *The Crucible,* because I made something lasting out of a violent but brief turmoil, and I think it will go on for a while yet, throwing some light. It also happens to be my most produced play, incidentally. I also get a big kick out of *The Price,* especially the old man in that play. I still enjoy him, and that I created him.

ROUDANÉ: Few American plays have exerted as much influence as *Death of a Salesman.* In terms of characterization, language, story, plot, and dramatic action, why do you think this play continues to engage audiences on a national as well as international level?

MILLER: Maybe because it's a well-told, paradoxical story. It seems to catch the paradoxes of being alive in a technological civilization. In one

From *Michigan Quarterly Review*, 24 (1985), pp. 373–389. Reprinted by permission of Matthew C. Roudané.

way or another, different kinds of people, different classes of people apparently feel that they're in the play. Why that is I don't really know. But it seems to have more or less the same effect everywhere there is a dominating technology, although it's also popular in places where life is far more pretechnological. Maybe it involves some of the most rudimentary elements in the civilizing process: family cohesion, death and dying, parricide, rebirth, and so on. The elements, I guess, are rather fundamental. People *feel* these themes no matter where they are.

ROUDANÉ: So you think that the plight of Willy and his family is as valid today as it was immediately after production?

MILLER: Who knows? People tell me that *Death of a Salesman* is more pertinent now than then. The suppression of the individual by placing him below the imperious needs of the society or technology seems to have manufactured more Willys in the world. But again, it is also far more primitive than that. Like many myths and classical dramas, it is a story about violence within a family.

ROUDANÉ: If *Death of a Salesman* is primitive in a Sophoclean sense, would you call it a tragedy?

MILLER: I think it does engender tragic feelings, at least in a lot of people. Let's say it's one kind of tragedy. I'm not particularly eager to call it a tragedy or anything else; the label doesn't matter to me. But when Aristotle was writing, there were various kinds of tragedy. He was trying to make definitions that would include most of them. There are tremendous differences between an *Ajax, Oedipus,* the *Theban Women*; they're all different and don't meet Aristotle's definition of tragedy in the same way. I suppose he was defining what he felt should be the ideal case.

ROUDANÉ: Throughout much of your theater you seem concerned with the notion of the American Dream, with its successes and failures. Could you discuss the influence of this Dream on your artistry?

MILLER: The American Dream is the largely unacknowledged screen in front of which all American writing plays itself out—the screen of the perfectibility of man. Whoever is writing in the United States is using the American Dream as an ironical pole of his story. Early on we all drink up certain claims to self-perfection that are absent in a large part of the world. People elsewhere tend to accept, to a far greater degree anyway, that the conditions of life are hostile to man's pretensions. The American idea is different in the sense that we think that if we could only touch it, and live by it, there's a natural order in favor of us; and that the object of a good life is to get connected with that live and abundant order. And this forms a context of irony for the kind of stories we generally tell each other. After all, the stories of most significant literary works are of one or another kind of failure. And it's a failure in *relation to* that screen, that backdrop. I think it pervades American writing, including my own. It's there in *The Crucible,* in *All My Sons,* in *After the Fall*—an aspiration to an innocence that when defeated or frustrated can turn quite murderous, and we don't know what to do with this perversity; it never seems to "fit" us.

ROUDANÉ: What is the relationship of form to content, and how have you arrived at the forms you've used in several of your plays which have a very inventive form—*Death of a Salesman, After the Fall,* which is almost cinematic, and the use of the narrator in *A View from the Bridge.* Did the form of these works come from the material or substance, or did the form come first? How does the creative process work for you?

MILLER: I think there is a dialectic at work. There are forces working in two directions. The central reality in my plays is the lead character. In one or two of them it would be the leading characters, like *Incident at Vichy* where, while there is one most important character, many others are on almost an equal rank. But basically the story is carried forward by one individual wrestling with his dilemma. I'm not sure I understand what element it is in the dilemma that moves me toward one form or another. *All My Sons* was actually an exception to a dozen or so plays that I had written in previous years which most people don't know about. Those were poetic plays; one or two were in verse; expressionist plays. Starting out I was never interested in being a "realistic" writer. I discovered the engine of the story at a certain point and *All My Sons* seemed a form that would best express it; and even though it was an unusual form for me to use, it best expressed what I was after, which was an ordinariness of the environment from which this extraordinary disaster was going to spring. The amoral nature of that environment; that is, people involved in cutting the lawn and painting the house and keeping the oil burner running; the petty business of life in the suburbs. So once I had that feeling about it, the form began to create itself. No, I am not really interested in "realism." I never was. What I'm very much interested in is *reality*. This is something that can be quite different. Realism can conceal reality, perhaps a little easier than any other form, in fact. But what I am interested in is the poetic, the confluence of various forces in a surprising way; the reversals of man's plans for himself; the role of fate, of myth, in his life; his beliefs in false things; his determination to tell the truth until it hurts, but not afterwards, and so on.

In an early play like *All My Sons* it was realism as we know realism; but I hope all my plays are realistic in the sense that the view of life is on the whole a useful, not a trivial, one. The form of *Death of a Salesman* was an attempt, as much as anything else, to convey the bending of time. There are two or three sorts of time in that play. One is social time; one is psychic time, the way we remember things; and the third one is the sense of time created by the play and shared by the audience. When I directed *Salesman* in China, which was the first time I had attempted to direct it from scratch, I became aware all over again that that play is taking place in the Greek unity of 24 hours; and yet, it is dealing with material that goes back probably 25 years. And it almost goes forward through Ben, who is dead. So *time* was an obsession for me at the moment, and I wanted a way of presenting it so that it became the *fiber* of the play, rather than being something that somebody comments about. In fact, there is very little comment verbally in *Salesman* about time. I also wanted a form that could sustain in itself the way we deal with crises, which is not to deal with them. After all, there is a lot of comedy in *Salesman*; people forget it because it is so dark by the end of the play. But if you stand behind the audience you hear a lot of laughter. It's a deadly ironical laughter most of the time, but it *is* a species of comedy. The comedy is really a way for Willy and others to put off the evil day, which is the thing we all do. I wanted that to *happen* and not be something talked *about*. I wanted the feeling to come across rather than a set of speeches about how we delay dealing with issues. I wanted a play, that is, that had almost a biological life of its own. It would be as incontrovertible as the musculature of the human body. Everything connecting with everything else, all of it working according to plan. No excesses. Nothing explaining itself; all of it simply inevitable, as one structure, as one corpus. All those feelings of a society falling to pieces which I had, still have, of being unable to deal with it, which we all know now. All of this, however, presented not with speeches in *Salesman*, but by putting together pieces of Willy's life, so that what we were deducing about it was the speech; what we were making of it was the moral of it; what it was doing to us rather than a romantic speech about facing death and living a fruitless life. All of these elements and many more went into the form of *Death of a Salesman*. All this could never have been contained in the form of *All My Sons*. For the story of *Salesman* is absurdly simple! It's about a salesman and it's his last day on the earth. There's very little ongoing narrative. It's all relationships. I wanted plenty of space in the play for people to confront each other with their feelings, rather than for people to advance the plot. So it became a very open form, and I believe a real invention. I initially titled it "The Inside of His Head" and had a set in mind, which I abandoned, of the inside of Willy's skull in which he would be crawling around, playing these scenes inside of himself. Maybe that throws some light on the kind of play I wanted it to be.

In *The Crucible* we see the fate of the society from a religious, moral point of view; its merged sublime and political powers forcing the transmission of a man's conscience to others, and then of the man's final immortal need to take it back. In the area of morals and society it had to be a more explicit and "hard" play, hence its form. You know we adopt styles when we speak. When you're speaking to your mother, you speak in a different tone of voice from when you're speaking to your class; you use different gestures when you speak to a friend and to the public; or to a policeman, or judge, or possibly a professor. So it's the kind of address that the play is going to make that also creates its form. The address in *The Crucible* was an insistence, hardly concealed in the play, that if the events we see in that play are not understood it can mean the end of social life—which is based primarily on a certain amount of shared trust. And when the government goes into the business of destroying trust, it goes into the business of destroying itself. So, saying this in *The Crucible*, what I believed at the time—the story of the Salem witch-hunt in 1692—was indeed saying it wanted that form. An aseptic form; it's less sensuous than *Salesman*. *The Crucible* is more pitiless, probably because power is at the bottom of it and because so much of the witch-hunt took place in a theocratic court. The witch-hunt was fundamentally a business of prosecutors and lawyers, witnesses, testimony. Literally the town of Salem did nothing anymore but attend court sessions in the church. It just about destroyed the town within the lifetime of those people.

In each of my plays the central creating force is the character, be it John Proctor or Willy Loman or Mr. Kelly or whoever. If I haven't got that, I haven't got anything. And the form comes as a result of the texture of what I feel about that person. I felt about Willy Loman that he talked endlessly, and in the play he talks endlessly. He had to seem to ramble, and yet be accumulating an explosive force, which is what happens when someone's talking a lot to himself and suddenly shoots himself. In *After the Fall* I wanted to confront somebody with his history, and rather than talk about it in a room in the third person, I wanted him to re-enact it. Maybe I can throw some light on *After the Fall* by saying this; it was done in India and the director came to see me and said that it had required no adaptation for the Indian theater. Now that was kind of a shock to me. He said, "In the old Indian plays the god comes forth and re-enacts his incarnations." And that's, formally speaking, what happens in *After the Fall*: the various paths circle around the same issues, which evolve into the person we finally see on the stage, striving toward a purer awareness of himself and the people in his life. To arrive at that it was necessary to break down some more walls of realistic theater.

I've paid probably an inordinate amount of attention to form because if it's not right, nothing works, no matter what. Form is literally the body that holds the soul of the play. And if that body doesn't maneuver and operate, you have an effusion of dialogue, a tickling of the piano keys, improvisation, perhaps, but you don't have music.

ROUDANÉ: How much revision do you go through when composing a play?

MILLER: Before I am finished with a play, I have normally written about a thousand to three thousand pages. I suspect that in the case of *After the Fall* it may have been more. So obviously I'm searching around all over the place for what the play wants to be. I have a feeling that a play, if it truly exists, makes an *a priori* demand that it be born with certain shapes and certain features. Sculptors know that feeling: that within the rock is the sculpture, and what they're doing is knocking off the excess stone to find the ordained shape. What I do is go up one dead end after another, picking up a little bit here and a little bit there until I discover where I ought to be and what it ought to look like. But, of course, the form depends a great deal upon how the play's going to end. If it's going to end in death, that has a tremendous effect on the way the play's going to be structured. It tends to draw it up tight because it limits time automatically. Form is a way of expressing the tempo on the stage. If we could sit for 25 hours, which some of our playwrights would like us to do, we would hardly need any form at all. You would just go on and on and on, letting the audience pick what they wished out of the scrambled eggs. I've often said that the best naturalism you could achieve would be to put a tape recorder on the corner of 42nd Street and Broadway and just leave it open! You would get a perfect absurd play, which would be interesting. I would contest that it isn't a play, but that's an academic point. It's not to my taste. Form is a choice, a selection of incident and feeling dictated by thematic considerations. That sounds like a definition! Maybe I better write that down!

ROUDANÉ: A *View from the Bridge* was first written as a one-act play, then a two-act play, but in the process the role of the narrator/chorus shifted. That's an unusual shift for you. Could you comment on this form-shift?

MILLER: This shift had to do with the circumstances of the play. That was a one-act play, in a time, incidentally, when you couldn't get a one-act play produced in New York. There wasn't an audience for one-act plays, so one wrote very few of them. But a friend of mine was in a Clifford Odets play—*The Flowering Peach*—which was failing on Broadway. He is Martin Ritt who later became a fine movie director. He called me one day and asked if I had any one-act plays because he had a cast of very good actors, and the producer was willing to let them use the theater on Sunday evenings to put on one-act plays. I didn't have any, but I wasn't doing anything and I thought, well, there *was* a story I'd known and loved for years but I could never figure out how to do a full-length play of it. So I said I'd try to do something, and I wrote *A View from the Bridge* in a week or two. That's how it started out; it had always seemed to me to be a one-act play. The form was also influenced by my own curiosity as to whether we could in a contemporary theater deal with life in some way like the Greeks did. Meaning that, unlike *Salesman*, it would not suck tons of water like a whale; everything that is said in the Greek classic play is going to advance the order, the theme, in manifest ways. There is no time for the character to reveal himself apart from thematic considerations. The Greeks never thought that art could be a crap-shoot. They thought art is form; a conscious but at the same time an inspired act. But anybody could be inspired; it was only the artist who had a conscious awareness of form, and this set him apart as the cultic, social voice. When I heard this story the first time—I never knew the man—it struck me even then how Greek it was. You knew from the first minute that it would be a disaster. Everybody around him of any intelligence would have told Eddie that it would be a disaster if he didn't give up his obsession. But it's the nature of the obsession that it can't be given up. The obsession becomes more powerful than the individual that it inhabits, like a force from another world. That to me was interesting. So I began *A View from the Bridge* in its first version with the feeling that I would make one single constantly rising trajectory, until its fall, rather like an arrow shot from a bow; and this form would declare rather than conceal itself. I wanted to reveal the method nakedly to everybody so that from the beginning of the play we are to know that this man can't make it, and yet might reveal himself somehow in his struggle. I must say the play was not cast in the best way; it had very good actors who didn't belong; some actors couldn't really handle the localized language, didn't have the timbre or feeling for it. It failed. Peter Brook saw it and thought that I might have been too relentless in the sense that some of the life of the family, the neighborhood, had been squeezed out. So as soon as I started to let that life back in, especially the dilemma as seen by the wife, it began to expand itself and become a two-act play. It was done in England as such for the first time. That change, however, came from internal considerations. It came because I could see on the stage that I could give those actors more meat, and let the structure take care of itself a little bit. I relaxed the play in the sense of allowing it to have its colors.

ROUDANÉ: Do you consider yourself a dramatic innovator?

MILLER: I can only confess that the most completely achieved form that I know about is that of *Death of a Salesman*. This is to accommodate the full flow of inner and outer forces that are sucking this man. I daresay I made it all seem so natural that people have accepted it as real. But it's the actors who understand the crush of condensation; they are, sometimes, at three places at the same time. The melting together of social time, personal time, and psychic time in *Death of a Salesman* is, for me, its unique power. I just directed it in China and it struck me all over again. I've always paid a great deal of attention to forms. I've never really written in the same form twice. The only mode that I haven't done much with, although a little of that too, is the absurd. But I did two one-act plays last year—*Elegy for a Lady* and *Some Kind of Love Story*—which are of a different form than I've ever tried before. *Elegy for a Lady* takes place in the space between the mind and what it imagines, and sort of turns itself inside out. *Some Kind of Love Story* concerns the question of how we believe truth, how one is forced by circumstance to believe what you are only sure is not too easily demonstrated as false. They were great fun to do, and were destroyed by the critics, but that doesn't matter—they'll be back one day.

ROUDANÉ: Several of your plays have been done at one time and received one way, and done at a later period and received quite differently; I'm thinking especially of *The Crucible, The Price, After the Fall*. How do you account for the changes in the audience's perception of the spectacle?

MILLER: We have to remember that, maybe more than any other art, the play lacks independence as an artifact. It is a set of relationships. There really are no characters in plays; there are *relationships*. Where there are only characters and no relationships, we have an unsatisfactory play. A work has to be supported by its time. It's an old story. A work can appear and the audience might not quite know what to make of it. They don't get the clues the work is sending them. It's a sociological and anthropological manifestation. The plays are not accessible to the audience. They haven't tuned into it yet by virtue of their own experiences. Time goes by, and a thousand social developments, and they see differently; they see the same thing now, but with different eyes. When *The Crucible* opened, we were at the height of the McCarthy period. There was simply a lot of fear and suspicion in the audience. This has been said a thousand times; you know the story, I'm sure. It was in many ways a disembodied theater. There was a fear of fear. Once they caught on to what *The Crucible* was about, a coat of ice formed over the audience because they felt they were being called upon to believe something which the reigning powers at the time told them they were not to believe. They would have to disobey very important social commands in order to believe in this play. Consequently the critics, who are merely registering their moment and, with few honorable exceptions, have no real independence from it, thought of *The Crucible* as a cold play. Now anyone who's seen *The Crucible* can level criticism, but that surely isn't a legitimate one anymore. It's that *they* felt cold; they were refrigerated by the social climate of that moment. I stood in the back of that theater after opening night and I saw people come by me whom I'd known for years—and wouldn't say hello to me. They were in dread that they would be identified with *me*. Because what I was saying in the play was that a species of hysteria had overtaken the United States and would end up killing people if it weren't recognized. Two years passed, Senator McCarthy died, the pendulum swung, and people began to recognize that he had been a malevolent influence. Some felt a little bit of shame, some felt angry that they had been taken, and others felt he was right—even though he was wrong. In any case, the heat was off. And the play was done again off-Broadway in a production that in many ways really wasn't as good as the original: the original had really fine, accomplished actors, and in the later one there was a much younger and more inexperienced cast. But the critics were overwhelmed with the play. That's because they allowed the play into themselves, whereas before they were afraid to. They suspected it of being propaganda that they had to defend their virgin minds against.

That was the most frightening change I have ever seen in the reception of a play, but of course there have been many other authors with similar fates. A play has to make an instantaneous connection with an audience made up of all sorts of people—some of them a little dumber than others. Some are smarter but less astute about the feelings they have. It's a mixed audience. That they should all be brought to the same feeling by looking at one play is really remarkable. It's almost too much to ask, but it happens all the time. A play's an arrangement by which the author speaks for himself and for his audience at the same moment. And for that to happen obviously takes a *lot* of luck—and a certain small amount of skill and talent.

ROUDANÉ: Reflecting upon Kate Keller in *All My Sons*, Elizabeth Procter in *The Crucible*, and, say, Linda Loman in *Death of a Salesman*, could you discuss the roles the women play in your drama?

MILLER: A production of *All My Sons* was on in England two years ago and was directed by Michael Blakemore, a very fine director, who had never seen it here. He saw Kate (Rosemary Harris) as a woman using the truth as a weapon against the man who had harmed their son. Kate Keller is pretty damn sure when the play begins that, in the widest sense of the word, Joe was "responsible" for the deaths of the Air Force men. She's both warning him not to go down the road that his older son is beckoning him to go, and rather ambiguously destroying him with her knowledge of his crime. She sees the horror most clearly because she was a partner to it without having committed it. There's a sinister side to her, in short. This actress caught it beautifully. The production was "dark" because of her performance of the mother who is usually regarded as ancillary, which she is not.

ROUDANÉ: Perhaps, then, there's more complexity to your female characters than critics have generally recognized.

MILLER: Critics generally see them as far more passive than they are. When I directed *Salesman* in China, I had Linda "in action." She's not just sitting around. She's the one who knows from the beginning of the play that Willy's trying to kill himself. She's got the vital information all the time. Linda sustains the illusion because that's the only way Willy can be sustained. At the same time any cure or change is impossible in Willy. Ironically she's helping to guarantee that Willy will never recover from his illusion. She has to support it; she has no alternative, given his nature and hers.

ROUDANÉ: So, in this context, Linda is supporting what Ibsen would call a "vital lie."

MILLER: That's right. The women characters in my plays are very complex. They've been played somewhat sentimentally, but that isn't the way they were intended. There is a more sinister side to the women characters in my plays. These women are of necessity auxiliaries to the action, which is carried by the male characters. But they both receive the benefits of the male's mistakes and protect his mistakes in crazy ways. They are forced to do that. So the females are victims as well.

ROUDANÉ: Do you try to get members of the audience to confront themselves and others about key issues?

MILLER: I am not a teacher in the theater, despite what you may have read. In the sense that a lesson is arranged on the stage that will give us a certain moral. The play is really an attempt to order life. Now I'm more than happy when people do arrange themselves on one side or the other of the argument of the play. And I think it may do their brain some good to move away from the anguish of daily chaos. But the theater is not an educational institution, certainly not primarily. If a play makes them feel more alive, it is more than enough.

ROUDANÉ: Regarding your adaptation of Ibsen's *An Enemy of the People*, in the preface you discuss some of the reasons for producing another version of Ibsen's work in terms of style, language, and so on. In light of the politics as well as the aesthetics of that play, can you discuss the different nature of "your" play—especially since it's so different a production for you personally.

MILLER: Let me tell you how it started. Early in 1951 Frederic March and Robert Lewis came to me—they wanted me to do *An Enemy of the People*. The versions that existed in English were very stiff, ungainly, and they didn't think they could do them. This might throw a little light on our theater history: at this time there was no off-Broadway theater. You had to do this on Broadway, complete with the usual Broadway merchandise. What they were interested in was some response to the crucifying of left-wingers. March and his wife were in the midst of a lawsuit against someone who had accused them of being pro-Communist. He was looking for some play which would clarify the principle behind his stand, and he found it in *An Enemy of the People*. I had never seen the play acted. Reading it again, I thought it would be a hell of a thing to do; the backer was a very wealthy young Norwegian who had a lot of love for the United States and was worried that it was turning fascist. He offered to supply me with a careful, word-for-word translation of Ibsen's original manuscript, done by him. It would simply set each word next to each word; there would be no attempt to write English, and, as you know, any foreign language translated that way is really not a language but a set of disconnected wooden blocks. So with that I wrote a version of the play, trying to generate some contemporary feeling. It was not to be a museum piece. It was to threaten us! The play was a very threatening play in its time. I had to reproduce that feeling of threat. You couldn't do it with the other language. It was basically a question of language. Also, the play is monstrously repetitive. Ibsen, in his later years, couldn't remember having written it! He had done it very quickly—in a few months—in response to violent criticism of him for *Ghosts*. He was portrayed as a pornographer, a dreadful antisocial mechanic. He wrote this as a self-defense, based on the idea fundamental to the play, as I saw it: that before many people can know something, one man has to know it. The majority in that sense is always wrong, always trailing behind that one man.

So do I feel the play's "mine"? Not really. Perhaps some of its humor, and a certain quickened throb not in the original. In any case before I did it, it was hardly ever produced here except by academic circles. Afterwards, it was put on fairly often, and still is, because I made the play more accessible, I believe, to a contemporary audience. The original, for example, had long arid debates about Darwinian questions which have been settled and nobody's particularly interested in anymore. Some of Ibsen's ideas seemed crackpot even then, however. He had in fact to go around explaining, especially to trade union meetings where he made speeches, that he hadn't intended to say that he believed in the superiority of an aristocracy. The play could lend itself to supporting the idea that an elite should be running the world because the average guy is rather an idiot—as he often is. But he was talking about the aristocracy of the intellect and the spirit, meaning those people who are prepared to disinterestedly venture into the future. They have to sacrifice for it, and they should be somehow protected so that they're not lost to society. But *An Enemy of the People* doesn't quite say that. In the original version it often sounds merely contemptuous of the ordinary citizen. But, on the other hand, maybe Ibsen really was.

ROUDANÉ: Earlier you commented that the central character often helps give shape or form to your play; but have you ever written a piece that was generated from a compelling thematic issue?

MILLER: *Incident at Vichy* is the closest I've ever come to that. The action originated from an actual event involving a group of men in Vichy, France. Incidentally, there's a man who's recently been arrested, Klaus Barbie, who ran the Gestapo in France; it was he who was running the program that I depicted in *Incident at Vichy*: the Germans hunting down Jewish people in the Vichy zone who were masquerading as French in order to escape the concentration camps. Barbie invented a lot of procedures. I'm very happy to say that in the play, written sometime in the sixties, one of the characters says, "These aren't the Germans, these are the French Police." And that's exactly where things are now. That is, yes, a thematic play. There's another element in *Incident at Vichy*, without which I wouldn't have written the play: that is, the time comes when somebody has to decide to sacrifice himself, and the act of sacrifice was interesting to me. And really the play comes down to that, the step from guilt to responsibility and action.

ROUDANÉ: When working with a director on a play, do you make many changes in the rehearsal procedure?

MILLER: I have, and most of the time to the detriment to the play. I'll tell you what happens. I've worked on Broadway where there's a very limited amount of time: three-and-a-half weeks and you're on. And we're dealing with a lot of overdone commercialization. And it costs a lot of money per day, so naturally you limit the day. The result? The power that now moves from the playwright to the director is inevitable because he's got to bring that curtain up. Sometimes, if I have a particularly sensitive and able director, this doesn't happen. But when you have a less than capable man, *you* have to make it possible for him to put that play on. So the playwright starts making up for his weaknesses. The playwright also has to consider what to do about actors who can't really sing on the pitch in which you wrote the music. The alternative is to let it stand there and know that they don't have a prayer: they can't hit certain notes and you've got to change the register. We have a very poor theater now, I'm afraid. It's poor in time: our theater doesn't have sufficient time to really stop and work on a difficult passage. Instead, the playwright is thrown the job of making the actor's or director's job pleasant, while at the same time protecting and defending his own work, as much as he can. Sometimes these things are contradictory and you don't always succeed. I've had that happen; there's hardly a playwright who hasn't from the beginning of time.

ROUDANÉ: Given all the economic, social, thematic, political, and aesthetic considerations that go into our theater today, and given all the problems our theater is facing today, what should or could or can theater be, and what in an ideal world should our theater try to accomplish?

MILLER: Well, that's a pretty big order. I think that a theater with the most vitality is a theater that confronts an audience made up of the whole people. We don't have anything like that. This is not merely a sentimentally democratic statement. When you break up society, as our theater audience largely does, into a very tiny fragment of the most well-to-do, it can only react in a certain way. I know when I go to Minneapolis or Dayton, there's a different atmosphere between the play and the people, because it costs next to nothing to get in—at least when compared to New York prices. A much wider group of people is in the theater, and I find this very stimulating. You see, Shakespeare had to address nobility, along with people who couldn't read and write; the whole gamut of society was in the theater, and that supported and invited the tremendous variety in his plays. As social and political revolutions took place in England after his passing, the audience got a more and more narrowly bourgeois ideological slant; it couldn't open itself to contradictions of its ideology. So the more you narrow your audience, the more you narrow the plays that serve it. The mechanics of it are quite obvious; if you hand a producer a piece that offends a significant portion of the Broadway audience, not to speak of the critics, he'll think two or three times before putting it on. You are in that way bound to one level of consciousness. It's not a new thing; my argument with our theater on that level is that it's constricted to a degree greater than I have ever known in my lifetime. It is very important that people not have to pay $40 to get into the theater, because if they pay $40, they're probably not going to want what I am writing.

Another element in a great theater is that it tried to place aesthetics at the service of its civic function. See how the plays that we call great have made us somehow more civilized. The great Greek plays taught the western mind the law. They taught the western mind how to settle tribal conflicts without murdering each other. The great Shakespearean plays set up structures of order which became parts of our mental equipment. In the immense love stories, the wonderful comedies, there's all sorts of color. But back of these great plays is a civic function. The author was really a poet-philosopher. A $40 ticket brooks no philosophies, tends toward triviality. I believe that if we had some means of expanding our audience it would take awhile but playwrights would respond to that challenge. They'd smell *blood* out there!

The biggest reason playwriting is in such dire straits is because the audience is gone; it's not there anymore. We've been talking about this for thirty years. Back in the early fifties I even got the Dramatists Guild to convene a meeting of playwrights, unions, and producers to try to reduce our take and lower our costs. That was over thirty years ago, when it was $10 or $8, something like that, for a ticket. But I saw it happening. I saw friends of mine who could no longer go to the theater, people who loved the theater. They didn't have the money. There are places in the world where this problem, if not solved, has been dealt with, steps have been taken. One of them is England. The National Theatre; the Arts-Council in England. That's one of the reasons there have been so many English plays around. There's an English audience for those plays. A writer might not be able to make a good living at it, but he could feed himself on a play that was written, not for the West End, not for Broadway, but for those three or four weeks of performances that he might get with very good actors. This is not amateur theater. Some of the best people in England are involved in this. So my great theater would be a poetic theater. It would have to be because once you're confronted with the Great Unwashed, well, the only image I have is when you go to a prize fight, a ball game, or a political rally. I was a delegate to the 1968 Democratic convention, and *there* was the American people. That's the audience I wish I had. You know: real ugly toughs from Chicago, professors from Massachusetts, southern crackers from Georgia, Alabama. I could talk to those people. But I can't get 'em! They're not in my theater. And if they ever got into the theater, you would have something! You would have fever!

From *Timebends: A Life*

MEMORY inevitably romanticizes, pressing reality to recede like pain. When the escaping Hebrews saw the waters rushing in to cover the God-dried seabed, drowning the pursuing Egyptian army, they sat down on the shore to catch their breaths and promptly forgot all their previous years of miserable argufying and internecine spitefulness.

Now, with only the serene blue sea before them, they were soon telling their children how wonderful life used to be, even under the Egyptians, when at least they were never allowed to forget they were all Jews and therefore had to help one another and be human. Not like now, when everybody's out for himself, etc. . . . The brain heals the past like an injury, things were always better than they are now.

Already in the sixties I was surprised by the common tendency to think of the late forties and early fifties as some sort of renaissance in the New York theater. If that was so, I was unaware of it. I thought the theater a temple being rotted out with commercialized junk, where mostly by accident an occasional good piece of work appeared, usually under some disguise of popular cultural coloration such as a movie star in a leading role.

That said, it now needs correction; it was also a time when the audience was basically the same for musicals and light entertainment as for the ambitious stuff and had not yet been atomized, as it would be by the mid-fifties, into young and old, hip and square, or even political left and middle and right. So the playwright's challenge was to please not a small sensitized supporting clique but an audience representing, more or less, all of America. With ticket prices within reason, this meant that an author was writing for his peers, and if such was really not the case statistically, it was sufficiently so to support an illusion that had a basis in reality. After all, it was not thought particularly daring to present T. S. Eliot's *The Cocktail Party* on Broadway, or Laurence Olivier in a Greek tragedy, or Giraudoux's *The Madwoman of Chaillot*, or any number of other ambitious works. To be sure, such shows had much shorter lives than the trash, but that was to be expected, for most people would much rather laugh than cry, rather watch an actor being hit on the head by a pig bladder than by some painful truth.

The net of it all was that serious writers could reasonably assume they were addressing the whole American mix, and so their plays, whether successfully or not, stretched toward a wholeness of experience that would not require specialists or a coterie to be understood. As alienated a spirit as he was, O'Neill tried for the big audience, and Clifford Odets no less so, along with every other writer longing to prophesy to America, from Whitman and Melville to Dreiser and Hemingway and on.

For Europe's playwrights the situation was profoundly different, with society already split beyond healing between the working class and its allies, who were committed to a socialist destiny, and the bourgeois mentality that sought an art of reassurance and the pleasures of forgetting what was happening in the streets. (The first American plays I saw left me wondering where the characters came from. The people I knew were fanatics about surviving, but onstage everyone seemed to have mysteriously guaranteed incomes, and though every play had to have something about "love," there was nothing about sex, which was all there was in Brooklyn, at least that I ever noticed.) An American avant-garde, therefore, if only because the domination of society by the middle class was profoundly unchallenged, could not simply steal from Brecht or even Shaw and expect its voice to reach beyond the small alienated minority that had arrived in their seats already converted to its aims. That was not the way to change the world.

For a play to do that it had to reach precisely those who accepted everything as it was; great drama is great questions or it is nothing but technique. I could not imagine a theater worth my time that did not want to change the world, any more than a creative scientist could wish to prove the validity of everything that is already known. I knew only one other writer with the same approach, even if he surrounded his work with a far different aura. This was Tennessee Williams.

If only because he came up at a time when homosexuality was absolutely unacknowledgeable in a public figure, Williams had to belong to a minority culture and understood in his bones what a brutal menace the majority could be if aroused against him. I lived with much the same sense of alienation, albeit for other reasons. Certainly I never regarded him as the sealed-off aesthete he was thought to be. There is a radical politics of the soul as well as of the ballot box and the picket line. If he was not an activist, it was not for lack of a desire for justice, nor did he consider a theater profoundly involved in society and politics, the venerable tradition reaching back to the Greeks, somehow unaesthetic or beyond his interest.

The real theater—as opposed to the sequestered academic one—is always straining at the inbuilt inertia of a society that always wants to deny change and the pain it necessarily involves. But it is in this effort that the musculature of important work is developed. In a different age, perhaps even only fifteen years later, in the sixties, Williams might have had a more comfortably alienated audience to deal with, one that would have relieved the pressure upon him to extend himself beyond a supportive cult environment, and I think this might well have narrowed the breadth of his work and its intensity. In short, there was no renaissance in the American forties, but there was a certain balance within the audience—a balance, one might call it, between the alienated and the conformists—that gave sufficient support to the naked cry of the heart and, simultaneously, enough resistance to force it into a rhetoric that at one stroke could be broadly understandable and yet faithful to the pain that had pressed the author to speak.

When Kazan invited me up to New Haven to see the new Williams play, *A Streetcar Named Desire*—it seemed to me a rather too garishly attention-getting title—I was already feeling a certain amount of envious curiosity since I was still unable to commit myself to the salesman play, around which I kept suspiciously circling and sniffing. But at the same time I hoped that *Streetcar* would be good; it was not that I was high-minded but simply that I shared the common assumption of the time that the greater the number of exciting plays there were on Broadway the better for each of us. At least in our minds there was still something approximating a theater culture to which we more or less pridefully belonged, and the higher its achievement the greater the glory we all shared. The playwright then was king of the hill, not the star actor or director, and certainly not the producer or theater owner, as would later be the case. (At a recently televised Tony Awards ceremony, recognizing achievement in the theater, not a single playwright was presented to the public, while two lawyers who operated a chain of theaters were showered with the gratitude of all. It reminded me of Caligula making his horse a senator.)

Streetcar—especially when it was still so fresh and the actors almost as amazed as the audience at the vitality of this theatrical experience—opened one specific door for me. Not the story or characters or the direction, but the words and their liberation, the joy of the writer in writing them, the radiant eloquence of its composition, moved me more than all its pathos. It formed a bridge to Europe for me, to Jouvet's performance in *Ondine*, to the whole tradition of unashamed word-joy that, with the exception of Odets, we had either turned our backs on or, as with Maxwell Anderson, only used archaically, as though eloquence could only be justified by cloaking it in sentimental romanticism.

Returning to New York, I felt speeded up, in motion now. With *Streetcar*, Tennessee had printed a license to speak at full throat, and it helped strengthen me as I turned to Willy Loman, a salesman always full of words, and better yet, a man who could never cease trying, like Adam, to name himself and the world's wonders. I had known all along that this play could not be encompassed by conventional realism, and for one integral reason: in Willy the past was as alive as what was happening at the moment, sometimes even crashing in to completely overwhelm his mind. I wanted precisely the same fluidity in the form, and now it was clear to me that this must be primarily verbal. The language would of course have to be recognizably his to begin with, but it seemed possible now to infiltrate it with a kind of superconsciousness. The play, after all, involved the attempts of his sons and his wife and Willy himself to understand what was killing him. And to understand meant to lift the experience into emergency speech of an unashamedly open kind rather than to proceed by the crabbed dramatic hints and pretexts of the "natural." If the structure had to mirror the psychology as directly as could be done, it was still a psychology hammered into its strange shape by society, the business life Willy had lived and believed in. The play could reflect what I had always sensed as the unbroken tissue that was man and society, a single unit rather than two.

By April of 1948 I felt I could find such a form, but it would have to be done, I thought, in a single sitting, in a night or a day, I did not know why. I stopped making my notes in our Grace Court house in Brooklyn Heights and drove up alone one morning to the country house we had bought the previous year. We had spent one summer there in that old farmhouse, which had been modernized by its former owner, a greeting card manufacturer named Philip Jaffe, who as a sideline published a thin magazine for China specialists called *Amerasia*. Mary worked as one of his secretaries and so had the first news that he wanted to sell the place. In a year or two he would be on trial for publishing without authorization State Department reports from John Stewart Service, among a number of other China experts who recognized a Mao victory as inevitable and warned of the futility of America continuing to back her favorite, Chiang Kai-Shek. *Amerasia* had been a vanity publication, in part born of Jaffe's desire for a place in history, but it nevertheless braved the mounting fury of the China lobby against any opinion questioning the virtues of the Chiang forces. At his trial the government produced texts of conversations that Jaffe claimed could only have been picked up by long-range microphone as he and his friends walked the isolated backcountry roads near this house. Service was one of many who were purged from the State Department, leaving it blinded to Chinese reality but ideologically pure.

But all that was far from my mind this day; what I was looking for on my land was a spot for a little shack I wanted to build, where I could block out the world and bring into focus what was still stuck in the corners of my eyes. I found a knoll in the nearby woods and returned to the city, where instead of working on the play I drew plans for the framing, of which I really had very vague knowledge and no experience. A pair of carpenters could have put up this ten-by-twelve-foot cabin in two days at most, but for reasons I still do not understand it had to be my own hands that gave it form, on this ground, with a floor that I had made, upon which to sit to begin the risky expedition into myself. In reality, all I had was the first two lines and a death—"Willy!" and "It's all right. I came back." Further than that I dared not, would not, venture until I could sit in the completed studio, four walls, two windows, a floor, a roof, and a door.

"It's all right. I came back" rolled over and over in my head as I tried to figure out how to join the roof rafters in air unaided, until I finally put them together on the ground and swung them into position all nailed together. When I closed in the roof, it was a miracle, as though I had mastered the rain and cooled the sun. And all the while afraid I would never be able to penetrate past those two first lines. I started writing one morning—the tiny studio was still unpainted and smelled of raw wood and sawdust, and the bags of nails were still stashed in a corner with my tools. The sun of April had found my windows to pour through, and the apple buds were moving on the wild trees, showing their first pale blue petals. I wrote all day until dark, and then I had dinner and went back and wrote until some hour in the darkness between midnight and four. I had skipped a few areas that I knew would give me no trouble in the writing and gone for the parts that had to be muscled into position. By the next morning I had done the first half, the first act of two. When I lay down to sleep, I realized I had been weeping—my eyes still burned and my throat was sore from talking it all out and shouting and laughing. I would be stiff when I woke, aching as if I had played four hours of football or tennis and now had to face the start of another game. It would take some six more weeks to complete Act II.

My laughter during the writing came mostly at Willy's contradicting himself so arrantly, and out of the laughter the title came one afternoon. *Death Comes for the Archbishop,* the *Death and the Maiden Quartet*—always austere and elevated was death in titles. Now it would be claimed by a joker, a bleeding mass of contradictions, a clown, and there was something funny about that, something like a thumb in the eye, too. Yes, and in some far corner of my mind possibly something political; there was the smell in the air of a new American Empire in the making, if only because, as I had witnessed, Europe was dying or dead, and I wanted to set before the new captains and the so smugly confident kings the corpse of a believer. On the play's opening night a woman who shall not be named was outraged, calling it "a time bomb under American capitalism"; I hoped it was, or at least under the bullshit of capitalism, this pseudo life that thought to touch the clouds by standing on top of a refrigerator, waving a paid-up mortgage at the moon, victorious at last.

But some 35 years later, the Chinese reaction to my Beijing production of *Salesman* would confirm what had become more and more obvious over the decades in the play's hundreds of productions throughout the world: Willy was representative everywhere, in every kind of system, of ourselves in this time. The Chinese might disapprove of his lies and his self-deluding exaggerations as well as his immorality with women, but they certainly saw themselves in him. And it was not simply as a type but because of what he wanted, which was to excel, to win out over anonymity and meaninglessness, to love and be loved, and above all, perhaps, to *count.* When he roared out, "I am not a dime a dozen! *I am Willy Loman, and you are Biff Loman!*" it came as a nearly revolutionary declaration after what was now 34 years of leveling. (The play was the same age as the Chinese revolution.) I did not know in 1948 in Connecticut that I was sending a message of resurgent individualism to the China of 1983—especially when the revolution had signified, it seemed at the time, the long-awaited rule of reason and the historic ending of chaotic egocentricity and selfish aggrandizement. Ah, yes. I had not reckoned on a young

Chinese student saying to a CBS interviewer in the theater lobby, "We are moved by it because we also want to be number one, and to be rich and successful." What else is this but human unpredictability, which goes on escaping the nets of unfreedom?

I did not move far from the phone for two days after sending the script to Kazan. By the end of the second silent day I would have accepted his calling to tell me that it was a scrambled egg, an impenetrable, unstageable piece of wreckage. And his tone when he finally did call was alarmingly somber.

"I've read your play." He sounded at a loss as to how to give me the bad news. "My God, it's so sad."

"It's supposed to be."

"I just put it down. I don't know what to say. My father . . ." He broke off, the first of a great many men—and women—who would tell me that Willy was their father. I still thought he was letting me down easy. "It's a great play, Artie. I want to do it in the fall or winter. I'll start thinking about casting." He was talking as though someone we both knew had just died, and it filled me with happiness. Such is art.

For the first time in months, as I hung up the phone, I could see my family clearly again. As was her way, Mary accepted the great news with a quiet pride, as though something more expressive would spoil me, but I too thought I should remain an ordinary citizen, even an anonymous one (although I did have a look at the new Studebaker convertible, the Raymond Lowey design that was the most beautiful American car of the time, and bought one as soon as the play opened). But Mary's mother, who was staying the week with us, was astonished. "*Another* play?" she said, as though the success of *All My Sons* had been enough for one lifetime. She had unknowingly triggered that play when she gossiped about a young girl somewhere in Central Ohio who had turned her father in to the FBI for having manufactured faulty aircraft parts during the war.

But who should produce *Salesman*? Kazan and I walked down Broadway from the park where we had been strolling and talking about the kind of style the production would need. Kazan's partnership with Harold Clurman had recently broken up, and I had no idea about a producer. He mentioned Cheryl Crawford, whom I hardly knew, and then Kermit Bloomgarden, an accountant turned producer, whom I had last seen poring over Herman Shumlin's account books a couple of years before when Shumlin turned down *All My Sons*. I had never seen Bloomgarden smile, but he had worked for the Group Theater and Kazan knew him, and as much because we happened to have come to a halt a few yards from his office building as for any other reason, he said, "Well, let's go up and say hello." When we stood across the desk from him and Kazan said he had a play of mine for him to read, Bloomgarden squeezed up his morose version of a smile, or at least a suggestion of one he planned to have next week.

This whimsical transforming of another person's life reminds me of a similar walk with Kazan uptown from a garage on Twenty-sixth Street where he had left his old Pontiac to be repaired. He began wondering aloud whom he should ask to head a new acting school to be called the Actors Studio, which he and Clurman and Robert Lewis and Cheryl Crawford were organizing. None of these founders was prepared to run the place, Kazan, Clurman, and Lewis being too busy with their flourishing directing careers, and Crawford with her work as a producer. "Lee Strasberg is probably the best guy for it. He'd certainly be able to put in the time." In due course Strasberg became not only the head of the Actors Studio but also its heart and soul, and for the general public its organizer. So his work there was made possible by his having been unemployable at the right moment. But that, come to think of it, is as good a way as any to be catapulted into world fame.

Willy had to be small, I thought, but we soon realized that Roman Bohnen and Ernest Truex and a few other very good actors seemed to lack the size of the character even if they fit the body. The script had been sent to Lee Cobb, an actor I remembered mainly as a mountainous hulk covered with a towel in a Turkish bath in an Irwin Shaw play, with the hilarious *oy vey* delivery of a forever persecuted businessman. Having flown himself across the country in his own two-engine airplane, he sat facing me in Bloomgarden's office and announced, "This is my part. Nobody else can play this part. I know this man." And he did indeed seem to be the man when a bit later in a coffee shop downstairs he looked up at the young waitress and smiled winsomely as though he had to win her loving embrace before she could be seduced into bringing him his turkey sandwich and coffee—ahead of all the other men's orders, and only after bestowing on his unique slice of pickle her longing kiss.

But while I trusted his and Kazan's experience, I lacked any conviction of my own about him until one evening in our Grace Court living room Lee looked down at my son, Bob, on the floor and I heard him laugh at something funny the child had said. The sorrow in his laughter flew out at me, touched me; it was deeply depressed and at the same time joyous, all flowing through a baritone voice that was gorgeously reedy. So large and handsome a man pretending to be thoroughly at ease in a world where he obviously did not fit could be moving.

"You know—or do you?—," Lee said to me one day in Bloomgarden's office a week or so before rehearsals were to begin, "that this play is a watershed. The American theater will never be the same." I could only gulp and nod in silence at his portentousness—which I feared might augur a stately performance—and hope that he would make Willy come alive anyway.

But as rehearsals proceeded in the small, periodically abandoned theater on the ratty roof of the New Amsterdam on Forty-second Street, where Ziegfeld in the twenties had staged some intimate revues, Lee seemed to move about in a buffalo's stupefied trance, muttering his lines, plodding with deathly slowness from position to position, and behaving like a man who had been punched in the head. "He's just learning it," Kazan shakily reassured me after three or four days. I waited as a week went by, and then ten days, and all that was emerging from Lee Cobb's throat was a bumpy hum. The other actors were nearing performance levels, but when they had to get a response from Lee all their rhythms slowed to near collapse. Kazan was no longer so sure and kept huddling with Lee, trying to pump him up. Nor did Lee offer any explanation, and I wondered whether he thought to actually play the part like a man with a foot in the grave. Between us, Kazan and I began referring to him as "the Walrus."

On about the twelfth day, in the afternoon, with Eddie Kook, our lighting supplier, and Jimmy Proctor, our pressman, and Kazan and myself in the seats, Lee stood up as usual from the bedroom chair and turned to Mildred Dunnock and bawled, "No, there's more people now. . . . There's more people!" and, gesturing toward the empty up-stage where the window was supposed to be, caused a block of apartment houses to spring up in my brain, and the air became sour with the smell of kitchens where once there had been only the odors of earth, and he began to move frighteningly, with such ominous reality that my chest felt pressed down by an immense weight. After the scene had gone on for a few minutes, I glanced around to see if the others had my reaction. Jim Proctor had his head bent into his hands and was weeping, Eddie Kook was looking shocked, almost appalled, and tears were pouring over his cheeks, and Kazan behind me was grinning like a fiend, gripping his temples with both hands, and we knew we had it—there was an unmistakable wave of life moving across the air of the empty theater, a wave of Willy's pain and protest. I began to weep myself at some point that was not particularly sad, but it was as much, I think, out of pride in our art, in Lee's magical capacity to imagine, to collect within himself every mote of life since Genesis and to let it pour forth. He stood up there like a giant moving the Rocky Mountains into position.

At the end of the act, Del Hughes, our sweet but hardheaded, absolutely devoted, competent stage manager, came out from a wing and looked out at us. His stunned eyes started us all laughing. I ran up and kissed Lee, who pretended to be surprised. "But what did you expect, Arthur?" he said, his eyes full of his playful vanity. My God, I thought—he really *is* Willy! On the subway going home to Brooklyn I felt once again the aching pain in my muscles that the performance had tensed up so tightly, just as in the writing time. And when I thought of it later, it seemed as though Lee's sniffing around the role for so long recapitulated what I had done in the months before daring to begin to write.

The whole production was, I think, unusual for the openness with which every artist involved sought out his truths. It was all a daily, almost moment-to-moment testing of ideas. There was much about the play that had never been done before, and this gave an uncustomary excitement to our discussions about what would or would not be understood by an audience. The setting I had envisioned was three bare platforms and only the minimum necessary furniture for a kitchen and two bedrooms, with the Boston hotel room as well as Howard's office to be played in open space. Jo Mielziner took those platforms and designed an environment around them that was romantic and dreamlike yet at the same time lower-middle-class. His set, in a word, was an emblem of Willy's intense longing for the promises of the past, with which indeed the present state of his mind is always conflicting, and it was thus both a lyrical design and a dramatic one. The only notable mistake in his early concept was to put the gas hot-water heater in the middle of the kitchen, a symbol of menace that I thought obvious and Kazan finally eliminated as a hazard to his staging. But by balancing on the edges of the ordinary bounds of verisimilitude, Jo was stretching reality in parallel with the script, just as Kazan did by syncopating the speech rhythms of the actors. He made Mildred Dunnock deliver her long first-act speeches to the boys at double her normal speed, then he doubled that, and finally she—until recently a speech teacher—was standing there drumming out words as fast as her very capable tongue could manage. Gradually he slacked her off, but the drill straightened her spine, and her Linda filled up with outrage and protest rather than self-pity and mere perplexity. Similarly, to express the play's inner life, the speech rate in some scenes or sections was unnaturally speeded or slowed.

My one scary hour came with the climactic restaurant fight between Willy and the boys, when it all threatened to come apart. I had written a scene in which Biff resolves to tell Willy that the former boss from whom Biff had planned to borrow money to start a business has refused to so much as see him and does not even remember his working for the firm years ago. But on meeting his brother and father in the restaurant, he realizes that Willy's psychological stress will not permit the whole catastrophic truth to be told, and he begins to trim the bad news. From moment to moment the scene as originally written had so many shadings of veracity that Arthur Kennedy, a very intelligent citizen indeed, had trouble shifting from a truth to a half-truth to a fragment of truth and back to the whole truth, all of it expressed in quickly delivered, very short lines. The three actors, with Kazan standing beside them, must have repeated the scene through a whole working day, and it still wobbled. "I don't see how we make it happen," Kazan said as we left the theatre that evening. "Maybe you ought to try simplifying it for them." I went home and worked through the night and brought in a new scene, which played much better and became the scene as finally performed.

The other changes were very small and a pleasure to make because they involved adding lines rather than cutting or rewriting. In Act I, Willy is alone in the kitchen muttering to himself, and as his memories overtake him the lighting brightens, the exterior of the house becomes covered with leaf shadows as of old, and in a moment the boys are calling to him in their youthful voices, entering the stage as they were in their teens. There was not sufficient time, however, for them to descend from their beds in the dark on the specially designed elevators and finish stripping out of their pajamas into sweaters and trouses and sneakers, so I had to add time to Willy's monologue. But that was easy since he loved talking to himself about his boys and his vision of them.

The moving in and out of the present had to be not simply indicative but a tactile transformation that the audience could feel as well as comprehend, and indeed come to dread as returning memory threatens to bring Willy closer to his end. Lighting was thus decisively important, and Mielziner, who also lit the show, with Eddie Kook by his side, once worked an entire afternoon lighting a chair.

Willy, in his boss's office, has exploded once too often, and Howard has gone out, leaving him alone. He turns to the office chair, which in the old days was occupied by Frank, Howard's father, who had promised Willy shares in the firm as a reward for all his good work, and as he does so the chair must become alive, quite as though his old boss were in it as he addresses him: "Frank, Frank, don't you remember what you told me? . . ." Rather than being lit, the chair subtly seemed to begin emanating light. But this was not merely an exercise in theatrical magic; it confirmed that we had moved inside Willy's system of loss, that we were seeing the world as he saw it even as we kept a critical distance and saw it for ourselves.

To set the chair off and make the light change work, all surrounding lights had to dim imperceptibly. That was when Eddie Kook, who had become so addicted to the work on this play that his office at his Century Lighting Company had all but ceased operations, turned to me and said, "You've been asking why we need so many lights. [We were using more than most musicals.] The reason is right there in front of you—it takes more lights to make it dark." With fewer lights each one would have to be dimmed more noticeably than if there were many, each only fractionally reduced in intensity to create the change without apparent source or contrivance.

Salesman had its first public performance at the Locust Street Theater in Philadelphia. Across the street the Philadelphia Orchestra was playing Beethoven's Seventh Symphony that afternoon, and Kazan thought Cobb ought to hear some of it, wanting, I suppose, to prime the great hulk on whom all our hopes depended. The three of us were in a conspiracy to make absolutely every moment of every scene cohere to what preceded and followed it; we were now aware that Willy's part was among the longest in dramatic literature, and Lee was showing signs of wearying. We sat on either side of him in a box, inviting him, as it were, to drink of the heroism of that music, to fling himself into his role tonight without holding back. We thought of ourselves, still, as a kind of continuation of a long and undying past.

As sometimes happened later on during the run, there was no applause at the final curtain of the first performance. Strange things began to go on in the audience. With the curtain down, some people stood to put their coats on and then sat again, some, especially men, were bent forward covering their faces, and others were openly weeping. People crossed the theater to stand quietly talking with one another. It seemed forever before someone remembered to applaud, and then there was no end to it. I was standing at the back and saw a distinguished-looking elderly man being led up the aisle; he was talking excitedly into the ear of what seemed to be his male secretary or assistant. This, I learned, was Bernard Gimbel, head of the department store chain, who that night gave an order that no one in his stores was to be fired for being overage.

Now began the parade of the visiting New York theater people to see for themselves, and I remember best Kurt Weill and his wife, Lotte Lenya, who had come with Maxwell Anderson's wife, Mab. We had coffee in a little shop, and Weill kept shaking his head and staring at me, and Mab said, "It's the best play ever written," which I dare repeat because it would be said often in the next months and would begin to change my life.

Of the opening night in New York two things stick to memory. At the back of the lovely Morosco, since destroyed by the greed of real estate men and the city's indifference, Kazan and I were sitting on the stairs leading up to the balcony as Lee was saying, "And by the way he died the death of a salesman . . ." Everything had gone beautifully, but I was near exhaustion since I acted all the parts internally as I watched, and suddenly I heard, " . . . in the smoker of the New York, New Hahven and Hayven." Surely the audience would burst out laughing—but nobody did. And the end created the same spell as it had in Philadelphia, and backstage was the same high euphoria that I had now come to expect. A mob of well-wishers packed the corridors to the dressing rooms. For the first time at a play of mine the movie stars had come out, but my face was still unknown and I could stand in a corner watching them unobserved—Lucille Ball and Desi Arnaz, Fredric and Florence March, and faces and names I have long forgotten, putting me on notice that I was now deep in show business, a paradoxically uncomfortable feeling indeed, for it was too material and real to have much to do with something that was air and whispers.

Finally, edging my way onto the stage, where I hoped to find a place to sit and rest, I saw as in a glorious dream of reward and high success three waiters in rich crimson Louis Sherry jackets arranging plates and silver on an extraordinarily long banquet table stretching almost the entire stage width. On its white linen table-cloth were great silver tureens and platters of beef, fowl, and seafood along with ice-filled buckets of champagne. Whose idea could this have been? What a glorious climax to the triumphant evening! Anticipating the heady shock of cold champagne, I reached for a gleaming glass, when one of the waiters approached me and with polite firmness informed me that the dinner had been ordered by Mr. Dowling for a private party. Robert Dowling, whose City Investing Company owned the Morosco along with other Broadway theaters, was a jovial fellow turning sixty who had swum around Manhattan Island, a feat he seemed to memorialize by standing straight with his chest expanded. I liked his childishness and his enthusiasms. I said that Mr. Dowling would surely not begrudge the play's author a well-earned glass of wine in advance of the celebration, but the waiter, obviously on orders, was adamant. I was dumbfounded, it must be somebody's joke, but a bit later, as Mary and I were leaving with the cast and their friends, we all stopped for a moment at the back of the theater to watch with half-hysterical incredulity as this rather decorous celebratory dinner proceeded literally inside Willy Loman's dun-colored Brooklyn house, the ladies in elaborate evening gowns, the men in dinner jackets, the waiters moving back and forth with the food under a polite hum of conversation suitable for the Pierre Hotel dining room, and the diners of course totally oblivious to the crowd of us looking on, laughing, and cracking jokes. It reminded me of scenes from Soviet movies of the last insensible days of the czarist court. Dowling, an otherwise generous fellow, was simply exercising the charming insensitivity of the proprietor, something Broadway would begin to see more and more of, but never perhaps on so grandly elegant and absurd a scale.

Secretly, of course, I was outraged, but sufficient praise was on the way to put offense to sleep. An hour or so later, at the opening-night party, Jim Proctor grabbed my arm and pulled me to a phone. On the other end was the whispered voice of Sam Zolotow, that generation's theatrical inside dopester and a reporter for the *Times*, who was actually reading our review directly off Brooks Atkinson's typewriter as the critic wrote it—I could hear the clacking of the typewriter on the phone. In his Noo Yawk voice he excitedly whispered word after word as Atkinson composed it under his nose—"Arthur Miller has written a superb drama. From every point of view, it is rich and memorable

. . ."—and as one encomium was laid upon another Sam's voice grew more and more amazed and warm and he seemed to reach out and give me his embrace. The conspiracy that had begun with me and spread to Kazan, the cast, Mielziner, and all the others now extended to Zolotow and Atkinson and the *Times*, until for a moment a community seemed to have formed of people who cared very much that their common sense of life in their time had found expression.

Driving homeward down lower Broadway at three in the morning, Mary and I were both silent. The radio had just finished an extraordinary program, readings of the play's overwhelmingly glowing reviews in the morning papers. My name repeated again and again seemed to drift away from me and land on someone else, perhaps my ghost. It was all a letdown now that the arrow had been fired and the bow, so long held taut, was slackening again. I had striven all my life to win this night, and it was here, and I was this celebrated man who had amazingly little to do with me, or I with him.

In truth, I would have sworn I had not changed, only the public perception of me had, but this is merely fame's first illusion. The fact, as it took much more time to appreciate, is that such an order of recognition imprints its touch of arrogance, quite as though one has control of a new power, a power to make real everything one is capable of imagining. And it can open a voraciousness for life and an impatience with old friends who persist in remaining ineffectual. An artist blindly follows his nose with hands outstretched, and only after he has struck the rock and brought forth the form hidden within it does he theorize and explain what is forever inexplicable, but I had a rationalist tradition behind me and felt I had to account to it for my rise.

I came to wish I had had the sense to say that I had learned what I could from books and study but that I did not know how to do what I had apparently done and that the whole thing might as well have been a form of prayer for all I understood about it. Simply, there is a sense for the dramatic form or there is not, there is stageworthy dialogue and literary dialogue and no one quite knows why one is not the other, why a dramatic line *lands* in an audience and a literary one sails over its head. Instead, there were weighty interviews and even pronouncements, and worst of all, a newly won rank to defend against the inevitable snipers. The crab who manages to climb up out of the bucket causes a lot of the other crabs to try to pull him back down where he belongs. That's what crabs do.

The fear once more was in me that I would not write again. And as Mary and I drove home, I sensed in our silence some discomfort in my wife and friend over these struggling years. It never occurred to me that she might have felt anxious at being swamped by this rush of my fame, in need of reassurance. I had always thought her clearer and more resolved than I. Some happiness was not with us that I wanted now, I had no idea what it might be, only knew the absence of it, its lack—so soon. In fact, the aphrodisiac of celebrity, still nameless, came and sat between us in the car.

And so inevitably there was a desire to flee from it all, to be blessedly unknown again, and a fear that I had stumbled into a dangerous artillery range. It was all an unnaturalness; fame is the other side of loneliness, of impossible-to-resolve contradictions—to be anonymous and at the same time not lose one's renown, in brief, to be two people who might occasionally visit together and perhaps make a necessary joint public appearance but who would normally live separate lives, the public fellow wasting his time gadding about while the writer stayed at his desk, as morose and anxious as ever, and at work. I did not want the power I wanted. It wasn't "real." What was?

Outlandish as it seemed, the Dowling party in the Lomans' living room came to symbolize one part of the dilemma; the pain and love and protest in my play could be transformed into mere champagne. My dreams of many years had simply become too damned real, and the reality was less than the dream and lacked all dedication.

V

Danger: Memory! to *Broken Glass*

"This country is being ruined by greed and mendacity and narrow-minded ignorance, and you go right on thinking there is hope somewhere."
> —Leonora in *I Can't Remember Anything*

"What you can't chase you'd better face or it'll start chasing you. . . ."
> —Detective Lieutenant Fine in *Clara*

"*Everybody's* persecuted. The poor by the rich, the rich by the poor, the black by the white, the white by the black, the men by the women, the women by the men, the Catholics by the Protestants, the Protestants by the Catholics—and of course all of them by the Jews. Everybody's persecuted—sometimes I wonder, maybe that's what holds this country together! And what's really amazing is that you can't find anybody who's persecuting anybody else."
> —Dr. Harry Hyman in *Broken Glass*

A Fabulous Appetite
for Greatness

To BEGIN with, these letters are essential to any understanding of Eugene O'Neill, if only because they demystify him. It is not merely the ordinary details of living that move him off his pedestal—income tax troubles and marital troubles and frustrations with productions of his plays. Far more powerfully, it is the sustained intensity of his feelings that brings him close, even though that may seem strange in a time of cool and campy fragmentation and disillusion. O'Neill's life-long naked anger with the American notion of a "Showshop" theater, for example, could be taken as a comment on the theater today—if anyone cared that much now.

"I stand for the playwright's side of it in this theatre," he wrote to the producer Kenneth Macgowan in 1926. "What's the use of my try-ing to get ahead with new stuff until some theatre can give that stuff the care and opportunity it must have in order to register its new sig-nificance? ... It makes me feel hopeless about writing except for my own satisfaction in a book."

Selected Letters of Eugene O'Neill, edited by Travis Bogard and Jack-son R. Bryer, who previously edited the letters of O'Neill to Mac-gowan (Mr. Bogard is also the editor of the *Complete Plays* of Eugene O'Neill in the Library of America series), is a collection of nearly 600 of his letters, many published for the first time. The volume could

From *The New York Times Book Review*, 6 November 1988, pp. 12–13. Reprinted by permission of Arthur Miller.

once again make his life and work instructive to a generation that needs the example of his integrity and grit, his vision and undying belief in what he called an art theater (something his Provincetown Playhouse ceased to be after a time).

His alienation from Broadway was total even at the height of his success. When he received the Nobel Prize in Literature in 1936, he wrote to Russel Crouse: "I have rec'd congratulations from all over the world . . . Hauptmann, Pirandello, Lenormand, etc. but none from home front playwrights with the exception of Ned Sheldon, Sam Behrman, George Middleton and your esteemed self." Then he applied an unprintable obscenity to his "U.S. colleagues" in general. (Actually, Sidney Howard wrote him a bit later.)

Journalists had him pegged as either a remote mystic or a drunken bum, but in this mass of correspondence he is an entirely different sort—several other sorts, in fact. Passionately involved in his time, a worried father, a canny theater agent for his own plays, an overwhelmed husband, a property owner, and a lifelong anarchist who in 1944 expressed "contempt for [Franklin D. Roosevelt's] sly hypocritical politician's tricks" (he favored the Socialist Norman Thomas), he was sufficiently conformist to advise Eugene Jr. at Yale "to have one fine, perfectly-fitting expensive suit of clothes where others will have three maybe but each minus the distinction."

O'Neill was the anarchist radical to the end. In June 1942 he wrote to his son Eugene: "It is like acid always burning in my brain that the stupid butchering of the last war taught men nothing at all, that they sank back listlessly on the warm manure pile of the dead and went to sleep, indifferently bestowing custody of their future, their fate, into the hands of State departments, whose members are trained to be conspirators, card sharps, double-crossers and secret betrayers of their own people; into the hands of greedy capitalist ruling classes so stupid they could not even see when their own greed began devouring itself; into the hands of that most debased type of pimp, the politician, and that most craven of all lice and job-worshippers, the bureaucrats."

But no other country, he felt, could match America for its spiritual possibilities. In the early 1920s he was not among the wave of disgusted American artists who fled from a mindless materialism to France. He wrote to the journalist Malcolm Mollan in 1921: "One critic . . . has said tragedy is not native to our soil, has no reason for being as American drama. . . . If it were true, it would be the most damning commentary on our spiritual barrenness. Perhaps it was true a decade ago but America is now in the throes of a spiritual awakening. . . . A soul is being born, and where a soul enters, tragedy enters with it. Supposing someday we should suddenly see with the clear eyes of a soul the true valuation of all our triumphant, brass band materialism, see the *cost*. . . . Why, we *are* tragedy the most appalling yet written or unwritten!" And from these letters his life seems, indeed, the work of creating a soul.

But in the end his grandiose, uncompleted cycle of plays about American history from its beginning would go to demonstrate "the bitter assertion," as the editors of this volume put it, that "to gain the world, the United States had sold its soul." He was a man divided, as he himself often said, and pointed to *The Great God Brown* as proof, between despair at a cynical materialism triumphant and his ever-renewing commitment to an ennobled human spirit. But he would never fuse the two conflicting sides excepting in his art, particularly in two of his final plays, *The Iceman Cometh* and *Long Day's Journey into Night*.

There are remarks in these letters that one cannot read without a sort of forlorn delight in the unchangingness of the torture that a playwriting life affords. To the critic George Jean Nathan about H. L. Mencken's criticism of his play *Welded*, O'Neill wrote: "I must confess the greater part of his comment seems irrelevant as criticism of my play. To point out its weakness as realism (in the usual sense of that word) is to confuse what is obviously part of my deliberate intention. Damn that word, 'realism!' When I first spoke to you of the play as a 'last word in realism,' I meant something 'really real,' in the sense of being spiritually true, not meticulously life-like." And finally the inevitable leaning on the last hope: "Well, just wait until you see it played! (if it's done right)."

His contempt for most critics is par for the course—"me that was born on Times Square . . . and have heard dramatic critics called sons of bitches . . . ever since I was old enough to recognize the Count of Monte Cristo's voice!" And "every paper ought to fire from their Drama Department anyone who has written a play. The boys look in the mirror and get bilious with envy." But what is unusual, to say the least, are his friendships with two or three critics—Joseph Wood Krutch, George Jean Nathan, Brooks Atkinson, the heavy hitters to whom he sometimes gave scripts before production so he could confute their opinions or sometimes follow their suggestions. Apparently critics were not always virgins of objectivity whose purity could not withstand the proximity of actual artists and their struggles to create life on the stage.

Belying the usual characterization of him as a total loner is the large number of letters to and about his children. And there is no more painful irony to contemplate in all the events of his life than the way his own "cursed" family evolved. In 1927 he wrote to his second wife, Agnes Boulton O'Neill, from their house at Spithead in Bermuda: "Our Home. *Our Home!* I feel that very much about Spithead, don't you? That this place is in some strange symbolical fashion our reward, that it is the permanent seat of our family—like some old English family estate. I already feel like entailing it in my will so that it must always be background for our children!" Two of those children would end in suicide and one he would in fury disown. And finally, beloved Agnes herself he would call the "idiot mother" of his children, a drunk and a "bigamist."

These letters confound a number of orthodox attitudes toward O'Neill's so-called unsophistication. In fact, he read widely, he knew Chinese and German philosophy, he began a serious study of ancient Greek, and he was far from being an inept writer of prose. Nor did he keep disdainfully apart from his peers—among them Padraic Colum and James Joyce, Sinclair Lewis and Sherwood Anderson, and his left-wing friends Mike Gold and Sean O'Casey, to whom he would exclaim, "I wish to God I could write like that!" He knew his work tended toward garrulousness but dreaded "leaving anything out"—his scenarios for three plays ran to 25,000 words each.

*   *   *

Despite the fifty-year period that these letters cover, a unity in O'Neill's life strikes the reader; from the beginning he had a fabulous appetite for greatness, and despite many personal and artistic lapses— of which he was helplessly aware—a noble quest emerges. As always, it is the spectacle of great courage that, in spite of his failings, merits a salute. "If we had Gods or a God, if we had a Faith, if we had some healing subterfuge by which to conquer Death, then the Aristotelian criterion might apply in part to our Tragedy," he wrote to Brooks Atkinson. "But our tragedy is just that we have only ourselves, that there is nothing to be purged into except a belief in the guts of man, good or evil, who faces unflinchingly the black mystery of his own soul!"

Toward the end, with his two greatest masterpieces in hand—*The Iceman Cometh* and *Long Day's Journey into Night*—in which at last he had fused character and theme, style and substance, he refused at first to let them be produced in the commercial Broadway theater. He wrote to Macgowan: "I dread the idea of production because I know it will be done by people who have really only one standard left, that of Broadway success.... The big fact is that any production must be made on a plane, and in an atmosphere to which neither I nor my work belongs in spirit, nor want to belong: that it is ... the Old Game, the game we used to defy in the P[rovincetown] P[layhouse] but which it is impossible for me to defy now, except in my writing, because there is no longer a theatre of true integrity and courage and high purpose and enthusiasm.... To have an ideal now, except as a slogan in which neither you nor anyone else believes but which you use out of old habit to conceal a sordid aim, is to confess oneself a fool who cannot face the High Destiny of Man!"

With his great and awesome hammer O'Neill kept striking the mountain to the bitter end, and this book is worthy of his struggle.

Again They Drink
from the Cup of Suspicion

I DID not write *The Crucible* simply to propagandize against McCarthyism, although if justification were needed that would have been enough. There was something else involved. I'll try to explain.

A writer friend was recently telling me about a Moscow theater producer who is interested in putting on a play about the Vietnam War. Why Vietnam? It turns out that what he would really like to illuminate is the Russian defeat in Afghanistan, but with feelings about Afghanistan still running so high he felt he needed a metaphor that would go to the dilemmas underlying such a war, rather than attempting an outright confrontation with the thickets of feeling surrounding Afghanistan itself.

That approach reminded me of my decision to write about the 1692 Salem witch trials, rather than trying to take on Joseph McCarthy and his cohorts directly. In the early fifties McCarthyism, so-called, began as a conservative Republican cavalry charge that in the name of anti-Communism helped scatter the left-liberal coalitions of Democrats and union people who had held together the only recently faded New Deal. But this was no ordinary political campaign. This time the enemy was not merely "The Democrat Party," as McCarthy sneeringly renamed it, but the hidden foreign plot which, naively but often knowingly, it shielded. Thus a certain sublime gloss—national secu-

From *The New York Times*, 26 November 1989, Sec. 2, pp. 5, 36. Reprinted by permission of Arthur Miller.

rity—was varnished over a very traditional grab for domestic political power.

With amazing speed McCarthy was convincing a lot of not unintelligent people that the incredible was really true, and that, say, General of the Army George Catlett Marshall was a Communist sympathizer, or that Senator Millard E. Tydings of Maryland was a buddy of Earl Browder, head of the American Communist Party. (A photo of both of them standing happily together would only much later be proved to have been a fake manufactured by Roy Cohn, McCarthy's right-hand bandido.)

For a time it began to seem that Senator Joe was heading straight for the White House, the more so when the sheer incredibility of his claims appeared to be part proof that they were real; if the Communists were indeed hidden everywhere, it followed that they would certainly be found where common sense indicated they could not conceivably be.

The case being circular, it was finally all but unarguable. Worse yet, you could not rely on the too-trusting police, the naively legalistic courts, or even the slow-moving F.B.I. to root out the conspiracy. As for the press, it was all but sold to Moscow, secretly, of course. Who then was absolutely reliable? McCarthy, naturally, and those who had his blessing.

This was colorful and fascinating stuff for the stage, but a play takes a year to write and months to see through production, and I could not imagine spending so much time on what seemed to me so obvious a tale. But as the anti-Communist crusade settled in, and showed signs of becoming the permanent derangement of the American psyche, a kind of mystery began to emerge from its melodramas and comedies. We were all behaving differently than we used to; we had drunk from the cup of suspicion of one another; people inevitably were afraid of too close an association with someone who might one day fall afoul of some committee. Even certain words vibrated perilously, words like organize, social, militant, movement, capitalism—it didn't do to be on too familiar terms with such language. We had entered a mysterious pall from which there seemed no exit.

Returning around that time to my alma mater, the University of Michigan, to do a story for *Holiday* magazine, I discovered that students were avoiding living in the co-op rooming houses because the very idea of a nonprofit organization was suspiciously pro-left. The F.B.I. was paying students at Michigan to report secretly on teachers' political remarks, and teachers to report on students.

Why was there so little real opposition to this madness? Of course there was the fear of reprisals, of losing jobs, or perhaps only bad publicity, but there was also guilt, and this seemed to me the main crippler, the internalized cop.

No doubt instinctually, McCarthy and Roy Cohn were handing around full plates of guilt which were promptly licked clean by people who in one way or another had brushed the sleeve of the Communist movement in the thirties—some by joining the party or supporting one of its front organizations, a left-wing union or professional guild, or in whatever manner had at some point in their lives turned to the left. Of course such people were used to being guilty—why else would they have bothered to worry about the poor, the blacks, the lynch victims, the Spanish Republicans, and so on when real Americans were only remotely aware of such inequities around them?

It was a charm, a kind of spell. McCarthy could call the Roosevelt New Deal "20 years of treason" with hardly a rejoinder from the vast multitude of Americans for whom New Deal measures, hardly more than a decade before, had meant the difference between living on the street or in their own homes, between hunger and real starvation. It was a sort of benighted miracle that just about anything that flew out of his mouth, no matter how outrageously and obviously idiotic, could be made to land in an audience and stir people's terrors of being taken over by Communists, their very religion in danger.

I had known the Salem story since college, over a decade earlier, but what kept assaulting my brain now was not the hunt for witches itself; it was the paralysis that had led to more than twenty public hangings of very respectable farmers by their neighbors. There was something "wonderful" in this spectacle, a kind of perverse, malign poetry that had simply swamped the imaginations of these people. I thought I saw something like it around me in the early fifties.

The truth is that the more I worked at this dilemma the less it had to do with Communists and McCarthy and the more it concerned something very fundamental in the human animal: the fear of the unknown, and particularly the dread of social isolation.

Political movements are always trying to position themselves as shields against the unknown—vote for me and you're safe. The difference during witch-hunts is that you are being made safe from a malign, debauched, evil, irreligious, wife-swapping, deceitful, immoral, stinking conspiracy stemming from the very bowels of hell. In Wisconsin in the early fifties a reporter went door to door asking residents if they agreed with certain propositions, ten in number, and discovered that very few people did, and that most thought the first ten amendments to the United States Constitution, unnamed of course in the inquiry, were Communistic. To propose that we should be free to express any idea at all was frightening to a lot of people.

The Colonial government in the 1690s saw itself as protecting Christianity (while unknowingly propagating a thrilling counter-religion of Satan worship) by seizing on the ravings of a klatch of repressed pubescent girls who, fearing punishment for their implicitly sexual revolt, began convincing themselves that they had been perverted by Satan. There were economic and social pressures at work, but the nub of it all as it appeared to the locals at the moment was that the Archfiend had been sneaked into the spotless town by an alien who, even better, was black, the Barbadian slave of the Lord's very own man, the church minister himself. Authority quickly converted the poor girls back to the true religion and made them celebrities for their agonizing bravery in pointing out likely adherents of the Devil.

But were there not really Communists, whereas there never were any witches? Of course. And there are also paranoids who are really being followed. There was a very real military face-off in the fifties between America and the Soviet Union, and we had only recently "lost" China, but were these grounds for blacklisting actors and writers in Hollywood, or destroying professionals in many other fields, and for turning the country into a whispering gallery? What research showed me, and what I hoped the play would show the country and the world, was the continuity through time of human delusion, and the only safeguard, fragile though it may be, against it—namely, the law and the courageous few whose sacrifice illuminates delusion.

In the 35 years since the play was written it has become my most produced work by far. I doubt a week has gone by when it has not been on some stage somewhere in the world. It seems to be produced, especially in Latin America, when a dictatorship is in the offing, or when one has just been overthrown.

There is so often a telltale social sidelight connected to its production. Years ago in South Africa, black Tituba had to be played by a white woman in blackface, but the director, Barney Simon, terrified though he was of attack, wanted the white audience to contemplate the story. Last year I happened to meet Nien Cheng, the seventy-year-old author of *Life and Death in Shanghai*, an account of her six-year imprisonment during the Cultural Revolution. Tears formed in her eyes when she shook my hand, tears, as it surprisingly turned out, of gratitude.

Released from prison, she had spent months recuperating when a director friend, Huang Tsolin, invited her to see his production of *The Crucible* in a Shanghai theater. She said she was astounded: "I could not believe the play was not written by a Chinese because the questions of the court were exactly the same ones the Cultural Revolutionaries had put to me!"

I saw the play in Tbilisi, Soviet Georgia, where John Proctor wore seventeenth-century Turkish pantaloons and a gorgeous wide moustache and was chased through a forest by a crowd waving scimitars. At Olivier's fabulous 1965 National Theatre production, with Colin Blakely and Joyce Redman, I overheard a young woman in front of me whispering to her escort, "Didn't this have something to do with that American Senator—what was his name?" I have to admit that it felt marvelous that McCarthy was what's-his-name while *The Crucible* was *The Crucible* still.

Simone Signoret and Yves Montand did a stirring French film, a version of their Paris stage performance, with a screenplay by Jean-Paul Sartre in which the New England farmers were, inexplicably, Roman Catholic. The Long Wharf Theater in New Haven is about to open it under Arvin Brown's direction—it was Long Wharf's first production 25 years ago—and the Roundabout Theater will be doing it later this season. An HBO film of it is to be made this winter for both television and theatrical distribution. In Glasgow recently two productions were running at the same time, one by a young Soviet company. The Schiller Theater in Berlin will have it on in a few months.

I have wondered if one of the reasons the play continues like this is its symbolic unleashing of the specter of order's fragility. When certainties evaporate with each dawn, the unknowable is always around the corner. We know how much depends on mere trust and good faith and a certain respect for the human person, and how easily breached these are. And we know as well how close to the edge we live and how weak we really are and how quickly swept by fear the mass of us can become when our panic button is pushed. It is also, I suppose, that the play reaffirms the ultimate power of courage and clarity of mind whose ultimate fruit is liberty.

Introduction to *The Golden Years* and *The Man Who Had All the Luck*

BOTH OF these plays came out of the years leading up to World War II, between 1938, my college graduation year, and 1944 when the fighting was raging. For me they are a kind of unadulterated evidence of my reactions to that time and it strikes me oddly that, as up to my neck as I was in the feverish anti-Fascism that swept my generation, the plays I chose to write were so metaphorical. This is especially strange when the only tradition in American theater of which I was aware was realism. I can't imagine what I thought I was doing.

Or, rather, I thought I knew that I was writing against the grain of the Broadway theater of the time, the only theater we had, which as usual was happily wallowing in its traditional sidewalk realism. My primary argument with this form was that I could not connect aspiration with it—it was too much like uninterpreted life. *The Golden Years* looked toward a non-existent poetic theater inspired by the Elizabethan models. Its lavish use of actors was no doubt encouraged by the fact that in the early months of its writing I was on the payroll, at $22.77 a week, of the expiring Playwriting Project of the WPA Theater, and at least in theory could call upon any number of actors for my cast. Unfortunately, before the play was finished, Congress had wiped out the WPA Theater and the play, like any play calling for several immense sets and a cast so large, was doomed as a possible com-

From *The Golden Years* and *The Man Who Had All the Luck*, Methuen, London, 1989, pp. 5–10. Reprinted by permission of Reed Books.

mercial enterprise. It was never produced until the BBC did a radio production in 1987.

Excepting for a revision of three pages at the end of *The Man Who Had All the Luck,* and some mild pruning of both plays, I have left them as they were. *The Man Who Had All the Luck* was given a regular Broadway production and lasted less than a full week after the critics, with one or two interested but puzzled exceptions, could make absolutely nothing of it. I recall at the time being unable to find the slightest connection between the production and the play I imagined I had written, and after watching but one bewildering performance fled back to my desk and began a novel, resolved never to write for the theater again. It was 45 years later, in 1988, that I began to understand the reason for my alienation from my own play, as well, very possibly, for the total incomprehension of the critics.

A staged reading of the play under the direction of Ralph Bell, an old friend who had always had a soft spot in his heart for this play, quickly revealed that it is, indeed, a fable with no relation to realistic theater. A fable, of course, is based on an obsessive grip of a single idea bordering on the supernatural and it is the idea that stands in the forefront, rather than the characters and the verisimilitudes of the tale. The coincidences are arrantly unapologetic in this play and so they should be played, rather than attempts made to rationalize them and dim them down.

I recall the original production lit in reassuring pink and rose, a small-town genre comedy. Given the threatening elements in the story, this atmosphere must indeed have been puzzling. The play is after all attacking the evaluation of people by their success or failure and worse yet, denying the efficacy of property as a shield against psychological catastrophe.

From a distance of half a century I am struck by a certain optimistic undercurrent in both plays, despite one being a tragedy and the other veering pretty close. I must say that, at the time, life at best seemed headed for a bloody showdown with Fascism, or at worst a hapless surrender to it, but while there is plenty of worry in these plays, there is no real despair or defeat of the spirit. This will strike some as perhaps a reflection of a callow Leftism, but in truth it was the way most Americans felt even after a very long decade of Depression. By the late thirties and early forties we had, of course, known much social violence and all kinds of vileness, but not yet a Holocaust, not yet the bursting of the banks of evil. I can still recall my incredulity at the daylight bombing of Guernica in the Spanish Civil War. As bombings go, it wasn't a very big one. The big ones were still on the way. But I simply could not believe that a European flying low in an airplane on a sunny day over an undefended town, could, whatever his politics, drop live bombs on women out shopping with their baby carriages, on old men sitting before their doorways, on young lovers strolling across the ancient square! It was hard to sleep for weeks afterwards. It was still possible to be shocked. At least within one's mind the lines of some sort of order of permissible human behavior still held.

In the West since the War of 1914–18 every period has known its main menace, some single force threatening life on the planet. For a long time now it has been Communism, and as this menace disintegrates, there are signs that ecological catastrophe is developing into a worldwide substitute. From the mid-thirties to the outbreak of war with the Axis powers it was the Fascist threat—and for some its promise—that pervaded every discussion. An important source of the energy in these plays was my fear that in one form or another Fascism, with its intensely organized energies, might well overwhelm the wayward and self-fixated Democracies. A reader today may find it strange that two such very different works could spring from the same source, or even, perhaps, that they are at all related to contemporaneous political events.

The telltale mark of this preoccupation, as I now see quite clearly, is much the same in both plays, even if one is a tragedy about the Cortés invasion of Montezuma's Mexico in 1522 and the other the tale of a very successful young man in a pastoral Ohio village. They are both struggling against passive acceptance of fate or even of defeat in life, and urge action to control one's future; both see evil as irrational and aggressive, the good as rational, if inactive and benign. Plainly, I was hounded at the time by what seemed the debility of Americans' grasp of democratic values or their awareness of them.

And I must recall—to fill out this picture—that these plays were written after a decade of Depression, which had by no means lifted with any certainty as yet, and that the Depression had humbled us, shown us up as helpless before the persistent, ineradicable plague of mass unemployment. Reason had lost a lot of her credentials between 1930 and 1940.

If as the decade ended, the devaluation of the individual—the main lesson of the Depression—was still spiked to the common consciousness, these plays are somewhat surprising testimony to me that I had not lost the belief in the centrality of the individual and the importance of what he thought and did. On this evidence I suppose I might even have been called an individualist—there is nothing like writing a play for unveiling one's illusions! *The Man Who Had All the Luck* tells me that in the midst of the collectivist thirties I believed it decisive what an individual thinks and does about his life, regardless of overwhelming social forces. And likewise, in *The Golden Years,* the fate of all Mexico hung on what an individual—Montezuma—believed about himself and his role in the universe. Indeed, if these plays are to be credited, there is no force so powerful, politically as well as personally, as a man's self-conceptions.

Hearing *The Man Who Had All the Luck* read after four decades, it only then occurred to me that I had written the obverse of the Book of Job. The story of a man who cannot come to terms with the total destruction of his property and all his hopes, when he has done nothing to earn such treatment from God or fate, is very much the same as that of a man who can't seem to make a mistake and whose every move turns out to be profitable and good. What had Job done to deserve such disasters? David Beeves has much the same question in mind, oppressed by his invariably good luck in everything he attempts. And he projects an imminent disaster that will even things up between himself and the rest of humanity. For both these characters the menace is much the same—anarchy in the high command of the universe, a yawning breach between effect and conceivable causation, and they are both an argument with God.

There is mitigation in the Book of Job, of course, since we are shown a purpose behind Job's catastrophe. God starts all the trouble by wagering with the Devil that nothing he can do will shake good Job's faith in Himself. So it is clearly the Evil One who strips Job of his good life in order to destroy his belief in God's justice. And indeed, it turns out that after much twisting and backsliding Job, despite everything, clings to God—and he is promptly rewarded with the return of all his wordly goods plus God's personal gratitude for his having kept the faith. Of course this won't do in our time if only because most of God's argument with Job consists of reminding the poor man of the incomprehensibility of his obscure powers—"Can you draw out the Leviathan with a fishook?" and so on. This sort of humiliation is less impressive now when we can press a trigger and destroy whales and might even lift them up with helicopters, and the atom in our hands has the power of a sun. It is the question of justice that we haven't come any closer to clearing up, and indeed the goal of achieving it may be moving further away, so perhaps there is still a little room for *The Man Who Had All the Luck.*

As for the ending of this play—which I am sure I have rewritten twenty times over the past half century, it is as satisfactory as it is possible to be, as complete, let's say, as Job's, which also doesn't quite come down on both feet. The simple fact is that, as moving and imperative as our questioning of our fates may be, there is no possibility of answering the main question—why am I as I am and my life as it is? The more answers one supplies the more new questions arise. David Beeves in this play arrives as close as he can at a workable, conditional faith in the neutrality of the world's intentions toward him. I would emphasize the conditional side of it, but it is better than shooting out your brains in sheer terror of what may happen tomorrow.

The Golden Years, its purplish passages notwithstanding, is a harder if earlier look at passivity and its risks, but here the society as well as an individual is at stake. Montezuma, like the Democracies facing Hitler, was as though hypnotized. Weakened by self-doubt, he looks to Cortés, manifestly a brute and a conqueror, as one who may nevertheless bear within him the seed of the future. Something has ended for Montezuma before Cortés ever arrived in Mexico, the heart-lifting glamor of what men call the future is gone out of his life and he can foresee only deadly and meaningless repetition. There was a metaphorical poetry in this in the late thirties when perfectly intelligent, respectable, even heroic folk like the great flier Charles Lindbergh and his wife Anne could return from a visit to Nazi Germany and call it "The Wave of the Future." I recall feeling myself surrounded in those times by a kind of drifting into cultural suicide and a self-blinded acceptance of murder in high places, and this play was written in alarm. A few years later I did believe that had the Japanese not been deluded enough to attack Pearl Harbor there might well have been sufficient isolationist sentiment in the American people to simply let Hitler have his way with a defeated England and Europe. In a word, our passivity seemed in reality a drift toward an unacknowledged arrangement with Fascism. So—perhaps despite appearances—these are two anti-Fascist plays that were written quite close to the abyss. But perhaps more importantly, they were one very young writer's wrestling with enormous themes.

Conditions of Freedom:
Two Plays of the Seventies—
The Archbishop's Ceiling and
The American Clock

I

It is pointless any longer to speak of a period as being one of transition—what period isn't?—but the seventies, when both these plays were written, seemed to resist any definition even at the time. *The Archbishop's Ceiling* in some part was a response to this indefinition I sensed around me. Early in the decade the Kent State massacre took place, and while the anti-Vietnam War movement could still mobilize tens of thousands, the freshness had gone out of the wonderful sixties mixture of idealism and bitterness that had sought to project a new unaggressive society based on human connection rather than the values of the market economy. There was a common awareness of exhaustion, to the point where politics and social thought themselves seemed ludicrously out of date and naively ineffectual except as subjects of black comedy. Power everywhere seemed to have transformed itself from a forbidding line of troops into an ectoplasmic lump that simply swallowed up the righteous sword as it struck. Power was also doing its own, often surprising thing.

At least as an atmosphere, there was a not dissimilar disillusion in Eastern Europe and, for different reasons, in France too. As presi-

From *The Archbishop's Ceiling* and *The American Clock*, Grove Press, New York, 1989, pp. vii–xx. Copyright © 1989 by Arthur Miller and Inge Morath as Trustee. Reprinted by permission of Grove/Atlantic Inc.

dent of International P.E.N, I had the opportunity to move about in Eastern Europe, as well as in the Soviet Union, and I felt that local differences aside, intellectual life in the whole developed world had been stunned by a common failure to penetrate Power with a more humane and rational point of view. It may have been that the immense sense of relief and the high expectations that rushed in with the defeat of Hitler and Mussolini's fascism had to end in a letdown, but whatever the causes, by the seventies the rational seemed bankrupt as an ultimate sanction, a bar to which to appeal. And with it went a sense of history, even of the evolution of ideas and attitudes.

The ups and downs of disillusionment varied with time and place, however. It was possible to sit with Hungarian writers, for example, while they talked of a new liberalizing trend in their country, at the very moment that in Prague the depths of a merciless repression were being plumbed. There, with the Soviet ousting of Dubček and the crushing of all hope for an egalitarian socialist economy wedded to liberal freedoms of speech and artistic expression, the crash of expectations was especially terrible, for it was in Prague that this novel fusion seemed actually to have begun to function.

The seventies was also the era of the listening device, government's hidden bugs set in place to police the private conversations of its citizens—and not in Soviet areas alone. The White House was bugged, businesses were bugging competitors to defeat their strategies, and Watergate and the publication of the Pentagon Papers (which polls showed a majority of Americans disapproved) demonstrated that the Soviets had little to teach American presidents about domestic espionage. The burgling of psychiatrists' offices to spy out a government official's private life, the widespread bugging by political parties of each other's offices, all testified to the fact that the visible motions of political life were too often merely distractions, while the reality was what was happening in the dark.

Thus, when I found myself in Eastern European living rooms where it was all but absolutely certain that the walls or ceilings were bugged by the regime, it was not, disturbingly enough, an absolutely unfamiliar sensation for me. Of course there were very important differences—basically that an Eastern writer accused of seditious thoughts would have no appeal from his government's decision to hound him into silence, or worse. But the more I reflected on my experiences under bugged ceilings, the more the real issue changed from a purely political one to the question of what effect this surveillance was having on the minds of people who had to live under such ceilings, on whichever side of the Cold War line they happened to be.

Vaclav Havel, the Czech playwright who was later to serve a long term in prison, one day discovered a bug in his chandelier when house painters lowered it to paint the ceiling; deciding to deliver it to the local police, he said that it was government property that he did not think rightfully belonged to a private person. But the joke was as unappreciated as the eavesdropping itself was undenied. Very recently, in the home of a star Soviet writer, I began to convey the best wishes of a mutual friend, an émigré Russian novelist living in Europe, and the star motioned to me not to continue. Once outside, I asked if he wasn't depressed by having to live in a tapped house. He thought a moment, then shrugged—"I really don't know how I feel. I guess we figure the thing doesn't work!"—and burst out laughing at this jibe at Soviet inefficiency. Was he really all that unaffected by the presence of the unbidden guest? Perhaps so, but even if he had come to accept or at least abide it fatalistically, the bug's presence had changed him nonetheless. In my view it had perhaps dulled some resistance in him to Power's fingers ransacking his pockets every now and then. One learns to *include the bug* in the baggage of one's mind, in the calculus of one's plans and expectations, and this is not without effect.

The occasion, then, of *The Archbishop's Ceiling* is the bug and how people live with it, but the theme is something different. There are a number of adaptations to such a life: one man rails furiously at the ceiling, another questions that a bug is even up there, a third has changes of opinion from day to day; but man is so adaptable—and anyway the bug doesn't seem to be reacting much of the time and may simply be one more nuisance—that resistance to its presence is finally worn down to nothing. And that is when things become interesting, for something like the naked soul begins to loom, some essence in man that is simply unadaptable, ultimate, immutable as the horizon.

What, for instance, becomes of the idea of sincerity, the unmitigated expression of one's feelings and views, when one knows that Power's ear is most probably overhead? Is sincerity shaken by the sheer fact that one has so much as *taken the bug into consideration?* Under such pressure who can resist trying to some degree, however discreet and slight, to characterize himself for the benefit of the ceiling, whether as obedient conformist or even as resistant? And what, in that case, has been done to one's very identity? Does this process not overturn the very notion of an "I" in this kind of world? It would seem that "I" must be singular, not plural, but the art of bureaucracy is to change the "I" of its subjects to "we" at every moment of conscious life. What happens, in short, when people know that they are—at least most probably, if not certainly—at all times talking to Power, whether through a bug or a friend who is really an informer? Is it not something akin to accounting for oneself to a god? After all, most ideas of God see him as omnipresent, invisible, and condign in his judgments; the bug lacks only mercy and love to qualify, it is conscience shorn of moral distinctions.

In this play the most unreconcilable of the writers is clearly the most talented. Sigmund really has no permanent allegiance except to the love of creating art. Sigmund is also the most difficult to get along with, and has perhaps more than his share of cynicism and bitterness, narcissism and contempt for others. He is also choking with rage and love. In short, he is most alive, something that by itself would fuel his refusal—or constitutional incapacity—to accept the state's arrogant treatment. But with all his vitality, even he in the end must desperately call up a sanction, a sublime force beyond his ego, to sustain him in his opposition to that arrogance; for him it is the sublimity of art, in whose life-giving, creative essence he partakes and shares with other artists whose works he bows to, and in the act transcends the tyranny.

In a sense *Archbishop* begs the question of the existence of the sacred in the political life of man. But it begins to seem now that some kind of charmed circle has to be drawn around each person, across which the state may intrude only at its very real economic and political peril.

Glasnost, which did not exist in the seventies, is to the point here, for it is at bottom a Soviet attempt, born of economic crisis, to break up the perfection of its own social controls in order to open the channels of expression through which the creativity, the initiatives, and the improvisations of individual people may begin to flow and enrich the country. The problem, of course, is how to make this happen in a one-party state that in principle illegalizes opposition. But the wish is as plain as the desperate need of the economy itself, indeed of the regime, for the wisdom of the many and the release of their energies. Finally, the question arises whether, after so many generations of training in submission, the habits of open-minded inquiry and independence can be evoked in a sufficient number of people to make such a policy work.

Late in 1986, when glasnost was a brand-new idea scarcely taken seriously as the main thrust of the new administration, a Russian writer expressing the pre-glasnost view said to me, "What you people in the West don't understand is that we are not a competitive society and we don't wish to be. We want the government to protect us, that is what the government is for. When two Western writers meet, one of them most likely asks the other what he is writing now. Our writers never ask such a question. They are not competing. You have been in our Writers Union and seen those hundreds of writers going in and out, having their lunches, reading newspapers, writing letters, and so on. A big number of those people haven't written anything in years! Some perhaps wrote a few short stories or a novel some years ago— and that was it! They were made members of the Union, got the apartment and the vacation in the south, and it is not so different in any other field. But this is not such a terrible thing to us!"

But, I countered, there were surely some highly talented people who produced a good deal of work.

"Of course! But most are not so talented, so it's just as well they don't write too much anyway. But is it right that they should be thrown out in the streets to starve because they are not talented? We don't think so!"

What he had chosen to omit, of course, was that the mediocrities, of which he was all but admittedly one, usually run things in the Writers Union, something the gifted writers are usually too prickly and independent to be trusted to do. And so the system practically polices itself, stifling creativity and unpalatable truth-telling, and extolling the mediocre. But its main object, to contain any real attempts at change, is effectively secured. The only problem is that unless the system moves faster it may be permanently consigned to an inferior rank among the competing societies.

And so it may well have come to pass that the sanctity of the individual, his right to express his unique sense of reality freely and in public, has become an economic necessity and not alone a political or aesthetic or moral question. If that turns out to be the case, we will have been saved by a kind of economic morality based on necessity, the safest morality of all.

II

The American Clock was begun in the early seventies and did not reach final form until its production at the Mark Taper Forum in Los Angeles in 1984, a version that in turn was movingly and sometimes hilariously interpreted in the Peter Wood production two years later at the British National Theatre. The seemingly endless changes it went through reflected my own search for something like a dramatic resolution to what, after all, was one of the vaster social calamities in history—the Great Depression of the thirties. I have no hesitation in saying that as it now stands, the work is simply as close to such a resolution as I am able to bring it, just as the experience itself remains only partially resolved in the hands of historians. For the humiliating truth about any "period" is its essential chaos, about which any generalization can be no more than just that, a statement to which many exceptions may be taken.

With all its variety, however, there were certain features of the Depression era that set it apart, for they had not existed before in such force and over such a long time. One of the most important of these to me, both as a person living through those years and as a writer contemplating them three decades afterwards, was the introduction into the American psyche of a certain unprecedented *suspense*. Through the twenties the country, for me—and I believe I was typical—floated in a reassuring state of nature that merged boundlessly with the sea and the sky; I had never thought of it as even having a system. But the Crash forced us all to enter history willy-nilly, and everyone soon understood that there were other ways of conducting the nation's business—there simply had to be, because the one we had was so persistently not working. It was not only the radicals who were looking at the historical clock and asking how long our system could last, but people of every viewpoint. After all, they were hardly radicals who went to Washington to ask the newly inaugurated President Roosevelt to nationalize the banks, but bankers themselves who had finally confessed their inability to control their own system. The objective situation, in a word, had surfaced; people had taken on a new consciousness that had been rare in more prosperous times, and the alternatives of fascism or socialism were suddenly in the air.

Looking back at it all from the vantage of the early seventies, we seemed to have reinserted the old tabula rasa, the empty slate, into our heads again. Once more we were in a state of nature where no alternatives existed and nothing had grown out of anything else. Conservatism was still damning the liberal New Deal, yearning to dismantle its remaining prestige, but at the same time the Social Security system, unemployment and bank insurance, the regulatory agencies in the stock market—the whole web of rational protections that the nation relied on—were products of the New Deal. We seemed to have lost awareness of community, of what we rightfully owe each other and what we owe ourselves. There seemed a want of any historical sense. America seems constantly in flight to the future; and it is a future made much like the past, a primeval paradise with really no government at all, in which the pioneer heads alone into the unknown forest to carve out his career. The suddenness of the '29 Crash and the chaos that followed offered a pure instance of the impotence of individualist solutions to so vast a crisis. As a society we learned all over again that we are in fact dependent and vulnerable, and that mass social organization does not necessarily weaken moral fiber but may set the stage for great displays of heroism and self-sacrifice and endurance. It may also unleash, as it did in the thirties, a flood of humor and optimism that was far less apparent in seemingly happier years.

When Studs Terkel's *Hard Times* appeared in 1970, the American economy was booming, and it would be another seventeen years before the stock market collapsed to anything like the degree it had in 1929. In any case, in considering his collection of interviews with survivors of the Depression as a partial basis for a play (I would mix my own memories into it as well), I had no prophecy of doom in mind, although in sheer principle it seemed impossible that the market could keep on rising indefinitely. At bottom, quite simply, I wanted to try to show how it was and where we had come from. I wanted to give some sense of life as we lived it when the clock was ticking every day.

The idea was not, strictly speaking, my invention but a common notion of the thirties. And it was a concept that also extended outward to Europe and the Far East; Hitler was clearly preparing to destroy parliamentary governments as soon as he organized his armies, just as Franco had destroyed the Spanish Republic, and Japan was manifestly creating a new empire that must one day collide with the interests of Britain and the United States. The clock was ticking everywhere.

Difficulties with the play had to do almost totally with finding a balance between the epic elements and the intimate psychological lives of individuals and families like the Baums. My impulse is usually toward integration of meaning through significant individual action, but the striking new fact of life in the Depression era—unlike the self-sufficient, prosperous seventies—was the swift rise in the common consciousness of the social system. Uncharacteristically, Americans were looking for answers far beyond the bedroom and purely personal relationships, and so the very form of the play should ideally reflect this wider awareness. But how to unify the two elements, objective and subjective, epic and psychological? The sudden and novel impact of the Depression made people in the cities, for example, painfully conscious that thousands of farm families were being forced off their lands in the West by a combination of a collapsed market for farm goods and the unprecedented drought and dust storms. The farmers who remained operating were aware—and openly resentful—that in the cities people could not afford to buy the milk for which they could not get commercially viable prices. The social paradoxes of the collapse were so glaring that it would be false to the era to try to convey its spirit through the life of any one family. Nevertheless the feeling of a unified theatrical event evaded me until the revision for the 1984 Mark Taper production, which I believe came close to striking the balance. But it was in the British National Theatre production two years later that the play's theatrical life was finally achieved. The secret was vaudeville.

Of course the period had much tragedy and was fundamentally a trial and a frustration for those who lived through it, but no time ever created so many comedians and upbeat songs. Jack Benny, Fred Allen, W. C. Fields, Jimmy Durante, Eddie Cantor, Burns and Allen, and Ed Wynn were some of the headliners who came up in that time, and the song lyrics were most often exhilaratingly optimistic: "Love Is Sweeping the Country," "Life Is Just a Bowl of Cherries," "April in Paris," "I'm Getting Sentimental over You," "Who's Afraid of the Big Bad Wolf?" It was, in the pop culture, a romantic time and not at all realistically harsh. The serious writers were putting out books like Nathanael West's *Miss Lonelyhearts*, Erskine Caldwell's *God's Little Acre*, Jack Conroy's *The Disinherited*, André Malraux's *Man's Fate*, Hemingway's *Winner Take Nothing*, and Steinbeck's *In Dubious Battle*, and Edward Hopper was brooding over his stark street scenes, and Reginald Marsh was painting vagrants asleep in the subways, but Broadway had O'Neill's first comedy, *Ah, Wilderness!*, and another comical version of the hard life, *Tobacco Road*, Noel Coward's *Design for Living*, the Gershwins' *Let 'Em Eat Cake*, and some of the best American farces ever written—*Room Service, Three Men on a Horse*, and *Brother Rat* among them.

In the Mark Taper production I found myself allowing the material to move through me as it wished—I had dozens of scenes by this time and was shifting them about in search of their hidden emotional as well as ideational linkages. At one point the experience brought to mind a sort of vaudeville where the contiguity of sublime and ridiculus is perfectly acceptable; in vaudeville an imitation of Lincoln doing the Gettysburg Address could easily be followed by Chinese acrobats. So when subsequently Peter Wood asked for my feeling about the style, I could call the play a vaudeville with an assurance born of over a decade of experimentation. He took the hint and ran with it, tossing up the last shreds of a realistic approach, announcing from the opening image that the performance was to be epic and declarative.

Out of darkness, in a brash music hall spotlight, a baseball pitcher appears and tosses a ball from hand to glove as he gets ready on the mound. The other characters saunter on singing snatches of songs of the thirties, and from somewhere in the balcony a man in a boater and striped shirt, bow tie and gartered sleeves—Ted Quinn—whistles "I Found a Million-Dollar Baby in a Five-and-Ten-Cent Store." At one side of the open stage, a five-piece jazz band plays in full view of the audience (impossible in the penurious New York theater), and the sheer festivity of the occasion is already established.

The most startling, and I think wonderful, invention of all was the treatment of the character of Theodore K. Quinn. This was the actual name of a neighbor of mine, son of a Chicago railroad labor organizer, who had worked himself up from a poor Chicago law student to the vice-presidency of General Electric. The president of GE, Quinn's boss through most of the twenties, was Gerard Swope, a world-famous capitalist and much quoted social thinker, who decided as the thirties dawned that Quinn was to succeed him on his retirement. Quinn, in charge of the consumer products division of the company, had frequently bought up promising smaller manufacturers for Swope, incorporating their plants into the GE giant, but had developed a great fear that this process of cartelization must end in the destruction of democracy itself. Over the years his rationalization had been that he was only taking orders—although in fact it was on his judgment that Swope depended as to which companies to pick up. Then the excuses were threatened by his elevation to the presidency, an office with dictatorial powers at the time. As he would tell me, "Above the president of General Electric stood only God."

The real Ted Quinn had actually been president of GE for a single day, at the end of which he put in his resignation. "I just couldn't stand being the Lord High Executioner himself," he once said to me. He went on to open an advisory service for small businesses and made a good fortune at it. During World War II he was a dollar-a-year head of the Small Business Administration in Washington, seeing to it that the giant concerns did not gobble up all the available steel. Particularly close to his heart was the Amana company, a cooperative.

Quinn also published several books, including *Giant Business, Threat to Democracy,* and *Unconscious Public Enemies*, his case against GE-type monopolies. These, along with his anti-monopoly testimony before congressional committees, got him obliterated from the roster of former GE executives, and the company actually denied—to journalist Matthew Josephson, who at my behest made an inquiry in 1972—that he had ever so much as worked for GE. However, in the course of time a film director friend of mine who loved to browse in flea markets and old bookstores came on a leather-covered daily diary put out by GE as a gift for its distributors, circa 1930, in which the company directors are listed, and Theodore K. Quinn is right there as vice-president for consumer sales. The fact is that it was he who, among a number of other innovations, conceived of the compact electric refrigerator as a common consumer product, at a time when electric refrigeration was regarded as a purely commercial item, the behemoth used in restaurants, hotels, and the kitchens of wealthy estates.

From the big business viewpoint Quinn's central heresy was that democracy basically depended on a large class of independent entrepreneurs who would keep the market competitive. His fear was that monopoly, which he saw spreading in the American economy despite superficial appearances of competition, would end by crippling the system's former ingenuity and its capacity to produce high-quality goods at reasonable prices. A monopoly has little need to improve its product when it has little need to compete. (First Communist China and then Gorbachev's Russia would be grappling with a very similar dilemma in the years to come.) He loved to reel off a long list of inventions, from the jet engine to the zipper, that were devised by independent inventors rather than corporations and their much advertised laboratories: "The basic things we use and are famous for were conceived in the back of a garage." I knew him in the fifties, when his populist vision was totally out of fashion, and maybe, I feared, an out-of-date relic of a bygone America. But I would hear it again in the seventies and even more loudly in the eighties as a muscle-bound American industrial machine, wallowing for generations in a continental market beyond the reach of foreign competition, was caught flat-footed by German and Japanese competitors. Quinn was a successful businessman interested in money and production, but his vision transcended the market to embrace the nature of the democratic system for which he had a passion, and which he thought doomed if Americans did not understand the real threats to it. He put it starkly once: "It may be all over, I don't know—but I don't want to have to choose between fascism and socialism, because neither one can match a really free, competitive economy and the political liberties it makes possible. If I do have to choose, it'll be socialism, because it harms the people less. But neither one is the way I'd want to go."

Perhaps it was because the style of the National Theatre production was so unashamed in its presentational declarativeness that the Ted Quinn role was given to David Schofield, a tap dancer with a brash Irish mug, for Quinn was forever bragging about—and mocking—his mad love of soft-shoe dancing. And so we had long speeches about the dire consequences of business monopoly delivered by a dancer uncorking a most ebullient soft-shoe all over the stage, supported by some witty jazz played openly before our eyes by a deft band. As Quinn agonizes over whether to accept the presidency of GE, a phone rings at the edge of the stage; plainly, it is as the new president that he must answer it. He taps his way over to it, lifts the receiver, and simply places it gently on the floor and dances joyously away.

It was in the National Theatre that I at last heard the right kind of straightforward epic expressiveness, joyful and celebratory rather than abashed and veiled, as economic and political—which is to say epic—subjects were in the mouths of the characters. In this antic yet thematically precise spirit, accompanied by some forty songs out of the period, the show managed to convey the *seriousness* of the disaster that the Great Depression was, and at the same time its human heart.

There was one more invention that I particularly prized. Alone in her Brooklyn house, Rose Baum sits at the piano, bewildered and discouraged by the endless Depression, and plays some of the popular ballads of the day, breaking off now and then to muse to herself about the neighborhood, the country, her family, her fading hopes. The actress sat at a piano whose keyboard faced the audience, and simply held her hands suspended over the keys while the band pianist a few yards away played the romantic thirties tunes. Gradually a triple reality formed such as I have rarely witnessed in the theater: first, the objective stage reality of the band pianist playing, but somehow magically directed by Rose's motionless hands over her keyboard; and simultaneously, *the play's memory* of this lost past that we are now discovering again; and finally, the middle-aged actress herself seeming, by virtue of her motionless hands suspended over the keys, to be recalling this moment from her very own life. The style, in short, had fused emotion and conscious awareness, overt intention and subjective feeling—the aim in view from the beginning, more than a decade before.

A Conversation with Arthur Miller

INTERVIEW BY JANET BALAKIAN

The following conversation took place on Tuesday, June 27, 1989 in Manhattan.

BALAKIAN: In some ways you seem to have begun a new phase in your career with plays like *The Creation of the World and Other Business, Some Kind of Love Story, An Elegy for a Lady, Danger: Memory!, The American Clock, The Archbishop's Ceiling,* and now your new screenplay, *Everybody Wins.* How would you compare these works to your earlier writing? Do you see them as different ventures from the earlier plays?

MILLER: I suppose that these last plays, with the big exception of the short play *Clara,* have a different view of life which is not an overtly tragic view. *The Creation of the World,* of course, is really the first tragedy in our religious mythology, a fratricide, but I treated it comedically, as man's groping his way to his own human nature with no instructions. The attempt underneath was to illuminate a kind of biological morality; that is, for the species to survive there had to be negatives in the world, there had to be prohibitions, there had to be a form, in short, because the race would destroy itself through narcissism and competitiveness. You can see it crudely in a litter of puppies where they're all fighting to get fed. The fluctuating moral conse-

From *Michigan Quarterly Review*, 29 (Spring 1990), pp. 158–170. Reprinted by permission of Janet Balakian.

quences of a given human nature are really what all my plays are about in a way, but this was an attempt to come closer to its most primitive, naked, and uncomplicated givens. So it's both continuous with the other plays and it's different.

BALAKIAN: The difference being?

MILLER: One difference I think is in tone; man is thrashing around blindly, yet, in a kind of a touching and moving way, toward some tolerable civilized form for his alienated feelings, which, he instinctively senses, are murderous. Parenthetically, it's interesting that the first story in the Hebrew Bible, and later in the Christian Bible, is of a murder, and I think what the old rabbis were after with this story was to show why the Bible was necessary.

A play like *Some Kind of Love Story*, which I very roughly based my new film on, is an offshoot in the sense that I present the appearance of reality, namely a woman who knows something about a murder; but she is soon revealed to be a fantasist. But the investigator has a sense that her fantasies don't necessarily negate her facts. Worse yet, he falls in love with her, further warping his hold on reality. So the question of what is real, how you measure the real, becomes the issue when the evidence seems outrageous.

BALAKIAN: Do you see the question of illusion and reality as something that concerns you more now than it did in your earlier plays?

MILLER: I always thought of the play as a lifting of the veil, as far back as *All My Sons*. That play took great pains to create a veritable backyard, and people sitting around having very ordinary conversations—the well-known norms of suburbia. And then the screen begins to tip over and we see what's behind it. So, it was always there: I begin with an equilibrium and something tips that equilibrium and interprets it as a result.

BALAKIAN: How the birds come home to roost.

MILLER: Right. The past reaches into the present, usually destructively, but leaving some illumination behind. I was thinking of that the other day in relation to China. These awful recent events are really China reasserting herself; it's that 6000-year history of feudalism catching up with this short-lived movement to enter a democratic civilization, and it's just [*Miller punches the palm of his hand with his fist, and makes the sound of an airplane crashing.*] The past is really the stubbornest problem of mankind. This is interesting to me, because a lot of our contemporary drama deals with characters who have no past. It's probably the nature of the film form, which after all is the single great cultural invention of this civilization. And you don't need a past in movies. The movie image is so overwhelming that it's convincing in itself; the person is *there*, simply by being photographed. The movie is eminently the art of the present tense. As soon as it slows down to give you the past you feel the urgency leaking out. It's true all over the West, not just here—this farewell to the past. I even wonder sometimes whether the theater as a form isn't in trouble, because it isn't sufficiently in the present tense and has to build up its effects by painfully accreting information through words. The Absurd drama made an attempt to escape all of that, but it left behind the psychological dialectic and created archetypes or cartoons, emphasizing situations rather than characters.

BALAKIAN: But *The Creation of the World* is an archetypal story. You're less interested in character in the conventional sense. Yet at the same time it's a play completely about the past.

MILLER: The play is set in the past, but the First Man and Woman and their sons, of course, have no past; they are all simply the essential human traits being assembled for the first disaster.

BALAKIAN: Would you say that you're becoming less naturalistic and more symbolic in your writing? You have said that if you live long enough that's the way it ends up.

MILLER: The time arrives when everything that happens has a certain backward-flowing echo, and little seems to be happening for the first time. You get carried off by the echo, and you see that life is cyclical, that human beings do repeat fundamental reactions. But that certain changes are made as a result of this repetition; it's a repetition and it's also an adventure, motion along a locus. For example, the whole sixties period. Having gone through the thirties, one couldn't help but notice the similarities and the differences. In the thirties it also came down to matters of style, the dress, the counterbourgeois clothing styles. This had all happened before. No Group Theater actor, for example, would be caught dead wearing a suit in a theater where everybody had always dressed like a British, Shakespearean star—conventionally. If you went up for a part to a producer, you dressed as though you were going to a bank. So the first thing that these rebels did was to dress like workers and, along with respect for the establishment, discard all of that clothing. Well, the same thing happened in the sixties *vis à vis* the fifties, and I found a certain futility in the repetition. Nevertheless, when it happened I was all for it—the rebellion—but I made a speech at Michigan telling the students that, while it's absolutely necessary that they do this, it's also a good idea to remember that somewhere down the line they were going to be held accountable for it, either by the F.B.I. spy who may be in the next seat, or simply by life. In other words, they were creating their past which they might have to face one day. Anyway, concerning your question about whether or not I've become less naturalistic and more symbolic. . . . I never really was the former. It's true that I wanted to make the characters as documented as was feasible, as parts of the social scene, but I wasn't interested in simply photographing types, that was only the beginning—the end in view was wonder. Maybe as a result people don't feel these plays belong to a different age; they can relate to these characters as not quite time-bound.

BALAKIAN: Do you see these later plays as being more metaphysical than the early ones, or can't you separate the metaphysical from the social?

MILLER: I have never been able to separate them. It's all one piece, one dream, sometimes real-looking, sometimes surreal. Back in 1949 I met Thomas Mann who had seen *Death of a Salesman* here in New York. He said that if a European had written the play, there would have been a discussion of the theme by the characters. And I think he was slightly disappointed about that. He felt the Lomans were like aborigines. I said, that's the greatest compliment I've had yet, although I'm not sure he meant it as a compliment. You see, I was not trying to create a work for academics to discuss. It's a very European idea, also an academic one, that if the characters don't directly discuss the theme, it hasn't got one. The point is that I hope the livingness of what I've written is there, and I let the audience make up its mind what this whole thing is about.

BALAKIAN: You seem to be more interested in myth than in psychology in these later plays, and it reminds me of your character Marcus in *The Archbishop's Ceiling* who says, "I'm not sure I believe in psychology anymore. That anything we think really determines what we're going to do or what we feel." Do you feel this way now?

MILLER: I do feel that way very often. Most decisions are made because it's five o'clock. After all, what is psychology? It is the depth to which we can presently reach into ourselves, and that may not turn out to be all that deep finally. [*We laugh.*] Freud started out as a neurologist more than a psychologist, as a "pure" scientist. He said it was all going to end with pharmacology and neurology. In other words, back to the chemistry. That's interesting. In other words, we may be in an intermediate stage between the sidewalk and the stars.

BALAKIAN: Doesn't Leo say in *I Can't Remember Anything* that he's just going to end up as a bunch of chemicals?

MILLER: Right. Of course he is taunting mysticism and religion.

BALAKIAN: Are there concerns that you have now at age 74 in 1989 as a playwright that you didn't have when you were launching your career?

MILLER: Of course. I'm working on a play that I started eleven years ago, one that I've tried to shake loose from at least 25 times! Formally speaking it's very free flowing, a little bit like *Salesman* was. But this one spills in all directions; time is rather plastic. While the story is moving forward, it's also moving sideways and out. That's probably one reason why it has taken me eleven years to find it and what it seems to be telling me.

BALAKIAN: When I was asking what concerns you have now that you didn't have when you began writing, is it connected to this new play in the sense of time that you're speaking about?

MILLER: It's viewing people from a tragic distance again, but with a certain forbearance, even a comic despair. But the play is still asserting that, while we are weak, the rules of life are powerful, and they exist. And that's a tragic view, and therefore hopeful.

BALAKIAN: You have voiced that view throughout your plays.

MILLER: Now it's funnier maybe. [*We laugh.*] I'm not sure whether this will end up a tragedy or a comedy. . . . I mean the theatrical impression it will make.

BALAKIAN: So your tragic perspective is becoming more humorous with time?

MILLER: Yes. Although what I think is funny has a tendency to make people cry.

BALAKIAN: Do you have a title for your play in progress?

MILLER: It's called *The Ride Down Mount Morgan.* But I can't begin to talk about it yet, beyond what I've just told you, because it's in the making.

BALAKIAN: You've said that the older you get the more you'd feel at home in Periclean Athens or Dickens' London. Would you elaborate on that statement?

MILLER: The Athens reference . . . if one can judge from the few plays we have, which are a fraction of the ones that were written, it seems as though the main business of life was to illuminate some coherent meaning to the whole human career. And for the plays to be involved so consistently in that kind of quest must indicate that the audience was also. At the same time we know that they were nuts about athletics, human beauty, a sensuous life. In other words, we're not dealing with a monastery. There was a wholeness of spirit that is enviable. We've got here now in New York and in America an enormous variety of experience, but there is also a pervading sense that it's all cornflakes, that it's all collapsing meaninglessly around our ears. I could be wrong about that, because there are millions of people who go to churches, but probably for ritualistic reassurance rather than philosophy; it seems to me that life is perceived as being just one thing after another until it stops.

BALAKIAN: Is this why you never felt at home in the mode of the Absurdists—Ionesco, Beckett, Pinter—to some extent? Their plays aren't trying to illuminate significance but rather confirming the fact that life is a chaotic mess.

MILLER: Yes. I think Beckett is different in the sense that, especially in later life, he's emphasizing a challenge that he implicitly hopes we can meet, the challenge of confronting the void without despairing of life. But it's true that I was rather uncomfortable with them. When people tend to celebrate the meaningless, it ends up with fascism. When they get too comfortable with the inevitable defeat of human hope, with man as a creature who is doomed to slip on a banana peel, I smell dictatorship around the corner; probably because I was born into the era when it was not an exaggeration to think that the hopeless could maybe turn out the lights on everything and kill you for being a Jew or a skeptic.

BALAKIAN: The bending of time has interested you since *Salesman* and continues to do so in *Danger: Memory!*, in *The American Clock*, and in your autobiography, *Timebends*. Would you discuss your interest in time and memory, in getting inside the head, as you have always been interested in doing, and the forms that best help you in this exploration?

MILLER: I think that a playwright, more than any other kind of artist, excepting possibly dance people, but in a very different way, is, by the nature of the art, involved with intense condensation. So, time is of the essence in everything he does.

BALAKIAN: You're using the word condensation. A poem is certainly condensed, but you're talking about physical movement.

MILLER: Theater is a dynamic form; it's going by you in a way that painting isn't but music is. In poetry, technically speaking, you can start and go back and keep combing the poem. To be sure, you can study a play endlessly, too, but for the audience it's in motion going past so that whatever has to be said through the play, has to be said in time. These days they've stretched the limits of performances beyond measure, going on six, seven, eight hours, but those aren't really dramas; they're performance pieces, like Robert Wilson's which are really set design displays, or special works like Peter Brooks' with *The Ik*, which I think of as a form of spiritual naturalism. He's trying to give you the feeling of what has happened by making you sit for a very long, eventless time. (This was an experimental work based on a book about a tribe in Africa called the Ik. It's fascinating, because it's a tribe whose social ties have been so destroyed that the people no longer have even a familial sense; they're so weakened that they can't do what we consider the fundamental actions of civilized people.)

Anyway, apart from these special events, you still have to work within some kind of time limit. So, consequently, time becomes an obsessive thing. It has become more mysterious with me over the years, possibly because I'm getting older, and as I said earlier, echoes of the past are loud in the present so that the idea of time as a circular motion becomes more and more realistic. For example, (my examples are political because we're all conscious of that) I think that ironically enough Ronald Reagan's master image was Franklin Roosevelt. He even went to the extreme of imitating his radio chats. In a time of television he did a weekly *radio* speech. This was literal miming of his father, because Reagan was growing up when this godlike leader was in power. In fact, he became a travesty of the original, favoring the rich over the poor. Now if you weren't aware of Roosevelt, I don't think you could see that dimension. So you need time or history, which is time-as-story.

BALAKIAN: So you need time to have it bend.

MILLER: I have become more and more obsessed with time. It's hard to avoid. If I walk down a street in New York, where I was born, I pass new buildings going up and I stand there and try to remember what was there before. In several cases the building they just tore down is the second one torn down on that lot in my memory.

BALAKIAN: That brings me to the question of memory, which is the subject of *Danger: Memory!*.

MILLER: And of *A Memory of Two Mondays* [*written in 1955*].

BALAKIAN: You've said that's the play closest to your heart!

MILLER: I tell in my book how I went back to that warehouse a few years later, but they didn't recognize me. But I recognized them! I knew all of them but when they looked at me, they saw nothing they recalled. That's a wonderful mystery.

BALAKIAN: It is. Although you liken your recent play *Danger: Memory!* to *Salesman* in the sense that the past spills into the present, these characters cannot remember.

MILLER: That's interesting. I hadn't thought of that. The past for her is obliterated.

BALAKIAN: Could you talk a little bit about that play? I'm intrigued by it because it seems like a new Arthur Miller phenomenon that I haven't encountered before in your work. It's certainly not a play that deals with social issues. What were you after in that play?

MILLER: I guess the play is looking at the phenomenon of time dying. All she's got left are immediate sensations. She sees deer, trees, things that evoke a sense of beauty in her. She wants to see beautiful things. But Leo does not accept the idea that time can die. He even doubts that she's forgetting all of this. He keeps prodding her to remember. Memory is time. He's a life force in a sense. You can interpret it in a lot of ways. One of the actors said that what she is really saying is that sex for her has ended. And he's saying, "It hasn't! You have just suppressed it all."

BALAKIAN: Right. Her husband has died, and Leo is trying to tell her "why don't you go on a trip, why don't you take up piano again!" Is it true that you rewrote the *Clara* play, which follows *I Can't Remember Anything*, for the London production?

MILLER: In my original version the adult murdered daughter comes in as a young girl and later as a young woman. Gregory Mosher, the director of the Lincoln Center production, convinced me that we couldn't do it that way here. So, in that version the father talks to her, but she isn't there. I never felt that succeeded, so I put it back the way it was: an actual young girl comes in. We had a very young girl of twelve or so in the New York production. In the London production they had an actress of twenty, but she was also able to be a very young child when required.

BALAKIAN: Would you talk more about your notion of time in this play?

MILLER: I guess what fascinated me about it was the idea of dropping out of time.

BALAKIAN: Dropping out of time is something Willy Loman does, but in a completely different way.

MILLER: Different. He's trying to get into his life, not out.

BALAKIAN: Leonora is dropping out of time, but Leo isn't.

MILLER: He's a direct contrast with her. He thinks the world is real. She was brought up in the New England tradition: life is earnest and has a purpose. And he's saying, "Look, I'm an engineer."

BALAKIAN: I noticed that in both of those plays you use bridge building as a kind of motif.

MILLER: I never thought of that. Many years ago I started a play I never finished called *The Half Bridge*, the dominant image being a bridge half finished, because it doesn't connect to the other side.

BALAKIAN: When you wrote *A Memory of Two Mondays,* was the way you dealt with time very different from your use of time in *Danger: Memory!*?

MILLER: The significant thing about *A Memory of Two Mondays* for me is that the people are being observed and are not aware that they're in time; only the observer knows.

BALAKIAN: It's like they're in purgatory.

MILLER: Yeah. It's the young boy, Bert, who knows they're in time. He's observing time as a pathetic user-up of people. He aches for them. He says there should be a statue in the park for these people to celebrate them, because they're being swept away by the clock. They don't know that they're in time, but he does. That's the pathos. They're involved in repetition; they do the same thing all the time, forever.

BALAKIAN: I know that the Greeks, Shakespeare, and Ibsen have been your models. Are there any contemporary or other novelists, playwrights, or poets whom you revere? I know that you keep very few books in the cabin where you write, one of which is the Bible. What else do you keep in there? Where do you go for fuel?

MILLER: There are some books I've found that fed me, but it's unsystematic. As far as plays are concerned, there's a very gorgeous play rarely done in this country, and I don't think it's done much anywhere else, called *The Playboy of the Western World* by Synge.

BALAKIAN: It was done here in New York during the winter.

MILLER: I didn't see it. I dread to see it, because I have such wonderful images of it. I don't know why I never mentioned it. When I was in college, that was an inspiration. It was a really lyrical conception. I love O'Casey, *Juno and The Paycock*.

BALAKIAN: I saw it last summer when it was here.

MILLER: I didn't like that production. They came over from Ireland. They went for the laughs too much, and it bothered me. I saw the original with Barry Fitzgerald and Sara Allgood, which was simply a masterpiece. These people were not in that league. [*Pause*] O'Casey has a defect—the integration of events is sometimes a little weak. But the lyricism makes up for everything. And the characters. There are important lapses in these plays, but his spirit meant a lot to me. I'm trying to think whether I'm still feeding off other works. I go back to Sophocles rather regularly; *Hamlet* and *Lear*—but it all vanishes by the time I sit down. In other words, I'm feeding off myself. There were books that simply fascinated me at one time when I was in school, a very formative time. *The Education of Henry Adams*. I remember writing in the flyleaf of that book after I finished it, "Read this book again after twenty years."

BALAKIAN: Did you?

MILLER: I did because I didn't understand a lot of it. *Moby Dick* had an impact on me too. And the Russians. The Russians meant a great deal to me.

BALAKIAN: Is it really true that you hadn't been a serious reader until after high school?

MILLER: Yes. My mother was a reader, one of those people who read everything. You'd give her the Sears Roebuck catalogue and she'd read the whole thing. Whatever was in the house.

BALAKIAN: In *The American Clock* she's reading all over the place. You have her reading *Coronet*.

MILLER: [*Laughs.*] She was totally naive but at the same time she had a discriminatory sense of what was high, low, or so-so.

BALAKIAN: Doesn't she say, "It's supposed to be literature but it's great anyway!"

MILLER: "But it's very interesting."

BALAKIAN: Would you discuss how the writers whom you mentioned have informed your work?

MILLER: The Russians were the most important of all. The mixture of enormous psychological and physical detail in Tolstoy, Gogol, Dostoevsky, with that realistic detail making everything palpable so that you could practically smell these people, with the metaphysical preoccupation—that's what I took from them. In other words, if you could find a way to penetrate the particles of matter, you can find the spirit.

BALAKIAN: That reminds me of your essay, "The Shadow of the Gods."

MILLER: You don't find the spirit by looking for the spirit; you find the spirit by looking at the way matter is organized, by the way experience asserts principles. In other words, hope to find what things mean by what they are.

BALAKIAN: It sounds scientific.

MILLER: In a way it is. My ambition used to be, and I guess it still is, that one could write so that the work would transcend science, so that any physicist with some sense of life, or psychiatrist, would stand before these works and realize that drama is presenting the original evidence and that analysis and criticism follow. It's a way of reasserting the primacy of the created work, the imagined architecture.

BALAKIAN: Organizing experience through language as opposed to the way scientists do it. Was Dostoevsky especially important to you?

MILLER: Yes. Well, that's a hard race. Tolstoy and Dostoevsky occupy different sides of the brain. I wouldn't put one above the other. I've got to simply worship both of them.

BALAKIAN: Do you still read them from time to time?

MILLER: Oh yeah. I read *Karamazov* only three or four years ago. It's simply like eating bread. I had an interesting discussion many years ago with a poet friend of mine, because I was talking the way I'm talking to you now about the primacy of matter, and we were also talking about Dostoevsky at the moment. He said, "You're carrying it too far, because Dostoevsky has long arias about the spirit." I said, "You try to think up a scene that has always stuck in your mind as poetic, spiritual, and we'll get the book out and see how it's constructed." He cited the scene in *Karamazov* where Alyosha is walking down the street of the village and is inspired by the "itness" of everything, the sheer existence of everything, which is a transcendent idea, that somehow it was created by God and shimmers in this space. We found the passage which, of course, was totally circumstantial. With that passage in your hand, if you were an invading army, you would know every street along that route, what each house and picket fence looked like. It's unbelievable. And that's what I'm thinking.

BALAKIAN: You've said that you don't consider yourself a realistic, naturalistic writer.

MILLER: Any more than Dostoevsky was.

BALAKIAN: In other words, you're not connecting naturalistic detail, like that window outside, with—

MILLER: It's just the opposite of Naturalism. Naturalism thinks that it's going to create reality by repeating reality. And that's impossible. It's the opposite of what I think I'm after, which is the interpretation of whatever I've seen, and the spirit in it, to use a religious notion. The means by which one gets to the spirit is through appearances. Appearances are the beginning of the quest, not the end of it.

BALAKIAN: This makes me think of *The Price*. That play is built on concrete detail, but at the same time that old furniture is the means to transcend itself. Critics call Arthur Miller a realistic writer when you aren't. Labels are terrible, but what could I call your writing? Maybe it's not necessary to call it anything.

MILLER: I don't know of a traditional label. The idea is to transcend. Very often in the contemporary theater and in novels too, there's the kind of dialogue, or in a novel, description, which is very stylish, namely, based on a mood, usually of a semi-disguised despair, and some smart remarks about it. When I watch this, very often I think, oddly enough, it's a form of Naturalism. The people aren't interpreting the despair; they're simply delivering it up again.

BALAKIAN: Like a Mamet play. That's naturalism. He is mimetically reproducing sleazy insurance salesmen. And you're after interpreting reality, and you use any form that works for you. You've said, "Fitting means to matter is the name of the game" for you.

MILLER: Right. How can you put a play like *Clara* anywhere near naturalism? How can you take *An Elegy for a Lady* . . . actually, how can you take *Incident at Vichy* as naturalistic? Because they all have stories? So does the Book of Job. I do present the surfaces of life, man in society. There's a whole other school that never wants to get near the surface of life and sometimes they are very successful doing it. Beckett is.

BALAKIAN: Although you and Beckett are using different means, your end is the same.

MILLER: The same. Maybe the question is whether a work simply exploits chaos or strives to resist it for survival's sake.

BALAKIAN: If you had to say what it is that you're after, what it is that you want to convey, or that you want to happen in your plays, what would you say? Is there an underlying thrust in your writing?

MILLER: It's to achieve a coherency out of the chaos, and, of course, the deeper the chaos, the more difficult it is to symbolize in a coherent, integrated symbol. It's a question of how deep the resistance to chaos is even as it is a pleasurable necessity to embrace it.

BALAKIAN: If I asked you what a play should do, could it be the same answer you would have given when you began writing?

MILLER: Maybe. It's really illumination. It's the light. We strike it in life rarely. There's endless talk, and then suddenly somebody says something or does something and that's all that has to be said. It's to arrive at that point of illumination.

Miller said he had not slept much the night before because he had his new play in his head, and he graciously offered to continue our conversation in Roxbury. Then he told me that there will be productions of The Crucible *at the Longwharf Theater and at the Roundabout Theater this year. In Budapest* The Archbishop's Ceiling, The American Clock *and* Salesman *are playing:* "There are 52 productions going on in Germany this year. Michael Blakemore is directing *After the Fall* at The National Theater in April. And *The Price* will be at The Young Vic in London," *he remarked.*

I asked him about his trip to Turkey with Harold Pinter to free imprisoned writers. "I'm told they freed some sixteen hundred after we left," *he said.*

I noticed a book of Havel's letters in his bookcase and asked him about the Czech playwright. "I have great admiration for Havel," *he remarked emphatically.*

As we were walking out together, I saw an Italian poster for The American Clock, *which he says is being done all over Europe, and a beautiful poster of a briefcase on a trunk.* "That's from the Flemish production of *Salesman*," *he said. We discussed the fact that Europe is much more receptive to his work than New York.* "I just don't know what's with New York. But I guess I shouldn't complain, because there will soon be two productions of *The Crucible* in the area."

We walked outside into one of those hot, humid Manhattan days. A tall, Lincolnesque Arthur Miller climbed into my Chevy whose ceiling isn't high enough for him. He tried to fix my air conditioner for me. Looking at those strong, large hands, I asked, "Do you still build furniture?"

"Just started a table yesterday."

"How's your daughter Rebecca?"

"She's great. She just acted in a film in Germany, and she wrote a wonderful screenplay."

I dropped him off on 57th and 6th where he was meeting someone for dinner and then going to a Terrence McNally play. And there was Arthur Miller walking along Sixth Avenue in a crowd of New Yorkers, waving good-bye.

Arthur Miller: An Interview

BY CHRISTOPHER BIGSBY

BIGSBY: *Death of a Salesman* is a contrast in a number of ways. It seems to me the most lyrical of your plays.

MILLER: That's true, yes. Well, I had always done that. Most of the plays I had written before had been reaching toward it. I was trying to find a poetic voice in the theater while at the same time making the scenes and the characters believable. Then I was also interested in time. We don't stop when we remember something; we go right on talking or doing whatever we're doing. Meanwhile, in another compartment of the brain the past is working. That was what I was trying for with that play. That was the form.

BIGSBY: Do you ever feel, in looking back, that there is a kind of rift in *Death of a Salesman*, in that our dramatic attention is on Willy Loman, but the play's moral resolution really turns on Biff's self-realization? Is that why some people thought of the play as pessimistic, because they were looking in the wrong place?

MILLER: Well, I'm sure that's why. There is a rift in it in that sense. You know, Thomas Mann saw that play, and he said, "You know, the thing about the play is that it is a lyric play, but you never tell them what to think. It is simply an experience that they can't escape." Now of course this is part of the reason that there's all this debate about the play. You see, I never allowed them to go beyond their intellectual and emotional capacity. There is no line in there that goes beyond

From *Arthur Miller and Company*, edited by Christopher Bigsby, Methuen, London, 1990, pp. 55–62. Reprinted by permission of Christopher Bigsby.

what they could possibly have realized. The consequence is that, unlike standard tragedy, where you have the right, so to speak, formally speaking, to make self-aware statements where the character is aware of the play he is in, I never let them become aware of the play they are in. All that was driven out, ruthlessly, because at that time I resolved that I was going to make that audience never escape, even at the risk of losing objectivity, if I could do it. Because, I believed in squeezing out all the self-consciousness in the play. Every scene in that play begins late. There are no transitions in the play. It starts with a man who is tired. He doesn't get tired. He's tired in the first second of the play. You can tell from the way he enters the play. On the first line she says, "What happened?" Nothing happened but he's exhausted. You know you're somewhere. The same is true of every scene in that play. I completely drove out the usual transitional material from the play. That's the form of the play, that I never allowed into it the self-conscious statements, which Mann wisely recognized. Now, he thought of it as a pessimistic play, but he loved the fact that the younger generation did not. You know, when I was writing that, there wasn't a younger generation. I was the age of Biff. I wasn't Willy's age. You don't regard yourself as the younger generation. But the key is in the requiem at the end, which everybody wanted me to cut out. They said the audience were never going to stay there because Willy Loman is dead; there's nothing more to say. Of course, they did want to stay there, just as you do want to go to a funeral. And what is the point of a funeral? You want to think over the life of the departed and it's in there, really, that it's nailed down: he won't accept this life.

BIGSBY: He had all the wrong dreams. But that's the dilemma, isn't it? Most of our attention has been focused on the man who has now gone and the moral resolution naturally comes from the character Biff, who's been less central.

MILLER: I think what is missing, if you want to look at it that way, is what is missing in *Lear*, which a lot of nineteenth-century commentators didn't like for the same reason. It's unalleviated, setting aside the beauty of the poetry which relieves us of the gloom. Lear is unredeemed; he really goes down in a sack, in a coal chute. *Hamlet* has relief, moral relief so to speak; there is a structure remaining.

BIGSBY: But you did say that there is a force that is in a race for Willy's soul, which is love. I am not quite sure what you mean by that, Linda's or Biff's, but do you in any way regret not giving Linda more resources to make the battle a bit more equal?

MILLER: I regretted it at the time but I couldn't honestly give her what I didn't think she would ever have. You see, if that woman were more articulate in terms of her ability to handle it, probably they would have broken apart earlier on; she couldn't have stood it. You know, he's a cruel son of a bitch, that guy; everybody is charmed by him, but if you objectively face some of those scenes in the bedroom, he just wipes the floor with her from time to time. You see, a woman who was thinking of herself more would simply not have been there one morning, or else she would have put up such a fight as to crush him because he would never be able to accept any independence around him. This is part of the disease.

BIGSBY: Is there something of a risk that in emphasizing the state of Willy's mind—and he is getting into a kind of deranged state, in which past and present are indistinguishable—the play might become a pathological case study?

MILLER: It depends how you do it. You see, they made a movie of it which did just that. I hated that movie. Let's talk about it for a minute, because it applies to some of the things we have been talking about. I wrote that play in 1948 and it was produced in 1949. It ran for years. They bought the film rights, let's say in 1950. The right wing had not yet taken over in the culture so they would buy a play of mine. They made the film, but as they were making it the country was swinging far over to the right. What did they do? They made Willy crazier and crazier. Interesting. Now I happen to have been a very good friend of Freddy March, who played Willy. We nearly cast him in the original play. He was a marvellous actor. Freddy was a real actor in the best sense; he was an animal and he knew that there was something wrong with making him so crazy. He knew that. I certainly didn't tell him. Of course, these people making the film had to make him crazy or they couldn't make the film. The social and moral dimensions of the picture had to be resolved in this pathological side. By this time I was being attacked left and right as a red and here they were stuck with this x million dollars that they had sunk into the film. They were threatened with boycotts from the American Legion, the Catholic war veterans, and all those yahoos. They came to me and said, "Would you make a statement to these people to placate them?" I said, "I'll placate nobody. You bought the picture, fellas, you're stuck with it."

You know what they did? Columbia Pictures had another film made, which they filmed at City College, New York City, the Business School of City College, about the life of a salesman. It was a short, like fifteen minutes, in which they interviewed professors of business administration and heads of corporations and other such people who were experts in this field who said that Willy Loman was absolutely an atypical American. Really! Well, they were using my title in and out of the film and they got nervous about a law suit, so they called me in. Now my picture had not been released yet and they said, "We'd like you to see this." So I saw it and I said, "Why did you do this? You've just destroyed the film you've made, because if this is true then my film must be some aberration of an idiot." "Well, we didn't think it would be bad." And I said, "Well, look, I'll sue you." They wanted to play it with my picture and I had a financial interest in my picture, I suppose, although I doubted if I could make it stick in court. But as far as I was concerned they were injuring my property rights and apparently they were worried about this too or they wouldn't have even consulted me. I convinced them that they would be laughed out of existence, which I doubt would have happened at that moment since nobody was laughing about anything. Anyway, productions of *Salesman* shouldn't be about pathology but it can happen if you play Willy like a real mad fellow, yes. But it would be bad acting and it would be a stupid way to do the show. However, I think that this is a real danger whenever you get into a highly charged personality like Lear. You can make *Lear* an absolutely meaningless play. In fact, you can do it easier than you can with Willy, because what kind of an idiot is it who cannot glimpse what we all see, the fact that he has a good daughter who he thinks is the bad daughter. Well, he's for the looney bin. The audience knew what *Salesman* was about. They knew he wasn't crazy. They were right up with him. See, let me not underestimate it, I was ironically stating all the things that they always state seriously. A man can get anywhere in this country on the basis of being liked. Now this is serious advice, and that audience is sitting there almost about to smile but the tears are coming out of their eyes because they know that that is what they believe. This man is obviously going down the chute and he's telling them exactly what they believe. So I don't have to make a speech that this is wrong. The irony of the whole situation is what is making it work.

BIGSBY: But it's not a play which only works in an American context.

MILLER: No. Let me put it this way. That play was a great success in Western Europe, Eastern Europe, Japan, it hardly mattered where it was done. You see all countries have people with reveries of how they're going to conquer life. It's just that in this particular situation he is a salesman.

BIGSBY: Incidentally, how far is Willy's brother, Ben, intended to be simply a product of Willy's mind and how far an independent character?

MILLER: He's a real brother but Willy has invested him already with the whole mythos of that vast brutal success which is larger than life. Nobody can be that successful. Ben is an expressionist figure; every time he opens his mouth he is talking about diamonds, or wealth, or the land, or exploitation of some kind, and that's the way it would be for Willy. Willy wouldn't think of him excepting as the one who won, the victor. *The Crucible* is built on what I would call autonomous characters, who bring on their personalities encased in their social roles as we do in real life: one is poor, one is rich, or whatever. *Death of a Salesman* was conceived literally on two dimensions at the same time. On one level there are autonomous characters while on another there are characters who exist as symbols for Willy Loman.

BIGSBY: You mean that Happy and Biff together are aspects of Willy's mind.

MILLER: Exactly. It was done up in Minneapolis by Guthrie and I sat with him and he said, "You know, I was never aware before but this is a lyric; this is a long poem by Willy." It is, you know. John Proctor's voice is not all the voices but in a certain sense Willy is all the voices.

BIGSBY: Is that why the play was originally to be called *The Inside of His Head*?

MILLER: Yes. I conceived it as taking place inside his head and that's why it is different from any other play.

BIGSBY: So, the gulf that I was suggesting existed between the physical attention on Willy and the moral resolution through Biff would not have occurred in the original because they would all have been aspects of Willy's mind.

MILLER: Yes, that's right. But at that point when he dies, his consciousness vanishes and there is a space between the requiem and the play. It takes place on the earth, so to speak. We've left Willy's head now; we're on the earth.

BIGSBY: You've seen, obviously, a lot of Willy Lomans over the years? What have the principal actors brought to that part that was different?

MILLER: Well, there have been three chief players, as far as I am concerned. One was Warren Mitchell, who played it marvellously in London. I didn't know Warren and I just saw him in the play and we chatted for a while but his Willy and Dustin Hoffman's are related. They are both small men, feisty fellows. They've got a large world that's trying to kill them and a small man reacts with a kind of nervosity. That is in the part. It is obvious that Willy is leaping from one contradictory attitude to another very rapidly, sometimes with hardly a line in between, and to me that also was the characteristic of a little man, a physically small man. And I wrote it for a small man, if I wrote it for anybody. Lee Cobb, who did the original, was a giant, he was six feet whatever and he weighed a lot and he looked like he was in mourning for his life. He had always been a sad sack and he had what we conventionally think of as a tragic air because he was so damn sad. When he laughed, you wept. He had a dark air about him. Dustin is of another order. First of all, because he is so diminutive, he has to create people, literally create them. I don't know how he gets into the skin of Tootsie or of Kramer or of any of the other parts he's done but he has a true actor's imagination. You see, Warren was playing closer to Lee Cobb. Dustin had to make Willy Loman happen as far as he was concerned and what I get from Dustin's Willy is tragic in a completely different sense. It isn't the tragedy of the portrait but of the idea. Probably Dustin's is the most lucid of all the Willys that I am aware of. I have been so closely involved with the production, maybe it seems so because I know what he is doing and how he arrived there, but he is a fantastically intelligent actor. That's a rare thing in anybody. Actors being feeling people, first of all, we don't normally think of them as being very intellectual. He's by no means intellectual and he doesn't want to be, thank God, but he's very bright and he can analyze his own feelings and know what part of himself he needs to use in order to become Willy.

BIGSBY: Have audiences changed, the audiences to *Death of a Salesman*? Do they respond to the same things?

MILLER: I tell you, I was just talking about that the other day. I don't see any change whatsoever, in 35 years. Everybody, including me, has been saying that that kind of a play isn't possible any more, purely and simply because nobody's going to sit there that long with that degree of attention. The television has destroyed them. They can only listen for ten minutes and then they start shifting around. Well, it's nonsense. They are doing exactly what they did, in my memory, in the beginning, and what they do in China and what they'd done in Germany and anywhere else I've seen the thing. I think their potential hasn't been used in some years.

BIGSBY: Willy Loman is a person who comes out of a different kind of time. He has a different sensibility. He wants to work with his hands. He looks back to the time before the city when things were simpler, relationships were simpler. I wonder if his nostalgia and Biff's nostalgia isn't also partly yours in that play?

MILLER: I am very sceptical about that, quite frankly, and I am one of the ones who does not think that in the Depression time people were better. You know, there's a whole romance going on about the Depression that because everybody was broke they were kinder to one another, because they understood that everybody was broke. Well, all I can remember was that I wanted to go to school outside New York because I thought that we were cutting each other's throats and that it would be nicer in a small town where I could breathe easier. I think the Depression time was a ferociously competitive period. There was idealism. There was radicalism, which gave a loftiness to some of the sentiments, but underneath it was murder.

BIGSBY: I don't think I was meaning quite so much the thirties as a period for which he was nostalgic, as the nineteenth century.

MILLER: That, of course, I share. But I have to say that one of our best writers was Thoreau and he trembled at the sound of the railroad. He thought that this was going to be the end of everything. Maybe it was. But intellectuals are always afraid of change. They are really the most conservative psychological types. They don't want it to change and they want to look back at some better era and what they're doing, of course, what I do, what I think everybody does, is look back to when you were young and you were so dumb and ignorant that you thought the world was full of hope.

BIGSBY: Doesn't the logic of that play almost confirm that nostalgia in that, at the end, we are left with Biff Loman who's come to an understanding of who he is and is presumably about to return to a farm in Texas, to light out for territory like Huck Finn. But the territory isn't, for the most part, there any more, is it?

MILLER: No, it isn't. But it would be wrong to say that it isn't. You see, there is a different life in certain parts of the United States still, as compared to the New York, Chicago, Los Angeles life. Life can be much more pleasant in a smaller place and Biff wants not to be an integer, a simple little factor, in this gigantic business and industrial operation that the United States is and like most other countries are. And there is an escape in that, of course, a desire to assert different values. He is a precursor of the hippy movement in a way. Vermont, the most remote northern part of the United States, is full of people, young people, very competent, professional people sometimes, who have simply given it all up and have gone up to these places to live a human life. That's really what he's doing. But I had no cultural tools at the time. Biff was not part of any movement.

BIGSBY: I wonder, though, if there isn't a sense of doubt on your part when you move on to *The Misfits* in which you have a person who is working with horses . . .

MILLER: And you see what it comes to.

BIGSBY: And you see what's happened.

MILLER: Oh yes, no doubt, it's directly connected with *Salesman*. Sure it is.

BIGSBY: Were you aware of that when you were . . .

MILLER: No. One of my failings is that I have a very short vision. When I am writing, I think that I am inventing it for the first time. I guess if I didn't, I wouldn't write it. But that's true, though. *The Misfits* is what happens when you are in the great outdoors. You are killing horses for dog food.

BIGSBY: I wonder also if there isn't a sense in which you yourself at this stage were feeling a misfit?

MILLER: Yes. Well, I've always felt a misfit. I've always identified with those fellows, even down in the middle of New York. I didn't have to go out to Reno, Nevada to feel that way. Yes. Sure. And not only identification with them but identification with the problem, which is to assert value apart from the society, to assert some kind of a human life apart from the society. That's pretty tough because it's got its own contradictions and its own paradoxes. I don't know whether you really can do it.

Introduction to *Plays: Three*

OBVIOUSLY there are two distinct kinds of theater in our time, the Majority one and the Other. The Majority includes the musicals, light comedies, melodramas of reassurance, and farces—anything that takes peoples' minds off their troubles.[1] The Other, in contrast, is devoted to generating anxiety rather than reassurance, or escape through hermetically circular ironies. Other comedy tends toward snarling parody of love or any similar implication of pure human intentions, and has far more prestige in academic circles. Other theater is most eager to become part of the future; the Majority is perfectly content with immediate acceptance at the highest possible ticket prices. Few seriously discuss the Majority theater; the Other gets written about in articles and books and its authors are treated as seers and philosophers. The Majority theater has only practitioners, no seers. In fact, the Majority theater practitioner who visibly aspires to become a seer is quickly thrown out of both camps and ends in poverty unless he has saved money in his pre-seer period.

How to tell a Majority work from the Other kind is often a tricky problem. A show is Majority when it runs a long time, although some

From *Plays: Three,* Methuen, London, 1990, pp. ix–xiii. Reprinted by permission of Reed Books.

---

[1] Of course, Shakespeare, the most-produced playwright of all time, is an anomaly. The Majority, by all laws inherent in such matters, should be too dull to enjoy him, but they persist in thinking he is a popular writer.

can close in a week or less (in New York). However, the Other kind may also run a long time but almost always in small theaters. One can only theorize that their audiences must abhor large crowds while Majority people like it best when surrounded by thousands in big halls or stadiums. Television they find most enjoyable of all, probably because they know they are watching along with millions of others, a fact which in itself is likely to raise suspicions of fraudulence in the Other audience.

There are differences as well in the receptivity of both audiences. The Majority expects to be reached by a play and to be able to understand what is taking place more or less when it is happening. The Other audience seems to prefer not to understand what is going on, at least not too precisely, probably in order to exercise their own imaginations, much as they have to in real life where most things people do are unanticipated, if not incomprehensible. It follows that the Other audience, disregarding its antipathy for naturalism, harbors an unacknowledged taste for it while the Majority audience prefers a theater based on the archaically formalized relationship to real-life behavior.[2] (One need only stand listening to snatches of conversation on a subway platform to realize the passengers are unknowingly performing what amounts to a real-life Other play.)

In general, life is a mystery to the Other no less than to the Majority theater, the difference being that the latter claims to have cleared it up in two hours. The very idea of clearing anything up is anathema to the Other theater; indeed, if in the course of time and repeated productions an Other play seems to have become clarified to the point of easy comprehensibility, it is gradually absorbed into the Majority repertoire and its author correspondingly becomes richer and richer until, slowly but surely, he is despised.[3]

Many ordinary people—people who never stop to analyze anything, are apt to wonder what the point is of having the Other theater when

---

[2]Namely, actors pretending to really feel emotions rather than mocking them—or pretending to mock them.
[3]Again, Shakespeare only serves to confuse analysis. The ambiguousness of his meanings is only that for scholars, the Majority audience remaining content to imagine they understand precisely what he is driving at.

it is attended by so ludicrously few people, and when even those who do show up cannot often agree on what it was they saw. But these people overlook a fundamental point about Other art—that its object is to analyze *them*, the Majority, in particular their middle-class stupidities, Puritanical or materialistic illusions about money, sex, and war, and general bourgeois dimness. So naturally the Majority is unlikely to catch on that it is, for example, a Rhinoceros, or that despite appearances of immense activity it is really standing around awaiting the non-arrival of the Lord, or that its idealistic patriotism is simply a clever means of enriching the ruling class through warfare. Those are some of the basic proposals of Other theater, and should one ask why, if Other theater is truly attempting to heal the Majority with its wisdom, it does not search out some way, difficult though this might be, to make itself Majority-comprehensible, one is likely to run into a philosophical conundrum; for if the Majority were ever convinced that it is a dangerous conformist Rhinoceros, or that all its worldly strivings, fanatical shopping, money-lust, automobile-fixations, etc., are futile attempts to escape the true and pointless conditions of existence, then—converted to the truth of these radical propositions— the Majority would cease to exist as such and would turn into the Other. In which case, one might ask, would the old Other separate itself from this new Other, detesting it as a *nouveau* or *faux* Other, while turning its back on the original Other theater as outmoded and passé, or historically exhausted, declaring that they, the original Others, are *not* Rhinoceroses and are *not* waiting around for a god who never shows up, thereby moving over inadvertently into former Majority positions? In other words, does the fundamental question finally come down to whether it is preferable to sit in a small theater with few people or a large theater with many?

The issue is complicated in addition by whether the definition of Other theater is or is not linked with immediate comprehensibility. There is—or was—no more Majority text than the Holy Bible whose stories have been drummed into immense mobs of people for close to two millennia. Indeed, whole wars have been launched against people who refused to accept it as God's truth, wars that mobilized hundreds of thousands of passionate Bible readers—or hearers—since most have been illiterate. Yet there is probably no book in whose narratives so much remains inexplicable. Why did Cain have to kill Abel? There is no straightforward explanation, it just happens. Where did Noah learn to build a veritable *Queen Mary*, especially having lived on a desert, no less? And if Adam and Eve were the first and only humans, with what people was Cain sent to live in exile in the land East of Eden so that they could curse him? Where did they come from? This is Other literature if there ever was any; indeed, the entire creation of the world takes less linear space than a cooking recipe, surely an example of Other condensation and elypsis. Yet most Other audiences are sure to consider it fit only for the Majority mentality and its lusting after clear and simple situations.

The possibility of some gross error would seem to open before us, a confusion of matter with manner, of the merely customary with the decrepit. In New York—to step aside from theater for illustration—a new architectural style has set Greek pediments and columns on top of fifty-story buildings in revolt, we are told, against the boring Bauhaus form-follows-function shibboleth. Instead, we are apparently to have form-tops-function since the working interiors of these immense buildings devoted to money-making and therefore impervious to useless add-ons, remain exactly the same as all other skyscraper designs of the past. One has to wonder whether the problem is not so much architecture as simple boredom. Since in other periods a large new building was a rare event, and in pre-industrial times one that took years and even generations to complete, perhaps we are so accustomed to immense new structures suddenly springing up that the sight of them is unlikely to inspire the effort to look up from the street, and so the architect's job, especially the Other architect, is to entertain and draw attention to his performance as much as to make something intrinsically unified and beautiful. In short, art now is an assault on the boredom of excess and the unnecessary with which life overflows, at least for the favored, in this, one of the longest periods of peace between the great-powers in all history.

Perhaps something similar is at work in theater where boredom, of course, has always been the cardinal sin. In Majority theater an event once strove above all for credibility, and to this end was carefully prepared for in advance, impressing the audience with the wonderful, or menacing, inviolability of cause-and-effect. In Other theater, in contrast, nothing is as valued as the unanticipated, the event which, if at all possible, violates every imaginable system of logic to the point of total arbitrariness. It is striking how this mode of perception more and more reflects like qualities that now glare forth from life. For example, the Soviet system, thought to be set in concrete, breaks up without foreign intervention, causing the implosion of vast edifices of Western armed war preparation without a shot being fired. The whole anti-Communist soufflé has simply slid down to the bottom of the pot just like the pro-Communist one. The Other style reflects the elevation to his country's Presidency of a playwright—of all things—who a few short months earlier had been jailed for his views. Other theater, the theater of the unanticipated, would seem to have its roots in the common, blatant world after all, would seem—ironically enough—not to have been as pure a flight of imaginative liberation as it would like to have seemed, but one quite as influenced, if not determined, by social and political circumstances as the Majority theater, with its boring enslavement to the logic of psychological-social-political realities. Other theater is hitched to a different cart, but it is hitched.

What does it all come to? The same old thing, of course—those radiating images, compact imitations of people that inflame the imagination with intimations of completeness; images of the self-defrauded Lear and Oedipus, of the abandoned Estragon, of fatuous Tartuffe, the infinite Alice, pining Bovary, God-hungry Ahab—the qualities of earthly existence, each bearing its self-contained interior system of logical inevitability. In such super-informing images the Majority and the Other merge, fall apart, in fact, into a mutuality of understanding that transcends the size of their theaters, the hipness of their audiences, or the modes they use to get themselves created—in short, despite everything. In the end, the long run, the informing human image—by whatever means it is brought to life—is. The rest is gossip.

On Screenwriting and Language: Introduction to *Everybody Wins*

A FUNNY thing happens to screenplays on the way to the screen. It isn't simply that they get changed, subtly or otherwise, from their earlier incarnations, but that they become brittle. This is only true for the writer, of course. He misses the lines that were merely shadings of meaning and would probably hold things up in a movie, which, after all, has to *move*. But in the final version of *Everybody Wins*, compared to earlier drafts, surprisingly little of the basic material was altered, although I agreed to cut a few scenes and revise the ending. In general, what I think happened—and this is probably usual in moviemaking—is that suggestion through words became rather more blatant indication through images.

I hasten to add that this is not a gripe, if only because it is, in my view, a generic quality of the form. A description in words tends to inflate, expand, and inflame the imagination, so that in the end the thing or person described is amplified into a larger-than-life figment. But something photographed is lifted out of the imagination and becomes simply what it really is, or less. It is montage, rather than the actual photograph itself, that gives the impression of an imaginary world larger than life. Words, unable to imitate reality, must in their nature serve it up in metaphoric guise, but film gives us the appearance of reality directly.

From *Everybody Wins*, Grove Press, New York, 1990, pp. v–xiv. Copyright © 1990 by Arthur Miller. Reprinted by permission of Grove/Atlantic, Inc.

If a telephone is photographed, isolated on a table, and the camera is left running, it becomes more and more what it is—a telephone in all its detail. Andy Warhol let the camera run on the Empire State Building for maybe an hour or more. I left before the "end" of this picture, so I'm not sure how long it lasted, but in the twenty minutes I watched, it never to my mind rose to metaphor, simply remaining what it was—the Empire State Building.

Things go differently on a stage. Set a phone on a table under a light and raise the curtain, and in complete silence, after a few minutes, something will accrete around it. Questions and anticipations will begin to emanate from it; we will begin to imagine meanings in its isolation—in a word, the phone becomes an incipient metaphor. Possibly because we cannot see its detail as sharply as on film or because it is surrounded by a much greater space, it begins to animate, to take on suggestive possibilities, very nearly a kind of self-consciousness. Something of the same is true of words as opposed to images. The word is not and can't be any more than suggestive of an idea or sensation; it *is* nothing in itself.

There is always too much dialogue. And it's true, there is, for one thing because dialogue cannot be seen. The contradiction, I suppose, is that movies—most of them, anyway—require a writer's sense of form while inherently rejecting his word-love. And so the writer, accustomed to forming sentences on which all his effects rely, ends up with something truncated and not quite his own on paper; with luck, however, it is paradoxically more his own on the screen. For it turns out—if he is lucky with director and actors—that the meaning of his lost lines is actually visible in pictures. I think that the quality of the final work is rougher and cruder, more brutally telegraphic, than when it was action described in words. But again, the word made flesh may *be* more and suggest less. It is a very mysterious business, and by no means a simple question of better or worse, but of differences of aesthetic feeling, of timbre and tissue, that always accompany differences of form. One need only recall the innumerable fine novels that simply could not be made to work on the screen because the quality of their language was removed; their story-essence vanished when their language was discarded.

Among "real" writers—novelists, playwrights, poets—screenwriting, when it is not regarded as a cousin of engineering, is seen as an art on a par with clothing design; the product has no life of its own until it is occupied by the wearer. I am afraid that this, at least in my view, is truer than one would wish, but it is necessary to add that there have been many more significant films over the past 25 years than plays or, proportionately, even novels. Nevertheless, screenplays, especially the good ones that work, tend by the nature of the art to be self-effacing, vanishing, as it were, into the total impression of the film, this in contrast to the play, which in the Western tradition has been assimilated to literature as a respectable form apart from performance (something that was not yet the case as late as Elizabethan times, when playscripts were tossed to managers and actors without reaching print). Except among technicians, the screenplay has little or no existence unless filmed, and the few exceptions, like Pinter's unproduced work for the screen, are precisely that—isolated examples that illuminate the rule.

The screenplay is the first element in a collaborative art, but only an element for all that, and not, like a stage play, a thing in itself. It is a sort of libretto for camera, its energies moving outward to serve the other elements in the film and to organize them for a common purpose. The forces in and around the stage play, in contrast, move in the opposite direction, for it is the play that is to be served—by director, actors, designer, costumer. An opera libretto is likewise content not to be noticed by the public, even as the singers and conductor know that it is their vital support, without which the music would fail to fly out to the audience's ear.

The screenplay may do many things, but one thing it must do, and that is give meaning to the pictures. In this sense it is equivalent to the words in a cartoon balloon or the titles sometimes given photographs or paintings. These may orient us as to the time and place a photo was shot or a picture painted, but there can't be many photos or paintings made memorable by their labels and dates. Indeed, the vitality of a screenplay, indispensable as it is to the finished film, springs from the life-giving structure by which the order of the images—the film's most affecting element—is organized.

The very invisibility of the screenplay accounts for the screen-writer's anonymity before the audience and most critics. To be sure, he alone was there when the pages were blank, it was his godlike hand that gave form to dust, but his occasional smart or touching line of dialogue notwithstanding, it isn't really words that people come to hear or long remember; it is actors and their mannerisms, their noses and hair and tones of voice, that really matter to them. And ironically, the more authority the actor has in performing his role, the further from sight the screenwriter recedes; in effect, the actor has eaten him. Indeed, when this happens, the movie is successful, since the actor seems to have originated his lines.

Except for the money, when there is any, screenwriting is a rather thankless profession compared with other forms of writing. The film medium belongs essentially to the director, its attraction for the public will always be the actor, and there will never be a way around that. There cannot be a Eugene O'Neill of the movies. Every element and person in the enterprise exists to serve the director's central purpose, which is to make the actors seem believable.

This may be why the most persuasive film acting is as close to word-less as possible. For a long time the idea that Gary Cooper might be an actor was thought a joke, and the same for Clark Gable, John Wayne, and their numerous heroic-type contemporaries who were "merely" personalities rather than actors. A Spencer Tracy, on the other hand, was certainly an actor because he could speak so well. This mis-taken judgment was historically determined by the fact that movies were originally offshoots of the stage, and stage acting was something for which these heroes were indeed unfit. Their way of speaking was either silly and boyish as in Wayne's case, whiny, as with Gable too much of the time, or monotonous, as with Cooper. But the point, which was missed because it was so new, was that all these heroes could show attitudes and feelings—usually simple and fundamental ones like anger or sexual desire, indignation or aggression—much bet-ter with their mouths shut than open. And even "show" is too strong a word—it is more accurate to say that they were eminently attributable actors. The mute human, like an animal, keeps all his possibilities in-tact, gives us nothing to make us doubt his reality while any speech is bound to narrow his plausibility dangerously. Thus, there is a peculiar pressure on words in film to contribute to silent communication rather than monopolizing communication as words do on the stage. Words must above all be utilizable, each one as unadorned a story-mover as possible. The director's first instinct when faced with a multi-sentence speech is to pick it apart with a question for each word: "Why do we need this?" Needless to say, confronted with such a question, no Shakespeare play would last more than an hour.

When an actor talks, he is more vulnerable to disbelief than when he is simply standing there. The very purpose of words in movies is to justify the silences that are the picture's main business. It is silence that creates an infinity of potential meaning that words can only diminish. This, I think, is also why very good prose writers do not usually prosper as screenwriters. Faulkner, Fitzgerald, Tennessee Williams, and a long line of eminent others discovered that their brightest stylistic inventions were precisely what movies reject like excrescences. Language tends to get in the way of the images, and the brighter the language, the more it draws attention to itself, the more it interferes.

The real poetry of a film lies first in its structure of meaning, distinctly a function of the screenplay, and second in the expressiveness of its images, which are realized by the director but have their root, if not more than that, in the writer's work. Language, nevertheless, cannot be more than a servant to the images in the final impression.

Inevitably, especially if one is not accustomed to writing films, the question arises as to exactly why words are in such rivalry with the image as to be nearly self-indulgences. Even the wordy films that come to mind—Huston's *The Dead*, Capra's *Mr. Smith Goes to Washington*, Wilder's *Some Like It Hot* (a brilliantly and eminently *written* film by the late I. A. L. Diamond in collaboration with Wilder)—endure in memory not primarily for their lines but for the snap and marksmanship of their visual moods, their portraits of actors and settings, the things they have let us *see*, and the image-driven story. In the final analysis, dialogue exists at all in film in order to justify images and bridge them to sustain continuity. Dialogue is the musculature of the gestalt, the combination of images whose interactions create meaning. Altogether unlike the novel and even the play, film simply will not stand for writing that is basically commentary, however, illuminating or beautiful or telling it may be. The closest one may safely verge on such adornment is in verbal wit, providing it is not convoluted, as it may be on the stage, but pithy and quickly understood. Otherwise, adornment and commentary are left to the director and his cinematographer, who indeed may elaborate through pleasurable explorations of things seen—locales, flesh, fingernails, eyes, all the wonders of the visible that film adores.

The reason or reasons for this image supremacy seem obvious: it is film's replication of dreams, or more precisely, of our relationship to dreams. The film scene, even the apparently legato one, is always secretly in a hurry, much like its unacknowledged matrix, the dream scene, which flashes up in the sleeper and dies away in a matter of seconds. Dreams (if the reader's are anything like mine) are almost never verbal. Sometimes a single emblematic word, or perhaps two, may emerge in a dream scene as a clue (most likely ambiguous) to its intent, but everyone knows the dream in which people are avidly talking, with no words coming from their mouths, thus creating the image of talk rather than talk itself. We all know, too, the dream in which we are shouting a warning or a plea to others, with no sound issuing forth. Yet we know the meaning of what was being said or shouted. The meaning, in short, stems from the situation and not from the words we are trying to say about it. The dreamer is essentially deaf, and this suggests that film's origins, like those of dream, reach back to archaic stages of our evolution, to a period antedating our capacity to understand language, when we communicated in the primitive sign language of infancy. Long before he can understand words, the infant is obviously moved by what he sees, made frightened or happy or curious or anxious by purely visual stimuli. After a mere few months of life he has all the mental capacities required to direct movies or to paint pictures—everything, that is, except a grasp of the coherency of theme that brings relevance and meaning to what he is so pleasurably staring at.

For coherency's sake words—whether spoken or printed on the screen—are indeed necessary, however brief and minimal they may be, and this needs a screenwriter, someone capable of using words efficiently in order to make some sense of pleasure, or, to put it differently, in order to provide a social justification of sensuousness. But coherency in film remains distinctly secondary in importance to the enticing infantile riddle of sheer image itself.

The primitiveness of the image-story, growing as it does primarily from our very earliest months of life, tends to thin out the filmed tale in comparison to the word-driven one. This is admittedly debatable and may be a purely personal reaction brought on by too many years in the theater, but it seems to me the brain needn't work hard before a film; it can coast along in neutral. And perhaps this absence of effort simply makes one's appreciation that much shallower, for dreaming and movie watching are essentially passive activities, something happening *to* us, rather than an active and willful participation in another's imaginary world, as is the case with reading or even watching stage plays built on words instead of pictures.

Before a play we are forced to do the chores of editing, of deciding what is more or less important, of shifting our attention from actor to actor on the stage. In reading any text we have to decide and sometimes puzzle out what the words themselves mean. At the movies we decide nothing, our treasured infantile inertia is barely nudged, for the editor, the director, the lighting, the orchestration, and the overwhelming size of the image itself hand us an unmistakable hierarchy of importance and lay before us the predigested results to wonder at and enjoy. In point of fact, a film is even more primitive than a dream if we consider how far more densely packed with ambiguity and insoluble mystery dreams are. But it is their dream-born primitiveness that accounts for the universal attraction of movies, and it is perhaps the passivity with which they are viewed that supplies the delights of release and escape for people everywhere. A movie is something being done to us, and this is very nice relative to the other forms, which by comparison are work.

So the screenwriter, charged as he is with creating and maintaining coherency in the film, stands in some contradiction to its real nature and fundamental sources of pleasure, which are incoherent, subconscious, sensuous. Indeed, it has long been standard procedure to disinvite screenwriters from the sets and locations of the films they have written (although not this one). They are like a guilty conscience arriving at the scene of a crime, necessary for upholding civilization but not really much fun. Their presence crowds the director, inhibits the actors. In the usual orgy of creative play that filmmaking is, with actors and director and cinematographer seeking to fabricate real feelings and marvellous accidents, the screenwriter—who started it all—represents the principle of good order without which all meaning is likely to escape the enterprise. Naturally, he is suspect.

But he has one final satisfaction. He may, if he so desires, contemplate the amazing fact that from this typewriter clicking away in his lonely room veritable armies of people have sprung forth—actors, makeup artists, food concessionaires, explosives teams, horse wranglers, plane pilots, chauffeurs, bankers, ushers, box office people, ad men and women, sign painters, costumers, hair designers, frogmen, attending physicians, dentists, nurses, truck drivers, mechanics, turbine experts, electricians, and people who know how to stretch shoes quickly or disguise a sudden pimple, plus their spouses and lovers. And all these regiments from the same typewriter ribbon and a few score sheets of paper with words on them. Magic.

Without in the least belittling screenwriting, I would say that it does not require one to write very well. The often agonizing stylistic effort that writing normally demands is obviated, if only because the work is not written to be read. So in this sense screenwriting is easier than other forms. On the other hand, the human relationships, the thematic coherency, and the story in a *good* screenplay are as tough to get right as they are in any other form. I must add my own (probably minority) view, however, that the screenplay requires much more of a shorthand approach to scene writing than the stage play or the novel. It wants things indicated, and as deftly as possible, rather than fleshed out in words, perhaps because the actor's image on the screen is so vast and omnipotent as to be overwhelming in its suggestive power. What in other forms must be written out or spoken may on the screen be achieved with a raised eyebrow, the movement of a mouth or a hand, or a mere mute stare. But the condensation of image demanded by screenwriting is reminiscent of poetry as opposed to the prose of the stage form. In all, then, writing screenplays has its own formidable challenges, not the least of which is the capacity to bear the pleasure and the pain of being a member of the orchestra—in the first section, perhaps, but a member nonetheless—rather than playwright-soloist or novelist-virtuoso. The good part is that if the screenwriter gets less of the credit than he deserves, he may also get less of the blame, so it evens out in the end, and that, one supposes, is fair enough.

We're Probably in an Art
That Is—Not Dying

IT HAPPENS to be a very bad historical moment for playwriting, because the theater is getting more and more difficult to find actors for, since television pays so much and the movies even more than that. If you're young, you'll probably be writing about young people, and that's easier—you can find young actors—but you can't readily find mature actors. They've either gone to the movies or weren't very successful, so they didn't stick with it. It's an extremely difficult thing in this country right now. It's never been worse.

That and the demise of the Broadway theater are probably part of a whole cultural shift. In New York, of course, it's a question of real estate and the costs of production. In a few weeks there will be only a couple of straight commercial plays on Broadway, and nineteen dark Broadway theaters. The theater culture in this city has been dispersed. It's been going on for about 25 years now, and I think it has almost completed its devolution.

People don't feel excited at the idea of going to the Broadway theater, even though occasionally a very good thing comes on. They've deserted it. They feel it's not for them. It's not up to date. It doesn't have any news to give them. And this was quite different some years ago. It was the most exciting thing in New York.

It's partly the price of the ticket. It's hard to get happy when you're going to lay out $100 to sit down for two hours with your friend—or

From *The New York Times*, 17 January 1993, p. H5. Reprinted by permission of Arthur Miller.

even your wife. People are willing to do it for a musical with a big orchestra and a lot of sets, but they're not so willing to do it for a straight play. Especially when some critic has said it's pretty good but not a masterpiece. Today the critic's power varies according to the price of the ticket. When the ticket is cheap, the critic's power is low. When the ticket is very expensive, the power of the critic is high. So we're probably in an art that is—not dying. I don't think it is ever going to die because it's so simple: all you need is a board and a man standing on it and a woman saying something interesting. You don't need machines. But it is going to have to develop a different way of production. The problem is not that people can't write plays anymore, the problem is that the audience's relationship to the theater has simply dribbled away. And the playwright is nothing without his audience. He is one of the audience who happens to know how to speak. We are a kind of church. And if the parishioners are no longer interested in that church, you know what happens. It becomes a garage or a grocery store.

It's different in other countries, especially with public subsidy. I just directed *Death of a Salesman* in Stockholm. They have many theaters, but in the main one, the Royal Dramatic Theater, they have six stages and ninety actors under permanent contract. In my case they had chosen a cast. There was one actor who I thought wasn't quite right for the role of Happy, and I told him. "It's all right," he said. "I'm playing Hamlet at the moment three times a week." So I asked the director of the theater if there were any other people at that age and general type. And he said, "We have some." The next afternoon we had *six* sitting in the room, all actors who were working in different plays in that building.

The Swedes, however, don't originate much drama. I don't know why, with all that encouragement. We do generate more plays in this hurly-burly, self-defeating system. Still, there's no comparison. They've got a couple of million people, and we're this mammoth society.

The problem for us is not that the plays are not there or that the playwrights are not there; it's that the audience is not in those Broadway seats. What the solution is, given the tremendous investment in real estate, I don't know. Maybe there is none, the way it stands.

Maybe we're just going to have to have a theater of the United States, where the work goes on in smaller places and occasionally is brought in to the city—which is what we do now.

The great excuse for commercial theater in America for a hundred years was that it was the only theater that *originated* anything. The theater outside New York City didn't originate very much, it copied what was here. Well, what they do now is bring in stuff from outside and therefore our Broadway theater is a cripple looking for a crutch. But nothing is going to change until this is recognized as a crisis that could turn out to be terminal for what we used to call professional theater in America.

About Theater Language:
Afterword to *The Last Yankee*

I

WHEN I began writing plays in the late thirties, something called realism was the undisputed reigning style in the American commercial theater—which was just about all the theater there was in this country. The same was more or less the case in Britain. If not a mass art, theater then could still be thought of at least as a popular one, although everyone knew—long before television—that something of its common appeal had gone out of it, and a lot of its twenties' glamor, too. One blamed the movies, which had stolen so much of the audience and thus theater's old dominance as a cultural influence. Notwithstanding the obvious fact that the audience was predominantly middle class, we continued to imagine that we were making plays for people of many different educational and cultural levels, a representative variety of the city and even the country. If this was never really true, there was certainly no thought of appealing to a clique of college graduates or to academics and their standards. A *New York Times* critic like George S. Kaufman had both feet in show business and became the most popular writer of comedies of the period, while Brooks Atkinson may have had one eye on Aristotle but understood that his readers were Americans impatient with any the-

From *The Last Yankee*, Penguin, New York, 1994, pp. 75–98. Reprinted by permission of Penguin Books USA, Inc.

atrical enterprise that required either education or patience. Outside New York there were at least the remains of the twenties' touring wheel, theaters in many smaller cities regularly attended by quite ordinary citizens eager for last year's Broadway hits, albeit with replacement casts. In New York, with a ticket price of 55 cents to four dollars and forty cents, one somehow took for granted that a professor might be sitting next to a housewife, a priest beside a skilled worker or perhaps a grammar-school teacher, a small or large business executive beside a student. This conception of the demotic audience, accurate or not, influenced the writing of plays directed at the commonsensical experience of everyday people. Missing were black or Asian or Hispanic faces, of course, but they were beyond the consciousness of the prevailing culture. As for production costs, even into the forties they were within reason; plays like *All My Sons* or *Death of a Salesman*, for example, cost between twenty and forty thousand to produce, a budget small enough to be raised by half a dozen modest contributors, who might lose all, with some embarrassment but reasonably little pain, or make a killing.

Radicals—people like myself, trying to convince ourselves that we were carrying on the age-old tradition of theater as a civic art rather than a purely commercial one—were in a conflict; to attract even the fitful interest of a Broadway producer, and subsequently to engage the audience, we had to bow to realism, even if the poetic forms were what we really admired or at least wished to explore. An Expressionist like the German Ernst Toller, for example, would not have been read past his sixth page by a Broadway producer or, for that matter, one in London. Among the playwrights one thinks of as important, not one was—or is now—welcome in the commercial theater. Not Chekhov, not Ibsen, not Hauptmann, not Pirandello, Strindberg, Turgenev—not even Shaw. To so much as think of performing a Beckett play like *Waiting for Godot* in the general proximity of Broadway a cast of movie stars and a short run are essential—Lincoln Center pulled it off in 1988—and things were probably a bit worse half a century ago. One need only read O'Neill's letters of complaint at the "showshop" of Broadway and the narrow compass of the American audience's imagination—or in Britain, Shaw's ridicule of his countrymen's provincialism—to understand the problem; for some mysterious reason the Anglo-Saxon culture regarded theater as an entertainment first and last, an art of escape with none of the Continental or Russian interest in moral and philosophical opportunities or obligations. Very occasionally in America there was an *Adding Machine* by the young Elmer Rice, but such a breakout from conventional realism was rare enough to be brought up in conversation for years after, like a calf born with five legs. The English-language theater was pridefully commercial, a profit-making enterprise which wed it to a form whose surfaces of familiar reality would be universally recognized. Captain Shotover's outcry, "I like to know where I am!" could have been sewn to the flag of this theater. Only musicals had the happy license to stretch reality, at least to some extent. But for straight plays, even satire was too strange to prosper; George Kaufman defined satire as what closes on Saturday night.

The point here is that what we think of as "straight realism" was tiresome half a century ago, indeed longer ago than that, but it was accepted by the audiences and almost all the reviewers as a reflection of life. Nonetheless, it should be remembered that realism has emerged at various moments to very capably express the essence of an era. At a time when "experimental" is all the virtue a play needs in order to gain serious consideration, it is not a bad idea to confess that an extraordinarily few such researches have achieved any kind of enduring life. It is not quite enough to know how to escape; one has also to think of arriving somewhere.

In the thirties, probably the single exception—at least that I was aware of—to realism's domination was the WPA's *Living Newspaper*, the one formal innovation of American theater. An epic in more or less presentational form, written like movies by groups of writers, rather than individually, it dealt in an overtly exuberant spirit with social issues like public ownership of electrical power, labor unions, agriculture, and medicine, and was extremely popular. Significantly, the WPA was government-subsidized, and did not have to make a profit. Using unemployed actors, designers, technicians, a show could call upon large casts and elaborate scenery and production elements. And the ticket was low-priced. The WPA could send Orson Welles, for example, into Harlem storefronts with a big cast playing *Doctor Faustus*, charging a quarter a seat. But theater-for-profit was hardly affected by what might be called this epic-populist approach—it was simply too expensive to produce.

I mention these mundane matters because they profoundly affect style in the theater, which, like politics, is always the art of the possible.

There were at least a dozen playwrights regularly feeding the commercial theater in the years before World War II, and all but perhaps Odets and Hellman would have pridefully declared that their sole purpose was to entertain. Those playwrights were sophisticated and no doubt knew all about the Continental theater tradition, and its aspiring to the philosophical condition, something like that of the Greeks or, in a different way, the Elizabethans. The Theater Guild, for one, had been started in the twenties in part to bring that kind of theater to America, the theater of Pirandello, Schnitzler, Ibsen, and Strindberg.

In the thirties, one American styled himself a political revolutionary, and that was Clifford Odets. O'Neill, of course, had been the aesthetic rebel but his socialism was private rather than informing his plays, although *The Hairy Ape* is surely an anticapitalist work. It was his formal experiments and tragic mood that set him apart. O'Neill was a totally isolated phenomenon in the Broadway theater as a maker and user of new and old theatrical forms.

Odets, on the other hand, while describing himself as "a man of the Left," was, with the possible exception of his first play, *Waiting for Lefty*, no innovator where form was concerned. He attempted a poetic realism but it was still trying to represent real people in actual social relationships. And this was perhaps inevitable given his actor's temperament as well as his Marxist commitment; he had the revolutionary's eye on the great public, on the reconstitution of power once a failed capitalism had been brought down—for such was the Marxist and non-Marxist Left position on the proper moral obligation of the artist. But by temperament he was a poet seeking words that would lift him into a takeoff, regardless of his realist political commitments. O'Neill, on the other hand, was not the revolutionary but the rebel with a despairing anarchism in his heart. If he glimpsed any salvation, it was not to arrive in a more benign reconstitution of political power but in the tragic cleansing of the life-lie permanently ensconced in the human condition. Since he took no responsibility in theory for a new and better policy to take the place of the corrupted present one, he was free to explore all sorts of theatrical means by which to set forth the situation of the damned. Moreover, if O'Neill wanted his plays to register, and he surely did, they need not be popular to justify his having written them, for he was hunting the sounding whale of ultimate meaning, and he expected to suffer for it; oppositely, a critical or box-office failure for Odets meant rejection of a very personal kind, a spit in the eye by an ungrateful, self-satisfied bourgeois society. A failed play for Odets was a denial of what he was owed, for he was chasing the public no differently from his bourgeois nonrevolutionary contemporaries. O'Neill could say, and he did, that he was not interested in relations between men, but between Man and God. For America, in his view, was damned and if there were a few individuals who behaved justly and well, it was not because they belonged to a particular social class or held a generous or unselfish political viewpoint, but by virtue of a grace whose source is beyond definition.

II

The realism of Broadway—and the Strand and the Boulevard theater of France—was detested by the would-be poetic dramatists of my generation, just as it had always been since it came into vogue in the nineteenth century. What did this realism really come down to? A play representing real rather than symbolic or metaphysical persons and situations, its main virtue verisimilitude, with no revolutionary implications for society or even a symbolic statement of some general truth. Quite simply, conventional realism was conventional because it implicitly supported the conventions of society, but it could just as easily do something quite different, or so it seemed to me. Nevertheless, we thought it the perfect style for an unchallenging, simpleminded, linear middle-class conformist view of life. What I found confusing at the time, however, was that not so very long before, the name "realism" had been applied to the revolutionary style of playwrights like Ibsen, Chekhov, and quite frequently Strindberg, writers whose thrust was in opposition to the bourgeois status quo and the hypocrisies on which it stood, or, in Chekhov's case, the futilities of the Czarist system.

My own first playwriting attempt was purely mimetic, a realistic play about my own family. It won me some prizes and productions, but, interestingly, I turned at once to a stylized treatment of life in a gigantic prison, modeled on Jackson State Penitentiary in Michigan—near Ann Arbor, where I was in school—the largest prison in the United States, which I had visited over weekends with a friend who was its lone psychologist. The theme of that play was that prisons existed to make desperate workingmen insane. There was a chorus of sane prisoners chanting from a high overpass above the stage, and a counterchorus of the insane trying to draw the other into their ranks. It was inevitable that I had to confront the problem of dramatic language, for it was impossible to engage so vast a human disaster with speech born in a warm kitchen. I gradually came to wonder if the essential pressure toward poetic dramatic language—if not of stylization itself—came from the inclusion of society as a major element in the play's story or vision. Manifestly, prose realism was the language of the individual and private life, poetry the language of man in crowds, in society. Put another way, prose is the language of family relations; it is the inclusion of the larger world beyond that naturally opens a play to the poetic.

But I wanted to succeed, I wanted to emerge and grip an audience. Minds might be illuminated by speeches thrown at them but it was by being moved that one was changed. And so the problem was that our audiences were trained, as it were, in a pawky realism and were turned off by stylistic novelty, by "art." How to find a style that would at one and the same time deeply engage an American audience, which insisted on a recognizable reality of characters, locales, and themes, while opening the stage to considerations of public morality and the mythic social fates—in short, the invisible?

Of course, this was not my preoccupation alone. I doubt there was ever a time when there was so much discussion about form and style. T. S. Eliot was writing his verse plays, and Auden and Isherwood theirs; the poetic mimesis of Sean O'Casey was most popular; and W. B. Yeats's dialogue was studied, if not very often produced. The impulse to poetry reached into the ex-newspaperman and realistic writer Maxwell Anderson, whose attempts to imitate Elizabethan prosody with contemporary characters and social themes were widely celebrated, as curious by some, as moving experiences by others.

To be just to Odets, it was he who challenged the Broadway theater's addiction to verisimilitude by his idiosyncratic dialogue. And he was surely the first American playwright to be celebrated—and more wildly and lavishly than any other before him—for his writing style. For younger writers such as myself, Odets for a couple of years was the trailblazer; he was bringing the suffering of the Great Depression onto the Broadway stage and making audiences listen. If he had not solved the problem of a contemporary American style, he had dared to invent an often wildly stylized stage speech. But I suppose that since his characters lacked elegance or strangeness, were, in fact, the very exemplars of realistic theater, Odets was called a realist—indeed, a kind of reporter of Jewish life in the Bronx. I may not have lived in the Bronx but the speech of Brooklyn Jews certainly bore no resemblance to that of Odets's characters.

> CARP [in *Golden Boy*]: I'm superdisgusted with you! . . . A man
> hits his wife and it's the first step to fascism! Look in the papers! On every side the clouds of war! . . . Ask yourself a pertinent remark; could a boy make a living playing this instrument [a violin] in our competitive civilization today?
> ROXY: I think I'll run across the street and pick up an eight-cylinder sandwich.

The audiences roared with delight at these inventions. It was as though Odets were trying to turn dialogue into jazz. And his devotees went to his plays especially to pick up his latest deliciously improbable remarks and repeat them to their friends. Had any Bronxite—or anyone else in the century—really exclaimed, "God's teeth, no!" "What exhaust pipe did he crawl out of?" Lorna: "I feel like I'm shot from a cannon."

Inevitably, in a theater bounded by realism, this had to be mistakenly labeled as accurate reportage, news from the netherworld. But, of course, it was an invented diction of a kind never heard before on stage—or off, for that matter. Odets's fervent ambition was to burst the bounds of Broadway while remaining inside its embrace, and if, as time went on, his lines began to seem self-consciously labored, no longer springing from characters but manifestly from the author and his will-to-poeticize, he at a minimum had made language the identifying mark of a playwright in America, and that was something that hadn't happened before.

Admittedly, I did not look at his style with objectivity but for its potential usefulness in breaking through the constricted realism of our theater then. Odets was tremendously exciting to young writers. I was troubled by a tendency in his plays toward overtheatricalized excess, however—lines sometimes brought laughter where there should have been outrage, or pity, or some deeper emotion than amusement—and at times the plots verged on the schematic. Odets often overrhapsodized at the climaxes when he should have been reaching to ancillary material that was not there. He wrote terrific scenes, blazing speeches and confrontations which showed what theater could be, but with the exception, perhaps, of *Awake and Sing* and the racy *Golden Boy* he never wrote a play that lifted inexorably to its climactic revelation.

I came out of the thirties unsure whether there could be a viable counterform to the realism around me. All I knew for sure was that a good play must move forward in its depths as rapidly as on its surfaces; word-poetry wasn't enough if there was a fractured poetry in the structure, the gradually revealed illuminating idea behind the whole thing. A real play was the discovery of the unity of its contradictions; the essential poetry was the synthesis of even the least of its parts to form a symbolic meaning. Of course, the problem had much to do with language but more primary was how to penetrate my own feelings about myself and the time in which I lived. Ideally, a good play must show as sound an emotional proof of its thesis as a case at law shows factual proof, and you can't do that with words alone, lovely as they might be.

Odets's contribution, ironically was not his realistic portrayal of society—his alleged aim—but his willingness to be artificial; he brought back artificiality, if you will, just as ten years later Tennessee Williams did with his birdsong from the magnolias. But Williams had an advantage—his language could be far more faithful to its sources in reality. Southern people did love to talk, and in the accents Williams captured (as in *The Glass Menagerie*):

> AMANDA: . . . But Laura is, thank heavens, not only pretty but also very domestic. I'm not at all. I never was a bit. I never could make a thing but angel-food cake. Well, in the South we had so many servants. Gone, gone, gone. All vestige of gracious living! Gone completely! I wasn't prepared for what the future brought me. All by gentlemen callers were sons of planters and so of course I assumed that I would be married to one and raise my family on a large piece of land with plenty of servants. But man proposes—and woman accepts the proposal!—To vary that old, old saying a little bit—I married no planter! I married a man who worked for the telephone company!—That gallantly smiling gentleman over there! (*Points to husband's picture.*) A telephone man who—fell in love with long distance! Now he travels and I don't even know where! . . .

This too was called realism, and it probably was in the sense that there were people who talked like this. But then how did it differ from the conventional realistic play? Clearly, it was that the very action of Williams's plays, certainly the best of them, was working toward the building of symbolic meaning that would embrace both the psychological development of his characters and his personal specter of a menacing America struggling with its own sexuality and the anomie born of its dire materialism. In a word, Williams's style arose from his pain and anxiety at being overwhelmed and defeated by a gross violence that underlay the American—one might say the whole Western—ethos.

Their obsession with words notwithstanding, it was their need to communicate their resistance to something deathdealing in the culture that finally pressed Odets and Williams to address the big public and made them playwrights rather than sequestered poets. Stylistic invention without an implicit commitment of some kind to a more human vision of life is a boat without rudder or cargo or destination—or worse, it is the occupation of the dilettante. Odets, when he began, thought his egalitarian Marxism would heal America and create its new community, but that ideology devolved into a rote religion before the thirties had even passed. Williams unfurled the banner of a forlorn but resisting heroism to the violence against the oddball, the poet, and sexual dissident. But it may as well be admitted that in their different ways both men in the end unwittingly collaborated with the monster they saw as trying to destroy them.

The plays these men wrote were shields raised against the many-arrowed darkness, but in the end there was little from outside to give them the spiritual support to complete their creative lives. Odets's best work ended with his rejection by Broadway and his move to Hollywood; Williams, likewise rejected, kept nevertheless to his trade, experimenting with forms and new methods that drew no encouragement from reviewers unable or unwilling to notice that the theater culture had boxed in a writer of greatness who was struggling to find an audience in the passing crowd of a generation other than his own. At his strongest he had spoken for and to the center of society, in a style it could relate to, an enhanced, visionary realism. In the end a writer has no one to blame for his failings, not even himself, but the brutally dismissive glee of critics toward Williams's last plays simply laid more sticks on his burden. Toward the end he was still outside, scratching on the glass, as he had once put it, and it was the shadowed edges of life that drew him, the borderland where how things are said is everything, and everything has been said before.

The advent of the Absurd and of Beckett and his followers both obscured and illuminated the traditional elements of the discussion of theater style. For O'Neill a good style was basically a question of the apt use of metaphor and argot. "God, if I could write like that!" he wrote to O'Casey, who, incidentally, would no doubt have labeled himself a realistic writer in the sense that he was giving his audiences the substance of their life conflicts. But like Williams, O'Casey came from a culture which loved talk and sucked on language like a sweet candy.

> MRS. GROGAN: Oh, you've got a cold on you, Fluther.
> FLUTHER: Oh, it's only a little one.
> MRS. GROGAN: You'd want to be careful, all th' same. I knew a woman, a big lump of a woman, red-faced and round-bodied, a little awkward on her feet; you'd think, to look at her, she could put out her two arms an' lift a two-storied house on th' top of her head; got a ticklin' in her throat, an' a little cough, an' th' next mornin' she had a little catchin' in her chest, an' they had just time to wet her lips with a little rum, an' off she went. (*Juno and the Paycock*)

Even in the most mundane of conversational exchanges O'Casey sought, and as often as not found, the lift of poetry. Indeed, that was the whole point—that the significantly poetic sprang from the raw and real experience of ordinary people. J. M. Synge, O'Casey's forerunner at the turn of the century, had struck a similar chord; Synge was in a supremely conscious revolt against the banality of most theater language. As John Gassner noted, in Ireland the popular imagination was still, according to Synge, "fiery and magnificent, and tender; so that those of us who wish to write start with a chance that is not given to writers in places where the springtime of local life has been forgotten, and the harvest is a memory only, and the straw has been turned into bricks."

Synge rejected the then-dominant Ibsen and Zola for the "joyless and pallid words" of their realism and as in *Riders to the Sea*, when the women are lamenting the deaths of so many of their men working the angry sea:

> MAURYA: In the big world the old people do be leaving things after them for their sons and children, but in this place it is the young men do be leaving things behind for them that do be old.

As far as style is concerned, the Beckett difference, as it might be called, was to introduce humble people—bums, in fact, or social sufferers—with the plainest of language, but arranged so as to announce and develop pure theme. His could be called a presentational thematic play, announcing what it was about and never straying very far from what it was conceived of to prove, or what his instinct had led him to confirm. Beckett had parted with inferential playwriting, where speeches inferred the author's thematic intentions while hewing to an apparently autonomous story building to a revelatory climax that united story and theme. In Beckett the story *was* the theme, inseparably so. Moreover, as will be shown in a moment, he interpreted the theme himself in his dialogue.

If—instead of the prewar poetic drama's requirement of an elevated tone or diction—the most common speech was now prized, it was not the speech of realistic plays. It was a speech skewed almost out of recognition by a surreal commitment to what at first had seemed to be the impotence of human hopes, and hence the futility of action itself. All but the flimsiest connections between speeches were eliminated, creating an atmosphere of sinister danger (in Pinter) or immanence (in Beckett). It was quite as though the emphatic absence of purpose in the characters had created a loss of syntax. It seems that in later years Beckett took pains to clarify this impression of human futility, emphasizing the struggle *against* inertia as his theme. In any case, however ridiculous so much of his dialogue exchanges are, the tenderness of feeling in his work is emphatically not that of the cynic or the hard ironist.

The dominating theme of *Godot* is stasis and the struggle to overcome humanity's endlessly repetitious paralysis before the need to act and change. We hear it plainly and stripped clean of plot or even incident.

ESTRAGON: Then adieu.
POZZO: Adieu.
VLADIMIR: Adieu.
POZZO: Adieu.
Silence. No one moves.

VLADIMIR: Adieu.

POZZO: Adieu.

ESTRAGON: Adieu.

Silence.

POZZO: And thank you.

VLADIMIR: Thank *you.*

POZZO: Not at all.

ESTRAGON: Yes yes.

POZZO: No no.

VLADIMIR: Yes yes.

ESTRAGON: No no.

Silence.

POZZO: I don't seem to be able ... (*long hesitation*) ... to depart.

ESTRAGON: Such is life.

This is a vaudeville at the edge of the cliff, but vaudeville anyway, so I may be forgiven for being reminded of Jimmy Durante's ditty—"Didja ever get the feelin' that you wanted to go? But still you had the feelin' that you wanted to stay?"

It is a language shorn of metaphor, simile, everything but its instructions, so to speak. The listener hears the theme like a nail drawn across a pane of glass.

So the struggle with what might be called reportorial realism, written "the way people talk," is at least as old as the century. As for myself, my own tendency has been to shift styles according to the nature of my subject. *All My Sons, The Crucible, A View from the Bridge, Death of a Salesman, The Price, The American Clock,* my earliest work, like *The Golden Years,* about the destruction of Mexico by the Spaniards, and the more recent plays, like *The Creation of the World, Some Kind of Love Story,* and *The Last Yankee,* differ very much in their language. This, in order to find speech that springs naturally out of the characters and their backgrounds rather than imposing a general style. If my approach to playwriting is partly literary, I hope it is well hidden. Leroy Hamilton is a native New England carpenter and speaks like one, and not like the New York working men and women in *A Memory of Two Mondays*, or Eddie Carbone, who comes out of a quite different culture.

So the embrace of something called realism is obviously very wide; it can span the distance between a Turgenev and a Becque, between Wedekind and your latest Broadway hit. The main thing I sought in *The Last Yankee* was to make real my sense of the life of such people, the kind of man swinging the hammer through a lifetime, the kind of woman waiting forever for her ship to come in. And second, my view of their present confusion and, if you will, decay and possible recovery. They are bedrock, aspiring not to greatness but to other gratifications—successful parenthood, decent children and a decent house and a decent car and an occasional nice evening with family or friends, and above all, of course, some financial security. Needless to say, they are people who can be inspired to great and noble sacrifice, but also to bitter hatreds. As the world goes I suppose they are the luckiest people, but some of them—a great many, in fact—have grown ill with what would once have been called a sickness of the soul.

And that is the subject of the play, its "matter." For depression is far from being merely a question of an individual's illness, although it appears as that, of course; it is at the same time, most especially in Patricia Hamilton's case, the grip on her of a success mythology which is both naïve and brutal, and which, to her misfortune, she has made her own. And opposing it, quite simply, is her husband Leroy's incredibly enduring love for her, for nature and the world.

A conventionally realistic play would no doubt have attempted to create a "just-like-life" effect, with the sickness gradually rising out of the normal routines of the family's life, and calling up our empathy by virtue of our instant identification with familiar reality. But while Patricia Hamilton, the carpenter's wife, is seen as an individual sufferer, the context of her illness is equally important because, for one thing, she knows, as do many such patients, that more Americans (and West Europeans) are in hospitals for depression than for any other ailment. In life, with such people, a high degree of objectification or distancing exists, and the style of the play had to reflect the fact that they commonly know a great deal about the social setting of the illness even as they are unable to tear themselves free of it. And this affects the play's style.

It opens by directly, even crudely, grasping the core of its central preoccupation—the moral and social myths feeding the disease; and we have a discussion of the hospital's enormous parking lot, a conversation bordering on the absurd. I would call this realism, but it is far from the tape-recorded kind. Frick, like Leroy Hamilton, has arrived for a visit with his wife, and after a moment's silence while the two strangers grope for a conversational opening . . .

FRICK: Tremendous parking space down there. 'They need that for?
LEROY: Well a lot of people visit on weekends. Fills up pretty much.
FRICK: Really? That whole area?
LEROY: Pretty much.
FRICK: 'Doubt that.

The play is made of such direct blows aimed at the thematic center; there is a vast parking space because crowds of stricken citizens converge on this place to visit mothers, fathers, brothers, and sisters. So that the two patients we may be about to meet are not at all unique. This is in accord with the vision of the play, which is intended to be both close up and wide, psychological and social, subjective and objective, and manifestly so. To be sure, there is a realistic tone to this exchange—people do indeed seem to talk this way—but an inch below is the thematic selectivity which drives the whole tale. Perhaps it needs to be said that this split vision has informed all the plays I have written. I have tried to make things seen in their social context and simultaneously felt as intimate testimony, and that requires a style, but one that draws as little attention to itself as possible, for I would wish a play to be absorbed rather than merely observed.

I have called this play a comedy, a comedy about a tragedy, and I am frankly not sure why. Possibly it is due to the absurdity of people constantly comparing themselves to others—something we all do to one degree or another, but in Patricia's case to the point of illness.

PATRICIA: There was something else you said. About standing on line.

LEROY: On line?

PATRICIA: That you'll always be at the head of the line because . . . *breaks off.*

LEROY: I'm the only one on it. . . . We're really all on a one-person line, Pat. I learned that in these years.

The play's language, then, has a surface of everyday realism, but its action is overtly stylized rather than "natural."

Finally, a conventionally realistic work about mental illness would be bound to drive to a reverberating climax. But repression is the cultural inheritance of these New Englanders and such theatricality would be a betrayal of *their* style of living and dying. Indeed, short of suicide, the illness, properly speaking, never ends in the sense of tying all the loose strings, nor should the play, which simply sets the boundaries of the possible. For the theme is hope rather than completion or achievement, and hope is tentative always.

A play about them should have a certain amplitude of sound, nothing greater or less, reflecting their tight yet often deeply felt culture. And in a play about them they should recognize themselves—and even possibly what drives them mad—just like the longshoremen who saw themselves in *A View from the Bridge* or the cops in *The Price* or the salespeople in *Death of a Salesman.* That would be a satisfactory realism as I saw it.

I suppose the form itself of *The Last Yankee* is as astringently direct and uncluttered as it is because these people are supremely the prey of the culture, if only because it is never far from the center of their minds—the latest film or TV show, the economy's ups and downs, and above all the endless advertising-encouraged self-comparisons with others who are more or less successful than they. This ritualistic preoccupation is at the play's dramatic core and, I felt, ought not be unclear or misted over, for it is from its grip they must be freed if they are ever to be free at all. Hence, the repeated references to ambition, to success and failure, to wealth and poverty, to economic survival, to the kind of car one drives and the suit one wears. In a word, the play could not be amorphously "realistic" if it was to reflect the obsessiveness of the characters in life. So if *The Last Yankee* is realism, it is of this kind resulting from an intense selectivity, which in turn is derived from the way these people live and feel.

But obviously, to make such a strictly thematic play demands intense condensation and the syncopating of idea and feeling and language. More than one actor in my plays has told me that it is surprisingly difficult to memorize the dialogue. It sounds like real, almost like reported talk, when in fact it is intensely composed, compressed, "angled" into an inevitability that seems natural but isn't. For it is always necessary to employ the artificial in order to arrive at the real. So that the question I bring to a play is not whether its form and style are new or old, experimental or traditional, but first, whether it brings news, something truly felt by its author, something thought through to its conclusion and its significance; and second, whether its form is beautiful, or wasteful, whether it is aberrant for aberrancy's sake, full of surprises that discover little, and so on.

Something called Realism can land us further from common reality than the most fantastic caprice. But in the end, if stylization in theater needs justification—and it does, of course—it is not in its novelty but in its enhancement of discovery of how life works in our time. How a thing is said is therefore only as important as what it is saying. The proof is the deep pile of experimental plays of two, three, five, ten years ago, which can be appreciated now only by the scholar-specialist, a pile, incidentally, no smaller than the one for so many realistic plays of the same era. So finding the truth is no easier now when we are totally free to use any stylistic means at hand than it was a century or half a century ago when a play had to be "real" to even be read, and had to make sense to sensible people.

Call it a question of personal taste rather than principle, but I think that in theater work there is an optimum balance between two kinds of approaches. One is the traditional attempt to fill characters with acknowledged emotion, "as in life." The other is, in effect, to evacuate emotion from characters and merely refer to it rather than acting it out. Brecht, for one, tried to do this and failed, excepting in his most agitprop and forgettable plays. Actually, the strict containment not of emotion but of emotionalism is the hallmark of the Greek tragic plays, of Molière and Racine and the Japanese No plays, while Shakespeare, it seems to me, is the balance, the fusion of idea and feeling. In short, it is by no means the abstracting of emotion I dislike; on the contrary, it is the lack of it and the substitution for it of fashionably alienated ironies.

As I am not a critic and would not do anything to make any writer's life harder, I will desist from naming names, but there has been a plethora of plays in recent years whose claim to modernity is based on indicated rather than felt emotion, on the assumption, I suppose, that this *sec* quality intellectualizes a work and saves it from the banality associated with writing aimed at the audience's belly rather than at its head. The devil to be avoided is, of course, sentimentality—emotion unearned. But emotion can be earned, of course. Yet a play that is not camp and moves people is in danger of dismissal. (Unless it appears in old films, which we allow ourselves to be moved by if at the same instant we can protect our modernity by feeling superior to their time-bound naïveté.) But if the pun can be pardoned, man lives not by head alone, and the balance between the two modes, one aimed at the mind and one at the flesh, as it were, is what will interpret life more fully, rather than headline it with conceptualizations that too often simply clump about on the stilts of dry irony that time and the shifts of cultural politics will make thoroughly disposable. After all, at least part of the aim of a modern play must be to show what life now *feels alike*.

Ultimately every assault on the human mystery falls back to the ground, changing little, but the flight of the arrow continues claiming our attention over more time when its direction is toward the castle rather than the wayward air.

Ibsen and the Drama of Today

In his introduction to the 1957 edition of his Collected Plays, *Arthur Miller singled out certain aspects of Ibsen's work for comment:*

There is one element in Ibsen's method which I do not think ought to be overlooked, let alone dismissed as it so often is nowadays. If his plays, and his method, do nothing else, they reveal the evolutionary quality of life. One is constantly aware, in watching his plays, of process, change, development. I think too many modern plays assume, so to speak, that their duty is merely to show the present countenance rather than to account for what happens. It is therefore wrong to imagine that because his first and sometimes his second acts devote so much time to a studied revelation of antecedent material, his view is static compared to our own. In truth, it is profoundly dynamic, for that enormous past was always heavily documented to the end that the present be comprehended with wholeness, as a moment in a flow of time, and not—as with so many modern plays—as a situation without roots. Indeed, even though I can myself reject other aspects of his work, it nevertheless presents barely and unadorned what I believe is the biggest single dramatic problem, namely,

From *The Cambridge Companion to Ibsen*, edited by James McFarlane, Cambridge University Press, New York, 1994, pp. 227–232. Reprinted by permission of Cambridge University Press.

how to dramatize what has gone before. I say this not merely out of technical interest, but because dramatic characters, and the drama itself, can never hope to attain a maximum degree of consciousness unless they contain a viable unveiling of the contrast between past and present, and an awareness of the process by which the present has become what it is. And I say this, finally, because I take it as a truth that the end of drama is the creation of a higher consciousness and not merely a subjective attack upon the audience's nerves and feelings. What is precious in the Ibsen method is its insistence upon valid causation, and this cannot be dismissed as a wooden notion.

This is the "real" in Ibsen's realism for me, for he was, after all, as much a mystic as a realist, which is simply to say that while there are mysteries in life which no amount of analyzing will reduce to reason, it is perfectly realistic to admit and even to proclaim that hiatus as a truth. But the problem is not to make complex what is essentially explainable; it is to make understandable what is complex without distorting and oversimplifying what cannot be explained. I think many of his devices are, in fact, quite arbitrary; that he betrays a Germanic ponderousness at times and a tendency to overprove what is quite clear in the first place. But we could do with more of his basic intention, which was to assert nothing he had not proved, and to cling always to the marvelous spectacle of life forcing one event out of the jaws of the preceding one and to reveal its elemental consistencies with surprise. In other words, I contrast his realism not with the lyrical, which I prize, but with sentimentality, which is always a leak in the dramatic dike. He sought to make a play as weighty and living a fact as the discovery of the steam engine or algebra. This can be scoffed away only at a price, and the price is a living drama.

Some 35 years after these words were written, Arthur Miller once again turned to the question of how one might assess Ibsen's influence today.

I am not scholar enough—or journalist either—to be able to say with any real certainty what Ibsen's influence is today. I have only impressions, which may or may not be accurate.

I don't believe that many of today's playwrights look to his methods as models, but his standing as a modern has nevertheless improved, I think, over the past thirty or forty years. When I began writing plays in the late thirties, he was a favorite of the Left for his radical politics and rebellious mind. His work, however, not often performed, was frequently regarded as quaintly methodical onion-peeling. If you had the patience to labor through it, an Ibsen play was more like argument in a legal case than an entertainment. Such was the prejudice and ignorance of the time, his most important lack was thought to be the poetic spirit; it was fashionable, as it still is in some places today, to call him more of a carpenter than the visionary architect that Shaw, among others, thought him to be. What the young avant-garde wanted in the thirties, positioned as ever against clunky Broadway realism, was the lyrical voice. Clifford Odets and Sean O'Casey specifically, were the more or less Marxist prophets while Saroyan, a premature or closet absurdist, sang basically for his supper. In the Broadway/West End mainstream Maxwell Anderson and Christopher Fry were trying to wring popular drama from unconventional word usage, reviving even Elizabethan iambics. These were very different writers but they were all attempting to sing the language on the stage, as Yeats had done for a more recondite audience and Eliot, too. All of these were self-conscious artists rather than stage shopsmiths, but they would all have no doubt thought that Ibsen's time had passed.

Ibsen's language, lyrical as it may sound in Scandinavia, does not sing in translation, although his ideas often do. Of course, they were only Ibsen's realistic social plays that were produced but these became his stamp, his mysticism having been more or less overlooked and his metaphysical side likewise. Probably his more social plays, like the genre itself, are fundamentally optimistic—demanding change, which is itself an upbeat notion and therefore easy to grasp, while his deepest personal thought is the opposite; symbolist, mythic, muffled in pessimism as it surveys the changeless sea, the sky, aging, cowardice, the classic brick walls against which philosophy has always broken its head.

It is the quasi-journalistic element therefore which came down to later generations, at least in America. He seemed to write about "issues," rather than circumstance. Especially in the Leftist tide of the thirties his stance was translated into an anti-capitalist militancy, but occasionally his apparent elitism seemed relevant to Fascism. For example, a small controversy developed over whether *An Enemy of the People* had a Fascistic tendency with its admittedly confusing claims for an elite of the intellect which must be trusted to lead ordinary folk. Nowadays the wheel has turned once more and probably something similar is happening now that political correctness is (again) in vogue. But *An Enemy of the People*, it seems to me, is really about Ibsen's belief that there is such a thing as a truth and that it bears something like holiness within it, regardless of the cost its discovery at any one moment entails. And the job of the elite is to guard and explain that holiness without compromise or stint.

For myself, I was deeply stirred by his indignation at the social lies of his time, but it was in his structures that I was thrilled to find his poetry. His plays were models of a stringent economy of means to create immense symphonic images of tragic proportions. It wasn't that things fit together but that *everything* fit together, like a natural organism, a human being, for example, or a rose. His works had an organic intensity making them, or most of them, undeniable. To me he was a reincarnation of the Greek dramatic spirit, especially its obsessive fascination with past transgressions as the seeds of current catastrophe. In this slow unfolding was wonder, even god. Past and present were drawn into a single continuity, and thus a secret moral order was being limned. He and the Greeks were related also through their powerful integrative impulse which, at least in theory, could make possible a total picture of a human being—character sprang from action, and like a spiritual CAT scan the drama could conceivably offer up a human being seen from within and without at the same. (In fact, my *Death of a Salesman* would proceed in that fashion.) Present dilemma was simply the face that the past had left visible. Every catastrophe was the story of how the birds came home to roost, and I still believe that a play without a past is a mere shadow of a play, just as a man or woman whose past is largely blank or ineptly drawn is merely a suggestion of a man or a woman, and a trivialization to boot.

I don't know what exactly has happened to the concept of the past in contemporary dramaturgy, but it is rarely there any more. Things happen, God knows why. Maybe we are just too tired of thinking, or maybe meaning itself has become an excrescence. But most likely it is that we have too often been wrong about what important things mean.

Perhaps it comes down to our loss of confidence in our ability to lay a finger on the inevitable in life; in the name of freedom and poetry it is now customary to declare, in effect, that our existence is itself a surprise and that surprise is the overwhelmingly central principle of life. Or maybe we are just surfeited with entertainment and prefer to lie back and let our brains enjoy a much needed rest.

The triumph of the past-less art is of course the film. A film persona requires no past or any other proof of his existence; he need only be photographed and he is palpably *there*.

The past keeps coming back to our art, however, if only in the parodistic form of the detective or crime story, probably our most popular fictional entertainment. The crime exists, or is about to happen, and we have to move backwards to find out whose general character fits the crime, who has dropped hints of his dire tendency, and so forth. It is the tragic event scrubbed clean of its visionary moral values, its sole job being the engendering of anxiety and fear. (Detective fiction also reassures us about the stability of our civilization, but that's another story.)

The so-called Absurd theater, in a different way, also helped make any obsession with the past seem quaint, and Ibsen with it. The proof of a character's existence was simply his awareness of his ironical situation, that was all and that was enough. Character itself, which surely must mean individuation, smacked of realism, and in its stead were interchangeable stickmen whose individuation lay in their varying attitudes and remarks about the determining force, the situation. Without a past the present, and its anxieties, was all that was left to talk about. And the situation of the stickman is of course so utterly overwhelming—war, or concentration camps, or economic disaster—that what individually he may have had, his will or lack of will, his self-doubt or assurance, his faith or cynicism is squashed out, leaving only the irony of humans continuing to exist at all.

So that the quality we instantly recognized as supremely human was not characterological definition, which requires a history, but its very absence; whatever his personality, it is without significance because it doesn't affect history—that is, his kindness, his dreams of a different kind of life, his love, his devotion to duty or to another human being simply do not matter as he is marched towards the flames. It may be the Holocaust clinched the case for reducing personality to a laughable affectation. I am inclined to believe this to be so, even for people who never think about the events in Eastern Europe directly. The Holocaust—the story of a great nation turned criminal on a vast scale—implicitly defeated us, broke confidence in our claims to being irrevocably in the camp of what was once securely called humanity, and left us with absurdity as the defining human essence.

Again, the concept of a gradually in-gathering, swelling, evidentiary, revelatory explosion is now reserved for thrillers, by and large; but instead of insights we have clues, mechanically dropped most of the time, to both lead us on and astray. We are given, if you will, the skeleton of the Ibsen form without the soul or the flesh.

The revolt—or rather the loss of interest in what is commonly thought of as Ibsenism—also imagines itself to be a revolt against the well-made play, quite as though Ibsen was not himself the first to attack that kind of play. Instead of being well-made his plays are true. That is the difference. They follow the psycho-moral dilemma, not the plot. But we have arrived at a point where, as indicated, the very notion of inevitability is itself highly suspect—in short, no one can know why great events happen, let alone why the shifts and changes in human attitudes take place. Under the rubric of a new freedom and a deeper wisdom we have turned against the rational, claiming the delightful license to simply express feeling and impressions, the more randomly the better to create surprise, the ultimate aesthetic value.

In short, Strindberg has won the philosophical battle with Ibsen and Ibsenism. The poet of instinct and the impromptu, of the paradoxical surprise, his mission is not to save anyone or a society, but simply to rip the habit of hypocrisy from the human heart and cant from the life of the mind. He is the destroying rebel chopping off the ever-growing heads of a thousand-armed dragon, a pessimistic labor to be sure. Ibsen, quite otherwise, is the revolutionary groping for a new system, an optimistic business, for when the old is destroyed, the new construct implies rational decisions, and above all hope.

And who can gainsay Strindberg any more? Apart from the Holocaust are we not witnesses to the implosion of the Soviet Union, the most "rationally" run society, falling in upon itself, a fraud and a farce? And what has survived but old, chaotic, irrational capitalism, blinding itself to its poor behind the glaring lights of its packed store windows, and hiding its spiritual starvation under the shiny bonnets of its marvellous cars? How to rationally account for *this* surprise— the victory of the decadent doomed and the disgrace of the historically "inevitable victors," the "new men" who stand revealed as medieval fief-holders when they were not actual gangsters and killers of the dream?

Compare this awesome moral chaos, this wracking collapse of the comfortably predictable, with Ibsen's methodical unravelling of motives and the interplay of social and psychological causation, all of it speaking of rational control! They cannot jibe, our reality and his. So he must seem outmoded, a picturesque mind out of a more orderly time.

Perhaps that is why he seems to be coming back, at least his prestige as a modern, if not precisely his methods. For while it is purely a sense of the new mood on my part, it does seem that the taste for "real plays" rather than only fun effusions has begun to stir again. Of course, there are still old-fashioned critics who think that anything that has a beginning and end is out of date, but there are young playwrights who would disagree and are looking to life rather than the theater for their inspiration, and life, of course, includes not only surprise but the consequences flowing from our actions or structure, in other words.

Perhaps I ought to add here that in these past dozen years my most Ibsen-influenced play, *All My Sons*, written nearly fifty years ago, is more and more frequently and more widely produced now and the reviewers no longer feel obliged to dismiss its structure as not-modern. I have had to wonder whether this is partly due to the number of investigations of official malfeasance in the papers all the time, and the spectacle of men of stature and social influence being brought down practically every week by revelations excavated from the hidden past. From the heights of Wall Street, the Pentagon, the White House, big business, the same lesson seems to fly out at us—the past lives! As does Ibsen, the master of the explosive force when it bombs in the present, and above all, with the soul-rot that comes of the hypocrisy of its denial.

Needless to say, I have not attempted in this short note to deal with Ibsen as poet and creator of mythic plays, beginning with the opening of his career. For one thing, those plays remain to be interpreted for modern audiences, their mythology having little obvious meaning for most people outside Scandinavia.

Appendix

Cast lists and production details are listed in this section for the following works:

The Man Who Had All the Luck (1944)
All My Sons (1947)
Death of a Salesman (1949)
An Enemy of the People (1950)
The Crucible (1953)
A View from the Bridge (one-act version, 1955)
A Memory of Two Mondays (1955)
A View from the Bridge (two-act version, 1956)
The Misfits (1961)
After the Fall (1964)
Incident at Vichy (1964)
The Price (1968)
The Creation of the World and Other Business (1972)
Up from Paradise (1974)
The Archbishop's Ceiling (1977)
Fame (1978)
Playing for Time (1980)
The American Clock (1980)
Elegy for a Lady (1982)
Some Kind of Love Story (1982)

Clara (1987)
I Can't Remember Anything (1987)
The Golden Years (1987)
Everybody Wins (1990)
The Last Yankee (one-scene version, 1991)
The Ride Down Mount Morgan (1991)
The Last Yankee (two-scene version, 1993)
Broken Glass (1994)

The Man Who Had All the Luck

A play in three acts with four scenes. Produced by Herbert H. Harris at the Forrest Theatre, New York, November 23, 1944. Staged by Joseph Fields; settings by Frederick Fox.

CAST (*in order of appearance*)

SHORY	Grover Burgess
J. B. FELLER	Forrest Orr
HESTER FALK	Eugenia Rawls
DAVID BEEVES	Karl Swenson
AUNT BELLE	Agnes Scott Yost
PATTERSON BEEVES	Jack Sheehan
AMOS BEEVES	Dudley Sadler
DAN DIBBLE	Sydney Grant
GUSTAV EBERSON	Herbert Berghof
HARRY BUCKS	James MacDonald
AUGIE BELFAST	Lawrence Fletcher

All My Sons

All My Sons was first presented by Elia Kazan, Harold Clurman, and Walter Fried (in association with Herbert Harris), at the Coronet Theatre on the evening of January 29, 1947, with the following cast:

JOE KELLER	Ed Begley
KATE KELLER	Beth Merrill
CHRIS KELLER	Arthur Kennedy
ANN DEEVER	Lois Wheeler
GEORGE DEEVER	Karl Malden
DR. JIM BAYLISS	John McGovern
SUE BAYLISS	Peggy Meredith
FRANK LUBEY	Dudley Sadler
LYDIA LUBEY	Hope Cameron
BERT	Eugene Steiner

The production was directed by Elia Kazan.
The setting was designed by Mordecai Gorelik.

Death of a Salesman

Staged by Elia Kazan

CAST (*in order of appearance*)

WILLY LOMAN	Lee J. Cobb
LINDA	Mildred Dunnock
BIFF	Arthur Kennedy
HAPPY	Cameron Mitchell
BERNARD	Don Keefer
THE WOMAN	Winnifred Cushing
CHARLEY	Howard Smith
UNCLE BEN	Thomas Chalmers
HOWARD WAGNER	Alan Hewitt
JENNY	Ann Driscoll
STANLEY	Tom Pedi
MISS FORSYTHE	Constance Ford
LETTA	Hope Cameron

The setting and lighting were designed by Jo Mielziner.
The incidental music was composed by Alex North.
The costumes were designed by Julia Sze.
Presented by Kermit Bloomgarden and Walter Fried at the
Morosco Theatre in New York on February 10, 1949.

An Enemy of the People

CAST *(in order of appearance)*

MORTEN KIIL	Art Smith
BILLING	Michael Strong
MRS. STOCKMANN	Florence Eldridge
PETER STOCKMANN	Morris Carnovsky
HOVSTAD	Martin Brooks
DR. STOCKMANN	Fredric March
MORTEN	Ralph Robertson
EJLIF	Richard Trask
CAPTAIN HORSTER	Ralph Dunn
PETRA	Anna Minot
ASLAKSEN	Fréd Stewart
THE DRUNK	Lou Gilbert
TOWNSPEOPLE	Lulla Adler, Barbara Ames, Paul Fitzpatrick, James Karen, Michael Lewin, Salem Ludwig, Gene Lyons, John Marley, Arnold Schulman, Robert Simon, Rod Steiger

Production directed by Robert Lewis.
Setting and costumes by Aline Bernstein.
Lighting by Charles Elson.
Presented by Lars Nordenson at the Broadhurst Theatre in New York on December 28, 1950.

The Crucible

Staged by Jed Harris

CAST (*in order of appearance*)

REVEREND PARRIS	Fred Stewart
BETTY PARRIS	Janet Alexander
TITUBA	Jacqueline Andre
ABIGAIL WILLIAMS	Madeleine Sherwood
SUSANNA WALCOTT	Barbara Stanton
MRS. ANN PUTNAM	Jane Hoffman
THOMAS PUTNAM	Raymond Bramley
MERCY LEWIS	Dorothy Joliffe
MARY WARREN	Jennie Egan
JOHN PROCTOR	Arthur Kennedy
REBECCA NURSE	Jean Adair
GILES COREY	Joseph Sweeney
REVEREND JOHN HALE	E. G. Marshall
ELIZABETH PROCTOR	Beatrice Straight
FRANCIS NURSE	Graham Velsey
EZEKIEL CHEEVER	Don McHenry
MARSHAL HERRICK	George Mitchell
JUDGE HATHORNE	Philip Coolidge
DEPUTY GOVERNOR DANFORTH	Walter Hampden
SARAH GOOD	Adele Fortin
HOPKINS	Donald Marye

The settings were designed by Boris Aronson.
The costumes were made and designed by Edith Lutyens.
Presented by Kermit Bloomgarden at the Martin Beck Theatre
in New York on January 22, 1953.

A View from the Bridge
(ONE-ACT VERSION)

Directed by Martin Ritt

CAST (*in order of appearance*)

LOUIS	David Clarke
MIKE	Tom Pedi
ALFIERI	J. Carrol Naish
EDDIE	Van Heflin
CATHERINE	Gloria Marlowe
BEATRICE	Eileen Heckart
MARCO	Jack Warden
TONY	Antony Vorno
RODOLPHO	Richard Davalos
FIRST IMMIGRATION OFFICER	Curt Conway
SECOND IMMIGRATION OFFICER	Ralph Bell
MR. LIPARI	Russell Collins
MRS. LIPARI	Anne Driscoll
TWO "SUBMARINES"	Leo Penn, Milton Carney

Production designed by Boris Aronson.
Costumes by Helene Pons.
Lighting by Leland Watson.
Presented by Kermit Bloomgarden and Whitehead-Stevens at the Coronet Theatre in New York on September 29, 1955.

A Memory of Two Mondays

Directed by Martin Ritt

CAST (*in order of appearance*)

BERT	Leo Penn
RAYMOND	David Clarke
AGNES	Eileen Heckart
PATRICIA	Gloria Marlowe
GUS	J. Carrol Naish
JIM	Russell Collins
KENNETH	Biff McGuire
LARRY	Van Heflin
FRANK	Jack Warden
JERRY	Richard Davalos
WILLIAM	Antony Vorno
TOM	Curt Conway
MECHANIC	Tom Pedi
MISTER EAGLE	Ralph Bell

Production designed by Boris Aronson.
Costumes by Helene Pons.
Lighting by Leland Watson.
Presented by Kermit Bloomgarden and Whitehead-Stevens at the Coronet Theatre in New York on September 29, 1955.

A View from the Bridge
(TWO-ACT VERSION)

Produced at the Comedy Theatre, London, England, on October 11, 1956. Directed and designed by Peter Brook.

CAST (*in order of appearance*)

LOUIS	Richard Harris
MIKE	Norman Mitchell
ALFIERI	Michael Gwynn
EDDIE	Anthony Quayle
CATHERINE	Mary Ure
BEATRICE	Megs Jenkins
MARCO	Ian Bannen
TONY	Ralph Nossek
RODOLPHO	Brian Bedford
FIRST IMMIGRATION OFFICER	John Stone
SECOND IMMIGRATION OFFICER	Colin Rix
MR. LIPARI	Mervyn Blake
MRS. LIPARI	Catherine Willmer
A "SUBMARINE"	Peter James

The Misfits

A John Huston Production presented by Seven Arts Productions and released by United Artists in New York in February in 1961. Screenplay by Arthur Miller. Produced by Frank E. Taylor and directed by John Huston.

CAST

GAY LANGLAND	Clark Gable
ROSLYN TABER	Marilyn Monroe
PERCE HOWLAND	Montgomery Clift
ISABELLE STEERS	Thelma Ritter
GUIDO	Eli Wallach
THE OLD MAN IN THE BAR	James Barton
THE CHURCH LADY	Estelle Winwood
RAYMOND TABER	Kevin McCarthy
YOUNG BOY IN BAR (LESTER)	Dennis Shaw
CHARLES STEERS	Philip Mitchell
OLD GROOM	Walter Ramage
FRESH COWBOY IN BAR	J. Lewis Smith
SUSAN	Marietta Tree
BARTENDER	Bobby La Salle
MAN IN BAR	Ryall Bowker
AMBULANCE ATTENDANT	Ralph Roberts

After the Fall

The play was directed by Elia Kazan and produced by Robert Whitehead for the Lincoln Center Repertory Company. It was first performed on January 23, 1964, at the ANTA–Washington Square Theatre, New York City.

THE CAST (*in order of appearance*)

QUENTIN	Jason Robards, Jr.
FELICE	Zohra Lampert
HOLGA	Salome Jens
DAN	Michael Strong
FATHER	Paul Mann
MOTHER	Virginia Kaye
NURSES	Faye Dunaway, Diane Shalet
MAGGIE	Barbara Loden
ELSIE	Patrica Roe
LOU	David J. Stewart
LOUISE	Mariclare Costello
MICKEY	Ralph Meeker
MAN IN PARK	Stanley Beck
CARRIE	Ruth Attaway
LUCAS	Harold Scott
CHAIRMAN	David Wayne
HARLEY BARNES	Hal Holbrook
PORTER	Jack Waltzer
MAGGIE'S SECRETARY	Crystal Field
PIANIST	Scott Cunningham
OTHERS	Clint Kimbrough, John Phillip Law, Barry Primus, James Greene

Incident at Vichy

The play was staged by Harold Clurman for the Repertory Theatre of Lincoln Center for the Performing Arts. It was first performed on December 3, 1964, at the ANTA–Washington Square Theatre, New York City.

THE CAST (*in order of speaking*)

LEBEAU	Michael Strong
BAYARD	Stanley Beck
MARCHAND	Paul Mann
POLICE GUARD	C. Thomas Blackwell
MONCEAU	David J. Stewart
GYPSY	Harold Scott
WAITER	Jack Waltzer
BOY	Ira Lewis
MAJOR	Hal Holbrook
FIRST DETECTIVE	Alek Primose
OLD JEW	Will Lee
SECOND DETECTIVE	James Dukas
LEDUC	Joseph Wiseman
POLICE CAPTAIN	James Greene
VON BERG	David Wayne
PROFESSOR HOFFMAN	Clinton Kimbrough
FERRAND	Graham Jarvis
PRISONERS	Pierre Epstein, Stephen Peters, Tony Lo Bianco, John Vari

The Price

The play was directed by Ulu Grosbard and produced by Robert
Whitehead. It opened on February 7, 1968, at the Morosco Theatre,
New York City.

THE CAST (*in order of appearance*)

VICTOR FRANZ	Pat Hingle
ESTHER FRANZ	Kate Reid
GREGORY SOLOMON	Harold Gary
WALTER FRANZ	Arthur Kennedy

Setting and costumes designed by Boris Aronson. Lighting
by Paul Morrison.

The Creation of the World and Other Business

The play was directed by Gerald Freedman and presented by Robert Whitehead on November 30, 1972, at the Shubert Theatre in New York. Settings by Boris Aronson; lighting by Tharon Musser; costumes by Hal George; music by Stanley Silverman.

CAST (*in order of appearance*)

ADAM	Bob Dishy
GOD	Stephen Elliott
EVE	Zoe Caldwell
CHEMUEL, THE ANGEL OF MERCY	Lou Gilbert
RAPHAEL, AN ANGEL	Dennis Cooley
AZRAEL, THE ANGEL OF DEATH	Lou Polan
LUCIFER	George Grizzard
CAIN	Barry Primus
ABEL	Mark Lamos

Up From Paradise*
(A THEATER PIECE SPOKEN AND SUNG)

Presented by The University of Michigan Theatre Programs at the Power Center for the Performing Arts, Ann Arbor, Michigan, on April 23, 1974. Book, lyrics, and direction by Arthur Miller; music by Stanley Silverman; settings by Alan Billings; costumes by Zelma Weisfeld; lighting by R. Craig Wolf.

CAST (*in order of appearance*)

NARRATOR	Arthur Miller
GOD	Bob Bingham
ADAM	Allan Nicholls
EVE	Kimberly Farr
LUCIFER	Larry Marshall
CAIN	Seth Allen
ABEL	Dennis Cooley

* A musical version of *The Creation of the World and Other Business.*

The Archbishop's Ceiling

The play was directed by Arvin Brown and produced by Robert Whitehead, Roger L. Stevens, and Konrad Matthaei on April 30, 1977, at the Eisenhower Theater, John F. Kennedy Center for the Performing Arts, Washington, D.C. Scenery by David Jenkins; costumes by Bill Walker; lighting by Ron Wallace.

CAST (*in order of appearance*)

ADRIAN	Tony Musante
SIGMUND	John Cullum
MAYA	Bibi Andersson
MARTIN	Josef Sommer
MARCUS	Douglas Watson
IRENA	Bara-Cristen Hansen

Fame

Written for television, *Fame* was presented on NBC on November 30, 1978.

CAST

MEYER SHINE	Richard Benjamin
FRANCESCO	José Ferrer
VINNY	Nipsy Russell
LUCIA	Shera Danese
MONA	Linda Hunt

The cast also included Raf Vallone, Robert Alda, Oliver Clark, Joe Bennett, Richard Libertini, and Tom Poston.

Playing for Time

An adaptation of Fania Fenelon's memoirs, Arthur Miller's screenplay *Playing for Time* was written for television and was first presented on CBS on September 30, 1980. Linda Yellen produced it for Syzygy Productions. Original music and synthesized sounds by Brad Fiedel.

CAST

FANIA FENELON	Vanessa Redgrave
ALMA ROSE	Jane Alexander
MARIANNE	Melanie Mayron
ELZVIETA	Marisa Berenson
LAGERFUHRERIN MANDEL	Shirley Knight
TCHAIKOWSKA	Elaine Bromka
LIESIE	Faith Catlin
COMMANDANT KRAMER	Clarence Felden
WOMAN ON TRAIN	Martha Schlamm
ESTHER	Marta Heflin
BERTA	Dorothy Sherwood
GRETA	Grace Stover
ASTHMATIC MAN	Sidney Sandness
BOY SCOUT	Thomas LaFleur
FIRST CHESSPLAYER	Svee Scooler
SECOND CHESSPLAYER	Thomas Everett
POLISH WOMAN	Mary Fay Fager
TATTOOER	Mary McGonical
BLOCKAWA	Phyllis Vanier
CANADA GIRL	Monica Merriman

LADISIAUS	Rovert Lucey
LADISIAUS' MOTHER	Lorraine Lucey
EDEK	Lee Jay Nelson
SS OFFICER	Robert Dannon
BRITISH RADIO MAN	Peter Phillips
SS SARGEANT	Spencer Waldron
GERMAN TROOPER	John Griesemer
EXECUTIONER	Huggy-Bear Fervis

The cast also included Maud Adams, Christine Baranski, Robin Bartlett, Verna Bloom, Donna Haley, Lenore Harris, Mady Kaplan, Will Lee, Anna Kluger Levine, Viveca Lindfors, Marcell Rosenblatt, and Max Wright.

The American Clock

A Harold Clurman Theater production presented by Jack Garfein, Warner Theater Productions, Inc., and Herbert Wasserman, *The American Clock* opened at the Spoleto Festival's Dockside Theater in Charleston, South Carolina on May 24, 1980, directed by Dan Sullivan. Under the direction of Vivian Matalon the play opened at the Biltmore Theatre in New York City on November 20, 1980. Karl Eigsti designed the scenery, Neil Peter Jampolis designed the lighting, Robert Wojewodski created the costumes, Charles LoPresto did the hairstyles, and Robert Dennis provided the incidental music.

CAST (*in order of appearance*)

LEE BAUM	William Atherton
MOE BAUM	John Randolph
CLARENCE, WAITER, ISAAC, JEROME, PIANO MOVER	Donny Burks
ROSE BAUM	Joan Copeland
FRANK, LIVERMORE, MAN IN WELFARE OFFICE, STANISLAUS	
	Ralph Drischell
GRANDPA, KAPUSH	Salem Ludwig
FANNY MARGOLIES, MYRNA	Francine Beers
CLAYTON, SIDNEY MARGOLIES, RALPH	Robert Harper
DURANT, SHERIFF, PIANO MOVER, TOLAND	Alan North
TONY, TAYLOR, DUGAN	Edward Seamon
WAITER, BICYCLE THIEF, RUDY, PIANO MOVER, RYAN	
	Bill Smitrovich
JOE, BUSH	David Chandler
DORIS, ISABEL, GRACE	Marilyn Caskey
IRENE	Rosanna Carter
JEANETTE RAMSEY, EDIE, LUCILLE, ATTENDANT	Susan Sharkey

Elegy for a Lady

On a twin bill with *Some Kind of Love Story, Elegy for a Lady* opened at the Long Wharf Theater in New Haven, Connecticut on October 26, 1982 under the title *2 by A.M.* The playwright also directed the production. Stanley Silverman provided original music. Hugh Landwehr designed the set, Bill Walker created the costumes, and Ronald Wallace designed the lighting.

CAST (*in order of appearance*)

MAN   Charles Cioffi
PROPRIETRESS   Christine Lahti

Some Kind of Love Story

On a twin bill with *Elegy for a Lady*, *Some Kind of Love Story* was presented at the Long Wharf Theater in New Haven, Connecticut from October 26, 1982 to December 5, 1982 under the title *2 by A.M.* The playwright directed the production, Hugh Landwehr designed the set, Bill Walker created the costumes, Ronald Wallace designed the lighting, and Stanley Silverman provided original music.

CAST (*in order of appearance*)

ANGELA   Christine Lahti
TOM   Charles Cioffi

Clara

In tandem with *I Can't Remember Anything*, *Clara* was staged as part of a double-bill entitled *Danger: Memory!* at the Mitzi E. Newhouse Theater, Lincoln Center, in New York City on February 8, 1987. Presented by the Lincoln Center Theater, *Clara* was directed by Gregory Mosher with Bernard Gersten as the executive producer. Michael Merritt designed sets, Nan Cibula created costumes, and Kevin Rigdon provided the lighting design.

CAST (*in order of appearance*)

ALBERT KROLL	Kenneth McMillan
DETECTIVE LIEUTENANT FINE	James Tolkan
TIERNEY	Victor Argo
CLARA	Karron Graves

I Can't Remember Anything

In tandem with *Clara*, *I Can't Remember Anything* was staged as part of a double-bill entitled *Danger: Memory!* at the Mitzi E. Newhouse Theater, Lincoln Center, in New York City on February 8, 1987. Presented by the Lincoln Center Theater, *I Can't Remember Anything* was directed by Gregory Mosher with Bernard Gersten as the executive producer. Michael Merritt designed sets, Nan Cibula created costumes, and Kevin Rigdon provided the lighting design.

CAST *(in order of appearance)*

LEO	Mason Adams
LEONORA	Geraldine Fitzgerald

The Golden Years

Directed by Martin Jenkins, *The Golden Years* received its world premiere on BBC Radio on November 6, 1987.

CAST

MONTEZUMA	Ronald Pickup
GUATEMOTZIN (*his nephew*)	Kim Wall
CUITLAHUA (*his brother*)	John Samson
CAGAMA (*Lord in Council*)	Brian Hewlett
TECUICHPO (*the King's daughter*)	Victoria Carling
PARACH (*the High Priest*)	Hugh Dickson
TALUA (*the history boy*)	Stephen Rashbrook
TAPAIA	Tim Reynolds
QUAUHOPOCA, JUDGE	Norman Jones
AN ASTROLOGER	David Timson
SACRIFICIAL BOY	Stephen Tompkinson
COURIER	Paul Sirr
HERNANDO CORTÉS	John Shrapnel
DONNA MARINA	Hannah Gordon
PEDRO DE ALVARADO	John Hollis
VELASQUEZ DE LEON	Paul Sirr
FRANCISCO DE MONTEJO	Paul Gregory
CRISTOBAL DE OLID	Michael Deacon
DIEGO DE ORDAZ (*older*)	John Bott
KING XICOTENGA	David Timson
ARBENGA	Steven Harrold
FR. OLMEDO	Norman Bird
MESA	Steven Thompkinson
PANFILO NARVAEZ	John Samson

Everybody Wins

A Jeremy Thomas production, *Everybody Wins* was released by Orion Pictures in February 1990. Karel Reisz directed Miller's screenplay with music by Mark Isham and Leon Redbone.

CAST

ANGELA CRISPINI	Debra Winger
TOM O'TOOLE	Nick Nolte
JERRY	Will Patton
CONNIE	Judith Ivey
AMY	Kathleen Wilhoite
JUDGE HARRY MURDOCH	Jack Warden
CHARLEY HAGGERTY	Frank Converse
FELIX	Frank Military
FATHER MANCINI	Steven Skybell
JEAN	Mary Louise Wilson
BELLANCA	Mert Hatfield
SONNY	Peter Appel
MONTANA	Sean Weil
DEFENSE ATTORNEY	Timothy D. Wright
JUDGE	Elizabeth Ann Klein
REPORTER	James Parisi
DRIVER	R. M. Haley
JUDGE #2	T. M. Nelson George
STUNT COORDINATOR	David Ellis
UTILITY STUNT	Tim Davison
UTILITY STUNT	Don Pulford
UTILITY STUNT	Richard Allison

The Last Yankee

The Last Yankee was originally performed as a one-scene play in June 1991. Presented by the Ensemble Studio Theater in New York City as part of the Marathon Annual Festival of New One-Act Plays, *The Last Yankee* was first directed by Gordon Edelstein.

CAST (*in order of appearance*)

LEROY HAMILTON   John Heard
JOHN FRICK   Biff McGuire

The Ride Down Mount Morgan

The Ride Down Mount Morgan was given its world premiere on October 11, 1991 at Wyndham's Theatre in London. Michael Blakemore directed and Robert Fox produced. Tanya McCallin created the set, Stephen Watson designed the lighting, Paul Arditti designed the sound, and Barrington Pheloung composed the music.

CAST (*in order of appearance*)

LYMAN FELT	Tom Conti
NURSE HOGAN	Marsha Hunt
THE FATHER	Harry Landis
THEO FELT	Gemma Jones
BESSIE	Deirdre Strath
LEAH FELT	Clare Higgins
TOM WILSON	Manning Redwood
HOSPITAL PORTER	Colin Stepney

The Last Yankee

Given its world premiere as a two-scene play at the Manhattan Theater Club in New York City on January 21, 1993, *The Last Yankee* was directed by John Tillinger. John Lee Beatty designed the set, Jane Greewood created the costumes, Dennis Parichy provided the lighting design, and Scott Lehrer created the sound.

CAST (*in order of appearance*)

LEROY HAMILTON	John Heard
JOHN FRICK	Tom Alredge
UNNAMED PATIENT	Charlotte Maier
PATRICIA HAMILTON	Frances Conroy
KAREN FRICK	Rose Gregorio

Broken Glass

Broken Glass was first produced at the Long Wharf Theater in New Haven, Connecticut in March 1994. Directed by John Tillinger, the play opened at the Booth Theater in New York City on April 24, 1994. *Broken Glass* was produced by Robert Whitehead, Roger L. Stevens, Lars Schmidt, Spring Sirkin, Terri Childs, Timothy Childs, and Herb Albert. Santo Loquasto designed the set and costumes, Brian Nason designed the lighting, T. Richard Fitzgerald provided the sound, and William Bolcom composed the music.

CAST (*in order of appearance*)

PHILLIP GELLBURG	Ron Rifkin
MARGARET HYMAN	Frances Conroy
DR. HARRY HYMAN	David Dukes
SYLVIA GELLBURG	Amy Irving
HARRIET	Lauren Klein
STANTON CASE	George N. Martin

Bibliography
of Works (1936–1996)
by Arthur Miller

All entries are listed chronologically by genre. With a few exceptions this listing includes first production and publication appearances only.

I. Plays (year of first major production is given in parentheses)

No Villain (unpublished; 1936, The University of Michigan), 1936. Microfilm copy in the Rare Book Room, Harlan Hatcher Library, The University of Michigan. The original manuscript has been retained by the Hopwood Room, 1006 Angell Hall.

They Too Arise (unpublished revision of *No Villain;* 1937, Lydia Mendelssohn Theater), 1936. Manuscript in the Billy Rose Theater Collection, New York Public Library.

Honors at Dawn (unpublished and unproduced), 1937. Microfilm copy in the Rare Book Room, Harlan Hatcher Library, The University of Michigan. The original manuscript has been retained by the Hopwood Room.

The Great Disobedience (unpublished; 1938, The University of Michigan), 1938. Manuscript in the Rare Book Room, Harlan Hatcher Library, The University of Michigan.

The Grass Still Grows (unpublished and unproduced revision of *They Too Arise*), 1939. Manuscripts in the Harry Ransom Humanities Research Center Manuscript Collection, Academic Center Building,

The University of Texas at Austin; and in the Rare Book Room, Harlan Hatcher Library, The University of Michigan. (First revised in 1938.)

Listen My Children (unpublished and unproduced), written with Norman Rosten, 1939. Manuscript in the Library of Congress.

The Golden Years (1987, BBC Radio), 1939–40. Published in the collection entitled The Golden Years *and* The Man Who Had All the Luck. London: Methuen, 1989. Manuscript in the Harry Ransom Humanities Research Center Manuscript Collection, Academic Center Building, The University of Texas at Austin.

The Half-Bridge (unpublished and unproduced), 1941–43. Manuscript in the Harry Ransom Humanities Research Center Manuscript Collection, Academic Center Building, The University of Texas at Austin.

That They May Win (1943). In *The Best One-Act Plays of 1944*, ed. Margaret Mayorga. New York: Dodd, Mead, 1945, pp. 45–60.

The Man Who Had All the Luck (1944, Forrest Theater). In *Cross-Section*, ed. Edwin Seaver. New York: L. B. Fischer, 1944, pp. 486–552. (1989 revision is published in the collection entitled The Golden Years *and* The Man Who Had All the Luck. London: Methuen, 1989.) The pre-Broadway preview of the original version of *The Man Who Had All the Luck* occurred in Wilmington, Delaware in 1944.

All My Sons (1947, Coronet Theater). New York: Reynal and Hitchcock, 1947. Also in *Arthur Miller's Collected Plays*, Volume 1. New York: Viking, 1957, pp. 57–127. The pre-Broadway preview of *All My Sons* took place at the Colonial Theater in Boston in 1947.

Death of a Salesman (1949, Morosco Theater). New York: Viking, 1949. Also in *Arthur Miller's Collected Plays*, Volume 1. New York: Viking, 1957, pp. 129–222. The pre-Broadway preview of *Death of a Salesman* took place at the Locust Street Theater in Philadelphia in 1949.

An Enemy of the People (1950, Broadhurst Theater). New York: Viking, 1951. Miller's adaptation of Henrik Ibsen's play.

The Crucible (1953, Martin Beck Theater). New York: Viking, 1953. Also in *Arthur Miller's Collected Plays*, Volume 1. New York: Viking, 1957, pp. 223–330. The pre-Broadway preview of *The Crucible* occurred in Wilmington, Delaware in 1953.

A Memory of Two Mondays (1955, Coronet Theater). Published in *A View from the Bridge: Two One-Act Plays by Arthur Miller*. New York: Viking, 1955. *A Memory of Two Mondays* is also in *Arthur Miller's Collected Plays*, Volume 1. New York: Viking, 1957, pp. 331–76.

A View from the Bridge (1955, Coronet Theater). Published in *A View from the Bridge: Two One-Act Plays by Arthur Miller*. New York: Viking, 1955.

A View from the Bridge (1956, London's Comedy Theatre, revised two-act version). New York: Dramatists Play Service, 1957. Published with Miller's new introduction to the two-act version in a paperback edition of *A View from the Bridge*. New York: Compass, 1960. The two-act version also appears in *Arthur Miller's Collected Plays*, Volume 1. New York: Viking, 1957, pp. 377–439.

Arthur Miller's Collected Plays (with an introduction), Volume 1. New York: Viking, 1957. Contains *All My Sons, Death of a Salesman, The Crucible, A Memory of Two Mondays*, and *A View from the Bridge* (two-act version).

After the Fall (1964, ANTA-Washington Square Theater, Lincoln Center). New York: Viking, 1964. *After the Fall* is also in *Arthur Miller's Collected Plays*, Volume 2. New York: Viking, 1981, pp. 125–242.

Incident at Vichy (1964, ANTA-Washington Square Theater, Lincoln Center). New York: Viking, 1965. Also appears in *Arthur Miller's Collected Plays*, Volume 2. New York: Viking, 1981, pp. 243–91.

The Price (1968, Morosco Theater). New York: Viking, 1968. *The Price* is also in *Arthur Miller's Collected Plays*, Volume 2. New York: Viking, 1981, pp. 293–373. The pre-Broadway preview of *The Price* took place in Philadelphia in 1968.

Fame (unpublished; 1970, The New Theater Workshop), one-act play in a double-bill with *The Reason Why*.

The Reason Why (unpublished; 1970, The New Theater Workshop), one-act play in a double-bill with *Fame*.

The Portable Arthur Miller, ed. Harold Clurman. New York: Viking, 1971. Includes *Death of a Salesman, The Crucible, Incident at Vichy*, and *The Price*. (Revised in 1995.)

The Creation of the World and Other Business (1972, Shubert Theater). New York: Viking, 1973. Also appears in *Arthur Miller's Collected*

Plays, Volume 2. New York: Viking, 1981, pp. 373–446. The pre-Broadway preview of *The Creation of the World and Other Business* took place at the Eisenhower Theater in the Kennedy Center in Washington, D.C. in 1972.

Up from Paradise (1974, The Power Center for the Performing Arts, Ann Arbor). New York: Samuel French, Inc., 1984.

The Archbishop's Ceiling (1977, Eisenhower Theater in the Kennedy Center). London: Methuen, 1984. Appears in The American Clock *and* The Archbishop's Ceiling: *Two Plays*. New York: Grove, 1989. Also included in *Plays: Three*. London: Methuen, 1990, pp. 87–176.

Fame (unpublished; 1978, NBC, revised two-act version).

Playing for Time (1980, CBS). New York: Bantam, 1981. Also appears in *Arthur Miller's Collected Plays*, Volume 2. New York: Viking, 1981, pp. 447–531. A two-act version of *Playing for Time* was first staged in 1985 at the Studio Theater, and the acting edition was published the same year in Chicago by the Dramatic Publishing Company.

The American Clock (1980, Biltmore Theater). New York: Dramatists Plays Service, 1982. Appears in The American Clock *and* The Archbishop's Ceiling: *Two Plays*. New York: Grove, 1989. Also included in *Plays: Three*. London: Methuen, 1990, pp. 1–86. *The American Clock* previewed at the Harold Clurman Theater before opening at the Spoleto Festival's Dockside Theater on May 24, 1980. After a short Broadway run in November 1980, it was revised and successfully produced at London's Cottesloe Theater in 1986.

Arthur Miller's Collected Plays (with an introduction), Volume 2. New York: Viking, 1981. Contains *The Misfits, After the Fall, Incident at Vichy, The Price, The Creation of the World and Other Business*, and *Playing for Time*.

Elegy for a Lady (1982, Long Wharf Theater), one-act play in a double-bill with *Some Kind of Love Story*. New York: Dramatists Play Service, 1982. Also appears in the collection entitled *Two-Way Mirror*. London: Methuen, 1984. Included in *Plays: Three*. London: Methuen, 1990, pp. 187–207.

Some Kind of Love Story (1982, Long Wharf Theater), one-act play in a double-bill with *Elegy for a Lady*. New York: Dramatists Play Service, 1983. Also appears in the collection entitled *Two-Way Mirror*.

London: Methuen, 1984. Included in *Plays: Three*. London: Methuen, 1990, pp. 209–251.

I Can't Remember Anything (1987, Mitzi E. Newhouse Theater, Lincoln Center), one-act play in a double-bill with *Clara*. Published in the collection entitled *Danger: Memory!*. New York: Grove, 1986.

Clara (1987, Mitzi E. Newhouse Theater, Lincoln Center), one-act play in a double-bill with *I Can't Remember Anything*. Published in the collection entitled *Danger: Memory!*. New York: Grove, 1986.

Plays: One. London: Methuen, 1988. This volume contains the famous 1957 introduction to *Arthur Miller's Collected Plays*, Volume 1, *All My Sons, Death of a Salesman, The Crucible, A Memory of Two Mondays*, and *A View from the Bridge* (two-act version).

Plays: Two. London: Methuen, 1988. This volume contains *The Misfits, After the Fall, Incident at Vichy, The Price, The Creation of the World and Other Business*, and *Playing for Time*.

Plays: Three. London: Methuen, 1990. This volume contains *The American Clock, The Archbishop's Ceiling, Elegy for a Lady*, and *Some Kind of Love Story*.

I Think about You a Great Deal (monologue). *Literary Cavalcade*, September 1990, pp. 24–25. First published in 1986 in *Vaclav Havel: Living in Truth*.

The Last Yankee (1991, Ensemble Studio Theater), one-scene version. New York: Dramatists Play Service, 1991.

The Ride Down Mount Morgan (1991, London's Wyndham's Theatre). London: Methuen, 1991. Also published in New York: Penguin, 1992.

The Last Yankee (1993, Manhattan Theater Club), two-scene version. London: Methuen, 1993. Also published in New York: Penguin, 1994.

Broken Glass (1994, Booth Theater). New York: Penguin, 1994. The pre-Broadway preview of *Broken Glass* took place at the Long Wharf Theater in New Haven in 1994.

The Portable Arthur Miller, ed. Christopher Bigsby. New York: Penguin, 1995. Includes *Death of a Salesman, The Crucible, After the Fall, The*

American Clock, The Last Yankee, Broken Glass, and an excerpt from *The Golden Years.*

II. Radio Plays

Grateful acknowledgement is made to Gerald Weales and Margaret Lynch for compiling information about the original performance dates of Miller's unpublished radio plays.

The Pussycat and the Expert Plumber Who Was a Man. In *One Hundred Non-Royalty Radio Plays,* ed. William Kozlenko. New York: Greenburg, 1941, pp. 20–30.

William Ireland's Confession. In Kozlenko's *One Hundred Non-Royalty Radio Plays,* pp. 512–21.

Joel Chandler Harris (unpublished radio play), June 23, 1941. Manuscript in the Library for Performing Arts, Lincoln Center.

Captain Paul (unpublished radio play), October 27, 1941. Manuscript in the Library for Performing Arts, Lincoln Center.

The Battle of the Ovens (unpublished radio play), June 22, 1942. Manuscript in the Library for Performing Arts, Lincoln Center.

Thunder from the Mountains (unpublished radio play), September 28, 1942. Manuscript in the Museum of Television and Radio in New York.

I Was Married in Bataan (unpublished radio play), October 5, 1942. Manuscript in the Library for Performing Arts, Lincoln Center.

Toward a Farther Star (unpublished radio play), November 2, 1942. Manuscript in the Library for Performing Arts, Lincoln Center.

The Eagle's Nest (unpublished radio play), December 28, 1942. Manuscript in the Library for Performing Arts, Lincoln Center.

The Four Freedoms (unpublished radio play), 1942. Manuscript in the Library of Congress.

Listen for the Sound of Wings (unpublished radio play), April 19, 1943. Manuscript in the Museum of Television and Radio in New York.

The Story of Canine Joe (unpublished radio play), August 21, 1944. Manuscript in the Library for Performing Arts, Lincoln Center.

Bernadine, I Love You (unpublished radio play), March 5, 1945. Manuscript in the Library for Performing Arts, Lincoln Center.

Grandpa and the Statue, March 26, 1945. In *Radio Drama in Action*, ed. Erik Barnouw. New York: Farrar and Rinehart, 1945, pp. 265–81.

The Philippines Never Surrendered (unpublished radio play), April 30, 1945. Manuscript in the Library for Performing Arts, Lincoln Center.

The Story of Gus. In *Radio's Best Plays*, ed. Joseph Liss. New York: Greenburg, 1947, pp. 303–19.

The Guardsman (by Ferenc Molnar; adaptation by Miller), September 30, 1945. In *Theatre Guild on the Air*, ed. H. William Fitelson. New York: Rinehart, 1947, pp. 69–97.

Pride and Prejudice (by Jane Austen; adaptation by Miller), November 30, 1945. Catalogued in the *Cavalcade of America* program log in the Library for Performing Arts, Lincoln Center.

Three Men on a Horse (by George Abbott and John C. Holm; adaptation by Miller), January 6, 1946. In Fitelson's *Theatre Guild on the Air*, pp. 207–38.

III. Autobiography

Timebends: A Life. New York: Grove Press, 1987.

IV. Books of Reportage

Situation Normal. New York: Reynal and Hitchcock, 1944.

In Russia (with Inge Morath). New York: Viking, 1969. An excerpt appears in *The Portable Arthur Miller,* ed. Harold Clurman. New York: Viking, 1971.

In the Country (with Inge Morath). New York: Viking, 1977.

Chinese Encounters (with Inge Morath). New York: Farrar, Straus & Giroux, 1979.

Salesman in Beijing. New York: Viking, 1984.

V. Fiction and Screenplays

The Man Who Had All the Luck (unpublished novel).

Focus (a novel). New York: Reynal & Hitchcock, 1945.

"The Plaster Masks." *Encore*, 9 (April 1946), pp. 424–32.

"It Takes a Thief." *Collier's*, 119 (February 8, 1947), pp. 23, 75–76.

"Monte Saint Angelo." Harper's, 202 (March 1951), pp. 39–47. Reprinted as "Monte Sant' Angelo" in *I Don't Need You Any More* (short story collection). New York: Viking, 1967.

The Hook (unpublished screenplay), 1951. Manuscript in the Harry Ransom Humanities Research Center Manuscript Collection, Academic Center Building, The University of Texas at Austin.

"The Misfits." *Esquire*, 48 (October 1957), pp. 158–66. Reprinted in *I Don't Need You Any More* (short story collection). New York: Viking, 1967. Also appears in *The Portable Arthur Miller,* ed. Harold Clurman. New York: Viking, 1971.

Bridge to a Savage World (unfinished screenplay). *Esquire*, 50 (October 1958), pp. 185–90.

"I Don't Need You Any More." *Esquire*, 52 (December 1959), pp. 270–309. Reprinted in *I Don't Need You Any More* (short story collection). New York: Viking, 1967.

"Please Don't Kill Anything." *The Noble Savage*, No. 1 (March 1960), pp. 126–31. Reprinted in *Redbook*, 117 (October 1961), pp. 48–49, and in *I Don't Need You Any More* (short story collection). New York: Viking, 1967.

The Misfits (a screenplay-novel). New York: Viking, 1961. Also appears in *Arthur Miller's Collected Plays*, Volume 2. New York: Viking, 1981, pp. 3–124. An excerpt appears in *The Portable Arthur Miller,* ed. Harold Clurman. New York: Viking, 1971.

"The Prophecy." *Esquire*, 56 (December 1961), pp. 140, 268–87. Reprinted in I *Don't Need You Any More* (short story collection). New York: Viking, 1967.

"Glimpse at a Jockey." *The Noble Savage*, No. 5 (October 1962), pp. 138–40. Reprinted in *I Don't Need You Any More* (short story collection). New York: Viking, 1967.

Jane's Blanket (a children's book). New York: Collier-Macmillan, 1963.

"The Recognitions." *Esquire*, 66 (July 1966), pp. 76, 118. Retitled as "Fame" in *I Don't Need You Any More* (short story collection). New York: Viking, 1967.

"Search for a Future." *The Saturday Evening Post*, 239 (August 13, 1966), pp. 64, 66–68, 70. Reprinted as "A Search for a Future" in *I Don't Need You Any More*. New York: Viking, 1967.

I Don't Need You Any More (short story collection). New York: Viking, 1967. Contains "Foreword: About Distances" by Miller; "I Don't Need You Any More"; "Monte Sant' Angelo"; "Please Don't Kill Anything"; "The Misfits"; "Glimpse at a Jockey"; "The Prophecy"; "Fame" (originally titled "The Recognitions"); "Fitter's Night" (previously unpublished); and "A Search for a Future."

"Kidnapped?" *The Saturday Evening Post*, 242 (January 25, 1969), pp. 40–42, 78–82.

"Lines from California" (a poem). *Harper's*, 238 (May 1969), p. 97. Also appears in *The Portable Arthur Miller*, ed. Harold Clurman. New York: Viking, 1971.

The Portable Arthur Miller, ed. Harold Clurman. New York: Viking, 1971. Includes the short story "The Misfits"; an excerpt from the cinema-novel, *The Misfits*; the short story "Fame"; "Fitter's Night"; an excerpt from *In Russia*; and the poem "Lines from California." (Revised in 1995.)

"Rain in a Strange City." *Travel & Leisure*, 4 (September 1974), p. 8.

"Ham Sandwich." *Boston University Journal*, 24, No. 2 (1976), pp. 5–6.

"The Poosidin's Resignation" (a play fragment). *Boston University Journal*, 24, No. 2 (1976), pp. 7–13. Includes a brief note by Miller on the political overtones of the fragment, and his feelings while writing it.

"White Puppies." *Esquire*, 90 (July 1978), pp. 32–36.

"1928 Buick." *Atlantic*, 242 (October 1978), pp. 49–51.

"The Misfits" and Other Stories. New York: Charles Scribner's Sons, 1987. Retitled publication of the collection of stories originally released as *I Don't Need You Any More*. New York: Viking, 1967.

"Bees." *Michigan Quarterly Review*, 29 (Spring 1990), pp. 153–57.

Everybody Wins (a screenplay). New York: Grove Weidenfeld, 1990. (Revised and expanded film version of the one-act play *Some Kind of Love Story*.)

Homely Girl (a novella). Illustrated by Louis Bourgeois. Two-volume set. New York: Peter Blum, 1992. Reprinted in the collection titled *Homely Girl, A Life*. New York: Viking, 1995. The Viking edition also includes the short stories "Fame" and "Fitter's Night."

VI. Articles and Essays

Autobiographical statement (untitled). In *Cross-Section,* ed. Edwin Seaver. New York: L. B. Fischer, 1944, p. 556.

"Their First Look at Live Bullets." *Science Digest*, 17 (April 1945), pp. 73–76. An excerpt from *Situation Normal*.

"Should Ezra Pound Be Shot?" *New Masses*, December 25, 1945, p. 6.

"Subsidized Theatre." *The New York Times*, June 22, 1947, Sec. 2, p. 1.

"Tragedy and the Common Man." *The New York Times*, February 27, 1949, Sec. 2, p. 1.

"Arthur Miller on 'The Nature of Tragedy.'" *The New York Herald Tribune*, March 27, 1949, Sec. 5, pp. 1, 2.

"The *Salesman* Has a Birthday." *The New York Times,* February 5, 1950, Sec. 2, pp. 1, 3.

"Ibsen's Message for Today's World." *The New York Times*, December 24, 1950, Sec. 2, pp. 3, 4.

"An American Reaction." *World Theatre*, 1 (1951), pp. 21–22.

"Preface" to adaptation of Henrik Ibsen's *An Enemy of the People*. New York: Viking, 1951, pp. 7–12.

"Many Writers: Few Plays." *The New York Times,* August 10, 1952, Sec. 2, p. 1.

"Journey to *The Crucible*." *The New York Times*, February 8, 1953, Sec. 2, p. 3.

"University of Michigan." *Holiday*, 14 (December 1953), pp. 68–71, 128–34, 136–37, 140–43.

"A Modest Proposal for Pacification of the Public Temper." *The Nation*, 179 (July 3, 1954), pp. 5–8.

"The American Theatre." *Holiday*, 17 (January 1955), pp. 90–98, 101–02, 104.

"A Boy Grew in Brooklyn." *Holiday*, 17 (March 1955), pp. 54–55, 117, 119–20, 122–24.

"Picking a Cast." *The New York Times*, August 21, 1955, Sec. 2, p. 1.

Short Reply (untitled) to John Gassner's article "Modern Drama and Society," which appears in the same issue. *World Theatre*, 4 (Autumn 1955), pp. 40–41.

Autobiographical statement (untitled). In *Twentieth Century Authors, First Supplement*, ed. Stanley J. Kunitz. New York: Wilson, 1955, pp. 669–70.

"American Playwrights Self-Appraised" (short answers by Miller and others to questionnaire), ed. Henry Hewes. *Saturday Review*, 38 (September 3, 1955), pp. 18–19.

"On Social Plays." Preface to the one-act original edition of *A View from the Bridge*. New York: Viking, 1955, pp. 1–18. Reprinted as "A View of One-Acters," *The New York Times*, September 25, 1955, Sec. 2, pp. 1, 3.

"Red and Anti-Red Curbs on Art Denounced by U.S. Playwright." *The New York Times*, February 13, 1956, p. 9.

"The Family in Modern Drama." *Atlantic Monthly*, 197 (April 1956), pp. 35–41.

"Concerning the Boom." *International Theatre Annual*, No. 1, ed. Harold Hobson. London: John Calder, 1956, pp. 85–88.

"The Playwright and the Atomic World." *Colorado Quarterly*, 5 (Autumn 1956), pp. 117–37. Reprinted in *Tulane Drama Review*, 5 (June 1961), pp. 3–20. Retitled for *The Theater Essays of Arthur Miller* as "1956 and All This."

"The Writer in America." *Mainstream*, 10 (July 1957), pp. 43–46. Based on a speech delivered to the National Assembly of the Authors League of America on May 7, 1957. Reprinted as "The Writer's Position in America" in *Coastlines*, 2 (Autumn 1957), pp. 38–40.

"Global Dramatist." *The New York Times*, July 21, 1957, Sec. 2, p. 1.

"Introduction" to *Arthur Miller's Collected Plays*, Volume 1. New York: Viking, 1957, pp. 3–55.

"Brewed in *The Crucible*." *The New York Times*, March 9, 1958, Sec. 2, p. 3.

"The Shadows of the Gods." *Harper's*, 217 (August 1958), pp. 35–43.

"My Wife Marilyn." *Life*, 45 (December 22, 1958), pp. 146–47.

"Arthur Miller on Adaptations." *The New York Times*, November 29, 1959, Sec. 2, p. 13. A letter to the Radio-Television editor.

"Art and Commitment." *Anvil and Student Partisan*, 11 (Winter 1960), p. 5.

"Introduction" to *A View from the Bridge* (two-act version). New York: Compass, 1960, pp. v–x.

"The Bored and the Violent." *Harper's*, 225 (November 1962), pp. 50–52, 55–56.

"A New Era in American Theater?" *Drama Survey*, 3 (Spring 1963), pp. 70–71.

"Eugene O'Neill: An Evaluation by Fellow Playwrights" (short answers by Miller and others to a questionnaire, ed. Edward T. Herbert). *Modern Drama*, 6 (Winter 1963), pp. 239–40.

"On Recognition." *Michigan Quarterly Review*, 2 (Autumn 1963), pp. 213–20. The 1963 Hopwood Lecture at The University of Michigan.

"Lincoln Repertory Theater—Challenge and Hope." *The New York Times*, January 19, 1964, Sec. 2, pp. 1, 3.

"Foreword" to *After the Fall*. *The Saturday Evening Post*, 237 (February 1, 1964), p. 32.

"With Respect for Her Agony—But with Love." *Life*, 56 (February 7, 1964), p. 66. Miller's reply to criticism of *After the Fall* as autobiography.

"How the Nazi Trials Search the Hearts of All Germans." *The New York Herald Tribune*, March 15, 1964, p. 24.

"Our Guilt for the World's Evil." *The New York Times Magazine*, January 3, 1965, pp. 10–11, 48.

"*After the Fall*: An Author's View." *New Haven Register*, April 25, 1965, p. 9.

"What Makes Plays Endure?" *The New York Times*, August 15, 1965, Sec. 2, pp. 1, 3.

"The Writer as Independent Spirit: The Role of P.E.N." *Saturday Review*, 49 (June 4, 1966), pp. 16–17.

"Arthur Miller: P.E.N., Politics and Literature." *Publisher's Weekly*, 190 (July 18, 1966), pp. 32–33. Excerpted from Miller's P.E.N. presidential address to the International Congress held on the Washington Square campus of New York University from June 12–18, 1966.

"Literature and Mass Communication." *World Theatre*, 15 (1966), pp. 164–67. A speech delivered before the P.E.N. International Congress in Bled, Yugoslavia on July 5, 1965.

"A Search for the Future." *The Saturday Evening Post*, 239 (August 13, 1966), pp. 64–68, 70.

"Foreword: About Distances." *I Don't Need You Any More*. New York: Viking, 1967.

"It Could Happen Here—And Did." *The New York Times*, April 30, 1967, Sec. 2, p. 17.

"The Contemporary Theater." *Michigan Quarterly Review*, 6 (Summer 1967), pp. 153–63. Published under the overall heading of "Arthur Miller Talks" along with "Freedom in the Mass Media" (a panel with Mike Wallace, Arnold Gingrich, and Arthur Miller), pp. 163–78, and "A Chat with a Class in Stage Directing," pp. 178–84.

"The Age of Abdication." *The New York Times*, December 23, 1967, p. 22.

"The New Insurgency." *The Nation*, 206 (June 3, 1968), p. 717. A talk given at Madison Square Garden on May 19, 1968.

"Writers in Prison." *Encounter*, 30 (June 1968), pp. 60–61.

"On the Shooting of Robert Kennedy." *The New York Times*, June 8, 1968, p. 30.

"The Battle of Chicago: From the Delegates' Side." *The New York Times Magazine*, September 15, 1968, pp. 29–31, 122, 124, 126, 128.

"On Creativity" (short answers by Miller and others to a questionnaire). *Playboy*, 15 (December 1968), p. 139.

"Are We Interested in Stopping the Killing?" *The New York Times*, June 8, 1969, Sec. 2, p. 21.

"Some Would Forge Ahead in Space, Others Would Turn to Earth's Affairs." *The New York Times*, July 21, 1969, p. 7.

"Arthur Miller in Russia." *Harper's*, 239 (September 1969), pp. 37–78.

"Broadway from O'Neill to Now." *The New York Times*, December 21, 1969, Sec. 2, pp. 3, 7.

Short comment (untitled) on the theater. *Theater1,* ed. Rosamond Gilder. New York: International Theatre Institute, 1969, pp. 4, 7.

"The Bangkok Prince." *Harper's,* 241 (July 1970), pp. 32–33.

"The War between Young and Old, or Why Willy Loman Can't Understand What's Happening." *McCall's,* 97 (July 1970), p. 32.

"Banned in Russia." *The New York Times,* December 10, 1970, p. 47.

"When Life Had at Least a Form." *The New York Times,* January 24, 1971, p. 17.

"Men and Words in Prison." *The New York Times,* October 16, 1971, p. 29.

"The Measure of Things Is Men." *The American Theatre, 1970–1971.* In Vol. 4 of *Theatre.* New York: Scribner's, 1972, pp. 96–97.

"Arthur Miller vs. Lincoln Center." *The New York Times,* April 16, 1972, Sec. 2, pp. 1, 5. Reprinted in *The Dramatists Guild Quarterly,* 8 (Winter 1972), pp. 6–11.

"In Hiding." *The New York Times,* July 9, 1972, Sec. 7, p. 1.

"Arthur Miller on *The Crucible.*" *Audience,* 2 (July-August 1972), pp. 46–47.

"Making Crowds." *Esquire,* 78 (November 1972), pp. 160–61, 216, 218, 220, 222, 224, 226, 228.

"Politics as Theater." *The New York Times,* November 4, 1972, p. 33.

"Miracles." *Esquire,* 80 (September 1973), pp. 112–15, 202–04.

Short comment (untitled) on the playwright's influence on the theater. *Yale Theatre,* 4 (Winter 1973), pp. 19–20.

"Introduction" to *Kesey's Garage Sale,* ed. Ken Kesey. New York: Viking, 1974, pp. xiii–xviii.

"Sakharov, Detente and Liberty." *The New York Times,* July 5, 1974, p. 21.

"What's Wrong with This Picture?" *Esquire,* 82 (July 1974), pp. 124–25, 170.

"The Limited Hang-Out: The Dialogues of Richard Nixon as a Drama of the Antihero." *Harper's,* 249 (September 1974), pp. 13–14, 16, 18–20.

"Authors on Translators" (brief comments by Miller and others). *Translation,* 2, nos. 1–2 (1974), pp. 5–8.

"On True Identity." *The New York Times Magazine,* April 13, 1975, p. 111.

"The Prague Winter." *The New York Times*, July 16, 1975, p. 37.

"U.S. Urged to Guarantee Freedom of All Writers." *The New York Times*, November 19, 1975, p. 25.

"Toward a New Foreign Policy." *Society*, 13 (March-April, 1976), pp. 10, 15, 16.

"A Genuine Countryman." *Country Journal*, (January 1978), pp. 34–38.

"The Sin of Power." *Index on Censorship*, 7 (May-June 1978), pp. 3–6.

"Our Most Widespread Dramatic Art Is Our Most Unfree." *The New York Times*, November 26, 1978, Sec. 2, p. 33.

"Legacy from a Simpler Time" (excerpt from *In the Country*). *Reader's Digest*, (June 1978), pp. 146–50.

"A Playwright's Choice of 'Perfect' Plays." *The New York Times*, January 14, 1979, Sec. 2, p. 10.

"Every Play Has a Purpose." *Dramatists Guild Quarterly*, 15 (Winter 1979), pp. 13–20.

"In China" (excerpt from *Chinese Encounters*). *Atlantic*, 243 (March 1979), pp. 90–103.

"Clurmania: Address, May 6, 1979." *The Nation* (May 26, 1979), p. 606.

"China Scenes, China Voices: Excerpts from *Chinese Encounters*." *Reader's Digest*, (July 1979), pp. 58–64.

"Arthur Miller Stirs the 'Melting Pot That Didn't Melt.'" *U.S. News and World Report*, (November 12, 1979), pp. 60–61.

"Saber and Me: Story of a Rare Friendship." *Vogue*, 171 (November 1981), pp. 211–12.

"The American Writer: The American Theater." *Michigan Quarterly Review*, 21 (Winter 1982), pp. 4–20. Miller's 1981 speech commemorates the fiftieth anniversary of the Avery Hopwood Awards at The University of Michigan.

"After the Spring." *House and Garden*, 155 (April 1983), pp. 104–05.

"Suspended in Time." *Life*, (May 1983), pp. 104–08.

"The Night Ed Murrow Struck Back." *Esquire*, 100 (December 1983), pp. 460–62.

"Tennessee Williams' Legacy: 'An Eloquence and Amplitude of Feeling.'" *TV Guide*, March 3, 1984, p. 30.

"School Prayer: A Political Dirigible." *The New York Times*, March 12, 1984, p. 31.

"Arthur Miller on McCarthy's Legacy: Address, April 30, 1984." *Harper's*, 269 (July 1984), pp. 11–12.

"The Face in the Mirror: Anti-Semitism Then and Now." *The New York Times Book Review*, October 14, 1984, p. 3.

"Thoughts on a Burned House." *Architectural Digest*, (November 1984), p. 44.

"Arthur Miller Speaks Out on the Election." *Literary Cavalcade*, (November 1984), pp. 4–5.

"The Mad Inventor of Modern Drama." *The New York Times Book Review*, January 6, 1985, pp. 1, 30.

"Arthur Miller's Rite of Spring." *Reader's Digest*, (April 1985), pp. 67–69.

"Dinner with the Ambassador." *The Nation*, (May 18, 1985), p. 577.

"A New Candor at Issyk-Kul." *Newsweek*, (January 19, 1987), p. 8.

"Okay, But Who Was I?" (excerpt from Miller's autobiography, *Timebends*). *Life*, 10 (November 1987), pp. 72–88.

"The Theater Must Be Bread, Not Cake." *U.S. News and World Report*, (January 11, 1988), pp. 54–55.

"A Note from Arthur Miller." *New Theatre Review*, (Winter 1988), p. 2.

"Arthur Miller Reports: P.E.N. Mission to Chile." *P.E.N. American Center Newsletter*, 66 (September 1988), pp. 1–5.

"A Fabulous Appetite for Greatness." *The New York Times Book Review*, November 6, 1988, pp. 12–13.

"Ibsen's Warning." *Index on Censorship*, 18 (July-August 1989), pp. 74–76.

"Arthur Miller on Rushdie and Global Censorship." *Authors' Guild Bulletin*, (Summer 1989), p. 5.

"Death in Tiananmen." *The New York Times*, September 10, 1989, Sec. 4, p. 31.

"Again They Drink from the Cup of Suspicion." *The New York Times*, November 26, 1989, Sec. 2, pp. 5, 36.

"On Screenwriting and Language." Preface to *Everybody Wins*. New York: Grove Weidenfeld, 1990, pp. v–xiv.

"Uneasy about the Germans." *The New York Times Magazine*, May 6, 1990, pp. 46–47.

"In the Ayes of the Beholder: With Congress Debating Obscenity in Federally Funded Art, What Will Happen to Free Expression?" *Omni*, 13 (February 1991), p. 10.

"The Measure of the Man." *The Nation*, (February 11, 1991), pp. 151–54.

"White Sole's Burden." *Travel Holiday*, 174 (June 1991), pp. 59–60.

"Get It Right. Privatize Executions." *The New York Times*, May 8, 1992, p. A31.

"Last Word." *American Theatre*, (July/August 1992), p. 68.

"We're Probably in an Art That Is—Not Dying." *The New York Times*, January 17, 1993. p. H5.

"The Parable of the Stripper." *The New Republic*, (January 3, 1994), p. 30.

"About Theater Language." Afterword to *The Last Yankee*. New York: Penguin, 1994, pp. 75–98.

"The One Thing That Keeps Us from Chaos." *New Choices for Retirement Living*, (October 1994), pp. 22–25.

"Ibsen and the Drama of Today." *The Cambridge Companion to Henrik Ibsen,* ed. James McFarlane. Cambridge: Cambridge University Press, 1994, pp. 227–32.

"To Newt on Art." *The Nation*, 261 (July 31-August 7, 1995), p. 118.

"Introduction." *The Oxford Mark Twain*, ed. Shelley Fisher Fishkin. New York: Oxford University Press, 1996.

VII. Testimony

"The Testimony of Arthur Miller, accompanied by Counsel, Joseph L. Rauh, Jr." United States House of Representatives, Committee on Un-American Activities. *Investigation of the Unauthorized Use of United States Passports, 84th Congress, Congressional Record*, Part 4, June 21, 1956. Washington: United States Government Printing Office, November 1956, pp. 4660–4690.

VIII. Interviews (selected)

Hutchens, John K. "Mr. Miller Has a Change of Luck." *The New York Times*, February 23, 1947, Sec. 2, pp. 1, 3. Collected in Roudané, pp. 3–5.

Schumach, Murray. "Arthur Miller Grew in Brooklyn." *The New York Times*, February 6, 1949, Sec. 2, pp. 1, 3. Collected in Roudané, pp. 6–8.

Wolfert, Ira. "Arthur Miller, Playwright in Search of His Identity." *The New York Herald Tribune*, January 25, 1953, Sec. 4, p. 3.

Griffen, John and Alice. "Arthur Miller Discusses *The Crucible*." *Theatre Arts*, 37 (October 1953), pp. 33–34. Collected in Roudané, pp. 24–26.

Samachson, Dorothy and Joseph. In *Let's Meet the Theatre*. New York: Abelard-Schuman, 1954, pp. 15–20.

Wain, John. "Arthur Miller." *The Observer* (London), September 8, 1957, p. 5.

Gelb, Phillip. "*Death of a Salesman*: A Symposium." *Tulane Drama Review*, 2 (May 1958), pp. 63–69. Collected in Roudané, pp. 27–34.

Gelb, Phillip. "Morality and Modern Drama." *Educational Theatre Journal*, 10 (October 1958), pp. 190–202. Collected in Roudané, pp. 35–51.

Allsop, Kenneth. "A Conversation with Arthur Miller." *Encounter*, 13 (July 1959) pp. 58–60. Collected in Roudané, pp. 52–55.

"Conversation at St. Clerans between Arthur Miller and John Huston." *Guardian*, February 25, 1960, p. 6.

Brandon, Henry. "The State of the Theatre." *Harper's*, 221 (November 1960), pp. 63–69. Collected in Roudané, pp. 56–67.

Anon. "Arthur Miller Ad-Libs on Elia Kazan." *Show*, 2 (January 1964), pp. 55–56, 97–98. Collected in Roudané, pp. 68–77.

Hyams, Barry. "A Theatre: Heart and Mind." In *Theatre: The Annual of the Repertory Theater of Lincoln Center*, 1 (1964), pp. 56–61.

Wager, Walter. "Arthur Miller." In *The Playwrights Speak*, ed. Walter Wager. New York: Dell, 1967, pp. 1–24. Collected in Roudané, pp. 137–151.

Gelb, Barbara. "Question: Am I My Brother's Keeper?" *The New York Times*, November 29, 1964, Sec. 2, pp. 1, 3. Collected in Roudané, pp. 78–82.

Fallaci, Oriana. "A Propos of *After the Fall*." *World Theatre*, 14 (January 1965), pp. 79, 81.

Morley, Sheridan. "Miller on Miller." *Theatre World*, 61 (March 1965), pp. 4, 8.

Gruen, Joseph. "Portrait of a Playwright at Fifty." *New York*, October 24, 1965, pp. 12–13. Collected in Gruen's *Close Up*. New York: Viking, 1968, pp. 58–63.

Carlisle, Olga and Styron, Rose. "Arthur Miller: An Interview." *Paris Review*, 10 (Summer 1966), pp. 61–98. Reprinted in *Writers at Work: The Paris Review Interviews*, Third Series, ed. George Plimpton. New York: Viking, 1968, pp. 197–230. Collected in Roudané, pp. 85–111.

"Arthur Miller Talks Again: A Chat with a Class in Stage Directing." *Michigan Quarterly Review*, 6 (Summer 1967), pp. 178–84. Collected in Roudané, pp. 128–36.

Barthel, Joan. "Arthur Miller Ponders *The Price*." *The New York Times*, January 28, 1968, Sec. 2, pp. 1, 5.

Martin, Robert A. "Arthur Miller—Tragedy and Commitment." *Michigan Quarterly Review*, 8 (Summer 1969), pp. 176–78. Collected in Roudané, pp. 173–76.

Evans, Richard I. *Psychology and Arthur Miller*. New York: E.P. Dutton, 1969. Collected in Roudané, pp. 152–172.

Martin, Robert A. "The Creative Experience of Arthur Miller: An Interview." *Educational Theatre Journal*, 21 (October 1969), pp. 310–17. Collected in Roudané, pp. 177–86.

Hayman, Ronald. *Arthur Miller*. London: Heinemann, 1970, pp. 1–14. Collected in Roudané, pp. 187–99.

Martin, Robert A. "Arthur Miller and the Meaning of Tragedy." *Modern Drama*, 13 (Summer 1970), pp. 34–39. Collected in Roudané, pp. 200–05.

Hills, Rust. "Conversation: Arthur Miller and William Styron." *Audience*, 1 (November-December 1971), pp. 6–21. Collected in Roudané, pp. 206–32.

Greenfield, Josh. "'Writing Plays Is Absolutely Senseless,' Arthur Miller Says, 'But I Love It. I Just Love It.'" *The New York Times Magazine*, February 13, 1972, pp. 16–17, 34–39. Collected in Roudané, pp. 233–48.

Anon. "Arthur Miller on *The Crucible*" (film version). *Audience*, 2 (July-August, 1972), pp. 46–47.

Buckley, Tom, "Miller Takes His Comedy Seriously." *The New York Times*, August 29, 1972, p. 22. Collected in Roudané, pp. 249–52.

Hayman, Ronald. "Arthur Miller." *Playback II*. London: Davis-Poynter, 1973, pp. 7–22.

"Symposium: Playwriting in America: Joyce Carol Oates, Arthur Miller, Eric Bentley." *Yale/Theater*, 4 (1973), pp. 8–27.

Gussow, Mel. "Arthur Miller Returns to Genesis for First Musical." *The New York Times*, April 17, 1974, p. 37.

Corrigan, Robert W. "Interview: Arthur Miller." *Michigan Quarterly Review*, 13 (Fall 1974), pp. 401–05. Collected in Roudané, pp. 253–57.

Schumach, Murray. "Miller Still a 'Salesman' for a Changing Theater." *The New York Times*, June 26, 1975, p. 32. Collected in Roudané, pp. 258–61.

Martin, Robert A. and Meyer, Richard D. "Arthur Miller on Plays and Playwriting." *Modern Drama*, 19 (December 1976), pp. 375–84. Collected in Roudané, pp. 262–72.

Gollub, Christian-Albrecht. "Interview with Arthur Miller." *Michigan Quarterly Review*, 16 (Spring 1977), pp. 121–41. Collected in Roudané, pp. 273–90.

Martine, James J. "'All in a Boiling Soup': An Interview with Arthur Miller." In *Critical Essays on Arthur Miller*, ed. James J. Martine. Boston: G. K. Hall, 1979, pp. 177–88. Collected in Roudané, pp. 291–306.

Unger, Albert. "Arthur Miller Talks of His Holocaust Drama." *Christian Science Monitor*, September 19, 1980, p. 19.

Atlas, James. "The Creative Journey of Arthur Miller Leads Back to Broadway and TV." *The New York Times*, September 28, 1980, Sec. 2, pp. 1, 32.

Terkel, Studs. "Studs Terkel Talks with Arthur Miller." *Saturday Review*, (September 1980), pp. 24–27. Collected in Roudané, pp. 307–14.

Kelly, Kevin. "Arthur Miller Emerges Again on Several Fronts." *Boston Globe*, October 12, 1980, pp. 81–82.

Moss, Leonard. "'The Absence of the Tension': A Conversation with Arthur Miller." In *Arthur Miller*. Boston: Twayne, 1980, pp. 107–22. Collected in Roudané, pp. 315–31.

Rajakrishnan, V. "After Commitment: An Interview with Arthur Miller." *Theatre Journal*, 32 (1980), pp. 196–202. Collected in Roudané, pp. 332–42.

"Learning from a Performer: A Conversation with Arthur Miller." *Gamut*, 1 (1982), pp. 9–23.

Allen, Jennifer. "Miller's Tale." *New York*, (January 24, 1983), pp. 33–37.

Wren, Christopher S. "Willy Loman Gets China Territory." *The New York Times*, May 7, 1983, p. 13.

Christiansen, Richard. "Arthur Miller's Verdict on Willy: He Has Elements of Nobility." *Chicago Tribune*, January 15, 1984, Sec. 13, p. 19.

Christiansen, Richard. "Dustin Hoffman and the Rebirth of a Classic *Salesman*." *Chicago Tribune*, January 15, 1984, Sec. 13, p. 18.

Centola, Steven R. "'The Will to Live': An Interview with Arthur Miller." *Modern Drama*, 27 (1984), pp. 345–60. Collected in Roudané, pp. 343–59.

Roudané, Matthew C. "An Interview with Arthur Miller." *Michigan Quarterly Review*, 24 (1985), pp. 373–89. Collected in Roudané, pp. 360–75.

Bigsby, Christopher. "Miller's Odyssey to a Brutal Decade." *Guardian*, August 4, 1986, p. 9.

Goode, James. *The Making of* The Misfits. New York: Limelight Editions, 1986.

Lamos, Mark. "An Afternoon with Arthur Miller." *American Theatre*, 3 (1986), pp. 18–23. Collected in Roudané, pp. 376–88.

Gussow, Mel. "Arthur Miller: Stirred by Memory." *The New York Times*, February 1, 1987, Sec. 2, pp. 1, 30.

Roudané, Matthew C., ed. *Conversations with Arthur Miller*. Jackson: University Press of Mississippi, 1987.

Carroll, James and Epstein, Helen. "Seeing Eye to Eye." *Boston Review*, 14 (February 1989), pp. 12–13.

Balakian, Janet. "A Conversation with Arthur Miller." *Michigan Quarterly Review*, 29 (Spring 1990), pp. 158–70.

Bigsby, Christopher. *Arthur Miller and Company*. London: Methuen, 1990.

Centola, Steven R. "'Just Looking for a Home': A Conversation with Arthur Miller." *American Drama*, 1 (Fall 1991), pp. 85–94.

Balakian, Janet. "An Interview with Arthur Miller." *Studies in American Drama, 1945–Present*, 6 (1991), pp. 29–47.

Wolf, Matt. "An Exile of Sorts Finds a Welcome." *The New York Times*, October 13, 1991, Sec. H, p. 6.

Kaplan, James. "Miller's Crossing." *Vanity Fair*, (November 1991), pp. 218–21, 241–48.

Centola, Steven R. *Arthur Miller in Conversation*. Dallas: Northouse & Northouse, 1993.

Simonson, Robert. "Values, Old and New: Arthur Miller and John Tillinger on *The Last Yankee*." *Theater Week*, (January 18–24, 1993), pp. 13–18.

Century, Douglas. "Miller's Tale of 'Tribalism': The Playwright Returns to His Roots." *The Forward,* April 22, 1994, pp. 1, 10.

Strickland, Carol. "Arthur Miller's Latest Message to Humanity." *Christian Science Monitor*, April 26, 1994, p. 12.

Lambert, Angela. "An Intellect at Ease." *The Independent*, August 2, 1994, pp. 17, 19.

Nathan, David. "Loman's Land." *The Jewish Chronicle*, August 5, 1994, p. 25.

Cheever, Susan. "The One Thing That Keeps Us from Chaos." *New Choices for Retirement Living*, (October 1994), pp. 22–25.

Centola, Steven R. "'The Last Yankee': An Interview with Arthur Miller." *American Drama*, 5 (Fall 1995), pp. 78–98.

Ratcliffe, Michael. "Miller's Crossing." *Observer Review*, October 15, 1995, p. 7.

IX. Recordings (arranged by play chronology)

Death of a Salesman. Decca DXA-102 (DL 9006-DL 9007) [1950]. Contains two long-playing records. Directed by Elia Kazan. With Thomas Mitchell, Mildred Dunnock, Arthur Kennedy, et al. (Not the original cast; Thomas Mitchell replaced Lee J. Cobb.)

Death of a Salesman. Caedmon TRS 310 [1966]. Contains three long-playing records. Directed by Ula Grosbard. With Lee J. Cobb and Mildred Dunnock, but without the other members of the original cast.

Death of a Salesman. Read by Lee J. Cobb, Mildred Dunnock. Sound recording, two cassettes. Harper Collins CPN 310.

Death of a Salesman. Sound recording, two cassettes. Recorded Books 20124.

Death of a Salesman. Read by Paul Douglas. Sound recording, one cassette. Mind's Eye.

Arthur Miller's Adaptation of Henrik Ibsen's An Enemy of the People. Caedmon TRS 349 [1971]. Contains three long-playing records. Directed by Jules Irving. With members of the Lincoln Center Repertory Company.

Arthur Miller Speaking on and Reading from The Crucible *and* Death of a Salesman. Spoken Arts 704 [1956]. Contains one long-playing record.

The Crucible. Caedmon TRS 356 [1972]. Contains four long-playing records. Directed by John Berry. With members of the Lincoln Center Repertory Company.

The Crucible: An Opera in Four Acts by Robert Ward. Composers Recordings, Inc., CRI 68-SD [1961]. Contains two long-playing records. Libretto by Bernard Stambler. With New York City Center Orchestra and cast.

A View from the Bridge. Mercury OCM 2 2212 (MC 21055-21056) [1966]. Contains two long-playing records. Directed by Ulu Grosbard. With the original cast.

A View from the Bridge. Caedmon TRS 317 [1967]. Contains two long-playing records. Directed by Ulu Grosbard. With Robert Duvall, Jeanne Kaplan, Linda Eskenas, et al.

After the Fall. Mercury OCM 4 2207 (MG 21000-21003) [1968]. Contains four long-playing records. Directed by Elia Kazan. With Jason Robards, Jr., Barbara Loden, Salome Jens, et al.

After the Fall. Caedmon TRS 326 [1968]. Contains four long-playing records. Directed by Elia Kazan. With the same cast as *After the Fall*, Mercury OCM 4 2207.

Incident at Vichy. Mercury OCM 2 2211 [1967]. Contains two long-playing records. Directed by Harold Clurman. With Hal Holbrook, David Wayne, Joseph Wiseman, and members of the Lincoln Center Repertory Company.

Incident at Vichy. Caedmon TRS 318 [1967]. Contains two long-playing records. Directed by Harold Clurman. With the same cast as Mercury OCM 2 2211.

X. Television Productions

Grateful acknowledgement is made to Margaret Lynch for assisting with the compilation of this list of important television productions.

Death of a Salesman. Director: Alex Segal. Producer: David Susskind. With Lee J. Cobb, Mildred Dunnock, George Segal, and James Farentino. CBS, May 8, 1966.

The Crucible. Director: Alex Segal. Producer: David Susskind. With George C. Scott, Colleen Dewhurst, Fritz Weaver, Tuesday Weld, and Melvyn Douglas. CBS, April 5, 1967.

A Memory of Two Mondays. Director: Paul Bogart. Producer: Jaqueline Babbin. Executive Producer: Jac Venza. With Kristoffer Tabori, Dick Van Patten, Estelle Parsons, and Jack Warden. PBS, *NET Playhouse*, 1971.

The Price. Director: Fielder Cook. Producer: David Susskind. With George C. Scott, Barry Sullivan, David Burns, and Colleen Dewhurst. NBC, *Hallmark Hall of Fame*, February 3, 1971.

Incident at Vichy. Director: Stacky Keach. Producer: Norman Lloyd. With Richard Jordan. PBS, 1973.

After the Fall. With Faye Dunaway and Christopher Plummer. NBC, December 10, 1974.

Fame. Director: Marc Daniels. Producer: Cates Brothers Production. With Richard Benjamin, José Ferrer, Nipsy Russell, Shera Danese, Linda Hunt, and Raf Vallone. NBC, *Hallmark Hall of Fame*, November 30, 1978.

Playing for Time. Director: Daniel Mann. Producer: Linda Yellen. With Vanessa Redgrave, Jane Alexander, Shirley Knight, and Melanie Mayron. CBS, September 30, 1980.

Arthur Miller on Home Ground. Produced by Canadian Broadcasting Company. Narrator: Harry Rasky. PBS, October 8, 1980.

"Willie Loman Comes to China." *Our Time with Bill Moyer.* Narrator: Bill Moyer. CBS, 1983.

Death of a Salesman. Director: Volker Schlondorff. Producer: Robert F. Colesberry. With Dustin Hoffman, John Malkovich, Stephen Lang, Kate Reid, and Charles Durning. CBS, September 15, 1985.

Private Conversations on the Set of Death of a Salesman. Director and Producer: Christian Blackwood. With Arthur Miller, Dustin Hoffman, Volker Schlondorff, Kate Reid, and John Malkovich. PBS, 1985.

All My Sons. Director: Jack O'Brien. Producer: Iris Merlis. With James Whitmore, Aidan Quinn, Joan Allen, and Michael Learned. PBS, *American Playhouse*, January 19, 1987.

An Enemy of the People (adaptation by Miller). Director: Jack O'Brien. Producer: David Griffith. PBS, *American Playhouse*, 1990.

Clara. Director: Burt Brinckerhoff. Producer: Nederlander Film and Television Productions. With William Daniels, Darren McGavin, and Jennifer Parsons. A&E Cable Network, *General Motors Playwrights Theater*, February 5, 1991.

Arthur Miller. Producer: Diana Lashmore. Interviewer: Alan Yentob. A&E Cable Network, February 5, 1991.

The South Bank Show. Director and Producer: Hilary Chadwick. Presenter: Melvyn Bragg. Bravo Cable Network, 1991.

The American Clock. Director: Bob Clark. Producer: Michael Brandman. With Mary McDonnell, Darren McGavin, David Strathairn,

John Randolph, and Rebecca Miller. TNT Cable Network, August 23, 1993.

The Charley Rose Show. Interviewer: Charley Rose. PBS, 1994.

XI. Videography

Death of a Salesman. CBS television [1966]. Three video cassettes. Director: Alex Segal. Producer: David Susskind. With Lee J. Cobb, Mildred Dunnock, George Segal, and James Farentino. Museum of Television and Radio, New York.

Death of a Salesman. CBS television [1985]. One video cassette. Director: Volker Schlondorff. Producer: Robert F. Colesberry. With Dustin Hoffman, John Malkovich, Kate Reid, Stephen Lang, and Charles Durning. Karl-Lorimar Home Video, 1986.

Private Conversations on the Set of Death of a Salesman. PBS documentary for television [1985]. One video cassette. With Arthur Miller, Dustin Hoffman, Volker Schlondorff, and John Malkovich. Karl-Lorimar Home Video, 1986.

All My Sons. PBS television [1987]. One video cassette. With James Whitmore, Aidan Quinn, Joan Allen, and Michael Learned. MCA Home Video, 1987.

XII. CD-Rom Diskettes

The Crucible. CD-ROM diskette. Developed by University of East Anglia/Norwich Technology Unit. New York: Penguin, 1994.

XIII. Manuscript and Typescript Collections

The University of Michigan, Ann Arbor. Four manuscripts: *No Villain* (1936) and *Honors at Dawn* (1937) in the Hopwood Room; *The Great Disobedience* (1938) and *The Grass Still Grows* (1939) in the Rare Book Room, Harlan Hatcher Library.

The University of Texas, Austin. Extensive holdings too numerous to list, consisting of notebooks, manuscripts, printers' copies, and typescripts in many versions. Harry Ransom Humanities Research Center, Academic Center Building.

The New York Public Library. Nine manuscripts: *They Too Arise* (1936); *The Man Who Had All the Luck*; *Death of a Salesman*; *The Crucible* (three versions); *A View from the Bridge*; *After the Fall*; and *Incident at Vichy*. Billy Rose Theater Collection.

American Academy of Arts and Letters, New York. Letters from Miller, plus other holdings.

The Viking Press, New York. Letters from Miller, plus other holdings.

XIV. Bibliographical References
(alphabetically by author)

Bigsby, Christopher. *File on Miller*. London: Methuen, 1988.

Carpenter, Charles A. "Studies of Arthur Miller's Drama: A Selective International Bibliography, 1966–1979." In *Arthur Miller: New Perspectives*. Ed. Robert A. Martin. Englewood-Cliffs: Prentice-Hall, Inc., 1982. pp. 205–19. Lists bibliographies, collections of essays, and critical essays.

Eissenstat, Martha. "Arthur Miller: A Bibliography." *Modern Drama*, 5 (May 1962), pp. 93–106. Contains works by and about Miller.

Ferres, John H. *Arthur Miller: A Reference Guide*. Boston: G. K. Hall, 1979. Lists reviews, interviews, and critical essays as well as works by the playwright.

Hayashi, Tetsumaro. *An Index to Arthur Miller Criticism*. 2nd Ed. Metuchen, New Jersey: Scarecrow Press, 1976.

Jensen, George H. *Arthur Miller: A Bibliographical Checklist*. Columbia, South Carolina: Faust, 1976. Contains illustrations of title pages, a full-length bibliography of Miller's writings, and the complete publishing history of all his books.

Moss, Leonard. *Arthur Miller*. Revised Edition. New York: Twayne, 1980.

Schlueter, June. "Arthur Miller." In *Contemporary Authors*. Vol. 3. *American Dramatists*, ed. Matthew C. Roudané. Detroit: Gale, 1989. pp. 189–270. Includes primary and secondary sources as well as a useful bibliographical essay.

Ungar, Harriet. "The Writings of and about Arthur Miller: A Check List 1936–1967." *Bulletin of the New York Public Library*, 74 (February 1970), pp. 107–34.

Index

Index to the Expanded Edition